www.wadsworth.com

www.wadsworth.com is the World Wide Web site for Thomson Wadsworth and is your direct source to dozens of online resources.

At www.wadsworth.com you can find out about supplements, demonstration software, and student resources. You can also send email to many of our authors and preview new publications and exciting new technologies.

www.wadsworth.com
Changing the way the world learns®

D1455830

POPULAR MUSIC IN AMERICA THE BEAT GOES ON

MICHAEL CAMPBELL

2nd Edition

THOMSON

™

SCHIRMER

Australia • Canada • Mexico • Singapore • Spain • United Kingdom • United States

THOMSON
™
SCHIRMER

Popular Music in America:
The Beat Goes On, Second Edition
Michael Campbell

Publisher: CLARK BAXTER
Senior Development Editor: SUE GLEASON
Senior Assistant Editor: JULIE YARDLEY
Editorial Assistant: EMILY PERKINS
Executive Technology Project Manager: MATT DORSEY
Executive Marketing Manager: DIANE WENCKEBACH
Marketing Assistant: RACHEL BAIRSTOW
Advertising Project Manager: PATRICK ROONEY
Project Manager, Editorial Production: TRUDY BROWN
Executive Art Director: MARIA EPES
Print Buyer: LISA CLAUDEANOS

Permissions Editor: CHELSEA JUNGET
Production Service: MELANIE FIELD, STRAWBERRY FIELD
  PUBLISHING
Text Designer: JOHN WALKER
Photo Researcher: MYRNA ENGLER
Copy Editor: ELIZABETH VON RADICS
Cover Designer: CUTTRIS AND HAMBELTON
Cover Image: © IMAGE 100/ROYALTY FREE/CORBIS
Compositor: TBH TYPECAST, INC.
Text and Cover Printer: TRANSCONTINENTAL
  PRINTING/LOUISEVILLE

Library of Congress Control Number: 2004112306

ISBN 0-534-55534-9

Thomson Wadsworth
10 Davis Drive
Belmont, CA 94002-3098
USA

Thomson Learning
5 Shenton Way #01-01
UIC Building
Singapore 068808

Australia/New Zealand
Thomson Learning
102 Dodds Street
Southbank, Victoria 3006
Australia

Canada
Thomson Nelson
1120 Birchmount Road
Toronto, Ontario M1K 5G4
Canada

Europe/Middle East/Africa
Thomson Learning
High Holborn House
50–51 Bedford Row
London WC1R 4LR
United Kingdom

To J. Bunker Clark (1931–2003), who helped make the study of American music as vibrant, eclectic, and democratic as the music itself

Popular Music in America: The Beat Goes On, second edition, is an introductory survey of popular music in the United States since 1840. In its attention to the kinship among its many musical styles and its organization around a coherent account of the evolution of popular music over the past century and a half, the book retains the overall emphasis of the first edition. But like a house that has been gutted and totally remodeled, this book has had a thorough makeover—in structure, content, pedagogical features, and ancillaries.

A New Structure

A quick tour of the table of contents will make the structural differences clear. A new, more pertinent, more accessible opening chapter introduces the elements of popular music through a Muddy Waters blues selection and Chuck Berry's "Maybellene." The balance of the text—thirteen chronological chapters—maps a historical journey that begins with the emergence of a distinctively American popular music in the middle of the nineteenth century and continues through the end of the twentieth century and into the present. There is proportionately greater emphasis on rock-era music, plus more attention to regional styles, such as Cajun and Tejano music, and to contemporary trends like techno and world beat. And in most cases, the narratives within the chapters cover narrower time spans so that there is less chronological backtracking.

With an eye to student success, each chapter begins with an introduction that addresses the significance and the direction of new developments, and each chapter ends with a new "Looking Back, Looking Ahead" summary that both reviews the developments of that chapter and anticipates those to come.

New Emphasis on Music in Context

This substantial revision places more emphasis on music's social context and on the connections between context and music. For example, it is one thing to catalog punk's style features; it is another to ask how punk musicians deliver the message of the music, and still another to trace how subsequent musicians (Devo, the Go-Go's) used the innovations of punk to send quite different messages. If style is a gateway to meaning, and I believe it is, a fuller awareness of musical style will not only strengthen students' listening skills but also make them aware of a work's intent. Both the narrative and the new Listening Guides for this edition's selections—in the text and on the Web—support listening for style.

Boxed features appear from time to time, highlighting trends and events in society, the music business, and technology and sometimes revealing behind-the-scenes stories. For example, a box in Chapter 4 tells the story of George Gershwin's composing *Rhapsody in Blue* in a week.

Learning to Listen

This edition's increased focus on listening may be its most important new feature. Each of the seventy-two audio selections discussed in depth—indicated by an icon plus CD and track numbers, where applicable—helps students develop listening skills in three ways. A **Listening Guide** enables students to navigate the selection by associating elapsed times in the recording with an outline of the form and noteworthy musical events. A **Style Profile** reviews the way each selection makes use of music's basic elements—rhythm, melody, instrumentation, performance style, dynamics, harmony, texture, and form—and associates them with a style. Using these elements students can listen more actively for style as well as develop a richer understanding of the connections and contrasts among popular styles. **Key Points** place the selection in its musical and social contexts and encourage student success in listening for style.

A logical progression moves the reader from each Listening Guide (get acquainted) through the Style Profile (notice these features) to Key Points (understand how they illustrate style and meaning) and **Terms to Know** (remember these key terms related to the style). Terms to Know repeat at the end of each chapter and reference the book's Companion Web site, where students can study the definitions using flashcards or a glossary.

None of this presumes any prior musical training—the book includes no musical notation, and the definitions of musical terms avoid technical jargon.

New Ancillaries

Active Listening Guides. The Listening Guides, Style Profiles, and Key Points appear in interactive multimedia form as free Active Listening Guide downloads (prepared by Thomas Smialek and L. A. Logrande) on the book's Companion Web site. They enhance those found in the text in three important ways:

o All sections of the Active Listening Guides—the visual fever bar tracking the audio CD, the style features, and the Key Points—contain audio links.

o Terms to Know link to glossary definitions, and many are augmented with a short audio clip.

o Key Points contain fuller discussions than those found in the text.

One of the major challenges for students in general studies courses is to connect words—definitions, observations, interpretations, and the like—to musical events. To assist students in this task, we have linked virtually all commentary on a selection's music to specific audio passages in the piece. For example, the Style Profile for Chuck Berry's "Maybellene" comments on the song's strong backbeat. Students can click on this comment and hear a short excerpt of the song in which the strong backbeat is clearly present. And to hear how the underlying rhythm shifts from a two-beat to a four-beat feel, students can click on two links to hear the contrast.

Book Companion Web site at *http://music.wadsworth.com/campbell_2e.* The book's Companion Web site gives students many more opportunities to test their understanding as they move through the text, by providing a glossary, flashcards, and a study outline and quiz for each chapter. Instructors have access to the *eBank Instructor's Manual/Test Bank* (prepared by John Keene, Xavier University and Wilmington College) on the instructor's Companion Web site.

Three-CD Set. Containing a recording of all but three of the Listening Guide selections in the text and on the Companion Web site, the CD set is more focused, more balanced—and more affordable for this edition, particularly when bundled with the text. The styles new to this edition range from tangos and Tejano music to reggae, newgrass, and techno.

As was the case with the previous edition, too many artists and record companies refuse to license their music at any price, much less one that results in an affordable CD package. We have addressed this dilemma on two fronts. A specific solution was to use recordings of Beatles songs by Rain, a top Beatles tribute band. Our feeling was that Rain's recordings are close enough to the originals to provide the basis for worthwhile discussion. A broader solution supplies **Web icons** in the text margins to indicate that a recording or album discussed in the text is available online through iTunes.™ We recognize that there are several online music services and that there will probably be many more before this edition has run its course. We have chosen to reference iTunes because it is, at this writing, the most comprehensive cross-platform online service. You can find the iTunes Web site at *www.apple.com/itunes.*

Acknowledgments

It has been nine years since the publication of the first edition of this book. In that time Schirmer Books has changed hands twice, and its college texts now make up the music division of Thomson Higher Education. For me this affiliation has been a special blessing because the new Schirmer has given this project such wonderful support. It starts at the top with Publisher Clark Baxter, who committed staff and resources to making the second edition of this book superior to the first and who has remained unfailingly gracious, encouraging, and positive. I owe special thanks to Sue Gleason, my development editor, whose patience and good humor have made the preparation of this new edition a pleasure and a terrific learning experience. Thanks also to the production team, especially Trudy Brown, the production project manager; Melanie Field, who supervised it all; and eagle-eyed copyeditor Elizabeth von Radics.

A number of teachers of American popular music provided immeasurably helpful advice, which led to the thoroughgoing revision that you hold in your hands. I am in debt to each and every one of them: Louis Abbott, Miami Dade College; Daniel F. Bakos, State University of West Georgia; T. Dennis Brown, University of Massachusetts; John Keene, Xavier University and Wilmington College; Barbara Rose Lang, University of Houston; Peter C. Matthews, John Jay College (CUNY); Gary Pritchard, Cerritos College; and Mark Sheridan-Rabideau, Millersville University.

I would also like to thank the many people to whom I am so indebted in so many different ways. I am grateful to the late Jan LaRue and to Allen Forte, professor emeritus of music theory at Yale University, for their example and their support. LaRue's seminal book *Guidelines for Style Analysis* has profoundly shaped every aspect of my musical life—research, writing, performing, composing, and teaching—and his support and advice over the many years of our friendship have been of inestimable value. My work with Allen Forte has opened up new areas of inquiry; the rigor of his thinking and the clarity of his vision have provided an admirable model.

I remain especially grateful to Maribeth Payne, who first acquired *And the Beat Goes On* for the original Schirmer books, and to Richard Carlin, who shepherded the book through its first publication. Thanks also to many of my former colleagues, especially John Murphy, now professor of jazz studies at the University of North Texas, and Paul Paccione and James Caldwell of Western Illinois University, for their willingness to share their time and expertise. Their suggestions and insights have been most welcome. And I would like to acknowledge my debt to three senior American music scholars: Richard Crawford, Charles Hamm, and H. Wiley Hitchcock. Separately and collectively, they have provided scholars and students with an inclusive and integrated view of American music. For me their work has been a source of information and inspiration.

The best for last! My heartfelt thanks to my family: my wife, Marie Jo De Maestri; her daughters, Eva and Helena Kranjc; and our son, Gabriel. They not only have made my work as easy as possible but also have given me the best possible motivation for doing it.

Michael Campbell

Michael Campbell is a writer and a pianist. A California native, he is a Phi Beta Kappa graduate of Amherst College and holds a doctorate from Peabody Conservatory, where he studied piano with Leon Fleisher. As a commercial musician, he has assisted such artists as Angela Lansbury, Gladys Knight and the Pips, Bob Hope, Redd Foxx, Ethel Merman, and Don McLean. As a concert pianist, he has performed a broad range of repertoire, including his own transcriptions of recordings by Art Tatum, Jelly Roll Morton, and other legendary jazz pianists. He has presented papers on Cole Porter, the evolution of popular music, and the search for the first rock-and-roll record and has contributed articles on Porter and Harold Arlen for a forthcoming book on popular song.

Campbell is the author of two music texts, *Popular Music in America: The Beat Goes On* and *Rock and Roll: An Introduction,* co-authored by James Brody. For many years Campbell taught a large course in popular music at Western Illinois University. He now lives in Rhode Island, where he devotes his time to research and writing.

The Elements and Identity
of Popular Music

In 1928, when Leonard Chess was eleven, his family emigrated from Poland to Chicago. Like so many before them, they had come to the United States to find a better life. By the time Leonard came of age, Prohibition had been repealed and he and his brother, Phil, went into the liquor business. During World War II, they acquired several nightclubs on Chicago's South Side, including the Macomba, a club that featured some of the best black performers in the city.

In 1947, sensing that the recording industry offered another good business opportunity, the Chess brothers bought into a newly formed independent label, Aristocrat Records. Like most other independents, Aristocrat concentrated on music outside of the pop mainstream. The first releases on the new label had featured **jazz** and **jump bands** (a jump band is a small R&B group that plays up-tempo music), but in 1947 the label recorded two sides by bluesman Muddy Waters.

MUDDY WATERS AND THE ELECTRIC BLUES

Muddy Waters (1915–1983), born McKinley Morganfield, grew up in Clarksdale, Mississippi, in the northwest part of the state in the heart of what is called the Delta region. The population was mostly black, and for the vast majority life was brutal. Both males and females worked as sharecroppers, often from childhood. Waters was a farm laborer as a boy. Some men made a little more money working as stevedores loading riverboats along the Mississippi, but there too the days were long, the work hard, and the pay meager. Most lived at a subsistence level, trapped in an unending cycle of economic dependence. From this harsh and isolated environment came what Robert Palmer called "deep blues," a powerful music that gave expression to, and release from, the brutal conditions of the Delta.

Waters heard this music while he was growing up and began to play it in his teens. He started on the harmonica, then took up the guitar because, "You see, I was digging Son House and Robert Johnson" (the great Delta bluesmen of the 1930s whom we meet in Chapter 3). By his late twenties, Waters had become a popular performer in the region.

Like many other southern blacks, Waters moved north during World War II, settling on Chicago's South Side. He continued to play, first at impromptu house parties and later at small bars. He recorded for Columbia Records in 1946, but the recordings were not released until many years later. It was not enough to pay the rent, and Waters was working as a truck driver when he approached Aristocrat Records about recording for the label.

Waters's first records did not make much of a splash. His 1948 recording, "I Can't Be Satisfied," however, found an audience, one that grew steadily over the next decade. "I Can't Be Satisfied" began a string of **rhythm and blues (R&B)** hits that included songs like "Rollin' Stone" and "Hoochie Coochie Man." By the early 1950s, Waters had become so popular in Chicago that one of his recordings sold out the day it was released; the first pressing never left town. In the meantime the Chess brothers had bought out Evelyn Aron, the woman who started Aristocrat Records. In 1950 they renamed the label Chess Records, and for the first half of the decade Muddy Waters was their top artist.

Waters brought the sound of the Delta blues north and transformed it. Performing in larger—and noisier—clubs, he needed more sound to cut through the noise of the crowd. His first step was to switch to **electric guitar**. As he became more successful, he pieced together a backup band for recordings and live performances. As his early recordings show, he added musicians in stages. By the early 1950s, his band included two guitars (Waters and Jimmy Rogers), harmonica, bass, drums, and piano. This more powerful version of Delta blues would define the sound of **electric blues**. We hear this sound in a memorable recording from 1952, "Standing Around Crying."

The Sound of Electric Blues

"Standing Around Crying," Muddy Waters (1952). Waters, vocal and guitar; Little Walter, harmonica.

Go to a blues bar anywhere in Chicago or to a blues festival anywhere in the world. If the band is playing in a "traditional" or "authentic" blues style, chances are the music will sound much like "Standing Around Crying." The song may be faster, it may be louder, but it will have essentially the same sound. The **blues** sound is familiar not only to blues fans but also to fans of the 1960s **rock** musicians who, immersing themselves in the blues, recorded cover versions of several Waters songs. (A **cover version** of a song is a recording by someone other than the original artist.) For more than fifty years, this has been the sound of the blues.

It's easy enough to figure out what the song is about. The words tell the story of a man who's lost his woman and is feeling the pain; the music seems to capture his mood. If we explore both words and music more deeply, we can better understand how we sense the meaning of the song and, by extension, of the blues and what they have to tell us about the people who created them.

The Message of the Lyrics

The story unfolds as a series of scenes, each scene presented in three lines of text. The first two lines are virtually the same (the second line repeating the first), and the third line rhymes with the first two. The two different lines form a **rhymed couplet**. In typical blues one full statement of the rhymed couplet is usually called a **chorus**.

Oh baby, look how you got me standin' 'round crying.
Oh baby, look how you got me standin' 'round crying.   rhymed ⎫ chorus
I know I don't love you little girl, but you're always restin' on my mind. ⎬ couplet ⎬

The rhymed couplet is the most basic of all poetic units. In the blues it is treated expansively: because of the repetition of the first line and the pauses between the lines, a lot of time passes before the rhyming line is sung. An inventive blues singer could easily make up additional choruses on the spur of the moment—and many did. As we listen to "Standing Around Crying," we have the feeling that Waters has more to tell us. And if we had heard Waters sing the song in person, we might have learned more. But blues musicians in the early 1950s recorded **singles**, which had a maximum length of about three minutes. So we never learn the rest of the story.

The relationship between words and music in "Standing Around Crying" might be summed up this way: the music tells us how Waters feels; the lyrics tell us why. We sense within a few seconds—well before Waters starts to sing—that we will hear a tale of woe in stark language and with deep feeling. Why? What are the musical clues that send this message?

The Message of the Music: Defining the Sounds

Let's step back for a minute to ask ourselves what we hear when we listen to a musical sound. Almost every musical sound has four qualities: timbre, pitch, intensity, and duration. **Timbre** (pronounced "*tam*-ber") refers to the tone color of a musical sound. It is the term we use to describe the characteristic sound of a voice or an instrument (the characteristic that helps you distinguish a friend's voice from a stranger's). The **flute**, for example, has a pure timbre. When we want to describe the different sounds of the same melody played on a piano and an electric guitar, we say that they have different timbres.

Pitch describes how high or low a musical tone sounds. We use **intensity** to describe how loud a musical sound is. In popular music simple descriptive terms like *loud* and *soft* usually suffice. **Duration** refers to the length of a musical sound. We typically relate the length of a sound to the beat and describe the length by saying, for example, "This note has a duration of two beats."

The elements of a musical performance grow out of these four qualities of sound. **Instrumentation** (meaning the different timbres) describes the voices and the instruments that perform the song. **Performance style** describes the way the musicians sing and play. In "Standing Around Crying," we would list electric guitar as part of the instrumentation and identify Muddy Waters's **slide**, or **bottleneck**, technique as an aspect of his performance style.

Pitches combine into melody and harmony. Intensity becomes **dynamics** on a large scale (the dynamic level of a typical heavy metal band is loud) and **inflection** on a smaller scale. When we say Little Walter's harmonica playing is "highly inflected," we mean that there is a lot of contrast between the loudest and the softest notes. Duration grows into **rhythm** as soon as more than one note is sounded.

Instrumentation and Performance Style. Using our basic music vocabulary, we can now return to the original question: what musical clues tell us that "Standing Around Crying" is a sad tale? Three sounds stand out: vocal, electric guitar, and harmonica. In the background are another guitar, a drum set, and a piano that we hear faintly on occasion.

The three background instruments—the second guitar, the drums, and the piano—form a **rhythm section**, the foundation of the band. The rhythm section supports the voice and the melody instruments by laying down (setting) the beat and laying out the harmony. (**Harmony** is the arrangement of chords; a **chord** is a group of notes considered a unit). The rhythm section typically contains at least one chord instrument, one **bass** instrument, and one **percussion** instrument. Waters's rhythm section contains no bass instrument, but the second guitar compensates by playing fragments of a bass line.

The three prominent sounds—vocal, electric guitar, and harmonica—are all melody instruments. We ask not only what instruments they are, but what is distinctive about their sounds. The voice is rough and highly inflected, as if singing for Waters is a more intense form of speech. The harmonica in the hands of Little Walter seems to moan, delivering a string of passionate sighs sustained over long phrases and commenting on, or responding to, the vocal line. On **lead guitar** Waters uses the slide, or bottleneck, technique to bend notes (when instrumentalists **bend notes,** they alter the pitch slightly to achieve greater expression) and intensify the sound by vibrating rapidly on a single note. This technique enables him to mimic the sound of his voice.

Dynamics and Intensity. All of the instruments are heavily inflected. That is, there is a lot of contrast between loud and soft within a phrase, from one note to the next, and at times on a single note. We can sense the intensity in the performance, especially in the harmonica and the slide guitar; and when Waters sings "Oh baby," we can hear the power and conviction in his voice. He delivers the lyric directly, without artifice, and with the art and heart of a skilled bluesman.

Melody. We hear a group of pitches in two ways: as melody and as harmony. A **melody** is a group of single pitches heard and understood as a series, one note after another. For example, the pitches that Waters sings to the words "Oh baby, look how you got me standin' 'round crying" form a series—a **melodic phrase.** By contrast we occasionally hear the guitarist and the pianist play chords that create harmony. (We discuss harmony in more detail later in this section.)

Three features of the melody of "Standing Around Crying" help express the mood of the song. The first is the pattern of rise and fall in pitch. Most of the melodic ideas—the opening guitar line, Waters's vocal line, and many of the harmonica comments—start high and end low. Why is this significant? Try saying with feeling these two phrases: "I just won the lottery!" and "Somebody broke into my apartment and stole everything I own." Listen to your voice at the end of each sentence. Chances are your voice will rise with joy at the end of the first sentence and drop in a sigh of despair at the end of the second. A phrase like Waters's "Oh baby" can be heard as an amplified sigh falling from a high to a low pitch that continues to fall in the subsequent phrase. (By contrast many of the instrumental melodies repeat a single note over and over as if to insist musically that what he's singing about is *real.*)

The second feature is the pacing of the melody. It flows with the rhythm of the words—a little drawn out for expressive purposes, perhaps, but still very much in the rhythm of speaking. Here the spoken rhythm of the words dictates the flow of the melody rather than the other way around. (Try reading the lyric with feeling, then compare your result with Waters's performance; they should move at much the same pace and rhythm.)

A third feature is the length, or duration, of the melodic phrases sung and played. Some melodic phrases linger over several beats, but others, like the opening "Oh baby" and the very first notes of the guitar, are short and set apart. Because of this they catch the ear. In addition there is a regular exchange of melodic ideas between the vocal and the instruments. The harmonica and the guitar respond to the vocal line in melody-like phrases suited to the instrument.

These devices of melody are simple yet powerful, conveying the strong, stark emotions of the blues. The falling melodic lines and the natural flow of the words help Waters convey the mood of the song directly and without pretense.

Rhythm. Although melody and inflection can amplify the emotional power of the lyric, and the sound of Waters's voice can make the performance personal, rhythm can be more powerful than any aspect of music because it controls our sense of time. Anything that happens over the course of the song—a string of pitches, the alternation of voice and instruments, the chord progression—forms some aspect of rhythm. Most music creates regular rhythms moving at a consistent speed. At the heart of these regular rhythms is the **beat**, the regular rhythm to which we can most easily respond—by tapping our foot, nodding our head, and so on. Other regular rhythms group and divide beats, much as minutes are grouped into hours and divided into seconds. Beats typically group into **measures**. Typically, measures contain two, three, or four beats; "Standing Around Crying" has four beats per measure.

The beat can match essential life rhythms—our pulse or our movement—and at times the beat can regulate them. Because of this, **tempo** (the speed of the beat) is powerfully evocative and influences our perception of mood in a song. "Standing Around Crying" has a very slow tempo. The song moves much more slowly than we would normally walk. This extremely slow tempo darkens the mood of the song because it evokes an image of a man whose heart is so heavy he can barely move.

Muddy Waters, deep into the blues. In this photo Waters is playing the conventional way rather than using a slide, as we heard on the musical example.

The beat is at the center of rhythm, but there is more to rhythm than the beat. "Standing Around Crying" features a **four-beat rhythm**—a rhythmic foundation in which each beat receives equal emphasis; it is the common rhythmic basis for jazz and many blues-based styles, including electric blues. But the song also gives a nice example of **rhythmic play** (sounds out of phase with the beat). Within the slow, walking beat, the drums and the backup guitar emphasize a rhythm that is three times as fast. Furthermore, Waters sings his vocal line in defiance of the beat; the rhythm of his delivery, especially in the longer phrases, seems more attuned to speech than to the steady rhythms of the instruments. This kind of rhythmic high-wire act is also part of Waters's expressive arsenal, as though his pain is too deep to be controlled by the relentless rhythms of the band. The beat may draw us into a song, but the ongoing rhythmic interactions keep us there.

So far we have identified musical features that we can latch onto within seconds. We find the beat, we hear Waters sing "Oh baby," and we notice the moaning harmonica and the edge on the sound of the slide guitar. All of these help set the mood of the song. Texture and harmony help sustain it. Form organizes it.

Texture. Throughout Waters's song the musicians play more or less continuously. Most of them play simple yet melodic lines. The harmonica and lead guitar lines stand out, but every instrument except the drums has something melodic to say. What's noteworthy is that vocal and instruments can all speak at the same time and still blend together to create a **texture**. (By contrast, try following several conversations simultaneously.) A significant aspect of texture is the **call-and-response** pattern, which is rapid exchange, usually of rifts, between two different timbres, such as solo voice (call) and guitar (response), or solo voice and choir.

Two aspects of the texture of "Standing Around Crying" stand out. First, much of the time there are many melodic strands. Not only the voice but also all the instruments play simple melodic figures, or fills. The instrumental lines are like a group of people who commiserate with Waters as he sings the blues. They don't say anything elaborate; they simply lend support. Second, the pitch of most of the lines occurs in a low or middle range. This makes the sound thick and helps darken the mood of the song.

Harmony. Like countless other blues songs, the harmony of "Standing Around Crying" is built on the typical blues chord progression. Recall that a chord is two or more notes sounded together. A **chord progression** is a sequence of chords that moves toward a goal—in this case, simply the end of the blues pattern. This **blues progression** is built on three chords, which we call **I, IV, and V**—Roman numerals for the numbers 1, 4, and 5 and referred to as "the 1, 4, and 5 chords." These three chords are like anchors that attach to a lyric line in this sequence:

The first vocal line: "Oh baby . . ."	begins on the I chord
The instrumental response	begins on the I chord
The second vocal line: "Oh baby . . ."	begins on the IV chord
The instrumental response	begins on the I chord
The third vocal line: "I know I don't . . ."	begins on the V chord
The instrumental response	begins on the I chord

The key points here are (1) each line of the chorus begins with its own chord and (2) the I chord returns at the beginning of each instrumental response.

A blues progression is like a pair of old jeans: both are durable and well broken in yet extremely flexible and adaptable, and neither goes out of style. Because the blues progression is so familiar and so comfortable, it helps ground a performance like the one we hear here.

Form. When we look at a photograph of Waters, we can take in the whole image in a glance. We can't do that with his music because it unfolds in time. Our sense of the organization of a musical performance—the **form**—comes gradually, as we hear clues that one section has ended and a new one has begun. Eventually, the clues coalesce into a pattern, and we grasp the performance as a whole.

"Standing Around Crying" uses the standard **blues form**: the 12-bar blues. What is a 12-bar blues? Each chorus of the song consists of a rhymed couplet presented as three lines of text. One line of text and music lasts four bars. (Recall that a measure, or **bar**, or is a regular group of beats and that in this song each bar contains four beats.) Because there are three lines of text, each chorus lasts twelve measures. So, **12-bar blues form** refers to the form of each chorus.

The form of the lyric is simple, the chord progression is regular, and the rhythm within the chorus is predictable. All of these qualities reinforce one another to make the blues form easy to hear and perform.

Blues form grows into a full performance by building one chorus after another into a complete song. In theory, the performance could go on as long as the bluesman had a story to tell. In practice, the performance is limited by the length of a single recording, the interest level of the audience, and the endurance of the performers.

Blues form, both within each chorus and overall, also contributes to the mood of the song although in a more subtle way. Within the chorus the rhythm of exchange between voice and

CD 1:1   **Early Electric Blues** (Muddy Waters; performed by Waters, vocal and guitar; and Little Walter, harmonica)

0:00	Introduction. Harmonica, lead guitar (playing single notes, slide guitar style), rhythm section.

1st Chorus ■ **Blues form; call-and-response between voice and harmonica/guitar**

0:22	Voice begins on I chord.
	Oh baby, look . . .
0:32	Harmonica response begins on (returns to) I chord.
0:42	Voice begins on IV chord.
	Oh baby, look . . .
0:52	Harmonica response begins on (returns to) to I chord.
1:02	Voice begins on V chord, moves to IV chord.
	I know I don't love you . . .
1:12	Harmonica response again begins on (returns to) I chord.

2nd Chorus ■ **Blues form; call-and-response between voice and harmonica/guitar**

1:22	*Oh baby, I ain't gonna be . . .*
1:42	*Oh baby, I ain't gonna be . . .*
2:02	*You got so many men . . .*

3rd Chorus ■ **Blues form; call-and-response between voice and harmonica/guitar**

2:22	*Oh baby, you ain't nothing . . .*
2:43	*Oh baby, you ain't nothing . . .*
3:04	*When I was deep in love . . .*
	Fade-out.

instruments becomes almost like slow breathing. It is as though Waters inhales during the instrumental breaks and exhales each vocal phrase in one long sigh. And simply because each chorus is self-contained, in both words and music, there is little suggestion of a higher level of organization. In each chorus we are in the here and now of a particular scene.

The Elements of a Style. How do we move from one example of a blues song to a more general understanding of blues as a style? In music **style** has to do with how musicians say what they are trying to say. When the same or similar features appear in song after song, a style begins to take shape and we come to expect those features. We have discussed these aspects of the music one by one to identify them and hear them in action, but we recognize that much of the power of this performance comes from the way they work together. Change any one of them dramatically—for example, give the song a bouncy beat, swap the rhythm section for strings, or give Waters the voice of an opera singer—and the impact of the performance diminishes. From all of the preceding elements we can create a sound image—a profile of style features—early electric blues.

STYLE PROFILE

"STANDING AROUND CRYING" (EARLY ELECTRIC BLUES)

Rhythm	*Very slow tempo.*
Style beat	*Four-beat rhythm.*
Beat keeping	*Steady in drums and guitar.*

Rhythmic play	*Waters's singing is independent of the beat and has the rhythm of intensified speech.*
Melody	*In the vocal line, characterized by short phrases that start high and end low.*
Instrumentation (timbre)	*Voice, harmonica, two electric guitars (lead and rhythm), piano, drums.*
Performance style	*Waters's rough, highly inflected vocal style is matched by Little Walter's moaning harmonica and Waters's slide guitar.*
Dynamics	*Moderately loud, but limited by acoustic instruments (piano and drums).*
Harmony	*Standard blues progression (I, IV, and V chords).*
Texture	*Active, dense texture: piano high, both guitars in the middle range, along with voice; harmonica above the voice. Voice, harmonica, and guitar sing/play melody-like lines, sometimes at the same time, sometimes in call-and-response style.*
Form	*Blues.*

Key Points

Blues feeling	*Rough, inflected vocal; high-to-low melody; and slow tempo reinforce lyric.*
Blues style	*Early electric blues: electric guitar, shuffle rhythm, and free-for-all interplay.*
Blues form	*12-bar blues: rhymed couplet with first line repeated; each phrase with four bars.*

Terms to Know

12-bar blues form	call-and-response	four-beat rhythm
blues form	chorus	I, IV, and V
blues progression	electric blues	rhymed couplet

We will use this checklist throughout the book as we listen to the other music that we explore. It will help us sense connections and contrasts among songs. For example, we will next hear how Chuck Berry uses the 12-bar blues form in a song that is not blues in other respects.

CHUCK BERRY AND THE ROOTS OF ROCK AND ROLL

Sometime early in 1955, Chuck Berry (b. 1926) "motorvated" (to adapt a Chuck Berry–ism) from St. Louis to Chicago to hear Muddy Waters perform at the Palladium Theater. Waters had been Berry's idol for years, although when Berry performed with the Johnnie Johnson trio, they played many different kinds of music. After the concert Berry went backstage to meet his idol. When he asked Waters how to find a record deal, Waters suggested that he get in touch with Leonard Chess. Two weeks later Berry was back in Chicago to give Chess a demo tape with four songs. Among them was Berry's remake of a song called "Ida Red," which he titled "Maybellene." Chess liked the song, Berry recorded it, and Chess released it on August 20, 1955.

"Maybellene" caught the ear of disc jockey Alan Freed, a strong and influential supporter of rhythm and blues and the man who gave rock and roll its name. Freed had begun using *rock and roll* in 1951, while a disc jockey in Cleveland, as code for *rhythm and blues*. The term caught on after Freed moved to New York in 1954. By the time "Maybellene" was released,

CD 1:2

"Maybellene," Chuck Berry (1955). Berry, electric guitar and vocal; Willie Dixon, string bass; Johnnie Johnson, piano; Jerome Green, maracas.

rock and roll was in the air and on the charts. Freed promoted "Maybellene" by playing it frequently on his radio show. With Freed's considerable help—legend has it that he played the song for two hours straight on one broadcast—"Maybellene" quickly jumped to number 5 on the *Billboard* "Best Seller" chart.

The success of "Maybellene" was a huge breakthrough for Chess Records. Leonard Chess had done quite well in the rhythm-and-blues market, especially in Chicago and the states directly to the south. But Chess wanted to expand into the larger—and far more lucrative—pop market, and Berry was his ticket. "Maybellene" was the first of nine Top 40 hits for Berry in the 1950s. Almost overnight he replaced Muddy Waters as the most popular Chess artist.

The changing of the guard at Chess Records prompts a number of musical questions: How does Berry's music compare with Waters's? In what ways did Waters influence Berry? Why did Berry's music cross over to the pop charts? We'll keep in mind that pop success is not a strictly musical matter—in this case, Freed's influence was important to Berry's breakthrough—but we'll try to identify musical factors as well.

The Message of the Lyrics

Once again let's begin with the lyrics. Here are the words to the first three sections of the song:

Chorus	*Maybellene, why can't you be true?*
	Oh Maybellene, why can't you be true?
	You done started back doin' the things you used to do.
Verse	*As I was motorvatin' over the hill*
	I saw Maybellene in a Coupe de Ville.
	A Cadillac a-rollin' on the open road,
	Nothin'll outrun my V8 Ford.
	The Cadillac doin' 'bout ninety-five,
	She's bumper to bumper rollin' side by side.
Chorus	*Maybellene, why can't you be true?*
	Oh Maybellene, why can't you be true?
	You've started back doin' the things you used to do.

Reprinted by permission of Isalee Music.

We recognize the pattern in the first section immediately. It's one chorus of a blues lyric (a rhymed couplet with the first line repeated). The next six lines group into three rhymed couplets, but the first line of each couplet does not repeat. The third section is a restatement of the opening couplet-chorus. The rest of the lyric alternates between the opening blues chorus and six-line verses.

Although both "Standing Around Crying" and "Maybellene" use blues form, there are significant differences in each song's form and content. Whereas Waters tells his story in three blues choruses, Berry uses the opening blues chorus as a new kind of chorus. (The word *chorus* has two distinct meanings, usually depending on the type of music. In blues styles, "chorus" commonly refers to one complete statement of the melody. In many nineteenth- and twentieth-century popular styles, however, "chorus" typically refers instead to that part of the song where both words and music are repeated. In certain kinds of music, especially postwar rhythm and blues, the same section of music may illustrate both meanings of *chorus*. That is the case here.) Sandwiched between statements of the chorus is a story that unfolds in three episodes. Each such episode is a **verse**.

In a song that uses verse and chorus, the chorus typically stresses the main theme of the lyric whereas the verses tell the story. But if we read the chorus of "Maybellene," we might expect yet another tale of woe about an unfaithful woman. While it's true that Berry is chasing Maybellene, the verses are really about a car chase. We never learn anything about Maybellene except her infidelity. We learn much more about the two cars—a Cadillac Coupe de Ville and a V8 Ford—and how fast they can go than we do about their drivers, and we never find out what happens when Berry finally catches Maybellene.

The lyrics are key to the success of Berry's song. They tapped into the fifties teens' enthusiasm for cars—this was the

Chuck Berry a-reelin' and a-rockin' and a-rollin' till the break of dawn, or at least into the night. This photo was taken in 1959, just before Berry was convicted of a felony for a Mann Act violation. After he served time in jail, smiles like this were less common.

CD 1:2　　**Early Rock and Roll** (Chuck Berry; performed by Berry, electric guitar and vocal; Willie Dixon, string bass; Johnnie Johnson, piano; and Jerome Green, maracas)

0:00	Introduction. Guitar riff.
0:03	Two-beat accompaniment prominent in drums and bass guitar.

Chorus ■ 12-bar blues form

0:05	1st riff on:
0:08	*Maybellene,*
	2nd riff on:
	why can't you be true?
	Combined and modified:
	Oh Maybellene, why can't you be true?
	You done started back doin' the things you used to do.

1st Verse

0:17	Proto-rap lyric is sung mainly on one note over one chord.
	As I was motorvatin'...

Chorus ■ 12-bar blues form

0:29	Listen for the piano.
	Maybellene,...

2nd Verse

0:41	*A Cadillac pulled up...*

Chorus ■ 12-bar blues form

0:53	Listen for vocal inflection on Maybell-*ene* and *true.*
	Maybellene...

Guitar solo over two choruses (both use blues form)

1:05	Bass shifts into four-beat rhythm.
1:17	Lots of bent notes in second chorus.

Chorus ■ 12-bar blues form

1:29	Return to two-beat.
	Oh Maybellene...

3rd Verse

1:42	*The motor cooled down...*

Chorus ■ 12-bar blues form

1:54	*Maybellene,...*
2:06	Tag. Guitar riff over one chord. Fade-out.

age of the so-called hot rod, after all (think *Grease!*). And the idea of a working-class car over-taking the far more expensive car of the era made the story even more appealing. (Ironically, Chuck Berry has a warehouse filled with vintage Cadillacs in pristine condition.)

Just as appealing is the way Berry tells the story. The verse is mostly car talk—as though the lyric captured an enthusiastic conversation between two auto buffs. In addition, the lyric also contains two instances of Berry's clever wordplay. One is the title: How many women named "Maybellene" do you know? The other is *motorvatin'*, a word Berry appears to have invented just for this song and that captures its meaning by its very sound. Both words are catchy, like the rest of the lyric.

The Message of the Music

Melody is a main feature of "Maybellene." The vocal line begins with two short phrases: one is three syllables ("May-bell-ene"), the other is five ("Why can't you be true?"). Both have a lot of empty space around them and are repeated immediately. Each phrase is a **riff**—a short, distinctive melodic idea that is separated from neighboring melodic material. In this setting the riffs stand out sharply, both in the chorus and in the song as a whole, because the verse is sung mostly to a single note. By keeping the main melodic idea short and isolated, Berry makes it easy to latch on to the riff. It's one of the hooks that caught listeners back in 1955.

As in "Standing Around Crying," rhythm plays a key role in shaping the mood of the song, but here the emotional effect is just the opposite. The quick tempo of "Maybellene" underscores the breakneck driving speeds. Unlike "Standing Around Crying," "Maybellene" has a danceable beat—brisk, but danceable.

Berry uses his **guitar** as an accompanying instrument when he sings; it is part of the rhythm section. He keeps the beat by strongly marking the bass note in a pattern that alternates bass note and chord. The rest of the rhythm section emphasizes this pattern: the bassist reinforces the bass note, while the drummer raps his snare drum on the chord.

An even stronger rhythmic feature, however, is the backbeat. A **backbeat** is a sharp, percussive sound on the second part of a beat or the second of a pair of beats. Especially in the verse, the backbeat almost overwhelms the bass notes. The clear marking of beat and backbeat invests the performance with a great deal of energy, very much in keeping with the spirit of the song.

This particular pattern—alternating bass and backbeat—is a clear **two-beat rhythm**. Berry's version of a two-beat is an aggressive reworking of the two-beat rhythm heard in **honky-tonk**, a country music style popular after World War II.

The easy-to-find beat and the strong backbeat are a foil for Berry's syncopated vocal and guitar riffs. **Syncopation** is a shift of accent in a song—when an accent does not line up with the beat. An **accent** is a note or a chord that is emphasized in some way so that it stands out. Often accents stand out because they are louder or longer than the notes around them. The opening riffs of the melody—"Maybellene" and "Why can't you be true?"—are out of phase with the beat, creating a kind of rhythmic play. As with the speech rhythm that Waters uses, Berry's syncopated riffs transcend the tyranny of the beat. Earlier we discussed how the (timekeeping) beat can regulate, even control, our sense of time; it invites—almost demands —that we get in step with it. The rhythmic play present in both recordings acknowledges the beat but refuses to be bound by it. This too is a source of excitement. Teens also seemed to resonate musically with "Maybellene." A profile of the song helps us discover why.

STYLE PROFILE

"MAYBELLENE" (EARLY ROCK AND ROLL)

Rhythm	*Fast tempo; two-beat rhythm (except in guitar solo, where it shifts into a four-beat rhythm); strong backbeat; syncopation mainly in lead lines heard in vocal or guitar.*

Melody	*Chorus in short riffs; verses in long stream of notes focused around one pitch.*
Instrumentation (timbre)	*Vocals, electric guitar, bass, drums, piano (making up a full rhythm section), and maracas.*
Performance style	*Berry sings with a gritty yet light and good-natured sound. In the verse, Berry finds a middleground between song and speech by singing most of the lyric on the same note. The guitar sound has an edge plus a little country twang; bent notes in guitar solo.*
Dynamics	*Loud, considering an unamplified backup band.*
Harmony	*Blues harmony in chorus and guitar solo; one chord in verses and* **tag** *(a short section added to the end of the song).*
Texture	*Melody with strong OOM-pah accompaniment; piano and maracas layered in (entering separately).*
Form	***Verse/chorus***; *12-bar blues in the chorus frames each verse. This is an ideal format for presenting a story in music. The chorus catches our ear and keeps us focused on the main idea. The verse reduces musical interest to focus attention on the story.*

Key Points

Blues-based music	*Blues form in the chorus; bent notes on guitar.*
Country influence	*Strong honky-tonk two-beat in the chorus.*
Rock and roll edge	*Slightly distorted guitar sound.*

Terms to Know

backbeat	riff	two-beat rhythm
bent notes	syncopation	verse/chorus form
chorus	tag	

Common Elements of Muddy Waters and Chuck Berry. Let's return to the three questions we raised at the beginning of this section: How does Berry's music compare with Waters's? In what ways did Waters influence Berry? Why did Berry's music cross over to the pop charts? If we place side by side the elemental features of "Standing Around Crying" and "Maybellene," we can begin by noting the common ground in both performances:

- Lyrics tell a story about an unfaithful woman.
- Rhythm section instruments make up the bands.
- Vocals are rough-edged.
- Electric guitar lines are prominent and have an edge to their sound.
- Melodic sections have a speechlike rhythm.
- Rhythmic play occurs.
- Harmony is a blues progression.
- Form is based on the blues.

Blues-based forms were used in a lot of postwar rhythm and blues (a point explored in greater depth in Chapter 9), but the common guitar sound and the use of backup bands made up mostly of rhythm-section instruments seem to point to specific Waters influences on Berry's music.

WATERS ELECTRIC BLUES AND EARLY ROCK AND ROLL

"Standing Around Crying"	**"Maybellene"**
RHYTHM	
Very slow tempo with a clearly marked four-beat rhythm, an insistently faster rhythm in the rhythm section, and a freer rhythm in the vocal line out of phase with the beat	Quick tempo with a strong two-beat rhythm and a strongly marked beat and backbeat; syncopation in the vocal line
MELODY	
Musical sighs in the vocal lines that start high and finish low	One-note verse; distinctive melodic riffs in the chorus
INSTRUMENTATION (TIMBRE)	
Voice, electric lead guitar, harmonica, and incomplete rhythm section (rhythm guitar, drums, and piano—no bass)	Voice, electric guitar, and full rhythm section (bass, drums, and piano)
PERFORMANCE STYLE	
Rough vocal sound, slide guitar, moaning harmonica; no-frills playing, with an edge to the sound	Rough, bright, vocal sound; sharp-edged guitar sound
DYNAMICS	
Strong playing (probably loud in live performance); voice, harmonica, and lead guitar are highly inflected	Strong playing (probably loud in live performance); infrequent inflection
HARMONY	
Standard 12-bar blues progression	12-bar blues progression in chorus; one-chord verse
Dense texture, made up of many simple melodic lines woven together	Thin and bright with high-pitched maraca percussion
FORM	
12-bar blues form in lyrics and harmony	Verse/chorus with 12-bar blues in chorus

We can best explain Berry's crossover success by examining the musical differences. The biggest overall difference is in mood and attitude. Waters's song is a tale of woe, and the music echoes the despair of the lyrics. Berry's song focuses more on the chase itself than on reclaiming Maybellene. We might easily understand why Maybellene left: she is clearly playing second fiddle to the two cars. The overall mood is upbeat. The words are fun and at times funny, and the music vibrates with energy. It's easy to imagine that teens—newly empowered, crazy about cars, ready to rock and roll, and not ready for bad news—would find Berry's lyrics especially appealing.

"Maybellene" is also more musically accessible, with its catchy riffs, chorus-based form, and bright, clear beat. The song brought a fresh vocal style and guitar sound into mainstream popular music that was different and engaging. Although it didn't hurt that Alan Freed promoted the song, the success of "Maybellene" lies in the song itself.

"Standing Around Crying" is a good example of fifties electric blues style, but what about the style of "Maybellene"? It is not electric blues, although the instrumentation of the rhythm section and Berry's performance owe a lot to the electric blues style. Neither the beat (two-beat rhythms were more common to postwar country music than to blues) nor the feeling of "Maybellene" typifies the blues. But as we will discover, neither is it a full-fledged example of rock and roll as Berry's later songs are.

The song is connected to both styles. The consensus view of the relationship between blues and rock as articulated by Muddy Waters is: the blues had a baby, and they called it rock and roll. Our discussion raises the question, Who was the other parent? "Maybellene" (and other early rock-and-roll songs) suggests that country music was in on its conception. We'll encounter other influences as well—most notably other blues styles, Latin, and even pop—when we explore the rock and the rhythm and blues of the fifties and sixties in Chapters 9 and 10.

TOWARD A DEFINITION OF POPULAR MUSIC

A hit blues record of the 1950s sold about 10,000 units. A hit rhythm-and-blues song might sell 100,000 units. "Maybellene" sold more than 1 million units. (We don't know exactly how many copies were sold because the Chess brothers apparently kept sloppy books.) If we define *popular music* as appealing to a large number of people, "Maybellene" is without question popular music. By contrast "Standing Around Crying" did not sell well enough to make the R&B charts. At the time he recorded it, Waters was barely known outside the black community in Chicago and points south. Yet we know that Waters was an important influence on sixties rock—a god to the Rolling Stones, Eric Clapton, and other blues-oriented British rockers. So he and his music are definitely part of the pop music world. We can reconcile this issue by taking a multilayered view of popular music.

Popular Music Appeals to a Large Percentage of the Population. Like *blues, pop, rock,* and many other words associated with popular music, the term *popular music* has acquired several different connotations. The most obvious is "music that appeals to a large percentage of the population." But if we stop here, we run into problems. Is a CD by a classical performer popular music if it goes platinum, as some have? Is punk a popular style even though such significant punk bands as the Sex Pistols and the Ramones never hit the Top 40 in the United States? Clearly, popular music embraces more than music that sells in large numbers. Popular music embraces an attitude—indeed, a group of attitudes—a family of sounds, and an industry that supports it. We will consider all of these connotations from a historical perspective.

Popular Music Is Familiar and Widely Heard. People make choices about everything—foods, friends, homes—and it would be very surprising if they did not make choices about the music they preferred. We know that certain songs were widely known to the Greeks and the Romans. Popular songs found their way into classical compositions; Mozart, for example, wrote variations on "Twinkle, Twinkle, Little Star." Some songs became well known because they served a larger purpose. Faithful Lutherans knew Martin Luther's hymns because he set out to compose simple words and melodies that everyone could remember and sing. This is just to say, however, that a component of popular music is familiarity—still a long way from an understanding of pop music as we know it.

Popular Music Is Profitable. Popular music began to take on the trappings of business—and the component of profitability as a measuring stick—with two important developments in the eighteenth century: the growth of the middle class in Europe and America and improvements in music publishing. The emergence of a middle class, especially in England, expanded the audience who would pay for entertainment at music halls. Publishers began to offer songs, dance music, and instrumental pieces for the amateur home performer, most often a pianist—pieces that were relatively easy to play and attractive to middle-class tastes. Profitable music tended to be appealing, simple, current, and unpretentious. Then as now the audience for more-sophisticated and difficult music was significantly smaller.

Almost all of the music of the eighteenth century was current, meaning contemporary compositions written and performed for their time. The notion of "classical music," that is, the continuing performance of music of the past, was an almost negligible part of the musical landscape for most of the century.

John Gay's *The Beggar's Opera*—a play with musical numbers woven into the plot—introduced the ballad opera, one of the most popular kinds of public entertainments. At the time the most esteemed musical **genre**, or stylistic category, was **opera**, and the most prestigious opera drew its plots from classical literature and mythology. The music of *The Beggar's Opera* came from several levels of society, from popular dances and songs to classical works and parodies of them. An "opera" about the seamy side of everyday life in London—an opera that lacked the grand themes explored in mythology—was a drastic change in 1729 and proved very popular.

These qualities—appeal, simplicity, currency, and lack of pretense—are still part of the pop music world. In the eighteenth century, however, the musical difference between aristocratic music and more-common music was one of degree, not kind. All of the music used the same musical language at varying levels of complexity; publishers simplified aristocratic music to make it accessible to a broader, less sophisticated, middle-class audience. Musical differences in kind did not appear until the next century.

A major trend in early-nineteenth-century music was the publication of folksong arrangements, particularly from the British Isles. Piano manufacturers served a rapidly growing middle class that aspired to more-cultivated values; especially for young ladies, this meant playing the piano with some facility. Until well into the twentieth century, the piano was an essential piece of domestic furniture and the center of home entertainment. Families would gather together in the parlor (the current living room), and one member would play the piano while others sang the popular songs of the day. These songs became known as **parlor songs** (home songs) or **piano bench music.**

Many people learned songs from **sheet music,** the primary means of spreading popular songs until the second quarter of the twentieth century. Publishing became a lucrative part of the music business, and the promise of financial gain enticed even Beethoven into arranging Scottish and Irish folksongs. Among the most popular music arrangers in England and America was Thomas Moore, who published ten volumes of Irish melodies between 1808 and 1834—arrangements that strongly influenced songwriters. American composer Stephen Foster based his new song "Jeanie with the Light Brown Hair" on Moore's Irish style.

The folksong settings by Moore, Beethoven, and others catered to middle-class taste by cleaning up folk music and smoothing the rough edges—as if it were a farm lad who got a bath, a haircut, new clothes, and a crash course in good manners. By the time the songs reached the marketplace, they had lost their country accents and spoke the same musical language as upper-class music.

Popular Music Is a Different Sound from Classical or Folk Music. The second major trend in nineteenth-century popular music was **blackface** entertainment—that is, whites "blacking up" to portray themselves as blacks. Dating back to the eighteenth century in both the United States and England, blackface coalesced in the 1840s into **minstrelsy**, a mix of song, dance, storytelling, jokes, parodies, and just about anything else that audiences found entertaining. The music for the minstrel show derived directly from folksong and dance and, as performed onstage, kept many of the rough edges. This sound represented a real departure from published music composed or arranged for the middle-class parlor. It was different in kind—a jarring break from the established style.

It is at this point that the idea of popular music as we know it begins to take shape. It is different from classical or folk music in sound, style, attitude, purpose, and audience. In the twentieth century, through the infusion of African-derived musical values and with the continued growth of the classical music industry, the differences increased. The former fostered innovation in the search for fresh sounds, and the other tenaciously preserved the past. Today, although each crosses over to the other's market, classical and popular music represent two different sound worlds and two different esthetics.

Thus, popular music can simply be music that appeals to a mass audience, it can be music intended to have wide appeal, and it can be music with a sound and a style distinct from classical or folk. When a particular song or piece of music has all three of these qualities, it is easy to classify as popular music. "Maybellene" is a good example. It was measurably popular (it had wide sales); both Berry and the Chess brothers intended that it be popular (they were looking for a hit); and its sound was new, distinctly different from folk music or stylized classical music. (Remember that it was Berry who asked Beethoven to roll over and "tell Tchaikovsky the news.")

"Standing Around Crying" was not as popular as "Maybellene," neither in number of sales nor in its appeal to a wide audience. Nor, apparently, did Waters intend it to be. Judging by his career, Waters had little interest in changing his style to attract a larger listenership. Still, the song has a distinct sound that connected it to the popular music of the time and to the next generation. So it is in the music itself that we can make the strongest case for classifying it as popular music.

Positioning Popular Music. Popular music is usually positioned between classical music on the one hand and folk or ethnic music on the other. A three-tiered musical world has developed that corresponds roughly to the social standing of the respective audiences. Classical music is associated with the upper class; it helps sell Swiss watches and luxury cars. Popular music is for the middle class—the largest portion of the population—and helps sell fast food and trucks. Folk music has been associated with isolated, largely rural, working-class people— those cut off geographically and economically from mainstream culture—and doesn't help sell anything. Ethnic music is similar in this respect, although the isolation may have more to do with cultural identity and language than geography or economics.

Some of the most interesting music in the popular tradition has arisen from musicians' exploring the boundaries between popular and classical music on the one hand and popular and folk/ethnic music on the other. Among its many virtues, **classical music** nurtures craft; its greatest artists are extraordinarily skillful in manipulating musical materials. Craft, whether in composition or performance, can become an end in itself. Musicians develop skill because it interests them to do so and it has become necessary to the full expression of what they have to say musically. How else does one account for the extraordinary and expressive virtuosity of guitarist Eddie Van Halen (heavy metal) or trumpeter Wynton Marsalis (jazz)?

When musicians working in popular styles like heavy metal and jazz assimilate some of the values of classical music, they may deliberately forsake a larger audience to preserve their artistic vision.

The goal of folk/ethnic–popular fusions is to broaden the audience, not leave it behind. The creative concern for the folk or ethnic performer is whether to add outside elements to his or her style. Muddy Waters's blues is a clear example of how a folk artist kept the essence of his home style, even as he urbanized and updated its expression. Because the connection between folk musicians and their audience is more immediate and less influenced by market values, the bond between the music and its culture is typically stronger. Numerous folklike styles have come from disenfranchised, largely poor populations, some in rural, isolated areas and more recently in cities. Both punk and rap are folklike because they emerged in urban areas within underprivileged populations that were outside the mainstream and because the music expressed the attitudes and emotions of their respective subcultures.

Popular Music as Synthesis. The popular music **mainstream**—that is, the prevailing popular style(s)—can have either a homogenizing or an energizing effect on the creative process. An artist typically moves toward the mainstream by taking on familiar musical elements that appeal to a wider audience. This homogenization may suppress or erase altogether the artist's defining qualities. For example, in the early years of rock and roll, white artists—including Pat Boone, who sang a notoriously bland version of Little Richard's raucous "Tutti Frutti"—made numerous cover versions of rhythm-and-blues songs. Although these homogenized songs often sold better than the originals, they so diluted the music with mainstream pop elements that they sacrificed the integrity of the new sound.

Alternatively, the mainstreaming process may create an exciting new synthesis—a new sound—as when British rockers absorbed the "deep blues" of Muddy Waters and others into their music, or when both British and American musicians integrated reggae rhythms and textures into pop music during the late 1970s and early 1980s.

There are plenty of examples of how artists or groups lost their edge when they moved away from their original styles. And there are purists who bemoan any departure from authenticity. But one generation's authentic style has often resulted from a previous generation's co-opting musical material. For example, folk revivalists of the 1960s regarded the Carter Family's recording of "Wildwood Flower" as authentic folk music. The song came into the world, however, as the parlor song "I'll Twine 'Mid the Ringlets," written by Maud Irving and J. P. Webster in 1860. When it moved from the city to the hills, it lost its printed sheet music and passed from one musician to the next by ear. Its lyrics changed, and it took on elements of the folk performance style. Although it became, in effect, a folksong, it didn't start out that way.

The Central Fact of Popular Music. Such debates obscure a central fact: popular music owes its identity and its evolution to a process of creative and open-minded synthesis. From its beginnings to the present, the new sounds in popular music have emerged from the blending of different kinds of music—often so different as to be opposite musically and culturally. Popular music blurs racial, economic, geographical, cultural, and class boundaries. Ultimately, the marketplace rules, for better or worse. We encounter this synthetic process in Chapter 2 in the music for the minstrel show and in Stephen Foster's "Old Folks at Home," arguably the most popular American song of all time. And we will encounter it again and again as we move toward the present. Popular music is an ever-expanding stream, as new styles join the mix and older styles linger. The most popular music of an era serves as our rudder as we navigate the stream, but we are also interested in what the tributaries add.

LOOKING BACK, LOOKING AHEAD

We had two main objectives in this opening chapter. The first was to provide a framework and a vocabulary for talking about music. The second was to define *popular music*. The story of popular music in America unfolds in the chapters that follow. We begin the story in the 1830s, more than half a century after the United States declared independence from Great Britain. How popular music has changed in the 170-plus years from then to now is a fascinating tale with a wealth of subplots: race relations, art versus commerce, how the pop music business has invented and reinvented itself, the impact of technology, and the happy and sad stories of the people who made the music.

TERMS TO KNOW

Test your knowledge of this chapter's important terms by defining the following. If you can't recall the meaning of a certain term, refresh your memory by looking up the boldfaced term in the chapter, turning to the Glossary at the back of the book, or working with the flashcards on the *Popular Music in America* Companion Web site: *http://music.wadsworth.com/ campbell_2e*

12-bar blues form	form	piano bench music
accent	four-beat rhythm	pitch
backbeat	genre	rhymed couplet
bar	guitar	rhythm
bass	harmony	rhythm and blues (R&B)
beat	honky-tonk	rhythm section
bent note	I, IV, and V	rhythmic play
blackface	inflection	riff
blues	instrumentation	rock
blues form	intensity	rock and roll
blues progression	jazz	sheet music
bottleneck	jump band	single
call-and-response	lead guitar	slide
chord	mainstream	style
chord progression	measure	syncopation
chorus	melodic phrase	tag
classical music	melody	tempo
cover version	minstrelsy	texture
duration	opera	timbre
dynamics	parlor song	two-beat rhythm
electric blues	payola	verse
electric guitar	percussion	verse/chorus form
flute	performance style	

Popular Music in the Nineteenth Century

Meet Henry Russell (1812–1900), the Elton John of the 1830s. Like John, Russell was an English singer-pianist-songwriter who was a smashing success in the United States. And, like John, Russell was apparently rather short and stout. Their music, however, was a (new) world apart.

HIGH-BROW, LOW-BROW IN AMERICA DURING THE EARLY NINETEENTH CENTURY

America declared political independence from Great Britain in 1776. Cultural independence in art, theater, literature, and especially music took quite a bit longer. Virtually all of the commercially produced music one might hear in the United States during the first decades of the nineteenth century came directly or indirectly from the British Isles: orchestral, **opera**, and choral music in public performance; music published for home performance; and hymnals for church use. So did much of the folk music, especially in the Appalachians.

America was mostly wilderness at the beginning of the 1800s. In 1790, New York, then as now the largest city in the country, had a population of about 33,000 people. By 1840 its population had grown almost ten times to about 312,000. The next-largest cities, Baltimore and New Orleans, had populations of just over 100,000. America remained mostly rural until well into the twentieth century, but its cities grew, and a cultural divide developed between the largely urban, literate, middle and upper classes and the poorly educated, less mannered, lower classes of city slums and rural counties. All forms of entertainment, including music, reflected this gulf. During the nineteenth century, the distinction was commonly expressed as *high-brow* (urban and cultivated) versus *low-brow* (rural and **vernacular**). Both the terms and the cultural division they identify persist into our own time.

Urban Music

From colonial times through the 1830s, the vocal music for the most discriminating audiences was Italian opera, Handel oratorios (like *Messiah*), and German *lieder* (art songs). Adaptations of opera **arias** with English texts and **sheet music** collections of folksongs from the British Isles, such as Moore's *Irish Melodies* and Robert Burns's Scottish songs (we still sing "Auld Lang Syne" once a year), found a wider audience in a less sophisticated but growing middle class.

Almost all of this music spoke the same musical language. Many of the most popular songs published in the United States before the Civil War differed from European opera arias more in difficulty and sophistication than in style. A genuinely American popular music had yet to appear.

Henry Russell. Having studied with three of the most important opera composers of the day —Gioacchino Rossini, Vincenzo Bellini, and Gaetano Donizetti—(or so he claimed), Henry Russell came to the United States in 1833. After hearing politician Henry Clay deliver a speech that left the audience spellbound, Russell decided to compose songs that would similarly enthrall his audiences. From 1837 through 1841, singing mainly his own songs, he toured the United States. He returned to England in 1845.

Russell's first big hit was "Woodman, Spare That Tree," published in 1837. A simplified version of the classical operatic style of his teachers, Russell's song evidenced the approach that brought him fame and success: the music sounded high-class, yet it was accessible. The instrumentation was voice and piano; the melody proceeded in regular phrases, flowing smoothly with only the occasional expressive leap; and the tempo was stately. As a result, the style resonated with cultivated audiences.

In the lyric, a poem written in 1830 by journalist George Pope Morris, the narrator begs a woodman not to chop down a tree under which he and his family played and rested when they were young. The song was the kind of sentimental, nostalgic journey into the past that audiences of the time craved.

Russell liked to tell the story of one performance of the song. After he had finished singing, an old gentleman, obviously moved by Russell's account, stood up, demanded silence, and said, "Mr. Russell, in the name of Heaven, tell me, was the tree spared?" When told that it was, the man said, "Thank God! Thank God! I breathe again!"

Rural Music: Anglo-American Folk Music

From colonial times most emigrants to the United States, drawn by the opportunity to own land in a vast new nation, found their way into rural areas. Some put down roots in the Appalachian Mountains that run from New England to the Carolinas. Most lost contact with the more-urban parts of the country. The world was their hollow or valley. Travel, especially in the mountainous regions, was difficult; often there were neither roads nor train service. There was no mass communication as we know it, only newspapers, which would have been of little value because most immigrants were illiterate. Families lived in the same area for many generations. The ancestors of Ben Jarrell, the fiddler whom we'll hear shortly, were in western North Carolina by the beginning of the nineteenth century.

These **Anglo-American** settlers from England, Ireland, and Scotland brought their music with them: fiddle tunes, songs, dances, and ballads. They passed on their music by ear: a child would hear her mother sing a song; a neighbor would learn a jig from the local fiddler. They made their own instruments and taught themselves how to play them. Over time the songs and dances evolved as musicians changed the details of the story or modified the melody, adding, subtracting, or altering parts of the tunes. One famous song, "Barbara Allen," which London diarist Samuel Pepys mentioned as early as 1665, survived into the twentieth century in countless versions, with almost a hundred variations documented in Virginia alone.

We have no direct evidence of how this folk music might have sounded. Still, because folk musicians like Jarrell were so isolated from change beyond their valley, and because they most likely passed their style of fiddle playing and singing from one generation to the next, we have good reason to believe that the sounds of early country music recordings are close to how such music would have sounded a century before. In a 1927 recording, we hear Ben Jarrell on the fiddle. His son, Tommy Jarrell, one of the most famous old-time fiddlers, sounds much like his father.

"Old Joe Clark," recorded in 1927, is a **breakdown**, an up-tempo fiddle tune for dancing. The tune had been around for generations when someone added words about Joe Clark, a rough-and-tumble store owner, Civil War veteran, and moonshiner (a person who makes his own liquor and sells it illegally). By the time Jarrell recorded it, the song existed in hundreds of versions (much like "Barbara Allen"). This version is one of the most humorous.

"Old Joe Clark" communicates directly, with skill but without artifice. The **chorus** ("Old Joe Clark . . .") alternates with a series of **verses**. Sometimes fiddle and banjo play the melodies of verse and chorus; at other times the singer carries the tune. The text paints an unflattering picture of "Betsy Brown," the female subject of the song. The instrumentation is voice, **fiddle**, and **banjo**. The vocal quality is nasal, and the fiddle has a scratchy, raw sound. This is music for the barn dance, not the concert stage.

STYLE PROFILE

BREAKDOWN

Rhythm	*Fast tempo, with active rhythms in both instruments; banjo and fiddle add extra notes to the melody or play* **drone notes** *to keep a steady stream of fast-flowing notes; no significant rhythmic play.*
Melody	*A two-phrase melody, repeated many times; both phrases are of moderate length; instrumental versions of the melody are elaborated with extra notes; uses* **modal** *scale in verse.*
Instrumentation (timbre)	*Voice, fiddle, and banjo.*
Performance style	*Nasal mountain twang in singing style; rough fiddle playing (not refined violin).*
Dynamics	*Moderately loud throughout (no amplification).*
Harmony	*None—there are no chords; voice and instruments perform different versions of the melody.*
Texture	*Jarrell and Jenkins play different versions of the melody simultaneously (heterophonic texture); there is no harmony.*
Form	***Verse/chorus.***

Key Points

Danceable song	*Dance music with a singable melody.*
Down-home lyrics	*Unsentimental, fun lyrics; the opposite of the parlor song.*
Verse/chorus form	*Verse = new words/same tune; chorus = same words and tune.*
Modal scale	*A seven-note* **scale** *different from scales used in other songs from this time.*

Terms to Know

banjo	drone notes	scale
breakdown	fiddle	verse
chorus	modal	verse/chorus form

CD 1:3   Breakdown (Traditional; performed by Ben Jarrell, vocal and fiddle; and Frank Jenkins, banjo)

Chorus ■ AA Instrumental

0:00	1st phrase
0:04	Repetition of 1st phrase, with a slightly different ending.
0:08	Chorus repeats; fiddle and banjo play different versions of melody.

1st Verse ■ B

0:15	Nasal twang in voice; modal scale.
0:04	*I went to see . . .*

Chorus ■ A

0:23	*Fare ye well, . . .*

1st Instrumental Interlude ■ A/BB/AA

0:30	A	Chorus.
0:37	BB	Verse played twice.
0:52	AA	Chorus played twice.

2nd Verse ■ B

1:07	*Never marry . . .*

Chorus ■ A

1:14	*Fare ye well, . . .*

2nd Instrumental Interlude ■ AA/BB

1:21	AA	Instrumental chorus, played twice.
1:36	BB	Verse played twice.

Chorus ■ AA Vocal, then instrumental

1:50	*Fare ye well, . . .*
1:58	Instrumental chorus.

3rd Verse ■ B

2:05	*Old Joe Clarks a . . .*

Chorus ■ AA Vocal, then instrumental

2:13	*Fare ye well, . . .*
2:20	Instrumental chorus.
2:27	Instrumental verse, then chorus.

Summary

Throughout most of the nineteenth century, a cultural gulf separated cultivated popular music ("Woodman, Spare That Tree") from vernacular music ("Old Joe Clark"). This gulf had to do with social standing, literacy, breeding, and taste. Middle- and upper-class society would have found both a rough-edged song like "Old Joe Clark" and its performers to be unacceptable. Its nasal singing style and the instrumentation would remain the exclusive property of folk and country music; but its fast tempo suggesting a dance rhythm, more-colloquial language, and the form of a recurring chorus found their way into nineteenth-century popular song. The new popular style would draw from both cultivated and vernacular traditions.

THE BIRTH OF AMERICAN POPULAR MUSIC

Minstrelsy was an American entertainment that set in motion the first revolution in American popular music. The songs of the early minstrel show, accompanied by scratchy fiddles and clacking **bones** (a folk percussion instrument), introduced new sounds with vitality, humor, and a lack of pretension. The introduction of these folk elements in a crude, unwashed form was its most revolutionary aspect.

If the revolution had been confined to just the minstrel show, however, it wouldn't have been much of a revolution. What made it far-reaching was the way in which the most popular minstrel songs wove themselves into the fabric of American life. Contemporary accounts tell us how everyone seemed to know and sing such Stephen Foster songs as "Oh! Susanna" (1848) and "Camptown Races" (1850). People couldn't seem to get enough of them. Dan Emmett's "Dixie," introduced in 1859 in a minstrel show, spread like wildfire through the South and quickly became the rallying cry of the Confederacy in the upcoming Civil War.

Two qualities distinguished the new songs: they were surpassingly popular, and they sounded homegrown. This represented a real shift in style. These were songs by Americans, with a recognizably American accent, that were better known to many Americans than almost any other songs. European music would continue to exert considerable influence on American popular music for the rest of the century, but with the minstrel songs of Foster, Emmett, and others, a distinctly American popular-song tradition took root in the 1800s and would flower in the next century.

America's Emerging Identity

The minstrel show and the beginnings of American popular song in the 1840s and 1850s constituted one aspect of a three-decade-long cultural awakening. It began in 1828 with the election of Andrew Jackson—the first so-called people's president. The previous six presidents had come from America's "first families" and were wealthy, well-educated easterners. Jackson, the orphan son of a poor North Carolina frontier family, was largely self-educated and self-made. He won the election primarily with support from the South and the West, where many shared his distrust of the eastern establishment.

Blackface entertainment—that is, entertainment using performers who smeared burnt cork on their faces to portray themselves as blacks—reflected these new Jacksonian values. It was informal, high-spirited, vigorous, and full of humor, bringing a breath of fresh air into the stuffy Victorian parlors of the nineteenth century. But it was also crude and cruel in its stereotyped portrayal of a racial minority. Americans have always shown contempt for the immigrant, and from the years of minstrelsy to the 1960s, ethnic and racial stereotyping was part of the entertainment world. Blacks, of course, were the most prominent target, but every ethnic or immigrant group was portrayed in caricature on-stage: Jews, Italians, Germans, French, Chinese, and others. Minstrelsy represented the best and the worst of this new American populism.

The decades before the Civil War also saw the beginning of the Industrial Revolution in the United States. Fed by cheap immigrant labor, industry grew rapidly as companies established themselves to manufacture the host of inventions and improvements in American lives. Trains and steamboats made travel easier, Samuel Morse's telegraph made rapid communication possible, and John Deere's plow and Cyrus McCormick's reaper (1831) helped settle the prairie. One industry in particular affected the music business: piano making.

In 1825 Alpheus Babcock patented a one-piece iron frame that made it possible to increase string tension and resulted in a richer, more projecting tone. Henry Steinway's new cross-strung metal frames, introduced in the 1850s, all but completed this most important development in the evolution of the modern piano. Pianos and sheet music spread widely to the parlors of the middle class, and popular music—the songs of Stephen Foster and others—moved into the home.

The Early Minstrel Show

The first minstrel show—billed as an "Ethiopian Concert"—took place in Boston in February 1843. It featured the Virginia Minstrels, four veteran blackface performers, none of whom were from the South. These all-around entertainers sang, danced, and played fiddle, banjo, **tambourine**, and bones, and their first evening of entertainment was an immediate success. Following their lead—and hoping to match their success—other minstrel troupes formed almost overnight. Within a few years, troupes crisscrossed the country, and many cities had their own resident troupe. The size of the minstrel troupe also grew (and would continue to grow after the Civil War). Christy's Minstrels, formed in 1844, soon added other performers and then an orchestra.

It is difficult to give a precise description of the minstrel show because it lacked a consistent form and evolved so quickly. In the twenty years prior to the Civil War, minstrelsy developed from small-group acts to a full evening's entertainment with a large troupe and orchestral accompaniment. Audiences at the early minstrel shows were the forerunners of today's raucous rock-concert or soccer-match crowds. Rowdy patrons provoked "minstrel programs [to list] 'Rules of Hall,' which pleaded with the audience not to whistle during the performances and not to beat time with their feet."

The show by its very nature was loosely structured (and remained loose even as the size of the troupe grew). There were at least three minstrels: the **interlocutor** and the two endmen, **Tambo and Bones**, so named for the tambourine and the bones that they played. The troupe sat in a semicircle, with the interlocutor in the center and the **endmen** at either side. The rest of the troupe filled the circle. There was no plot or storyline, although there were stock routines and consistent characters. The subject matter provided the continuity in a string of comic exchanges between the interlocutor, who spoke with a resonant voice, proper diction, and a rich vocabulary (think cultivated here), and the endmen, who spoke in an exaggerated African American speech (think vernacular). These exchanges bonded together a varied assortment of songs and dances. The interlocutor controlled the pacing of the show. According to the mood and the response of the audience, he would allow routines to continue or cut them off.

The first minstrel shows simply strung together into a full-length show various routines about the two most popular blackface characters. The opening section portrayed the city slicker, and the closing section portrayed the country bumpkin. Although stage impersonation of African Americans predated the American Revolution, these stereotypes began with George Washington Dixon, who first introduced them on-stage in New York in 1827.

1st Statement of Complete Song

0:00   Instrumental.

2nd Statement

0:25   A   1st chorus
            Vocal, in harmony.
            Hi row, . . .

0:32   B   Verse
            Listen for the descending five notes of the song's pentatonic scale in the 2nd and 4th lines.
            1. De boatman dance . . .
            2. De boatman up . . .
            3. And when de boatman . . .
            4. He spends his cash . . .

0:40   C   2nd chorus
            Vocal, in unison.
            Notice how 1st and 2nd choruses bracket the verse.
            Den dance, . . .

3rd Statement

0:48   A   *Hi row, . . .*
0:55   B   *Wen on board . . .*
1:03   C   *Den dance, . . .*

The country bumpkin was the first to acquire a name. In 1832, Thomas Dartmouth Rice observed (or claimed to have observed) an African American street entertainer in Cincinnati doing a song and dance with a peculiar hop step, which he called "jumping Jim Crow." He copied the man's routine and introduced it on-stage shortly thereafter with great success.

The city counterpart acquired a name two years later, when in 1834 Bob Farrell, another blackface entertainer, introduced the song "Zip Coon" on-stage. With the success of Farrell's portrayal, the two stock characters of the minstrel show were in place: Zip Coon was the urban dandy, and Jim Crow was the naive, uneducated slave.

Within a few years, the show had grown into three distinct parts. The opening section alternated highly ritualized minstrel material with a balladeer singing popular parlor songs. The second section, called the **olio** (an Anglicization of the Spanish word *olla* for "stew"), was the variety portion of the show and featured a wide range of acts. Many of these were novelty routines; others were **burlesques** (humorous parodies) of cultivated material—Shakespeare's plays or Italian operas, for example. The final section was an extended skit. Originally based on idealized plantation life, the skits later became topical comedy sketches. The show concluded with a **walkaround**, which featured the entire minstrel troupe in a grand finale of song and dance.

Dan Emmett. Dan Emmett's "De Boatmen's Dance," heard here in a contemporary performance by Robert Winans, illustrates the sound of early minstrel show music. Emmett (1815–1904) was a blackface entertainer in the 1830s and one of the founding members of

4th Statement

1:10   Instrumental version of complete song.

5th Statement

1:31   A   *Hi row,...*
1:40   B   *When de boatman...*
1:48   C   *Den dance,...*

6th Statement

1:56   A   *Hi row,...*
2:03   B   *De boatman is a...*
2:11   C   *Den dance,...*

7th Statement

2:18   Instrumental version of the melody.

8th Statement

2:41   A   *Hi row,...*
          B   *When you go to de...*
          C   *Den dance,...*

9th Statement

3:04   A   Vocal.
3:11   BC   Instrumental.

the Virginia Minstrels. He also composed (or adapted from folk repertory) a number of songs for the minstrel show, including "Dixie." Among his contemporaries, only Foster surpassed him as a minstrel show songwriter. "De Boatmen's Dance" was one of the songs in the first Virginia Minstrels show in 1843.

Even a quick first impression makes clear the affinity between "De Boatmen's Dance" and Ben Jarrell's "Old Joe Clark." Both have lyrics that describe a series of "scenes" in down-home language. They share the same instrumental nucleus—voice, fiddle, and banjo—an upbeat tempo with a clear beat, alternation of singing and playing the melody, and a form that alternates verse and chorus. In this song there are two choruses: one is sung in harmony, the other in **unison**—that is, more than one voice and/or instrument performs the same melody. The use of a chorus, in which both words and music are repeated again and again, would become more common in popular music after the Civil War, when songwriters and publishers deliberately set out to create popular songs.

It is easy to imagine the song supporting action on-stage as the troupe acts out the scenes described in the song or simply dances. Perhaps the most crucial difference between "Old Joe Clark" and "De Boatmen's Dance" is the latter's use of harmony. Clearest in the chorus and implicit throughout the rest of the song, the use of harmony connects "De Boatmen's Dance" to the cultivated parlor songs of the period. This addition of urban harmony to folk content and rhythm created a mix with a different sound and attitude. So did the use of African American images and sounds.

CD 1:4

"De Boatmen's Dance," Dan Emmett (1843). Robert Winans, vocal.

STYLE PROFILE

MINSTREL SHOW SONG

Rhythm	*Bright, steady tempo; fast rhythms in banjo; syncopated patterns in fiddle and bones; quick-paced vocal line.*
Melody	*Simple, three-phrase melody based on **pentatonic** (five-note) **scale**. The last phrase (the chorus) is the simplest and catchiest.*
Instrumentation (timbre)	*Voices, fiddle, banjo, tambourine, and bones.*
Performance style	*Down-home, up to a point. (This recording is a modern re-creation of the song as it might have been sung by a minstrel show troupe. The performance is probably not as rough and ready as the original would have been.)*
Dynamics	*Moderately loud, with little nuance.*
Harmony	*Simple: all I-IV-V.*
Texture	*Some harmony in the first segment of the chorus; otherwise, voices and pitched instruments sing and play different versions of the melody.*
Form	*Verse/chorus.*

Key Points

For stage entertainment	*Song is part of an all-around show, with singing, dancing, and joke-telling.*
Chorus-based form	*Two refrains: one at the beginning and one at the end of each melody statement.*
Dance rhythms	*Song uses a bright dance rhythm.*
Minstrel show lyrics	*Pale imitation of black speech brings earthier element into popular song.*

Terms to Know

banjo	chorus	tambourine
bones	fiddle	

Black Faces and Black Sounds. Without question African American music influenced the sound of early minstrel performers. Bones and tambourine formed the first "rhythm section," and the banjo developed from African instruments. But the music of minstrel songs had little relation to authentic African American music; in fact, it had much more in common with the folk music of rural settlers, and many minstrel songs passed into the oral tradition of country music. "Zip Coon," for example, became the fiddle tune "Turkey in the Straw." The song lyrics were not authentic either, but were written in pseudo-dialect. A line from "Zip Coon" shows the inconsistency in language: "I went the udder arter noon to take a dish ob tea." Some words are in alleged dialect; others remain unchanged.

Although it is clear from drawings and accounts of the period that at least some white minstrels keenly observed the appearance, speech, and dancing of black Americans, "Jim Crow," "Zip Coon," and other minstrel songs were in fact crude parodies of the African American life that minstrels attempted to capture in song and dance. In the years before the Civil War, minstrel performers had only incidental contact with the African Americans—and the African American music—whom they supposedly portrayed. Most minstrel troupes resided permanently in northeastern cities—New York especially—that were far from southern plantations.

There is compelling, if indirect, evidence to suggest that white minstrels did not capture the *quality* of African American music making. After the Civil War, performances by black minstrels were far more successful than the white minstrel shows, and white minstrels all but conceded to black Americans the right to perform the traditional minstrel show.

"De Boatmen's Dance" was popular music for mass audiences (low-brow taste); "Wood-man, Spare That Tree" was a popular song for the cultivated audience (high-brow). At the time, the two were worlds apart, but we hear them come together in the next song, arguably the most popular American song of all time.

Stephen Foster and the Development of a New American Style

Stephen Foster (1826–1864) was the most important songwriter in nineteenth-century American popular music. He was versatile and skillful, and his songs were well written and often inspiring and innovative. Success came early with minstrel tunes like "Oh, Susanna" and "Camptown Races," which remain popular to this day. Particularly in the 1850s, at the apex of his career, Foster was a composer of real skill. His best songs far outshine the work of his contemporaries and successors. The relative simplicity of his style came about by choice, not default, as he sought to create a specifically popular style. From the beginning of his career in the mid-1840s, he was equally active composing for the minstrel stage and the parlor.

Intended primarily for home entertainment, **parlor songs** were simple, genteel songs for voice and piano, simple in both melody and accompaniment so that amateur musicians could play them. It is a safe bet that the stack of sheet music on the piano in the parlor of the 1860s included a copy of Stephen Foster's "Jeanie with the Light Brown Hair" or "Beautiful Dreamer."

By contrast, the more respectable members of American society looked down their noses at "the Ethiopian business." They considered the early minstrel show and anything associated with it to be low-class entertainment, even while some patronized the shows. John Sullivan Dwight, whose *Journal of Music* served as the semiofficial arbiter of good taste among the cultivated, admitted that "Old Folks at Home" was popular but likened

---

LISTENING GUIDE: "OLD FOLKS AT HOME"

CD 1:5 **Plantation Song** (Stephen Foster; performed by Richard Lalli, vocal; and Michael Campbell, piano)

0:00	Piano introduction.
0:18	1st verse, 1st phrase
	The melody is pentatonic, based on a five-note scale.
	Way down upon de . . .
0:36	1st phrase repeated, with different words. The notes of the pentatonic scale are numbered by syllable.
	All [3] up [2] and [1] down [3] de [2] whole
	[1] cre- [1 (high)] a- [5] tion, [1 (high)]
	Sad- [4] ly [3] I [1] roam [2] . . .
0:55	Chorus
	All de world . . .
1:18	Piano interlude.
1:37	2nd verse
	All round de . . .
1:56	*When I was . . .*
2:16	Chorus
	All de world . . .
2:41	Piano postlude.

Foster's song to a "morbid irritation of the skin." As it turned out, Foster's minstrel show songs were the clearest signal that a distinctive new musical style, one that was both popular and American, had emerged. His songs have remained part of our collective memory for almost a century and a half, while much of the more-genteel music that Dwight championed is long forgotten.

Foster's Plantation Songs. Stephen Foster's most significant innovation was the creation of a new popular genre, the plantation song. The **plantation song** was a hybrid: in songs like "Old Folks at Home," Foster merged the minstrel show and parlor song styles.

The music finds a middle ground between the minstrel show and the parlor, as the Style Profile makes evident.

STYLE PROFILE

PLANTATION SONG

Rhythm	*Moderately slow tempo; simple beat keeping in piano accompaniment.*
Melody	*Long, flowing lines, forming three big sighs that reach a peak early, then gradually descend; melody derived from pentatonic scale.*
Instrumentation (timbre)	*Voice and piano.*
Performance style	*Variable; this performance is from the sheet music; in the **oral tradition**, it was performed in countless ways.*
Dynamics	*Moderate.*
Harmony	*Simple tonal harmony: only I-IV-V.*
Texture	*Melody plus accompaniment.*
Form	*Verse/chorus.*

Key Points

Plantation song	*Parlor song sentiment + minstrel show theme = plantation song.*
Pentatonic scale	*Used here, as in both Irish and minstrel show songs.*
Focus on melody	*Simple but distinctive melody; no dance rhythm underneath.*

Terms to Know

oral tradition

plantation song

Foster's Legacy. Foster left an enduring musical legacy. His work, and especially his minstrel and plantation songs, was influential and widely known. Much of it is memorable, and many songs remain familiar after 150 years. Two are official state songs—for Florida and Kentucky. No other nineteenth-century American songwriter comes close to him in esteem or influence.

The minstrel show was the catalyst for the development of an American popular-song tradition, but it was Stephen Foster who, almost single-handedly, created the tradition. Before minstrelsy there had been popular music in America, but after its emergence there was a genuinely *American* popular music. Because of Foster's musical inspiration and his instinct for the middle ground between styles, his songs transcended class boundaries. They became familiar to many Americans and were recognized as American outside of the United States.

Unfortunately, Foster's death in 1864 at age thirty-eight sapped the musical revolution of its energy. No one was musically equipped to replace him.

African American Entertainers After the Civil War

Before the Civil War, it had been almost impossible for African Americans to perform professionally, as minstrels or in any other capacity. There were isolated instances of black minstrel troupes in the 1850s, but they enjoyed limited success. After the Civil War, however, black Americans found two main outlets for their talents: jubilee choirs and the minstrel show.

Jubilee Choirs. Jubilee choirs were a success born of desperation. In 1871 a group of students from the newly formed Fisk University in Nashville, Tennessee, set out on a tour of the North to raise money for their school. Along the way their director, George L. White, named them the Fisk Jubilee Singers to distinguish them from minstrel troupes. In their concerts the Fisk Jubilee Singers performed **spirituals**—African American religious songs—as well as popular songs of the day. A successful appearance at Gilmore's 1872 World Peace Jubilee in Boston made the group's reputation. Although singing groups from other black colleges and professional choirs soon followed in their wake, jubilee choirs were a peripheral part of the popular-music world even during their heyday. Overall, the minstrel show provided much greater opportunities for African American performers, and black minstrels began to have a commercial and musical impact.

African American Minstrels. Minstrel shows co-opted the spiritual almost immediately, integrating it into the scenes of plantation life. According to American music scholar Charles Hamm, "From 1875, ensemble numbers featuring the entire cast singing pseudo-religious songs regularly opened and closed the performances of many minstrel troupes." A new kind of song, the **minstrel-spiritual**, grew out of the assimilation of the spiritual into the minstrel show. Its most distinguishing feature was the occasional use of **call-and-response**. The minstrel-spiritual was the most important new song style of the 1870s and 1880s.

When black minstrel troupes took the stage right after the end of the Civil War, they were popular from the start, drawing crowds as big as, or bigger than, the white troupes did. During the 1870s there were at least twenty-eight professional African American minstrel troupes, none more successful than the one owned by Charles Callendar, a tavern owner turned entrepreneur. Callendar's Georgia Minstrels (in the minstrel show, at least, *Georgia* was synonymous with *colored*) was the best-known black minstrel troupe of the decade.

The presumed authenticity of African American troupes was a large part of their appeal. Even as the white minstrel show moved away from "the Ethiopian entertainments" of early minstrelsy, black minstrel shows, ironically enough, stayed closer to the original. Promoters billed African American performers as **delineators**, or authentic portrayers of plantation life. Rather than compete, white performers chose to move away from the stereotypes. Although blacks were certainly capable of portraying plantation life more accurately than whites, to satisfy white audiences they had to perpetuate the stereotypes created by white blackface performers.

These stereotypes even extended to their appearance. Bert Williams, the great African American vaudeville performer of the early twentieth century, complained that he and other black performers had to appear in blackface so that they looked the way white people thought they should. As the lingering stereotypes suggest, the minstrel show changed very little in sentiment following the Civil War. Postwar minstrel-song lyrics suggest that the Civil War did little to foster more-realistic and enlightened racial perceptions among minstrels, songwriters, and their audiences. Lyrics continued to portray the lives of African Americans during slavery as idyllic. The "happy darkie" myth had considerable staying power.

James Bland. Of all the black minstrels, James Bland (1854–1911) left the most enduring legacy. Although famous as a performer, singer, comedian, and banjoist during the 1870s and 1880s, he is best remembered as a songwriter. Bland was the most successful composer of minstrel songs after Stephen Foster and the first African American songwriter to achieve commercial success. Like Foster before him, Bland was fluent in all the popular styles of the day. His most famous song, "Carry Me Back to Old Virginny," became the Virginia state song in 1940. Unlike most of the black artists discussed in this book, however, Bland's African heritage had no evident impact on his musical style.

Sheet-music covers of minstrel songs and, later, so-called coon songs pictured African Americans in exaggerated caricatures. One particularly interesting cover has both a realistic portrait of black songwriter James Bland and an imaginary scene of African Americans singing, dancing, and praying. There was a huge gap between whites' perception of African Americans and the reality of their persons and lives. Whites, at least those involved with the minstrel show, made no apparent effort to close that gap.

Despite continuing indignities on- and off-stage, the minstrel show gave African American performers, according to Eileen Southern, "their first large-scale entrance into show business." W. C. Handy, himself a minstrel in the 1890s, noted that "All the best [African American] talent of that generation came down the same drain. The composers, the singers, the musicians, the speakers, the stage performers—the minstrel show got them all."

Coon Songs. The late-nineteenth-century minstrel show created a vogue not only for the cake-walk, which we discuss later, but also for the **coon song**. There had been coon songs in the minstrel show prior to 1890, but the genre reached its peak in mid-decade with the popularity of such songs as May Irwin's "Bully Song" and "All Coons Look Alike to Me," written by black minstrel star Ernest Hogan.

Hogan was the Randy Newman of the 1890s: both wrote songs that were too easily misunderstood as prejudiced. In the 1970s listeners misinterpreted Newman's "Short People" as an attack on short people, rather than an attack on those who scorn them. Likewise, today's readers could misinterpret Hogan's title. In fact, the lyrics of the song are romantic in tone; they describe a young man who has eyes for only one girl; all other girls "look alike" to him.

Coon songs of the 1890s gently introduced syncopation into popular song; the piano accompaniment of Hogan's "All Coons Look Alike to Me" anticipates the style of piano ragtime. Coon songs evolved smoothly into the ragtime songs of the 1900s.

The Legacy of the Minstrel Show. The minstrel show was America's first indigenous popular music and its first musical export. It brought a freshness to America's cultural life. Because of this it is doubly unfortunate that its most indelible image is its demeaning stereotypes of African Americans. Minstrelsy cultivated prejudice and ignorance in some and reinforced it in others. Still, the positive contributions of the minstrel show include four important firsts, all of which figure prominently in subsequent generations of popular music:

- It was entertainment for the masses. Its primary purpose was to entertain, not uplift or educate.
- It made use of vernacular speech and music. Members of the upper class (lawyers, doctors, politicians, and the like) of both races were among minstrels' favorite targets for parody, assigning to the northern African Americans malapropisms and bad grammar and to the whites a shifty, sly craftiness—and ridiculing both for their pretensions.
- The music of the minstrel show introduced a synthesis of the middle-class urban song (derived from European classical) and folk music. The process of forging a new style

from several, often dissimilar, sources would become a trademark of American popular music.

o The minstrel show was the first instance of a pattern in American popular music that has continued to the present day: the periodic infusion of energetic, often danceable music that invigorated the popular mainstream.

DIVERSITY IN POPULAR STAGE ENTERTAINMENT AFTER THE CIVIL WAR

Stage entertainment with music exploded after the Civil War. The spark came from the minstrel show, whose appeal made it clear that there was a market for popular entertainment. Improvements in everyday life, from elevated trains in cities to electric lights in theaters and streets, made it easier to draw audiences and made the theaters safer venues. And the potential audience grew dramatically as immigrants from all over Europe poured into the United States. In just a few decades, stage entertainment with popular music went from a happy accident to a significant industry.

By 1870 three entertainment genres incorporated popular music: the minstrel show, vaudeville, and musical comedy. Musical theater historian Gerald Mast suggests that the three new forms of stage entertainment that became popular after the war grew out of the three independent sections of the prewar minstrel show. In his view the opening section became the black minstrel show of the 1880s and 1890s, the olio transformed into vaudeville, and the half-hour sketches grew into full-length musical comedies.

A grand scale became a bigtime preoccupation. At least some of the productions were gargantuan spectaculars, featuring huge casts and lasting for several hours. In this respect they were in step with American attitudes of the time. In the late 1800s, Americans admired bigness, whether it was the tallest building, the personal fortune of a Rockefeller or a Carnegie, or one of Patrick Gilmore's colossal band spectaculars (which we discuss later in this chapter).

Vaudeville, which began directly after the Civil War, grew quickly from a small-scale variety show into the most popular form of stage entertainment from the 1880s through the 1920s. The minstrel show diversified with the entry of African Americans into professional entertainment. And by most accounts, the first American musical comedy was staged in 1866, marking the beginning of the most enduring form of stage show.

Vaudeville

Vaudeville was a variety show, pure and simple. It featured a series of acts—singers, dancers, comics, acrobats, magicians, jugglers, and the like—without any pretense of dramatic unity. Acts came on-stage, did their routines, and left, not to return for the rest of the show.

Vaudeville had its roots in New York City. Tony Pastor, a performer turned promoter, opened Tony Pastor's Opera House in New York's Bowery section in 1865. It flourished, and by the time he opened another theater farther uptown on 14th Street in 1881, his was one of many vaudeville houses in New York. Vaudeville quickly became much more than a local phenomenon. Chains of theaters, managed by impresarios like B. F. Keith and E. F. Albee, created a touring circuit of major cities across the country. In the decades around the turn of the century, vaudeville replaced the minstrel show as the most popular form of live entertainment in the United States. It remained popular until about 1930, when the

Great Depression made times hard for its audience, and radio and talking films became cheaper alternatives. Although vaudeville was not exclusively musical entertainment, it was a major performing outlet for popular song.

The Revue

The slow demise of the minstrel show at the end of the nineteenth century created a void for a breezy, loosely jointed show with lots of song and dance and a skimpy plot to hold it all together. The public craved shows that were topical, upbeat, aimed at the masses, and full of comedy, song, and dance. The **revue** filled that void for more than twenty-five years.

Florenz Ziegfeld's *Follies of 1907* put the American revue on the track that it would follow for the next two decades. Ziegfeld, the greatest theater impresario of the era and the self-styled "glorifier of the American girl," combined promotional acumen, an eye for talent, and a sharp sense of public taste. His shows featured the top comics and singers of the day, along with lots of female dancers, dressed as revealingly as public taste would allow. Unlike earlier revues, Ziegfeld's *Follies* had a **libretto**, or script (however flimsy)—a believable story line was not the focal point of the show.

The "Follies" title had two connotations: it evoked the French Folies Bergére with its leggy female dancers, and it referred to the foolish actions of the famous people of the day. Ziegfeld's shows lampooned celebrities, politicians, rich businessmen, and stars, rather than the stock ethnic stereotypes. Perhaps unconsciously reflecting the reform spirit in the air and his own ethnic background, Ziegfeld's shows moved away from comedy based on crude parodies toward a more sophisticated kind of humor.

Beyond Minstrelsy. Bert Williams joined the *Ziegfeld Follies* in 1909. A year later he was one of the headliners in Ziegfeld's enormously popular revue, and he remained one of its stars until 1919. Williams's stardom gave evidence of the gradual, if often grudging, acceptance of black performers into show business. But around 1900 African Americans in entertainment faced good news and bad. The bad news was the decline of the minstrel show, which put many black performers out of work. The good news was the greater range of opportunities. Many of the leading African American minstrel performers, like Bert Williams and Ernest Hogan, found work in vaudeville, musical comedy, and revues.

An African American vaudeville theater circuit, organized in 1913, became the famous—and notorious—Theater Owners Booking Association (TOBA), nicknamed "tough on Black Artists" because of the low pay and the poor conditions offered to African American entertainers on the circuit. Several black vaudevillians moved on to the major white vaudeville circuits or to Broadway.

Musical Comedy

Today the minstrel show, vaudeville, and the revue exist mainly in memory, old film footage, and the occasional revival. The one form of early stage entertainment that is still very much with us is **musical theater**. Its origins in **musical comedy** go back almost 150 years.

By most accounts the opening of *The Black Crook* in 1866 marked the beginning of American musical comedy. Popular musical-dramatic entertainments had been staged in America as early as the late eighteenth century, most notably watered-down versions of European operas. In this respect *The Black Crook* followed their lead: its story line and char-

Bert Williams in blackface. This is how Williams often appeared to vaudeville audiences and on film. Although minstrelsy was no longer a popular entertainment, performers, black and white, continued to appear in blackface through the first half of the twentieth century.

© Corbis

The "real" Bert Williams, in a far more distinguished pose. The comedian W. C. Fields described Williams as the funniest man he had ever seen and the saddest he had ever known. Comparing Williams the man with Williams the minstrel helps us understand why.

© Bettmann/Corbis

acter types come from sources like Johann Goethe's *Faust* and Carl Maria von Weber's *Der Freischütz*.

The qualities that made *The Black Crook* more American than European were its irreverence, its seemingly improvisatory style—in which unrelated acts are linked by the thinnest of dramatic threads—and its high spirits. All were qualities associated with, if not borrowed from, the minstrel show. A landmark because of its popularity, *The Black Crook* ran for 475 performances in New York, which made it one of the longest-running shows of the century. Touring companies spread its popularity throughout the country, and periodic revivals kept it alive well past 1900.

Operetta

As musical comedy was taking root in the United States, operetta was flourishing abroad, especially in England and German-speaking Europe. In England, Sir William Schwenck Gilbert and Sir Arthur Seymour Sullivan—commonly identified simply as Gilbert and Sullivan—created a string of successful operettas, including *H.M.S. Pinafore* and *The Mikado*.

These remain popular with cultivated audiences to this day in both England and the United States. Several operetta composers settled in the United States around 1900. Among the most successful were Irish composer Victor Herbert, Czech composer Rudolph Friml, and Hungarian composer Sigmund Romberg.

Operettas typically told tales that took place long ago or far away in exotic locales. Some involved fairy tale–like settings, with handsome princes and beautiful princesses. The music was the most accessible form of late-nineteenth-century "classical" and was light entertainment for the cultural elite.

By contrast, the stories of early musical comedies usually dealt with the here and now. Plots were often topical, comprising stories and incidents that, but for their exaggeration, could have come from the daily lives of the audience members. In the same spirit, many characters were stereotypes of the various ethnic groups that flooded New York in the latter part of the century. As in vaudeville, musical comedy featured stock portrayals of the Irish, Germans, Italians, Jews, and African Americans who emigrated or migrated to New York.

Operetta and musical comedy also diverged in their integration of music and plot. In operettas the plot usually had a dramatic continuity, and the songs highlighted important moments in the story. In musical comedy, plots were at the mercy of song hits and star performers. A common practice was **interpolation**, or incorporating songs into a show because they were hits, because star performers liked them, or because producers were paid by the publishers or songwriters to include them.

Today we expect songs in musicals to serve a dramatic purpose, even though the song may become popular outside of the show. The idea of introducing a song into a show just because it is popular, or in the hope that it will become popular, seems a crude practice. Viewed as a transitional step on the way to dramatically credible musical theater, however, or as a way to connect popular song and popular stage entertainment after the Civil War, interpolation is more understandable. Compared with the minstrel show, which had a deliberately loose story line (when it had one at all), and vaudeville, which was a plotless variety show, the surprise is not that the plot of a musical comedy was fair game for interpolation but that it had a plot at all.

Summary

Popular song found its way on-stage in several venues: vaudeville, the minstrel show, the revue, musical comedy, and operetta. The connection between song and story ranged from none at all (vaudeville) to somewhat (the revue and early musical comedy) to quite a bit (operetta). At the beginning of the twentieth century, sound recordings were primitive, expensive, and hard to reproduce; movies were silent; and commercial radio was still a dream, so the stage was the best way—indeed, almost the only way—to hear professional performances of popular songs. From the 1880s through the 1920s, there was more variety and more opportunity to hear popular music on-stage than at any time before or since.

TIN PAN ALLEY

The two decades before the Civil War saw the birth of popular music; the three decades after the Civil War saw the birth of the **popular-music industry**. Musical comedy and vaudeville competed with the minstrel show for audiences. Charles Harris's 1892 hit, "After the Ball," confirmed what music publishers already suspected: the existence of a large market for popular song. By 1895 the popular-music industry was flourishing.

The Birth of Tin Pan Alley. In the 1880s a different breed of music publisher opened for business in New York City. Whereas traditional publishers issued music of all kinds, the new publishers sold only popular songs and marketed them aggressively. They hired **song pluggers**, house pianists who could play a new song for a professional singer or a prospective customer. At first the publishers congregated in the theater district around Union Square (14th Street), but most soon moved uptown to 28th Street, still near enough to the theaters to have access to performers. Writer Monroe Rosenfeld dubbed 28th Street "**Tin Pan Alley**" because the sound of several song pluggers auditioning songs at the same time reminded him of crashing tin pans.

New York City became home to both popular stage entertainment and popular-music publishing. The new flood of immigrants, among them Irish, Germans, and then Jews, plus the migration of African Americans into the city, swelled New York's population. Many immigrants found work in show business, as performers or songwriters or as theater owners, agents, or publishers. New York would be the center of popular music for decades, challenged only by Hollywood after the advent of talking movies.

African American songwriters found wider acceptance for their work. In the 1890s Gussie Davis became the first black songwriter to achieve success on Tin Pan Alley. The songwriting team of Bob Cole and the brothers J. Rosamund Johnson and James Weldon Johnson supplied music for their own shows and for interpolation into other productions. African American musicians of the time usually wore many hats. For example, the most lasting contribution of the Johnson brothers was not popular songs but their arrangements of Negro spirituals. They published two sets of them, in 1925 and 1926. Will Marion Cook, musical director for the Walker-Williams Company in the 1900s, also composed songs in a style influenced by African American folksong. Later he directed one of the leading syncopated dance orchestras of the time.

"After the Ball." Charles Harris's 1892 popular song "After the Ball" was the first big Tin Pan Alley hit, eventually selling more than 5 million sheet-music copies. An early recording of "After the Ball," sung by George Gaskin, one of the Irish tenors who were so popular around the turn of the century, was a bestseller in 1893. (*Bestseller* is a relative term, however: commercial recording was only three years old at the time, distribution was difficult, and record players were expensive.) The story of its road to success tells us a lot about the growth of stage entertainment and music publishing, the way they operated, and the extent to which they intertwined.

Harris was a self-taught songwriter and performer (on the banjo). He never learned to read or write music and had to hire a trained musician to notate his songs. But he made up for his lack of training in determination, nerve, and business savvy. While living in Milwaukee, he wrote "After the Ball" for a friend. Harris then approached several popular singers whose tours with vaudeville took them through Milwaukee, and he asked them to perform the song in their shows. The first three, two vaudeville stars and a **ballad** singer in a minstrel show, unceremoniously turned him down. He finally convinced the fourth—who was starring in a touring production of *A Trip to Chinatown,* one of the most popular musical comedies of the 1890s—to interpolate the song into the show. Reportedly, Harris convinced the star by representing himself as a correspondent for the New York *Dramatic News,* promising a glowing review, and paying the star $500.

"After the Ball" was such a great success in the show that Julius Witmark, one of the new breed of Tin Pan Alley publishers, offered Harris $10,000 for the rights to the song. Instead, figuring that he could make more money publishing it himself, Harris set up his own publishing house. As it turned out, he was correct. He understood public taste and had a knack for spotting potential hits. Although he never wrote another song as successful as "After the Ball," Harris made a fortune publishing his own songs and those of other songwriters.

"After the Ball" and the Music Business. From the story of Harris's song we can infer much about changes in the popular-music industry between the first minstrel show in 1843 and the success of "After the Ball" in 1893. The publishers along Tin Pan Alley, like Witmark and Harris, no longer cluttered their catalogs with items that had little chance of brisk sales. "After the Ball" was the first song to demonstrate the full commercial potential of this new direction in music publishing. In the wake of its success, even more publishers hopped on the bandwagon, and by 1900 very few hit songs were published away from Tin Pan Alley. Harris's decision to go into business for himself suggests that the songwriter realized the least fame and fortune: it was the publisher who saw most of the profits, and the singers who enjoyed the celebrity.

Part of a publisher's profits went toward recruiting singers to perform the publisher's songs. Then as now the surest route to popularity was performance by a star of the day, even when the song was intended primarily for the home market. It was standard practice to secure performances with gifts and bribes, just as record companies bribed disc jockeys sixty years later. The principle—or lack of principle—was the same; only the players and the terms of the deals differed.

By the 1890s popular stage entertainment and music publishing had become closely intertwined. Professional performers promoted new songs. Sheet music, which enabled people to learn the song at home, kept songs popular. Each fed off the other to a much greater extent than they did in Stephen Foster's day.

DANCE RHYTHMS IN POPULAR SONGS

Dance rhythms had been a part of American popular song since the rise of blackface entertainment. Songs like "De Boatmen's Dance" had the energy of a reel; the rhythm of the polka was widely used in postwar minstrel songs, such as James Bland's "De Golden Wedding." The majority of popular songs, however, were of the slow, sentimental sort. That changed in the 1890s. Dance rhythms were in the air, and songwriters set songs to them—even songs with sentimental texts.

CD 1:6

"Take Me Out to the Ball Game," Albert von Tilzer, music; Jack Norworth, lyrics (1908). Harvey Hindermeyer, vocal.

Waltz Songs. The waltz was the first dance rhythm to enjoy widespread use in popular song. Many of the most memorable songs of the 1890s and 1900s had a waltz beat, hence the term **waltz song**. In *Yesterdays,* his chronicle of popular song, Charles Hamm lists sixteen commercially successful songs (most had sales of at least 1 million copies of sheet music) from these two decades—thirteen of which have a waltz beat. The most familiar of the turn-of-the-century waltz songs is the 1908 hit "Take Me Out to the Ball Game."

"Take Me Out to the Ball Game" is a true product of Tin Pan Alley. Its composer, Albert von Tilzer, was the younger brother of Harry von Tilzer, the most successful songwriter of the

CD 1:6   **Waltz Song** (Albert von Tilzer, music; Jack Norworth, lyrics; performed by Harvey Hindermeyer, vocal)

0:00	Instrumental introduction.
0:10	1st verse, 1st section
	Katie Casey was...
0:23	1st verse, 2nd section
	Begins like the first phrase, but melody takes a new direction toward the chorus.
	On a Saturday...
0:37	Chorus, 1st section
	Notice how the long notes in the melody line up with the bass notes.
	Take me out...
0:50	Chorus, 2nd section
	There is no syncopation.
	Let me root,...
1:06	2nd verse, 1st section
	Katie Casey saw...
1:19	2nd verse, 2nd section
	When the score...
1:33	Chorus
	Identical words and music every time.
	Take me out...

period and a partner in a very profitable music-publishing firm. The younger von Tilzer worked for his older brother's publishing house.

The song itself shows how the industry was changing. The lyric is fun and very much in the present, neither sentimental nor nostalgic. The language is simple, direct, and slightly slangy, and it tells the story of the imaginary Katie Casey.

The music is as jaunty as the lyrics. The band's *OOM-pah-pah* **waltz rhythm** gives the song a bounce, and the rhythm of the melody swings from one strong beat to the next. Like the parlor song and the plantation song, "Take Me Out to the Ball Game" is all about melody; once the voice enters, everything else stays in the background. The rhythm of the melody governs the rhythm of the lyrics, which is quite different from speech rhythm.

The song uses a verse/chorus form: the verse tells us about Katie; the chorus states and restates the song's main theme. This form was more widely used than any other from the 1860s through the 1910s. Gradually, however, perhaps because the chorus was more memorable and central to the song, performers began to ignore the verse. The verses of "Take Me Out to the Ball Game" and "Yankee Doodle Boy" (Chapter 6) all but disappeared from our collective memory decades ago. One rarely, if ever, hears the verses of these and other songs from the period.

In time and in topic, "Take Me Out to the Ball Game" is a long way from the minstrel songs "De Boatmen's Dance" and "Old Folks at Home." Still we find in this song the legacy of the minstrel show and the revolution it sparked. It is apparent in the everyday language of the lyric, the dance rhythm that supports the melody, and the verse/chorus form—the most far-reaching influences of minstrel show songs.

WALTZ SONG

Rhythm	*Waltz, no syncopation (the long notes of the melody line up with the first beats in a measure).*
Melody	*Flowing phrases, each four measures long, with a rest at the end; one big leap ("Take me"), then mostly by step; no riffs.*
Instrumentation (timbre)	*Male voice plus band.*
Performance style	*Overenunciated singing typical of early recordings; quasi-operatic voice.*
Dynamics	*Moderately loud (taking into account recording limitations).*
Harmony	*Basically I-IV-V, with extra chords for variety.*
Texture	*Melody plus accompaniment, with instrumental interludes and countermelodies.*
Form	*Verse/chorus, each having two phrases; each phrase begins the same but ends differently.*

Key Points

Acoustic recording	*Very early commercial **acoustic recording**; poor fidelity.*
Expanded verse/chorus form	*Bigger verse/chorus form; chorus can stand alone.*
Waltz songs	*Not for dancing, but with a clear dance rhythm in accompaniment.*

Terms to Know

acoustic recording

waltz rhythm

Summary. The 1890s and 1900s saw several dance rhythms invigorate popular song. The most popular was the waltz, although George M. Cohan set many of his most memorable melodies to march rhythms. The syncopated rhythms of ragtime and related styles also found their way into popular song and dance music, as we discover later in this chapter and in the next.

The use of dance rhythms was an important stage in the imminent merger of popular song and dance music. When the merger occurred in the late teens and the early twenties, however, the rhythms came from African Americans, not whites.

BANDS AND BAND MUSIC

The most popular instrumental ensemble in late-nineteenth-century America was the **concert band**. In an era without radio or television, the touring concert bands as well as the hometown band was a primary source of musical entertainment.

The Emergence of the Concert Band. Bands had been a part of life in the United States since the American Revolution. Almost every city and town, large or small, had a municipal band and a band shell on the village green or town square. Bands performed on most public occasions and gave concerts in season. After the Civil War, some of the bands that had formed in major cities became professional ensembles, playing concerts and dances and enhancing public occasions. The most famous of these professional bands before 1890 was that of the Twenty-second Regiment of New York, renamed the Gilmore Band when Patrick Gilmore became its director in 1873.

Patrick Gilmore. Although he initially made his mark as a skilled performer on the cornet (a close relative of the trumpet), Gilmore, an Irish immigrant, was best known for organizing "monster concerts," particularly the National Peace Jubilee of 1869 and the World Peace Jubilee of 1872, which featured choruses of thousands, bands and orchestras of hundreds, and world-famous soloists. He also increased the level of musicianship by arranging visits to the United States of the leading European bands and by raising the standard of performance in his own band. Gilmore's band toured annually throughout the United States until his sudden death in 1892. His success set the stage for the great era of American bands.

John Philip Sousa

From the 1890s until well into the 1920s, the most popular concert band in the United States was a civilian, professional band directed by John Philip Sousa. Sousa (1854–1932) was the most prominent bandleader and band composer of his era. He established his reputation as a composer and a conductor with the United States Marine Band, which he directed for twelve years before forming his own band in 1892. For the remainder of his career, Sousa led his band on annual tours throughout the United States, as well as several tours to Europe and one world tour, giving more than 10,000 concerts. Sousa's band was known for its precision and musicianship and for the excellence of its soloists, several of whom subsequently led bands of their own.

A typical Sousa band concert included marches, original works for band, solos featuring the band's virtuoso instrumentalists, arrangements of familiar orchestral compositions, and the popular music of the day. The latter included the latest in syncopated music. In fact, many European audiences first gained exposure to ragtime's syncopated rhythms through Sousa's performances.

The role of professional bands in American musical life around 1900 was much like that of the contemporary pops orchestra. Concerts mixed familiar classical and popular music and featured star soloists. In an interview, Sousa made the distinction between his band and a symphony orchestra: comparing himself to Theodore Thomas, the esteemed nineteenth-century orchestra conductor, he noted that Thomas "gave Wagner, Liszt, and Tchaikovsky [classical composers], in the belief that he was educating his public; I gave Wagner, Liszt, and Tchaikovsky with the hope that I was entertaining my public."

Sousa's Marches. The most popular and memorable music that the Sousa band performed was the **march**, a composition in regularly accented, duple meter that is appropriate to accompany marching. Although he composed other kinds of works—songs, operettas, and band suites—Sousa made his reputation as a composer of marches. Their popularity earned him the title "The March King" and made him America's best-known composer during his lifetime. Sousa wrote 136 marches between 1876 and 1931. Most of the best known, however, were written between 1888 and 1900: among them are "Semper Fidelis" (1888), "Washington Post" (1889), and Sousa's most famous march (possibly the most famous march of all time), "The Stars and Stripes Forever" (1897).

Sousa's Legacy. Sousa's marches are the instrumental counterpart to Stephen Foster's songs. They share three important qualities.

A poster from 1898, showing a couple doing the cakewalk. What's interesting is that the couple is white, not black or whites in blackface. This shows that the cakewalk had moved from the minstrel stage to become the dance fad of the 1890s.

© Corbis

- The most famous works by both composers were immediately popular and have remained among the best-known music from the nineteenth century.

- The best works of both composers are musically significant. They are the finest examples of their genres.

- Their music is (almost indefinably) American but shows no obvious African American influence.

Marches for Dancing: The Cakewalk. Other instrumental music, especially piano rags and early jazz compositions, drew heavily on the march, as we discover in Chapter 3. And around the turn of the century, marches and marchlike music began to accompany social dancing. During the 1890s Sousa's "Washington Post" march was the preferred music for a newly popular dance, the **two-step.** Instead of marching, dancers twirled around the ballroom floor. It was a vigorous couple's dance.

This dance fad passed, but virtually all of the ragtime and jazz dances popular for several decades after the turn of the century had their basis in the march. They started with its basic rhythm, tempo, form, and at least some of the instruments, and they added syncopation—a little or a lot. The first of these dances set to march-based **syncopated dance music** was the cakewalk.

The **cakewalk** came out of the postwar minstrel show. By most accounts it originated as a contest among slaves: couples danced for a prize, generally a cake. The winners were the "pair that pranced around with the proudest, high-kicking steps." After the war the cakewalk served as the finale to the minstrel show. In the 1890s it became a dance fad, moving from the stage to the dance floor, where couples competed in contests for prizes larger than a cake.

LOOKING BACK, LOOKING AHEAD

The period from the end of the Civil War to the close of the century was one of great change in American popular music. The boom in professional songwriting, centered in New York's famous Tin Pan Alley, showed that there was a strong desire for real, American songs. The favored form was the verse/chorus song, set to a lively waltz beat, such as the still-beloved "Take Me Out to the Ball Game." Meanwhile, black performers began to find more opportunities to work for urban white audiences, thanks to the popularity of jubilee choirs and "authentic" minstrel troupes. Although much of the material they performed was demeaning or perpetuated stereotypical images, the music began to more accurately reflect African

American rhythms and melodies. Stage entertainment also reached a new level of sophistication, with everything from variety shows to light operetta drawing its own audiences.

As the nineteenth century drew to a close, American popular music had grown into an independent industry, headquartered in New York. The minstrel show, a stage entertainment specifically associated with America, had flourished for half a century and had only recently begun to decline in popularity. Vaudeville and an identifiably American musical theater had begun to take its place.

America had produced two composers, Stephen Foster and John Philip Sousa, whose music remains popular and identifiably American, if only by association. All of this was a prelude to the more distinctively American music that would emerge in the first part of the twentieth century.

TERMS TO KNOW

Test your knowledge of this chapter's important terms by defining the following. If you can't recall the meaning of a certain term, refresh your memory by looking up the boldfaced term in the chapter, turning to the Glossary at the back of the book, or working with the flashcards on the *Popular Music in America* Companion Web site: *http://music.wadsworth.com/ campbell_2e*

acoustic recording	interlocutor	revue
Anglo-American	interpolation	scale
aria	jubilee choir	sheet music
ballad	libretto	song plugger
banjo	march	spiritual
blackface	minstrel-spiritual	syncopated dance music
bones	minstrelsy	Tambo and Bones
breakdown	modal	tambourine
burlesques	musical comedy	Tin Pan Alley
cakewalk	musical theater	two-step
call-and-response	olio	unison
chorus	opera	vaudeville
concert band	operetta	vernacular
coon song	oral tradition	verse
delineator	parlor song	verse/chorus form
drone notes	pentatonic scale	walkaround
endman	plantation song	waltz rhythm
fiddle	popular-music industry	waltz song

The Emergence of African American Music

Sometime in 1914, Jim Europe sat at the piano during a break between dance numbers. He was playing a song that he'd played many times before, W. C. Handy's "Memphis Blues." Irene and Vernon Castle, who had heard him play it over and over, approached him and asked him to turn it into a dance number. Europe did, and the Castles created a new dance, the fox trot. The Castles' casual request marked the beginning of the modern era in popular music.

This new music sounded modern because it incorporated unmistakable elements of African American music. In the first twenty-five years of the twentieth century, African American music exploded into American life. Ragtime, syncopated dance music, blues, and jazz—all found an audience among blacks and whites and eventually blended with the mainstream styles to produce a new kind of popular music. These new sounds surfaced after more than thirty years of bubbling under the surface of the minstrel show, vaudeville, and other venues. We survey them below.

RAGTIME

Ragtime began as an obscure folk-dance music played up and down the Mississippi valley in the last quarter of the nineteenth century. Before it faded away, it would significantly alter the sound of popular music. It was through ragtime that white Americans finally discovered the rhythmic vitality of a real African American music. Whites would have encountered black performers in minstrel shows or touring jubilee choirs, but because authentic ragtime could be performed from sheet music, whites now had a chance to study and savor it. As a result, its influence was far more extensive than that of earlier African American styles. Ragtime was the catalyst for the revolutionary changes in popular music that marked the beginning of its modern era.

The Emergence of Ragtime. The heyday of ragtime lasted about two decades, from just before the turn of the century to the end of World War I. Its history begins earlier, however, in the years after the Civil War. Black musicians in the Midwest had been playing ragtime—or at least syncopated music—well before the first rags were published in the 1890s. According to several accounts of the period, black pianists in bars and bordellos up and down the East Coast played what would soon be called "ragtime."

In the 1890s blacks and whites in search of jobs flocked to national and international expositions, particularly Chicago's 1893 World Columbian Exposition. African American entertainers, especially ragtime pianists, found employment and valuable exposure in the restaurants, saloons, and brothels in the vicinity of the exposition. Most of the St. Louis ragtime pianists, Scott Joplin among them, migrated to Chicago in search of work during the Chicago World's Fair.

Toward the end of the century, composers and songwriters began to use the terms *rag* and *ragtime* to identify a new style. Ernest Hogan's 1896 song "All Coons Look Alike to Me" makes reference to a Negro "rag" accompaniment; the song is the first published example of a raglike piano style. The first published rags appeared a year later. With the publication of Joplin's "Maple Leaf Rag" in 1899, *ragtime* became a household word.

Joplin's "Maple Leaf Rag" was the first commercially successful **piano rag**. It did not start a craze for syncopated music so much as give it a major push along two lines: it introduced more-complex African rhythms to popular music, and it made them available in sheet-music form. The rhythms of Joplin's early rags were more complex than the syncopated songs and dances of the 1890s. Rhythmically, they found a midpoint between the improvised style of black ragtime pianists and the cakewalks and ragtime songs of the period. By doing so his rags steered popular music in the direction of the more syncopated rhythms of the 1910s and 1920s.

Furthermore, ragtime was the first African American music that looked on paper the way it sounded in performance. Any competent pianist, black or white, who was able to read music could buy the sheet music to Joplin's "Maple Leaf Rag" and perform it in a reasonably authentic manner. At a time when recordings were limited, radio and television nonexistent, and live entertainment, especially by African American performers, relatively rare outside of the big cities, sheet music was the best way to absorb new music.

Scott Joplin. The classic piano rags of Scott Joplin (1868–1917) are the most enduring music of the ragtime era. Several have remained familiar, especially since the ragtime revival of the 1970s; Joplin's piano rags remain the core of the ragtime repertoire. A professional musician from his teenage years, Joplin played in saloons and clubs along the Mississippi valley and eventually in Missouri. (The "Maple Leaf Rag" is named after the Maple Leaf Club in Sedalia, Missouri, where he worked from 1894 until the turn of the century.) He also received formal musical training in the European tradition, principally through study at George R. Smith College in Sedalia, and was a fluent composer and arranger in the popular white styles of the day. After the turn of the century, Joplin devoted most of his professional efforts to legitimizing ragtime. In addition to a steady stream of piano compositions, mostly rags, he composed a ballet, *The Ragtime Dance,* and two operas, *Treemonisha* and the now-lost *A Guest of Honor.* (Joplin received a posthumous Pulitzer Prize for *Treemonisha* in 1976 on the occasion of its revival.)

The Sound of the Piano Rag. In Joplin's own performance of "Maple Leaf Rag," we can hear virtually all the significant features of traditional piano ragtime. Like so many other African American musical styles, the piano rag emerged from the reinterpretation of an established idiom, in this case the march. (At this time marches were almost as popular on the dance floor as in a parade.) Joplin and his peers simply transformed the march into ragtime by adding an African rhythmic conception—**syncopation**—and adapting the style to a single

CD 1:7

"Maple Leaf Rag," Scott Joplin (1899). Joplin, piano (piano roll, 1916).

CD 1:7	**Piano Rag—Multisectional AABBA/CCDD** (Scott Joplin; performed by Joplin, piano)

0:00	A	1st strain
		Notice the characteristic ragtime figuration: a series of arpeggiated chords, timed so that the top-note accents are often syncopated.
0:08		Nice stop-time effect where the *OOM-pah* stops briefly.
0:22	A	1st strain repeats.
0:43	B	2nd strain
		Underlying melody is relatively simple; ragtime patterns animate it.
1:04	B	2nd strain repeats.
1:25	A	1st strain repeats.
1:46	C	A 3rd strain in a new key (this would be the trio in a march).
2:07	C	3rd strain repeats, with a more decisive ending; nice call-and-response pattern in the melody.
2:28	D	4th strain and a fourth new melody.
2:49	D	4th strain repeats, with a decisive ending.

instrument, the piano. The Listening Guide details both the connection with the march and the ragged syncopation that sets it apart.

STYLE PROFILE

PIANO RAG

Rhythm	*March rhythm* in accompaniment; syncopated ragtime patterns in melody; dance beat.
Melody	*Instrumental-style melody, idiomatic to piano. Most of the patterns are arpeggiated chords set to syncopated rhythms. (An* **arpeggio** *is a chord in which the notes are played one after another rather than all at once.) There are four different melodies, or* **strains** *(sections of a* **march** *or a marchlike piece); the presence of a C strain indicates the insertion of a* **trio**, *which occurs in* **march forms**.
Instrumentation (timbre)	*Piano (this recording is from a piano roll).*
Performance style	*As Joplin notated it, in the main; there are a few extra "smears" (handfuls of notes run together) in the left hand.*
Dynamics	*Moderate throughout.*
Harmony	*Basically I-IV-V but with some prominent chords that are not I, IV, or V.*
Texture	*Melody and accompaniment: chords under the melody in the right hand, OOM-pah pattern in the left hand.*
Form	**Multisectional** *march form: AABBA/CCDD.*

Key Points

The march connection	*Piano rag is like a march with syncopation played on the piano.*
Ragtime, publishing, and the spread of African American music	*The first authentic African American music that could be faithfully notated, then bought and learned by anyone.*
The sound of the piano rag	*The most characteristic sound is the syncopated figuration.*

Ragtime Enters Popular Culture. Although initially referring to piano music, the word *ragtime* quickly came to identify almost any syncopated music and even some that was not. (For example, Irving Berlin's 1911 hit "Alexander's Ragtime Band" is a thoroughly modern song for the time, but it does not have even the modest syncopation of earlier ragtime songs.) Ragtime songs, written and performed by both blacks and whites, were often interpolated into Broadway shows. "Under the Bamboo Tree," a hit song by black musicians James Weldon Johnson, J. Rosamond Johnson, and Bob Cole, first appeared in the show *Sally in Our Alley,* sung by Marie Cahill, an Irish American singer. (It is difficult to imagine how they worked the lyrics—about a jungle maid—into the plot and how Cahill passed herself off as an African queen.)

Ben Harvey, a ragtime pianist who enjoyed great success on the vaudeville stage after moving from the Midwest to New York, illustrated in his *Ragtime Instructor* how to "rag" the familiar music of the day. Harvey and other ragtime pianists often transformed classical compositions and other well-known works into ragtime. Harvey's approach was probably similar to that used by ragtime pianist and songwriter Eubie Blake, who demonstrated in a television documentary how he used to rag a Wagner overture. It was also possible to rag popular song: "That Mesmerizing Mendelssohn Tune," a big 1912 hit for the comedy team of Arthur Collins and Byron G. Harlan, was a ragged version of Felix Mendelssohn's "Spring Song."

Reactions Against Ragtime. Ragtime met with resistance from virtually every corner of the establishment. It was considered immoral, fit only for the saloons and brothels where it was played. It was deemed musically déclassé—the product of an inferior race incapable of the musical sophistication that Europeans had achieved. And it was considered a cause of moral decay. According to one writer, the "Ragtime Evil" should not be found in Christian homes. There were, of course, overtones of racial prejudice in virtually all of these arguments. During this low point in race relations, few whites accepted blacks as equals, so it is not surprising that many found ragtime's mix of black and white influences unacceptable.

Critics foretold the demise of ragtime almost before it began, as this comment from 1900 suggests: "Thank the Lord [that ragtime pieces] have passed the meridian and are now on the wane." Eighteen years later they were still singing the same song: "It is gratifying to observe that this one-time doubtful feature [ragtime syncopation] is gradually losing favor and promises to be eventually overcome." Of course, it would not be overcome but replaced with music that was even more syncopated.

Serious musicians stood divided on the question of ragtime's worth. Daniel Gregory Mason, one of the guardians of the cultivated tradition, sought to demean ragtime by drawing an unfavorable comparison between its syncopated rhythms and those found in Beethoven's and Schumann's music. Charles Ives, the most important American classical composer of that generation and an after-hours ragtime pianist, responded that the comparison showed "how much alike they [ragtime and Schumann] are." In retrospect the reaction against ragtime (and the African Americans who created it) was even stronger than the reaction would be against rock and roll a half century later.

The Legacy of Ragtime

Ragtime's legacy to American music includes three contributions:

o   A body of music of enduring value and appeal

o   A number of firsts in the history of African American music

o   The catalyst for the revolution that produced the modern era in popular music

The Classic Piano Rag. The classic piano rags of Scott Joplin and other distinguished composers represent a repertoire of real artistic worth and individuality; there is no other music like it. From musical evidence in Joplin's works, we can also infer his dedication to bringing ragtime under the European classical music umbrella. The later rags are more melodious and less syncopated. For example, the first half of the opening strain of "The Cascades" (1904) contains a flowing stream of fast notes and a cascade in reverse (in which both hands play an arpeggio that goes up, not down) but no syncopation at all. And in both his tempo indications for rags and his written commentary on the correct performance of ragtime, Joplin constantly admonishes pianists against playing ragtime too fast: ragtime played at a slower tempo gains dignity.

As his later compositions showed, Joplin saw ragtime as a vehicle for serious artistic expression as well as entertainment. Accordingly, he thought of himself as a composer of **art music** in the tradition of the nineteenth-century nationalist composers. He believed that he had elevated a folk-dance music to concert status, in much the same way that Polish composer Frédéric Chopin had elevated the mazurka (Polish folk dance) and Viennese composer Franz Schubert the *ländler* (Austrian folk dance) in classical compositions.

Joplin's disciples approached ragtime composition with a similar seriousness of purpose, and his publisher, John Stark, identified him as a composer of "classic" rags. In keeping with his purpose, the classic ragtime style of Joplin and his disciples was the most conservative, or European, of the ragtime piano styles current around 1900. The East Coast ragtime of Eubie Blake and the New Orleans style of Jelly Roll Morton are considerably more syncopated than Joplin's music.

Ragtime and the Preservation of African American Culture. Ragtime, or at least the classic ragtime of Joplin and his peers, enabled African Americans to become more aware of their own culture. Eileen Southern describes the process in this way:

> At last the black composer was involved in writing down the music he had been playing for his own people for many years. An improvisational music would be transformed into a notated music; a functional music, intended for dancing and entertainment, into a concert music intended for listening; a folk-style music, into the music of the individual composer, upon which he stamped his unique personality.

Prior to ragtime, African American folk music had been passed on through oral tradition: each new generation of African Americans would learn the songs, dances, and religious music of their culture by hearing them and singing or playing along. It is frustrating to read pre-twentieth-century descriptions of African American music; attempts by interested white musicians to capture black folk music in notation fall far short of the mark, no matter how sincere they may have been. Joplin's work marked the beginning of a movement among historically conscious African American musicians to preserve their musical heritage. W. C. Handy, the "father of the blues," began collecting blues melodies and assembling them into songs, just as Joplin had done with rags. James Weldon Johnson and J. Rosamond Johnson, brothers who were also active Broadway composers, assembled and arranged spirituals, fitting them with piano accompaniments for performance at home, at church, and even in the concert hall.

Ragtime also represented the first documented instance of African Americans' filtering through their own musical heritage the European music to which they had been exposed. By comparing pieces in rag style with their original versions and models, it is possible to identify the specifically African elements in the rag.

Ragtime as the Catalyst for Change. Ragtime had a widespread impact on other musical styles. It loosened up popular music (both song and dance), helped shape jazz in its early years, and aroused the interest of several of the most important classical composers in the early twentieth century. Ragtime also made popular music more lively. Its beat had more of a bounce, and its syncopated rhythms permitted a rapid yet relatively natural delivery of the words.

There is such a smooth continuum between ragtime and other syncopated styles that early jazz can be thought of as a dialect of ragtime. Jelly Roll Morton, the self-proclaimed "inventor of jazz" and its first great composer, identified his jazz version of "Maple Leaf Rag" as New Orleans ragtime (as opposed to Joplin's St. Louis style). Handy's "Memphis Blues" is more rag than blues, and syncopated dance picks up where ragtime left off.

Summary. Even at the peak of its popularity, and despite its notoriety, ragtime was never the dominant popular style. Mainstream popular music remained largely unsyncopated, as we discovered in "Take Me Out to the Ball Game." But no music from its era was more influential, and no music of the period remains more popular. Even more important it opened the doors of popular music to real African American music. Syncopated dance music, blues, and jazz would soon follow ragtime's path toward the popular mainstream.

SYNCOPATED DANCE MUSIC

From the second decade of the twentieth century through the mid-1920s, Americans went dance crazy. The series of dance fads that had begun with the cakewalk continued with the notorious animal dances, including the fox trot, and ended with the vigorous dances of the early 1920s, most notably the Charleston (which we hear in Chapter 4). Early on, much of the music that they danced to was ragtime, but over time the music lost some of its rough edges and became more clearly danceable—it was simply syncopated dance music. More important, however, was the growing acceptance by mainstream audiences of this new syncopated music—which led to a social and musical revolution.

Ragtime Dance. Almost as soon as it appeared, ragtime became music for social dancing. Piano rags were scored for the dance orchestras of the period. Joplin's famous "Red Book" (so called because it had a red cover), a collection of dance-orchestra arrangements of his popular rags, is the best-known example. Original dance music in a syncopated style also appeared throughout the late 1890s and into the 1910s.

Animal Dances. As the cakewalk fad faded away, other dances took its place, most of them adapted or borrowed from African American folk dances. The most infamous of these new dances was a group of animal dances. The grizzly bear, the chicken glide, and the turkey trot all became popular in certain circles around 1910. "Respectable" citizens reacted violently to these dances, which were associated with sleazy establishments and disreputable people. As recounted in Sylvia Dannett and Frank Rachel's book, *Down Memory Lane: The Arthur Murray Picture Book of Social Dancing:*

> A Paterson, New Jersey, court imposed a fifty-day prison sentence on a young woman for dancing the turkey trot. Fifteen young women were dismissed from a well-known magazine after the editor caught them enjoying the abandoned dance at lunchtime. Turkey trotters incurred the condemnation of churches and respectable people, and in 1914 an official disapproval was issued by the Vatican.

The **turkey trot** was one of the most popular dances. By all accounts it was simple and awkward, but it permitted "lingering close contact," a novelty at the time. Body contact between couples (presumably) delighted the dancers but scandalized the more conservative segments of American society and provoked a hostile backlash. A more refined dance, the fox trot, soon replaced it.

The Fox Trot

The story of the **fox trot** begins in 1908, when W. C. Handy composed his first blues, and continues for several decades.

W. C. Handy and the First Fox Trot Song. In its first incarnation, "Memphis Blues" was "Mr. Crump," a protest song of sorts. The lyric criticizes a certain Mr. Crump, a politician who was trying to restrict nightlife in the black sections of Memphis. Ironically, Crump hired Handy to play the song during Crump's campaign for mayor, and one wonders whether Crump ever heard the lyrics. If he did, it didn't bother him; Crump liked the music, at least as a political tool, and so did the voters—he won.

Handy had formed a band/dance orchestra in Clarksdale, Mississippi, in 1902 and published "Memphis Blues" in 1912 as a song with new words and piano accompaniment. In its notated form, it was a far cry from the Muddy Waters blues heard earlier. Like a march it had several sections; most of them featured **blues form** and a touch of blues style. It was the third blues song published that year. It might well have been the first, if Handy hadn't had so much trouble finding a publisher (he eventually founded his own publishing firm). When he did get the song into print, it sold all over the country and caught the ear of Jim Europe.

James Reese Europe. James Reese Europe (1881–1919) had come to New York in 1905 from Washington, D.C., and quickly immersed himself in the popular music world. By 1910 he had organized the Clef Club, an organization for black musicians that was part union and part booking agency. In 1912 he directed the 150-piece Clef Club Orchestra in a concert at Carnegie Hall, then as now America's musical mecca. Designed to showcase the achievements of African American musicians, the concert impressed members of New York's high society, and soon Europe and his Society Orchestra were in demand for parties given by the Rockefellers and other wealthy families.

Jim Europe's life ended abruptly, when one of his musicians, angry about Europe's discipline of the band, attacked him and severed his jugular vein. At the time, Europe was probably the most popular and highly respected black musician in the United States. Although newspapers eulogized him as the "jazz king," he wasn't (just as the later figure Paul Whiteman wouldn't be); but he was important for his music and his seemingly tireless efforts to raise the stature of African American musicians.

Many writers have speculated that if Europe hadn't died, popular music would have been quite different. The skimpy musical evidence that survives does not lend much support to this notion. Two circumstances argue against it. One was the proliferation of dance orchestras, both black and white, beginning the year of Europe's death and continuing into the 1920s. The other was the emergence of two other African American musical styles: blues and jazz.

Irene and Vernon Castle. In 1914 Jim Europe began an association with Irene and Vernon Castle, a husband-and-wife dance team who brought style and elegance to syncopated social dancing. The Castles had just returned from Paris, where they had ridden the crest of the tango fad (see Chapter 8). They began dancing at teas in a New York restaurant and soon appeared in a Broadway stage show, *The Sunshine Girl*, where they danced the turkey trot. Shortly after, they invented the fox trot, setting it to James Reese Europe's version of Handy's "Memphis Blues." Within a year the dance was more popular than all the other dances in their repertoire, and the Castles were the toast of New York high society.

The Castles' success signaled a fundamental shift in popular taste. For the first time, social dancing to a clearly African American beat became acceptable to a significant portion of the population. Fox trotting caught on with all levels of society, from the Rockefellers on down. Although it may not have been condoned in all quarters, dancing to syncopated music was no longer a criminal offense. By the mid-1930s dancing "cheek to cheek," as Fred Astaire and Ginger Rogers did so often on-screen, not only was socially acceptable, it was the epitome of elegance.

By the late 1910s, the new dance even affected fashion. Following the lead of Irene Castle, who wore her hair short and dressed in looser-fitting garments (the better to dance the more vigorous syncopated steps), the more emancipated women bobbed their hair and cast off their corsets, floor-length skirts, and any other clothing designed to obscure their shape.

Summary. The successes of Handy's song and Europe's dance music were milestones in the mainstreaming of African American popular music. Both the song and its performance by Europe found an audience among the tastemakers in white society. At least some African American music did not have to hide behind the mask of minstrelsy. Still, it was only a step toward equal opportunity, equal treatment, and dignity. Handy had to struggle to get his song published, and Europe got dance engagements in part because white bands refused to play the new syncopated music—they considered it beneath them.

Origins of the Fox Trot

This story is one of several conflicting accounts of the origins of the fox trot. It was told by Noble Sissle, a close associate of Jim Europe, a fine musician very much part of that world, and one of the leading African American musical figures of the early twentieth century. Another account links its birth to a vaudeville performer named Harry Fox, who apparently included a sprightly step across the stage in his act—hence the fox trot. In spite of the obvious association of name and step, the Sissle account seems more credible. There were dozens of "animal dances" in the 1900s and 1910s; the foxtrot would have been yet another. And the Castles were *the* dance team of the teens, the trendsetters of the decade not only in dance but also in appearance and etiquette. So it shouldn't surprise us that they would be responsible for the most popular social dance of the era.

BLUES

Beginning as a folk music sometime after the Civil War, the **blues** became a commercial music around the turn of the nineteenth century. In the 1910s and 1920s, blues filtered into popular music in several stages, first as songs and instrumentals distributed mainly through sheet music, then in jazz, and finally as recorded vocal music—the classic blues of the 1920s. In these years blues came in several shades.

The Origins of the Blues. Folk and country blues flourished in isolated regions of the rural South from the Carolinas and Virginia to Texas and Oklahoma. To the extent that blues had a home, it was the Mississippi Delta, in the northwest part of the state. Many important bluesmen, including Robert Johnson and Muddy Waters, called the Delta home.

In the first half of the century, the Mississippi Delta was mostly black. Jim Crow laws enforcing rigid segregation throughout the South had particular force there because so few African Americans had any economic, legal, or political leverage. Sharecropping, with its poor wages, few rights, and high prices at the company store, kept many blacks almost as dependent as they had been during slavery. Some men—roustabouts and stevedores—worked on the river, building up the levees or moving cargo on and off the riverboats. Pay for this work was marginally better than for sharecropping—although it would make today's minimum wage seem like a fortune—but working conditions were harsher. White overseers carried guns to enforce discipline, and men labored long hours and lived in squalid work camps.

Most black Americans had little direct contact with white society, and none of it was on an equal footing. Moreover, in these days before television, few had much awareness of the outside world. Perhaps because they were so isolated in every way, blacks rediscovered, or perhaps reinvented, many aspects of the cultures their ancestors had left behind in Africa. We sense this when Muddy Waters, a Delta native, sings about "mojo"; or when we discover that Bo Diddley's stage name refers to the diddley bow, an instrument similar to those found in West Africa; or when we hear a group of laborers singing a work song. It is in the South that we find what Robert Palmer called "deep blues"—the starkest, most powerful expression of blues feeling.

The bluesman was a part of life in the Delta, yet apart from it. Performing for his own amusement rather than for an audience—or at least a paying audience—he entertained on street corners and at almost any social occasion—fish fries, parties, picnics, and the like. In his songs he told stories about life in the Delta—memorable events, hard times, and the local take on the universal theme of love gained and lost. This solitary aspect of folk blues differen-

The *Griot* and the Bluesman

In West African culture, the **griot** fulfills many roles. He is the healer (the witch doctor), the tribe historian (he preserves its history in his songs), and, along with the master drummer, its most important musician. Although the *griot* is respected for his abilities, he is sometimes feared, or at least distrusted. As a result, he often stands outside of tribal life. The *griot*'s incarnation in African American culture has been the bluesman. Like the *griot,* he told stories through songs and earned admiration and respect for this ability, but he also lived on the fringes of society. Many bluesmen traveled around in search of work and company. The bluesman led a life much different from the sharecropper and the roustabout—working when others played, and playing around when others worked.

tiates it from most other African American folk styles, including work songs and spirituals, which are based on collective music making.

Traveling from town to town, the bluesman would stay long enough to earn some money and entertain the ladies, especially when their men were off working on the river. For roustabouts, the bluesman was often the notorious "backdoor man," sneaking out the rear of the house as the man came home. Many viewed the bluesman's arrival in town as a mixed blessing.

Early Blues Singers. As African Americans migrated to urban areas in both the North and the South, they took the blues with them. After the move to the city, what had been private or small-group entertainment in the rural South became music for public performance. In the first decades of the twentieth century, a group of blues singers, most of them women, toured on the black vaudeville circuits and performed wherever they got paid. Ma Rainey was among the first; Bessie Smith joined her in the teens. They and other blues singers remained unknown to most Americans (both white and black) until the 1920s. In the meantime, however, white America got its first taste of the blues.

Blues in Print. Because so much of the power of the blues lies in the style of the performer, it is ironic that the first widely known blues songs reached their audience via sheet music. These published blues songs were hybrids. "Memphis Blues" is as much rag as blues. Handy's "St. Louis Blues" (1914), the most frequently recorded song in the first half of the twentieth century, inserts a tango between two blues choruses. Neither the sheet music nor the recordings of the time communicate what we have come to regard as authentic blues; they are a pale imitation of the blues that Ma Rainey and Bessie Smith were singing in tent shows and on the black vaudeville circuit. Still they mark the entry of the blues into popular music; it was this distinction that enabled Handy to claim with some justification that he was the "father of the blues." Although he certainly didn't invent the blues, he codified many of its conventions, such as the 12-bar form, and brought it into the world of popular music.

Race Records. It was an advance in technology that brought country and classic blues singers like Ma Rainey and Bessie Smith into the recording studio. But it was Mamie Smith who first put bluesy, distinctively black singing on disc. Her 1920 recording "Crazy Blues" caused a sensation and encouraged record companies to seek out other, similar singers.

What really spurred them into action was the competition from radio. Commercial radio began in 1920 with a single station. It mushroomed into big business almost overnight, crippling the recording industry in the process: people didn't want to pay for what they could get for free. To make up for the losses in the mainstream market, record companies sought out smaller markets—blacks, southern whites, and various ethnic groups—where they would not face competition from mainstream radio.

Style Labels

Mamie Smith's "Crazy Blues" is not a blues song in the full sense of the term. Rather, it is a blues-influenced popular song sung in a blues-influenced style. *Ragtime, jazz, blues, swing, rock and roll, rock, soul, funk*—when a new African American–derived sound enters the mainstream, its style label is used to identify almost any music with even a hint of the new sound. We encountered this with ragtime, and we encounter it here with the blues and later with many other styles. Only in retrospect does the essence of the music come into focus.

Chief among these new markets was the race record market. **Race records** were recordings of black performers, targeted at a black audience. The featured styles were blues and jazz. Blues recordings covered a wide range of styles: country blues, which we'll hear in Robert Johnson; the more commercial classic blues of Bessie Smith; and **boogie-woogie**, a blues piano style characterized by repetitive bass figures, usually in a shuffle rhythm.

These blues styles differed from one another in the mood and the power that each projected, in the content and the style of the lyrics, and in the instrumental accompaniment. Styles served different purposes—dance music, party music, self-expression to anyone who cared to listen—but all blues styles shared common ground:

- Blues, in form and style
- Rooted in the South
- Outside of the mainstream

Some blues musicians were folk musicians; some were semi-professional, playing locally; others did well enough to work more or less full-time—but they all made much less money than the successful popular musicians of the time. Much of the African American music created during this time slipped under the popular music radar.

Columbia Records, the company that recorded Bessie Smith, was a major label; Paramount, which recorded Blind Lemon Jefferson, was a sideline for a Wisconsin furniture manufacturer. The recordings remain obscure, although they are more available now than they were at the time of their release. With few exceptions the artists who recorded them were not popular in any measurable way. Their recordings remain valuable contributions because of their inherent expressiveness and interest and because of their influence on popular music. We begin with Robert Johnson and country blues.

This publicity shot is one of only two verified photos of bluesman Robert Johnson. The other is a candid in which he glares into the camera. The contrast between these two photographs, and the fact that there are only two, only add to the mystery that surrounds his life.

The Sound of Country Blues

For many serious students of the blues, the purest blues has been the **country blues** of artists like Robert Johnson. Its purity lies in its freedom from commercial influences. We hear no pop, no jazz, no horns in country blues—just a man and his guitar.

Robert Johnson. Robert Johnson (1911–1938), the most esteemed of the early Delta bluesmen, is a strong contender for the most mysterious figure in the history of popular music. He lived and worked in obscurity, virtually unknown outside

CD 1:8   **Country Blues** (Robert Johnson; performed by Johnson, vocal and guitar)

0:00	Guitar introduction.

1st Chorus ■ **Conventional blues form**

0:09	1st phrase
	I got to keep movin'...
0:24	1st phrase repeats.
	Notice how Johnson's guitar playing mimics his voice.
	Mmmmmmmmm, blues fallin' down...
0:36	Rhyming phrase, with guitar response.
	And the days keeps...

2nd Chorus

0:51	There are two quite different guitar sounds here: high chords behind the voice and two-part response figure (bass sounds plus riff on higher strings).
	If today was Christmas...

3rd Chorus

1:25	Notice how the vocal line starts high and ends low.
	You sprinkled hot...

4th Chorus

1:58	*I can tell the wind...*

of the Delta region during his lifetime. Although he spent most of his life in the Mississippi Delta, he made his only recordings—a CD's worth of tracks (including alternate takes)—in Texas: San Antonio in 1936 and Dallas in 1937. There are at least three different versions of his death, the most likely being that he drank whiskey poisoned with strychnine (by the jealous husband of a woman he'd been visiting) and died soon after from pneumonia.

Columbia reissued Johnson's recordings on a single LP during the folk and blues revival of the late 1950s and early 1960s. The album was instrumental in helping a generation of rock musicians discover Johnson's music. His playing was a major influence on many important blues and rock musicians, including the Rolling Stones, who covered his songs "Love in Vain" and "Stop Breakin' Down," and Eric Clapton, who covered many Johnson songs, including "Hellhound on My Trail," in his 2004 album, *Me and Mister Johnson*.

In Johnson's 1937 recording, "Hellhound on My Trail," the lyrics are filled with vivid images—"blues fallin' down like hail," "hellhound on my trail"—and he delivers them straight. We listen to what the words have to say and how Johnson delivers them. His guitar playing is extraordinary. Johnson can make his guitar mimic his voice, provide strong accompaniment, or serve as another voice. We hear all of these qualities in this important recording.

CD 1:8

"Hellhound on My Trail," Robert Johnson (1937). Johnson, vocal and guitar.

STYLE PROFILE

COUNTRY BLUES

Rhythm	*Lazy tempo; guitar keeps intermittent shuffle rhythm (a **shuffle** rhythm divides each beat into two unequal parts; the first is long, the second is short).*

Melody	*Long musical phrases that start high and end low; set to short bursts of lyrics; smooth continuum between sung and spoken words.*
Instrumentation (timbre)	*Voice and acoustic guitar.*
Performance style	*Raw, harsh, high-pitched vocal sound; guitar part often contains both strummed chords and a melodic answer to the vocal phrase.*
Dynamics	*Soft, but loud for unamplified voice and acoustic guitar.*
Harmony	***Blues progression.***
Texture	*Melody plus widely varied accompaniment.*
Form	*Blues form with some irregular pacing.*

Key Points

Lyrics	*Dark images ("hellhound . . .") evoke the world of the Delta bluesman.*
Singing	*Strong, unfiltered, raw, powerful, acrid.*
Guitar roles	*Accompanist, responder, reinforcer: sometimes two at a time.*

Terms to Know

shuffle

The Sound of Classic Blues

The recordings of Bessie Smith (1894–1937) epitomize **classic blues.** They feature Smith's rough, full-voiced singing supported by jazz musicians. The accompaniment varies, from just a pianist to a full jazz band. Most of her recordings are conventional 12-bar blues, with call-and-response between singer and an instrumentalist. We hear a famous example below, recorded in 1928 at the peak of her career.

In "Empty Bed Blues," Smith begins by singing about her man troubles. For most of the song, she describes their lovemaking, sometimes in metaphor ("coffee grinder," "deep sea diver") and sometimes directly. All of this makes his two-timing (or, more likely, multi-timing) infidelity even more painful.

Particularly since the emergence of punk and rap, we are used to music being "real"—a no-nonsense, no-holds-barred representation of our lives. In popular music this is where *real* begins.

CD 1:9

"Empty Bed Blues," Bessie Smith (1928). Smith, vocal; Charlie Green, trombone; Porter Grainger, piano.

Courtesy Morgan Collection

This photo, shot when Bessie Smith was about thirty, shows her looking both elegant and vulnerable. Smith was a big woman with a big voice; other publicity shots show a more rambunctious side of her personality.

0:00	Instrumental introduction: piano and trombone.
0:11	1st Chorus
	Hear the blues harmony underneath the voice and the trombone response.
	[I] I woke up . . . [I response]
	[IV] I woke up . . . [I response]
	[V] My new man . . . [I response]
0:44	2nd Chorus
	Call-and-response between voice and trombone.
	Bought me a . . .
1:18	3rd Chorus
	Notice the "blue" notes on "can't" and "stay."
	He's a deep sea diver . . . [twice]
	He can stay . . .
1:52	4th Chorus
	Melody starts high and ends low.
	He knows how . . .
2:26	5th Chorus
	Lord, he's got that sweet . . .
	End of the first side of the disc.
3:01	Break, with piano and muted trombone.
3:08	6th Chorus
	Trombone continues using a mute.
	When my bed . . .
3:42	7th Chorus
	Sometimes Smith "talks" the words; the rhythm is independent of the beat ("bought him a blanket").
	Bought him a . . .
4:16	8th Chorus
	Smith's inflection on words like "beret" is typical of "deep blues."
	He came home . . .
4:50	9th Chorus
	He give me . . .
5:24	10th Chorus
	He poured my first . . .
5:58	11th Chorus
	This chorus is shortened—probably to fit on the recording.
	When you git good . . .

Not only the subject of the lyrics but also the range of emotions they describe and the frankness with which Smith sings them were without precedent. She tells us how good it is with her man and how devastated she is when he's with someone else.

Smith's singing is comparably direct. She has a rough, rich, powerful voice. Most phrases start high and end low. She inflects key words to intensify their emotional power; her delivery is speech intensified into song. In all these respects, her singing is comparable to that of Muddy Waters (whom we heard sing "Standing Around Crying" in Chapter 1).

Smith is backed by two good jazz musicians of the time: trombonist Charlie Green and pianist Porter Grainger. Green in particular tries to emulate and extend the blues vocal style: his playing is full of swoops, smears, and bent notes—all of which mimic the expressive inflection heard in great blues singing.

The sound of this recording is quite different from "Standing Around Crying." Why is it considered classic blues? We find the answer in three places: the earthy, direct lyrics; Smith's singing; and the use of several blues conventions—the 12-bar form, call-and-response between voice and instrument, and phrases that start high and end low. Of these the most essential are the words and Smith's singing. That is where the expressive power resides.

STYLE PROFILE

CLASSIC BLUES

Rhythm	*Four-beat feel, but with two-beat accompaniment in piano; syncopation in voice and trombone.*
Melody	*In voice; medium-length phrases in a narrow range that start high and finish low.*
Instrumentation (timbre)	*Voice, **trombone**, and piano.*
Performance style	*Smith's singing has a rough, gravelly quality; it is a strong voice. She sings with a lot of inflection and subtle timing, moving ahead or behind the beat. Green, the trombonist, tries to emulate her style with his own gravelly sound. He also uses a mute in the second part.*
Dynamics	*Loud but unamplified singing and playing.*
Harmony	*I-IV-V, standard blues harmony.*
Texture	*Melody with piano accompaniment, plus trombone line; **call-and-response** between voice and trombone.*
Form	*Blues.*

Key Points

Racy lyrics	*Talking about the sexual act via metaphors like "deep sea diver."*
Essence of blues style	*Big, rough voice; high-to-low phrases; subtle timing and inflection.*
Standard blues form	*Several choruses of a classic 12-bar blues.*

Terms to Know

call-and-response
classic blues
trombone

Smith's audience included not only black Americans but also a small, devoted group of white fans. She was admired enough to appear in a short film, an extremely unusual circumstance for a black blues singer in the late 1920s. The blues that she epitomized penetrated almost every aspect of popular music.

The Great Depression hit Americans hard—and African Americans especially hard. Too few could afford to buy records or attend the theaters and clubs where these blues singers performed. As a result, the market for this kind of commercial blues singing had all but dried up by the early 1930s.

The Legacy of Blues Style. In the next chapter, we encounter Louis Armstrong's "West End Blues." Both the idea and the sound of the blues had entered the popular mainstream, touching popular song, jazz, and even pop-based concert music. We even find evidence of blues in musical theater. When composer Jerome Kern wanted to tell the audience of his landmark musical *Show Boat* that the character who sings "Can't Help Lovin' Dat Man" is a light-skinned mulatto passing for white, he adds blues touches to the song. What ragtime and syncopated music did for dance, blues did for the heart and soul. All of this filtered into popular music. The music of the 1910s and 1920s was the first generation of popular music to be shaped by the blues. It would not be the last. We will hear the blues again and again.

EARLY JAZZ

Legend has it that Buddy Bolden was already blowing everyone away in New Orleans before 1900. Bolden was the first of the great New Orleans cornetists. (A **cornet** is a close cousin of the **trumpet**.) But we don't know what Bolden's music sounded like, or what jazz might have sounded like around the turn of the century, because we have no recordings of him or any other jazz musician from that time.

The Roots of Jazz. We do know that New Orleans was the birthplace of **jazz** and that contemporary accounts date its beginnings sometime around the turn of the twentieth century. It flourished in the rich cultural mix that was New Orleans: whites of English and French descent, African Americans, immigrants from the Caribbean and Europe, plus many citizens of mixed race. (New Orleans bordellos were famous for octoroon and quadroon prostitutes—those who were one-eighth and one-quarter black.) Then as now New Orleans liked to celebrate, most famously at Mardi Gras, but also for almost any occasion—for example, the trip back from the cemetery after a "jazz funeral" was usually a high-spirited affair. Music was part of this mix: brass bands for parades, and pianists and small groups for the bars, honky-tonks, and houses of prostitution, which was then legal in New Orleans. New Orleans and its visitors simply let the good times roll.

The Jim Crow laws enacted in the wake of *Plessy v. Ferguson* (the 1892 Supreme Court ruling in favor of racially segregated schools) had a profound impact on the development of jazz. Throughout much of the nineteenth century, New Orleans had been a relatively hospitable environment for African Americans. During slavery Congo Square (now Louis Armstrong Park) was the only part of the South where people of African descent could legally gather and play drums and other percussion instruments. Before the Emancipation Proclamation, there were more free blacks in New Orleans than anywhere else in the United States, and New Orleans developed a complex social structure. It assigned social status by race and ethnic heritage—not just whites and blacks but also those of mixed race. "Creoles of color," those with ancestors from both France and Africa, enjoyed a higher social standing than ex-slaves. They lived in better neighborhoods, were better educated, and had more freedom. An aspiring Creole musician received traditional classical training, whereas black musicians typically learned to play by ear. Creoles of color tended to look down on the ex-slaves. They emulated white culture rather than black.

This all changed in the wake of Jim Crow legislation. Race in New Orleans became simply "white" and "colored." Grouped together with no legal difference between them, black and

In 1864 a "quadroon bill," which proposed that anyone with one-fourth or less African blood be considered white, was introduced into the state legislature. It was defeated after lengthy debate. A majority of whites took action in response to the "threat" of a truly interracial, color-blind society. Louisiana eventually developed codes for determining race that rival those of South Africa during apartheid. Quite simply, if a person had *any* African blood, he or she was considered a Negro. As late as 1970, Louisiana enacted a law stating that a person with one-thirty-secondth African ancestry was to be considered colored/Negro/black. This means that if one of your great-great-great grandparents was black, so are you. This kind of law documents the obsession of some whites with "racial purity." By contrast, there is no Louisiana law documenting the "Frenchness" of its white citizens, although by the same logic those with one-thirty-secondth French ancestry would be considered Cajun.

Creole musicians began to work with one another. Jazz gained the spontaneity of improvisation and the feeling of the blues from the blacks, and the discipline and the traditional virtuosity of classical training from the Creoles.

Storyville and the Spread of Jazz. In 1898 a New Orleans alderman named Sidney Story proposed that legal prostitution be restricted to a relatively small section of the black part of the city. Prostitution, and the low life that goes with it, had spread throughout the city, and Story wanted to curb it. Story's proposal became law, and the section of the city where prostitution was legal became known, ironically, as Storyville. Jazz flourished in Storyville, which was where most jazz musicians found work. In 1917 a series of unsavory incidents involving sailors of the U.S. Navy brought Storyville to the attention of the Secretary of the Navy, who threatened to shut down the New Orleans naval base if the city fathers didn't close Storyville. They did.

The closing of Storyville put jazz musicians out of work and forced them to look elsewhere. Many moved out of town, and Chicago became a prime destination. Among those who moved north were the members of the Original Dixieland Jazz Band (ODJB). A group of five white musicians, the ODJB was the first jazz band to record. (Freddie Keppard, an African American who was one of the notable New Orleans cornetists, turned down the chance to make the first jazz record, allegedly because he was afraid that other musicians would steal his licks—his musical ideas.) The ODJB recordings, released in 1917, were a novelty success. They put the word *jazz* on people's lips and a jazzlike sound in people's ears.

The New Orleans Jazz Band. The early history of jazz that we can document begins in the early twenties, when African American jazz bands began to record with some frequency. The traditional **New Orleans jazz** band has two parts: the front line and the rhythm section. The **front line** (so called because the musicians stand at the front of the bandstand) is typically three instruments: clarinet, trumpet or cornet, and trombone. The standard **rhythm section** consists of banjo, piano, **brass bass** (or **tuba** the lowest-pitched of the brass instruments), and drums. The front-line instruments play melody-like lines. The rhythm section has two jobs: to mark the beat and to supply the harmony.

The standard New Orleans jazz band blended the instrumentation of three key popular music genres. From the marching band came the clarinet, cornet, trombone, tuba, and drum line. From the minstrel show came the banjo, and from the saloons and bordellos (and other places where one could hear professional ragtime pianists) came the piano.

The three front-line instruments usually play within a well-defined range and work within well-defined limits, particularly when playing together.

The Drum Set

The **drum set** (also called *drum kit* and *trap set*) essentially puts an entire drum line at the service of a single player. The two key inventions necessary for a usable one-man drum set were a bass drum pedal and a hi-hat. The **bass drum pedal** dates back to 1888, but the big breakthrough was the invention of a spring-activated bass drum pedal by William Ludwig in 1909. The **hi-hat** is a pair of **cymbals** mounted on a stand that the drummer operates with his foot. The "Snow Shoe Sock Pedal," which appeared during the 1920s, was the first of these devices (hence the other name for the hi-hat: the **sock cymbal**). The modern hi-hat, however, didn't come into widespread use until the mid-1930s.

- The cornet (trumpet) is the midrange instrument that usually carries the melody.
- The **clarinet** takes the highest part, playing a fast-moving countermelody to the main part.
- The trombone carries the lowest melodic part, usually in the form of "commentary" on the melody and the clarinet part.

All three (or four, when there's an extra cornet or saxophone) melody instruments typically play at the same time, a procedure known as **collective improvisation. Improvisation** means that the performers make up the music as they play, rather than playing music that they or someone else has already written. *Collective* simply means that they do it simultaneously.

Collective improvisation requires teamwork: everyone has to know not only his or her own role but the others' roles as well. In this respect collective improvisation in jazz is much like a well-executed fast break in basketball: the cornet or trumpet player is like the ball handler. Both are located in the center of the action: midrange melody for the musician, center court for the basketball player. Other players flank the center and react to what the player controlling the action does. In both cases the process is spontaneous, but it occurs within prescribed and well-understood boundaries.

The two most important New Orleans bands were those led by King Oliver and Jelly Roll Morton, both of whom became nationally known.

King Oliver's Creole Jazz Band. Joe "King" Oliver (1885–1938) was one of the major figures of early jazz. His reputation rests on his achievements as a bandleader and a cornet player. Like many New Orleans musicians, he emigrated to Chicago in search of better-paying jobs following the closing of Storyville. By 1920 he had assembled several of his New Orleans expatriates into King Oliver's Creole Jazz Band, the finest traditional New Orleans–style jazz band preserved on record.

Although in "Dippermouth Blues," Oliver and clarinetist Johnny Dodds play solos, most of the performance proceeds with all instruments playing simultaneously, with no one instrument completely dominant. This is the quintessential New Orleans jazz sound.

"Dippermouth Blues" is a blues song in form and style. Each section is twelve measures long, with the characteristic harmonic pattern of the blues. It is also a blues song in style, which is nowhere more evident than in Oliver's famous cornet solo. As a cornet player, Oliver developed an influential style deeply rooted in the blues. His solo in "Dippermouth Blues" was one of the most frequently imitated jazz solos of his generation. His playing parallels the heightened inflection, narrow range, and unconstrained rhythmic delivery of a blues singer. The manner in which he slides in and out of important notes is an instrumental counterpart to blues vocal style.

King Oliver's Creole Jazz Band in 1922. From left to right: Johnny Dodds, clarinet; Baby Dodds, drums; Honore Dutrey, trombone; Louis Armstrong, second cornet; King Oliver, lead cornet; Lil Hardin (Armstrong's wife), piano; and Bill Johnson, banjo. Notice that Johnson is holding a bass that he doesn't play and that Dodds's drum set is primitive by modern standards.

CD 1:10

"Dippermouth Blues," Joe Oliver. King Oliver's Creole Jazz Band (1923), featuring Oliver, cornet, and Johnny Dodds, clarinet.

"Dippermouth Blues" shows the "deep blues" roots of early jazz. Most early jazz recordings show at least some influence of blues style, and many of them—almost half, it would seem—are based on blues form. From the beginning, jazz musicians have liked to improvise on the blues chord progression because the chords are simple and change relatively slowly. This gives the musicians plenty of time to invent ideas—blueslike riffs (as in Oliver's solo), faster running lines, or whatever strikes their fancy. (In Chapter 4 we hear a spectacular demonstration of improvisation over blues harmony in Louis Armstrong's "West End Blues.")

STYLE PROFILE

NEW ORLEANS JAZZ

Rhythm	*Fast tempo;* **four-beat rhythm** *(kept by the banjo and felt by the entire band); a strong backbeat at times from the drummer; lots of syncopation and other forms of rhythmic play, especially anticipating or lagging behind the beat; active lines in cornet and clarinet.* **Stop time***, the periodic interruption of steady timekeeping, is a special effect; it occurs during the clarinet solo.*
Melody	*Active, instrumental-style melody with little repetition; differs from chorus to chorus because of improvisation. Cornet solo is like a blues melody: narrow range, downward direction, and repeated, slightly varied riffs.*
Instrumentation (timbre)	*Front line: two cornets, clarinet, and trombone.*
	Rhythm section: piano (barely heard), banjo, and drums/percussion.

Performance style	*Instrumental counterpart to blues vocal style: lots of bent notes and slides into notes, imitating the voice.*
Dynamics	*Consistently loud.*
Harmony	*Blues progression throughout.*
Texture	*Classic New Orleans sound: in most choruses, collective improvisation in the front line (three independent lines, all improvised); the rhythm section keeps time.*
Form	*Improvised variations over blues form, with introduction and **tag**.*

Key Points

Jazz rhythm	*Rhythm section chunks out steady four-beat rhythm.*
Blues influence	*12-bar blues harmonic progression; blues style, especially in Oliver's solo.*
New Orleans instrumentation	*Standard New Orleans jazz band: front line (clarinet, cornet[s], trombone) plus rhythm section (here, banjo, piano, and drums).*
Collective improvisation	*Front-line players improvise at the same time.*

Terms to Know

collective improvisation	four-beat rhythm	stop time
cornet	New Orleans jazz	tag

LISTENING GUIDE: "DIPPERMOUTH BLUES"

CD 1:10 **New Orleans Jazz** (Joe Oliver; performed by King Oliver's Creole Jazz Band, featuring Oliver, cornet, and Johnny Dodds, clarinet)

0:00	Introduction.
0:05	1st Chorus
	Full band; clarinet, cornet, and trombone engage in collective improvisation.
0:19	2nd Chorus
	Notice how each instrument stays in a particular register: clarinet, high; cornet, medium high; trombone, midrange.
0:34	3rd Chorus
	Clarinet solo; notice the stop time in the rhythm section.
0:49	4th Chorus
	Clarinet solo continues.
1:03	5th Chorus
	Full band again, playing different material over the same blues progression; the drummer can be heard marking the beat, especially the backbeat, here and in most of the choruses.
1:18	6th Chorus
	Oliver's famous and widely imitated cornet solo.
1:32	7th Chorus
	Oliver's solo continues.
1:46	8th Chorus
	Full band returns, with stop time (rhythm section stops playing); break at the end.
	Oh, play that thing!
2:00	9th Chorus
	Ends with tag.

Improvisation Versus Composition in Jazz. "Dippermouth Blues" also illustrates the central place of improvisation in jazz. All of the African American styles discussed in this chapter accept, even encourage, some spontaneity in performance. Although the basic feel and the musical content of a blues or a piano rag would be established before it was performed, each performance could be—and often was—different. We know this through comparisons of alternate recorded versions of the same song or piece. In jazz, however, improvisation often plays a bigger role; there would be more variation from one performance of a piece to the next, and the improvisations tended to be more elaborate, as we hear in both solos.

Although improvisation may be central to jazz performance, it is not essential—many memorable jazz recordings exist in which there is little or no improvisation. Because we don't know exactly what's coming, improvisation gives a musical performance a sense of immediacy, a sense of being in the moment, a sense of anticipation, Composition, where the musical events are planned in advance and rehearsed, trades spontaneity for structure and discipline.

Jelly Roll Morton. One of the most colorful figures in the history of jazz, Ferdinand "Jelly Roll" Morton (1890–1941) claimed to have "invented" jazz. Although he may simply have been bragging (he was famous for that), Morton has as much right to the claim as any single person. He was certainly its first great composer and its first great pianist. In a largely improvised music, Morton's best compositions highlight the role of the composer in creating a formal design and varying the texture through changing instrumentation. In the work of Morton and the other great jazz composers, composition does not necessarily eliminate improvisation; it simply controls the context in which it takes place.

The Spread of Jazz. With the influx of New Orleans jazz musicians like King Oliver and Jelly Roll Morton into northern cities and the recording of both white and black musicians, jazz became a national music in the early 1920s. Chicago was its crucible. The city was wide open—Al Capone and other gang leaders all but ran it—and musicians found ample employment opportunities in speakeasies and ballrooms. A generation of white musicians, among them Bix Beiderbecke and Benny Goodman, absorbed the sound of the New Orleans musicians firsthand, much as white rockers absorbed Chicago blues style in the sixties.

Jazz, Ragtime, and Blues. Most early jazz recordings were blues- or rag-based compositions. Perhaps for this reason, jazz historians have discussed ragtime, blues, and occasionally syncopated dance music as if they were tributaries that fed into the river that became jazz. A less jazz-centric view of the African American musical landscape in the first part of the twentieth century might be this: these four styles, performed by blacks and whites, are more or less parallel streams that often intersect, not only with one another but also with popular song.

The "Jazz Age." What ragtime and syncopated dance music did for dance, and what blues did for the heart and soul, jazz did for the spirit. The jazz of the early 1920s was exuberant, optimistic, spontaneous, and fast paced. It suggested illicit pleasures, if only because it so often accompanied good times that might include smoking, drinking, sex, and the like. In these respects it captured—and often inspired—the mood of the country, which accelerated through the decade until everything came crashing down in 1929. More than any other music, jazz would become the soundtrack of the decade. Small wonder that novelist F. Scott Fitzgerald and others called the 1920s the **Jazz Age.** We visit this heady time in Chapter 4.

LOOKING BACK, LOOKING AHEAD

The first quarter of the twentieth century saw the emergence of four important African American musical styles. Ragtime was first; it caught on at the turn of the century. Syncopated dance music grew out of the ragtime dances of the 1900s and became popular in the early teens. Blues (as published songs) and jazz (as performed by white musicians) caught on shortly thereafter.

Because ragtime was disseminated via publishing and piano rolls, both black and white audiences could encounter the music in its authentic form. During the teens syncopated dance orchestras played for white audiences in ballrooms and hotels. It wasn't until the 1920s that jazz musicians moved away from New Orleans to other parts of the country; Chicago was a prime destination. Race records, a new direction in the recording industry that took off in the early 1920s, gave more listeners the opportunity to hear not only jazz but also the classic blues of Bessie Smith, Ma Rainey, and others.

All of these new sounds would transform popular music, beginning in the teens and really catching on during the twenties. They would be the primary cause for the popular music revolution of the 1920s, which we encounter in the following chapter.

TERMS TO KNOW

Test your knowledge of this chapter's important terms by defining the following. If you can't recall the meaning of a certain term, refresh your memory by looking up the boldfaced term in the chapter, turning to the Glossary at the back of the book, or working with the flashcards on the *Popular Music in America* Companion Web site: *http://music.wadsworth.com/ campbell_2e*

. . . .

arpeggio	drum set	piano rag
art music	four-beat rhythm	race record
bass drum pedal	fox trot	ragtime
blues	front line	rhythm section
blues form	*griot*	shuffle
blues progression	hi-hat	sock cymbal
boogie-woogie	improvisation	stop time
brass bass	jazz	strain
call-and-response	Jazz Age	syncopation
clarinet	licks	tag
classic blues	march	trio
collective improvisation	march form	trombone
cornet	march rhythm	trumpet
country blues	multisectional form	tuba
cymbal	New Orleans jazz	turkey trot

. . . .

The Modern Era in Popular Music

On January 4, 1924, George Gershwin was shooting pool with his brother, Ira, and Buddy DeSylva, Gershwin's lyricist at the time, when Ira happened to read an article in the New York *Tribune* about an upcoming concert. Presented by Paul Whiteman, who led one of the popular dance orchestras of the time, the concert was billed as an "Experiment in Modern Music." Among the featured pieces on the program would be a "jazz concerto" by George Gershwin.

The announcement threw Gershwin into a panic. He had had an informal and rather vague conversation with Whiteman about the project but hadn't imagined that Whiteman took the discussion as a commitment. Working at a white heat, he finished the piece, by then titled *Rhapsody in Blue*, in time for the premiere on February 12. Gershwin's jazz concerto was the highlight of the concert and a critical success. It remains the most popular instrumental concert piece ever written by an American.

Most of the music on Whiteman's program was not modern in any sense of the term. Gershwin's rhapsody *was* modern; it captured the spirit of the times as well as any music has been able to. We consider how and why in this chapter.

THE MODERN ERA

The fifteen years between 1914 (the start of World War I) and 1929 (the start of the Great Depression) marked the beginning of the modern era, not only in popular music but also in art, literature, and American life. To be modern in America during the 1920s meant moving and living at a faster pace. It meant believing in progress, especially material progress. It meant moving out of the country and into the city. It meant taking advantage of new technologies, from automobiles and air conditioning to the zippers that were now featured on clothing, luggage, and a host of other products. It meant buying into fashionable intellectual ideas and artistic trends. And it meant listening—and dancing—to a new kind of music.

The emergence of a distinctively American popular music expressed both the fact and the nature of America's coming of age. With its intercession in World War I, the United States had become a world power, a player on the world stage. Business, applying the assembly-line pro-

Gershwin, describing his method of composition and his source of inspiration: "No set plan was in my mind, no structure to which the music would conform. . . . I was on the train [to Boston], with its steely rhythms, and its rattlety-bang that is so stimulating to a composer. . . . And then suddenly I heard—even saw on paper—the complete construction of the *Rhapsody* as a sort of musical kaleidoscope of America." He finished it in a week.

cedures used so successfully by Henry Ford and the management techniques of Frederick Winslow Taylor, grew in size and efficiency. New products, particularly electrically operated home appliances, made domestic chores significantly easier. Skilled workers had more money to spend and more time to spend it.

As a result, the entertainment industry flourished. Much of this entertainment, particularly popular music and films, projected a uniquely American cultural identity and a distinctly modern attitude. Politically, economically, and culturally, the United States relied much less on Europe for inspiration and guidance.

Sex, Booze, and All That Jazz

The teens and twenties saw enormous social change in America. Immigration and migration, Prohibition and its consequences, and a sexual revolution that dramatically redefined the place of the woman in American society—all reshaped life in the modern era.

People on the Move. Immigration from abroad, especially during the teens, and internal migration within the United States, especially by African Americans, swelled cities like New York and Chicago. The biggest influx of people from abroad came in the teens. A backlash against this new wave of immigrants resulted in laws severely restricting immigration. By 1931 more people were leaving the United States than entering it.

Large ethnic and minority populations in such cities as New York and Chicago helped support their resident musicians and entertainers. Most of the great songwriters of the period between the wars were Jewish or African American: Irving Berlin, Jerome Kern, Harold Arlen, George Gershwin, Duke Ellington, and Thomas "Fats" Waller. So were many vaudeville stars: Eddie Cantor, Al Jolson, Bert Williams, and Fanny Brice. African American musicians supplied dance music and entertainment for all levels of society in the 1910s and '20s, although bands remained segregated until the late 1930s.

Prohibition. In an effort to eliminate workers' "blue Mondays" (worker absenteeism or poor performance caused by excessive weekend drinking), among other alcohol-related social problems, the Temperance movement succeeded in getting the Eighteenth Amendment passed. Although it didn't stop Americans from drinking, Prohibition did make it illegal (specifically, purchasing alcohol). The 1920s became the era of bathtub gin (and other kinds of homemade liquor) and **speakeasies**—clubs that required a softly spoken password for admission.

Prohibition meant work for many popular musicians. Jazz spread from New Orleans throughout the country by way of Chicago's speakeasies, as Joe "King" Oliver, Louis Armstrong, and other early jazz greats moved north in search of more and better-paying work. Benny Goodman, the "king of swing," also got his professional start in a Chicago speakeasy.

The New Woman. The passage of the Nineteenth Amendment, which gave women the right to vote, ended a long and difficult chapter in the history of women's rights. It also signaled a major shift in American attitudes toward women and their place in society. One product of this change was a new kind of young woman.

This "new woman" appeared in the 1920s. Freed to some extent from the drudgery of housework by a wave of new appliances and with more cash in hand, she consumed—and became a target of advertisers. Liberated from Victorian morality by trendy interpretations of Freudian ideas, she indulged in "petting parties" with all-too-eager young men. She cut her hair and dressed in short, loose-fitting dresses. Tempted by illicit liquor, cigarettes, and other accoutrements of fast living, she partied hard. She was called a "flapper," and she danced, and danced, and danced to the new syncopated music. Her parents were, not surprisingly, horrified by this behavior. And, then as now, popular music was judged one of the causes of her moral degradation. To cite just one example, an article appeared in a 1921 issue of the *Ladies Home Journal* entitled, "Does Jazz Put the Sin in Syncopation?"

Compared with the suffragists who had fought so hard for the right to vote, and the members of the Women's Christian Temperance Union who decried the evils of alcohol, the flappers seemed frivolous and hedonistic. But what they represented—women who had the power to make choices, however misguided or silly they might seem in retrospect—was not frivolous. The battle for equal rights had a long way to go, but the flappers reaped the benefits of a significant victory and the change in attitude it symbolized.

Flappers were too-easy targets. Young men in the 1920s were certainly just as frivolous as their female counterparts. And how to label the fiscal foolishness of so many of their parents who hopped on the stock market bubble until it burst in 1929? Jazzy, bluesy, get-up-and-dance-to-it popular music was the soundtrack to all these changes. How people heard it is the next part of our story.

The First Technological Revolution: From Radio to Talking Pictures

In 1919, if you were living in Omaha or Oklahoma City and wanted to hear a hit song, you had few choices. You could buy the sheet music and play it yourself—or get a friend to play it for you. That was a popular choice; sheet music sales peaked in the teens. Or you could buy an **acoustic recording**, like the one by King Oliver. Or you could pay to see a vaudeville show passing through town, where you might hear one of the acts sing the song. Otherwise, you'd have to go out of town—to places like New York or Chicago.

In 1929 you had many more choices. You could still buy the sheet music and go to the theater to hear a vaudeville act. But you could also turn on the radio and find a local musician playing the song or tune in to a network broadcast of one of the top hotel bands from New York City. You could go into Woolworth's and buy a record of the song; it would sound a lot better than the recording from ten years earlier. And if a movie musical featured the song, you could go downtown to the local movie theater.

At no time—not even our own—has the way in which popular music reached its audience changed so fundamentally. In 1919 the majority of the audience learned pop songs by looking at them—that is, by playing through the sheet-music versions. In 1929 more people learned songs by ear: on the radio, on record, at the movies, and in live performances. The advances in our own time—MP3s, streaming audio, worldwide access, and the like—don't change the way we learn the music. We listen to it through the media, just like our parents and grandparents did. The shift from eye to ear happened in the 1920s.

The new media appeared in stages: first radio, then electric recordings, followed by amplified live performances, and finally talking films. We begin in Pittsburgh, Pennsylvania, in 1920.

Radio Broadcasting. In 1920 the first commercial radio station, KDKA in Pittsburgh, began broadcasting. Within two years the number of commercial stations had grown from one to more than 200. With few exceptions each radio station, hiring local musicians and personalities to provide entertainment, generated its own programming.

Important technological advances accompanied the rapid growth of commercial radio. None was more important than the conversion from acoustic to electric broadcasting. Many of the earliest radio studios were equipped with long, conical horns similar to those used in acoustic recordings, into which performers spoke, sang, or played. These horns soon gave way to **microphones** that converted sound into electric impulses, which were then converted into the broadcast signal or transmitted to network affiliates for local broadcast. **Amplifiers** and loudspeakers were used to reconvert the electric impulses into sound. This new technology improved quickly.

In 1925 the National Broadcasting Company (NBC) began broadcasting simultaneously on twenty-five affiliates throughout the Northeast and the Midwest with a gala concert. Although American Telephone and Telegraph (AT&T) had already experimented with broadcasts over several stations from one source, it was NBC's debut that celebrated the birth of a new industry: network radio. Soon performances emanating from one location could be broadcast throughout the country and provide the nation with an unprecedented sense of unity.

Electric Recording. Microphones, amplifiers, and speakers found immediate application elsewhere, in recording, live performance, and instrument manufacture. In 1925 the recording industry converted from acoustic to **electric recording** almost overnight. As in broadcasting, microphones replaced the cumbersome and inefficient horns used for acoustic recording. The result was a dramatic improvement in recorded sound.

Amplified Live Performance. The most obvious benefit of **amplification** was greater volume in performances both live and recorded. Amplification had an even more far-reaching effect, however, on the *sound* of popular music, first by enabling small-voiced singers to record and perform and then by boosting and transforming the sound of existing instruments and making possible an increasingly broad array of electronic instruments.

Before commercial radio, popular singers performed in theaters and auditoriums without any amplification. Many had classically trained, quasi-operatic voices suitable for the operettas fashionable in the early part of the century and for the more serious and conservative popular songs. Others, like Sophie Tucker, Bessie Smith, and Al Jolson, belted out their songs in a full voice that filled the theater.

The new electric technology spawned new kinds of singers: those whose voices would not otherwise project in a theater or record well using acoustic-recording techniques. Almost overnight this new generation of singers broadened the spectrum of vocal styles heard in popular music. By 1929 listeners could choose from the intimate crooning of Bing Crosby; the jazz-inflected, conversational style of Louis Armstrong; the patter of Fats Waller; the faint sounds of "Whispering" Jack Smith; and many others who would not have succeeded in live performance or recording before the electric revolution of 1925.

Talking Films. On October 6, 1927, *The Jazz Singer,* starring Al Jolson, premiered. Although there had previously been other films with sound, this was the first talking picture. Jolson sang, talked, and acted over the soundtrack. The public loved it, and soon Hollywood was churning out talking pictures, even as theater owners were scrambling to add sound systems to the theaters.

Soon popular music was firmly entrenched on the screen. Vaudeville performers filmed their acts. Broadway stars trekked off to Hollywood, and in the 1930s songwriters would follow. By 1929 moviegoers could have seen the first film versions of *Show Boat, Rio Rita* (a spectacular adaptation of another Broadway musical), and *Broadway Melody of 1929,* the first musical and the first sound film to win an Academy Award for best picture.

The sound technology, called Vitaphone by Warner Brothers, the film studio that developed it, was good enough to make the sound realistic. Earlier attempts to merge sound and film had failed because the sound quality was so poor. This was yet another adaptation of the technology that had transformed radio, recording, and live performance.

The changes in the entertainment industry during the 1920s were staggering: radio, network radio, amplification in live performance, decent recording quality, and talking pictures. All of these dreams of 1919 were reality in 1929. The closest parallel might be the Internet explosion in the 1990s; at no other time has so much world-transforming technology appeared in such a short period.

SONG AND DANCE IN THE MODERN ERA

The early twenties saw a dramatic shift in the popular-music landscape, triggered by a new round of energetic dances, whose rhythms had already begun to filter into popular song. During the same time, mainstream popular song and its performance increasingly reflected the spirit of the times. We hear examples of each in the following discussion.

Dance Fads of the 1920s

The 1920s began with a second wave of dance crazes: the black bottom, the shimmy, the blues (yes, the blues was also a social dance), and, above all, the Charleston. Like the ragtime dances of earlier decades, these began as African American social dances and found a new home among younger whites. Dancing to syncopated music had become commonplace and socially acceptable, but these new dances were the cutting edge, a more energetic alternative to the fox trot.

African Americans On-stage

The 1920s saw a resurgence of musical productions by black Americans in New York, both uptown and downtown. *Shuffle Along,* a 1921 musical that featured Noble Sissle and Eubie Blake as songwriters and performers, made the first big splash. Other shows soon followed; most were revues. Both the new social dances and the all-black stage productions were signs of a growing African American presence in American musical life, especially in New York. At various times during the 1920s, intrepid and tireless New Yorkers could dance to Fletcher Henderson's band at the Roseland Ballroom; go uptown to Harlem to hear Duke Ellington at the Cotton Club; visit a theater for the annual edition of Lew Leslie's *Blackbirds,* where they might hear Ethel Waters; or visit the right record store to buy recordings by Bessie Smith and Louis Armstrong.

CD 1:11   **1920s Fox Trot** (James P. Johnson; performed by Paul Whiteman and His Orchestra)

0:00	Introduction. Full band.	
0:07	Vocal interjections.	
0:11	Verse.	

1st Chorus ■ **Two-note "Charle-*ston*" riff**

0:29	A	Full band; strumming banjo keeps the beat.
0:34	B	
0:39	A	
0:42	C	Woodblock percussion accents.
0:47	Sax leads 1st chorus, repeats with variation in the last two phrases.	
1:04	Tag slightly extends the chorus.	
1:06	Interlude. Muted trumpet calls.	
1:08	Clarinet responds.	
1:10	Vocal interjections.	
1:20	Tag.	

2nd Chorus ■ **Variation**

1:24	Saxes play variation on the original melody.
1:38	Trumpets take over.
1:43	Piano takes over.
1:58	Tag.

3rd Chorus ■ **Stop time**

2:03	Clarinet swooping solo.
2:17	Sax solo takes over B phrase.
2:21	Vocal interjections.
2:37	Tag brings the song to a close.

The Charleston. The most popular and enduring of these new dances was the **Charleston**. The dance goes back to at least the early twentieth century, and there is apparently a connection to Charleston, South Carolina. It was danced in Harlem as early as 1913, but it didn't become well known until 1923, when it was introduced on-stage, most notably in an all-black musical production, *Running Wild*.

The dance was done to the song of the same name, "Charleston," written by James P. Johnson (1894–1955), who is much better known as a superb stride pianist. (**Stride piano** is a jazz piano style with deep roots in ragtime.) "Charleston" was Johnson's most memorable hit. It had lyrics by Cecil Mack, but they are seldom sung. Then and now we almost always hear it as an instrumental strictly for dancing.

Johnson's song is the textbook for the new syncopated **fox trot**. The chorus presents not only the **two-beat rhythm** that is the rhythmic foundation of the dance but also its signature syncopation. It consists of a two-note riff over two beats, with the accent on the second note. We hear the riff all by itself at the beginning of the chorus; the words are "Charle-*ston*," "Charle-*ston*." The first note comes with the first beat, and the second note comes just *before* the second beat (**syncopation**). This riff, either in the most basic form heard here

CD 1:11

"Charleston," James P. Johnson (1923). Paul Whiteman and His Orchestra.

or in various elaborations, was the rhythmic key to countless songs of the late teens and twenties, including "After You've Gone," which we hear at the end of this chapter.

The recording heard here, by Paul Whiteman and His Orchestra, documents the emergence of the modern dance orchestra. The two important developments are the prominent role of the **saxophone** and the use of a complete rhythm section. Tuba and banjo lay down the *OOM-chuck* rhythm of the two-beat throughout most of the song.

STYLE PROFILE

1920s FOX TROT

Rhythm	*Fast tempo. This song introduces both the basic fox trot rhythm (bass note and **backbeat** in alternation) and the most popular syncopation ("Charle-" on the first beat; "ston" just before the second beat).*
Melody	*In both the verse and the chorus, the melody grows out of riffs; the chorus riff is the famous two-note "Charleston" riff. Other riffs appear later in the chorus. The second chorus features an elaborated version of the melody.*
Instrumentation (timbre)	*Dance orchestra: rhythm section (brass bass, banjo, piano, and drums); saxes **doubling** (switching from one instrument to another) on clarinets, trumpets, and trombones, all grouped by section; violin reinforcing the melody; an occasional hot vocal.*
Performance style	*Vocal interjections, a real novelty; melody instruments played with the clipped articulation characteristic of the 1920s.*
Dynamics	*Moderate throughout.*
Harmony	*Enriched I-IV-V harmony; many extra chords, all connected to I and V.*
Texture	*Harmonized melody over a (usually) steady rhythm section.*
Form	*Introduction/verse/chorus (three statements)/interlude/tags. The chorus of the song has four phrases, in an **ABAC form** (B starts like A but ends differently). Each statement of the chorus is different from the others. All of this helps introduce variety into the performance of a song that has a repetitious rhythm.*

Key Points

Fox trot rhythm and its signature syncopation	*Fox trot = bass alternating with backbeat.* *Signature syncopation = "Charle-ston."*
Rhythm section	*Rhythm section (banjo, tuba, piano, and drums), a new sound in 1920s music, lays down the beat.*
Saxophone	*Warmer and fuller-sounding than the clarinet; the new sound of the 1920s.*
Dance orchestra	*Modern dance orchestra formed by creating a rhythm section and grouping melody instruments into sections.*

Terms to Know

ABAC form	doubling	two-beat rhythm
backbeat	fox trot	

The Formation of the Rhythm Section. It is in the early 1920s that the rhythm section takes shape. We heard it in the recording by Oliver, and we can hear it even more clearly in this recording. It is an essential part of the sound of the dance orchestras of the 1920s, and it is a key element in the new, more modern sound of popular music. Since that time the instrumentation of the rhythm section has changed, but its basic components have not. A complete

rhythm section always has at least one chord instrument, a bass instrument, and a percussion instrument. The rhythm section's role—to supply the beat and the harmony—also remains essentially the same.

The Dance Orchestras of the 1920s. The rhythm section was the foundation of the dance orchestras that serenaded dancers in ballrooms, hotels, and roof gardens and eventually on record and radio. During the teens black groups like Jim Europe's Society Orchestra provided most of the syncopated dance music. By the end of the decade, white bands were offering this jazzy new music. Among the first was the orchestra of Paul Whiteman. Whiteman and his band were part of an unprecedented success in the music business: "Whispering" (1920), one of Whiteman's first recordings, was the first song to top 1 million in sheet music and record sales.

By the early 1920s, Whiteman had plenty of company. Dance orchestras led by Guy Lombardo, Fred Waring, and Isham Jones (who was also a fine songwriter, "It Had to Be You") found work in hotels in resorts and major cities. Black bands also modernized: among the best was the Fletcher Henderson Orchestra, which performed at the Roseland Ballroom, one of New York's hotspots.

There were other major changes in the sound of the dance orchestra besides the consolidation of the rhythm section. Orchestras got larger, and the instruments were grouped into sections: not only rhythm but also **brass** (trumpets and trombones), **winds** (clarinets and

Paul Whiteman and His Orchestra in their natural environment: the ballroom of the Hotel Biltmore (1934).
Notice the large size of the orchestra, with strings and an accordion, plus rhythm, brass, and saxophones.

saxophones), and **strings** (mostly violins). Typically, the musical spotlight would shift from one section to the next, often quickly, as if the two were talking back and forth. These changes are evident in Whiteman's recording. What's missing is the singer. Singers certainly did record, as we hear below, but not yet with dance orchestras.

The Saxophone: A New Sound of the 1920s. The saxophones that are so prominent in the recording of "Charleston" represent the most enduring new sound of the 1920s. There were other new sounds during the same time: the ukulele was an even bigger novelty when Hawaiian music was intermittently in vogue during the decade. But it was the sax that would ultimately become an integral part of the sound of popular music. James Reese Europe was the innovator: his was one of the first dance orchestras to feature the saxophone. But it did not become a staple in the dance orchestra until arrangers began to group instruments into sections in the 1920s. The more massive sound and the broader range of the saxophone family (most bands used three different saxes, alto, tenor, and baritone) made them a more effective counterpart to the brass instruments than the clarinets that were popular in jazz bands and early dance orchestras.

THE NEW POPULAR SONG AND THE INTEGRATION OF SONG AND DANCE

A new kind of popular song flooded the market in the late 1920s. It was upbeat and uptempo. You could sing it and you could dance to it. It captured the high spirits of the age. In it you could hear the influence of the new African American music and the impact of the new technology. We hear a classic example below: Jean Goldkette's recording of "Sunday," but first we consider the issues in recording popular song.

The Record, the Recording, and the Integration of Song and Dance. For the first half of the twentieth century, almost all pop records were released on 10-inch records that played at 78 rpm (revolutions per minute). These records could hold about three minutes of music. Consequently, musicians had to structure their performances so that they would finish around the three-minute mark.

Recordings of popular songs increasingly involved compromise. Nineteenth-century verse/chorus songs typically had several verses; a complete performance might take six minutes or more. To record the same song in three minutes, they cut extra verses and songs got shorter.

The electric revolution created an entirely new relationship between singer and band as well as between song and dance. Prior to 1925 one heard either singer or band. Without microphones it would have been just about impossible to hear a singer over a vigorous dance

Albums

Twelve-inch records, which could hold four minutes, were used mostly for classical music. Because most classical works last longer than four minutes, a recording of a Beethoven symphony or a Tchaikovsky ballet would be spread over several discs. These discs were packaged in an *album,* with a cover, binding, and sleeves for each disc. The invention of the LP (long-playing record) made it possible to record entire pieces on one disc instead of several. Despite this LPs were still called *albums;* the term persists even with CDs.

orchestra in a live performance, and it would have been just as impossible to find a workable balance between singer and band in the recording studio. With amplification, however, singers could perform *with* bands, and they began to do so sometime after 1925. Whiteman claimed to have been the first; he was certainly among the earliest, as was Jean Goldkette.

A New Kind of Song. "Sunday" was a hit in 1927 for the songwriting team of Clifford Gray and J. Fred Coots. (Coots is best remembered for the Christmas evergreen "Santa Claus Is Coming to Town.") The song first appeared in the revue *The Merry World,* and when it caught on several bands recorded it, among them the one led by Goldkette.

CD 1:12

"Sunday," Clifford Gray and J. Fred Coots (1927). Jean Goldkette Orchestra, with the Keller Sisters, vocals.

The song is up-to-date in both words and music. The lyrics are simple and tell us about the life of a young person working long hours. (Among other things, we learn that the 1920s had a six-day workweek.) From the words the mood could be either up or down, depending on whether the focus is on Sunday or the rest of the week. In either event the lyrics are full of the exaggerated feelings that so often accompany infatuation.

One of the novel features of this recording of the song is the absence of a sung verse. We hear a fragment of the verse played by the band just before the voices come in, but we never hear it sung.

AABA Form. The chorus of the song resonates with the faster pace of life in the 1920s. It consists of four short sections. The first, second, and last sections are just about the same (there are minor differences between the first and the second sections); the third is different. We usually refer to this form as **AABA form**: A is the first section of the chorus and any repetition of it, and B is a new section. AABA form was not new to popular music, but it was not widely used before 1925. After that year, however, a decided majority of popular songs used AABA form or some variant of it until well into the rock era.

The A section consists of three phrases: two that are rather short and a third that's about twice as long. The first phrase is built from two riffs: "I'm blue" and "every Monday." The other two alter the scheme a little. The B section starts with the same rhythm as the A section but with a different melody. The music moves fast, both within and among the sections. The phrases within each section are short and snappy. Performed at the brisk, Charleston-like tempo heard here, the song flies by.

Even at first hearing, we notice a big difference between this recording of "Sunday" and all the others that predate it. The song begins like a dance number, with the band playing the melody over a strong, jazz-inflected two-beat rhythm. Midway through, however, we hear the song sung by a female trio. The band returns for a final chorus. From the late teens on, almost all new pop songs were fox trots. (Sheet music covers and record labels make this clear.) In this sense they were for both singing and dancing. Prior to 1925 performances went one way or the other: you either sang the song or you played it for dancing. After 1925 the performance could cover both bases: you could dance to it and still hear someone sing it. The practice of sandwiching a vocal between dance-oriented instrumental statements of the melody remained popular through the early 1940s.

It is around this time that the verse virtually disappears from pop-song recordings. The idea was to get the chorus, which contained the catchiest musical ideas, into the ear of the listeners as frequently as possible. In this recording we hear the chorus four times and just a fragment of the verse.

Jean Goldkette's Orchestra. This recording of "Sunday" dates from 1927. It features the Jean Goldkette Orchestra. Born in France and trained as a concert pianist, Jean Goldkette (1899–1962) came to the United States in 1911 and found work in Chicago as a musician

CD 1:12   **1920s Popular Song** (Clifford Gray and J. Fred Coots; performed by the Jean Goldkette Orchestra, with the Keller Sisters, vocals)

1st Chorus ■ AABA form

0:00	A	Instrumental, full orchestra.
0:09	A	A section repeats.
0:17	B	Full orchestra.
0:26	A	Full orchestra.
0:34		Short tag before the second chorus.

2nd Chorus ■ AABA

0:38	A	Trombone and violin improvise solos.
0:55	A	Saxophones play the bridge.
1:04	B	Trombone returns.
1:11	A	Transition to the verse.

Verse

1:16		Full orchestra.
1:35		Guitar break, tag (the most extended and prominent of the section tags).

3rd Chorus ■ AABA

1:43		Voices enter, guitar accompaniment.
	A	
		I'm blue every . . .
	A	
		It seems that I sigh . . .
	B	Bridge.
		And then comes . . .
2:17	A	
		But after payday . . .
		Highly syncopated tag.
		Wanna see you . . .

4th Chorus ■ AABA

2:21	A	Trumpets play variation on the melody (written-out, not improvised).
2:38	A	
2:48	B	Clarinet solo on the bridge.
2:56	A	A section repeats.
		Tag.

during his teens. In 1915 he heard a Dixieland jazz band and started playing in, then leading, dance orchestras. By the mid-1920s, he had put together what many considered the best jazz orchestra of the time. Among the band members were several of the top white jazz musicians in Chicago, including Bix Beiderbecke. They did well on record ("Sunday" almost reached the top of the charts), but not well enough in the ballrooms. (It was probably an early example of an age-old problem among jazz musicians: playing music that's too hip for the room.) Goldkette disbanded his orchestra in 1927, and most of the top players soon joined Paul Whiteman's band.

1920s POPULAR SONG

Rhythm	*Two-beat rhythm with a jazz feel: two-beat in bass, banjo on the backbeat, then four-beat rhythm in banjo or guitar (during vocal). Bright tempo—for dancing the fox trot. Syncopated version of the melody; syncopation in solos and arrangement (especially at the end of the vocal).*
Melody	*The song is based on two pairs of riffs: one for the A section, the other for the B section, or **bridge** (the contrasting section of a song in AABA form). In both, the melody spins out from the riff and its continuation. The second and fourth choruses are more elaborate forms of the melody.*
Instrumentation (timbre)	*1920s dance orchestra: rhythm section of banjo/guitar, bass (drums and piano are not audible but were certainly present); trumpets, trombones, and saxophones in sections, plus solo violin and vocals.*
Performance style	*Cartoonish singing (imagine the Powerpuff Girls as flappers). Trombone solo features jazz inflections.*
Dynamics	*Moderate.*
Harmony	*Enriched I-IV-V harmony.*
Texture	*Rhythm section gives a strong foundation: **horns** grouped together (first chorus, verse), separated into sections (saxophones in the bridge of the second chorus) or spotlighted (trombone solo).*
Form	*Verse/chorus; the chorus of the song uses AABA form. The recorded performance features four choruses, with the vocal in the middle, plus one statement of the verse, just before the vocal chorus.*

Key Points

AABA popular song	*Older form newly revived around 1925.*
Sound of a snappy fox trot	*Two-beat rhythm in rhythm section; orchestration showcases sections and soloists.*
Integration of song and dance	*Finally, a danceable popular song!*

Terms to Know

AABA form

bridge

two-beat rhythm

The Sound of the Band (and Singers). Goldkette's band offers a jazzier version of the dance orchestra sound of Paul Whiteman. Again we hear the band grouped into sections: the first half of the last chorus has a particularly nice stretch for the trumpet section. There are also improvised solos for trombone and clarinet. The vocal trio that sings the third chorus sounds like flappers look: the nonsense syllables "vo-de-o-do" are a sound of the times, much like Gene Vincent's "Be-Bop-A-Lula" belongs to the early years of rock and roll. It is not a particularly ingratiating sound; we'll hear better examples below.

A special feature of Goldkette's band was the use of both banjo and guitar in the rhythm section. The tuba and the banjo lay down a straightforward two-beat rhythm, while the guitar (Eddie Lang, whom we hear later) plays the four-beat rhythm so basic to jazz. This combination of rhythms is a main source of the song's bounce.

Summary. With recordings like "Sunday," the revolution that produced the modern era in popular music is just about complete. The interaction of black music with white popular song and the integration of new technology comprehensively reshaped the mainstream popular style. Among the most significant and evident changes were the following.

- *The merger of song and dance.* Popular songs before 1910 had used dance rhythms but were not sung as music for social dancing. By 1920 popular song had become dance music. By the late twenties, performances of popular songs were singable and danceable.

- *The formation of the syncopated dance orchestra.* Although dance orchestras had existed in America since colonial times, none sounded like those of Jim Europe in the teens and Whiteman, Goldkette, and so many others in the twenties. Two key differences in the instrumentation distinguished these new dance orchestras: the full rhythm section and the use of the saxophone. Violins, long the main melody voice of the dance orchestra, lost status during the twenties. In orchestras like Paul Whiteman's, they played a less prominent role. In the jazz-influenced dance bands like those of Henderson and Ellington, they disappeared altogether.

- *Light-voiced singing styles.* With the electric revolution of 1925, new kinds of singers entered the popular-music business. Light-voiced singers like Gene Austin, Cliff "Ukulele Ike" Edwards, and even "Whispering" Jack Smith joined song belters like Al Jolson as popular recording and performing artists.

- *A fox trot beat.* Most songs in the twenties were fox trot songs. In performance a two-beat rhythm, played by tuba and banjo (or other bass and chord instruments) in alternation, supported the melody. The two-beat rhythm, with its crisp backbeat, was the first of the African American rhythms to reshape popular music.

- *New instrumental styles.* Popular instrumentalists, especially wind and brass players, cultivated ways of playing their instruments that distinguished them from band and orchestra performers. Brass players used **mutes**, **plungers**, and other timbre-altering devices. All wind (brass, sax, and clarinet) players used **vibrato**, a subtle alteration of the pitch of a note. All this came from jazz and blues.

- *Snappy, riff-based melodies.* Blues and ragtime influenced the melodies of popular song even more directly. The influence is evident in three characteristics: the use of riffs, rhythms that flow like speech, and syncopation. All three in combination created melodic rhythms that closely corresponded to the natural inflection and rhythm of American vernacular speech.

- *Conversational lyrics.* Lyrics matched the spirit and the feel of the melodies. More often than not, words were one syllable; phrases and sentences were short. Colloquial expressions replaced the more formal language of nineteenth-century song.

- *A chorus-oriented form.* Except in musical theater, verses were all but scrapped. A performance of a song consisted primarily of several statements of the chorus. A fragment of the verse might be used as an interlude, particularly in dance-band arrangements. Further, the form of the chorus was itself fast paced: four short sections, almost always in AABA form.

Any one of these changes would have been significant. Taken together they represent a comprehensive transformation of popular music. Certainly, they are on a par with the changes that took place during the early years of the rock era. Add to that the advent of electric technology and its impact on how the music reached its audience, and you end up with a revolution in popular music.

POPULAR MUSIC AS ART

We tend to think of classical music and popular music in opposition to each other—a continuation of the high-brow/low-brow divide that began musically with the emergence of **blackface** entertainment. We can begin to explore how a work of popular music can be art by considering what it probably isn't. It won't be music to do something to: march, dance, exercise, and so on. It won't be music to do something else by: work, study, read, eat, shop, ride elevators, and so on. And it won't be music with a job: set the mood in a film or sell a product. Instead it will be music that asks listeners to sit in respectful silence and actively listen. It promises listeners something that will stimulate their minds and touch their hearts and souls. We value it by how well it engages its listeners.

In the nineteenth century, the idea took hold that music, especially instrumental music (that is, the symphonies of Beethoven and the like), could provide a sublime aesthetic experience for a person of culture. Institutions emerged to support the idea: beautiful theaters and concert halls where resident symphony orchestras and opera companies performed, university music departments where scholars researched and taught, and conservatories where musicians learned their craft. Largely because of this, by the early part of the twentieth century in both Europe and America the idea of **art music** became associated with music by European composers (most of whom were dead). In the minds of the cultural elite, one could enjoy a completely fulfilling aesthetic experience only by listening to certain kinds of music, the so-called classics, in a certain way. This is still a strongly held opinion today. But those who take this position overlook two facts: music can communicate expressively in many different ways, and these ways are learned.

Rhapsody in Blue and jazz challenged this prevailing view—and succeeded. They did it by creating a new kind of music—music with a "classical" connection but that was popular and indigenously American. New music appeared in the 1920s because imaginative musicians took obvious pleasure in exploring the fresh, new sounds from ragtime, jazz, blues, and dance music. The best of the new music became classics because, despite the passage of years and the shift in cultural attitudes, they still communicate powerfully. And this makes them art by almost any measure.

George Gershwin's *Rhapsody in Blue*

Previous efforts to mix classical and popular music had been pop versions of classical pieces. Irving Berlin's 1910 hit, "That Mesmerizing Mendelssohn Tune," was a take on Felix Mendelssohn's "Spring Song"; and several bands had charted in 1918 with a pop version of a Chopin melody, "I'm Always Chasing Rainbows." In the opinions of high-minded critics, these pop versions lowered classical music to the level of popular music; they had a point.

Whiteman too had had classically derived hits in the early 1920s, among them the soon-to-be jazz standard "Avalon." ("Avalon" was adapted from "E lucevan le stelle," a well-known aria from Giacomo Puccini's opera *Tosca*. The resemblance was close enough that Ricordi, Puccini's publisher, sued the songwriters for plagiarism and won.) In 1924 he attempted the reverse—to raise jazz (which really meant the new dance music) to the stature of classical music. His concert "An Experiment in Modern Music" carried the subtitle "Symphonic Jazz." It was an audacious claim, implying as it did that jazz was ready to leave the speakeasy for the concert stage. Most of the music in his Aeolian Hall concert did not live up to Whiteman's advance billing. The centerpiece of the concert, however, Gershwin's "jazz concerto" succeeded beyond anyone's expectations.

Underwood & Underwood/Corbis

George Gershwin at the piano, a place where he felt very much at home. This photo was probably taken around the time Gershwin composed and recorded *Rhapsody in Blue;* his hair has not yet begun to recede.

CD 1:13

Rhapsody in Blue, George Gershwin (1924). Paul Whiteman and His Orchestra, featuring Gershwin, piano.

Rhapsody in Blue certainly approaches the symphonic in scale, length, and sound. A complete performance of the piece will last about fifteen minutes, the approximate length of the first movement of a standard classical piano concerto. (The performance heard here, by Whiteman's orchestra and Gershwin, is an abridged version of the original.) Similarly, Whiteman's good-sized orchestra approaches the sound of a symphony orchestra but with a pop twist. The string section is, by classical standards, quite small, and Whiteman's orchestra includes three saxophones and a banjo. (A revised orchestration of the work for piano and full symphony orchestra appeared soon after the 1924 premiere.) All this is very much in the classical style in intent and result.

It's what Gershwin did within this framework that was so remarkable. The piece bubbles over with fresh musical ideas. Almost all of them are stylized reworkings of the sounds, rhythms, and melodies of the ragtime, jazz, blues, and dance music that African Americans had contributed over the prior twenty-five years. Gershwin created rich harmonies by blending twentieth-century French harmony with commercial blues sounds. The virtuosic piano writing, however, is Gershwin's own. There is no real precedent for it, not in classical, ragtime, or jazz piano playing.

Rhapsody in Blue is a **rhapsody** in the way it moves freely from section to section, as if it were cutting or fading between scenes in a film. And it is blue from the first notes—the famous clarinet solo that takes off from New Orleans–style jazz clarinet playing.

LISTENING GUIDE: *RHAPSODY IN BLUE* (abridged version)

CD 1:13   **Symphonic Jazz** (George Gershwin; performed by Paul Whiteman and His Orchestra, featuring Gershwin, piano)

Notes

1. Gershwin built his Rhapsody mainly out of several melodic fragments, which he transformed and recontextualized as the piece unfolded. Here we use letters (A, B, C) to identify the fragments and letters with exponents (A^1, A^2, A^3) to identify variations on those fragments.
2. A rhapsody is, by definition, free in form. Gershwin seems to use cadenza-like passages as sectional dividers. The timeline reflects this.

1st Section

0:00	Cadenza	Famous clarinet solo.
0:11	A	Bluesy melodic idea; only the first part of this idea returns later.
0:37	B	A more active melodic idea.
0:47	A^1	The beginning of A, played by muted trumpet.
0:53	C	What seems like an improvised interlude for the piano.
0:57	A^2	A again, played by the full orchestra.
1:05	C^1	Expanded version of C, piano, then orchestra, leading to . . .
1:21	1st piano cadenza	Built on two syncopated patterns; the first outlines a chord, and the second repeats the chord before shifting.

2nd Section

1:43	A^4/C	Languid version of A, by the piano, answered by C, played on the bass clarinet.
1:53	A^4/C	As before.
2:02	D	A bridgelike interlude.
2:09	A^5	Another, more playful version of A, in a new key.
2:17	C^1	Development of C, leading to . . .
2:34	2nd piano cadenza	A slightly different version of the first cadenza.

3rd Section

2:48	A^6/C^2	A brisk orchestral version of A; oboe, rather than bass clarinet, plays C.
2:55	A^6/C^2	Played more rhythmically, this time by saxophones.
3:01	D^1	Like A^5 except orchestrated: trombones play the melody, high winds answer with offbeat accents.
3:07	A^7	(2:48–3:14 = orchestral version of 1:43–2:16).

4th Section

3:15	E	A new melodic idea without the blues/jazz overtones of the earlier themes.
3:21	E	Repeated almost exactly (notice the piano figuration in the background).
3:27	F	This section's bridgelike interlude.
3:33	E	As before, but leading to cadenza-like piano arpeggios.
3:38	B^1	A cadenza-like passage: clarinet plays new version of B, and piano answers with more fast arpeggios.

5th Section

3:50	B^2/A^8	Raucous version of B; piano answers with a fragment of A.
3:55	B^2/A^8	Almost identical to the previous phrase.
4:00	G	A new melodic idea, and a new answer from the piano; it serves as a bridge.

4:05	B³	This phrase begins like the earlier version of B but dissolves into another cadenza-like passage.
4:09	B⁴	Clarinet, trumpet, then muted trombone develop the second part of the original B, which leads to the third piano cadenza.
4:23	3rd piano cadenza	The first part is arpeggios; the second develops from a fragment of B.

6th Section

4:41	B⁴/A⁹	Capricious piano solo version.
4:50	B⁴/A⁹	Repeated.
4:59	G¹	A different version of the bridge.
5:05	B⁴/A⁹	Reprise of this version of B, leading to . . .
5:12	Sudden transition to . . .	(except for the end, 4:41 – 5:11 = 3:50 – 4:08)

7th Section

5:19	H/I	The "love" theme, played on saxophones, with horn obbligato (5:23).
5:33	H¹/I	A more intense version of H (it ends higher).
5:43	H²	The third statement of the melodic idea, which rounds off this section.

8th Section

6:02	H	Full orchestra playing the theme; piano has the obbligato part this time.
6:14	H¹	
6:22	H³	A different ending, with bells playing the theme and piano and other instruments supplying chords underneath.
6:39	Cadenza	The piano develops I, the obbligato answering figure to H.

9th Section

6:53	H	Solo piano version of this section, in free rhythm, leading to a dramatic change.
	H¹	
	H	
7:26	J (fragment)	Preview of the "Latin" section.
7:30	J	Cadenza-like solo piano section with Latin rhythmic patterns.

10th Section

7:38	H³	Trombone has the melody now, a fragment of H in a fast tempo.
7:44	H⁴	Still another version of H, played by orchestra (trumpets in the lead), with piano playing the Latin obbligato part.
7:56	H⁵	A continuation of the orchestra, with an even smaller fragment; it intensifies, then ends with a dramatic chord.
8:05	C³	Piano plays a more animated version of C, while the orchestra plays moving chords.

11th Section

8:26	B⁵	A grand version of B, played by the piano with orchestral accompaniment.
8:33	A⁹	An even grander version of A, full orchestra.
8:41	C³	Piano answers with a majestic version of C that brings the *Rhapsody* to a close.

Ferde Grofé was the top arranger on Whiteman's staff. As such he was the unsung hero in Gershwin and Whiteman's triumph. Gershwin composed only a piano score of the *Rhapsody*. He passed it on to Grofé, who worked as quickly as Gershwin to get the work ready for the premiere. The relationship between Gershwin's and Grofé's roles in the preparation of *Rhapsody in Blue* was much like that between two visual artists, one who creates a black-and-white drawing and the other who colors it. The drawing contains the form and line of the artist's conception, but the coloring adds the texture.

The *Rhapsody* was absolutely unique. It created a new language for concert music, one that was based on the progressive popular music of the early twentieth century. It inspired many other jazz—or at least jazzy—concert pieces, including several by Gershwin. But none has challenged *Rhapsody in Blue* as the most successful and popular work of its kind. Its premiere was a defining moment in the history of popular music as well as of twentieth-century music of all kinds.

STYLE PROFILE

SYMPHONIC JAZZ

Rhythm	*Tremendous variation in tempo, steady versus free rhythm, fast versus slow speed; strong syncopation in most themes; nonmetrical groupings create out-of-phase patterns (see Listening Guide).*
Melody	*Gershwin uses several main **melodic ideas** of varying length; the most prominent are more than a riff or a motive but less than a phrase with a beginning and an end; they either stop or dissolve, but they don't resolve. Most of the melodic ideas include blue notes; they are stylized versions of blues and jazz melodies. Gershwin often modifies his ideas—slowing them down or speeding them up, snipping off fragments, or moving them higher or lower.*
Instrumentation (timbre)	*Solo piano, plus a good-sized orchestra with a small string section, winds (including a bass clarinet and an oboe), trumpets and trombones, plus percussion.*
Performance style	*Solo wind players emulate jazz horn styles—slides into notes,* wah-wah *trumpet sound, use of mutes.*
Dynamics	*Strong contrasts from soft to loud; no regular pattern.*
Harmony	*Enriched harmony: many changes of key, exotic chords, and repetition of chord progressions in a new key.*
Texture	*Varies from full orchestra to solo piano. Consistent features are the use of **obbligato** (a second melody or syncopated figure playing under the main melody) and **response** (a second melody or figure answering a phrase).*
Form	*Rhapsodic, **modular**—one section does not necessarily imply what follows; frequent use of cuts and dissolves, piano **cadenzas** (virtuoso solo performances) that bridge sections; varied repetition of melody links one section to the next.*

Key Points

Symphonic jazz, part I: Classical and jazz elements	*Classical influence = big work, sprawling form, reworking of rifflike ideas.* *Jazz/blues influence = saxophones, slides and slurs, syncopations.*

| Symphonic jazz, part II: Two strategies | *1. Modular units assembled into larger entities.* *2. Constant dialogue between instruments.* |
| Uniqueness of *Rhapsody in Blue* | *No other similar works, by Gershwin or any other composer, were comparably individual.* |

Terms to Know

cadenza	modular form	response
melodic idea	obbligato	rhapsody

Louis Armstrong and Jazz as Art

Scholars frequently describe jazz as America's art music. The seminal contribution to this new art was the music of Louis Armstrong, the first great jazz soloist. Armstrong elevated and transformed jazz into a music that was valuable on its own artistic terms—fascinating, challenging, and uplifting. Playing with feeling and flair, Armstrong brought virtuosity, creativity, and artistry to spontaneous improvisation.

Louis Armstrong. Like so many New Orleans musicians, Louis Armstrong found his way north after Storyville closed. Joe Oliver had left in 1919; and at Oliver's invitation in 1922, Armstrong followed him to Chicago, where he joined Oliver's band. Early in 1924 Armstrong married Lil Hardin, the pianist with Oliver's band. Soon after, they moved to New York, where Armstrong joined Fletcher Henderson's hot dance orchestra. In New York, Armstrong was a regular in the studio as well as on the bandstand, recording with Henderson, a host of blues singers (including Bessie Smith), and pianist Clarence Williams, who doubled as Okeh Records's A&R (**artists and repertoire**) man. Williams noticed that the recordings on which he used Armstrong sold better than others, so in 1925 he offered Armstrong the chance to record as a leader rather than a sideman. Armstrong, who had returned to Chicago, proceeded to record with what amounted to a studio band of his New Orleans friends plus his wife, Lil, and, somewhat later, pianist Earl Hines. Okeh billed them as Louis Armstrong's Hot Five (or Hot Seven, depending on the number of players). Armstrong's groups made dozens of recordings over the next four years, and made jazz—and music—history in the process.

Louis Armstrong's "West End Blues." Many of Armstrong's "hot" recordings are treasures, but perhaps the most spectacular of them is "West End Blues," which Armstrong recorded in 1928. It begins with an Armstrong solo flourish, a free-flowing cascade spanning in two big swoops almost the entire usable range of the trumpet. One would be hard pressed to find anywhere in the history of music before 1928 a trumpet solo that displays the exuberance of this opening flourish. It must have shocked listeners expecting to hear the Oliver brand of New Orleans jazz. That was a group music. This was one man showcasing his mastery and imagination, and it transformed jazz into a new kind of music.

A textbook example of how to play jazz with imagination and deep feeling, "West End Blues" is a blues in both style and form (like "Dippermouth Blues," it is based on the blues harmonic progression). But halfway through the first chorus (after the opening flourish), Armstrong departs from the blues melodic form in a series of well-defined melodic and rhythmic ideas. The progress of this opening chorus, from blueslike riffs to the more elaborate musical ideas at the end, brings into focus one of the primary distinctions between blues and jazz: jazz

CD 1:14

"West End Blues," Joseph Oliver and Clarence Williams (1928). Louis Armstrong's Hot Five: Armstrong, trumpet and vocals; Earl Hines, piano; Fred Robinson, trombone; Jimmy Strong, clarinet; Mancy Cara, banjo; Zutty Singleton, drums.

CD 1:14 **1920s Jazz** (Joseph Oliver and Clarence Williams; performed by Louis Armstrong's Hot Five: Armstrong, trumpet and vocals; Earl Hines, piano; Fred Robinson, trombone; Jimmy Strong, clarinet; Mancy Cara, banjo; and Zutty Singleton, drums)

0:00   Introduction. Opening trumpet flourish; Armstrong, alone, out of time, displaying revolutionary artistry.

1st Chorus ■ **12-bar blues form**

0:15   Trumpet (Armstrong) in the lead states the melody but soon moves away from it; trombone comments.

2nd Chorus ■ **Blues form**

0:50   Trombone solo (Robinson).

3rd Chorus

1:24   Clarinet and Armstrong vocal—call-and-response. Clarinet (Strong) makes the most straightforward statement of the melody.

4th Chorus

1:58   Piano solo, elaborates melody (Hines).

5th Chorus

2:31   Armstrong sustains one note for four measures.
2:43   The four-note riff, never the same twice.
2:49   A melodic swoop, down, then up, and peaking with a rip to the top note.
2:55   Piano takes over, then everyone returns to finish the chorus—Armstrong again the lead voice.

tends to be more elaborate melodically, even jazz steeped in the blues. Notice also that the chord instruments (banjo and piano) "chunk" out a steady four-beat rhythm. The front-line instruments, rather than balanced against each other, are subordinate to Armstrong's trumpet.

Armstrong returns on the third chorus as a vocalist. The chorus begins with a call-and-response exchange between clarinet and voice; but as in the opening chorus, Armstrong soon breaks out of the limited melodic framework of the blues. His first few responses are relatively simple paraphrases of the clarinet riff, but after the fifth riff he sings several wide-ranging phrases that quickly surpass the relatively simple and regular clarinet part. Armstrong's musical conception remains the same, regardless of whether he plays or sings; when he sings he simply offers the same kinds of musical ideas in a different package.

There are no words to Armstrong's vocal; this kind of nonverbal vocalizing was soon called **scat singing**. Reputedly, Armstrong invented scat singing during a recording session when he forgot the words to a song and sang a series of nonsense syllables with his characteristic expression. The style became enormously popular, both for its expressiveness and its humorous sound.

The fourth chorus is a piano solo by Earl Hines. Hines was Armstrong's most important musical collaborator and the only musician of the period who could keep up with Armstrong. Especially interesting is the second phrase of the chorus, beginning a third of the way through, when Hines suddenly implies a tempo twice as fast as before. In his solo Hines sounds like Armstrong might have if he had played piano instead of trumpet; we hear it most clearly from this point on.

Armstrong's final chorus is one of the great moments in the history of recorded jazz. He begins with a sustained tone at the top of his range that lasts for more than ten seconds. Next he plays five rhythmically varied statements of a simple four-note riff, none of which conforms exactly to the underlying beat; this shows the subtlety of his sense of swing. He breaks out of the riff with another of his patented top-to-bottom-to-top melodic flourishes, which he ends with a **rip**—a kind of slide up into the last high note.

STYLE PROFILE

1920s JAZZ

Rhythm	*Slow tempo; steady four-beat rhythm, laid down by the rhythm section, except for the opening fanfare and the ending; much rhythmic play, especially in solos by Hines (piano) and Armstrong (vocal and trumpet).*
Melody	*Blues melody, as heard in the clarinet solo, is a simple* **riff***. The improvisations by Armstrong and Hines are considerably more active and flamboyant; Armstrong's often move in big sweeps through the full range of the instrument.*
Instrumentation (timber)	*Small, New Orleans–style group: trumpet, clarinet, trombone in front line; piano, banjo, and drums in rhythm section (no bass).*
Performance style	*Armstrong revolutionized trumpet playing in recordings like this, with an absolutely distinctive sound. A wordless vocal is unusual. Strong's playing typifies the bluesy New Orleans clarinet style. Hines's piano style is the equivalent of Armstrong's trumpet.*
Dynamics	*Wide range, from soft in clarinet solo to loud in Armstrong's opening and closing solos.*
Harmony	*Blues progression, except for the opening.*
Texture	*Solo-oriented New Orleans style with soloist dominant; clarinet below trumpet and less active; rhythm in the background.*
Form	*Blues form.*

Key Points

Jazz as art	*More substantial than dancing or drinking music.*
Jazz and blues	*"Deep blues" roots, but more virtuoso and melodic.*
Jazz as a soloist's music	*Armstrong's virtuosity and range overwhelm other front-line instruments, making jazz a solo-oriented music.*
Armstrong's influence	*Armstrong taught jazz musicians how to swing and pop singers how to sing in a more personal way.*

Terms to Know

riff

rip

scat singing

In his book *Early Jazz*, Gunther Schuller identifies four qualities that distinguish Armstrong's playing. In this final chorus, Armstrong presents them one by one:

o *A gorgeous, distinctively personal sound.* Armstrong sustains a beautiful high note for what seems like forever.

o *The ability to swing.* **Swing** is rhythmic play over a four-beat rhythm. Here, Armstrong plays a four-note riff repeatedly, all the time dancing over the steady pulse of the rhythm section. No two statements of the riff are exactly alike.

Legend has it that Armstrong had to stand outside the recording studio during his sessions with Joe "King" Oliver because he overpowered everyone else, and primitive, acoustic-recording techniques provided no other way to balance the sound.

- *Melodic invention.* Armstrong follows the riff with another of his down-and-up flourishes.
- *Varied and expressive inflection of the sound.* The flourish ends with a rip that gives the last high note extra oomph.

With recordings like this, Armstrong raised the bar for jazz improvisation. The rest of the jazz world spent the next ten years assimilating what Armstrong taught them. Armstrong transformed jazz from a group music to a soloist's music. His excursions into the upper range of the instrument and the power and beauty of his sound destroyed the delicate balance among the front-line instruments of the New Orleans jazz band.

Improvisation and Composition in Jazz. When we compose music, we create it mentally, then write it down. At some later time, we or another group of musicians will perform what we wrote. When we improvise music in spontaneous performance, we create it in the moment. The difference is similar to the difference between reading a prepared speech and having a conversation. **Composition** gives us the chance to organize our thoughts and state them in the most appropriate way. **Improvisation** gives us the opportunity to express inspirations and react to situations.

Both are part of the world of jazz, but improvisation has enjoyed a higher stature by far. Some writers have claimed that the essence of jazz lies in improvisation. This simply isn't true, as the Duke Ellington recording that we hear in Chapter 5 demonstrates. What is true, however, is that the ability to improvise fluently and creatively is an essential requirement for any jazz musician.

Most popular styles allow for some improvisation. A pop singer may reshape a melody. A blues singer may invent a new lyric or a completely new song. A rock guitarist may play a great solo. But no music demands as much improvisational skill from a performer as jazz. As we heard with Armstrong, jazz improvisation requires virtuosity, melodic inventiveness, personality, and the ability to swing. (Serious heavy metal comes closest, certainly in virtuosity although not in harmonic complexity.)

The most influential jazz musicians have been its master improvisers. Louis Armstrong, Charlie Parker, Miles Davis, and John Coltrane—these are the musicians who have shaped the sound of jazz and charted its evolutionary path.

So where does that leave the composition? In fact, composition and improvisation are constantly shifting points on the continuum of a jazz performance. At one end of the continuum is the complete predetermination of composition; at the other end is "free jazz" with virtually no prior planning. Most jazz performances fall somewhere in between these extremes.

Given the complementary relationship between improvisation and composition, why do musicians (jazz and otherwise) and critics seem to value improvisation over composition?

First, we appreciate the skill: it is hard to improvise competently and even harder to improvise expressively. Second, we tend to value individual brilliance over team effort: highlights on Sports Center showcase spectacular dunks, home runs, catches, and the like; they seldom show an effectively run play or an efficient team defense. Third, and most important, skilled improvisers play music in performance that may never be duplicated. With their inspired ideas and interactions, they create an absolutely electric atmosphere of anticipation. For these reasons improvisation is central to jazz, more so than any other popular music. But it is not essential, or we would have to dismiss the music of Jelly Roll Morton, Duke Ellington, and many other noteworthy jazz composers.

Summary

Both *Rhapsody in Blue* and "West End Blues" are quintessentially American. From the time of their creation to the present, musicians, critics, and audiences have recognized their distinctively American character. More slowly—and, in some cases, reluctantly—they have acknowledged their substance, their artistic value. It was the infusion of an African American sensibility into a European musical language that gave the music of Gershwin and Armstrong an American sound. We hear in both works the expressive gestures of the blues and the energy and play of jazz syncopations. Their importance and identity underscore the significant role of African American culture in creating music that sounds distinctively and uniquely American.

JAZZ, BLUES, AND THE BIRTH OF MODERN POPULAR SINGING

The latter part of the 1920s saw the total integration of song and dance in performance, not only through the use of a fox trot rhythm in support of the song but also through the alternation of instrumental and vocal versions of the chorus.

Two other noteworthy developments were the blending of jazz into popular-song performance and the birth of modern popular singing. Popular dance bands like Paul Whiteman's orchestra included some of the top white jazz musicians of the day. Whiteman also took the lead in featuring singers—among the first was a young Bing Crosby. Crosby was part of a new generation of popular singers. Their singing was intimate and conversational because the microphone eliminated the need to belt out a song. And it was more personal because they adapted the freedom of jazz and the expressive inflection of the blues. We hear a fine early illustration of this new singing style in a 1929 recording of "After You've Gone."

Written in 1918 by a black songwriting team, Henry Creamer and Turner Layton, by 1929 "After You've Gone" was already a **standard** (a song that remains popular well after its initial appearance). The song is a very early example of the new modern style of constructing a melody from a riff. It has a dance orchestra accompaniment, with a rhythm section anchored by a banjo and a tuba playing a fox trot beat.

The jazz influence is most evident in the solos. Violinist Joe Venuti's hot solo, supported only by guitarist Eddie Lang, stands out. During his solo the underlying rhythm shifts from a two-beat fox trot to the four-beat swing of jazz. (Like several other members of the Whiteman band, Venuti and Lang had joined when Jean Goldkette's orchestra broke up.)

CD 1:15

"After You've Gone," Henry Creamer and Turner Layton (1918). Paul Whiteman and His Orchestra, with Bing Crosby, vocal.

CD 1:15 **Modern Popular Song** (Henry Creamer and Turner Layton; performed by Paul Whiteman and His Orchestra, with Bing Crosby, vocal)

1st Chorus ■ ABAC form

0:00		Brief introduction, then . . .
	A	Saxophones play the melody; fox trot rhythm with tuba and banjo.
0:09	B	Saxes continue.
0:15	A	Strings.
0:21	C	Strings continue, then short interlude played by clarinets.

Verse

0:32	Strings lead, with background accompanying riffs from saxes.

2nd Chorus ■ Crosby sings, with guitar accompaniment

0:56	A	*After you've gone . . .*
1:02	B	*You'll feel blue . . .*
1:08	A	*There'll come a time . . .*
1:14	C	*Some day . . .*
		Short interlude derived from verse follows.

3rd Chorus ■ ABAC form

1:28	Trumpet, then trombone (at C), solos, followed by another interlude (early jazz style).

4th Chorus

2:00	Violin and guitar duet, plus drummer on the backbeat (jazz style continued).

5th Chorus

2:30	Full orchestra, with trumpets playing the melody (return to fox trot style, but with more syncopation).

STYLE PROFILE

MODERN POPULAR SONG

Rhythm	*Medium two-beat tempo. Jazz-influenced two-beat rhythm at the beginning and the end of the song; strong four-beat rhythm in the middle. Rhythm of the melody is active and syncopated, with distinct pauses between phrases; jazz solos are more elaborate.*
Melody	*Melody grows from a short, syncopated riff; it proceeds in a series of short phrases.*
Instrumentation (timbre)	*Vocal, plus full dance orchestra with violins and extra percussion (chimes).*
Performance style	*The conversational, microphone-aided singing of Crosby stands out. So does the hot playing of violinist Venuti.*
Dynamics	*Loud in the choruses featuring the full band; nice contrast with the vocal and violin choruses.*

Harmony	Enriched I-IV-V harmony; lots of extra chords (a nice feature of this arrangement).
Texture	Varied: from rich orchestration—melody, obbligatos, and rhythm section—to voice, guitar, and drums.
Form	Song: ABAC. Performance: multiple choruses, with verse and vocal chorus interpolated.

Key Points

Early modern song	Syncopated melody and ABAC form suggest a date around 1920.
Standards and covers	Standard: song that remains popular. Covers did not exist during twenties.
Conversational lyrics, conversational singing	Everyday language, with Crosby's easy delivery.
Moderate tempo	Slower tempo a trend from 1920s to 1930s.
Jazzy two-beat, jazz four-beat	Two rhythmic feels, one based on two-beat, the other on four-beat swing.

Terms to Know
standard

Bing Crosby's Approach to Popular Singing. The truly novel element here is Bing Crosby's singing. Crosby had joined Whiteman in 1926 as part of a vocal trio, the Rhythm Boys. (Whiteman claimed to be the first to use singers with a dance orchestra.) During his three years with Whiteman, Crosby sang as part of the group and in the solo spotlight, as he does here.

Those who remember Crosby mainly for his recording of "White Christmas" might be surprised by his singing here. This is not the crooning that made his reputation in the thirties, but real jazz singing. Crosby was cool before it was cool to be cool and hip before it was hip to be hip. He learned how to swing from Louis Armstrong by frequenting the clubs where Armstrong performed. (In the thirties, after he had become a big star, he repaid this musical debt by insisting that Armstrong be included in the film *Pennies from Heaven*.)

Many writers have observed that Crosby was the first singer to really use the microphone well. It's true that he was certainly among the first and was the most successful at it. He developed a low-key style that was as conversational as the lyrics he sang. Coming through the radio or phonograph, he sounded as though he were in the same room as his listeners. The new technology made this kind of intimacy possible; Crosby was the first to capitalize on it in a big way. He soon had many imitators.

This recording captures him early in his career, when he was primarily a jazz singer. After he left Whiteman in 1929, he diversified his repertoire and became known mainly for his comfortable crooning of ballads; "White Christmas" was the most famous of his more than 300 hits and his 4,000-plus recordings. He was the most popular singer in the first half of the century.

Al Jolson may have starred in *The Jazz Singer,* but he didn't sing jazz. Crosby did: his singing was more relaxed and swinging than the histrionic style used by Al Jolson and the aggressive style of song belters like Sophie Tucker. As heard here it displays the freedom of jazz, a tinge of the blues (which came to him mainly through Armstrong), and the easy delivery that the microphone made possible. It was a brand-new sound and an essential transitional step between the big-voiced singers of the acoustic era and the song interpreters that we hear in Chapter 5.

LOOKING BACK, LOOKING AHEAD

The five examples included in this chapter help document perhaps the most eventful decade in the history of popular music. Compared with the music from the first part of the century, almost every aspect of this music—and the business surrounding it—had been significantly altered.

A media revolution transformed the way audiences encountered popular music: through radio, electric recording, and film, Americans learned popular music by listening to it more than they did by reading the sheet music. Moreover, it opened the door to a host of new sounds—sounds that could be preserved on recordings or broadcast over the air, but not transmitted very faithfully via sheet music. These include not only the new singing styles of Crosby and others and the jazz of Oliver, Armstrong, and others but also a variety of blues and blues-based styles and country music (which we hear in Chapter 7).

Most of the new sounds emerged through the wholesale infusion of African American elements into popular styles. Most fundamental were the rhythmic changes. First came the transformation of the march into the fox trot, mainly by converting the afterbeat (*pah*) into a crisp backbeat. Also important was the prominent syncopation, as we heard in "Charleston" and "After You've Gone." In addition, the more active and swinging rhythms of jazz and the relaxed, free delivery of the blues soon penetrated popular song and its performance, as we heard especially in "After You've Gone."

Song and dance, separate at the turn of the century (although songs often had a dance rhythm), came together in the 1920s, first with the performance of popular songs by dance orchestras and then by interpolating vocals between instrumental sections. Popular songs also changed, not only in rhythm and melodic style but also in form. Performances typically consisted of several statements of the chorus; the verse was ignored or used as an interlude between choruses. AABA form, which repeated the catchiest part of the melody many times, largely displaced earlier forms. Listeners often heard the opening riff of the melody ten or more times because fast tempos permitted four or five statements of the melody. The newly formed rhythm section provided the beat underneath the melody; the newly popular saxophone often played it.

Music connected to the popular tradition also emerged as a new kind of art music, in concert works such as Gershwin's *Rhapsody in Blue*, in the inspired jazz of Louis Armstrong, and in the groundbreaking musical *Show Boat*, which we encounter in Chapter 6.

The infusion of blues and jazz into mainstream music also produced a small but measurable improvement in race relations: Jolson still blacked up, bandstands were not yet integrated, stereotypes persisted in the media, separate but equal remained the law in the South and the rule elsewhere; but the numerous black musicals and revues, black dance orchestras like those of Henderson and Ellington, the jazz of Armstrong and Oliver, Kern and Hammerstein's sympathetic portrait of Joe in *Show Boat*, the emergence of such entertainers as Ethel Waters and Fats Waller—all of these developments moved public perception of African Americans away from the minstrel show stereotypes and toward real people. Moreover, many acknowledged not only their person but also their genius: Crosby found in Armstrong and his music something that he could find nowhere else.

Perhaps because it is an art of the ear, music has been the most colorblind facet of the entertainment world. The majority of good musicians have been most concerned with only one thing: how well one sings or plays the music that they like. Partly because of this, racial barriers came down faster in popular music than in any other segment of American society. The best music, black and white, helped speed this process along. There was still a long way to go in 1930, but the popular-music business had at least started down the road, with American society following along.

In the early 1930s, the popular-music mainstream would split in two. One branch continued the infusion of African American elements, and the other retreated to a gentler, more melodious style. By the middle of the decade, the boundaries were clear: it was swing versus sweet, as we explore in the next chapter.

TERMS TO KNOW

Test your knowledge of this chapter's important terms by defining the following. If you can't recall the meaning of a certain term, refresh your memory by looking up the boldfaced term in the chapter, turning to the Glossary at the back of the book, or working with the flashcards on the *Popular Music in America* Companion Web site: *http://music.wadsworth.com/campbell_2e*

A&R (artists and repertoire)	doubling	riff
AABA form	electric recording	rip
ABAC form	fox trot	saxophone
acoustic recording	horn	scat singing
amplification	improvisation	speakeasy
amplifier	melodic idea	standard
art music	microphone	stride piano
backbeat	modular form	string section
blackface	mute	swing
brass section	obbligato	syncopation
bridge	plunger	two-beat rhythm
cadenza	response	vibrato
Charleston	rhapsody	wind section
composition	rhythm section	

Swing and Sweet

After his sister, Adele, broke up their long partnership in 1932, Fred Astaire returned to Hollywood to try to break into the movies. Four years earlier a screen test had netted this verdict from an executive at Paramount Studios: "Can't act. Can't sing. Balding. Can dance a little." Undaunted by this lukewarm appraisal, Astaire—whom some have called the greatest American dancer—persevered and signed a contract with RKO Pictures. First appearing on-screen in 1933, Astaire returned later that year in *Flying Down to Rio*. Although he and his new partner, Ginger Rogers, had only supporting roles, with a sensational dance number they stole the show from the stars. So the next year RKO headlined them in a film adaptation of Cole Porter's 1932 musical *The Gay Divorce*. (The film version was titled *The Gay Divorcée*, apparently because the censors wouldn't approve a title that glorified divorce.) This was the beginning of a string of nine feature movies for the pair. The third of these films was *Top Hat*, which came out a year later. It featured music by Irving Berlin—most notably, "Cheek to Cheek."

FRED, GINGER, AND THE ACCEPTANCE OF THE MODERN POPULAR SONG

In almost all of the Fred and Ginger films, the plot followed a predictable pattern: boy sees girl and is immediately infatuated with her; girl rejects boy because of some kind of misunderstanding; boy ardently woos girl, using song and dance; girl succumbs to boy's charm and dancing ability; the misunderstanding is cleared up, and boy and girl live happily ever after, or at least until the next film.

In *Top Hat* and their other films, Fred and Ginger are living the lifestyle of the rich, if not always famous. They wear beautiful clothes, stay in fancy hotels, drive nice cars (or have someone else drive them), and travel extensively—they are jetsetters before the jet age. Nowhere is this more evident than in the big scene from *Top Hat*.

The setting is a posh supper club, with tables adjacent to a large dance floor, where an orchestra plays in the background. Dressed formally in white tie and tails, Fred asks Ginger, in her long evening gown, to dance. Ginger reluctantly agrees. At the beginning of the number, Fred sings "Cheek to Cheek" while they're dancing. Initially, Ginger keeps her distance, but by

CD 1:16   **1930s Popular Song** (Irving Berlin; performed by Fred Astaire, vocal)

0:00		Instrumental introduction.

1st Chorus ■ AABBCA (more than double the length of a typical AABA song)

0:06	A	Listen to the clear fox trot rhythm underneath; obbligato in violins.
		Heaven...
0:29	A	Notice how the phrase "Heaven" unfolds slowly.
		Heaven...
0:53	B	Notice the shift to a four-beat rhythm.
		Oh! I love to climb...
1:04	B	The rise and fall of the melody outlines mountains.
		Oh! I love to go out...
1:16	C	
		Dance with me...
1:29	A	
		Heaven...

2nd Chorus

1:53	A	Strings take the melody; notice the shift from a clear two-beat to a four-beat rhythm at the end.
2:16	B	Trumpets take over the melody with the shift to a more swinging style.
2:28	B	Saxophones, then trumpets play a more syncopated version of the melody.
2:40	C	Fanfarelike brass for "Dance with me . . ."
2:52	A	Solo violin.

1:16

"Cheek to Cheek,"
Irving Berlin
(1935). Fred
Astaire, vocal.

the time Fred has finished singing and the orchestra has taken over, they have drifted off to their own private ballroom to perform a dance that's far more elaborate than the fox trot they danced earlier in the scene. By the end of the number, Ginger is completely smitten with Fred. Shortly after, she comes to her senses, slaps him, and flounces away.

The scene tells us a great deal about popular song in the 1930s, its place in society, and its role in daily life. "Cheek to Cheek" is an elegant, expansive fox trot. Compared with the songs in Chapter 4, "Cheek to Cheek" is longer, more melodious, and less syncopated. It has a more moderate tempo, and the basic fox trot that Fred and Ginger dance at the beginning is far less vigorous than the Charleston—Fred can easily sing to Ginger as they dance. That he can do both at the same time emphatically confirms the integration of song and dance.

Their dancing makes clear how far up the social ladder the fox trot song has moved. Recall that a mere twenty-five years earlier, people were outraged over the "lingering close contact" that the animal dances required. In this film dancing elegantly and cheek to cheek requires that other parts of the body also touch. The setting, their dress, the music, and everything else strongly suggest that cheek-to-cheek dancing is now not only socially acceptable but also admired. And here art and Hollywood are imitating life: the scene could have been shot in any swanky hotel, without the need to hire extras.

Everything about the scene is more mature and upscale than the frantic flappers of the twenties: Ginger is twenty-four and clearly a woman. Fred is thirty-six and looks as if he were never an adolescent. Their clothes must have cost a fortune, especially by thirties' standards.

Fred and Ginger at the end of their spectacular dance number to "Cheek to Cheek." Note in particular the elegant setting—Fred in white tie and tails and Ginger in a long gown—and the almost "cheek to cheek" pose, although they are in the middle of a tricky maneuver.

Elegance replaces energy; Ginger is wearing an evening gown instead of a flapper dress. The rough edges and vigorous movements of the Charleston are gone; the gliding movements of the fox trot and the artistic dancing at the end of the scene take their place. The song offers a gentle "Heaven" instead of the syncopated "Charleston."

Irving Berlin (born Israel Baline, 1888–1989) had huge hits over four decades, including "Alexander's Ragtime Band" (1911), one of the very first modern songs; "White Christmas" (1942), arguably the most popular song of the first half of the twentieth century; and "Cheek to Cheek" (1935), the top candidate for the most popular song of the thirties.

STYLE PROFILE

1930s POPULAR SONG

Rhythm	*Moderate tempo; two-beat rhythm with discreet **backbeat** through most of the song (the introduction, end of the A section, and the B section have a stiff four-beat rhythm). Little syncopation. Melodic rhythm has long pauses between short, then long, bursts of notes.*
Melody	*Melody grows cleverly out of simple two-note riff ("Hea-ven"). The A section is a long arch. The B section melody has a rapid rise and fall. The C section has dramatic skips.*

Instrumentation (timbre)	*Vocal, with dance orchestra featuring violins plus rhythm section (string bass and guitar stand out; piano plays fills), muted trumpet, saxophones, and extra percussion.*
Performance style	*Astaire has a soft, reedy voice. He is best remembered as a terrific dancer, but many songwriters favored his singing because of his faithful approach to the melody and his subtle phrasing.*
Dynamics	*Moderate.*
Harmony	*Rich harmony-enhancing I-IV-V.*
Texture	*Melody, rhythm section accompaniment, plus at least one obbligato melody (in the beginning, strings behind the vocal).*
Form	*Expanded song form: AABBCA. The A sections are sixteen measures each, twice normal length; the entire song is seventy-two measures, more than double the length of a typical popular song of the 1930s. The recording omits the second A section during the instrumental version (probably to fit it on the record).*

Key Points

Classy cheek-to-cheek dancing	*Classy song and classy dancing mean that modern popular music is socially acceptable.*
Long song	*"Cheek to Cheek" is more than double the length of the typical popular song.*
Melodic economy	*Berlin builds big phrases out of a two-note riff.*
Words and melody	*The melody of all three sections reinforces the meaning of the lyric.*

Terms to Know
backbeat

If you had to select one song to signal the end of the revolution that ushered in popular music's modern era, "Cheek to Cheek" would probably be the top choice. It was arguably the most popular song of the decade, and the Fred and Ginger films were among the most successful films of the thirties. The title, the lyrics, the lush setting, the elaborate dancing, and Berlin's wonderful song—all send the same message: it's not only okay to dance cheek to cheek but, as done by Fred and Ginger, it's about as classy as popular culture gets. The deep penetration of this suave and sophisticated sound into all levels of society essentially marginalized those who found popular music and its social setting objectionable. "Cheek to Cheek" demonstrates, as convincingly as any song of the era could, that the revolution that produced modern popular song was complete.

"Cheek to Cheek" and so many songs like it helped people dream, to escape the harsh reality of Depression-era America and experience vicariously the lifestyle depicted in *Top Hat*. For many people of this era, melodious popular song was the music of romance. Just like Fred and Ginger, couples often had "their" song—the song they fell in love to. Granted, it didn't pay the rent or feed the children, but it allowed people to forget about their day-to-day cares, at least for a few minutes.

There was also music that confronted and commented on this reality: the music of Woody Guthrie (Chapter 8) stands out. And even as Fred and Ginger seduced so much of America with their graceful moves and sensuous music, a generation of young people, black and white, sought out a new, more high-spirited sound. They found it in the music of Benny Goodman, Tommy Dorsey, Glenn Miller, and the other bands of the era that played a new kind of dance music: swing.

FLETCHER HENDERSON AND THE ROOTS OF BIG-BAND SWING

The early 1930s were the worst years of the Great Depression. Times were very tough: one person in four was out of work. The devastation of the Dust Bowl—severe droughts that paralyzed agriculture and uprooted families—reached its peak. The adversity affected African Americans disproportionately because so many doors were already closed to them. In spite of this, a few black bands, among them those led by Fletcher Henderson, Bennie Moten, and Edward "Duke" Ellington, managed to find enough work to keep their bands together. From their work came the sound of big-band swing.

The man most responsible for shaping the sound of big-band swing was Fletcher Henderson (1897–1952). Henderson is one of the shadow figures of popular music. We know that he came from a black middle-class family in Georgia and got his musical training from his mother, a piano teacher. He came north in 1920 to study chemistry, but soon found work with the Pace-Handy music company, first as a song plugger in its publishing business, then as a jack-of-all-trades for Harry Pace's Black Swan Records. We know that during the 1920s he led one of the top bands in New York; they performed at the Roseland Ballroom and made it *the* place to go for great dancing. But hard times and Henderson's lack of business and leadership skills made it difficult to keep his band together. Still he continued to find work for the band through the early years of the Depression.

We have conflicting accounts of Henderson the person and Henderson the musician. Most agree that he was far from a dynamic leader. Some accuse him of laziness; more claim that he was a terrible businessman. He owes his fame to his skill as an arranger, but even his musical contributions have been subject to doubt. Some scholars deflect credit to other musicians, notably Don Redman, who arranged for Henderson's band in the late 1920s, and Benny Carter, who did the same in the early thirties. We will probably never know the truth.

Nevertheless, Henderson was a major player behind the scenes for more than twenty years. He attracted to his band some of the best black jazzmen of the time, from Louis Armstrong to Coleman Hawkins to Lester Young. And, most important, he was the musician most responsible for the sound of big-band swing. We discover why in his 1934 recording "Wrappin' It Up."

Henderson's "Wrappin' It Up." This 1934 recording conveys the essence of how to compose and play big-band swing. The first few seconds describe **swing**: syncopation over a steady four-beat rhythm. The rhythm section, by this time composed of piano, acoustic guitar (instead of banjo), string bass (instead of tuba), and drums, lays down the beat. The horns (brass and saxophones) play a simple **riff** that is out of phase with the beat. The swing results from the conflict between the beat and the syncopated riff.

The melody of the song grows out of another simple riff. In this respect it's like so many of the songs from the twenties. What's different is the way it proceeds: instead of developing the melody by varying the riff, Henderson simply repeats it one or more times, then shifts to another riff. Creating a melody by repeating a riff, rather than developing it, is one of the trademarks of big-band swing.

Another common feature is the **call-and-response** among the sections. Henderson's band features a four-man saxophone section, plus three trumpets and two trombones. Often saxes and brass exchange riffs; in the opening the brass "comment on" or "respond to" the sax riff, as if they were saying, "Yeah!" Call-and-response has been an integral part of African American music throughout its history. We heard it in the blues, and we hear it again and again in

CD 1:17

"Wrappin' It Up," Fletcher Henderson (1934). Fletcher Henderson and His Orchestra.

| 0:00 | | Introduction. The essence of swing: syncopated chords by the horns over a steady four-beat rhythm from the rhythm section. |

1st Chorus

0:09	A	Repeated riff in saxes with response in brass.
0:19	B	New riff in saxes.
0:28	A	Full band.
0:37	C	More elaborate than a riff.

2nd Chorus ■ ABAC

| 0:48 | | Alto sax solo, with sustained brass chords. |

3rd Chorus

1:25	A	Trumpet solo with sax riff behind.
1:34	B	Full band playing a new riff.
1:44	A	Trumpet solo resumes.
1:53	C	Trumpet solo continues.

4th Chorus

2:02	A	New brass riff, answer by clarinets (sax players switched instruments).
2:12	B	Clarinet solo, with low brass chords.
2:22	A	Written out "solo" for sax section (the melody is like an improvised solo).
2:32	C	Full band.

swing. With arrangements like this one, Henderson laid the groundwork for **big-band swing:** saxes and brass exchanging riffs over a propulsive four-beat rhythm.

STYLE PROFILE

BIG-BAND SWING

Rhythm	*Bright tempo; clear four-beat rhythm laid down by the rhythm section, with lots of syncopation in the horn parts.*
Melody	*Melody constructed from a series of short, repeated riffs, especially the A and B phrases.*
Instrumentation (timbre)	*Small-scale swing band: 3 trumpets, 2 trombones, 4 saxophones (doubling on clarinet), plus full rhythm section (acoustic guitar, piano, string bass, and drums).*
Performance style	*Highly inflected playing in the horns; Armstrong-like effects in the trumpet solo.*
Dynamics	*Nice contrasts between the subdued accompaniment behind the soloists (beginning of the second chorus) and the loud sound with the full band (end of the song).*
Harmony	*Beyond I-IV-V harmony.*
Texture	*Extensive use of call-and-response; in ensemble sections, harmonized riffs over rhythm; in solo sections, background chords or riffs, all over rhythm.*
Form	*A string of four choruses; form of the chorus is **ABAC**.*

Henderson's Legacy. Fletcher Henderson contributed more than just a model for swing. Desperate for cash, he sold arrangements to Benny Goodman, whose late-night radio show *Let's Dance* was broadcast all over the country. After the contract for the radio show expired, Goodman and his band embarked on a cross-country tour, just to keep working. By the time they reached Los Angeles, they were disheartened. At almost all of their previous stops, the managers of the ballrooms had wanted sedate waltzes and fox trots; swing had not yet made it to the heartland.

Gun-shy from the road trip, Goodman began the evening playing the syrupy music they'd been forced to play on the tour. But the capacity crowd that greeted Goodman's band at the Palomar Ballroom came from their radio audience (midnight in New York meant nine o'clock in Los Angeles), who loved the band's new, swinging sound. The crowd was perplexed and gave the band a lukewarm response. Sensing their indifference, Goodman and the band decided to go down in flames—they pulled out a swing tune, started to play, and the crowd went wild. This was the music that they'd come to hear, and they let the band know it. The concert at the Palomar Ballroom was a huge success, broadcast across the country. Many cite this concert as the event that kick-started the swing era.

Critics and fans climbed on the Goodman bandwagon. Goodman went on to become the "king of swing," while Henderson remained very much in the background. Henderson's arranging style, however, was the central component of big-band swing. It remained only for Goodman, Tommy Dorsey, William "Count" Basie, Glenn Miller, and many others to bring it to the popular radio show *Your Hit Parade*.

SWING AND SWEET

We call the years between 1935 and 1945 the **swing era**—and with some justification. Certainly, swing was the fresh new sound in popular music, and it seemed to capture—and even help create—the increasingly optimistic mood of the country as it fought off the Depression.

Swing as a noun—meaning big-band swing—was a style of music. *Swing* as a verb was a way of playing. Swing and music that swung made up about half of the popular music scene in the late 1930s. The other half was the music called *sweet*. Like swing, sweet was both a type of music and a way of playing. A wave of slow, romantic songs, or **ballads**, flooded the market in the late 1930s. Singers sang them with a soothing voice; bands played them in a slow, smooth, subdued style. In essence sweet music was a thoroughly tamed fox trot. The key

SWING AND SWEET

Swing	Sweet
RHYTHM	
Moderate or fast tempos; four-beat (swing); lots of syncopation	Slow to moderate tempos; two-beat (fox trot); little or no syncopation
MELODY	
Songs created by repeating riffs	Songs develop from short riffs, usually without syncopation
INSTRUMENTATION (TIMBRE)	
Standard big band: trumpets, trombones, saxophones, and rhythm section	Big band, often with strings added
PERFORMANCE STYLE	
Brassy, bright, jazzy, with lots of inflection	Soft, smooth, intimate, crooning; generally less inflected
DYNAMICS	
Loud	Soft
HARMONY	
Swing tunes often based on simple progressions (like blues), to make improvising easier	Richer harmony more likely
Call-and-response patterns common; multiple layers, especially under solos	Melody is primary; other horn lines are more in the background
FORM	
Blues or simple riff tunes	Popular-song forms, often with more individual touches

component of the sweet sound was melody. Whereas swing jumped, sweet flowed. We see the contrast between the two styles in the above table. And we hear the differences between swing and sweet in the next pair of examples.

The Sound of Swing: Glenn Miller's "Chattanooga Choo Choo"

Pure big-band swing with no vocal was a relatively small corner of the popular-music landscape. There were big hits in this style; Glenn Miller's "In the Mood" and Count Basie's "One O'Clock Jump" stand out. But relatively few instrumental swing tunes found their way onto the hit parade. Far more common were popular songs played in a swing style. Also popular were swing-based novelty numbers—vocals where the melody resembles a riff-type swing melody.

Glenn Miller (1904–1944) led the most popular band of the era. Goodman was the "king of swing," and Count Basie and Duke Ellington were among its royalty, but no band was more

CD 1:18   Big-band Swing (Glenn Miller; performed by Glenn Miller and His Band, with Tex Beneke and the Modernaires, vocals)

0:00	Instrumental introduction. Notice the mix of real and imitation train sounds.
0:22	Introduction continues; final A section. This is an unusual beginning (perhaps because of the three-minute time limit): we hear only the last A section (in the vocal it's at 2:04). The melody leaves room for not one but two responses per riff: clarinets high and trombones low.

Verse

0:48	Spoken/sung:
	Hi, there Tex . . .

Chorus ■ AABBAA

1:08	A	Tex and the vocal group in effect function like a fourth section; there are answering riffs in the saxes and occasionally the brass.
		Pardon me, boy . . .
1:21	A	
		Can you afford . . .
	B	Note the shift to a strong two-beat rhythm with a clear backbeat (still with a swing feel) at the beginning of the chorus, then the shift back to a four-beat rhythm.
		You leave the Pennsylvania . . .
1:47	B	2nd bridge
		When you hear . . .
2:04	A	
		There's gonna be . . .
2:17	A'	
		She's gonna cry . . .
		Fade-out seems to signal the end of the song, but . . .

Ending

2:46	New instrumental melody enters, based on the chords of the A section.
2:59	Another new melody, this time expanded into a tag.

popular than Miller's. One reason was his ability to move effortlessly between swing and sweet. For every "In the Mood" hit (swing), there was a "Moonlight Serenade" (sweet).

Among the band's biggest hits was a 1941 recording, "Chattanooga Choo Choo." Miller's band performed the song in a now-obscure film entitled *Sun Valley Serenade*. The film quickly faded away, but the song caught on, selling more than a million copies in less than a month.

The recording is a real period piece that can belong only to the swing era. The song sounds like an instrumental riff-based song ("Pardon me, boy") that acquired words along the way. In particular, the melody of the B sections moves quickly and skips around (it's easier to play than it is to sing). Although there's the obligatory sweetheart at the end, the song is about a train ride.

Tex Beneke, one of the saxophone players in Miller's band, sings the lead vocal. The Modernaires, a close-harmony vocal group that had joined Miller in 1939, back up Beneke and occasionally step into the spotlight. Close-harmony groups like the Modernaires and the Andrews Sisters were also part of the sound of swing-based popular music.

1:18

"Chattanooga Choo Choo," Glenn Miller (1941). Glenn Miller and His Band, with Tex Beneke and the Modernaires, vocals.

Instrumental sections frame the long vocal. The clever train sounds give way to a **walking bass** (a bass player playing one note per beat). Bass and drums lay down the four-beat swing rhythm; the rest of the band pile syncopated riffs on top. Miller's band is bigger than Henderson's: four trumpets, four trombones (Miller, who played beautifully, and three others), five saxophones (switching over to clarinets at times, a practice called **doubling**), and a full rhythm section. The extra brass instruments allow both trumpets and trombones to stand alone as sections. As a result, the call-and-response among sections makes for a three-way exchange, rather than the dialogue we heard in the Henderson recording.

With its vocal, special effects, riffs, syncopation, and growled/smeared/bent notes in the horns—all sounding over a firm four-beat rhythm at a brisk tempo—"Chattanooga Choo Choo" epitomizes swing as a popular style. The music is exuberant. It's fun in both words and sounds: the kind of sound that put smiles on peoples' faces and got them out on the dance floor.

STYLE PROFILE

BIG-BAND SWING

Rhythm	*Moderate tempo (slower than a typical swing song, but faster than a sweet song); strong four-beat swing rhythm presented clearly at the beginning; lots of syncopation—in the melody where all the phrases end on an offbeat and in many of the answering riffs.*
Melody	*The A section grows out of a riff; the continuation includes a longer, instrumental-style line, then two more riffs; the B section also includes an instrumental-style melody (big skips, fast pace) and riffs.*
Instrumentation (timbre)	*Lead singer and close-harmony vocal group plus a full **big band**: saxes/clarinets, trumpets, trombones, and rhythm; plus train noises at the beginning.*
Performance style	*Tex Beneke's vocal style has neither the personality of Billie Holiday nor the suaveness of Fred Astaire or Connee Boswell ("Heart and Soul," the next song we hear); still his "stepped-out-of-the-band" sound works well here. Note also the extra inflection in saxes and horns on certain notes for more swing and the frequent use of mutes in the brass.*
Dynamics	*Generally moderately loud, but with some effective variations, especially the fade-out ending, then full-bore instrumental sections at the end.*
Harmony	*Mostly I-IV-V chords, but in a rarely used progression (neither the blues progression nor the "Heart and Soul" progression).*
Texture	*Layers of riffs, generally in a call-and-response arrangement, with rhythm section underneath.*
Form	*AABBA, an expanded version of the typical popular-song form in the vocal heart of the song; an introduction, a verse (by this time, it's rare to hear the verse or even to write a song with a verse), instrumental versions of the A sections, and a tag frame the vocal.*

Key Points

Novelty song	*A swing tune about a train ride, not love.*
Instrumental song	*Instrumental-style swing tune with lyrics added.*
Imaginative design	*Bigger-than-usual form (two statements of the **bridge**, B), train sounds, pause before end—all distinctive touches.*
Swing as a popular style	*Swing as a comfortable, commercial, and fun music.*

Terms to Know

bridge
doubling
walking bass

The energy of swing is not just a function of tempo. For example, "Cheek to Cheek" actually moves at a faster tempo, at least in relation to the backbeat. But the bass moves more slowly, and there is little syncopation in "Cheek to Cheek." The combination of walking bass and lots of syncopation invests the performance with more drive despite its slower tempo. This pattern will repeat itself when rock and roll surfaces in the 1950s and the basic rhythm of popular music shifts from four to eight beats.

The Sound of Sweet: "Heart and Soul"

The music that went in the opposite direction—toward a more conservative and comfortable style—was **sweet**. Perhaps the most popular piano duet of all time is the first phrase of "Heart and Soul." It's the one song that almost everyone who has fooled around on the piano seems to know.

1:19

"Heart and Soul," Frank Loesser and Hoagy Carmichael (1929). Connee Boswell, vocal.

Hoagy Carmichael (1899–1981), who also wrote "Stardust" and "Georgia on My Mind," composed "Heart and Soul" in 1938. It was an immediate hit for several bands. Many other top artists followed suit, including Connee Boswell, the singer heard here. "Heart and Soul" is accessible: what could be easier to grasp than the three notes of the title phrase—or the way it climbs up a **scale**, stopping along the way to repeat "heart and soul"?

The song is also skillfully crafted: at first hearing, it might seem as though "Heart and Soul" is yet another of the thousands of AABA songs popular during this time. But each of the A sections ends differently, as Carmichael works magic with the scales that are so much of the raw material of the melody. In particular, the second A section continues upward so that the bridge (the B section) is the melodic high point of the song and its most intense part.

Connee Boswell (1907–1976) was one of the more unusual stars of the 1930s and '40s in that she sang from a wheelchair. As a child she had contracted polio (this happened all too frequently before Jonas Salk developed a vaccine in 1952), which left much of her body paralyzed. Despite this limitation Boswell and her two sisters toured on the vaudeville circuit, beginning around 1930, and began to record steadily the next year. After all three married, she pursued a solo career, which lasted into the 1960s.

Boswell was one of the most popular singers of the era. Her fans included songwriter Irving Berlin, who called her "the finest ballad singer in the business," and jazz vocalist Ella Fitzgerald, who acknowledged her as one of her influences. Boswell mastered an easy, seemingly effortless singing style, comparable to the delivery of Bing Crosby and the other

CD 1:19	**Sweet/Romantic Ballad** (Frank Loesser and Hoagy Carmichael; performed by Connee Boswell, vocal)

0:00		Instrumental introduction: clarinets play the famous arpeggiated accompaniment figure.

1st Chorus ■ AABA

0:10	A	Note how the melody grows out of successively higher repetitions of the title riff.
		Heart and soul . . .
0:28	A¹	Clarinets behind the vocal play the chords of the "Heart and soul" progression as arpeggios.
		Heart and soul . . .
0:46	B	Bridge
		Four-measure phrase is built by extending the two notes sung to "thrilling" (rather than repeating) riff.
		Oh! but your lips . . .
1:04	A²	Final A section ends differently; melody stays afloat on the word "stole" before coming to rest on "soul."
		But now I see . . .
1:22		Instrumental interlude. Pianist plays a fragment of the A section.

2nd Chorus

1:33–2:09	A and A¹	
2:10	B	Shifts from a two-beat to a four-beat rhythm.
2:28	A²	Vocalist interpolates extra words and music; brief shift to swing rhythm highlights it.
		But now I see . . .

crooners; she was in effect a female crooner. We sense her ease in the timing of the words; she is not swinging, but she is not locked onto the beat, either.

Boswell's singing is a key component of the sweet sound, as it should be, because the focus is on melody—*sung* melody. The band simply frames the two choruses Boswell sings. A gentle two-beat rhythm with the familiar **broken chord**, or **arpeggio**, in the accompaniment supports it. The tempo is slow, just right for slow dancing and dreaming.

STYLE PROFILE

SWEET/ROMANTIC BALLAD

Rhythm	*Moderately slow tempo; mainly a two-beat rhythm, except during the bridge and at the very end of the song; strong syncopation only in the final phrase. Boswell subtly alters the timing of the original version of the song.*
Melody	*A section grows out of a simple three-note motive: "heart and soul"; the melody forms a graceful arch. The B section contains two identical four-measure phrases that spin out a two-note idea.*
Instrumentation (timbre)	*Vocal, plus dance orchestra (rhythm section, saxes/clarinets, and brass), with trumpets, clarinets, and piano most prominent.*
Performance style	*Boswell's singing is a fine example of crooning—a sweet voice, with easy delivery (no sense of straining) and subtle nuances in timing to make the rhythm more speechlike.*
Dynamics	*Soft.*

Harmony	*The four-chord progression that repeats throughout the A section is the famous "Heart and Soul" progression; it was used not only in other pop songs (Rodgers and Hart's "Blue Moon") but also in pop-derived rhythm-and-blues and rock-and-roll songs like "Earth Angel."*
Texture	*Three layers: melody, arpeggiated accompaniment in the clarinets (in an arpeggio, or broken chord, the notes of the chord are presented one after another, instead of all at once), plus rhythm.*
Form	*Two choruses of an **AABA** song, plus introduction, interlude, and tag.*

Key Points

Focus on the voice	*New development: a dance number that is all vocal.*
"Heart and Soul"	*A more complex song than the amateur version might suggest: the ends of the three A sections work hard to link the sections instead of predictably coming to rest. No reference to the verse. Outside of musical theater and film, the verse has all but disappeared in favor of greater emphasis on the chorus.*
Crooning	*Boswell sings with a pretty sound and an easy delivery—a match for conversational lyrics.*
Swing versus sweet	*Mostly two-beat sweet, with a little swing during the bridge and at the end.*

Terms to Know

AABA form	bridge	sweet
arpeggio	broken chord	

Romantic Ballads. As its title implies, "Heart and Soul" is an unabashedly romantic song. The lyric tells us about love at first sight, much as did "Cheek to Cheek" and so many other sweet songs of the 1930s and '40s. This is the era of the **romantic ballad**. Such songs are a curious mix of the personal and the impersonal. Despite their use of personal pronouns ("I'm in heaven"), we don't get a clear sense of who the people are. There are several reasons for this. Most came from shows or films, where the singer is playing a character. Hit songs produced multiple recordings, almost overnight, and the listener heard different singers describing the same romantic encounter. Most important, the creative process involved several steps: the songwriter writing the song, the arranger preparing it for performance, and the singer performing it.

Paradoxically, faithful performances of popular songs, such as we heard from Astaire and Boswell, distance us from a sense of identity because they emphasize the song over the singer. As a result, we don't have the same sense of personal connection between song, singer, and listener that we had with Bessie Smith—or that we will enjoy with singer-songwriters like Bob Dylan. What we do get is an invitation to escape into a world of romantic infatuation, longing, and, often, heartbreak. A new, more personal approach to singing popular songs would soon emerge.

Summary. We have contrasted swing and sweet. Swing was more about rhythm than melody; sweet was more about melody than rhythm. Swing was both instrumental and vocal; sweet was vocal as a rule, spotlighting the singer. Both were popular styles in about equal measure. Some bands played swing almost exclusively; others played only sweet. Still others, like Glenn Miller's, moved easily between the two. The battle between the two genres was over around the time the bigger battle of World War II ended in 1945. Changing tastes and the high cost of operating a big band signaled the end of the swing era.

Swing led to the future, its rhythms spreading to a host of postwar styles, including rhythm and blues, bebop, and jazz-flavored popular singing. Sweet connected with the past and to musical styles that looked to the past, especially musical theater.

MAINSTREAMING THE BLUES

Despite their influence blues and blues singing remained distinctly different from popular song and singing. There are obvious differences in musical approach: the form of the song; the melodic range (popular songs tend to span a wider range than blues songs); the use of repetition and response that we heard in "Empty Bed Blues," as opposed to the development that we heard in "Cheek to Cheek"; and the vocal quality and timing of the singers. All of these qualities highlight the more fundamental difference: intent.

Blues singing focuses attention on the *singer*. As we listen to Bessie Smith describe her empty bed, we feel that she intends to share a chapter in her life. It is a personal account. Popular song focuses attention on the *song;* the feeling is more generic, the singing a more detached crooning as popularized by such singers as Crosby, Astaire, and Boswell. Popular songs are more impersonal. Those who write popular songs cannot make their songs as autobiographical as a blues because they are writing songs that others—many others, they hope —can and will perform.

In the 1930s, however, there emerged a new, more personal way of singing popular songs. It became more personal because of a blues-influenced reshaping of the song and its message. Its two most important and influential models were Louis Armstrong, whom we heard in Chapter 4, and Billie Holiday, whom we hear next.

Billie Holiday and the Next Major Step in Popular Song

Billie Holiday claimed that her two biggest influences were Bessie Smith and Louis Armstrong. She admired Smith's power and Armstrong's style. Smith and Armstrong, along with Bing Crosby and Ethel Waters, helped chart a new path to popular singing. It was Billie Holiday, however, who took the next major step.

Born Eleanora Harris, Billie Holiday (1915–1959) led an unimaginably difficult life. Both she and her mother were born out of wedlock, and both were arrested for prostitution in 1929, when Holiday was only fourteen. Shortly after, she started her musical career singing at tables in Harlem nightclubs. These were not glamorous places like the Cotton Club, but rough bars where the girls were expected to do more than just sing. She became an alcoholic and a drug addict, and she died at age forty-four after a steady decline in her ability to perform.

At her peak during the late 1930s and '40s, Holiday was a unique voice in popular music. We hear her ability to transmute popular song into personal statement in her 1940 recording of "All of Me." A small band led by Eddie Heywood and featuring saxophonist Lester Young provides accompaniment.

"All of Me," written in 1931 by Seymour Simons and Gerald Marks, is a standard; it remains one of the most popular songs of the 1930s, and over the years hundreds of artists have recorded it. Billie Holiday's version shows how she brought the deep feeling of blues and

CD 1:20

"All of Me," Seymour Simons and Gerald Marks (1931). Eddie Heywood and His Orchestra, with Billie Holiday, vocal, and featuring Lester Young, tenor saxophone.

CD 1:20   **Jazz/Blues Song** (Seymour Simons and Gerald Marks; performed by Eddie Heywood and His Orchestra, with Billie Holiday, vocal, and featuring Lester Young, tenor saxophone)

0:00		Instrumental introduction

1st Chorus

0:18   A   Listen for the blues-derived expressive inflection (the second "All of me," "I'm no good").

All of me, why not take all of me,
Can't you see, that I'm no good without you.

0:36   B   By this time Holiday has in effect begun to create a new melody to the song—same words, same harmony underneath, but a melody quite different from the original.

Take my lips,
I want to lose them,
Take my arms,
I'll never use them.

0:54   A

Your goodbye
Left me with eyes that cry,
How can I
Go on dear without you,

1:11   C

You took the part
That was once my heart,
So why not take all of me.

Instrumental interlude.

1:24   Tenor saxophone (Lester Young).

2nd Chorus

1:47   A   Same words, but a reworked melody. Notice how Holiday compresses the melody into a narrower range.

2:05   B   The vocal inflection tells us what the lyrics are trying to say.

2:23   A   Her continual reshaping of the original melody shows the influence of jazz practice on her singing.

2:42   C   Holiday's ad-libbed lyrics are the climax of the performance:

You took the best, so why not take the rest . . .

Permission of Marlong Music Corp., Berkley, Michigan.

the swing of jazz into popular singing. In essence, she projects *herself* through the song. As we listen to her recording, we are less concerned with the words than with how she delivers them. Her performance transcends the sentimental lyrics to express the real and almost universal pain of lost love, with an immediacy that the song by itself can't begin to attain. As written, words and music send one message; her voice sends a second, much deeper one. Hers is not a pretty sound, but it remains one of the most individual timbres ever to emerge in the popular tradition.

We notice this most clearly in the second chorus, as Holiday transforms this straightforward popular song into a blues song. The melody's range narrows considerably, and most phrases begin high and end low. She sings this chorus in the top part of her range, giving her voice a particular urgency. The inflection of the melodic line becomes more intense, especially on the words "lips," "eyes," and "cry." The note values lengthen and the rhythm becomes

Billie Holiday in a scene from *New Orleans* (1946). It was her only film appearance. In the film she plays a maid; she is the girlfriend of Louis Armstrong, seen here playing a cornet (not a trumpet).

freer, suggesting even more strongly than before that Holiday sings because simple speech cannot convey the emotion she wishes to express. She saves the very top note in the song for the climactic phrase, "why not take the rest"; as her voice descends, we can feel her despair. Her performance transcends the lyrics to express the real anguish of lost love.

Billie Holiday's art is not one of technical virtuosity. In one of the most fascinating paradoxes of jazz history, this great jazz singer was never known as a scat singer (recall that this means singing a wordless vocal that imitates jazz instrumental style). Nor is it a style of conventional beauty. Instead, she communicates her feelings directly, unfiltered by stylistic conventions, a preferred vocal sound, or a literal adherence to the original melodic shape of the song. Like other great performers, she is a style unto herself, instantly recognizable, broadly influential, and widely, if unsuccessfully, imitated.

STYLE PROFILE

JAZZ/BLUES SONG

Rhythm	*Moderate tempo; swing (four-beat) rhythm marked by guitar and bass; lots of rhythmic play in Holiday's singing, Young's sax solo, and the backing riffs.*
Melody	*Develops from a three-note riff; succeeding versions of the riff keep the rhythm but assume a different melodic shape. During the second chorus, Holiday reshapes the melody, flattening it out to make it more blueslike.*
Instrumentation (timbre)	*Holiday's vocal, backed by a band featuring a trumpet, three saxophones, and a full rhythm section (guitar, piano, bass, and drums).*
Performance style	*Holiday's unique vocal timbre and her expressive blues-tinged inflections give her singing a distinct personality.*

Dynamics	Moderate throughout; strong contrast within the vocal line.
Harmony	Enriched I-IV-V harmony; many chords are not I, IV, or V.
Texture	Melody dominant, with discreet rhythm-section support and background melodic figures and riffs in the horn parts.
Form	ABAC popular song form in two choruses, with introduction, instrumental interlude, and a very brief tag.

Key Points

Holiday, blues, jazz, and pop	Holiday sings pop songs with the feeling and style of blues and the swing and freedom of jazz.
Holiday's voice	A unique, unconventional vocal sound that set her apart.
Pop singers versus song interpreters	Holiday was among the first important **song interpreters**, using songs to project her experience—and reshaping them in the process.

Terms to Know

song interpreter

Summary

Armstrong and Holiday brought blues style and blues feeling into the singing of popular songs. Their work showed how to use a popular song as a window to a singer's heart and soul. In essence they made popular singing a more autobiographical art, bringing a jazzlike freedom into their reshaping of a melody and the timing of their delivery. With them jazz singing goes beyond the easy swing we heard from Crosby in "After You've Gone."

JAZZ IN THE SWING ERA

Jazz flirted with popularity between the two world wars. The first of the Original Dixieland Jazz Band recordings—in 1917—was a sensation; jazz and a lot of music that passed for jazz made the 1920s the **Jazz Age**. With swing, jazz came even closer to the popular-music mainstream. There were hits by Benny Goodman, Count Basie, Duke Ellington, Jimmy Lunceford, Artie Shaw, and others that were unquestionably jazz. And there is a smooth continuum between swing songs like "Chattanooga Choo Choo" and big-band jazz.

We don't think of jazz as a popular music, however. As jazz became an established and distinctive music, jazz musicians developed what might be considered an anti-popular attitude. It wasn't so much that they didn't want their music to be popular; rather, they wanted it to be popular on their own terms. Instead of catering to their audience, jazz musicians wanted listeners to come to them.

The crux of the issue was creativity and artistry. Musicians wanted to play for themselves —to express their creativity without worrying about commercial appeal. This attitude put them at odds with the people who ran popular music: then as now, it was a business as well as a creative endeavor, and the purpose of a business is to turn a profit on a product.

The career of Louis Armstrong during the twenties and thirties epitomizes the difficult relationship between jazz and popular music. As we heard in "West End Blues," Armstrong's

Hot Five and Hot Seven recordings thoroughly divorced jazz from mainstream popular music. The most influential jazz recordings of the era, they showed that jazz could be an expressive, artistic music on its own terms, and they set a standard against which other musicians' work would be measured. But just before 1930, Armstrong changed his musical direction. He sang, played, and began to record popular songs instead of jazz compositions. This made him a much more popular figure to the general public. Within jazz circles, however, his star fell. Many dismissed him as old-fashioned or accused him of selling out, trading creativity for commercial success.

This attitude still prevails. Jazz historians tend to place the greatest value on "pure" jazz recordings; that is, recordings without evidence of artistic compromise or mainstream connections. This jazz is almost always instrumental, strictly for listening. The main melodic material will be jazzlike, either by using a melody specifically composed for jazz performance or by thoroughly transforming an existing blues or popular melody. It will swing, but it won't be for dancing. The attitude took root in the 1930s and early '40s, as we hear in Duke Ellington's "Ko-ko," a twentieth-century masterpiece.

Duke Ellington's "Ko-ko"

It used to bother Duke Ellington that people tried to put labels on everything. Speaking about race relations, he said, "I don't believe in categories of any kind, and when you speak of problems between blacks and whites in the USA you are referring to categories again." His dislike of categories certainly extended to music; he liked to say that there were only two kinds of music: good and bad.

Certainly, his career and music resist categorization. Almost from the beginning, Ellington was apart from the main currents in jazz. While most jazz musicians were playing in ballrooms or speakeasies, Ellington was writing "jungle" music for floorshows at the Cotton Club, the famous Harlem nightclub. By the early 1930s, he and his band gained a national following through radio broadcasts from the Cotton Club. The swing-era years were a creative and commercial high point for Ellington. After the end of World War II, when so many big bands folded, Ellington kept his going. He continued to tour, write hit songs, and take on new challenges, such as film scoring and church music. Although we associate Ellington with the swing era, his career—like his music—transcends the boundaries of time and style.

Ellington's music is both a part of jazz and apart from it. His music is an esteemed part of American music, yet he stands apart from other esteemed American musicians. He is a composer in a genre that values **improvisation**, and he composed jazz, rather than "classical" music or even classical/popular hybrids like *Rhapsody in Blue*. He is universally revered as jazz's greatest composer, and some authoritative commentators have called him America's greatest composer. We get some sense of his art in "Ko-ko," a 1940 composition.

1:21

"Ko-ko," Edward "Duke" Ellington (1940). Duke Ellington and His Orchestra.

In "Ko-ko" Ellington uses big-band swing style as a point of departure. His orchestra has a standard instrumentation—three high brass, three low brass, five saxophones, and a four-man rhythm section, with Ellington at the piano—with two differences: Ellington substitutes a then-unfashionable cornet for one of the trumpets in the high-brass section, and a valve trombone for one of the slide trombones in the low-brass section. These unconventional instruments hint at one of the keys to Ellington's art: his sound imagination.

The sound resources in Ellington's orchestra went beyond the choice of instruments. Almost every member of the band developed a signature sound. For example, trumpeter Cootie Williams became a master of mutes and the sounds they could create, to the extent

CD 1:21   **Swing-era Jazz** (Edward "Duke" Ellington; performed by Duke Ellington and His Orchestra)

0:00	Introduction. Call-and-response between baritone sax and trombones.

1st Chorus (blues form)

0:12	Call-and-response riffs between valve trombone (low) and saxophones (high).

2nd Chorus

0:31	Riff in high trombone (with plunger mute), with offbeat figure in lower brass underneath.

3rd Chorus

0:50	Another high trombone sound, with offbeat answers continuing.

4th Chorus

1:09	Repeated riff in the saxes, jagged responses in brass, piano fills. Note the quicker riff rhythm that repeats every four beats instead of eight.

5th Chorus

1:27	After riff, in trumpets, with two responses: high saxes/clarinets and trombones.

6th Chorus

1:45	A short four-note riff, handed from saxes to trombones to trumpets to clarinets; then walking bass solo. Instrument order varies with each repetition.

7th Chorus

2:04	Massive brass chord, followed by sax riff.

Ending

2:23	Introduction returns, but this time leads to a climactic end.

that Ellington wrote a concerto that showcased that ability. We also hear this timbral play in "Ko-ko": there is a striking contrast between the relatively neutral valve trombone sound of Juan Tizol at the beginning and the high-trombone sound of Joe Nanton, who uses a (toilet) plunger to make his instrument talk.

Because his band had relatively little turnover, Ellington was able to experiment with various sound combinations. Sometimes he would showcase individuals; other times he would blend unusual combinations of instruments instead of grouping the band into sections. Ellington seemed to delight in his bold experiments with sound.

Just as Ellington's choice and combinations of instruments go well beyond conventional big-band arranging, so does his melodic material. His basic unit of melodic thought is the riff, but he gives his riffs a personal twist. Individually and in combination, they sound different from the kinds of riffs we heard in "Wrappin' It Up" and "Chattanooga Choo Choo": less predictable and more varied. These and other features, like the exploiting of extreme high and low registers, help give "Ko-ko" a darker, more ominous character.

Compositions like "Ko-ko" set Ellington and his music apart from other bands and musicians of the era. This music is making a statement. It goes well beyond the lindy-hopping, jitterbugging riff tunes played by Fletcher Henderson, Count Basie, Benny Goodman, and so many others. This is not to say that swing wasn't great music but that Ellington is operating on a different, more artistic level.

SWING-ERA JAZZ

Rhythm	*Moderately fast tempo; four-beat swing rhythm in rhythm section, with synco-pated riffs pushing against the beat. Of particular interest is the "exchange" rhythm—the rhythm created by the call-and-response between sections. Initially, it is eight beats per call/response pair, but it alters at various times during the performance.*
Melody	*The opening chorus is a stylized call-and-response blues heard in a rising riff in the trombone, answered by a longer descending riff in the saxophones; subsequent choruses also build from riffs.*
Instrumentation (timbre)	*Full big band: two trumpets and a cornet, two slide trombones and a valve trombone, five saxophones, and a rhythm section (guitar, bass, drums, and piano).*
Performance style	*Many of the band members either used alternate versions of standard instruments (Juan Tizol's valve trombone) or cultivated distinctive sounds (trombonist Sam Nanton's use of a plunger mute).*
Dynamics	*Considerable contrast, from solo bass to full-band piles of sound.*
Harmony	***Minor blues**, a darker version of the basic blues progression; however, Ellington blends in many exotic harmonies, some almost unique to his personal style.*
Texture	*Multilayered texture over a steady rhythm section; considerable variation in **density**—the number and the spacing of parts—and register; effective use of extremes in both features.*
Form	*Blues form, with the introduction and its reprise.*

Key Points

Ellington, the painter in sound	*Band members' sounds are like colors; Ellington "paints" with them by using unusual combinations, first as sections, then individually. Timbre and register change from chorus to chorus.*
Ellington's use of register	*Ellington uses register to create energy and excitement. It starts low, then gradually ascends; shifts back down close to the end, then rises quickly for a strong finish.*
Ellington: beyond swing	*Ellington approaches art through imaginative and sophisticated treatment of the swing style.*
Jazz as composed music	*"Ko-ko," which Ellington wrote complete, contains no improvised solos, showing that improvisation is not essential to jazz.*

Terms to Know

density
"exchange" rhythm
minor blues

SONG INTERPRETATION: POPULAR SINGING AFTER WORLD WAR II

We call the enduring popular songs of the modern era **standards**. These are the songs that live on in recordings, films, and live performances. We have heard a few, from "After You've Gone" to "Heart and Soul," and there are hundreds more. Most of these songs appeared before 1945, but the most memorable *performances* of these songs appeared after 1945. Most of the great names in popular singing—Frank Sinatra, Nat "King" Cole, Sarah Vaughan, Ella Fitzgerald, Tony Bennett, Peggy Lee, and Rosemary Clooney—reached the height of their careers between 1945 and 1965. Some, like Sinatra and Fitzgerald, started with swing bands, but the bulk of their legacy comes from recordings that date from the fifties and sixties.

The distinguishing feature of all of these singers is the way in which they put their personal stamp on a song performance. It begins with a distinctive vocal style. None of the song interpreters has a conventionally pretty voice. For example, Sinatra's voice at the beginning of his career, when he sang with Tommy Dorsey's orchestra, was silkier: he was a real crooner. Years of fast living, cigarettes, and alcohol took away the sweetness and added a heavy dose of grit.

Like Armstrong, Holiday, Crosby, and a few others, the song interpreters project a personality. They do it with their own sound, inflection, and timing. All are masters of pacing; they are not bound by the beat. Typically, they will reshape the melody. Sometimes they reconceive the song completely: an up-tempo song becomes a ballad; a Latin song swings.

All of this transforms the relationship between song and singer. When we listened to Astaire sing "Cheek to Cheek," the focus was on the song. He delivered it impeccably, in a way perfectly suited to his film character (it must have delighted composer Irving Berlin), but he did not open a window to his soul. The new generation of popular singers reversed this dynamic. When they sing a song, we sense that they are using the song to share their feelings and life experiences. In so doing they make the impersonal song personal. We hear this clearly in Tony Bennett's exuberant remake of the swing-era hit, "Taking a Chance on Love."

Tony Bennett: Swing as a Vocal Style. "Taking a Chance on Love" first appeared in the Broadway musical (1940) and film (1943) *Cabin in the Sky*. Ethel Waters sang the song beautifully in the film version. Benny Goodman's version, which featured vocalist Helen Forrest, was a number 1 hit, also in 1943. Bennett's 1962 version is a joyous romp through the song. Like Armstrong, Bennett personalizes the melody, reshaping it to help project the optimistic message he finds in the song—we can almost see the smile on his face when he sings.

A wonderful studio big band supports him. Although it's true that the swing era ended around 1945, the sound of swing lived on. A few big bands stayed together, but many of the top musicians left the ballroom bandstands for the recording studios in New York and Los Angeles, where they played for films, television, and top singers like Bennett. This is the most direct continuation of the sound of big-band swing. And it's clear that they have the style down. The biggest difference is in the rhythm section. Here the drums, bass, and guitar lock into a wonderful swing groove and drive Bennett and the band in a way that only a handful of thirties' rhythm sections could.

 CD 1:22

"Taking a Chance on Love," Vernon Duke (1940). Tony Bennett, vocal.

STYLE PROFILE

SONG INTERPRETATION

Rhythm	*Fast tempo. Clear swing rhythm with a crisp backbeat (in the drums). Frequent syncopation in Bennett's vocal and the horn riffs.*
Melody	*The melody of the A section grows out of the opening five-note riff. The B section, like many bridges, is made up of two similar four-bar phrases set at different pitches. Bennett reshapes both the rhythm and the pitches of the original melody, especially in the second chorus.*
Instrumentation (timbre)	*Voice, plus full big band.*

| 0:00 | Instrumental introduction |

Chorus

0:06	A	Bennett alters the timing of the melody to make its rhythm more speechlike.
		Here I go . . .
0:17	A	The rhythm section lays down a swing groove behind Bennett.
		Here I slide . . .
0:28	B	The sax section switches from short riffs to sustained chords behind Bennett.
		Now I thought . . .
0:39	A	
		Things are mending . . .

Chorus

| 0:49 | A | Trumpets play opening riff. |
| | | *I hear those trumpets . . .* |

STYLE PROFILE *(cont'd)*

Performance style	Bennett has a warm voice of remarkable range (evident at the end). The horns play at times with exaggerated inflection—to help the swing. The trumpet shakes and slides are part of Armstrong's legacy.
Dynamics	Nice contrasts between the loud sections featuring the full band and the quieter moments with just voice and rhythm.
Harmony	Enriched I-IV-V.
Texture	Mainly melody over steady rhythm, with background parts in the saxes and brass; call-and-response in the second chorus.
Form	Two choruses of an AABA song, plus a short tag.

Key Points

Song interpretation	Bennett in effect rewrites the melody of the song, not once but twice.
Rhythm section	Easy to hear: guitar and bass on every beat, drummer's **ride cymbal** (long/long-short/long/long-short pattern), and piano **comping** (playing chords in an irregular, often syncopated rhythm).
Maturity of swing style	Updated, better-executed version of '40s swing style.

Terms to Know

comping

ride cymbal

There is an interesting difference between recordings like this and swing-era songs. Big-band swing is largely an exercise in nostalgia. Songs like "Chattanooga Choo Choo" identify a certain time, place, and mood. By contrast, pop standards sung in a swing style by a top singer represent an essentially timeless sound: whether it's recordings by Bennett, Sinatra, and their

Trumpets again

And we're taking...

The trumpets take the first and third phrases of the melody to set up call-and-response with the vocal.

1:00   A   Trumpets

About to take that ride again,

Trumpets

Taking a chance.

Compare the phrases in this chorus with the matching phrases in the first chorus to hear how Bennett reshaped the melody.

1:11   B

Now I walk around...

1:26   A   Bennett pushes to the climax of the performance by going into a very high range.

On the ball...

---

contemporaries or versions by a new generation of singers. This is how it's been done for more than half a century.

The End of the Modern Era of Popular Song. Bennett's "Taking a Chance on Love" comes from his 1962 album *I Left My Heart in San Francisco.* With this album and the title-song single, Bennett became even more popular; in a career that began shortly after World War II, the album was a peak, reaching number 2 on the charts. Ahead of it was the soundtrack to the film version of *West Side Story,* which stayed at number 1 for more than a year.

The previous year, Frank Sinatra had wriggled out of his contract with Capitol Records and formed his own label, Reprise. Recording at a frantic pace, he put six albums on the charts. All of this attests to the continuing presence of modern era–type music: ballads, swing tunes, venerable standards, and new songs written in an older style. It was very much part of the popular music landscape, even though the Beach Boys were giving America a sales pitch for surfing and the Shirelles were wondering whether he would love them tomorrow.

Despite its success, Bennett's album marks the end of an era that had spanned fifty years. The British bands began invading the next year, and by 1965 rock had taken over the marketplace. In fact, it was a rock-era icon who pointed modern-era music in a new direction: Ray Charles's 1960 recording of Hoagy Carmichael's "Georgia on My Mind," which Carmichael had written in 1931, showed a new and quite different way to sing this music. Although Bennett, Sinatra, and others remained popular, they were no longer current. Rock had taken over.

LOOKING BACK, LOOKING AHEAD

In the previous chapter, we saw how everything came together—song and dance, popular song, jazz, and blues—to foment the revolution that produced modern popular song. In this chapter we have traced its strongest reverberations. "Cheek to Cheek" exemplified the mellower, more mature form of the fox trot song—with an occasional hint of swing. Its length, the extended dance number, and the setting of the song in the musical—all suggest its ascent up the social ladder. The more moderate tempo, the less frequent syncopation, and Fred Astaire's restrained singing style suggest a retreat from the more hectic music of the 1920s; in this respect "Cheek to Cheek" is an evolutionary about-face, a partial return to a more melodious past.

Even as Fred and Ginger delighted millions in films like *The Gay Divorcée* and *Top Hat*, jazz got a second infusion of the blues. Repeated riffs, call-and-response, and intense inflection traveled from the blues to mix with the strong four-beat rhythm and heavy syncopation of jazz to create a new kind of dance music: big-band swing. The architect of this new sound was Fletcher Henderson, whose arranging style became the model for the swing bands of the late 1930s.

By 1935 it was clear that popular music was going in two different directions. In the late thirties, swing became a popular style; during that same period, the fox trot song became even slower and smoother. These two trends split popular music into two camps, as we heard in our comparison between "Heart and Soul" and "Chattanooga Choo Choo."

The powerful influence of Louis Armstrong is evident in two other important musical trends. One was jazz as concert music; the other was a more personal kind of popular singing. Duke Ellington's music, as we hear in "Ko-ko," does not connect directly to Armstrong. By the time Armstrong made his small-group recordings, Ellington had begun developing his unique style, which he brought to a peak around 1940. The common ground is their artistry —an artistry specific to jazz: Ellington did for jazz composition what Armstrong had done for improvisation.

Billie Holiday brought the expressive vocabulary of the blues and the swing of jazz to her singing. More than any other singer of the late thirties and early forties, she was able to transform popular songs into deeply personal statements. Her more interpretive approach would influence an entire generation of stellar singers: Frank Sinatra, Nat "King" Cole, Peggy Lee, Sarah Vaughan, and Tony Bennett among them.

By the end of World War II, the swing era was over. A few bands continued to operate in the postwar years, but none enjoyed the kind of popularity they'd had in the late thirties and early forties. The sound of swing did not disappear, however. Many swing-era musicians found steady employment in recording studios, where they played behind the top pop singers of the postwar era. We heard a fine example of this in Tony Bennett's rendition of "Taking a Chance on Love."

This kind of singing was the most popular continuation of swing—but it was not the only one. In the postwar years, swing split off in three directions: one was jazz/swing–influenced popular singing. Another was bebop, a daring new jazz style just for listening that fostered the first counterculture. A third was an upbeat brand of rhythm and blues. Jump bands—pocket-sized versions of swing-era big bands—posterized swing: a stronger beat, more riffs, and more blues. We hear a nice example of this sound in Chapter 9.

Sweet and swing made up the popular music mainstream in the late 1930s and early '40s, but there was other music that periodically intersected with this mainstream. We encounter examples of these intersections in the next three chapters. We will discover musical theater becoming more arty and musically conservative: songs like "Oh, What a Beautiful Morning," from Rodgers and Hammerstein's landmark 1943 musical *Oklahoma!*, return to the past, both within the musical and stylistically. In Chapter 7 we hear country takes on popular dance music in Bob Wills's western swing and the honky-tonk of Hank Williams; both sport a countrified two-beat rhythm. And in Chapter 8, we hear the mainstreaming of Latin music in Xavier Cugat's recording of Cole Porter's "Begin the Beguine." We turn next to musical theater.

TERMS TO KNOW

Test your knowledge of this chapter's important terms by defining the following. If you can't recall the meaning of a certain term, refresh your memory by looking up the boldfaced term in the chapter, turning to the Glossary at the back of the book, or working with the flashcards on the Popular Music in America Companion Web site: *http://music.wadsworth.com/campbell_2e*

. . . .

AABA form	comping	romantic ballad
ABAC form	crooner	scale
arpeggio	density	song interpreter
backbeat	doubling	standard
ballad	"exchange" rhythm	sweet
big band	improvisation	swing
big-band swing	Jazz Age	swing era
bridge	minor blues	walking bass
broken chord	ride cymbal	*Your Hit Parade*
call-and-response	riff	

. . . .

Musical Theater

Sometime after eight o'clock on the evening of December 27, 1927, Paul Robeson (1898–1976), a young African American actor-singer, stepped into the spotlight of the Ziegfeld Theater in New York to sing a song about a river. Robeson was one of the most multitalented men of the twentieth century. He graduated as class valedictorian from Rutgers University after winning letters in four sports and twice earning All-America honors as a football player. He went on to law school at Columbia and took his degree in 1923. Despite these academic credentials, Robeson decided to go on-stage as a singer and actor. His appearance on December 27 was a breakthrough for him—and for American musical theater.

Robeson portrayed Joe, a stevedore, one of the thousands of faceless black men who worked long hours for little money along the Mississippi River and who liked their liquor a little too much. He spoke and sang in a pseudo-black dialect that rang with the unmistakable echoes of the minstrel show. It was not the most dignified role, although it was certainly several steps up from blackface minstrelsy, and Robeson invested it with great dignity.

Had he been born a half century later and held views politically closer to the center, he might well have become our first black president. But after a trip in the 1930s to the Soviet Union, where he received red-carpet treatment, he embraced communistic ideals and continued to support communism even after he learned of Stalin's atrocities. He devoted much of his life and all of his heart to causes that benefited the disadvantaged of all kinds, particularly African Americans, as well as causes that promoted a united, peaceful world. The McCarthy-era witch hunts devastated his career and his life; after 1950 he faded from the public spotlight.

Robeson recorded his river song with Paul Whiteman and His Orchestra. It was a hit—quite different from almost all of the hits of that era. He would sing it for the rest of his career, changing the words to fit the circumstances.

Robeson's role and subsequent career tell us a lot about race relations in the United States during his lifetime. *Show Boat,* the musical in which he appeared, played a small but noteworthy role in moving white perceptions of African Americans from minstrel stereotypes toward a more authentic, humane image—all of which underscores the close connection between popular music and life in America. But it doesn't answer the intriguing question:

Paul Robeson, toting that bale. This is a still image from the scene in the film shown during the bridge of the song. Even this staged photo gives us some insight into the hard life of a stevedore on the Mississippi.

why was Robeson singing a song about a river (rather than, say, romantic love)? To explore this question, we consider the role of song in musical theater.

POPULAR SONG AS A DRAMATIC TOOL

Throughout the history of popular music, songwriters have intended that their songs be appealing—that they be both accessible and artful. The best ones succeed on both counts, as we have heard in songs ranging from "Old Folks at Home" to "Cheek to Cheek." Those who write for musical theater productions, or any dramatic situation, must also factor in another important expectation: a song must be not only appealing but also dramatically effective.

In a musical comedy, operetta, or a musical play, most of the words are spoken, not sung. Because of the power of song, it is a special moment when a character begins to sing. Still, there are pros and cons to song in drama. Although singing projects the message of the text with a power and an expressiveness beyond speech alone, it slows down the action—sometimes to a standstill.

So, we ask: What, if anything, can song accomplish *dramatically* that words cannot? Why do the librettist and the composer choose to incorporate a song at a particular point in the story? What dramatic purpose does song serve? In musical theater a dramatically effective song usually fulfills one (or more) of three functions:

- It helps establish the mood of a situation.
- It advances the plot.
- It gives the audience greater insight into the character singing the song.

We explore these functions of song by looking at five productions that are milestones in the history of musical theater.

GEORGE M. COHAN: TOWARD AN AMERICAN MUSICAL COMEDY

James Cagney made his reputation on-screen as a tough guy. In films from the 1930s, he often played a gangster, the head of a mob. He also earned a reputation as a tough guy off-screen. Chafing at the restrictions in his contract with Warner Brothers and wanting to be his own boss, he formed his own production company, with his brother William as producer. Cagney served as president of the Screen Actors Guild, supported union activities in general, and championed Franklin D. Roosevelt's New Deal programs. In the process he antagonized his bosses as well as political conservatives. Some accused him of communist sympathy—not as big a crime as it would be after World War II but still damaging to his reputation. They questioned his patriotism, so Cagney sought out a part that would squelch any questions about his loyalties. He found it in the lead role of a 1942 film, *Yankee Doodle Dandy,* a biography of George M. Cohan. Cagney was enormously successful portraying Cohan. Critics loved it; audiences loved it. Cohan, who was gravely ill at the time, received a private screening of the film at home. After it was over, someone asked him what he thought of Cagney's portrayal. Reportedly, he grinned and said, "My God, what an act to follow!"

Music On-stage in the Early Twentieth Century

Two things stand out about song on the American stage around the turn of the century: most songs had little dramatic connection to their context, and most songs did not sound particularly American. Recall that vaudeville had no plot, just a sequence. The minstrel show had songs but not much of a story. Revues used some kind of story line to hook a string of songs together with comedy and dance routines. Although it generally began with a real plot, musical comedy wasn't much better. **Interpolation** was the rule of the day; plots accommodated songs, not the other way around. Only in operetta do we find a consistent connection between song and story.

Moreover, with the exception of the occasional coon song or ragtime song, most songs lacked a recognizably American musical character. Although the lyrics were often American in subject and style (recall "Take Me Out to the Ball Game"), the music was less so. Operetta songs came from Europe or were composed in the United States by European immigrants (Victor Herbert, Sigmund Romberg, and Rudolf Friml among them). **Waltz songs**, the most popular kind of song around the turn of the century, owed more to Europe than to America. Most other songs from musical comedies and even the minstrel show had little music that said, "*This* is American." And then came Cohan.

George M. Cohan

Born into a family of vaudeville performers, George M. Cohan (1878–1942) came into prominence around 1900 with a string of successful musicals that included many still-familiar songs and were more tightly knit dramatically than their predecessors. Cohan was a one-man entertainment industry, adept at all phases of the theatrical business: songwriting, performing, directing, and producing. He was among the most important and versatile entertainers of his age.

But it is as a patriotic songwriter that Cohan's legacy endures. His **patriotic songs** have the energy of a great march, a vigorous melody, a hint of syncopation, and clever lyrics without a trace of nineteenth-century sentimentality. With the exception of Irving Berlin, no American songwriter before or since has embodied patriotic sentiment so successfully in words and music.

In addition to their memorable songs, Cohan's musicals were also noteworthy because their **books** (scripts for nonmusical sections) and song lyrics used everyday speech, a practice that Cohan readily defended. As musical theater historian Gerald Bordman notes:

> A number of traditional reviewers assailed [Cohan's] excessive dependence on slang. Cohan retorted that that was the way his characters would talk could they have come to life on stage. He was not writing "literature," he was creating an entertainment about people with whom his audience could identify.

Cohan's musicals were a people's music, written for "the plumber and his lady friend in the last balcony." We see this in the lyric of "Yankee Doodle Boy" from Cohan's musical *Little Johnny Jones* (1904). The verse contains several slang expressions that give the song an easy familiarity: "all the candy"; "ain't that a josh"; and "phony"—early twentieth century street talk.

"Yankee Doodle Boy" is one of the most memorable of Cohan's patriotic songs. In the musical it helps establish the character of Johnny Jones, a jockey who has come to England to ride in the Derby. Jones, played by Cohan in the original production, is, in Bordman's words, "the cocky, slangy, identical twin of his creator." These qualities certainly come across in the song. It is an early example of the best kind of theater song—one that enhances the action on-stage but that has a life apart from the show as well.

CD 2:1

"Yankee Doodle Boy," George M. Cohan (1904). Richard Perry, vocal.

STYLE PROFILE

MARCH SONG

Rhythm	*Brisk march tempo, faster than the waltz songs that were so popular during this period. March-style (OOM-pah) accompaniment throughout most of the song. Quick rhythms in the melody, with a little syncopation.*
Melody	*Both verse and chorus begin with fairly long phrases. The verse is a patchwork of preexisting melodies. The chorus develops simply from the opening phrase.*
Instrumentation (timbre)	*Here, voice, piano, and drums. This recording is based on the sheet-music version of the song; the drums (not notated) enhance the song's marchlike aspect. (There are drums as well as piano in the accompaniment because this performance simulates a modestly produced theater production.)*
Performance style	*Singer* **belts** *the song, in Broadway-style singing.*
Dynamics	*Loud, given the instruments used.*
Harmony	*Mainly I-IV-V, but with a few extra chords.*
Texture	*Melody and accompaniment, plus percussion.*
Form	*Verse/chorus. Extended verse; chorus has two quite similar sections.*

STYLE PROFILE *(cont'd)*

Key Points

Sampling, 1904 style	*Cohan's* **sampling** *(inclusion of fragments of other songs) of several patriotic tunes includes "Dixie" and "The Star-Spangled Banner."*
The common touch	*Colloquial lyrics and a bright catchy tune.*
Patriotic character	*Patriotic tunes, plus a crisp march rhythm.*
Cakewalk rhythm	*The simple syncopation of the* **cakewalk** *is used throughout: "ain't that a josh."*

Terms to Know

belt	patriotic song
cakewalk	sampling

LISTENING GUIDE: "YANKEE DOODLE BOY"

CD 2:1   **March Song** (George M. Cohan; performed by Richard Perry, vocal)

0:00   Introduction.

1st Verse

0:12   1st section
Cohan uses the opening of "Yankee Doodle" as the beginning of his verse.
I'm the kid . . .

0:26   2nd section
In this section of the verse, Cohan quotes three more songs: "Dixie," "The Girl I Left Behind Me," and "The Star Spangled Banner."
I love to listen . . .

Chorus

0:44   A   Notice the cakewalk rhythm on the phrase "Born . . . July."
I'm a Yankee . . .

0:59   A^1 Another quotation from "Yankee Doodle."
I've got a . . .

2nd Verse

1:22   1st section
Father's name was . . .
The cakewalk rhythm can be heard in "Yanks" through "blue."

1:36   2nd section
My mother's mother was . . .
Most of the verse has new words; only "The Star-Spangled Banner" quotation remains the same.

Chorus

1:54   A
I'm a Yankee . . .

2:08   A^1
I've got a Yankee . . .

James Cagney in a scene from *Yankee Doodle Dandy*. The 1942 film was a biography of singer-songwriter-playwright George M. Cohan. Cohan, who was ill at this time, was delighted with Cagney's on-screen portrayal of him.

Cohan's musicals are seldom produced today—indeed, they might be hard to reconstruct. Still, his music has survived. Other than Stephen Foster's songs, Cohan's are the oldest still around in our time. Songs such as "Yankee Doodle Boy," "Give My Regards to Broadway," and "You're a Grand Old Flag" are still very much in the air. Cagney's portrayal in *Yankee Doodle Dandy* (1942), and the musical *George M.* (1968), have helped keep Cohan and his music alive and in the public eye.

Cohan's Legacy. As a songwriter for musical comedy, Cohan succeeded on three fronts. First, he created a body of memorable songs—songs that live on in the present day. Second, he gave many of them a distinctly American character. In both of these respects, he was the vocal counterpart to John Philip Sousa and his music. His patriotic songs have the vigor of Sousa's marches, yet they are certainly singable. Third, he put the song at the service of the story, rather than bend the story to the song. Even without seeing the show, we can easily imagine the character of Johnny Jones when we hear "Yankee Doodle Boy." In connecting song and show, Cohan helped lay the groundwork for Kern and Hammerstein's "musical play" *Show Boat* a quarter century later.

SHOW BOAT: AN AMERICAN MUSICAL PLAY

Jerome Kern (1885–1945), whose first hit was a song interpolated into a musical comedy, was already a well-established songwriter in 1926, when he read Edna Ferber's best-selling novel *Show Boat*. Convinced that it would make a superb musical, Kern persuaded Oscar

Hammerstein II (1895–1960) to supply the libretto (a **libretto** is the text for a sung stage production, from opera to musical comedy).

We can't know how clearly Kern envisioned a new, more substantial kind of musical, but we know from his previous work that he wanted to integrate music and drama more thoroughly than was common practice at the time. In the words of Gerald Bordman, Jerome Kern's series of shows for the small Princess Theater, beginning in 1915, "brought American musical comedy into the twentieth century." *Show Boat,* an "American musical play" created by Oscar Hammerstein II and Jerome Kern, opened at the Ziegfeld Theater in New York on December 27, 1927.

Music On-stage in the 1920s

The twenties were the heyday of musical stage entertainment in the United States. Vaudeville was still going strong. Revues—the grandest of which were the Ziegfeld shows—were doing well. Florenz Ziegfeld produced his first *Follies* in 1907, followed by annual editions (called the *Ziegfeld Follies* from 1911 on) until 1925. Other annual revues also flourished, including Lew Leslie's *Blackbirds* series, which featured African American performers. Cohan-style musical comedies continued to appear, competing with operettas. Theatergoers could attend stage productions of unprecedented variety, lavishness, and quality.

Still, virtually all stage shows were dramatic fluff. **Operettas** had fantasy plots in the long-ago-and-far-away. The plots for musical comedies were lighthearted, comparable in emotional depth to an average sitcom. Shows included a lot of singing and dancing—they generally opened with a string of chorus girls kicking away—and there was lots of comedy. These productions were fun; they were designed to entertain and occasionally titillate, but they didn't go much deeper than that.

Stage entertainment served as the primary outlet for popular songs, especially those by songwriters of high caliber. The songs would eventually become popular apart from their shows and make up the majority of the hits in the twenties and thirties. Typically, however, songs written for revues or musical comedies did little dramatic work. Some were fine songs that have become standards, while their musical comedy sources have been forgotten. For example, we might hear jazz musicians play George Gershwin's "Lady Be Good" but be hard-pressed to find a production of the 1924 musical of the same name—and that was one of the best.

The Novelty of Show Boat

Ziegfeld, who had stopped producing revues in favor of musical comedies, was reluctant to produce a show that departed dramatically from other kinds of stage entertainment. Only when Kern and Hammerstein convinced Ziegfeld to bill the production as an "American musical play" did he agree to throw his considerable resources behind its production.

Why was Ziegfeld so reluctant? Ferber's novel dealt seriously with difficult social issues in chronicling the life of the Hawkes family over a period of about forty years and three generations. The patriarch, Captain Andy, runs a showboat, a riverboat cruising up and down the Mississippi and stopping at river cities to put on theatrical productions. The plot centers around the marriage between Magnolia, the Hawkes' daughter, and Gaylord Ravenal, a good-looking, good-for-nothing gambler. They go through hard times, including a separation that lasts years, before they are reunited at the end, when any happiness is certainly tempered by heartache. A key subplot involves the principal actors in the showboat's productions: Julie, a light-skinned mulatto, and her white husband, Steve. A jealous suitor exposes Julie as non-white, and a law against interracial marriage forces the couple to leave the showboat. Later in the musical, we encounter Julie working as a cabaret singer and obviously suffering from alcoholism. Another recurrent theme is the life of the stevedores along the Mississippi, a commentary on the hard lot of African Americans after the Civil War.

For all its seriousness, *Show Boat* was ultimately entertainment, albeit with a message. From our current perspective, it may seem politically incorrect. There are reverberations of the minstrel show in the lyrics to "Ol' Man River," the song Joe sings. A white singer, Helen Morgan, played Julie, although many light-skinned African Americans were certainly capable of playing the role in 1927 (and in the 1936 and 1951 film versions). But this was the 1920s. Jim Crow segregation laws were still on the books in the South, lynchings were all too frequent, professional baseball remained segregated, and there had been a strong backlash against the few increased opportunities for black Americans. Less than three months before *Show Boat*'s premiere, Al Jolson had blacked up for the opening of *The Jazz Singer*. Against this backdrop *Show Boat* made a major statement simply by addressing difficult issues.

 CD 2:2

"Ol' Man River," Jerome Kern and Oscar Hammerstein II (1927). Paul Robeson, vocal.

"Ol' Man River." To the extent that *Show Boat* was a vehicle for hits songs—"Ol' Man River," "Can't Help Lovin' Dat Man," "Bill," and "Make Believe"—it was very much in step with other musicals. Where the songs differed was in how they worked in the show. For Kern, songs in a play were not simply something for actors to sing. Songs also had to function dramatically, enhancing the action or revealing character. Kern's self-imposed task was to take the popular

LISTENING GUIDE: "OL' MAN RIVER"

CD 2:2   **Musical Theater Solo** (Jerome Kern and Oscar Hammerstein II; performed by Paul Robeson, vocal)

1st Verse

0:00	A	Although this a "popular" song, notice that there is no dance rhythm.
		Dere's an ol' man . . .
0:24	B	This is also the bridge in the chorus.
		Don't look up . . .

2nd Verse

0:46	A	Note the spiritual-inspired reference to the river Jordan in the lyric.
		Let me go 'way . . .

Chorus

1:13	A	The first eleven notes use the five different notes of the pentatonic scale.
		Ol' Man River . . .
1:39	A^1	Although the melody grows out of a rifflike idea, it forms just one big arch. In this restatement of A, the peak of the arch is a little higher.
		He don't plant taters . . .
2:03	B	Bridge
		The melody is more active here.
		You an' me . . .
2:26	A^2	In this last version of A, Kern creates a climax for the entire song by keeping the last part of the section in a high register.
		Ah gits weary . . .

song to a new, higher level. It must not only appeal but also be appropriate to the dramatic situation.

In *Show Boat* Kern composed several memorable songs, the best known of which is "Ol' Man River." Sung by the stevedore Joe (portrayed in the stage musical and the first film version by Paul Robeson), the song appears early in the show. The lyric blends three themes: the grueling and thankless labor of the stevedores, the desire to escape it, and the constancy of life on the river personified as "Ol' Man River," who "just keeps rollin' along."

The lyrics are a gentle form of the dialect that we first encountered in the minstrel show. This dialect had recently found a new, more dignified home in the arrangements of Negro spirituals published in 1925 by James Weldon Johnson and J. Rosamund Johnson. The brothers had enjoyed some success as two-thirds of a songwriting team earlier in the century and had become active figures in the Harlem Renaissance, a flowering of cultural activity among African Americans in New York in the 1920s. During this time collections of **spirituals** were generally regarded as among the most cultured expressions of an African American sensibility. The reference in the verse to the "river Jordan" makes clear the verbal connection to the spiritual.

By connecting the song musically to the spiritual—most evident in the slight syncopation of the title phrase—Kern projects the dignity of the black stevedores and, by extension, of all African Americans who worked hard for little pay and even less respect. Clearly, this is a song *for* the show. It doesn't transfer easily to vaudeville or the cabaret. It was popular, without question, and it grew out of the popular style of the time, but it was not a conventional popular song. "Ol' Man River" is twice as long as "Sunday" (Chapter 4), and, with a wide range that extends from very low to quite high, the song requires an accomplished singer. Paul Robeson sang about a river because Kern and Hammerstein believed that it was dramatically necessary.

Kern used musical associations to portray character elsewhere in the show. In one poignant example, Julie reveals her racial heritage by singing the song "Can't Help Lovin' Dat Man," a song that has the occasional **blue note** (an African-inspired alteration of certain conventional scale tones) to show its African American roots.

STYLE PROFILE

MUSICAL THEATER SOLO

Rhythm	*Slow tempo, with much beat stretching (in this authoritative performance). Slow-moving melody and even slower rhythms in the accompaniment. Slight syncopation in the melody (the cakewalk rhythm).*
Melody	*Both the A and B sections of the refrain develop from rifflike figures ("Ol' Man River" and "you an' me"), using the **pentatonic scale**. The A section forms a long arch. This in turn sets up the climax in the last statement of A. The bridge and the verse (which includes the bridge) are more active.*
Instrumentation (timbre)	*Bass voice, plus orchestral accompaniment. Orchestra includes strings, harp, trumpets, trombones, saxophones; strings are most prominent. Rhythm-section instruments are very much in the background.*
Performance style	*Robeson sings with a full, somewhat classical-style voice. Strings play in classical style (not fiddling).*
Dynamics	*Starts softly and builds to the end.*
Harmony	*Opening sections of both verse and refrain use mainly I, IV, and V, with a slow rate of chord change. The bridge is more active and begins in a different key.*
Texture	*Melody plus lush accompaniment.*

| Form | Verse/chorus. Verse uses ABA form; chorus uses the newly popular **AABA form**. The A section reaches progressively higher peaks before descending at the end. The B section (bridge) is the same in both verse and chorus. |

Key Points

Show Boat and race	Show Boat *presents racial issues, especially interracial relationships, sensitively, although it was a touchy subject.*
"Ol' Man River": spiritual as popular song	*The song evokes the Negro spiritual in both words ("river Jordan") and music.*
Expansive song	*Weightier lyric needed a slower, longer popular-song setting.*

Terms to Know

AABA form

pentatonic scale

The Legacy of *Show Boat*. *Show Boat* in effect integrated the two popular forms of music and theater: musical comedy and operetta. Like operetta, it began long ago and far away (the story begins in the 1880s along the Mississippi—a time and place far removed from New York in the late 1920s). Like musical comedy, it was American.

Above all, the show aspired to be more than just entertainment, and it succeeded. The premiere was a milestone in American music—the night musical comedy became American **musical theater**. *Show Boat* was the first of the great modern musicals. Audiences would wait more than fifteen years for another musical of comparable dramatic integrity and appeal.

After *Show Boat*. One might expect *Show Boat* to have spawned a new genre, an endless string of like-minded productions, but that was not the case. Talking films and the Great Depression were a one-two combination that brought musical theater to its knees and changed its audience. Broadway became more of an elite entertainment, simply because fewer could afford it; film musicals offered a cheaper and more accessible alternative.

There were a few attempts to follow the course charted by Kern and Hammerstein. George Gershwin's three political satires in the early thirties stand out in this regard. The second of them, *Of Thee I Sing,* won the 1931 Pulitzer Prize for best play, one of only a few musicals to do so. Gershwin followed these shows with an even more spectacular achievement: his opera *Porgy and Bess* (1935). In its enduring popularity and special place straddling the boundary between classical and popular music, it is Gershwin's vocal counterpart to *Rhapsody in Blue.* Rodgers and Hart's musicals of the late 1930s also sought to bring more realism and greater integration of story and song to the Broadway stage; their 1940 musical, *Pal Joey,* was the capstone of their Broadway career.

Rodgers and Hart. For almost a quarter century, Lorenz (Larry) Hart (1895–1943) and Richard Rodgers (1902–1979) had been songwriting partners. They first worked together in 1919 and had their first hit six years later, a song entitled "Manhattan." Hart wrote the words. With Cole Porter, he was the cleverest lyricist of the era. (The opening phrase of "Manhattan," with its witty internal rhyme "I'll take Manhat*tan* and Sta*ten* Island, too," is a famous early demonstration of Hart's style.) Rodgers wrote the music. For more than fifteen years, they turned out hit after hit. Many of their best songs are standards: "My Funny Valentine," "Isn't It Romantic?" and "Little Girl Blue" are just a few of their many great songs.

They stayed together because they were good and because they were successful. It was difficult: Rodgers was a workaholic, and Hart was an alcoholic, whose undependability strained their relationship. The split came shortly after *Pal Joey*. Hart, whose health was deteriorating, declined an offer from Rodgers to turn a play by Lynn Riggs, *Green Grow the Lilacs* (1931), into a musical. Rodgers then turned to Oscar Hammerstein II, who had enjoyed great success with *Show Boat* but little since then. Out of their first collaboration came *Oklahoma!*. It was the beginning of their long and extremely successful career together, and it was the end of Hart's career; he died in 1943, shortly after the premiere of *Oklahoma!*.

The musicals of Gershwin and of Rodgers and Hart were the exception. In general, audiences wanted relief, not reality. Musicals like Cole Porter's *Anything Goes*, produced in 1934, offered escapist entertainment for the theatergoing elite. Film musicals, such as the Fred and Ginger series, offered it for the masses. The 1930s and early '40s were difficult times for musical theater. That would change almost overnight in 1943.

OKLAHOMA! AND THE GOLDEN ERA OF MUSICAL THEATER

When he teamed up with Hammerstein, Rodgers became a different songwriter. The difference lies not only in the songs themselves but in their relationship to the musicals for which they were written. We remember the *songs* of Rodgers and Hart; we remember the *shows* of Rodgers and Hammerstein. This difference is apparent from the first notes of "Oh, What a Beautiful Mornin'" as the curtain goes up on *Oklahoma!*.

Oklahoma! The Musical as Drama

Oklahoma! embeds two romantic triangles in a frontier setting at the turn of the century. The more significant triangle involves Curly, a cowhand, and Jud, the hired hand on Aunt Eller's farm, who compete for the favor of Laurey, Aunt Eller's niece. The two men personify a central tension in the play's tale of frontier life: the opposing interests of ranchers, who want their cattle to roam freely, and of farmers, who want to fence their land to keep cattle from grazing on their crops. The second triangle, connecting Will Parker, Ado Annie, and an "Egyptian" peddler, Ali Hakim, provides comic relief.

A quick take on the story line leaves the impression that this is simply another "good guy wins/bad guy loses" plot. But Jud (the bad guy) is a complex character, the most complex in the musical. Aunt Eller praises him for his hard work, but he has a sinister side. In a departure from strict good guy/bad guy, Jud is in many ways the most sympathetic character in the musical simply because he is doomed. We know from the outset that Curly will marry Laurey. Jud's death—as a precondition for Curly and Laurey's honeymoon—is a grisly touch, at least for a Broadway musical of the time.

CD 2:3

"Oh, What a Beautiful Mornin'," Richard Rodgers and Oscar Hammerstein II (1943). Gordon MacRae, vocal.

Song as a Dramatic Tool

In *Oklahoma!* we sense the power of song right from the start. The play opens with Curly, the male lead, singing "Oh, What a Beautiful Mornin'." The song immediately establishes a mood and begins to sketch in Curly's character. The text of the song is a commentary on the weather and rural life—the most commonplace of topics in everyday conversation: "Great day, isn't it?"; "Yep, sure is"; "Corn's sure growin'." Rendered in speech instead of song, such a

CD 2:3   **Musical Theater Song** (Richard Rodgers and Oscar Hammerstein II; performed by Gordon MacRae, vocal)

0:00	1st verse
	The violins help depict the haze with a high tremolo.
	There's a bright…
0:29	Chorus
	"Mornin'" and "feelin'" contain melodic and harmonic surprises that keep the melody from becoming predictable.
	Oh, what a beautiful mornin'…
0:51	2nd verse
	The tempo slows at the end of the verse, confirming that this waltz song is not for dancing.
	All the cattle…
1:14	Chorus
	Both verse and chorus are short: half the length of a typical popular song.
	Oh, what a beautiful mornin'…
1:36	3rd verse
	All the sounds…
2:00	Chorus
	Rodgers wrote the melody, but Robert Russell Bennett provided the sensitive orchestration, as he did for hundreds of Broadway musicals in a long career.
	Oh, what a beautiful mornin'…

commentary would almost certainly have a limited impact. It takes only a few seconds to evaluate the weather and life on the farm, and any speech as rich in metaphor as the song lyric would probably be inconsistent with the character speaking the lines.

But "Oh, What a Beautiful Mornin'" allows Curly to project the sentiments of the text with an exuberance that transcends speech. We share Curly's delight in the weather and farm life, learning why he thinks it's a wonderful day. Phrases like "cattle are standin' like statues" and "corn is as high as an elephant's eye" give details that help paint an idyllic picture of rural life. The swing of the chorus's melody communicates Curly's sunny disposition; we are surprised to encounter a dark side to his personality later on in the play.

What the song costs the play in pace it gives back in expressive impact. We can stand to hear the chorus of "Oh, What a Beautiful Mornin'" over and over because the melody to which it's set draws us in and carries us along. The song establishes an upbeat mood right from the start and sustains it for several minutes; the intensity of this mood and the insight into Curly's personality more than compensate for the relatively slow rate at which the play unfolds.

STYLE PROFILE

MUSICAL THEATER SONG

Rhythm	*Moderate waltz tempo. Considerable variation in timekeeping: from **tremolo** (time kept in the melody only) to clear* OOM-pah-pah *rhythm in the accompaniment. The beat is elastic at times. There is no syncopation.*
Melody	*Both verse and chorus consist of long phrases. Within verse and chorus, the phrases are similar in rhythm. Both verse and chorus melodies have a swing because of the pattern of rise and fall.*

Instrumentation (timbre)	*Voice plus orchestra—mainly strings and woodwinds (piccolo, a high-pitched relative of the flute, is featured).*
Performance style	*Refined but friendly vocal style.*
Dynamics	*Moderate, with a prolonged fadeaway at the end.*
Harmony	*The outline is I-IV-V, but there are surprise chords in the refrain (under "mornin'" and "feelin'").*
Texture	*Melody with rich and varied accompaniment, from single-note tremolos to chordal accompaniment plus obbligato.*
Form	*Verse/chorus form, with slight extension at the end.*

Key Points

New way to begin a musical	*A casual yet beautiful comment on the weather—a much more laid-back beginning—rather than the usual rousing number designed to grab the audience's attention.*
Cowboys, waltz rhythm, and turning back the clock	*Waltz rhythm, flowing melody, and simple verse/chorus form evoke both the cowboy songs of the thirties and the ca. 1900 waltz songs.*
New kind of musical theater	*American operetta (long-ago-and-far-away plot, more "classic" style), no longer influenced by contemporary trends.*

Terms to Know

operetta

tremolo

waltz rhythm

The immediate appeal of "Oh, What a Beautiful Mornin'" has a dramatic purpose within the play. By the time the song has ended, we like Curly and we like the Oklahoma Territory. The music invests the lyric with power and impact. The tune has a waltz rhythm that seems to connect it in a general way to cowboy folksongs like "Home on the Range" and "Oh, My Darlin' Clementine." But Rodgers's tune is far more sophisticated than these. Curly may not be an urban cowboy, but "Oh, What a Beautiful Mornin'" is certainly an urbanized cowboy song. Rodgers has written a wonderful song that works dramatically, simply because it is so good that it draws us in.

***Oklahoma!* and *Show Boat*.** *Oklahoma!* was a landmark musical. Critics loved it. Theater critic Stanley Green sums up its special quality like this:

> Everything fit into place. . . . Not only were songs and story inseparable, but the dances devised by Agnes de Mille heightened the drama by revealing the subconscious fears and desires of the leading characters.

Audiences loved it even more: *Oklahoma!* ran on Broadway for more than five years; its 2,248 performances far exceeded any previous run.

Show Boat was the most direct precursor of *Oklahoma!* Similarities between the two musicals went beyond their enormous popular appeal and emphasis on dramatic integrity. Both shows drew their plots from existing literature. This practice, a new approach in 1927, had become increasingly common by the early 1940s. Both musicals featured stories set in America, but in a time and place far removed from contemporary New York.

Most important, both incorporated significant innovations in the depth of character portrayal; the seriousness of the plot; the integration of song into the story line; a disregard for convention; and, in the case of *Oklahoma!*, the dramatically purposeful use of dance. The extraordinarily enthusiastic public support for a dramatically credible musical inspired a wholesale shift in values, by both creators and audience.

The Legacy of *Oklahoma!* Rodgers and Hammerstein followed *Oklahoma!* with several more musicals. Most were successful and many were memorable: *Carousel* (1945), *State Fair* (1947, their only musical written specifically for film), *South Pacific* (1949), *The King and I* (1951), and *The Sound of Music* (1959). Their partnership, the most successful in the history of musical theater, ended only with Hammerstein's death in 1960.

Because of their innovative approach to musical theater and their tremendous critical and popular success—almost all of their Broadway musicals also became extremely popular films—Rodgers and Hammerstein's musicals were a major influence on other Broadway productions and the standard by which all other musicals were measured. This is reflected in such key matters as the choice and the source of subjects, dramatic integrity, and the musical language.

As in *Show Boat* and *Oklahoma!*, plots of musicals from the forties and fifties explored the long-ago-and-far-away, and many drew on classics of one kind or another. Cole Porter remade Shakespeare's *Taming of the Shrew* for his musical *Kiss Me, Kate;* Alan Lerner and Frederick Loewe did the same with George Bernard Shaw's play *Pygmalion* for their long-running musical *My Fair Lady;* and *Carmen Jones,* an African American show, adapted the music of Georges Bizet's opera, *Carmen.*

The music also reached back to the past. Even as rhythm and blues, mambo, bebop, and honky-tonk were bringing not only vigorous new sounds but also strong beats and complex rhythms to American ears, Broadway musicals all but abandoned the innovations of the modern era. Syncopation disappeared, as did the propulsive swing beat that underlay it. Melody reigned supreme. Similarly, the performance of the musicals often featured performers with classically trained voices singing in a quasi-operatic style. Theater orchestras sounded more like symphonies than swing bands.

In dramatic substance Rodgers and Hammerstein's musicals were a big step above the movie musicals of the thirties. In *Top Hat,* for example, Fred and Ginger are stock characters, and "Cheek to Cheek" is a great song in a great scene. But it's as if the story is an excuse to present the song. By contrast, "Oh, What a Beautiful Mornin'" is not just an engaging song; it also tells us something about Curly. One reason why *Oklahoma!* and the other Rodgers and Hammerstein musicals have endured is that the main characters are real people.

Hammerstein worked to be "real" in another significant way: in almost all of the major musicals to which he contributed, he took on difficult social issues. In *Show Boat* the sympathetic portraits of Julie and Joe, and Julie's banishment because of a mixed marriage, address racial injustice. Conflict between farmers and cowboys was a real issue in the turn-of-the-century Southwest; in real life it often erupted in violence. By any absolute standard, it is treated lightly in *Oklahoma!* ("The Farmer and the Cowman"); still, Hammerstein mentions it, and the scene ends in a brawl.

But the almost universal conservatism of Broadway—in Rodgers's music, the attitudes of producers, the conventions of the genre, and the expectations of audiences—necessarily sugarcoated these issues, on-stage and even more in the film versions, to present wholesome family entertainment. In this respect Rodgers and Hammerstein were very much in step with white America's postwar image of itself as portrayed in the media.

As a kind of American operetta, in that they took place in different times and places (Oklahoma Territory, the South Pacific, Siam/Thailand), the Rodgers and Hammerstein musicals were escapist entertainment. They gave audiences the chance to put aside their day-to-day concerns for a few hours and enter the world of Curly and Laurey or of the von Trapp family. In this sense they were not truly "real." And during the time that Rodgers and Hammerstein created their long string of hit musicals, Woody Guthrie was chronicling the hard times of the working class and speaking out against social injustice; Charlie Parker and others were creating bebop, an aggressively rebellious new jazz style; and Alan Freed was launching rock and roll.

It is against this backdrop that we consider another landmark musical, *West Side Story*.

BEYOND THE BROADWAY MUSICAL: WEST SIDE STORY

West Side Story grew out of the collaboration of composer Leonard Bernstein, **lyricist** Stephen Sondheim, **choreographer** Jerome Robbins, and **librettist** Arthur Laurents. The key player was Bernstein. By the time he composed *West Side Story*, Leonard Bernstein (1918–1990) had established himself as America's renaissance musician. He had an active career as a conductor and would become music director of the New York Philharmonic in 1958. He had already composed three Broadway musicals, an opera, two ballets, two symphonies, film soundtracks, and numerous other works. He was an excellent pianist, whether performing the classical repertoire or his own compositions. He would become best known to the general public as a commentator on music, through television programs such as the *Young People's Concerts*, which began in 1959. (Remember, these were the days when most viewers had only three or four channels to choose from.) He also wrote several widely read books on music.

As his career makes clear, Bernstein brought a different background to composition for Broadway. Most Broadway composers were mainly songwriters (Richard Rodgers is a prime example). The breadth of Bernstein's training and interests—he had strong affinities for jazz and theater music—is evident throughout the musical.

The Innovations of *West Side Story*. *West Side Story*, staged in 1957 and filmed in 1961, was the landmark musical of the 1950s, a great success in both the stage and film versions. It was creative and innovative in its plot, music, and use of dance. Its inventiveness begins with its book, which puts a new twist on an old practice: instead of using a long-ago time or an exotic locale, the collaborators took a timeless story—Shakespeare's *Romeo and Juliet*—and set it in contemporary New York.

Bernstein and his team turned the Capulets and Montagues into two street gangs, the white Jets and the Puerto Rican Sharks, but kept the essence of Shakespeare's drama intact. As a result, the musical portrayed a contemporary issue with a realism unprecedented in a Broadway show.

Two other distinctive features of the show stand out: Bernstein's music—both the songs and the dance music—and the total integration of dance into the show. In *West Side Story*, Bernstein brings his compositional range to bear in ways that songwriters, even those as skilled as Jerome Kern and Richard Rodgers, couldn't. In as conservative a genre as postwar musical theater, his musical language is generally up-to-date. He wrote contemporary jazz for the Jets' dance numbers, and for the Sharks he wrote Latin, or at least Latinate, numbers. (There is a **mambo**, a Latin dance popular during the 1950s, for the dance in the gym, but

CD 2:4	**Musical Theater Ensemble** (Leonard Bernstein, music; Stephen Sondheim, lyrics; original motion picture soundtrack)
0:00	Music under dialogue.
	Note: The first three notes of this movement are also the opening three notes of "Maria," the love ballad of the musical.
0:14	A
	Boy, boy, crazy boy . . .
0:38	Instrumental section begins. Suspenseful part (1:07)—just drums playing the hi-hat and finger-snap on the backbeat.
1:00	Melodic fragments, in a seemingly random sequence. This is the beginning of the dance.
1:14	Here the music gets more complex, with a slow-moving line and a jazzy, faster-moving line going against each other.
1:34	A
	Boy, boy, crazy boy . . .
2:09	Slow-moving melodic idea in the strings, growing louder and more dense. Pows accompany the dance movements.
3:01	Return of the opening idea in a new key.
3:12	Instrumental version of the song, expanded and reorchestrated for a big band.
3:40	A
	Boy, boy, crazy boy . . .
3:55	*Just play it cool, boy . . .*
	Then fade away.

other music for Puerto Rican characters, like "America," seems derived more from classical music by Latin composers than Puerto Rican popular music.

The love songs ("Maria," "Tonight," "One Hand, One Heart," and "Somewhere") use the Tin Pan Alley popular-song conventions as a point of departure but abandon them as necessary. For example, "Maria" has its roots in Tin Pan Alley song—it develops from a rifflike melodic idea—but it clearly transcends it. On the other hand, it is not a classical aria; it unfolds much too quickly for that. Almost uniquely within the popular tradition, "Maria" and its companions are poised somewhere between Tin Pan Alley and the opera house.

West Side Story was also exceptional for its use of dance. In this musical, dance is functional, not decorative; choreographer Jerome Robbins was a full partner in the collaboration. No scene shows the integral role, the dramatic necessity, of dance better than "Cool." In the film version of the musical, the dance features the Jets, who have reassembled in a garage after scattering to avoid the police. They have just finished a "rumble" with the Sharks that has left the rival gang leaders dead. Some of the Jets are almost boiling over in their urgency to gain revenge on the Sharks, but the de facto new leader, Ice, cautions "Cool." In this scene dance speaks louder than words or song. The dance captures the repressed emotion of the gang, ready to explode at the slightest provocation and kept under wraps only by the force of Ice's will.

"Cool," Leonard Bernstein, music; Stephen Sondheim, lyrics (1957). Original motion picture soundtrack.

STYLE PROFILE

MUSICAL THEATER ENSEMBLE

Rhythm	*Medium tempo. Four-beat rhythm (but without walking bass), crisp backbeat, evident especially in fingersnap/drum sections. Lots of syncopation, from the opening riff on. Considerable variation in rhythm: from slow values in a single line to many different rhythms simultaneously.*

Melody	Melody grows out of three notes—the same three notes that open "Maria" in the musical. Both the melody of the vocal section and the new melodies in the central instrumental section tend to be angular with frequent melodic skips.
Instrumentation (timbre)	Voice (speaking and singing), full orchestra plus rhythm section and big-band instruments. Woodwinds (flutes and clarinets) featured.
Performance style	"Everyday" voice, no special quality, such as classical, bluesy, or belter. Orchestral musicians play with a jazz feel.
Dynamics	Wide range, from very soft to very loud. Sudden changes underscore movements in the dance.
Harmony	Complex chords far removed from I-IV-V.
Texture	Considerable variation, from just percussion to full big band. Central section often has two or more melodic lines sounding simultaneously.
Form	A two-section melody: AA. The overall form is **free**; it does not conform to any of the standard forms that we have encountered.

Key Points

Hip talk, ca. 1957	Fifties' slang ("cool" and "daddy-o") gives lyrics a contemporary sound.
Importance of dance	Dancers' movements powerfully express the characters' agitation.
Cool music	Bernstein evokes cool jazz (the hippest music of the fifties) in the music for "Cool."
Jazz/classical fusion	Jazz feel, classical form; melody sometimes rifflike, sometimes angular.

Terms to Know

free form

Summary

West Side Story marks another important step in the transformation of the musical. At the turn of the century, musical comedy and its siblings were a primary form of mass entertainment. Audiences came from all strata of society. Over the next fifty years, other forms of entertainment, musical and otherwise, gradually drew much of this mass audience. Films in the teens, followed by talking films in the late twenties; phonograph records and broadcast radio after World War I; nightclubs and ballrooms in the twenties and thirties; and television after World War II—all provided cheaper and more accessible mass entertainment. The revue, the heart and soul of Broadway in the 1920s, was all but dead; about three revues per season were produced in the 1950s, down from an average of fourteen per season in the 1920s.

As a result, rather than being a part of mass entertainment, musical theater became an *alternative* to mass entertainment. Its audience became increasingly elite, although not necessarily elitist. Ticket prices escalated; as early as 1927, scalpers' prices for *Show Boat* tickets reached $100 per seat. For most people, attending a Broadway show became a special event, enjoyed only occasionally. Despite the regular appearance of Broadway show tunes on the pop-music charts, musical theater had moved out of the popular-music mainstream. Broadway was a still an important source of popular song, but much less so than before.

MUSICAL THEATER IN THE ROCK ERA

Broadway began the rock era on top of the popular-music world. The decade between 1955 and 1965 was a commercial and artistic high point. Four shows, beginning with Lerner and Loewe's *My Fair Lady* in 1956, exceeded the record for the longest-running show set by *Oklahoma!* in 1943. *Fiddler on the Roof,* which featured Zero Mostel, began its record-breaking run of 3,242 performances in 1964. Original cast recordings dominated the album charts through the early 1960s. By the end of the decade, however, film and television had largely supplanted Broadway as a source of hits. Of the fifty original cast albums (recordings of Broadway shows) that made the Top 40 lists between 1955 and 1990, only eight were released after 1965, and only two of these eight after 1975.

Soundtrack recordings of film musicals showed a similar trend. During the late 1950s and early '60s, most of the best-selling soundtrack albums were from film versions of current Broadway shows like *West Side Story* and *The Sound of Music* as well as older shows like *Oklahoma!* and *South Pacific.* After 1963, however, far fewer soundtracks came from film versions of musicals. Soundtracks instead featured music written specifically for a film rather than the stage—*Saturday Night Fever* is a spectacular example. They often featured rock-era pop stars rather than musical theater performers: Simon and Garfunkel's songs in the 1968 movie *The Graduate,* the Bee Gees' hits in *Saturday Night Fever,* and Prince's songs for *Batman* are representative examples.

The fame of composer-songwriters like Henry Mancini, John Williams, and Quincy Jones suggests the extent to which film and television supplanted Broadway as the primary visual media for popular music after 1960. In the prerock generation, Broadway-type composer-songwriters (Gershwin, Berlin, Kern, and Rodgers and Hammerstein) were the marquee names, even when they wrote for films. Those who created background music were relatively unknown outside the industry. After 1960 composers with no Broadway affiliation became household names. Henry Mancini was the first. His breakthrough came in the late 1950s with his jazz-based theme and background music for *Peter Gunn,* a television series about a detective. Mancini developed into one of the most versatile composers of the time. Michel Legrand followed suit with a series of successful scores in the 1960s.

John Williams and Quincy Jones have enjoyed comparable recognition since the 1970s. Williams composed music for several blockbuster films, including *Jaws,* the *Star Wars* epic, the *Indiana Jones* series, and *Superman.* In addition, he maintained a high profile as the conductor of the Boston Pops from 1980 to 1994. Jones, who has worn many hats in his career, made his commercial mark with music for the television show *Sanford and Son,* the landmark miniseries *Roots,* and *The Wiz,* the 1978 film remake of *The Wizard of Oz;* he has also served as the producer of many of Michael Jackson's best-selling recordings, including the album *Thriller.*

Rock on Broadway

There were several popular and important shows in the 1960s that reflected the spirit and the style of rock. Many rock-era shows were focused squarely on the present or the recent past, which they viewed forthrightly. Just as rock songs had abandoned Tin Pan Alley "moon/June" love lyrics for singer-songwriter slices of contemporary life, rock-influenced musical theater traded in an often rose-colored "there and then" for a sometimes bittersweet "here and now."

Four shows from the late sixties and early seventies—*Hair; Promises, Promises; Company;* and *Jesus Christ Superstar*—demonstrated the nature and the range of rock's influence. The most revolutionary was *Hair.* Billed as an "American tribal love-rock musical," *Hair* portrayed the counterculture lifestyle. Although its notorious parts, like the nude and flag-burning scenes, got most of the press, *Hair*'s revolution went deeper than this surface sensationalism. The **rock musical** embodied counterculture attitudes in almost every aspect of its design: the ambiguity and relative insignificance of its plot, the absence of Broadway stars, and the racially integrated cast.

Burt Bacharach and Hal David's *Promises, Promises* (1968) also showed the influence of rock attitude and style. Like *Hair,* the show dealt with thorny issues in contemporary urban life rather than a fantasyland or a historical event. The musical, adapted from Neil Simon's film *The Apartment,* told the story of a young businessman who let his bosses use his apartment for extramarital affairs in return for job advancement.

This more modern approach continued through the 1970s and '80s. Two noteworthy instances came from director Michael Bennett. *A Chorus Line* (1975) gave its audience an unsentimental glimpse into Broadway's life behind the curtain. His 1981 show, *Dreamgirls,* did the same for black girl groups of the sixties. Both offered a comparatively frank, unglamorous dramatization of the ostensively glamorous showbiz lifestyle.

A spectacular incursion of rock onto the stage—although it barely got there—was Randy Newman's *Faust* (1993/1995). Newman, respected as one of the most provocative and original rock songwriters and film composers of the rock era, reset Goethe's *Faust* in modern-day Indiana. Henry Faust is an unmotivated student at the University of Notre Dame. In true rock fashion, the recording appeared before the stage production (typically, it's the other way around with Broadway shows). It featured an all-star cast, including James Taylor as God, Don Henley (of the Eagles) as Faust, and Linda Ronstadt as Margaret. Newman's retelling of the Faust legend captures a rock sensibility at its most cynical and worldly. It is truly amoral: the devil's smile at the end is the happy ending.

In a continuing trend, most of the significant new musicals have not only been bolder and more open in their choice of subject but also more worldly in their treatment—with considerable success. *Chicago,* a film version of Bob Fosse's 1975 musical, won six Oscars, including best picture in 2003. The plot makes stars, if not heroines, out of two chorus girls who shoot their lovers and gain notoriety in the process.

Contemporary Musical Theater

No theater composers have been bolder or more imaginative in their choice of subjects than Stephen Sondheim and Sir Andrew Lloyd Webber. Both started spectacularly in the early 1970s. In musical theater at least, Sondheim and Lloyd Webber epitomize the difficult balancing act between art and commerce. Sondheim has received better press; Lloyd Webber has done better—much better—at the box office. Their different routes to success stand out because of their common ground as well as the contrast in their approach. Both are extremely adept at evoking any style—Tin Pan Alley, rock, contemporary classical—and they use this skill for dramatic purposes.

Both compose musical stage works that defy category. Each has created a novel approach to music on-stage: their works are neither traditional musicals nor conventional opera. Lloyd Webber's works are operatic in their grandeur and the absence of spoken dialogue. His musical vocabulary is eclectic in the extreme. Sondheim's works are more sophisticated dramatically and musically than much eighteenth- and nineteenth-century opera, but their musical languages seem to occupy a special place between classical and pop. We consider an early example of Sondheim's unique approach next.

Stephen Sondheim. Stephen Sondheim (b. 1930) is the most versatile and esteemed American musical theater composer of the past century. Like few other theater composers, he has written both words and music for his shows. Moreover, he is musical theater's grand eclectic: the master of virtually every twentieth-century musical style.

Although thoroughly trained as a musician, Sondheim began his career as a lyricist. His first collaborations were three of the major musical theater events of the 1950s: a musical version of *Candide* in 1956, *West Side Story* in 1958 (both scored by Leonard Bernstein), and the 1959 musical *Gypsy,* with music by Jules Styne. The first Broadway show for which he wrote both lyrics and music was *A Funny Thing Happened on the Way to the Forum* (1962).

With the opening of *Company* in 1970, Sondheim's career took off. *Company* portrayed a contemporary situation in mostly contemporary (for 1970) musical language. It revealed many of the qualities that would characterize Sondheim's work: his fondness for concepts; his psychological insight; his willingness to dig below the surface, even when it's not pretty; the complexity of his thinking—musically as well as dramatically; and his sense of humor. Sondheim seems to revel in complexity, virtuosity, surprise, and a subtle, occasionally acerbic humor. The complexity in his work grows out of the multiple layers of meaning present in some aspect: a song, a turn of phrase, even the title of a show.

Company hints at several of these qualities. The plot, such as it is, takes place in modern-day New York. It revolves around a thirty-five-year-old, eligible bachelor (Robert/Bobby), unable or unwilling to commit to a relationship, and the efforts of three couples to find him a partner. Bobby is far from the heroic leading man; indeed, he is a kind of anti-hero or anti–leading man. His leading lady is conspicuous by her absence; instead of a single partner to be wooed and won, there are three candidates, none of whom fit the bill. There is no hierarchical arrangement of roles, no "star" in the show. The title *Company* means at least three things: company that a partner will give Bobby; company, as in visitors—the couples who drop in to see Bobby; and company as in theatrical troupe. Most of Sondheim's titles are a play on words: typically they have multiple meanings, as they do here.

We get a glimpse of Sondheim's ability to give us insight into a character in one of the numbers from *Company,* "Another Hundred People." It is sung by Marta, one of Bobby's prospective partners. It begins frenetically, first with the **keyboard** figuration, then in the vocal line, which moves at patter-song speed. At the outset Marta is simply observing, as though she were a television reporter on-location. It's detached emotionally, if somewhat breathless; we can sense from the words and music the fast pace of life in Manhattan. Suddenly, the music changes when she sings, "It's a city of strangers." This underscores the shift in perspective, injecting a personal element into her commentary. The music shifts again, this time into a higher gear, as the words describe the difficulty of connecting with people in a crowded city; we sense that when she describes the frustration of finding a suitable partner she is speaking from long experience. One can almost imagine the camera starting out with a wide-angle shot of a busy street and gradually focusing in on Marta: the shift from third person to first person and the musical shifts that highlight the changes convey much the same impression.

Sondheim's music for a particular work typically tells listeners something about the work. Because he is fluent in so many styles, he can craft the music to evoke the setting or the story. "Another Hundred People" belongs to *Company;* it would be horribly out of place in other Sondheim musicals.

2:5

"Another Hundred People," Stephen Sondheim (1970). Pamela Myers, vocal.

0:00		Instrumental introduction. The raglike keyboard figuration stands out here.
0:05	A	Marta reports breathlessly about all the people arriving in Manhattan. It's seemingly a rather detached, third-person account.
		Another hundred people . . .
0:21	B	Marta switches from reporting to interpreting. The music gets more personal too, with a slower melodic rhythm and rich string chords.
		It's a city of strangers . . .
0:35	C	The music resumes its frenetic pace, suggesting the hectic urban lifestyle. Marta's critical remarks deepen the personal connection. The dry accompaniment (percussion sounds, plucked strings) helps convey the sense of the words.
		Can find each other . . .
0:52	C¹	The lyric becomes personal. Warmer orchestration suggests a hope of finding Mr. Right in these brief encounters. The harmony's slide back to the home key while the singer holds the last note seems to indicate that Marta has failed.
		And they meet at . . .
1:13	A	The title phrase,
		And another hundred people . . .
1:19	B	
		It's a city of strangers . . .
1:36	C	
		Or they find . . .
1:53	C¹	
		And they meet . . .
2:15	A	
		And another hundred people . . .

STYLE PROFILE

ROCK-ERA MUSICAL THEATER

Rhythm	*Quick tempo. Latin- and/or rock-influenced rhythm in the accompaniment and the vocal line, especially in A section. Syncopation and rhythmic conflict are built into the melody and the fast-moving accompaniment figures.*
Melody	*A section: a **patter song**—streams of notes, gradually climbing. B section: grows out of a riff. C section: a longer phrase made up of three syncopated rifflike figures.*
Instrumentation (timbre)	*Voice, plus an orchestra including electric keyboard, strings, winds, and percussion.*
Performance style	*Belt-style singing.*
Dynamics	*Overall, moderately loud, building toward the C¹ section, then tapering off to the title phrase.*
Harmony	*Rich, complex harmony, with several surprising chords (note "City of strangers" and the change of harmony under "explain" at the end of the form).*

Texture	*Melody with varying accompaniment: dramatic shifts in texture highlight new sections (A = light, open; B = rich; C = more transparent; C^1 = most active and complex).*
Form	*A long song form—ABCC—that repeats once.*

Key Points

Contemporary show	Company *presents an old problem (how to find a mate) in a contemporary way: almost no plot and an anti-star for a lead character.*
Character's changing perspective	*From seemingly objective third-person reporting to frantic first-person perspective.*
Contemporary sound	*Electric keyboard and Latin/rock-influenced rhythm make the song sound contemporary.*
Sondheim's sophisticated style	*Rooted in popular music but more elaborate and sophisticated than traditional musical theater songs.*

Terms to Know

patter song

Many commentators have called *Company* the first modern musical. They point to its lack of plot, the absence of stars, the candid portrayal of urban life, and the sophisticated up-to-date music. Since then Sondheim has looked in all directions: he has chosen such diverse subjects as the history of Japan from its first American encounter (*Pacific Overtures,* 1976), the grisly tale of a mad barber in England (*Sweeney Todd,* 1979), and a French painting (*Sunday in the Park with George,* 1984).

Sondheim was not alone in his use of style to evoke time and place. It was very much a part of rock-era music, whether in the songs of the Beatles or Paul Simon, the film music of John Williams, or the theater compositions of Sondheim's contemporary, Andrew Lloyd Webber. We encounter Lloyd Webber's quite different approach next.

Andrew Lloyd Webber. Andrew Lloyd Webber (b. 1948) grew up in a musical family; his father was a composer, and his brother is a highly regarded cellist. Lloyd Webber apparently gained most of his training by osmosis: despite a short stint at the Royal Academy of Music, he is largely self-taught.

Although he has composed for films, he has devoted most of his professional energy to musical theater. Single-handedly, he has returned London to musical-theatric prominence that it hasn't enjoyed since the days of Gilbert and Sullivan in the late 1800s. In addition to writing musical theater works, Lloyd Webber has formed his own production company, the Really Useful Company, and bought and refurbished a theater.

Lloyd Webber made a splash with *Jesus Christ Superstar* in 1970. He followed that with an expanded version of an earlier musical, *Joseph and His Amazing Technicolor Dreamcoat* (originally produced in 1968). His next big hit was *Evita* (1976). It was *Cats* (1981), however, that secured his position as the pre-eminent British composer of musical theater. *Cats* is the most commercially successful musical of all time: it enjoyed a run of eighteen years in New York and twenty-one years in London. Lloyd Webber followed that with several other hit shows, some nearly as successful. As an illustration of his commercial impact: in the 1990s Lloyd Webber productions accounted for more than half of Broadway ticket sales, and it was much the same in London.

Some commentators have attributed the appeal of Lloyd Webber's musicals to the striking and novel concepts out of which they grow (people costumed as cats or depicting trains on roller skates) as well as their spectacular stage effects. Although these elements are certainly part of the story, there are also good musical reasons for his success.

Lloyd Webber uses a formula that has worked from the beginning of his career: start with the familiar and accessible and follow it with a surprise twist or two. Dramatically, Lloyd Webber uses style to establish a character or set a mood. In *Cats*, for example, rock and roll immediately types Rum Tum Tugger, whereas the ponderous bass line at Grizabella's entrance darkens the mood in an instant. The musical materials tend to be rather generic, especially at the outset. This would seem to have two interrelated purposes: First, it makes them instantly recognizable so that listeners can easily associate the style or musical gesture with its most familiar contexts. Second, it focuses attention on the dramatic situation by virtue of its evocation of time, place, and mood.

Everything in a Lloyd Webber work is painted in bold strokes and basic colors. In *Cats* there is no plot to speak of; the show proceeds mainly as a series of portraits. Nevertheless, the core issue to be resolved—the only issue, really—is whether Old Deuteronomy will choose Grizabella to enter cat heaven. The music sets up the tension: the dark music of Grizabella's entrance, which conveys her problematic past, versus the tunefulness elsewhere in the show. This opposition carries through the diversions that follow, especially the abduction and return of Old Deuteronomy. It sets up one of the most enduring and heartwarming themes in western culture: the triumph of the underdog. We wait for the moment when Grizabella returns for the last time and reprises "Memory"; we know it is going to happen, and we know how it will all end, but it is still an affecting moment because of "Memory" and because it so neatly resolves the central dramatic tension. It doesn't really matter that we never learn why Old Deuteronomy chose her.

In its final reprise, "Memory" leaves rock and roll behind; at its peak it soars, like an **aria** from a Puccini opera. The progress of the song—and in particular its elevation from rock-and-roll ballad to Italian aria—seems to encapsulate Grizabella's rise in stature: the other cats scorn and reject her at the beginning and defer to her at the end. There is no ambiguity, in story, words, or music. The subtlety is very much in the background, but it is there—almost subliminally.

Cats mixes simple and subtle, known and novel. It has a timeless theme, which Lloyd Webber underscores with music whose meaning is clear. It evidences his undeniable craft and range as a composer and dramatist. The basic premise—a musical about some special, Jellicle cats—is novel and fun. It makes excellent use of technological wizardry. All of these qualities, in combination, certainly help account for its appeal.

Andrew Lloyd Webber has been musical theater's one-man counterpart to the British rock invasion of the 1960s. There are striking parallels between the Beatles and Lloyd Webber that extend well beyond their British citizenship and their status as the commercially dominant artists in their genres. Both updated an established genre: the Beatles revitalized popular song; Lloyd Webber reenergized musical theater. And both brought their respective genre into the realm of art by drawing on classical models. The Beatles created beautifully crafted miniatures and concept albums that echoed the art songs and song cycles of nineteenth- and twentieth-century classical music. Lloyd Webber's compositions moved away from the alternation of dialogue and song in musical comedy to completely sung stage works: operas with a pop-music language.

Contrasting Sondheim and Lloyd Webber. The musical and dramatic differences between Sondheim and Lloyd Webber may help explain why the former is more popular with critics and the latter more popular with audiences. Lloyd Webber hides his skill behind musical materials that can be cartoonishly obvious (the "phantom" music in *Phantom of the Opera*). But that is precisely the point: the audience does not have to work hard to decode the meaning of the music. Similarly, "Memory" sounds like hundreds of other songs for the first few seconds; it is only when we are into the song that Lloyd Webber takes the tune down a highly personal path.

By contrast, we have to grow into Sondheim. The drama contains many more layers. Characters are more complex. Unlike the beginning of "Memory," Sondheim's phrases sound different from those in other pop songs and classical arias, in both melodic construction and orchestral setting, and they respond most directly to the lyric. In every respect Sondheim asks his audience to pay attention right from the start. He rewards the effort, certainly, but he does not supply the easy entry into either story or music that the familiar provides.

Summary

Musical theater reinvented itself during the rock era. The transformation began in the late 1960s, when it absorbed elements of rock's worldview and musical style. This process had already begun. *West Side Story, Gypsy,* and *Fiddler on the Roof* offered richer characterization and tougher plot lines than most earlier musicals. But *Hair, Jesus Christ Superstar,* and *Company* were a big step forward.

In the 1970s and '80s, Sondheim and Lloyd Webber essentially created a new genre. The old categories—musical, operetta, and opera—no longer described their work either dramatically or musically. Each in his own way occupies a unique position: using quite different approaches, they have created forms of musical drama that integrate pop and classical elements seamlessly. *Cats* is like opera in that there is no dialogue, but its musical languages come mainly from pop. In *Company* Sondheim creates musical structures far more sophisticated than one finds in early-nineteenth-century Italian opera, yet his provenance comes through the musical, and so does much of his musical language. Moreover, Sondheim has put music strictly at the service of drama; it is hard to imagine "Another Hundred People" having a life apart from its parent work.

LOOKING BACK, LOOKING AHEAD

The transformation of the genre is evident in the marketplace and in the relation of musical theater to the larger musical world. Musical theater is still a vital part of cultural life in both the United States and Great Britain, but it no longer occupies a central place: the steady stream of hits from Broadway to the pop charts has dwindled to a trickle.

Musical theater has become a new kind of art music. This is evident not only in newer works but also in the presence of revivals. In the same way that symphonic orchestras play from the classical repertoire, Broadway reproduces earlier masterpieces, such as Hal Prince's splendid 1994 production of *Show Boat*. The audience for musical theater has changed, as have the ticket prices. Still, despite more-elaborate productions and escalating costs, musical theater, both old and new, should continue to thrive in the foreseeable future.

TERMS TO KNOW

Test your knowledge of this chapter's important terms by defining the following. If you can't recall the meaning of a certain term, refresh your memory by looking up the boldfaced term in the chapter, turning to the Glossary at the back of the book, or working with the flashcards on the *Popular Music in America* Companion Web site: *http://music.wadsworth.com/campbell_2e*

AABA form	keyboard	pentatonic scale
aria	librettist	rock musical
belt	libretto	sampling
blue note	lyricist	spiritual
book	mambo	tremolo
cakewalk	musical theater	waltz rhythm
choreographer	operetta	waltz song
free form	patriotic song	
interpolation	patter song	

Country and Folk Music, 1920—1955

efore there were country music and folk music, there was folk music from the country—that is, the southern Appalachians. The music that spawned both country and folk came originally from the British Isles: England, Scotland, Wales, and Ireland. America's first **Anglo-American** settlers brought their music with them. Some found their way into the mountains of Virginia and the Carolinas, where they preserved many of the songs and dances from their home countries and created new ones like "Old Joe Clark," which we heard in Chapter 2.

There was—and is—a timelessness to this music. When we listen to a recording like "Old Joe Clark," we sense that it would have sounded much the same in 1825 or 1875. The fieldwork of English folklorist Cecil Sharp confirms this impression. In trips through the southern Appalachians between 1916 and 1918, he discovered songs that went back centuries (and which were no longer sung in England).

When Sharp visited the United States, there was no such thing as country music or folk music. The music that he heard and transcribed for posterity was a real **folk music**; that is, it was music made by members of a group for their own entertainment and passed down—and around—by ear. The musicians were not professional, and there was no industry to support and promote this music. It just was. That would all change within a decade.

THE EMERGENCE OF COUNTRY AND FOLK MUSIC

Look at a map of the southeastern United States and you'll find a web of interstate highways crisscrossing Virginia and West Virginia, the Carolinas, Tennessee, Alabama, Mississippi, Kentucky, and Louisiana. Were you to drive down one of these interstates and pull off, chances are you would find modern gas stations with minimarkets, chain motels, and a belt-stretching array of fast-food restaurants. There would be cable or satellite TV in the motel rooms and probably phone service to anywhere as well as a modem hookup for your laptop. This is the twenty-first-century American South.

So it may be difficult to imagine a time and place where there were only dirt roads, few cars, no phones, no electricity, no running water, no indoor plumbing, no television or radio, and no CD players. Whole regions lacked most if not all of the conveniences that we associate with modern life. People who lived in the southern Appalachians had little knowledge of the outside world. A trip to the nearest large city produced severe culture shock.

Technology Creates Country Music from Folk

It is a sweet irony that country music, which reflects the traditional values of southern culture, is the product of a modern technology. The folk music of white southerners became **country** music when commercial radio came on the air. Clear-channel AM radio—50,000-watt stations like WSM in Nashville—covered most of the country when the sun went down. WSM became the radio home to the *Grand Ole Opry* in 1928. Radio's impact on what would become known as country music was enormous. Almost immediately, radio forced record companies to seek out niche markets to compensate for the huge drop in record sales when people chose to listen to the radio for free. The **race records** of African Americans like Bessie Smith were one such market. **Hillbilly** records were their country counterpart.

The new technology helped create a class of professional, or at least semi-professional, musicians. Appearances on radio and records led to opportunities for live performances. Bands or solo acts with a weekly radio show would fill in the days between broadcasts with engagements in cities and towns within the listening area of their radio station.

Records helped spread the sound of **old-time music** beyond the South. By 1930 a guitar player in Oklahoma could learn Virginian Maybelle Carter's distinctive accompanying style simply by buying a record and copying it. Just as important, this new technology helped connect rural southerners to the outside world. They could share their own music and discover other kinds. This contact with one another and the outside would become the main impetus for the evolution of country music.

In little more than a decade, what had been simply a folk music transplanted from the British Isles had split into country and folk, two worlds that were almost mutually exclusive. (It took Bob Dylan to bring them together again.) And each world divided further into several streams, some creating paths to the mainstream, others running counter to the trend. At the heart of it all were the central tensions of this music: between commerce and culture, between innovation and preservation, between old and new, between inside and outside, and between staying home and roaming far and wide.

Ralph Peer and the Lomaxes: Country and Folk Music

Three men—Ralph Peer, John Lomax, and Lomax's son Alan—helped chart the divergent paths of country and folk music. None was a musician of distinction, but all played key roles in developing country and folk music.

Ralph Peer. At the center of early country music, yet behind the scenes, was a man named Ralph Peer (1892–1960). Peer grew up in Missouri, and as a young man he helped his father sell sewing machines and phonographs. He went to work for Columbia Records, moved to Okeh Records in 1920, and moved again in 1925 to Victor. As a talent scout and producer, Peer would go from town to town, setting up temporary recording studios wherever he could. Word would spread that he was coming, and musicians would come down from the hills to record for him.

Music Licensing

The radio industry had laid the groundwork for increased diversity before World War II by forming its own licensing organization. Music licensing was the mechanism by which those who created the music received payment from those who made money from it.

In 1914 a group of songwriters and publishers banded together to form a society that would protect their rights when their songs were performed. Together they formed **ASCAP**, the American Society of Composers, Authors, and Publishers, a membership organization that protects the rights of its members by licensing and distributing royalties for the public performances of their copyrighted works. Twenty-five years later, what had begun as a grassroots organization had become an exclusive club. A key requirement for membership in ASCAP was five hit songs. In effect, this excluded almost everyone who was not part of the pop-music inner circle. In particular, country music songwriters and African American musicians were on the outside, looking in. So were most of those just starting their careers.

In the 1930s radio became the most popular form of mass entertainment. Most homes had a radio, and it was free (like television before cable). So in 1932 ASCAP entered into a licensing agreement with broadcast companies for the use of music on radio programs: broadcasters would pay royalties on songs played over the air, either in live performance or on record. (During the 1930s live performance over the radio was far more common; recall that radio gained a national audience for Bing Crosby, Duke Ellington, Benny Goodman, and hundreds of other musicians through live broadcasts.)

Five years later ASCAP proposed a massive increase in royalties. In response, broadcasters formed their own organization. They chartered Broadcast Music Incorporated in 1939; **BMI** opened its doors early the next year.

Unlike ASCAP, BMI accepted all aspiring songwriters. Overnight, all musicians had a potential stake in the music industry. That was good news for those who had been on the outside, looking in, especially jazz, country, and blues musicians. Many joined BMI, which gave the organization some much-needed leverage.

Peer always seemed to be at the right place at the right time. He was responsible for the first on-location recording and the first country recording to be released, "Fiddlin'" John Carson's "The Little Log Cabin in the Lane" (1923). A few years later, he helped give old-time music a new name: hillbilly music. The term *hillbilly* had been in use since the turn of the century to identify rural white southerners, but its musical association dates from a 1925 recording session with Al Hopkins, leader of a four-man **string band** (a small group consisting mainly of string instruments of various types). Peer, who was running the session, asked Hopkins to give his band a name. Hopkins replied, "Call the band anything you want. We are nothing but a bunch of hillbillies from North Carolina and Virginia anyway"; they became Al Hopkins and His Hillbillies. Peer's biggest coup, however, came in August 1927, when he recorded the Carter Family and Jimmie Rodgers, the two biggest acts of early country music, in Bristol, Tennessee.

Peer was an astute businessman. He negotiated a split of the publishing rights to the songs he recorded for Victor and created his own publishing firm, Southern Music, in 1928. Southern Music grew into one of the leading publishers of country music and made Peer a rich and powerful man.

In 1940 Peer created a new publishing company, Peer International, which joined the newly created BMI (Broadcast Music Incorporated; see "Music Licensing" above). His support helped get BMI off the ground. (He still retained his ASCAP connection through Southern Music.)

Peer's musical and business interests extended well beyond country music. Almost as soon as he began working for Okeh Records, he set up the first race record recording session, which produced Mamie Smith's "Crazy Blues," and he negotiated the rights to Victor's race records along with the hillbilly music he had been recording. By the early 1930s, he had branched into popular music; and after a trip to Mexico, he secured the rights to several Latin hits. He continued to diversify his catalog after World War II by signing up rockabilly and rhythm-and-blues artists.

John and Alan Lomax. Even as country music began to absorb new sounds and styles, folklorists sought to preserve—capture on record and in notation—the traditional music of the South. John Lomax (1867–1948) spent his life going in and out of the South. He was born in Mississippi and grew up in Texas. He interrupted a teaching career to do graduate studies at Harvard. There he met George Kittredge, an eminent folklorist who encouraged his longstanding interest in cowboy songs. Lomax returned to teaching but was fired in 1917, when he came out on the wrong—and wrongful—end of a tug of war between the president of the University of Texas and the governor of Texas (who was later impeached). Moving to Chicago, Lomax went into banking for the next fifteen years.

About the time most people think about retirement, Lomax returned to the music that had been his passion since childhood. In 1932 he secured a contract for an American folksong anthology. The next year he made the first of his field trips through the South, where he recorded folksingers—most notably Huddie "Leadbelly" Ledbetter—on equipment mounted in the trunk of his car. By 1934 he had become the first curator of the Archive of American Folk Song at the Library of Congress. His son Alan (1915–2002) accompanied him on his trips and collaborated with him on many projects, including folksong collections. Together they were able to preserve elements of America's cultural heritage that would have otherwise disappeared.

New Versus Old; Profit Versus Preservation. Peer and the Lomaxes were among the very first to seek out folk musicians—Peer through his on-location recordings, and the Lomaxes through their field recordings. Although they became associated with country and folk music, respectively, they embraced a wide range of music: African American, Hispanic, and, in the case of Alan Lomax, music from around the world. Their careers highlight the central creative tension in the evolution of country and folk. While the Lomaxes worked to preserve folk music, Peer worked to profit from country. Profit was good not only for Peer but also for country music. Among other things, it enabled musicians to work steadily and, as a result, develop new musical directions. We can hear a big difference between Ben Jarrell's old-time fiddling (Chapter 2) and Bob Wills's modern western swing (later in this chapter). Peer's business paralleled—even anticipated—the evolutionary direction of country music as it drew on blues, pop, and jazz.

If Peer looked to the future, John Lomax clung to the past. He feared that an important part of American heritage would be lost because the new media—radio, recordings, and films —would change the cultures that had previously been so isolated. He was right, of course. They did change. But by using the same technology that disrupted the long-established cultures of the rural South, Lomax was able to capture on disc a good sampling of white and black folk music before it disappeared.

Peer and the Lomaxes represent the two poles of the cultural value system that informed and shaped the styles evolving out of folk music after 1920. Musically and socially, the Lomaxes stood for preservation; Peer represented ongoing change. Philosophically, John Lomax looked back, whereas Peer tried to anticipate the future.

By recording folk musicians, the Lomaxes froze folk music in time. By cannily expanding his business and broadening its base, Peer helped show country music the direction it could take. The man who cut country music's first slice of the pop market was a light opera singer from west Texas named Marion Slaughter, aka Vernon Dalhart.

COUNTRY MUSIC HITS THE POP CHARTS

Dalhart is a town of about 8,000 people in the northwest corner of the Texas panhandle—about as far north as you can go and still be in Texas. Vernon is another Texas small town, which lies about 250 miles southeast of Dalhart. No interstate connects the two, but they are linked in popular music history by the first big country music star.

Vernon Dalhart and "The Prisoner's Song"

Vernon Dalhart, born Marion Slaughter (1883?–1948), grew up near Jefferson, Texas, a small town about 20 miles east of the Louisiana state line and 50 miles south of the Oklahoma border. Slaughter's father killed his mother's brother during a saloon fight when Slaughter was ten; perhaps as a consequence, Slaughter changed his name, not once but many times. The first time, in 1912, shortly after he moved to New York, he took the stage name Vernon Dalhart, after the two west Texas towns where he had allegedly been a cowboy as a young man. He began his professional career as an opera singer and made his first recordings in 1916. By the end of the teens, he was recording many different kinds of music, from opera to minstrel-like popular songs (billing himself as Bob White). Because he never signed a contract with any one company, he probably made more recordings during the 1920s and '30s than any other singer (well over a thousand by the end of his career), for virtually every record label in business at the time and under some two dozen names, although Vernon Dalhart remained his first choice.

"The Prisoner's Song," traditional (1924). Vernon Dalhart, vocal; Carson Robison, guitar.

The song that has secured his place in history is "The Prisoner's Song." Dalhart recorded it in 1924 as the **B side** (flip side) of a popular event song, "The Wreck of the Old 97." (**Event songs** have a long history in folk and country music. This one is about a train wreck, but there have been others about floods, fires, and hurricanes.) The two sides represented a return to his Texas roots while at the same time showing how far he had moved away from them.

LISTENING GUIDE: "THE PRISONER'S SONG"

CD 2:6   **Early Country Song** (Traditional; performed by Vernon Dalhart, vocal; and Carson Robison, guitar)

0:00	Instrumental version of the melody.
0:25	The first section, with two distinct phrases.
	Oh! I wish . . .
0:38	This phrase parallels the first: the only difference between the two is at the very end.
	Oh! I wish . . .
0:51	Same melody, different words.
	Oh! Please meet me . . .
1:18	Viola plays the melody.
1:43	*I'll be carried to . . .*
2:09	The violist plays an obbligato.
	Now I have . . .
2:35	*Now if I had . . .*

"The Prisoner's Song" song is simple, episodic, and confusing. The melody consists of a single phrase with alternate endings. A simple three-chord accompaniment supports it, the same three chords that we encounter in the blues (I, IV, and V) but in an even simpler sequence. We hear a violist play the melody when Dalhart doesn't sing, and play an **obbligato** (a second, secondary melody) toward the end. That's what's simple about it.

The confusion lies in its history, its style, and its success. Dalhart claimed that he heard the song from his cousin, Guy Massey, and insisted that it was a folksong that had been around for years—as it almost certainly was. But others involved in the recording, guitarist Carson Robison and producer Nat Shilkret, each claimed some share of its authorship.

As Dalhart sings we hear traces of his east Texas accent, but we also hear a trained voice far different from the harsh twang of early country singers. And instead of a fiddle, we hear a viola played in a classical rather than a country style; and instead of a banjo, we hear a guitar. This is a country song that has been cleaned and polished.

STYLE PROFILE

"THE PRISONER'S SONG" (EARLY COUNTRY SONG)

Rhythm	*Moderate tempo. Simple rhythm: no style beat or syncopation. Melody moves in a slow rhythm; accompaniment steady on each beat.*
Melody	*Four phrases, in a question/answer pattern. Pronounced rise and fall. Slow pace.*
Instrumentation (timbre)	*Voice, viola, and guitar.*
Performance style	*Dalhart's singing shows his operatic training and Texas roots. It's a richer sound than the harsh country heard in Ben Jarrell's "Old Joe Clark," but there is a trace of a twang in Dalhart's delivery of the words. The viola sound is from the classical tradition, not country.*
Dynamics	*Moderately soft throughout.*
Harmony	*Three chords, in a simple I-IV-V-I pattern, throughout the song.*
Texture	*Melody plus simple accompaniment, with viola obbligato at the end.*
Form	**Strophic** *(two or more verses sung to the same melody).*

Key Points

Focus on the story	*The lyric, which promises a "sad tale," is the main source of interest here.*
Simplicity of the song	*A folklike song designed to tell a story. Unlike "Old Joe Clark," it is not a dance tune with words added.*
Dalhart's singing	*Full, somewhat refined voice with a little twang.*
Mainstreaming of country music	*The formula for country crossover success: borrow elements from other styles (e.g., viola, not fiddle) and adapt them to country.*

Terms to Know

event song
obbligato
strophic

Success Versus Identity in Country Music. "The Prisoner's Song" was a huge success—perhaps the second-best-selling song from the first half of the century behind Bing Crosby's rendition of "White Christmas." And it seemed to come out of nowhere. Dalhart was popular enough;

he had already made 400 recordings by 1924, but this song represented a new direction for him. We don't know why it was popular, but we know that it was; and because it was, "The Prisoner's Song" showed country musicians the surest path to commercial success: blend country with other, more popular styles. From Dalhart's **citybilly** through the singing cowboys of the thirties and forties, Eddy Arnold's syrupy **Nashville sound** in the 1950s, Glen Campbell's 1960s hits, and Kenny Rogers's 1970s **countrypolitan** (all three being urbanized, slickly produced country styles) to the mainstreaming of contemporary country performers like Garth Brooks and Shania Twain, the route to fame and fortune led out of the country and into the city.

This conflict—between remaining true to one's roots and moving toward fame and fortune in the contemporary mainstream—has been the central tension in country almost from the start. If it wasn't present before Dalhart's hit, it certainly was afterward, and it remains a hotly debated topic to this day. We see a different form of this opposition in the next pair of examples.

August 1927, Bristol, Tennessee

At the tail end of July 1927, Ralph Peer got off the train with his recording equipment and set up a temporary studio in a hotel on State Street in Bristol, Tennessee. Over the next four days, he recorded two of country music's most important and influential acts: the Carter Family on August 1 and 2 and Jimmie Rodgers on August 4. Country music historian Bill Malone described the event in this way:

> Rodgers brought into clear focus the tradition of the rambling man which had been so attractive to country music's folk ancestors and which ever since fascinated much of the country music audience. This ex-railroad man conveyed the impression that he had been everywhere and had experienced life to the fullest. His music suggested a similar openness of spirit, a willingness to experiment, and a receptivity to alternative styles. The Carter Family, in contrast, represented the impulse toward home and stability, a theme as perennially attractive as that of the rambler. When the Carters sang, they evoked images of the country church, Mama and Daddy, [and] the family fireside . . . Theirs was a music that might borrow from other forms, but would move away from its roots only reluctantly.

The Carter Family and "Wildwood Flower." The Carter Family, one of the most influential groups in the history of country music, consisted of Alvin Pleasant "A. P." Carter (1891–1960); his wife, Sara (1898–1979, after 1933, his ex-wife); and his sister-in-law, Maybelle (1909–1978). All three sang, Sara played guitar and autoharp, and Maybelle developed one of the most widely imitated guitar styles in the history of country music. A. P. had grown up playing the fiddle, learning **ballads** and other songs from his mother, and he never lost his love for the traditional songs he heard as a youth. The Carter Family performed and recorded traditional songs that A. P. had collected and arranged. Among the best known was their 1928 recording of a song they called "Wildwood Flower." It had started out as a commercially published parlor song, composed in 1860 by Maud Irving and J. D. Webster, entitled "I'll Twine 'Mid the Ringlets"; but like so many nineteenth-century commercial songs, it had found its way into **oral tradition**. (The popular Stephen Foster songs have become so familiar that we forget their composer and think of them as timeless, anonymous folksongs.)

The sound of the Carter Family was an intriguing mix of old and new. Certainly the song was old, although not nearly as old as those Cecil Sharp had heard in 1918. Maybelle's singing exemplifies the **traditional country vocal** sound—flat, nasal, and without much inflection.

Meridian/Lauderdale County Tourism Bureau

Jimmie Rodgers in a pensive mood. This unusually candid portrait shows Rodgers picking his guitar. Note his name inlaid in the neck of the guitar.

It is the accompaniment that begins the break with the past. There is no fiddle, just guitar. The clear separation of melody and accompaniment is more like Dalhart's "The Prisoner's Song" than it is like "Old Joe Clark." The most important and influential feature of the accompaniment is Maybelle's **thumb-brush style.** She plays the melody on the lower strings and, between melody notes, brushes the chords on the upper strings. We will hear this style in a Woody Guthrie song later in this chapter.

The Carters' professional career lasted from their discovery by Ralph Peer in 1927 until 1943. After World War II, Maybelle and her daughters continued to tour as the Carter Family, and subsequent incarnations of the group performed through the 1960s.

Jimmie Rodgers's "Blue Yodel No. 11." Jimmie Rodgers (1897–1933) had a brief but extraordinarily influential career. His musical legacy, preserved primarily through recordings, inspired an entire generation. According to Bill Malone, "Ernest Tubb estimated that perhaps 75 percent of modern country music performers were directly or indirectly influenced to become entertainers either through hearing Rodgers in person or through his recordings."

Born in Mississippi, Rodgers spent much of his childhood and early adult life around the railroad, at first accompanying his father, a gang foreman, and then working off and on as a railroad man, before contracting the tuberculosis that was to end his life so prematurely at age thirty-six.

Rodgers's first recordings for Peer, in Bristol, Tennessee, and later that year in Camden, New Jersey, made him one of country music's first stars. Almost immediately he was making

0:00	Introduction
0:09	1st Chorus
	I've got a gal...
0:34	[Yodel.]
0:39	2nd Chorus
	Now looka' here...
1:02	[Yodel.]
1:07	3rd Chorus
	You want furs...
1:29	[Yodel.]
1:34	4th Chorus
	I believe...
1:55	[Yodel.]
2:00	5th Chorus
	You may call...
2:23	[Yodel.]
2:28	6th Chorus
	Listen here...
2:51	[Yodel.]

$2,000 a month in record royalties alone. For the rest of his life, he enjoyed great popularity throughout the South in personal appearances, radio broadcasts, and frequent recordings. Forced to move to Texas because of his illness, he gained an especially strong following in the Southwest. The greater receptiveness of southwestern country music to outside influences is surely due in part to Rodgers.

The image of the rambling man roaming far and wide that Rodgers carefully cultivated in his songs had great appeal for his fans. Musically, Rodgers borrowed liberally from all the styles with which he came into contact; there are elements of Tin Pan Alley song, blues, and jazz in many of his recordings.

"Blue Yodel No. 11," one of thirteen blue yodels that Rodgers recorded, is a blues, pure and simple—in its lyrics, melodic style, harmony, and form. More significant, it is a blues in style. Rodgers sounds natural and very much at ease singing a blues. He has captured essential elements of the blues singing style: a rhythmically free and unstilted delivery of the text, a highly inflected phrasing (listen to the extra emphasis on the word "presents" in the third phrase of the first section), and a vocal style more expressive than pretty.

CD 2:7

"Blue Yodel No. 11," Jimmie Rodgers (1929). Rodgers, vocal and guitar.

STYLE PROFILE

"BLUE YODEL NO. 11" (COUNTRY SONG)

Rhythm	*Lazy four-beat rhythm. Rodgers's singing plays off the beat, as is common in blues singing. Sometimes it's expressive; on a few occasions, however, there is some confusion with the guitarist who accompanies him; they are not always in sync because Rodgers takes liberties with the beat on occasion.*

Melody	*Short phrases that start high and finish low; most are derived from the* **pentatonic scale***.*
Instrumentation (timbre)	*Voice and two guitars (Rodgers and an anonymous partner).*
Performance style	*Blues inflections—stressed syllables, sliding into notes, and conversational pacing. The yodeling at the ends of sections is a Rodgers trademark.*
Dynamics	*Moderate, with little change.*
Harmony	*Basic* **blues progression***, with occasional modification of the timing.*
Texture	*Melody and accompaniment; some responses in the guitar.*
Form	*Blues.*

Key Points

Lyrics	*Common blues subject: man/woman problems.*
Rodgers's idiomatic style	*Rodgers sings the blues naturally and idiomatically.*

Terms to Know
blues progression
pentatonic scale

Summary. Bill Malone's description of the Carter Family and Jimmie Rodgers contrasts their values. The difference is clearest in the songs. The Carters recorded traditional songs or songs written by A. P. Carter in the traditional style. Rodgers, drawing on the blues, pop, jazz, and country music of the time, wrote his own songs. The Carters preserved the past; Rodgers showed the way to the future.

COUNTRY'S NEW DIRECTIONS IN THE 1930s

Country music became a regional music with an international following, spreading geographically and musically yet retaining its home base. It remains rooted in southern culture and values. Nashville, Tennessee, is the most obvious evidence of country's strong southern roots. As the home of the Grand Ole Opry, Nashville became the most important city in country music. Now also home to the Country Music Foundation and major recording studios, Nashville remains the spiritual, economic, and promotional center of country music. Country music did not shift its operational base to New York or Los Angeles when it entered the popular-music mainstream; the music industry came to Nashville.

During the 1930s hard times compelled people from the South and the Southwest to look elsewhere for work. Especially during the Dust Bowl of the early 1930s, they went west and north and took their music with them. The sound of country music spread to Hollywood and onto the screen. Radio played an even more important role. In 1924 NBC began broadcasting its *National Barn Dance* on WLS in Chicago, supplementing Nashville's WSM's *Grand Ole Opry.* In the thirties, Mexican radio stations, which exceeded the 50,000-watt limit imposed by the Federal Communications Commission (FCC) in the United States, also broadcast country music.

The new sounds of the 1930s in both country and folk music came from the Southwest in an almost vertical line that connects Kosse, Texas; Tioga, Texas; and Okemah, Oklahoma. These three towns were home to key figures in country and folk music. Bob Wills, the man most responsible for western swing, the hottest country sound of the 1930s, came from Kosse, a small town almost directly south of Dallas. Tioga, another small town, due north of Dallas, was the birthplace of Gene Autry, the first of the singing cowboy movie stars. Woody Guthrie, the man who made folk a contemporary music, was born in Okemah, mostly north and a little east of Dallas (and Tioga). Autry died in Los Angeles, Wills in Tulsa, and Guthrie in New York. And therein lies the story.

Bob Wills: Putting the Swing in Country

Bob Wills (1905–1975) was a maverick. In a genre that valued tradition and respected success, Wills took the bold step of blending the country string-band sound with pop, blues, and jazz into a new style called **western swing.** The blues and jazz influence was most often evident in the heavier beat, the fuller instrumentation, and the styles of many of the soloists in Wills's band, the Texas Playboys. Wills, a fine fiddle player as well as a bandleader and all-around entertainer, surrounded himself with good musicians.

"Steel Guitar Rag," a 1936 recording, features Leon McAuliffe playing the then-novel electric steel guitar. The **steel guitar** stands alone among contemporary popular instruments as the signature instrument for two—and only two—kinds of music: Hawaiian and country. These are two different musical worlds, yet the instrument sounds equally at home in both.

During the 1920s there was a tremendous vogue for Hawaiian music. Hawaiian guitarists, playing the lap steel guitar, were a vaudeville staple, and most of the bigger music publishers published learn-at-home methods. In search of a more powerful sound, instrument makers created the **dobro,** a guitar with a built-in steel resonator, also played on the lap. (The term *dobro* reportedly comes from *Do*pyera *Bro*thers, a family of Czech immigrants who created the first dobros in 1928; *dobro* also means "good" in Czech). The **electric steel guitar,** invented in the early thirties, soon replaced the dobro as the instrument of choice for lap guitarists. As with the steel guitar, the origins of the electric steel guitar are cloudy, but it seems safe to say that the steel guitar was the first **electric guitar.**

A strictly instrumental song featuring an almost brand-new instrument is innovative enough, but Wills's "Steel Guitar Rag" featured a host of country music innovations, most of which were borrowed from other genres. Wills and the Texas Playboys were not responsible for all of them, but, as the most popular band in the Southwest during the late 1930s and '40s, they did more than anyone else to popularize them.

 2:8

"Steel Guitar Rag," Leon McAuliffe (1936). Bob Wills and the Texas Playboys, featuring Leon McAuliffe, electric steel guitar.

Origins of the Steel Guitar

The steel guitar—played on the lap rather than in an upright position—apparently came about by accident. This is the most widely told account: In the late nineteenth century, a young boy named Joseph Kekuku was walking along the railroad tracks with his guitar when he picked up a loose bolt and slid it along the strings. Delighted by the sound, he replaced the bolt with the back of a knife and transferred the guitar's position to flat on his lap to facilitate moving the knife up and down the strings. The steel bar, now in use, soon replaced the knife. (Note how the early history of the steel guitar parallels the development of the bluesman's slide guitar.)

CD 2:8   **Western Swing** (Leon McAuliffe; performed by Bob Wills and the Texas Playboys, featuring Leon McAuliffe, electric steel guitar)

| 0:00 | | Introduction. Leon's steel guitar and Bob's voice. |

1st Chorus

0:07	A	Leon's bent notes give his performance a bluesy touch.
0:25	B	A clear two-beat rhythm underneath McAuliffe's solo.
0:43	C	The chord progression here serves as the basis for the two solos.

2nd Chorus ■ Solos

1:00	C	Piano solo: not very country sounding.
1:17	A	An interlude between solos.
1:34	C	Saxophone solo.

3rd Chorus ■ Reprise of the first chorus

1:52	A	Steel guitar, with Wills's voice-over.
2:09	B	Identical with the earlier B.
2:26	C	Identical with the first C except for the short tag at the end.

STYLE PROFILE

"STEEL GUITAR RAG" (WESTERN SWING)

Rhythm	Fast tempo. **Two-beat rhythm** with a strong backbeat. Occasional shift to a four-beat rhythm (e.g., piano solo). Some syncopation, mostly in the horn riffs.
Melody	The melody mixes long gestures with **arpeggios** (the "rag" aspect of the song). The first section is close to a vocal-style melody; the other two sections are more instrumental because of the frequent arpeggios (easier to play on the steel guitar than to sing).
Instrumentation (timbre)	Steel guitar in the spotlight, plus a small horn section (trumpets and saxophones stand out) and a rhythm section (including piano, bass, and drums).
Performance style	Occasional blues-influenced **bent notes** in steel guitar line. Chordal piano style. Early instance of honking saxophone.
Dynamics	Moderately loud throughout.
Harmony	The three-part rag is based on a bluesy version of I-IV-V; only one chord is not from these three.
Texture	Melody or solo over strong rhythm section.
Form	Raglike three-section form presented at the beginning and then repeated at the end. The middle contains the first section, sandwiched by piano and sax solos on C.

Key Points

Blues influences	A few **blue notes** in the melody and a few bentnotes in McAuliffe's playing.
Jazz influence	Most apparent in the piano solo; less so in the sax solo.
Expanded instrumentation	Wills augments the traditional country band with a full rhythm section and a small horn section, plus the steel guitar.
Use of drums	Wills was the first important country bandleader to use drums.

Honky-tonk beat	A **honky-tonk beat** is a countrified two-beat: clear OOM-pah rhythm with a crisp backbeat.
Countrifying influences	Country-style adaptations of borrowed features (e.g., two-beat rhythm acquires a harder edge).
Bob Wills, country progressive	Western swing would influence honky-tonk, rockabilly, and **country rock**.

Terms to Know

arpeggio	country rock	honky-tonk beat
bent note	dobro	steel guitar
blue note	electric steel guitar	two-beat rhythm

Most of these novel features eventually wove their way into the fabric of country music. For example, the sound of a country rhythm section playing a honky-tonk two-beat (or a **country rock beat**, which merges the honky-tonk beat with a rock rhythm) is the traditional country rhythm these days.

In his receptiveness to other styles, Wills certainly drew on Jimmie Rodgers's legacy. His stage demeanor, with his frequent words of encouragement to his musicians and his yodeled expressions of pleasure, also recalls Rodgers's occasional spoken asides. In turn Wills too left an enduring legacy of stylistic innovation. No one did more to popularize the sound of western swing than Bob Wills, and few other musicians have played such a significant role in charting the future of country music.

Gene Autry: Putting the "Western" in "Country and Western"

It was inevitable that there would be musical westerns. America had long had a love affair with cowboys and the Wild West. Kids idolized not only the good guys like Wyatt Earp and William "Buffalo Bill" Cody (at least we *thought* he was a good guy), but also bad guys like outlaws Jesse James and William "Billy the Kid" Bonney. Cowboy songs like "Home on the Range" and "Git Along, Little Dogies" were as much a part of everyday life as Foster's minstrel songs, patriotic anthems, and current hits. It simply remained for Hollywood to put everything together. Beginning in 1935, it did.

The first singing cowboy on-screen was Gene Autry (1907–1998). As a young man, he got a job as a telegraph operator. In one of those happy coincidences that never seem to happen anymore, Autry was passing the time singing and playing the guitar one day in 1926 when a man walked in to send a telegram. The man was Will Rogers, the most popular humorist of the twenties and thirties. Rogers asked Autry to keep singing, then suggested that he get a job in radio. After an unsuccessful audition for Victor in 1927, Autry landed a radio show in 1929. This led to a recording contract later that year. After much success on radio and record —he was featured on the *Grand Ole Opry* and *National Barn Dance;* Sears sponsored his radio show and promoted his records—Autry made his way to Hollywood in 1934.

The next year he starred in the film *Tumbling Tumbleweeds*. The film is generally considered to be the first musical western (or **horse opera**) because the plot depends on the singing ability of Autry's character. The success of the film created a demand for singing cowboys. Autry became one of the most popular Hollywood stars, and other singing cowboys, like Roy Rogers and Tex Ritter, were not far behind.

Autry's most popular musical western was the 1939 film *South of the Border*. The title track, "South of the Border," was the work of Jimmy Kennedy, an Irish lyricist, and Michael Carr, a British songwriter. The song sounds like what it is—a pop songwriter's take on a pop country song. **Western songs** like "South of the Border" were country music's first crossover style. Like Dalhart's, Autry's singing has a distinct southwestern flavor, pleasant but without much of the twang we associate with country music. The featured instruments are the accordion, which evokes Mexico, and the steel guitar, which gives it the new country flavor. For many Americans in the 1930s and '40s—especially those who went to the movies but didn't listen to the *Grand Ole Opry*—this was country music.

Much as "The Prisoner's Song" did, western songs followed the formula for country **crossover** success:

o Begin with a vocal sound that is recognizably country but not intensely so.

o Sing a simple melody with a simple accompaniment based mainly on three chords.

o Add in some country instrumental sounds, then mix in a little pop sophistication: more-complex chords, melodic lines, and forms.

o Package it with an appealing personality.

The formula worked for Autry, and for generations to come it would work for many more country and western singers. It still works today.

Summary

Musical westerns cultivated a shared heritage, a romance with the frontier that Americans had pursued through the nineteenth century and much of the twentieth. As opposed to the West, the South had remained isolated from the North after the Civil War. For many Americans the earliest country music—the songs of Jimmie Rodgers and the Carter Family—was exotic. When country went west, Gene Autry, Roy Rogers, and the other singing cowboys upgraded country's image—no longer hillbillies, they were heroes. And even though almost everyone who saw musical westerns knew they were make-believe stories, audiences still bought into the value system woven into the plot lines and their characters. Their success put western music in America's ear. This was the first pop style with evident country roots. Whereas Dalhart made a splash with one song, Autry and his peers made a long string of hits in roughly the same style.

Bob Wills also expanded country music beyond its southern boundaries. But whereas the pop elements in Autry's song (and Dalhart's) essentially dilute its country essence, Wills brought new sounds and styles into country music—he countrified them; that is, he gave them a new identity specific to country music. In Leon McAuliffe's hands, the steel guitar takes on a completely different character; there is no trace of Hawaii. The same countrification is true of the rhythm section's accompaniment and the saxophone solo.

By putting a country spin on blues and jazz, Wills built on Jimmie Rodgers's legacy more extensively than any other country musician of his time. Because of this his significance extends beyond his key role in shaping the sound of western swing. His innovations would also help shape honky-tonk and rockabilly, two significant post–World War II country styles.

WOODY GUTHRIE: FOLK SPLITS FROM COUNTRY

Whether it's riding a horse on the range, hopping on a train, or driving an eighteen-wheeler down the interstate, one of the enduring images in country music is the traveling man. But you wouldn't find America's greatest musical wanderer on the stage of the Grand Ole Opry, even though he was born in a small town in Oklahoma and borrowed his guitar style directly from Maybelle Carter. Instead, he forged a new path—one that created the contemporary folk movement.

For Woody Guthrie (1912–1967) growing up was hard. His parents were pioneers. His sister died when a stove exploded; his father rode the oil boom, then went bust; and his mother ended up in a mental institution with an undiagnosed case of Huntington's chorea, a congenital disease that would curtail Guthrie's career and claim his life. He left home at sixteen, just before the stock market crash and a few years before the Dust Bowl drove so many Oklahomans west in search of a better life.

His first stop was Pampas, Texas, where his uncle, Jack Guthrie, nurtured his interest in country music. Before long he had assembled the Corncob Trio and was doing what so many other country bands were doing. But his music soon went in a different direction, and in the early thirties he started writing songs. Here is how he described them in *Bound for Glory,* his novel-like autobiography of the early years of his life:

A young Woody Guthrie serenading the camera. Note that Guthrie is dressed to roam; most other performers—pop, jazz, or country—would be wearing tuxedos or some kind of dress clothes.

> Some people liked me, hated me, walked with me, walked over me, jeered me, cheered me, rooted me and hooted me, and before long I was invited in and booted out of every public place of entertainment. But I decided that songs was a music and a language of all tongues.
>
> I never did make up many songs about the cow trails or the moon skipping through the sky, but at first it was funny songs of what all's wrong, and how it turned out good or bad. Then I got a little braver and made up songs telling what I thought was wrong and how to make it right, songs that said what everybody in that country was thinking.
>
> And this has held me ever since.

Guthrie makes clear that he is the champion of the working class. In the course of his career, he wrote songs—more than a thousand of them—told stories, and authored articles (for a Communist Party newspaper) that commented on social injustice, the lives of the poor and the unknown, and anything else that caught his sharp eye. He spent most of the 1930s crisscrossing the United States, sometimes hopping trains to get from one place to the next.

In 1940 he made his way to New York, where Alan Lomax discovered him singing at a "Grapes of Wrath" rally for farmworkers. Within a year Lomax recorded him at the Library of Congress and featured him on his radio show. Pete Seeger was also part of the liberal/radical circle in which Lomax moved, and Guthrie joined Seeger and two others in 1941 to form the Almanac Singers.

In "Do-Re-Mi," a song Guthrie wrote in 1937, we can hear what drew Lomax, Seeger, and working-class folk to his music. We don't listen to Guthrie's songs for the beauty of his singing; what Robert Christgau calls his "vocal deadpan" was the opposite of the crooning of

CD 2:9

"Do-Re-Mi,"
Woody Guthrie
(1937). Guthrie,
vocal and guitar.

CD 2:9	Topical Folksong (Woody Guthrie; performed by Guthrie, vocal and guitar)
0:00	Introduction. Guitar, thumb-brush technique (melody in the single notes, higher chords thumb-brushed).
0:17	Verse *Lots of folks . . .*
0:43	Chorus *Oh, if you ain't got . . .*
1:14	Interlude. Guitar, thumb-brush style.
1:31	Verse *You want to buy . . .*
1:55	Chorus *If you ain't got . . .*

Bing Crosby, whom Guthrie openly despised. And we don't listen for the sophistication of the accompaniment; Guthrie was fond of saying that three chords were one too many. We listen for the words.

With no sugarcoating, Guthrie tells the tough-times story of the desperate people who migrated west in search of a decent life. He gets his point across with a wry humor that, if anything, intensifies the grim circumstances that he describes. This is a funny song that isn't funny at all.

Guthrie's music is centuries old and brand-new at the same time. In his music are echoes of British broadside ballads, a tradition that dates back to the sixteenth century. (A **broadside** is a topical text sung to a well-known tune. Broadsides were, in effect, an urban folk music with printed words.) In fact, Guthrie occasionally fashioned new words to familiar songs, in true broadside and folk tradition. But in the musical context of the 1930s—the world of silver-screen pop, swinging big-band jazz, singing cowboys, and crooners—Guthrie's songs stood apart. From the late 1930s through the end of World War II, there was no sharper musical commentator on the inequities of life in America, no more persistent musical voice for social justice, and no more prolific musical advocate for the cause of the working class than Woody Guthrie.

He wrote and delivered his songs in a folk style, but the songs were new. In so doing he made folk a commercial music—even if much of the time his songs had an anti-commercial message. He also made folk a living music. Others, most notably the Weavers, would follow in his footsteps. It remained for Bob Dylan, however, to fully realize Guthrie's legacy.

STYLE PROFILE

"DO-RE-MI" (TOPICAL FOLKSONG)

Rhythm	*Moderate tempo; light beat keeping in regular accompaniment rhythm (no syncopation or rhythmic play).*
Melody	*Long phrases at a quick pace, narrow melodic range.*
Instrumentation (timbre)	*Voice and guitar.*
Performance style	*Twangy singing style; easy delivery of words; the Carter thumb-brush guitar style (melody low, accompanying chords above).*
Dynamics	*Moderate throughout.*

Harmony	Three chords (I-IV-V).
Texture	Voice and active guitar accompaniment.
Form	**Verse/chorus.**

Key Points

Topical song	Guthrie brought topical songs into Depression-era American life.
Folk-style accompaniment	Guthrie adapted Maybelle Carter's thumb-brush accompanying style.

Terms to Know

thumb-brush style
verse/chorus form

Guthrie essentially left country music behind, or at least a country music audience, to forge a new direction. The difference between Guthrie's folk music and country music had more to do with politics and social issues than with the music itself. Folk music found a new home in New York's Greenwich Village and a new, politically liberal, and largely urban audience. Country music kept its home base, in the South and the Southwest, and retained its conservative values. Country and folk were like two brothers who grew up together but followed paths so different that they became estranged. Their reconciliation came only in the 1960s.

ON THE CHARTS: COUNTRY AFTER WORLD WAR II

Billboard magazine, the preeminent trade journal of the entertainment business, published its first country music **chart** on January 8, 1944. It was called the "Most Played Juke Box Folk Records." It was the first of three country-related charts. *Billboard* added the "Best Selling Retail Folk Records" in 1948 and "Country and Western Records Most Played by Folk Disk Jockeys" a year later. Only in 1958 did *Billboard* drop the word *folk* and bring the three country charts together as "Hot C&W Sides."

Billboard's charts indicate the growing—and broadening—audience for country music. Other clues include the offer of a movie contract to Hank Williams (who died before he could fulfill it) and **cover** versions of country hits by pop artists; Patti Page's 1950 version of Pee Wee King's "Tennessee Waltz" was a huge hit, with sales of more than 6 million records.

We look at two acts: Bill Monroe and the Blue Grass Boys, and Hank Williams. Each epitomizes an important development in postwar country music.

Bill Monroe and the Birth of Bluegrass

Bill Monroe (1911–1996), a singer and mandolin player, is known as the "father of bluegrass." He was responsible not only for the sound but also the name: Kentucky, where he was born, is the bluegrass state. Monroe grew up surrounded by skilled folk musicians, including his uncle Pendelton Vandiver (whom he would remember in the song "Uncle Pen"). He took up the mandolin because no one else in the family played it.

Monroe began to build his career in the 1930s and arrived on the stage of the Grand Ole Opry in 1939. By that time he was well on his way to assembling the sound of bluegrass. It would come together in 1945, when virtuoso banjo player Earl Scruggs joined Monroe's group.

Monroe's **bluegrass** music descends directly from the early string bands. The **acoustic instrumentation** (no electric instruments or amplification) and the **mountain vocal style** (the "high lonesome" sound) preserve important country music traditions. But there are some important differences as well:

- *Expanded instrumentation.* Monroe and the Blue Grass Boys offered a complete array of acoustic string instruments: fiddle, guitar, banjo, **mandolin**, and string bass.

- *Chop-chord mandolin style.* Bill Malone calls Bill Monroe's mandolin style "chop-chord." The **chop-chord style**, a percussive sound occurring in alternation with the bass, is the bluegrass answer to the honky-tonk backbeat.

- *Earl Scruggs's virtuoso banjo playing.* Scruggs updated the Appalachian three-finger banjo style. It combined the continuous stream of notes found in earlier banjo styles with the syncopated groupings of ragtime and the occasional blues lick—all at breakneck tempos.

- *Collective improvisation.* The texture and the form of a bluegrass recording have close parallels with New Orleans jazz. In both there is a dense, active texture resulting from simultaneous **improvisation** on several melody instruments over a timekeeping rhythm section, with occasional interruptions for a featured soloist. This collective improvisation harks back to the thoroughly blended texture of the string band, but there are more parts and their roles are more varied.

- *Exceedingly fast tempos.* String-band music was often dance music, but the tempos in many bluegrass songs are much too fast for all but the most agile dancers. This is listening music, although it invites a physical response. Part of the excitement of bluegrass is the skill with which its best performers reel off streams of notes at very fast speeds.

We hear all of these features in "It's Mighty Dark to Travel," a 1947 recording by Bill Monroe and the Blue Grass Boys. The recording features Earl Scruggs on banjo, Lester Flatt on guitar, and Bill Monroe on mandolin. Flatt and Scruggs would leave the following year to form their own group. By the end of the 1940s, other musicians were copying features of Monroe's music, and it remains the standard by which bluegrass groups are measured.

CD 2:10

"It's Mighty Dark to Travel," Bill Monroe (1947). Bill Monroe and the Blue Grass Boys: Monroe, mandolin and vocal; Earl Scruggs, banjo; Lester Flatt, guitar and vocal; Chubby Wise, fiddle; Howard Watts, bass.

STYLE PROFILE

"IT'S MIGHTY DARK TO TRAVEL" (BLUEGRASS)

Rhythm	*Very fast tempo. Strong two-beat rhythm with crisp off-beat chords. Guitar and banjo move at double-time speed; vocal and fiddle lines move at a slower speed.*
Melody	*Vocal line consists of short phrases. Instrumental solos generally move at a faster pace and with more skips.*
Instrumentation (timbre)	*Vocals, banjo, fiddle, and mandolin.*
Performance style	*"High lonesome" mountain vocal sound.*
Dynamics	*Moderate throughout.*
Harmony	*I, IV, and V only.*
Texture	*Three distinct levels of activity: melody (vocal or instrumental), bass/chord accompaniment, and one or more obbligato parts—runs, more-elaborate accompaniments (e.g., mandolin in chorus), or secondary melodies.*
Form	*Verse/chorus, with verse and chorus using the same melody.*

CD 2:10   **Bluegrass** (Bill Monroe; performed by Bill Monroe and the Blue Grass Boys: Monroe, mandolin and vocal; Earl Scruggs, banjo; Lester Flatt, guitar and vocal; Chubby Wise, fiddle; and Howard Watts, bass)

0:00	Instrumental statement of the melody.
0:13	Chorus
	The vocal harmony has a traditional sound because the intervals between the two voices are different from pop vocal harmony; they have a more open sound.
	It's mighty dark . . .
0:26	Fiddle plays the melody.
0:40	Verse
	Notice the fast mandolin chords behind the vocal.
	To me she was . . .
0:53	Chorus
	It's mighty dark . . .
1:12	Banjo solo. Notice the syncopation produced by the accents in Scruggs's line and the blue notes. We hear echoes of ragtime in some of the figuration.
1:18	Verse
	There is a lot going on underneath the vocal: Flatt's guitar runs, Monroe's busy mandolin part, Wise's sustained fiddle harmonies, and Scruggs's picking.
	Many a night . . .
1:31	Chorus
	It's mighty dark . . .
1:44	Mandolin solo. Monroe embeds the melody into the fast chords he's playing.
1:56	Verse
	Traveling down . . .
2:08	Chorus
	It's mighty dark . . .
2:22	Violin solo. Notice how Wise decorates the melody with harmony notes (like the vocal) and the occasional quick run.
2:33	Chorus
	It's mighty dark . . .

Key Points

Bluegrass instrumentation	*The core bluegrass instrumentation: all strings, no drums or horns.*
Influence of black music: ragtime, blues, and jazz	*Banjo lines have raglike figuration and a few blue notes; interaction among instruments recalls New Orleans jazz.*
Tempo and text	*Very fast tempo versus mournful lyric.*

Terms to Know

acoustic instrumentation	blue note	mountain vocal style
bluegrass	chop-chord style	

Bluegrass was part of a larger movement throughout all popular music to hold on to the past and bring it to life. Reflecting that segment of the country music world, including the powers at the Grand Ole Opry, bluegrass was the first important neo-traditional style in

Country music and blues have played opposing roles in the development of popular music. African American music has led the way in creating new styles. Country music has been reactive, absorbing into a traditional base musical influences from myriad sources. But from their beginnings to the emergence of rock, the commercial development of country music and African American music, especially blues and blues-influenced styles, ran along remarkably parallel paths.

Each served a minority population assumed to be lower class by most of the mainstream majority. The popular-music industry identified both styles by names with strong pejorative overtones. Recordings by black Americans were called race records; early country came to be known as hillbilly music.

Because country and blues were transmitted aurally, radio and records were essential to widespread dissemination. At midcentury both blues and country stood apart from the popular-music mainstream, although they had moved closer to the center. But like many country songs of the late 1940s and early '50s, cover versions of "Your Cheatin' Heart" hit big before Williams's version became nationally popular. From both country music and rhythm and blues came songs that mainstream white audiences found appealing but more palatable when sung by pop singers.

The movement of the two styles toward the mainstream and vice versa was evident in their more complimentary and musically accurate names. Hillbilly had become country and western; race had become rhythm and blues. Crossover hits appeared on the pop charts with increasing frequency.

There are musical parallels as well. Both blues and country music embraced the electric guitar almost as soon as it came on the market. And they gradually filled out the instrumental accompaniment to include a complete rhythm section—blues in the 1940s, country in the 1950s.

Finally, in both genres the most traditional and authentic vocal styles were instantly recognizable and far from the sound of pop crooners. Their vocal sound was not pretty but was powerfully communicative. Writing about Hank Williams, Bill Malone says:

> Williams sang with the quality that has characterized every great hillbilly singer: utter sincerity. He "lived" the songs he sang. He could communicate his feelings to the listener and make each person feel as if the song were being sung directly and only to him or her.

Change *hillbilly* to *blues,* and Malone's statement accurately describes a great blues singer or a blues-influenced pop singer, as we have heard in Billie Holiday's "All of Me."

country music. (A **neo-traditional** style offers a new take on an established, or traditional, style.) Based on traditional country music elements, Monroe and the Blue Grass Boys produced a new yet old-fashioned sound.

Bluegrass was one of several tradition-oriented trends to emerge during the 1940s. The Dixieland revival of the forties was the jazz counterpart to bluegrass. Rodgers and Hammerstein returned to a simpler, more melodic musical past in *Oklahoma!* and the musicals that followed it. And the Weavers, while spurring a revival of folk and folk-style music, took a third route—into the mainstream, as we discover presently.

Hank Williams and the Redefinition of Country Music

A *honky-tonk* is a working-class bar. Honky-tonks catering to white audiences typically featured country music, often performed by a live band. After the repeal of Prohibition in 1933, bars and dancehalls catering to a working-class clientele sprang up all over the South and the Southwest, but particularly in Texas and Oklahoma. These bars were usually rough, noisy establishments, and musicians who performed in them needed a musical style that could be heard above the din. At the same time, their songs needed to articulate the problems and pleasures of the audience. Most of the traditional country repertoire, particularly sentimental or religious songs, would have been wildly inappropriate for a honky-tonk.

Hank Williams performing at a square dance with his band. Note Williams's dress cowboy outfit, standard attire for many country singers.

Out of this environment came a new kind of country music, called (appropriately enough) **honky-tonk**. By the early 1940s, it had taken shape, and by the end of the decade it had become the most popular style in country music.

One big reason for its success was Hank Williams (1923–1953), the quintessential country singer. Williams was born into a poor family in rural Alabama. While still in his teens, he performed in rough honky-tonks near his home and later in southern Alabama. His career received a boost from Fred Rose, a Nashville-based pianist, songwriter, and music publisher and one of the most successful promoters in the history of country music. Williams gained widespread exposure throughout the South and the Southwest through appearances on two radio shows: the *Louisiana Hayride* and the *Grand Ole Opry.*

Williams suffered from spina bifida, a birth defect affecting his back. Throughout his life he was in constant pain, which may have contributed to his alcoholism and which cost him his life before his thirtieth birthday.

The music of Hank Williams embodies the essence of country music. In "Your Cheatin' Heart," which he recorded in 1952, shortly before his death, we hear the mixture of old and new that distinguishes country music from the folk music from which it emerged. As in traditional country music, the fiddle plays a prominent role; but the band behind Williams also includes a full rhythm section, including drums, plus the "newly traditional" country instrument, the steel guitar. They lay down a two-beat rhythm with a crisp backbeat; it is in essence a country take on the fox-trot. (We heard this rhythm previously in Bob Wills's "Steel Guitar Rag.")

 2:11

"Your Cheatin' Heart," Hank Williams (1952). Williams, vocal.

0:00	Introduction. Steel guitar lead; drum kit keeps the beat.
0:07	A
	Vocal enters, fiddle comments after each phrase.
	Your cheatin' heart [fiddle] will make you weep. [fiddle]
	You'll cry and cry, [fiddle] and try to sleep. [fiddle]
0:22	A
	Vocal; steel guitar comments after each phrase.
	But sleep won't come [steel guitar] the whole night through. [steel guitar]
	Your cheatin' heart [steel guitar] will tell on you. [steel guitar]
0:38	B Bridge
	When tears come down . . .
0:54	A
	You'll walk the floor . . .

Bridge—Instrumental

1:08	Steel guitar solo, first two phrases.
1:24	Fiddle solo completes bridge.
1:38	A Vocal returns.
	Your cheatin' heart . . .
1:52	A
	The time will come . . .
2:07	B
	When tears come down . . .
2:22	A
	You'll walk the floor . . .
2:36	Steel guitar tag.

Williams's singing also blends old and new. It has a uniquely country timbre. It is thin, nasal, and flat yet intensely expressive, as plaintive or high-spirited as the song demands. It is also tinged by the blues that Williams heard from street-corner blues singers when he was growing up. In particular, he credited Rufus Payne, a local blues singer whom he befriended, with giving him "all the music training I ever had." Indeed, Williams referred to his own singing as "moanin' the blues." This fusion of country and blues was Williams's own synthesis, one that made him perhaps the most easily recognized singer in country music.

Even more important, Williams unlocked the expressive potential of country music. Like Billie Holiday and Frank Sinatra, he is one of the great **song interpreters**. When performed by a pop singer, his songs can seem banal. It is the intensity of Williams's rendition that brings to life the pain behind the words. He conveys it with the contrast between the inherent fragility of his vocal sound—it comes close to breaking several times—and the intensity with which he emphasizes the long notes of the melody.

Williams does not have a conventionally pretty voice, but that seems to be an advantage. He cuts through pop vocal conventions to communicate directly with his audience. He's not just singing the song—he's reliving the experience that prompted it.

"YOUR CHEATIN' HEART" (HONKY-TONK)

Rhythm	*Moderate dance tempo; honky-tonk beat (two-beat rhythm with strong, crisp backbeat); subtle alternations in timing in the delivery of the melody.*
Melody	*Melody constructed from short phrases (like a riff but without syncopation).*
Instrumentation (timbre)	*Voice, fiddle, steel guitar, guitar, bass, and drums.*
Performance style	*Williams's "moanin' the blues," a country twang with blueslike inflections.*
Dynamics	*Moderate.*
Harmony	*I-IV-V almost all the way through.*
Texture	*Melody (vocal and instrumental response; instrumental lead) and rhythm-section accompaniment.*
Form	*AABA popular song.*

Key Points

Moanin' the blues	*Williams adapted the blues that he had heard growing up into a straightforward, intense vocal style.*
Defining country instruments	*Fiddle (old) and steel guitar (new).*
Honky-tonk and country's move toward the mainstream	*Complete rhythm section and two-beat rhythm = country adaptation of mainstream pop feature.*
Country pop song	***AABA** form and melodic style (build from a riff) show pop influence.*

Terms to Know

AABA form

honky-tonk

honky-tonk beat

The Sound of Honky-tonk. In large part because of Williams, honky-tonk quickly became an important country style after World War II. A host of new singing stars emerged: Lefty Frizzell, Hank Thompson, Patsy Cline, Kitty Wells, Ray Price, and more. Most remain well known and well loved.

Honky-tonk was the avant-garde of country music in the postwar years. Today it is country's traditional, almost timeless style. Its chief musical features remain the key qualities of country music today, the ones that preserve its identity:

o   Song texts that speak plainly and personally about everyday life: love, alcohol, hard times, loneliness, work, or life on the road

o   A nasal, often twangy vocal style

o   Straightforward melodies, delivered plainly and directly

o   Simple accompaniments, usually built from the three basic chords: I, IV, and V

o   The old and new country instruments: fiddle and steel guitar

o   A full rhythm section playing a countrified version of a popular dance beat

With honky-tonk, country music redefined itself. With the exception of bluegrass, it left the old-time roots of country's first 1923 recording in the past. The two clearest links to the past were the singing and the fiddle playing. Still, the expressive intent in the singing was more personal, its vocal sound showing influences of blues and pop. And the fiddle playing lost its rough edges. Everything else about honky-tonk was new: the full rhythm section, the honky-tonk beat, and the steel guitar. Country songs were freshly written and had contemporary themes.

Country music remains a genre with a strong sense of tradition. But tradition is relative. Honky-tonk, the new sound in country music during the 1940s, has become the traditional sound in contemporary country music. Country music's more distant past is a much dimmer memory.

FOLK GOES POP (BY ACCIDENT)

Although *Billboard* called its country charts "folk" music until 1949, folk performers like the Weavers and Burl Ives appeared more frequently on the pop charts than they did on the "folk" charts. And in 1958, the year the country charts consolidated, the Kingston Trio sparked the folk revival with their number 1 pop hit, "Tom Dooley." Groups like the Weavers and the Kingston Trio—no matter how well intentioned—were some distance musically from the kind of folk music that the Lomaxes were recording.

The Weavers. After Woody Guthrie joined the merchant marine in 1943 and left the Almanac Singers, Seeger and Hays continued to sing together. In 1949, joined by Veronica "Ronnie" Gilbert and Fred Kellerman, they formed the Weavers. They all sang, and the three men played the accompanying instruments: Seeger on the banjo, Kellerman on guitar, and Hays on bass.

The Weavers' breakthrough as a pop act came at the end of 1949 during an engagement at the Village Vanguard, a nightclub in New York. Booked for two weeks, they stayed for six months. They had begun recording for a small independent company, but their success caught the attention of the major record labels. The Weavers eventually signed with Decca Records, where Gordon Jenkins, one of the top pop arrangers of the day, provided lush string backgrounds.

The Weavers were the first ambassadors of folk music. Among their hit songs were folk and folklike songs from the United States as well as other cultures around the world. Their first and biggest recording coupled a folklike Israeli song, "Tzena, Tzena," with "Goodnight, Irene," a folklike song associated with Leadbelly, the African American folk and blues singer who had been discovered in a Louisiana prison by John Lomax. A later hit, "Wimoweh," was their version of a South African Zulu song.

CD 2:12

"This Land Is Your Land," Woody Guthrie (1963). The Weavers: Pete Seeger, vocal and banjo; Fred Kellerman, vocal and guitar; Lee Hays, vocal and bass; Ronnie Gilbert, vocal.

They also sang more politically oriented songs—songs with lyrics that advocated a particular stance. They recorded several songs by Woody Guthrie as well as by Pete Seeger, such as the familiar "If I Had a Hammer." It was their longtime association with leftist politics and causes that made them a target of the McCarthy-era witch hunts that grounded their career not long after it took off. They continued to work through the fifties—a 1955 Carnegie Hall concert was the highpoint—but they never recaptured their early success.

In their 1963 version of Woody Guthrie's "This Land Is Your Land," we can hear the qualities that made their music attractive to a larger audience. They sing close harmony in a warm, hearty, upbeat way. (In **close harmony** singing, the other notes of the chords are near in pitch to the melody note; all parts typically move in the same rhythm.) Their singing exudes an optimistic, "everything's all right with the world" spirit, and the accompaniment

CD 2:12   Popular Folksong (Woody Guthrie; performed by the Weavers: Pete Seeger, vocal and banjo; Fred Kellerman, vocal and guitar; Lee Hays, vocal and bass; and Ronnie Gilbert, vocal)

0:00	Chorus
	Notice the close harmony with some expressive harmony notes.
	This land is . . .
0:22	1st verse
	Solo voice: notice the change in the banjo from strumming to picking.
	As I was . . .
0:45	Chorus
	No significant change from opening chorus.
	This land is . . .
1:07	2nd verse
	Accompaniment shifts back to lighter picking sound.
	I roamed and . . .
1:30	Chorus, 2nd phrase
	Harmonica and rhythm.
1:41	3rd verse
	Note the sung bass part (Hays) under Ronnie Gilbert's singing.
	The sun comes . . .
2:04	Chorus
	No significant change from opening chorus.
	This land is . . .
2:27	Tag.
	This land was . . .
	Gradual fading away.

has much the same feel—in particular, Seeger's banjo jangles along. There is a big difference between the Weavers' singing and Guthrie's laconic, dead-voiced style, or the pure sound of Maybelle Carter's singing, or the "high lonesome" sound of Bill Monroe's group. Both the harmony and the richness of their voices bring the sound closer to pop. The simple accompaniment also helps make the music accessible; it too is a far cry from the intricate, high-energy picking of bluegrass.

STYLE PROFILE

"THIS LAND IS YOUR LAND" (POPULAR FOLKSONG)

Rhythm	*Moderate tempo. Simple two-beat rhythm in the accompaniment;* **shuffle***-style strumming in banjo during the chorus, but not with the feel of dance music. No syncopation in the melody.*
Melody	*The melody grows out of a short phrase; it forms two almost identical four-phrase sections. The rhythm remains pretty much the same from one phrase to the next; the melodic shape changes from phrase to phrase, with a gradual descent.*
Instrumentation (timbre)	*Voices, both solo and harmony; harmonica, bass, guitar, and banjo.*
Performance style	*Hearty singing; no trace of a country twang, blues influence, or pop smoothness.*

Dynamics	*Moderate, with a fadeaway at the end.*
Harmony	*I-IV-V, in the following progression: IV-I-V-I // IV-I-V-I.*
Texture	*Melody is dominant. Three levels of support: vocal harmony, bass and guitar accompaniment, and banjo strumming and picking (in solo sections).*
Form	*AA. Verse/chorus, with verse and chorus using the same melody.*

Key Points

Inspiring lyric	*Guthrie's celebration of America's beauty.*
"Folk" versus folk	*Song is modern, not traditional; singing doesn't relate to a traditional folk style.*
"We" music	*Lyric, simple tune, and hearty singing invite the audience to sing along.*

Terms to Know

shuffle

The Weavers' importance lies more in their influence than in their music. The folk revival of the late 1950s and early '60s was a revival in two senses. The more obvious was the recapturing and updating of traditional folk music. But it was also a re-energizing of the Weavers' attempt to use the accessibility of folklike music to advance their political and social agenda —to address the inequities of American life and the need for social justice—by taking it to a broader audience. Guthrie was the first to bring folk-style singing into the present; the Weavers were the first to take it to a big audience.

They had another, more long-range impact on popular music, one that would not be fully evident for several decades. Their versions of international folksongs, which find a middle ground between conventional singing and the authentic style of the song, planted the seed that would grow into the world music movement of the latter part of the twentieth century. The Weavers and their music served as a bridge not only between folk traditions and the pop mainstream but also between the social commentaries of Guthrie and important rock-era artists like Bob Dylan and Paul Simon.

LOOKING BACK, LOOKING AHEAD

In 1922 country music wasn't. That is, the musical styles that we now identify as country music did not exist, and there was no industry in place to support what would become country. By 1952, however, the year before Hank Williams's untimely death, country music had acquired a name: country and western, not folk. It had also acquired an array of styles— honky-tonk, western swing, bluegrass, the Nashville sound—and a sizeable share of the popular-music marketplace, not only within the loyal country music market but also with country songs and singers crossing over to the pop charts. Country mutated from the folk music that was its primary source by absorbing elements of other traditions: pop, blues, and even jazz.

During the same period, folk music came out of the hills and out of a timeless past to become a contemporary, urban, and often topical music. It too was transformed thoroughly, acquiring an old/new sound and a new audience.

Both country and folk began as styles completely off the popular-music radar. Early country music was a niche music—and a small one at that, save for the occasional break-through, like Dalhart's "The Prisoner's Song." Folk was so off the beaten path that preservationists like the Lomaxes scoured the South to record it. Both had become popular styles after World War II by gradually assimilating mainstream elements, such as a rhythm section in country music and pleasant voices in Weavers-style folk. And despite their differences, both would play a crucial role in defining the sound and the sensibility of rock.

From one perspective, country and folk followed the opposite path of stage entertainment. Country and folk moved from the exotic to the familiar, from the unknown to the known, in the three-plus decades surveyed in this chapter. Stage entertainment began the twenties at the center of the popular-music industry; after World War II, it became a more elite, if still popular, segment of the popular-music industry—and one that was increasingly out of touch with other developments in popular music.

In the next chapter, we encounter another family of musical styles that began as exotic alternatives. These developed beyond the borders of the United States, mainly in Cuba and Brazil, but found a home, and distinctive new sounds, in North America. We consider Latin music in the United States next.

TERMS TO KNOW

Test your knowledge of this chapter's important terms by defining the following. If you can't recall the meaning of a certain term, refresh your memory by looking up the boldfaced term in the chapter, turning to the Glossary at the back of the book, or working with the flashcards on the *Popular Music in America* Companion Web site: *http://music.wadsworth.com/ campbell_2e*

. . . .

AABA form	countrypolitan	obbligato
acoustic instrumentation	country rock	old-time music
Anglo-American	country rock beat	oral tradition
arpeggio	cover version	pentatonic scale
ASCAP	crossover	race record
ballad	dobro	shuffle
bent note	electric guitar	song interpreter
Billboard	electric steel guitar	steel guitar
bluegrass	event song	string band
blue note	folk music	strophic
blues progression	hillbilly	thumb-brush style
BMI	honky-tonk	traditional country vocal
broadside	honky-tonk beat	sound
B side	horse opera	two-beat rhythm
chart	improvisation	verse/chorus form
chop-chord style	mandolin	western song
citybilly	mountain vocal style	western swing
close harmony	Nashville sound	
country	neo-traditional	

. . . .

Latin Music in the United States

In the late 1850s, Louis Moreau Gottschalk (1829–1869), a composer and pianist who was America's first classical music star, toured South America and the Caribbean. On his return Gottschalk, a native of New Orleans, composed several piano pieces—the first noteworthy American music to show Latin influence. Native Latin music was not widely known in the United States, and Gottschalk's pieces were exotic novelties. But no one of importance followed Gottschalk's lead; other American musicians stayed home or turned to Europe for inspiration.

A hundred years later, in the 1950s and '60s, the biggest break a pop star could get was an appearance on *The Ed Sullivan Show*—the television show most remembered for introducing Elvis and the Beatles to the huge American audience. When rhythm-and-blues artist Bo Diddley got the chance to appear on the show in 1955, he agreed to perform "Sixteen Tons," a big hit at the time for popular country singer Tennessee Ernie Ford. But when the curtain opened, Diddley and his band played their hit song "Bo Diddley." It had been a number 1 R&B hit for them in 1955, they felt most comfortable with it, so they played it, even if it cost them a return engagement on the show.

The most distinctive musical feature of "Bo Diddley" (which we hear in Chapter 9) is the "shave and a haircut, two bits" rhythm in the guitar's response to each phrase of the lyric. This rhythm had been around for a while before Bo Diddley built his song around it. Some called it the **hambone rhythm**; others have connected it to **patting juba**, a practice among slaves in which they tapped out tricky rhythms on their thighs, chest, and almost any other part of their body that they could slap. But the rhythm is much more familiar to Cubans than it is to Americans.

Also familiar to Latin listeners of "Bo Diddley" is the sound of **maracas**, a percussion instrument made by putting handles on dried, seed-filled gourds; the shaking of seeds against the interior walls of the gourd makes the distinctive sound. Jerome Green, a longtime associate of Bo Diddley, played maracas in his band. One can find homemade percussion instruments throughout the Delta, but maracas are not one of them. They are, however, a staple in Latin bands, such as those led by bandleader Ricky Ricardo.

Ricardo was a main character in another extremely popular CBS show, *I Love Lucy*. The show featured the real-life husband-and-wife team Desi Arnaz and Lucille Ball, portraying husband and wife Ricky and Lucy Ricardo. Ricky led a Latin band at the Tropicana nightclub; Lucy was a show-business wannabe. The commercial viability of a white woman married to a Latin musician was a hard sell to CBS executives. Lucy and Desi spent $5,000 of their own money to make a pilot showing that the couple would be believable. CBS finally bought the idea, the show went on the air in 1951, and the result was the popular, now classic, sitcom of the 1950s (still showing on cable stations).

What *I Love Lucy* and Bo Diddley's appearance on *The Ed Sullivan Show* have in common is the blending of Latin music and Latin musicians into American life. There was little sense of the exotic in *I Love Lucy,* and the Latin influence in Bo Diddley's song is seldom acknowledged. Yet the **Bo Diddley beat** is his (unintentional) take on the **clave** (pronounced "*clah-vay*") **rhythm** of **Afro-Cuban** music.

Almost certainly, he learned the rhythm indirectly, but it was explicitly a part of New Orleans rhythm and blues from the late 1940s. Similarly, the maracas are one of many Afro-Cuban instruments that have become commonplace in popular music. Think of the cowbell sound that starts the Rolling Stones' "Honky Tonk Women" or the conga drums that can be heard on so many Motown recordings, such as Marvin Gaye's version of "I Heard It Through the Grapevine."

By 1955 Latin music had become a subtle seasoning in popular music, jazz, and rhythm and blues, and it had become an acceptable alternative to more-conventional American music. In fact, the biggest hit of 1955 was a Latin song, Perez Prado's "Cherry Pink and Apple Blossom White." In about a century, the place of Latin music in the United States had changed dramatically from exceptional oddity to part of the mix. To explore the place of Latin music in the United States, we ask two questions: *What is Latin music?* and *How did it flow into the mainstream?*

LATIN MUSIC

In the first half of the twentieth century, *Latin music* was the American umbrella term for music with a "Spanish tinge" (as Jelly Roll Morton liked to say). It identified three related types of music. One was popular music that originated in countries in the New World where Spanish or Portuguese was the native language. Most of this music first arrived in the United States as music for social dancing. Among the most popular Latin dances were the Argentine tango, the Cuban rumba and cha-cha-cha, and the Brazilian samba and maxixe.

The other two kinds of Latin music originated in the United States but came from either inside or outside the Latin community. The former came from Hispanic musicians—in Cuba, Puerto Rico, and other islands in the Spanish Caribbean—who had immigrated to the United States and created new kinds of Latin music. The latter was the product of Americans without a Latin heritage who adapted Latin elements—particularly the rhythms—into popular songs, dance music, and jazz.

We encounter all of these in the following brief survey of Latin music in the United States.

The Roots of Latin Music

The slave trade that brought Africans to the United States also brought them to other parts of the New World, particularly the Caribbean islands and Brazil. Like popular music styles in the United States, Latin styles grew out of the interaction between African and European musical traditions. Unlike their counterparts in the American South, however, slaves in Latin America and the Caribbean kept much of their culture. They merged their tribal religions with the various forms of Christianity introduced by European colonialists. They created Creole dialects—hybrid languages that were part European, part African. And because drums (banned in the slave-holding American South) were permitted in most other parts of the New World, folk music from these regions remained much closer to its African roots than almost all African American music. Afro-centric folk music from Latin America typically features more percussion instruments and a denser, more complex rhythmic texture.

From country to country, these folk and popular styles vary considerably, reflecting most directly differences in the language and the culture of the European nations that colonized them. The most dramatic instance of this variety would seem to be the contrast between Afro-Cuban and Afro-Brazilian music. Both have dense, rhythmically complex textures rich in percussion instruments. But whereas the rhythm of Cuban music is sharply articulated, Brazilian rhythm flows more smoothly from beat to beat. The contrast seems to parallel the difference between the harder consonants of Spanish (Spain colonized Cuba) and the softer consonants of Portuguese (Portugal colonized Brazil).

Latin Music in the United States

The most influential Latin dances and dance music in the United States have come primarily from Cuba and Brazil. Although these dances originated outside the United States, their sounds and rhythms have become part of the vocabulary of American popular music. Their assimilation parallels native **outsider musics** as they progress from exotic novelty to integral element. (Consider that in the first half of the century, old-time fiddle music or country blues would have been at least as alien to urban American ears as Latin popular music.)

Proceeding gradually over the twentieth century, the assimilation of Latin elements into popular music took place in three stages. They followed a roughly chronological progression, with considerable overlap, particularly in the decade around 1960.

- In the first stage, lasting until the early 1940s, Latin styles emerged as exotic novelties, usually dance fads that departed from mainstream fare. As they became popular in America, they moved away from their native forms, especially when played by the most popular bands.

- The second stage, lasting from the 1930s through the 1950s, saw the emergence of hybrid or transformed styles. These grew out of the interpretations of Latin music by American musicians—and, more significant—the incorporation of American music into Latin styles. Because of their different rhythms and instrumentations, these Latin-influenced or Latin-derived styles remained distinct from mainstream pop music until well into the rock era (as we discover later in this chapter).

- In the third stage, surfacing in the 1950s, elements of Latin music became part of the fabric of dominant styles. Latin rhythms helped shape the rhythms of rock-era popular music, and, consequently, Latin instruments now appeared routinely in a broad range of musical styles. Latin music still stood apart from American popular styles, but the line distinguishing Latin from mainstream was, and is, not nearly so clear as it had been before rock.

THE FIRST STAGE: LATIN DANCES AS EXOTIC NOVELTY

The story of Latin dance music in the United States begins more than a century ago with the Cuban **habanera**. Its name is probably an abbreviated form of *contradanza habanera*—that is, a *contredanse* (a European ballroom dance) from Havana. Its characteristic rhythm is one of the first recorded instances of African influence on European music. Developing during the early part of the nineteenth century, the habanera spread beyond Cuba after 1850, traveling to Europe, the United States, and South America. In Europe the habanera caught on not only in Spain but also in France. The French composer Georges Bizet composed a habanera for his immensely popular opera *Carmen* (1875).

The habanera entered the United States by way of Mexico, where it had become popular in the 1870s. A Mexican military band performed the dance at an international exposition held in New Orleans in 1884–1885. The band was the musical hit of the event, and its popularity led to the publication of several of the most popular pieces in its repertoire. By the end of the century, the influence of the habanera was evident in more-mainstream American popular music. The rhythmic signature of cakewalks and many ragtime songs is virtually identical to the habanera.

The first of the twentieth-century Latin dance fads in the United States was the Argentine tango. Irene and Vernon Castle, the creators of the fox trot, brought the tango to New York from Paris in 1913. They were a sensation, and the tango (suitably Americanized) became a fixture in popular culture, especially in musicals and films. We explore the tango at greater length below, in conjunction with a discussion of a beautiful contemporary tango by Astor Piazzolla.

Don Azpiazú and the Cuban Rumba

The surprising success of Don Azpiazú's 1930 recording of "El Manisero" ("The Peanut Vendor") triggered the second of the Latin dance crazes in the United States—the **rumba** (also spelled *rhumba*). Its success touched off widespread enthusiasm for Latin music, sending publishers back to their catalogs for Latin numbers and inspiring a number of Latin songs by American songwriters. When performed by Latins, the rumba was a spectacular exhibition dance, but simplified rumbas were also widely used for social dancing. It remains the most popular of the Latin ballroom dances.

The rumba grew out of an Afro-Cuban dance called the *son*. Developing from African and Hispanic elements, the *son* apparently originated in eastern Cuba. Brought to Havana around the turn of the century, it flourished in the 1920s among all classes with the growth of Cuban commercial radio. Many Cuban radio shows featured live performers; and because they were heard but not seen, Cubans of African descent gained access to audiences who would not normally have heard them perform.

The Cuban influence in Don Azpiazú's recording of the rumba "El Manisero" is most evident in the vocal, the prominent Latin percussion, and the reverse clave rhythm. (Clave rhythm, in either regular or reverse form, is to Cuban popular music what the backbeat is to American popular styles: a consistent point of rhythmic reference. In **reverse clave rhythm**, the second half of the pattern comes first.) In other respects, the recording shows the necessary accommodation of Cuban music to American pop styles of the period (swing and sweet). The trumpet is muted, and the piano style is halfway between Cuban and cocktail piano. Still, it is a milestone. It marked the first incursion of authentically

CD 2:13

"El Manisero" ("The Peanut Vendor"), Sunshine Marion, Gilbert Wolfe, and Simons Moises (1930). Don Azpiazú and His Havana Casino Orchestra.

CD 2:13 **Rumba** (Sunshine Marion, Gilbert Wolfe, and Simons Moises; performed by Don Azpiazú and His Havana Casino Orchestra)

0:00	Instrumental introduction. First piano, then maracas, then clarinet and horns (layers); the long notes in the clarinet riff match up with the reverse clave rhythm.
0:06	Muted trumpet plays fragments from vocal line.

A Section

0:19	Three phrases—two calls and a spun-out melody.
	Maní, maní...
0:41	Instrumental interlude.

B Section

0:52	Two parts; short, active phrases.
	Qué calentico y rico está...
1:11	Instrumental interlude.
1:18	A variations.
	Dame de tu maní...
1:43	B variations.
	Cuando la calle sola está...
2:10	A variations.
	Dame de tu maní...
2:43	Calls from A; ending fades.

Latin-sounding music into popular music. "El Manisero" was a Cuban song, Don Azpiazú was Cuban, and His Havana Casino Orchestra recorded it with a complete Cuban rhythm section.

STYLE PROFILE

"EL MANISERO" ("THE PEANUT VENDOR") (RUMBA)

Rhythm	*Moderate tempo; reverse clave rhythm; other rhythms line up with clave pattern; steady activity in percussion accompaniment.*
Melody	*Two melodic phrases, either long notes or active lines whose accents line up with clave rhythm.*
Instrumentation (timbre)	*Voice, piano, guitar, clarinets, trumpet, and a battery of percussion instruments —most prominent: maracas, **claves** (cylindrical sticks about an inch in diameter used to tap out the clave rhythm), and **timbales** (shallow, single-headed drums tuned to different pitches).*
Performance style	*Use of **mute** by the trumpet player.*
Dynamics	*Moderate.*
Harmony	*Just two alternating chords.*
Texture	*Melody with rich, percussion-heavy accompaniment.*
Form	*Open form: alternation of two sets of phrases, with variation in pitches and phrase length.*

The song and the style were enormously influential for the better part of two decades, until an even more rhythmically complex Afro-Cuban style—the mambo—developed in the United States. The 1930s began with the sound of the rumba and continued with a wave of Latin music by both Latins and Americans. Next we discover how it merged with American music and culture.

THE SECOND STAGE: HYBRIDS AND TRANSFORMATIONS

American-generated Latin Hybrids: Porter, Cugat, and the Latin Song

By the 1930s songs by American songwriters, like Irving Berlin's "Heat Wave" (1933), showed a greater sensitivity to Latin style; and songs by Latin composers, such as Cuban Nilo Melendez's "Green Eyes," were on their way to becoming pop standards. Both stage and film musicals featured Latin music more prominently. Bandleaders like Xavier Cugat and Desi Arnaz popularized Latin music in a hybrid style—rhythmically simplified and commercially acceptable to white audiences. They gave the most visible evidence of a growing Latin musical presence in the United States, especially in New York.

Xavier Cugat (1900–1990), a Spanish-born violinist raised in Cuba, came to the United States in 1921 and worked as a violinist before forming his own bands. As the most filmed bandleader in Hollywood—signed to long-term engagements at the Waldorf Hotels in New York and Los Angeles and, along with Benny Goodman's band, featured on the network radio show *Let's Dance*—Cugat helped establish a commercial Latin style.

Cole Porter. Among Cugat's biggest fans was Cole Porter, then living at New York's Waldorf Hotel. Of the great Tin Pan Alley songwriters, Porter was the most open to the sound of Latin music, or at least the commercial Latin music that Cugat played. Porter wrote several Latin songs, beginning in the 1930s, identifying the rhythm variously as "rhumba" or **beguine** ("beh-*geen*"). What is noteworthy about most of these songs is that their lyrics have nothing to do with Latin culture. Apparently, Porter simply liked the feel of the rhythm. A spectacular exception is his most famous Latin song, "Begin the Beguine" (1935): the lyrics would make great ad copy for a Caribbean getaway.

In addition to its Latinesque rhythm, "Begin the Beguine" is remarkable in another way: it is a very long song. Most of the phrases are twice as long as the entire A section of a typical pop song. Although songs did indeed get longer in the thirties ("Cheek to Cheek" is another

CD 2:14		Beguine (Cole Porter; performed by Xavier Cugat and His Orchestra)
0:00		Introduction.
0:32	A	First phrase of the melody.
0:54	A	First phrase, varied.
1:17	B	Contrasting phrase.
1:41	A	First phrase, varied again.
2:03	C	Second contrasting phrase.
2:26	C'	Second contrasting phrase, repeated with extension.
2:54		Tag.

example), the song seems to imply, not only by its length but also by its sophisticated melodic construction, that popular song can be more than just a catchy tune.

Xavier Cugat. Among the first recordings of "Begin the Beguine" was Xavier Cugat's with his band. Cugat was Latin music's Paul Whiteman. Both wore moustaches and were rotund. Both were string players who became bandleaders. Both hired the best musicians. Whiteman's band included top jazzmen of the 1920s; Cugat's bands included top Cuban musicians. Both were showmen, but Cugat put more emphasis on the show—and on showing off. The band wore ridiculous uniforms, played corny arrangements, and did campy routines. Still, each bandleader was responsible for bringing his music into the mainstream. Whiteman was instrumental in making jazz and the dance orchestra popular during the twenties, whereas Cugat was making Latin music for the masses in the thirties, forties, and fifties.

CD 2:14

"Begin the Beguine," Cole Porter (1935). Xavier Cugat and His Orchestra.

Cugat's recording of "Begin the Beguine" was a hit—one of three for him that year. Although the song has a lyric, Cugat's orchestra performs it as an instrumental. Only two short vocal sections frame an instrumental statement of the melody. It is elegantly done. Violins play the opening phrase of the melody, while the rest of the orchestra supports the melody with the Americanized Latin rhythm and Porter's original accents. The rich overlay of percussion instruments gives the performance a more authentic Latin sound; among these instruments are the claves.

STYLE PROFILE

"BEGIN THE BEGUINE" (BEGUINE)

Rhythm	*Moderate tempo; beguine rhythm in the accompaniment (slight syncopation in the pattern); long notes in the melody; the beguine rhythm—four beats per measure—can be represented like this:*
Chord:	*x x x x Plays on every afterbeat*
Bass:	*X X X Plays on beats 1, 3, and 4*
	The silent second beat gives the rhythm its characteristic lift.
Melody	*Unfolds slowly from rifflike ideas that float over the beat rather than bounce off it; builds gradually toward the final climactic phrases.*
Instrumentation (timbre)	*Full downtown Latin orchestra with the most audible being vocal (only to intone the title phrase), strings, rhythm section with piano, bass, and many Latin percussion instruments (**bongos**, maracas, and **claves**), trumpets, **accordion**, and **marimba** (a pitched percussion instrument featuring wooden bars*

	laid out like a piano keyboard, with resonators under each bar; the bars are struck with mallets).
Performance style	No exceptional features with its musical style.
Dynamics	Moderate throughout.
Harmony	Enriched I-IV-V.
Texture	Dense texture because of the overlay of percussion instruments; otherwise, melody plus accompaniment and countermelody in piano.
Form	AABACC, expanded song form, with each phrase double the normal length.

Key Points

Porter's long song	A very long, well-integrated song, three times the length of a typical pop song.
Latinesque song	Porter's take on Latin rhythms, delivered in Cugat's commercial Latin style.
Latin orchestra	A sweet band (note the violins) with Latin instruments, plus accordion and marimba.

Terms to Know

accordion	bongos	marimba
beguine	claves	

American Versus Latin Rhythms. For songwriters like Porter, "Latin" meant mostly a change in the rhythm, from an uneven division of the beat to an even division. In a typical fox trot, like "After You've Gone," the beat is divided into a long/short rhythm: "Af-" is longer than "ter." So when syncopation occurs, as it does on the syllable "gone," the accent is stronger because it's playing off the beat.

The same is true of swing rhythm: listen to Tony Bennett sing the title phrase of "Takin' a Chance on Love." The unequal division of the beat links two- and four-beat rhythms, despite the difference in the rhythmic feel. The rhythm of the bass part is different: two beats per measure versus four beats. As a result, the emphasis is different. But fast-moving values typically divide unequally in both. That sets up the contrast with Latin rhythm. The American-ized Latin rhythm in "Begin the Beguine" divides the beat into equal parts. In Porter's Latin songs, the bass line typically has notes on the first, third, and fourth beats, while the accompaniment chords all come on off-beats. (The Listening Guide explores this point in greater detail.) This pattern becomes the generic Latin rhythm of the 1930s and beyond.

The melody flows over this subtle, sinuous rhythm. Unlike "El Manisero," the clave pattern does not govern the accentuation of the melody; in fact, the melody actually soars over the underlying rhythm with long notes and slow triplets that do not line up with the Latin accompaniment (a **triplet** divides the beat or other rhythmic unit into three equal parts). In Cugat's recording, one of his percussionists plays the claves and allows us to hear the clave rhythm and the melody moving independently. Here the clave rhythm is simply a strand in the rich tapestry of percussion sounds; it does not serve as the rhythmic reference point as it did in "El Manisero."

"Begin the Beguine" remains the best known of Porter's many Latin songs, although iron-ically Artie Shaw's swing version of the song was a much bigger hit. But Cugat's recording shows one important way in which Latin elements filtered into American popular music. American composers borrowed from the Latin music that they heard and interpreted it through their own musical understanding. Latin bandleaders like Cugat accommodated the

American composer and played to the American public. Most American musicians (Porter excepted) couldn't hear the clave rhythm because it was so foreign to their musical experience, but they found the rippling beguine accompaniment, with patterns similar to more familiar music, easy to adapt.

Even as Porter, Cugat, and others were creating Latin pop, Latin musicians in New York were approaching the assimilation process from the opposite direction. They took elements of American music—most specifically big-band swing—and adapted it to Afro-Cuban music. Those New Yorkers who wanted more than just a taste of Latin music had to head to New York's uptown clubs, at least until after World War II.

Latin-generated Transformations

The establishment of a Latin district, or *barrio*, in New York dates back to the turn of the twentieth century, when, as a consequence of the 1898 Spanish-American War, Spain ceded Puerto Rico to the United States. Puerto Ricans were allowed to emigrate to the United States without restriction. Latins from other parts of the Caribbean soon followed, and by the late 1920s a substantial community of Cuban musicians resided in the United States. Some appeared in vaudeville or worked in society dance orchestras, but many also played for clubs and recorded for companies catering to the growing Latin community. New York was the most popular destination. Most Latins settled in upper Manhattan's east Harlem—the Spanish Harlem of Ben E. King—and passed on their musical styles to Americans of Cuban and Puerto Rican descent.

Among the Cuban musicians and, later, the Puerto Rican musicians who copied them, a clear division separated downtown and uptown music (just as it did among African American jazz musicians). The **downtown Latin style** was intended for the white American market. The **uptown Latin style** served the musical needs of the ever-growing Latin community in New York. This music was more African, with much heavier percussion and denser, more complex rhythmic textures. In the 1940s uptown Manhattan would be home to the mambo and **cubop**, the first sustained experiment in Latin jazz. Both represented the second stage of development of Latin music in the United States.

The Mambo: An American Afro-Cuban Music.
The **mambo** was the third of the twentieth-century Latin dance fads but the first to develop on American soil. It merged authentic Afro-Cuban *son,* as performed in New York by musicians like Arsenio Rodriguez, with big-band horns and riffs. The style was born in 1940, when Machito (Frank Grillo), New York's first important *sonero* (lead singer in a *son* band), formed his own band, Machito's Afro-Cubans, and hired fellow Cuban Mario Bauza as musical director. Bauza had worked in the African American swing bands of Cab Calloway and Chick Webb and wanted to combine Cuban rhythms with the horn sound of swing. Their new style provided an uptown alternative to the commercial Cugat sound.

By the late 1940s, the mambo had begun to attract notice outside of uptown New York. Downtown ballrooms like New York's Palladium Dance Hall served as venues for this new dance fad. The mambo caught on with the non-Latin audience, first as dance music, then as popular song. Top singing stars occasionally dabbled in it. Both Perry Como and Nat "King" Cole recorded a song called "Papa Loves Mambo"; it was a million-seller for Como in 1954. The mambo fad was not limited to pop music, however. Rhythm-and-blues bands of the

1950s typically included a few mambo tunes in their repertoires and created the most important point of entry for Latin influence on rock-era music.

The dilution of the mambo as it entered the mainstream paralleled the watering down of the rumba in the early 1930s or, for that matter, almost any outsider style in the first half of the century. What differentiated the fate of the mambo from the rumba was the presence of a stable, enthusiastic U.S. audience for Afro-Cuban-inspired music. In the 1930s the audience for authentic Cuban music had been too small to support expatriate Cuban musicians who, to attain any commercial success, modified Latin music to fit popular taste. Twenty years later that audience had grown large enough to support the undiluted Afro-Cuban sounds of the mambo.

The presence of two "mambo kings" in the 1950s brings to light the deep division between commercial and authentic Latin music. For white audiences pianist/bandleader Perez Prado was king. His recordings, many of them called simply Mambo No. 1, 2, and so on, offered the commercial sound of the mambo for the masses. The extent of his entry into the mainstream market can be gauged by the success of his biggest hit, "Cherry Pink and Apple Blossom White," which topped the pop charts in early 1955 for ten weeks. But his style often had little to do with authentic Afro-Cuban music. In many of his recordings, Afro-Cuban rhythms and instrumentation are severely diluted or completely absent.

Tito Puente performing at a Hispanic gala in Miami, 1996. Note the expanded timbales setup: several drums, all about the same size as a drum, plus two cowbells and a cymbal.

For Latins the "king of the mambo" was Tito Puente. Born in New York of Puerto Rican parents, Puente was an alumnus of Machito's band, in which he played timbales. By the early 1950s, he had formed his own band, for which he also composed and arranged. His style, with its heavy brass and full Cuban rhythm section, appealed much more strongly to Latin audiences than Prado's music did.

"Complicacion," recorded in 1958 by Tito Puente, shows a successful blend of American and Afro-Cuban elements. The instrumental accompaniment mixes big-band-style horns (brass and saxes playing riffs and sustained chords) with a full Latin percussion section.

 2:15

"Complicacion," Francisco Aguabella (1958). Tito Puente and His Band.

Particularly in the second section, it is possible to hear key elements of Afro-Cuban rhythm. The repeated riff conforms to the clave rhythm, and several layers of percussion produce a dense texture with considerable rhythmic conflict. The bass plays the offbeat *tumbao* pattern, while the piano plays an active pattern, called a *montuno*, that recalls ragtime figurations but is even more syncopated. There is little stylistic difference between this and the salsa of twenty years later.

Like country music, the Afro-Cuban mambo exemplified here by Tito Puente was a regional music; in this instance the region was a slice of Manhattan and the Bronx. Also like country music, the mambo was gaining a national presence in the years after World War II (most popularly in diluted forms), and it would play a significant, but not primary, role in shaping rock.

"COMPLICACION" (MAMBO)

Rhythm	*Fast-moving rhythms in percussion parts. No instrument consistently marking the beat. Lots of syncopation: in percussion, vocal lines, tumbao and montuno patterns, and horn riffs. Clave rhythm evident in vocal chorus.*
Melody	*A series of short riffs, usually repeated, in the instrument and group vocal lines. Solo vocal part has longer phrases.*
Instrumentation (timbre)	*Big-band horn section (full trumpet and sax sections) plus piano, bass, and full Afro-Cuban percussion section:* **conga drums**, *claves,* **cowbell**, *and timbales, among others.*
Performance style	*Group vocal has a rough sound; solo vocal a somewhat strained sound. Trumpet and sax sounds also have a rough edge.*
Dynamics	*Loud all the way through.*
Harmony	*Two chords, for the most part: I and V.*
Texture	*Thick, with several layers: lots of rhythmic activity in percussion parts, plus chords in horns.*
Form	*Multisectional form with two similar choruslike sections.*

Key Points

Mambo	*Afro-Cuban rhythm (full percussion section and complex rhythms) plus big-band swing (horn sections playing riffs).*
Clave rhythm	*Hear it clearly at 0:28—* **Yo la que**-ri-**a** (**x**) *(bold syllables = clave rhythm).*
Rhythmic floating	*Piano and bass often play against time rather than marking the beat; other instruments play fast patterns.*
Inspiracion	**Inspiracion** = *Latin jamming; big band jazz = horn soloists; mambo = percussion solos.*

Terms to Know

clave rhythm	*inspiracion*	timbales
conga drums	mambo	*tumbao*
cowbell	*montuno*	

LISTENING GUIDE: "COMPLICACION"

CD 2:15　　**Mambo** (Francisco Aguabella; performed by Tito Puente and His Band)

0:00	Introduction. Big band brass riffs over Latin rhythm.
0:14	1st verse
	Yo no quiero complicacion . . .
0:28	Chorus
	The rhythm of this phrase lines up with the clave rhythm.
	Yo la queria . . .
0:37	2nd verse
	Solo singer. Notice the sustained sax chords underneath the vocal.
0:51	Instrumental interlude. Brass and sax riffs.
1:12	Chorus
	Yo la queria . . .

The other Cuban-inspired dance fad in the 1950s was the **cha-cha-cha**. It became popular among white Cubans in the 1950s, and its popularity quickly spread to the United States. Both the rhythm and the dance step of the cha-cha-cha were simpler than the mambo, and its tempo was slower. As a result, it replaced the mambo as the Latin dance of choice in the United States.

Latin Music and Jazz. The impact of Latin music on jazz dates from the time of its origins. Jelly Roll Morton, the self-styled inventor of jazz and one of its early greats, claimed that it was a "Spanish tinge" that differentiated jazz from ragtime. The presence of a "Spanish tinge" in early jazz is not surprising because New Orleans had Spanish settlers and more contact with the Caribbean islands than did any other American city during the nineteenth and early twentieth centuries.

Latin sounds and rhythms surfaced again in the swing era. For example, Duke Ellington made extensive use of Latin rhythms and percussion in compositions like "Caravan." When **bop** jazz musician Dizzy Gillespie formed a big band in the late 1940s, he hired Chano Pozo, a Latin percussionist. This sparked the development of cubop, a true Latin jazz style. At about the same time, Stan Kenton, who composed for and directed an innovative postwar big band, also incorporated Latin rhythms and instruments into extended jazz compositions.

Throughout the 1950s Latin-influenced jazz maintained a consistent if modest presence. Gillespie continued to experiment with Latin/jazz fusions, as did the popular British jazz pianist George Shearing. In the early fifties, Shearing formed a combo that included three Latin percussionists as well as vibraphonist Cal Tjader. Cuban Mongo Santamaria, who played conga with Shearing, would play an important role in bringing jazz, rock, and Latin music together in the sixties. Other prominent jazz musicians, among them Sonny Rollins, Clifford Brown, and Horace Silver, also explored Latin-influenced rhythms.

The Latin/jazz fusions of the 1940s and '50s mixed jazz with Afro-Cuban elements. The sixties would usher in another major Latin/jazz fusion by way of Brazil. The fusion began with the bossa nova fad of the early sixties but soon encompassed the rhythmically richer samba as well. This fusion would not simply provide an alternative to straight-ahead jazz; it would play a major role in creating the new jazz style of the seventies and eighties.

1:22	3rd verse
	Solo singer.
1:35	2nd chorus
	This chorus is a variant of the first chorus, different mainly because of the words. Notice tumbao bass and piano montuno.
	Yo no quiero complicacion . . .
1:58	Inspiracion. Repeated riff over two chords: percussionists jam over sax and brass riffs.
2:21	2nd chorus
	Afro-Cuban section.
	Yo no quiero complicacion . . .
2:43	Two chords: riff based on chorus. With vocal, a series of similar riffs.

THE THIRD STAGE: LATIN AND CARIBBEAN MUSIC IN THE ROCK ERA

On New Year's Day 1959, Fulgencio Batista y Zaldívar, Cuba's corrupt dictator for most of the forties and fifties, fled to the Dominican Republic. A week later Fidel Castro, leader of Cuba's revolution, arrived in Havana and assumed power. The violent transfer of authority marked the end of the cozy relationship among Cuba, the United States, and organized crime. Soon the two countries severed all political connections, and they remain at odds to this day.

For Latin musicians in New York, the Cuban revolution would sever the link between Afro-Cuban music and its roots. The steady flow of ideas, sounds, and musicians from Cuba abruptly stopped. But by 1959 Afro-Cuban music in the United States rested firmly in musical identities that blended Cuban and American musical influences (as we heard in Tito Puente's "Complicacion"). Even as musical contact between Cuban and American-based musicians abruptly stopped, musical exchanges between the United States and countries in the Caribbean and Latin America increased dramatically.

The first significant import came from the island of Trinidad in the Caribbean. Harry Belafonte launched a **calypso** craze in 1956 with an enormously successful album that included authentic calypso songs like "Banana Boat (Day-O)." At about the same time, Jamaican sound-system operators flew to the United States to buy the newest rhythm-and-blues releases to play back home as they drove around in their speaker-equipped trucks. Much farther south, Brazilian musicians were falling in love with American jazz and incorporating its harmonies into their songs. In 1959 the world heard the fruits of their labor. *Black Orpheus,* a film that retold the Orpheus legend in Rio de Janeiro during Carnaval (the Brazilian Mardi Gras), won first prize at the Cannes Film Festival. The soundtrack for the film introduced bossa nova, a new Brazilian style, to new audiences in both Europe and North America.

Herb Alpert and the Tijuana Brass gave Mexican **mariachi** music a slick makeover in the mid-sixties. At about the same time, Tejano, a Tex-Mex country music, was building a strong regional base, even as it continued to absorb outside influences. The 1960s also saw the rapid evolution of a new Jamaican music: first ska, then rock steady, and, by the end of the decade, reggae.

The stronger presence of Latin and Caribbean music in the United States grew out of several related factors. National musical styles flourished as expressions of emerging national identities. For example, both Jamaica and Trinidad-Tobago gained political independence in 1962. Improvements in technology, especially in tape recorders, made it easier to produce recordings and made them more accessible over the air. Immigration, especially from Mexico and the Spanish Caribbean, broadened American audiences for Latin music. Television and radio shrank the world, and Americans could not help but become more aware of other cultures.

Americans also became more sympathetic. One of the consequences of the civil rights movement was a greater sensitivity to minorities and minority issues (the Chicano rights movement, for example, in the 1970s). More specific, rock's international presence and openness to new sounds made listeners more receptive to music outside the mainstream. In the discussion that follows, we sample several Latin and Caribbean styles, including an expatriate Cuban music. We begin with bossa nova.

Music from Brazil

For American audiences, Brazilian music has meant almost exclusively music from just one part of Brazil: the southern part, especially Rio de Janeiro. Rio is home to the samba and the bossa nova (Ipanema is a famous beach in Rio). This is particularly evident at Carnaval, Rio's

João Gilberto and Stan Getz. This performance was at the Rainbow Grill in New York's Rockefeller Center in the early seventies, well after the release of their landmark album.

last big splurge before Lent. It is a huge street party that culminates in a massive parade. **Samba** schools, each featuring hundreds of musicians, many of them percussionists, work almost the entire year preparing for the parade.

Most Americans first encountered samba rhythms in the films of Carmen Miranda (1909–1955). For moviegoers in the 1940s, Miranda *was* Brazilian music. Born in Lisbon, Portugal, she grew up in Brazil and came to the United States in 1939. Her Hollywood debut came in *Down Argentine Way* (1940), in which she appears as a high-class nightclub performer. In the film she sings "Bambu-Bambu," a traditional samba performed as it might have been heard in a Rio café. But the samba did not get Americanized during the 1940s. Its busy rhythms were so different from the sweet and swing rhythms of the time that American musicians did not assimilate them into mainstream music. Samba, like swing, was a rhythmically infectious music. But whereas swing drove dancers with its strong, bass-anchored beat and syncopations, samba rhythms caressed them with subtle rhythms that sped along. An even subtler Brazilian style would evolve before samba would merge with American musical styles.

Bossa Nova and Its Impact. *Bossa nova* is Brazilian slang for something new and different. The music emerged in Rio de Janeiro during the late fifties as a sophisticated alternative to samba, the dominant music in southern Brazil for decades. A small nucleus of musicians, notably songwriters Antonio Carlos Jobim (1925–1994), Luis Bonfa, singer/guitarist João Gilberto (b. 1931), and songwriter-guitarist Baden Powell, fell in love with American jazz, especially jazz-influenced pop singing and West Coast–based cool jazz. They blended the harmonic sophis-

CD 2:16 **Bossa Nova** (Antonio Carlos Jobim; performed by João Gilberto, guitar; Stan Getz, tenor saxophone; Jobim, piano; and Astrud Gilberto, vocal)

0:00		Vocal introduction. Notice the almost total syncopation of the guitar chords.
0:07	A	Just voice and guitar. João Gilberto sings the lyric in Portuguese.
0:22	A	Rhythm section enters. Note the rhythmic relationship between drums and bass: the drums keep a steady rhythm four times as fast as the bass.
0:37	B	Bridge. Notice the shift to longer phrases, which shift surprisingly. The bridge is twice the length of the A section.
1:06	A	As before.
1:21	A	The vocalist is Astrud Gilberto, the wife of João Gilberto at the time.

Tall and tan...

A

When she walks...

B

Oh, but I watch her...

A

Tall and tan...

2:34	Saxophone solo by Stan Getz. Complete statement of the melody (AABA).
3:47	Piano solo by Jobim, the first two A sections. Note the rich harmonies under the melody.
4:17	Astrud Gilberto sings the bridge and the last A section, with an obbligato line from Getz.
4:59	Gradual fade-out.

CD 2:16

"The Girl from Ipanema," Antonio Carlos Jobim (1963). João Gilberto, guitar; Stan Getz, tenor saxophone; Jobim, piano; Astrud Gilberto, vocal.

tication and cool of West Coast jazz with the rhythms of Brazil to produce this new style. The **bossa nova** craze peaked in the midsixties with authentic music by Jobim and Gilberto, Sergio Mendes' Brazilian crossover music, and the inevitable travesties, such as "Blame It on the Bossa Nova."

The landmark bossa nova recording appeared in 1963; it was a collaboration between singer/guitarist João Gilberto and jazz saxophonist Stan Getz. The signature track was "The Girl from Ipanema," which charted as a single the following year. The recording featured not only Getz and João Gilberto, but also Astrud Gilberto, his wife at the time, singing an English translation of the lyric. The opening of the song contains two keys to the style and the sound of bossa nova: João Gilberto's cool, flat, low-pitched voice and the complex off-beat rhythms of the guitar chords. Bass and drums flesh out the rhythmic texture, with bass on every slow beat and drums marking a steady rhythm four times as fast as the bass. Jobim plays the occasional fill on piano and takes a brief solo toward the end.

Jobim's song takes its form from a pop model. It has the AABA form heard in so many pop songs of the twenties, thirties, and forties. The first phrase of the melody is deceptively simple: a simple riff that gently slides down over smoothly shifting chords. The bridge is more complex: bold harmonies support a sinuous melody. Jobim's songs favored both subtly shifting melodies and exotic, jazz-derived harmonies that were an ideal complement to the subtle rhythm of the guitar and Gilberto's low-key, almost monotonic singing. This song offers an especially accessible example. Getz's playing is straightforward and lyrical; his sound has the restrained quality and smooth edge that the Brazilians admired so much. His contribution underscores the affinity between jazz and bossa nova.

"THE GIRL FROM IPANEMA" (BOSSA NOVA)

Rhythm	*Moderately slow tempo. Bass and drums establish a slow **16-beat rhythm**. Highly syncopated guitar chords conflict with this rhythm. Both Gilbertos anticipate the beat, which adds more rhythmic conflict.*
Melody	*The A section spins out from three notes repeated several times. The B section repeats a long, winding phrase three times before closing with a new idea.*
Instrumentation (timbre)	*Voices, acoustic guitar, saxophone, piano, bass, and drums.*
Performance style	*Both Gilbertos, but especially João, sing with flat, uninflected voices.*
Dynamics	*Soft, for the most part.*
Harmony	*Rich chords shift underneath the repetitive melody; far removed from I-IV-V in the bridge.*
Texture	*Distinct layers: voice, guitar, bass, drums, and the occasional obbligato. Syncopation of the guitar part makes it more interesting than a typical chordal accompaniment.*
Form	*Four choruses of a long **AABA** song.*

Key Points

Bossa nova and jazz	*Jazz, especially jazz harmonies, influenced Jobim and Gilberto.*
Cool Latin music	*Hot Latin music is loud, fast, dense, and busy; bossa nova is slower, softer, and leaner.*
Samba, bossa nova, and American acceptance	*Carmen Miranda was an exotic; bossa nova fit better with rock-era music.*
Brazilian music and 16-beat rhythms	*The first 16-beat rhythms popular in the United States; a "lite" alternative to rock rhythm.*

Terms to Know

16-beat rhythm	bossa nova
AABA form	samba

The bossa nova fad lasted only a few years, but its impact touched American music in several important ways. Most obvious was the continuing presence of Brazilian musicians. Sergio Mendes and Brazil '66 had a strong following for more than a decade; their biggest successes were Latin-tinged versions of pop hits. Bossa nova rhythms became the pop alternative to rock rhythm; Dusty Springfield's version of Bacharach's "The Look of Love" is one example. And jazz easily absorbed Brazilian rhythms.

Summary. Bossa nova and samba are close musical relatives: bossa nova is, in effect, an offshoot of samba style, but they send quite different musical messages. Bossa nova is melodic popular song flavored with jazz harmonies and samba-inspired rhythms. Sambas can also have beautiful melodies, and many do, but the greater emphasis is on rhythm. With its long history, its African roots, its central place in an Afro-centric culture, and its range of expression, samba plays a role in Brazilian culture that is comparable to the blues in American life. They are quite different musical styles, of course, but they occupy similar places in their respective cultures.

Hispanic Music: Tango, Salsa, and Tejano

Most people living south of the United States are Hispanic. From Mexico and Cuba to the southern tip of Argentina, one hears Spanish more than any other language. Increasingly, one also hears Spanish within the United States. As of the 2000 U.S. census, Hispanics replaced African Americans as America's largest minority population. Especially in some parts of the United States, Hispanics are a significant presence: New Mexico is 42% Latino; East Los Angeles is 97% Hispanic; Mexicans make up the majority of San Antonio's population—about 55%; there are twice as many Puerto Ricans living in New York as there are in San Juan, Puerto Rico's largest city; and Miami has a Cuban population of almost 900,000, larger than the population of any Cuban city other than Havana.

Musical life in the Hispanic part of Latin America has reflected the varied cultures in which it has developed. We consider relatively recent expressions of three traditions with a long history in the United States: the Argentine tango, salsa, and Tejano music.

The Argentine Tango in the United States. The **tango** is a dance from Argentina and the music for that dance—the first of the Latin dance crazes in the United States. Its home is Buenos Aires, much as New Orleans is home to jazz. Both jazz and the tango began as dance music in low-life environments—brothels, bars, and the like—but grew in status and sophistication during the course of the twentieth century. And both are considered the "signature" music of their home countries; the tango is as strongly identified with Argentina as jazz is with the United States—and for an even longer time.

The tango dates back to late-nineteenth-century Cuba and its African-influenced habanera. Musical evidence suggests that the habanera went south to Argentina, where it became the rhythmic basis of the tango. It arrived in America in 1913 from Argentina by way of Paris, where Irene and Vernon Castle had captivated audiences with their dancing of the tango. Upon their return to the United States, they introduced it in a Broadway show, *The Sunshine Girl*, where it was an immediate success. Tin Pan Alley songwriters featured occasional tangos in Broadway shows until well into the 1950s. Richard Alder and Jerry Ross's 1954 musical *The Pajama Game* features the tango "Hernando's Hideaway." It occasionally also filtered into popular songs: W. C. Handy's "St. Louis Blues" (1914), the most recorded song of the first half century, sandwiches a tango/habanera middle section between two blues sections.

Although it never approached the popularity of the fox trot—compared with other social dances of the early twentieth century, the tango is elaborate and exhibitionistic—the tango became the first Latin dance to achieve a permanent place in American popular music. In its authentic form, the dance movements are violent and erotic, reflecting the tango's origins.

The first tango bands were small, typically violin, guitar, and flute; but as the dance gained favor, in Argentina and elsewhere, these small groups grew in size. They added more strings and the **bandoneón,** an accordion imported from Germany. The bandoneón would become the sound most identified with the tango.

In the 1950s the tango went through a revolution led by Astor Piazzolla (1921–1992). Piazzolla was born in Argentina but grew up in New York City. At thirteen he heard authentic tangos for the first time when Carlos Gardel, the leading performer of tango-based songs, appeared in New York. The experience sparked a love affair between Piazzolla and the tango. As a composer, however, Piazzolla chafed at the restrictions of tango style and explored jazz and contemporary classical composition. In 1954 he went to Paris to study with Nadia Boulanger, who had coached so many young classical composers, including Americans Aaron

CD 2:17   **Tango** (Astor Piazzolla; performed by Piazzolla, bandoneón)

0:00	A	1st phrase.
0:23	A^1	1st phrase, developed. The essential tango rhythm continues in the bass throughout "Oblivion."
0:47	A^2	Climax of the 1st phrase.
1:10	B	Orchestral strings play the melody, supported by close harmony.
1:33	B	Repeated with bandoneón.
1:58	A	1st phrase, with slightly different version of the melody.
2:21	A^1	Developed as before, with Piazzolla's slight changes.
2:46	A^2	Climax of the phrase.
3:06	Tag.	

Copland and Elliott Carter. She assured him that his music spoke most powerfully and personally through the tango. With that, Piazzolla returned to Argentina and began creating what he called **tango nuevo**, or new tango.

From the 1960s on, Piazzolla stretched the boundaries of the tango, not by merging it with contemporary popular styles but by moving it closer to concert music. His reputation grew, first in Argentina, then throughout the world. Toward the end of his life, he enjoyed an international following, with successful and acclaimed appearances in the United States during the 1980s. We hear the results of Piazzolla's revolution in "Oblivion," a beautiful tango from his last years.

The setting, mainly a sumptuous string orchestra underpinned by a plucked string bass, supports Piazzolla himself playing bandoneón. The bass plays the fundamental rhythm of the tango throughout, while Piazzolla weaves his melancholy melody over the cushion of sound from the strings.

In this recording we can hear how the tango became such an expressive music in Piazzolla's hands—figuratively and literally. The bass part is the rhythmic link to the tango; it remains as constant as a heartbeat—the pulse of the music. Piazzolla's melody is made up of short melodic fragments daisy-chained together by sustained notes into a single long phrase. The descent of the melody helps project a mood of seemingly bottomless despair. (In this respect we hear its kinship to the blues.) There are no words, but the mood is unmistakable.

The most personal expression of this mood is found in Piazzolla's playing. He plays the melody with such freedom—darting ahead, laying back, changing articulation and dynamics in a flash—that it sounds spontaneous. Because he can sustain notes on the bandoneón, his performance has a vocal-like quality that is reminiscent of the expressive devices of the best blues and jazz musicians.

"Oblivion," Astor Piazzolla (1984). Piazzolla, bandoneón.

STYLE PROFILE

"OBLIVION" (TANGO)

Rhythm	*Slow (below dance tempo). Still, tango rhythm (heard in the bass) underpins everything:* DUM ... da dum dum. *Melody alternates long notes with faster-moving rhythms. Piazzolla's playing avoids regular division of the beat: an expressive device.*

STYLE PROFILE *(cont'd)*

Melody	*Melodies of both the A and the B sections grow out of the opening idea: a long note followed by faster-moving notes. Both make extensive use of **sequence**—repeating a melodic idea at a higher or lower pitch.*
Instrumentation (timbre)	*Bandoneón (an accordion of German invention popular in Argentina), string orchestra, bells, and double bass.*
Performance style	*Piazzolla dances around the beat—anticipating, lagging behind—when he plays by himself. He extracts a great variety of sounds from his instrument.*
Dynamics	*Soft throughout.*
Harmony	*Based on I-IV-V, but a very rich harmonic palette.*
Texture	*Melody plus lush accompaniment: countermelody in strings under bandoneón.*
Form	*ABA, with three different but related phrases in the A section.*

Key Points

Tango rhythm	*The basic tango rhythm:* DUM ... da dum dum.
Sad melody	*Like many blues, phrases begin high and slowly descend.*
Piazzolla: composer and performer	*Piazzolla composed the melody but plays it more freely than he composed it.*
Between classical and popular	*Accordion and symphonic strings: pop-song form with classical dimensions.*

Terms to Know

bandoneón

sequence

tango

Perhaps it is because the tango owes more to Europe than to Africa. Perhaps it is because Buenos Aires is farther away from the United States than any other major city in the New World. Perhaps it is because so few Argentineans have emigrated to the States. Perhaps it is because the sensibility of the tango—what it depicts and how it depicts it—is foreign to American culture. Whatever the reason(s), the tango has remained an exotic sound throughout the century, despite its long history in the United States—longer than any other Latin dance. In the music of Piazzolla and others, however, it is also a beautiful sound, one cherished by many American listeners.

Salsa. Salsa (Spanish for "sauce") is a Latin musical style of American origin. It has been the dominant Latin style since the early 1970s. Its parent style, the mambo of the late 1940s and '50s in New York, was already a music of two worlds, with roots in both Afro-Cuban music and big-band swing. Fundamentally a "return to roots" movement, salsa successfully reinvigorated the uptown mambo style that went out of favor during the ascendancy of rock. Salsa updated this fifties sound mainly by assimilating elements of other styles, both Latin (Puerto Rican music, for example) and American (jazz and R&B). Nevertheless, according to accounts by both older and younger musicians, salsa retained its Cuban core, even though few of the musicians were Cuban or of Cuban descent. Essentially, salsa has become a Cuban-derived style nurtured on foreign soil and thereby transformed.

The purest form of salsa, that is, the sound and style closest to the music's Afro-Cuban roots (such as "Ojos," recorded in 1978 by trombonist Willie Colón and vocalist Ruben

Blades) had a limited audience, mainly Latinos and a small minority of non-Latinos drawn to the music. By the time of this recording, however, *salsa* had also acquired a more generic connotation: it referred to music with a Latin flavor, but not Afro-Cuban in the most important respects. For example, "Salsation," one of the songs on the *Saturday Night Fever* soundtrack, has a Latin sound because of the brass riffs, the Latinesque rhythm, and the Latin percussion, but its rhythmic foundation owes more to disco than to Afro-Cuban music. This gave the song more crossover appeal but diluted its essence.

Like so many other outsider styles—jazz, country, blues—salsa has wrestled with the conflict between artistic freedom and commercial success. As in these other styles, there are artists in both camps. Musicians like Colón, vocalist Celia Cruz (the "queen of salsa" until her passing in 2003), and pianist/bandleader Eddie Palmieri have remained true to the Afro-Cuban roots of salsa even as they absorb other influences. Palmieri has been especially bold in his exploration of new possibilities and has enjoyed the acclaim of both critics and aficionados.

Commercial success usually means blending the outside with pop, and that is certainly what has happened in Latin music. Currently, Latin music is more popular than it has ever been. The Latin Grammys began in 2000; Gloria Estefan and Miami Sound Machine have been going strong for almost two decades; Ricky Martin is one of this decade's male heart-throbs, and even pop diva Christina Aguilera rerecorded in Spanish several of her hits to acknowledge her Latin heritage. Still, most of this pop Latin music owes more to Michael Jackson and Madonna than it does to mambo.

The neo-traditional salsa in "Ojos" remains the most distinctive sound in Latin music. Its flowing, floating rhythms and percussive interplay—as in the music of contemporary Latin stars like La India—set it apart from more pop-oriented Latin music and Latin-tinged jazz. And, like contemporary blues that moved from Mississippi to Chicago, salsa has flourished after moving from Havana to its new home in New York. Both remain a window into the soul of important musical cultures.

Tejano Music. Tejano music is salsa's country cousin. Whereas salsa's home is densely populated New York, the home of Tejano music is South Texas, with its wide-open spaces. A *Tejano* is a male Texan of Mexican descent; it is also the name for the music that Tejanos developed. **Tejano** music blends Mexican music with outside influences—at first local but more recently wide-ranging.

The country connection is more than a matter of geography; Tejano music closely parallels American country music. Like early country music, and very much *unlike* Cuban music, early Tejano music seldom featured percussion, drums, or their complex rhythms. The closest American parallel to much prerock Tejano music was the cowboy song, such as Gene Autry's "South of the Border." The most obvious differences were the language and the instruments.

The two most characteristic instrumental sounds of early Tejano music were the accordion and the *bajo sexto*. The **bajo sexto** is an oversized Mexican twelve-string guitar that typically served as a bass instrument in small groups (or **conjuntos**). (In recent Tejano music, it more often serves as an extra rhythm instrument.) The accordion, like the bandoneón played by Piazzolla, has its roots in central Europe. Its use in Tejano music tells us something about immigration patterns in Texas.

Mexicans are the most visible ethnic group in Texas, in part because so many have retained their language and much of their culture. People of German descent are a less widely acknowledged but still significant ethnic group; today, people of German descent compose about one-sixth of Texas's population. From about 1830 through the end of the nineteenth century, a steady stream of German immigrants settled in Texas. They created enclaves and established towns—New Braunfels, for example—across south central and southeast Texas. Even today, there are still a few parts of Texas where German (that is, Texas German) is still spoken in everyday language.

The Germans who settled in Texas ranged from farmers (the majority) to middle-class business- and craftspeople to a few professionals. They were drawn by the promise of cheap land and the chance to escape the political upheavals of nineteenth-century Germany. Upon arrival, to the extent that they could, they re-created the lifestyle they had enjoyed in their homeland. This included such German staples as beer (Texas Germans founded the breweries that make Pearl and Shiner, two popular Texas beers) and polkas, a popular dance in central Europe. Polka bands, then as now, included an accordion, an instrument that developed in German-speaking Europe during the middle of the nineteenth century.

Instruments tend to travel from one culture to the next: the steel guitar's path from Hawaii to Nashville via vaudeville is a spectacular example. So it is not surprising that the accordion found a home among Spanish-speaking Texans from Mexico.

In the early years, the accordion was the key instrument in Tejano music. It went out of favor in the 1960s and '70s, as Tejano began to incorporate contemporary influences, especially country, rock, and disco. The music of Little Joe y La Familia, one of the leading Tejano bands of the sixties and seventies, typified this approach: their music includes a full and modern rhythm section, a full horn section, and, at times, rhythms from other kinds of music. But by the midseventies, Tejano music also experienced a "return to roots" movement.

Flaco Jiménez. Accordionist Flaco Jiménez (b. 1939) is typical of this more recent generation of Tejano musicians. He is the son, and student, of Santiago Jiménez Sr., one of the pioneers of Tejano music (who learned accordion from his father, who learned it from a German immigrant). As a young man, Flaco mastered the traditional Tejano accordion style. His musical curiosity led him to explore other styles, and he was discovered by Ry Cooder, a fine rock guitarist with a deep interest in traditional music of many cultures. Jiménez and Cooder first recorded together in 1976. Since that time he has recorded with a host of pop music stars, including country singer Dwight Yoakum, Linda Ronstadt, and even the Rolling Stones. He has also recorded more traditional Tejano music. Over the years his stature as a musician and a representative of Tejano culture has grown steadily. Currently, he is the "squeeze-box king," the most renowned Tejano accordionist and the best-known ambassador for his music.

As Jiménez's career attests, both traditional and more-modern Tejano styles have coexisted, often side by side, for the last quarter century. We hear a recent example with a traditional orientation: a fun-loving party song that updates the sound of a Tejano-style polka with two contemporary instruments: electric guitar and electric bass. The lyrics repeat the same message in three languages: Spanish, English, and Dutch.

STYLE PROFILE

TEJANO MUSIC

Rhythm	*Moderate tempo. Steady* OOM-pah *rhythm throughout.*
Melody	*Vocal phrases are short and simple. Accordion passages feature lively running patterns.*
Instrumentation (timbre)	*Two singers in close harmony, accordion, electric guitar, electric bass,* bajo sexto, *and drums.*
Performance style	*Full, plain vocal style in both parts.*
Dynamics	*Moderate.*

Harmony	Mostly I-IV-V, with a few other chords interpolated once in a while.
Texture	Harmonized melody with simple accompaniment; bajo sexto provides occasional counterpoint.
Form	Several choruses, with instrumental interludes.

Key Points

Sound of the accordion	The most distinctive sound in Tejano music.
Mexican close harmony	Whether it's vocals or a pair of trumpets in a mariachi band, close harmonization of the melody is a sound associated with Mexican music.
Polka	The OOM-pah rhythm, accordion, short melodic phrases, and simple harmony —all connect this song to the polka.
Party music	This is Tejano-style party music: a good-time song with a tongue-in-cheek lyric.

Terms to Know

accordion

bajo sexto

Tejano

LISTENING GUIDE: "EN EL CIELO NO HAY CERVEZA" ("IN HEAVEN THERE IS NO BEER")

CD 2:18   **Tejano Music** (Jose Morante; performed by Flaco Jiménez, accordion and lead vocal)

0:00	Introduction. This turns out to be an instrumental version of the chorus.
0:16	1st chorus (in Spanish)
	En el cielo no hay cerveza que beber
	Por eso ando tomando noche y día
	Porque ya cuando se me llegue el día
	En el mundo seguir la ferrusquilla
0:32	Interlude: active accordion figuration.
0:39	2nd chorus
	In heaven there is no beer
	That's why we drink it here
	And when we're gone from here
	All my friends will be drinking all the beer
0:57	3rd chorus (instrumental)
	Begins like the introduction, then proceeds as a variation on the melody.
1:12	4th chorus
	The beer lament, this time in Dutch.
1:29	Interlude: still more accordion.
1:30	5th chorus
	Once again in Spanish.
1:50	Interlude: accordion featured, plus nice *bajo sexto* countermelody.
1:58	6th chorus
	And once again in English.
2:15	7th chorus
	Instrumental, with a decisive ending.

Summary. Like country music (its Anglo counterpart), Tejano music is not one style but several. There are the traditional waltz songs, polkas, and fox trots and the traditional instruments—*bajo sexto* and accordion; both reflect the mixed heritage of the music. There are outside influences, coming from both Anglo and Hispanic sources. These can mix in varying proportions, as our single example can only begin to suggest. Tejano music carries a strong sense of regional identity associated with Texas (and by extension the entire border area between Mexico and the United States). And, like country music at midcentury, it is just beginning to find a broader audience. As the Hispanic population increases (and as schools place more emphasis on bilingual education), Tejano music may well find an audience among those seeking country music–type values but in Spanish.

LOOKING BACK, LOOKING AHEAD

In 1909 Scott Joplin published his one Latin-flavored piece, "Solace," which he subtitled, "A Mexican Serenade." The third strain became familiar to a new generation of listeners in 1973, when it was incorporated into the soundtrack for the film *The Sting.* Joplin's "Mexican" sound was actually an adaptation of the tango rhythm. It was far from the first instance of a "Spanish tinge" in American popular music; the tango rhythm and habanera syncopation appear occasionally in popular songs and dance music of the 1890s and 1900s.

Joplin's still-familiar serenade and its unique place in his output imply a good deal about the state of Latin music in the United States at the turn of the twentieth century. The Latin influence is barely evident—there are no percussion instruments, and the rhythms are transparent and only lightly syncopated. "Mexican" seems to have been the all-purpose Latin label, at least for Joplin. All this suggests that Americans did not hear much Latin or Latin-influenced music around 1900, that what they heard was filtered through American composers' ears, and that most of the sounds and rhythms that we now associate with Latin music were not in the air.

That began to change in the next decade with the tango craze. The Cuban rumba, an even more popular Latin dance fad, introduced Cuban rhythms and instruments into American popular music. It led to American takes on Latin music, such as Cole Porter's "Begin the Beguine," and to new American-influenced Latin styles, most notably the mambo. Especially after World War II, these new Latin sounds gained greater prominence, in both commercial and Afro-Cuban versions, and insinuated themselves into popular music, especially rhythm and blues. Also during the 1940s, Carmen Miranda introduced an authentic upscale Brazilian music to Americans. Her café-style sambas were exotic, even as Cuban-influenced music took on more Americanized forms.

With the emergence of rock and new rhythm-and-blues styles, Latin instruments and rhythms were subtly woven into the fabric of popular music. At the same time, music imported from Latin America—bossa novas and sambas from Brazil, tangos from Argentina, and mariachi music from Mexico—has found receptive American audiences. So did regional fusions, most notably Tejano music in Texas and salsa in New York. At the turn of the twenty-first century, Latin music was a significant segment of the popular music industry; it had even acquired its own Grammy awards ceremony. Its influence is pervasive: from the barely noticed conga drums heard in so much contemporary pop to the use of 16-beat rhythms, it has helped shape the popular music of the past fifty years while preserving Latin styles and forging new Latin/American hybrids, as we discover in the next several chapters.

TERMS TO KNOW

Test your knowledge of this chapter's important terms by defining the following. If you can't recall the meaning of a certain term, refresh your memory by looking up the boldfaced term in the chapter, turning to the Glossary at the back of the book, or working with the flashcards on the *Popular Music in America* Companion Web site: *http://music.wadsworth.com/campbell_2e*

. . . .

16-beat rhythm	conga drums	patting juba
AABA form	*conjunto*	reverse clave rhythm
accordion	cowbell	rumba
Afro-Cuban	cubop	salsa
bajo sexto	downtown Latin style	samba
bandoneón	habanera	sequence
beguine	hambone rhythm	*son*
Bo Diddley beat	*inspiracion*	*sonero*
bongos	mambo	tango
bop	maracas	tango nuevo
bossa nova	mariachi	Tejano
calypso	marimba	timbales
cha-cha-cha	*montuno*	triplets
clave rhythm	mute	*tumbao*
claves	outsider music	uptown Latin style

. . . .

Rhythm and Blues
and Rock and Roll, 1945—1960

As the 1950s began, there was only rhythm and blues (R&B). As they ended there was still only rhythm and blues, or so it seemed. In between was rock and roll's wild roller-coaster ride: starting slowly, gathering steam in mid-decade, peaking between 1956 and 1958, and then apparently dying away in the wake of death, scandal, and defection. Although rock and roll made the bigger splash, rhythm and blues also strengthened its toehold in the popular-music marketplace. This would culminate in the early sixties: *Billboard* suspended its R&B chart for more than a year, beginning in 1963, because the R&B chart and the Top 100 chart were virtually identical. In this chapter we examine the rise and fall of rock and roll and the ascendancy of rhythm and blues.

POSTWAR RHYTHM AND BLUES, 1945—1955

In 1947 Jerry Wexler graduated from Kansas State with a degree in journalism. After return-ing home to New York, he helped his father wash windows while he tried to land a job as a reporter with one of the New York papers. He failed but did manage to find a position with *Billboard,* the trade journal that charted record sales in the music industry.

By the early 1940s, the race record market had grown enough that *Billboard* began to sur-vey sales. The journal published its first **chart** in October 1942, as "Harlem Hit Parade." In 1945 *Billboard* changed the name of the chart to "Race Records." Wexler, by now at *Billboard,* coined the more musically accurate term *rhythm and blues* to identify the new music by African American artists directed at African American audiences. The term caught on, and in 1949 *Billboard* began monitoring the success of these artists on a "Rhythm and Blues" chart. The term is still in use today.

Rhythm and blues (R&B) arose out of the evolution of the music itself, significant changes in the entertainment industry, and an increase in its audience. Even as the music became more diverse, the audience for it broadened and became more affluent, technology improved, and the music industry went through a shakeup that would continue into the rock era.

The Audience. World War II mixed soldiers from all over the country. To some extent it also mixed the races. (More important culturally, it made many African Americans wonder why the country they defended abroad granted them second-class citizenship when they returned.) The common experience of the war prompted soldiers and civilians to share music. Louis Jordan's "G. I. Jive," an unadulterated rhythm-and-blues song, was a huge pop hit in 1944. The song was a prelude to the growing presence of rhythm and blues in the decade after World War II.

The postwar recovery put more money in most Americans' pockets. To a lesser extent, black Americans shared in the prosperity, but all Americans found new ways to spend. One of them was on television sets.

Television and Radio. The television industry mushroomed shortly after the war ended. In 1946 the industry was in its infancy and had sold only 6,000 television sets. Three years later there were 2 million sets. By the mid-1950s television was a household staple, and the first color sets were on the market. Television quickly took over radio's role as the primary source of all-purpose entertainment. Soap operas, situation comedies, variety shows, mysteries—all of these and more moved from radio to television.

As a result, radio redefined itself as a medium. To fill the void left by the migration of these shows to television, radio stations began programming recorded music—most prominently pop. Some stations, however, offered an alternative to the bland pop fare. It was usually scheduled at odd hours—late at night or early in the morning. Still, the alternative music was different. Disc jockeys chose the recordings that they played in the early days of recorded programming. By 1951 Alan Freed was playing rhythm and blues over WJW in Cleveland. He called himself Moondog and billed his show as *Moondog's Rock and Roll Party*.

Records and the Rise of the DJ. After World War II, the major record companies fought a format war. For decades shellac 78 rpm recordings had delivered about three minutes of popular music on 10-inch discs and about four minutes of classical music on 12-inch discs. In 1948 Columbia Records (now Sony) began issuing 33 rpm long-playing records, or LPs. These vinyl discs held more than a half hour of music and didn't break when you dropped them. The next year RCA (now BMG) introduced the 7-inch 45 rpm **single**. This disc was also vinyl and, despite its much smaller size, also held about three minutes of music.

It took a while for these new formats to catch on because they required new record players. By the midfifties, however, the new 45 rpm format had caught on. Record companies used the 45 for singles targeted at teens, who liked the convenience and the durability of the new format and had the disposable income to buy records. To an unprecedented extent, music became accessible to listeners as *sound;* rock-and-roll 45s found their way into teenage bedrooms, jukeboxes, and radio stations, where disc jockeys like Alan Freed played them for eager listeners. The record, whether bought outright or heard on the air, was becoming the primary document of a song. Increasingly, the recording was not simply a version of the song —it *was* the song. The notion of a cover version is a rock-era concept; a pop song of, say, the 1930s and '40s existed independent of any particular version of it.

Indies. The music market was there, thanks to the postwar economic boom. The way to make money was there, thanks to radio, jukeboxes, and record stores. The way to collect it was there, thanks to BMI (see "Music Licensing" in Chapter 7). All that was needed was someone to record the music.

The growth of **indie** music today, in opposition to the major recording companies, relives the rise of independent labels in the late 1940s and early '50s. The technology is different:

sophisticated, inexpensive, digital technology versus primitive tape recorders. The distribution is different: Internet and cooperative download sites versus selling records from the trunk of a car (as 1940s indie Leonard Chess did). And the music is different. Many of today's indie bands, mostly white, explore peripheral retro styles and style fusions, like ska and punk. A half century ago, legendary independent labels recorded black Americans whose sound was on the cutting edge of popular music.

What the indies of yesterday and today have in common is an entrepreneurial spirit and a desire to bring to a larger audience the music to which they are passionately devoted—and to make some money in the process. The story of Chess Records (Chapter 1) was replicated with some variation in cities around the country. Ahmet Ertegun, a Turkish immigrant living in New York, founded Atlantic Records in 1947; Jerry Wexler bought in six years later. Art Rupe's New Orleans–based Specialty Records, Lew Chudd's Imperial Records based in Los Angeles, Syd Nathan's King Records based in Cincinnati—all helped preserve and disseminate the sound of rhythm and blues (and country western). So did Sam Phillips's Sun Records. His recording studio, the only place African Americans could record in Memphis, also recorded top rockabilly acts, beginning with Elvis Presley. Starting and running an independent label was risky business. Some folded, but labels such as Chess, Imperial, and King carved a niche in the market on the strength of a few good acts. Only Ahmet Ertegun's Atlantic grew into a major label. Still, all the independent labels left later generations an impressive legacy, which we sample here.

The Sounds of Rhythm and Blues

Rhythm and blues was not one sound but several sharing some common ground. Many R&B songs had a strong beat, usually based on a four-beat, long/short **shuffle** rhythm. The songs were rich in **riffs**—in the melody, in the backup parts, and occasionally in the bass line. The differences between styles—electric blues versus doo-wop, for example, perhaps the most pronounced contrast—is a matter of emphasis: a strong blues influence in electric blues versus a strong pop influence in doo-wop. These new styles—jump bands, electric blues, doo-wop, and countless variations and combinations—emerged and evolved in the decade between 1945 and 1955. We explore some representative examples next.

Jump Bands. The end of the war brought an end to the swing era. Musically, the style had run its course. But the more significant reason for its decline was economic: less demand plus higher costs made it just about impossible to keep a big band together. Only a few survived.

One important offshoot of swing was the jump band. **Jump bands** stripped down and souped up the sound of big-band swing. They kept the rhythm section but reduced the horn sections drastically, paring down three full sections to a couple of saxophones and a trumpet. They strengthened the beat by converting the four-beat swing rhythm to a shuffle. They built songs on repeated riffs, usually over a blues or blues-based form. The songs typically took a medium tempo because shuffle rhythm put the more frenetic swing tempos out of reach. Jump bands also emphasized singing more than swing had. The vocalist was the key figure in the group, and the lyrics typically told a funny story or allowed the singer to brag a little, or both. A blend of hokum, boogie-woogie, and big-band swing, jump band music was different from all of them.

Our jump band example, "Choo Choo Ch'Boogie," was a big hit in 1946 for Louis Jordan and His Tympany Five. Louis Jordan (1908–1975) first made his mark as a saxophonist in

"Choo Choo Ch'Boogie," Louis Jordan (1946). Louis Jordan and His Tympany Five.

0:00   Introduction. Mixed horns (trumpets and saxophones) act as a single section. Riffs over blues harmonic progression.

1st Statement of the Verse/Chorus Form

0:17   1st verse
         Uses 12-bar blues progression but has six lines of text instead of three.
         Headin' for the station . . .
0:34   Chorus
         Simple harmony, but not blues form.
         Choo choo . . .

Instrumental Interlude

0:45   Piano solo, boogie-woogie style, based on 12-bar blues progression. Shuffle rhythm in the left hand.

2nd Verse/Chorus Statement

1:02   2nd verse
         You reach your destination . . .
1:19   Chorus
         Choo choo . . .

3rd Verse/Chorus Statement

1:30   Jordan's sax solo (verse and chorus). Jordan builds his solo out of a series of riffs. Background riffs by the horns.

4th Verse/Chorus Statement

1:59   3rd verse
         I'm gonna settle down . . .
2:14   Chorus
         Choo choo . . .
2:26   Tag

Chick Webb's fine swing band. He played for Webb from 1936 through 1938, then formed his own smaller group a year later. Unlike many later rhythm-and-blues artists, Jordan got a record deal with a major label, Decca, with whom he signed a contract in 1939. This undoubtedly helped build his audience.

The song is all of a piece. It begins with the pianist laying down a boogie-woogie bass while the horns play a simple riff. The first part of Jordan's vocal is a series of six short phrases, all of which rhyme, and all of which develop from a simple repeated riff. Although the words happen over a blues harmonic progression, they do not follow the standard form of the blues lyric. Instead they serve as a storytelling verse to the catchy chorus that follows. The theme, of course, is life on the railroad—certainly a common topic for songs of that era. (Note the reference to "ballin' the jack," that is, getting the train moving.) As with "Maybellene" (Chapter 1), "Choo Choo Ch'Boogie" adapts the conventional blues form to a verse/chorus pattern; the hook of the chorus provides an easy point of entry into the song.

In a jump band like Louis Jordan and His Tympany Five, the roles of the musicians are clearly defined: the bass walks; the drummer plays a shuffle beat; the guitar and/or the piano also helps keep the beat—the pianist may also play fills and solo; the saxophone honks riffs, either behind the vocalist, in response to him, or in a solo; and the other horns join the sax in creating harmonized response riffs. There is a clear hierarchy.

The tone of the lyric is humorous and self-deprecating; we sense that the "I" in the song is a happy-go-lucky kind of fellow. (The wanderer has pretty much disappeared from our twenty-first-century lives; but even a half century ago, hoboes—men who "rode the rails" from place to place (stowed away on trains), working odd jobs in exchange for food, a roof, and maybe a little cash, or simply begging—were more common. Their mystique, a holdover from the Great Depression, was still powerful.) The music—with its bouncy shuffle beat, catchy riffs (not only in the vocal parts but also in both the piano and the sax solos), and pleasant vocal style—helps capture the mood of the lyric.

This became the formula for Jordan and many of the jump bands that followed him. The appeal of these songs, to black Americans and gradually to whites as well, grew out of the easy points of entry: upbeat lyrics; repeated riffs, either sung or played on a honking saxophone; a clear beat, usually in a shuffle rhythm; and a chorus-based form.

STYLE PROFILE

"CHOO CHOO CH'BOOGIE" (JUMP BAND SONG)

Rhythm	*Fast tempo. Shuffle rhythm (an intensified four-beat rhythm), with a light backbeat. Vocal and horn parts move in tandem with the shuffle rhythm, with an occasional strong syncopation.*
Melody	*Verse is built from a long stream of notes that ends in a syncopation—almost like bebop but not as fast or aggressive. The chorus grows out of a short riff.*
Instrumentation (timbre)	*Vocal, rhythm section (piano, bass, drums—using **brushes**—and guitar), and small horn section.*
Performance style	*Relaxed vocal (good-humored) and honking saxophone (lots of inflection, an occasional rough edge to the sound).*
Dynamics	*Moderately loud; no contrast.*
Harmony	***Blues progression** in the verse; chorus = last two-thirds of a blues chorus (IV-I-V-I).*
Texture	*Melody plus background riffs and rhythmic accompaniment during vocals; instrumentals much the same, except the melody is harmonized.*
Form	*Blues-based verse/chorus form.*

Key Points

Jump band	*Essentially a streamlined swing band: a full rhythm section plus a mixed horn section—trumpet(s) and saxophones.*
Blues-based verse/chorus form	*Integrating blues form into a verse/chorus pattern common in postwar R&B, then rock and roll.*
Riff-heavy sound	*Both melody and solos are built mainly from riffs.*
Shuffle rhythm	*A four-beat rhythm in which each beat is divided into a long/short pattern. Bass and guitar keep the beat, while the lower part in the piano plays the shuffle rhythm.*
Trains	*Popularity of trains reflects not only the useful sounds but also their importance to transportation.*

Electric Blues. Muddy Waters (Chapter 1) played a key role in creating the sound of **electric blues.** His legacy, and that of other bluesmen who followed in his footsteps, like Elmore James, Buddy Guy, and Otis Rush, has made Chicago the spiritual home of electric blues.

Whereas the music of jump bands was bright, electric blues was dark. Electric blues urbanized and amplified country blues (Chapter 3). As with boogie-woogie (later in this chapter) and honky-tonk (Chapter 7), these changes were born of necessity. As the music moved into noisy bars and **amplification** became available, bluesmen like Muddy Waters fleshed out their bands with full rhythm sections and plugged in their guitars. Occasionally, a leader would add another melody instrument to the mix. Little Walter, whom we heard earlier and who worked with Waters for many years, was an integral part of the Waters sound. The addition of other rhythm instruments and the use of amplification brought this new electric blues closer to the more commercial blues styles of the era. Adapted to the changing tastes of audiences, it became a much more popular music. Although Muddy Waters was never a pop presence in the 1950s, his relative popularity among African Americans certainly indicates a shift in taste.

Even as the additional instruments moved electric blues closer to other R&B styles, the interaction among the instruments helped set electric blues apart. As opposed to the defined instrument roles in a jump band, electric blues is often a free-for-all. In the Waters recording, the two guitars, the piano, and the harmonica compete melodically with riffs and vocal-like lines. The result is a dense mass of sound, mostly in the lower registers of the instruments, with the harmonica as the highest voice. This thick, deep sound fabric helps give the music its dark hue.

The sound of electric blues would have little immediate influence on later African American styles (both Motown and soul borrowed more directly from other R&B styles); but it eventually trickled down to the white community via the blues revival that began around 1960 and would prove to be a powerful influence on sixties rock. Both the prominence of the rhythm instruments and their free interaction heralded the blues-tinged rock of groups like the Rolling Stones, Cream, Jimi Hendrix Experience, and Led Zeppelin.

Another important, if less pervasive, influence was Latin music. Latin rhythms and instruments appeared with increasing frequency in rhythm and blues in the latter part of the fifties. We survey some of these important new developments next.

 1:1

"Standing Around Crying," Muddy Waters (1952). Waters, vocal and guitar; Little Walter, harmonica.

The Latin Tinge

The connection between Latin music and R&B goes back to the beginning of rhythm and blues. To cite just one obscure but noteworthy example, "Longhair's Blues Rhumba," a 1949 recording by the New Orleans pianist Professor Longhair (whose real name was Roy Byrd), layered a clave rhythm—played on **claves,** cylindrical sticks about one inch in diameter used to tap out the rhythm—over a boogie-woogie-style piano blues. During the fifties several R&B artists began to include Latin-influenced songs in their shows. A successful example is Ruth Brown's 1954 recording "Mambo Baby," which was a number 1 hit for her on the rhythm-and-blues charts. Toward the end of the decade, some used Latin rhythms as an alternative to the eight-beat rhythm of rock and roll. Perhaps the most familiar example of this trend is Ray Charles's classic 1959 recording, "What'd I Say." The most overt, and distinctive, link between **Afro-Cuban** rhythm and blues, however, was Bo Diddley.

Bo Diddley. The enigma of Bo Diddley begins with his name. He was born in McComb, Mississippi, in 1928. His father's name was Bates, but he was adopted by a relative, Gussie McDaniel; by most accounts his real name is Elias McDaniel. In the mid-thirties the McDaniels moved to Chicago and settled on the South Side. He acquired his stage name from his schoolmates in his teens. As he tells it, students started calling him "Bo Diddley" and it stuck. (How it connects to the diddley bow, a homemade instrument popular in Mississippi, remains unknown.)

The enigma persists when we consider the extent of his influence compared with his lack of commercial success. In his fifty-year career, he has had only one Top 40 hit—his 1959 recording, "Say Man." Yet he is without question a rock icon; among his many distinctions, he was a second-year inductee into the Rock and Roll Hall of Fame (1987).

Bo Diddley was fascinated by rhythms and percussion. (The story goes that he added **maracas** to his street-corner band because he wanted a percussive sound but didn't want to lug a drum set around town. Still, he kept the maracas when he added drums.) Not surprisingly, his most important and memorable contribution to popular music is not a song but a beat—the Bo Diddley beat—which appears in the aptly titled 1955 song "Bo Diddley," the first of his R&B hits. The **Bo Diddley beat** is a distinctive rhythm that is virtually identical to the clave rhythm we encountered in the rumba example ("El Manisero") in Chapter 8.

The song "Bo Diddley" is all about rhythm. It consists mainly of rifflike vocal fragments alternating with the Bo Diddley rhythm, played (more or less) on guitar and drums. All of this happens over one chord. The lyric is pure stream of consciousness; there is no story. Bo

CD 2:20

"Bo Diddley," Bo Diddley (1955). Diddley, guitar and vocal; Jerome Green, maracas.

LISTENING GUIDE: "BO DIDDLEY"

CD 2:20   **Latin-tinged Rhythm and Blues** (Bo Diddley; performed by Bo Diddley, guitar and vocal; and Jerome Green, maracas)

0:00	Instrumental introduction.
0:09	The Bo Diddley beat continues underneath the voice.
	Bo Diddley bought his babe a diamond ring,
	If that diamond ring don't shine,
	He gonna take it to a private eye,
	If that private eye can't see,
	He'd better not take the ring from me.
0:36	Instrumental interlude. Two alternating chords around the introduction material.
0:47	*Bo Diddley caught a nanny goat,*
	To make his pretty baby a Sunday coat,
	Bo Diddley caught a bear cat,
	To make his pretty baby a Sunday hat.
1:06	A more extended interlude. One chord several times, then a series of three-chord riffs.
1:42	*Mojo come to my house, and rack that bone,*
	Take my baby away from home,
	Ask that mojo (?) where he's been,
	Up your house, and gone again.
	Bo diddley, bo diddley have you heard?
	My pretty baby said she was a bird.
2:12	Repeated chord (like earlier interlude), then fade-out.

Diddley's self-titled song was the first big R&B hit to feature Latin-inspired rhythms and instruments so prominently. Rock musicians would borrow the beat; we encounter a remarkable example below.

STYLE PROFILE

"BO DIDDLEY" (LATIN-TINGED RHYTHM AND BLUES)

Rhythm	*Three insistent rhythms dominate the song: the maracas rhythm (twice as fast as the beat), the drums rhythm (four times as fast as the beat), and the famous Bo Diddley beat (a rhythmic pattern close to the clave rhythm of Afro-Cuban music). The vocal lines move at the same speed as the drum part but include some syncopation.*
Melody	*Short phrases, with one-chord guitar responses.*
Instrumentation (timbre)	*Vocal, electric guitar, drums, maracas, and perhaps bass.*
Performance style	*Hawaiian guitar–like effects on the guitar. The drummer plays on low-tuned drums; no cymbals.*
Dynamics	*Consistently loud.*
Harmony	*Most of the song is just one chord. Some changes of harmony in the instrumental interludes—a simple shift between chords, not a progression.*
Texture	*Three layers around voice: low-sounding drums, midrange guitar, and high-pitched maracas.*
Form	*Freely strophic, with instrumental interludes, plus intro and fade-out ending.*

Key Points

Bo Diddley beat and other Latin influences	*Bo Diddley beat close to clave rhythm; maracas are a Latin percussion instrument.*
Different approach to harmony	*Basically one chord, with a few simple shifts down.*
Different kind of song	*Many distinctive features: beat, harmony, bizarre lyrics, insistent rhythm, **tremolo** effect.*
Window to the future	*Many features—one-chord harmony, insistent rhythm, extra percussion—anticipate important directions in rock-era music.*

Terms to Know

Bo Diddley beat

maracas

tremolo

Another new black style emerged in the late forties. Although listed under rhythm and blues, it was often neither strongly rhythmic nor bluesy. By the end of the fifties, it was called doo-wop. We consider it later in this chapter.

Summary

In the decade after World War II, a broad spectrum of new African American musical styles emerged. By the end of the 1940s, most people, from Jerry Wexler on down, were calling these new sounds "rhythm and blues." The styles grouped under R&B were, in varying proportions, energetic, earthy, and powerfully expressive. Their creators drew on the rich heritage of prewar African American styles and numerous black takes on popular song. From this they forged some of the most vibrant new music of the 1950s.

Rhythm and blues found an ever-expanding audience, first within the black community and later among white teenagers who had time and money and who sought a music livelier and more pertinent to their lives than the music of their parents. Like the songs already discussed, we value rhythm and blues because it remains fun to listen to, even after a half century, and because it helped lay the foundation for the music of the rock era.

ROCK AND ROLL

What is rock and roll? It depends on whom and when you ask. If you had asked a blues singer in the 1920s, she'd have said that *rock and roll* is a euphemism for sex. If you had asked a teenager in Cleveland in 1951, he'd have said that's what disc jockey Alan Freed plays on the radio. If you had asked an adult in 1955, she'd have told you that it's that trashy music all the kids are listening to. If you had asked Fats Domino around the same time, he would have told you it's the music he's been playing in New Orleans since the early forties. And if you asked the Rolling Stones today, they'd tell you it's the music that they play better than anyone else.

In the first part of the fifties, *rock and roll* was simply another term for rhythm and blues. Alan Freed began using the term in 1951, but it didn't catch on until he moved to New York in 1954 and began broadcasting on WINS. At about the same time as Freed's move, white artists began to cover R&B hits (remember that a **cover version** of a song is a recording by someone other than the original artist). An early and successful example of this practice was a 1954 recording of "Sh-Boom" by the Crew Cuts, a white singing group from Toronto, Ontario. Their version of the song followed quickly on the heels of the original version by the Chords, one of the countless doo-wop groups from New York. The Crew Cuts' cover version climbed to number 1 on the charts, far outselling the original Chords recording.

A year later Chuck Berry and Fats Domino had songs on the pop charts, and Bill Haley's "Rock Around the Clock" rose to the top of the charts. By 1956 Elvis Presley was a huge success. During these early years, almost any music by and for teens was considered rock and roll. Because both performers and audience had such recognizable identities, it was easy, even natural, to lump under one label—**rock and roll**—all the music that teens listened to. (There are precedents for this: whenever a new African American–based style becomes the hot new sound, its label identifies any music with even a hint of the style. In this regard *rock and roll* simply followed *ragtime, blues,* and *jazz.*)

Rock and roll began as **outsider music**. Its first stars were mostly African Americans or southern whites. But when the music tapped into the newly enfranchised teenage audience, rock and roll became insider music. As teenagers in the fifties created an identity, rock and roll became as much a part of it as their dress, their speech, and their cars. By 1956 rock and roll was for real. Little Richard woke up the nation with "Tutti Frutti," and Elvis had eleven Top 40 hits that year, four of which reached number 1. By the end of the year, *rock and roll* was a household phrase and Elvis was a household name.

The Rhythmic Roots of Rock and Roll

Much of what was called "rock and roll" in 1956 was either rhythm and blues, as Fats Domino pointed out; white takes on R&B, like Pat Boone's cover of Little Richard's "Tutti

Frutti"; or Elvis's hits, which featured "a white man with the Negro sound and the Negro feel" as Sam Phillips once put it. But if we look at rock and roll "back from the future"—that is, if we view rock and roll as the music that led directly to 1960s rock, it becomes clear that rock and roll and R&B diverged. The key musical distinction is the beat. Rock and roll has a more active and assertive beat, which would soon develop into the rhythmic foundation of rock. Chuck Berry put together this new beat, but he borrowed it from boogie-woogie, a blues piano style that had been on record since the 1920s. We trace the connection between them next.

Boogie-woogie. **Boogie-woogie** is a blues piano style that chases the blues away. It is typically exuberant, even boisterous, loud, and strong. Originating in the rural South during the early years of the century, boogie-woogie was born of necessity. Its creators were pianists who performed in noisy working-class bars and clubs, variously called juke joints, barrelhouses, and honky-tonks. To be heard over the crowd, pianists created a powerful two-handed style in which they played an active left hand pattern in the lower part of the instrument and repeated riffs on the upper part. By the late 1920s, pianists were playing boogie-woogie in such urban centers as Chicago, New York, and Kansas City. It flourished in the 1930s and '40s, spreading beyond black neighborhoods into mainstream America. The Andrews Sisters scored a hit with "Boogie Woogie Bugle Boy." Tommy Dorsey's "Boogie Woogie" (a recording of "Pine Top's Boogie Woogie") was his biggest instrumental hit.

Among the most famous boogie-woogie performances is the 1936 recording of "Roll 'Em, Pete," featuring blues shouter Joe Turner (1911–1985) and pianist Pete Johnson (1904–1967), one of the kings of boogie-woogie piano. Turner grew up in Kansas City and started his career by singing after hours at the club where he tended bar. After teaming up with Johnson through the early 1940s, Turner became a prominent figure in the postwar rhythm-and-blues scene. Among his biggest hits was the 1954 jump song "Shake, Rattle, and Roll."

CD 2:21
"Roll 'Em, Pete," Joe Turner and Pete Johnson (1936). Turner, vocal; Johnson, piano.

"Roll 'Em, Pete" is a straightforward blues in form, the kind that Turner could have made up on the spot. (The title of the song apparently came from the patrons of the club where Turner and Johnson worked. They would shout, "Roll 'Em, Pete," as Johnson played chorus after chorus.) In its power Turner's singing is reminiscent of Bessie Smith's classic blues ("Empty Bed Blues," Chapter 3), but "Roll 'Em, Pete" is good-time music. There's a smile in Turner's voice that matches the exuberance of Johnson's playing.

In this recording Pete Johnson sets up a steady rhythm in the left hand that divides each beat into two parts. And Johnson builds piles of riffs on top of the steady left hand. In a medium-tempo boogie-woogie song, the division of the beat is uneven: a long/short pattern, like we heard in "Choo Choo Ch'Boogie." At really fast tempos, however, it is difficult if not impossible to sustain the long/short rhythm in the left hand. So, in "Roll 'Em, Pete," the rhythm tends to even out so that each beat is divided in two halves of equal length. This even **eight-beat rhythm**, also referred to as **eight-to-the-bar**, is even more powerful than the loping rhythm of medium-tempo boogie-woogie.

STYLE PROFILE

"ROLL 'EM, PETE" (BOOGIE-WOOGIE)

Rhythm	*Fast tempo; even division of the beat in the pianist's left hand (eight-to-the-bar). Lots of syncopation in vocal line and piano riffs.*
Melody	*Short riffs, with frequent repetition. Some longer lines during piano solos.*

STYLE PROFILE *(cont'd)*

Instrumentation (timbre)	*Voice and piano.*
Performance style	*Rough, powerful voice; two-fisted piano style.*
Dynamics	*Loud.*
Harmony	*Blues harmony.*
Texture	*Voice plus driving accompaniment figure; call-and-response—answering riffs in upper piano part.*
Form	*Standard blues.*

Key Points

Boogie-woogie beat	*Left-hand boogie-woogie pattern divides the beat into two equal parts.*
Big-voiced singing	*Joe Turner was one of the first blues shouters.*
Two-fisted piano style	*Continuous, vigorous left hand + riff-heavy right hand.*

Terms to Know

boogie-woogie

eight-beat rhythm

eight-to-the-bar

LISTENING GUIDE: "ROLL 'EM, PETE"

CD 2:21 **Boogie-woogie** (Joe Turner and Pete Johnson; performed by Turner, vocal; and Johnson, piano)

0:00	1st chorus
	Piano solo—starts high, then settles into boogie-woogie pattern.
0:15	2nd chorus
	Well, I've got a gal …
0:30	3rd chorus
	She got eyes …
0:46	4th chorus
	You so beautiful …
1:01	5th chorus
	Roll it boy …
1:16	6th chorus
	Piano.
1:31	7th chorus
	Piano solo.
1:46	8th chorus
	Well babe …
2:01	*Yes yes [five times]*
	Sung at two-measure intervals.
	Yes I know …
2:16	Sung every two bars.
	Well all right then …
2:32	*Bye bye …*

And it would prove to be more influential. After years of working with Johnnie Johnson, another fine boogie-woogie pianist, Chuck Berry would transfer this pattern to the guitar. Through this connection boogie-woogie would become the foundation for rock rhythm. But there was more to rock than just the beat. There was the sound and the look, which Elvis helped provide. We follow his path to rock-and-roll stardom via rockabilly.

Rockabilly

Carl Perkins, perhaps the truest of the rockabilly stars, once explained his music this way: "To begin with . . . rockabilly music, or rock and roll . . . was a country man's song with a black man's rhythm. I just put a little speed into some of the slow blues licks." As Perkins described it, rockabilly was the latest in a long line of country takes on black music. We have already heard Jimmie Rodgers's blue yodels, Bob Wills's western swing, and Hank Williams's honky-tonk. Rockabilly simply continues that trend.

Rockabilly began as a white southern music. Its home was Memphis, more specifically Sam Phillips's Sun Records. Perkins and Jerry Lee Lewis recorded there; so did Elvis. Even today the style retains this strong southern identity. The sound of rockabilly, however, was not confined to Memphis or even the South. Just as earlier country styles and their popular appeal had spread throughout North America, so did the idea of countrifying rhythm and blues.

 2:22

"Rock Around the Clock," Max Friedman and James Myers (1954). Bill Haley and His Comets.

Bill Haley's "Rock Around the Clock." The first big hit in rockabilly came from an unlikely source, by way of an unlikely place, and took an unlikely path to pop success. Bill Haley (1925–1981), who recorded it, grew up in Pennsylvania listening to the *Grand Ole Opry* and dreaming of country music stardom. By the late 1940s, he had begun fronting small bands—one was called the "Four Aces of Western Swing"—and enjoyed some local success. Over the

---

LISTENING GUIDE: "ROCK AROUND THE CLOCK"

CD 2:22   **Rockabilly** (Max Friedman and James Myers; performed by Bill Haley and His Comets)

0:00	Introduction.
	One two three o'clock . . .
0:12	1st chorus
	Put your glad rags on . . .
0:28	2nd chorus
	When the clock strikes two . . .
0:44	3rd chorus
	Guitar solo.
1:00	4th chorus
	When the chimes ring five . . .
1:16	5th chorus
	When it's eight . . .
1:32	6th chorus
	Instrumental: big-band swing-type riff, syncopated and on one note.
1:48	7th chorus
	When the clock strikes twelve . . .
2:02	Tag.

next few years, he began to give his music a bluesier sound and chose—or wrote—songs with teen appeal. "Crazy, Man, Crazy" (1953) was his first hit. In 1954 he had some success with a song called "Rock Around the Clock." (This was not the first time he had used *rock* in a lyric; an earlier song entitled "Rock-a-Beatin' Boogie" talked about rocking and rolling.)

A year later "Rock Around the Clock" resurfaced in the film *The Blackboard Jungle.* The connections among film, song, and performer were tenuous. The film portrays juvenile delinquents in a slum high school, but "Rock Around the Clock" is exuberant rather than angry, and Haley, at almost thirty, looks nothing like a rebel. But it was music for and about teens (parents weren't likely to rock around the clock), and that was enough for the producers. With the release of the film, the song skyrocketed to number 1. It was Haley's big moment. He had a few other minor hits, but he never repeated his chart-topping success.

Was "Rock Around the Clock" the first rock-and-roll record? It depends on your point of reference. It certainly was the first big hit clearly associated with rock and roll. And it was a different sound—at least for pop. But it connects more to the past than to the future. The sound is a light version of jump band rhythm and blues. Haley's voice is bright, but it has little of the inflection that we associate with blues singing. The band supports Haley's voice with a small rhythm section that includes a guitar played in a high register (compare this with the Muddy Waters recording) and drumsticks tapping out a brisk shuffle rhythm. The band plays riffs underneath Haley, then alone. This is much closer to rockabilly than it is to the rock and roll that came later in the decade.

STYLE PROFILE

"ROCK AROUND THE CLOCK" (ROCKABILLY)

Rhythm	*Fast tempo. Shuffle rhythm (heard in bass and especially drums). Syncopation in vocal line, guitar riff, and instrumental riff in chorus 6.*
Melody	*The first phrase of the melody seems derived from the standard R&B bass line of the time. The second phrase is a riff that's repeated with a little variation. The third is a longer answering phrase.*
Instrumentation (timbre)	*Voice, electric guitar, acoustic bass, drums, and saxophone (accordion).*
Performance style	*Haley's voice is light and friendly but not bluesy or country—and not pop crooning either. The guitar solo features the double-speed picking that would be the staple of surf-music guitarists.*
Dynamics	*Moderately loud, given the mostly acoustic instrumentation.*
Harmony	*Blues harmony, except for introduction and tag.*
Texture	*Somewhat layered, although the melody is the most important line; prominent backup riff and rhythm section make for a more balanced relationship between the parts.*
Form	*Blues-based chorus form. Instead of the typical rhymed couplet and melody to match, the form features a verselike section in the first four bars and a chorus in the last eight. This is the lyric and melodic style of the sung choruses.*

Key Points

Sound of rockabilly	*A "lite" version of rhythmic R&B: faster tempo, higher register, less rough-edged vocal.*
Rockabilly and rock and roll	*Shuffle beat does not lead to rock and roll; Chuck Berry's music does.*
Playing with blues form	*Another kind of verse/chorus **blues form**: first four bars = verse; last eight bars = chorus.*

Elvis. "I Don't Sound Like Nobody." Back in Memphis, in the summer of 1953, a young truck driver named Elvis Presley walked into the Sam Phillips Recording Service to make a demo record. Phillips wasn't in, so his assistant, Marion Keisker, handled the session. Perhaps to make him feel at ease, she asked him about himself. The conversation went something like this:

Marion: *"What kind of singer are you?"*
Elvis: *"I sing all kinds."*
Marion: *"Who do you sound like?"*
Elvis: *"I don't sound like nobody."*
Marion: *"Hillbilly?"*
Elvis: *"Yeah, I sing hillbilly."*
Marion: *"Who do you sound like in hillbilly?"*
Elvis: *"I don't sound like nobody."*

This now-legendary encounter gives us some insight into Elvis's success. Imagine yourself —barely out of high school and with no professional experience—having such a clear sense of who you are and what you can do. Elvis truly didn't sound like anyone else; he was the "white man with the Negro feel" that Sam Phillips had been seeking for several years.

Elvis Presley (1935–1977) recorded his first local hit for Phillips's Sun Records in 1954. The record, a cover of bluesman Arthur Crudup's "That's All Right," sparked interest on country-western radio (although some stations wouldn't play it because Elvis sounded too black). Within a year he had reached number 1 nationally on the country-western charts with "Mystery Train"—one of Elvis's most enduring early hits.*

Elvis's Sun sessions are quintessential rockabilly, in large part because of his singing. In both its basic timbre and its variety, his sound is utterly unique—the purest Elvis. Equally remarkable is his ability to adapt his sound to suit the material. He could emulate almost any style—pop, country, gospel, R&B—and still sound like himself. Although he didn't play much guitar, he played the radio really well. He was an equal-opportunity listener with an insatiable appetite for music. And what he heard, he used.

Elvis's sound brought him radio attention, but it was his looks and his moves that propelled him to stardom. In late 1955 he signed a personal management contract with Colonel Tom Parker, who arranged a record contract with RCA. Within a year Elvis had become a national phenomenon. Within two years he had recorded several number 1 hits and appeared on TV's *The Ed Sullivan Show* as well as many others. He had become the symbol of rock and roll for millions, for both those who idolized him and those who despised him. With his

www

Elvis Presley,
"Mystery Train"

---

*We regret that we are unable to include this song on our CD set; the licensing fees set by the copyright holders would make the CD set prohibitively expensive. Please go to *http://music.wadsworth.com/campbell_2e* for information about online availability.

Elvis and Bill Haley. A backstage meeting between Bill Haley and Elvis Presley in October 1958. Haley is about to give a concert in Frankfurt, Germany; Elvis had just been transferred to Germany as a U.S. soldier.

totally uninhibited stage manner, teen-tough dress, greased pompadour, and energetic singing style, Elvis projected a rebellious attitude that many teens found overwhelmingly attractive.

In *Jailhouse Rock*—one of the films he made before he went into the army—his seeming lack of inhibition when he sings the title song contrasted sharply with white pop singers standing in front of microphones and crooning. To the audiences of today, jaded by the antics of Prince, Madonna, Britney Spears, Christina Aguilera, and too many others, Elvis seems almost wholesome. But in his day, this was bold stuff, and he took a lot of heat for it. We can also admire Elvis's courage: he refused to tone down his style despite the criticism. In sticking to his guns, Elvis gave rock and roll a sound and a look—both of which immediately set the style apart from anything that had come before. He was rock and roll's lightning rod. For teens he was all that was right with this new music; for their parents he symbolized all that was wrong with it. And for all intents and purposes, he stood alone.

The *Billboard* charts reflect Elvis's singular status. Except for Elvis hits, rock and roll represented only a modest segment of the popular-music market. The top-selling albums during this time were mostly soundtracks from Broadway shows and film musicals. Even sales of singles, which teens bought, show that rock and roll did not enjoy the unconditional support of America's youth. Besides Elvis, the top singles artists during the same period were either prerock stars like Frank Sinatra and Perry Como; younger artists singing in a prerock style (Andy Williams and Johnny Mathis); teen stars like Pat Boone, who covered early rock and roll songs; or vocal groups like the Platters, whose repertoire included a large number of reworked Tin Pan Alley standards. Among the lesser figures—from a commercial perspective—are such important and influential artists as Buddy Holly, Chuck Berry, Little Richard, and Ray Charles. Elvis was by far the most important commercial presence in rock and roll; no one else came close.

The musically significant part of Elvis's career lasted only three years. It ended in 1958, when he was inducted into the U.S. Army. Although still a major public figure in the sixties and seventies, he seldom recaptured the freshness of his earlier years. His fans still call him the "king of rock and roll," but to what extent was it the image and to what extent was it the music? Certainly, he brought a new vocal sound into popular music. In his various blends of blues, R&B, country, gospel, and pop, Elvis summarized the musical influences—and epitomized the musical direction—of this new music. But his musical significance stops there. He neither wrote his own songs nor used the rock-and-roll beat copied by so many late-fifties and early-sixties bands. That would come from another source.

Rock and Roll Versus Rhythm and Blues

At some point during the mid-fifties, rock and roll broke off from rhythm and blues. The first —and easiest—distinction was racial. Rock and roll usually featured white performers and catered to a white audience. Rhythm-and-blues artists were black and so was their core audience. But this division, although accurate up to a point, is fundamentally flawed, if only because Chuck Berry, the architect of the rock-and-roll sound, was an African American. By 1957, however, it was possible to make a clear musical distinction, one that helps explain why we consider the music of Berry and Little Richard to be rock and roll, not rhythm and blues.

The distinction grows out of two features that, above all, define rock and roll as a style distinct from rhythm and blues: the beat and the sound of a rock guitar. We encounter the first in the music of Little Richard. We encounter both in the music of Chuck Berry.

Little Richard. Born Richard Penniman (1932) in Macon, Georgia, Little Richard was on the road in black vaudeville shows by the time he was fourteen. He made a few records in the early fifties, but none of them did much. In 1955 Lloyd Price (of "Lawdy Miss Clawdy" fame) suggested that Little Richard send a demo to Art Rupe, who ran Specialty Records, one of the many independent labels recording rhythm and blues. He did, and a few months later Bumps Blackwell set up a recording session at Cosimo Matassa's J&M studio in New Orleans. The house band included some of the legends of New Orleans rhythm and blues, including drummer Earl Palmer and saxophonist Lee Allen. The session got off to a slow start because Little Richard sang mostly slow blues songs, which were not his strength. During a break in the recording session, they went to a local club, where Little Richard began to sing a "blue" song, a naughty novelty number that he'd featured in his act. Blackwell realized that that was the sound they wanted, so on the spur of the moment they recruited local songwriter Dorothy LaBostrie to clean up the words. At the time, her new lyrics didn't make any more sense than they do now, but they were enough to get Little Richard his first hit, "Tutti Frutti."

Little Richard continued to record for Specialty through the first phase of his career. Among his biggest hits was "Lucille," which topped the R&B charts and almost reached the Top 20 on the pop charts in 1957. In this song we hear Little Richard's two biggest contributions to the sound of rock and roll: a clear, locked-in rock rhythm and a vocal sound that was as outrageous and outlandish as his appearance. The song begins with bass and guitar playing a boogie bass line, the most prominent sound until Little Richard starts singing. Drummer Earl Palmer keeps an absolutely pure rock rhythm—a steady rhythm moving twice as fast as the beat with a strong backbeat—perfectly in sync with the rest of the band. As the song unfolds, the piano line reinforces the rock rhythm with repeated chords. All this is the backdrop to Little Richard's vocal.

From Little Richard's first screamed "Lucille," one would be hard put to find a more abrasive sound in fifties music of any genre. No one's voice, not even Jerry Lee Lewis's, grated quite so much. The lyrics become meaningless; they're simply an excuse to present his voice.

In his sound and persona, Little Richard officially put rock and roll over the top. He was openly, flagrantly gay in an era when *gay* meant "happy" and the vast majority of homosexual men buried themselves in the backs of closets. And he was a black man. When Little Richard performed, he made the outrageous seem routine. In a favorite pose—one leg up on the lid of the piano, hands beating out a boogie beat, and a smirk on his face—there was no way you could avoid noticing him. Generations of rockers—gay, straight, androgynous, and cross-dressing—have followed his example. Mick Jagger, Jimi Hendrix, Elton John, Kiss, David Bowie, and Prince are just a few of the artists for whom performance is—or can be— a spectacle.

Little Richard has claimed that he was responsible for the new beat of rock and roll. He was right, up to a point. However, it took someone else to show how to play this new beat on the guitar.

Chuck Berry. Chuck Berry (b. 1926) was the true architect of rock and roll. More than any other musician of the 1950s, he spoke to its audience and defined its sound. The lyrics of his songs captured the newly emerging teen spirit. He talks about them ("School Days" and "Sweet Little Sixteen"), to them ("Rock and Roll Music"), and for them ("Roll Over, Beethoven"). His music enunciates the core elements that make rock and roll so distinctive.

Berry's first big hit was "Maybellene," which charted in the summer of 1955. As we noted in Chapter 1, "Maybellene" was Berry's take on honky-tonk. Except for its strong backbeat, twangy guitar, and motorvatin' lyrics, there is little to connect it to rock and roll. But over the next thirty months, step-by-step, Berry assembled the sound of rock and roll. Finally, in "Johnny B. Goode" (1958), he put all the pieces together.

In this song we can hear how Berry forged this revolutionary new style. Berry's voice is lighter and more transparent than Muddy Waters's, Joe Turner's, or even Elvis's. It is neither bluesy nor sweet, but it's well suited to deliver the rapid-fire lyrics that are a trademark of his songs.

The basic instrumentation of "Johnny B. Goode" is conventional enough. It is Berry's **overdubbing**—recording an additional part onto an existing recording—that is the breakthrough and the key to the sound of rock and roll. (We can assume that one of the guitar parts was overdubbed because both lead and rhythm guitar styles are Berry's and no other guitarist is credited in the album notes.) The two guitar lines, the rhythm section—a walking bass, drums (here adding a heavy backbeat), and a steady rhythm guitar—and an active piano **obbligato** create a dense texture. Lead guitar plays solo choruses and the response line in dialogue with the vocal.

To create the rhythm guitar line, Berry took the patterns he learned from working with Johnnie Johnson and made two innovations. He adapted the standard boogie-woogie left-hand pattern to the guitar (moving it up into a slightly higher register), and he evened out the rhythm so that each beat is divided into two equal parts.

The lead guitar lines are radically new. He borrows the double notes from the boogie-based rhythm lines and blends them with repeated notes and running lines—all played with the twang heard in "Maybellene." The **lead guitar** sound is forceful and compelling.

0:00	Famous guitar intro.
0:17	Verse
	Deep down in Lou'siana . . .
0:34	Chorus
	Go go . . .
0:51	Verse
	He used to carry his guitar . . .
1:08	Chorus
	Go go . . .
1:25	Guitar break. Stop time in the other instruments at the beginning of each chorus.
2:00	Verse
	His mother told him . . .
2:17	Chorus
	Go go . . .

In "Johnny B. Goode" we hear the three main influences on rock and roll come together. From electric blues Berry took the instrumentation, the thick texture, and the prominent place of the guitar. From boogie-woogie he took the eight-beat rhythm. From more rhythmic and up-tempo R&B styles, he took the blues-based verse/chorus form (*à la* "Choo Choo Ch'-Boogie") and the heavy backbeat.

At the same time, it's clear that the song is more than just the blending of these influences. The guitar work, Berry's voice, the content and style of the lyrics—all of these features were new elements, and all would prove extraordinarily influential. Berry's guitar breaks and solos are on the must-learn list of every serious rock guitarist. His lyrics, among the first to discuss teen life, are humorous, irreverent, and skillful.

Both the content and the style of his songs were widely copied. The surfing songs of the late fifties and early sixties are an especially good example of Berry's influence on song lyrics and musical style. No rock-and-roll artist was more covered by the creators of rock—the Beach Boys, the Rolling Stones, and the Beatles—than Chuck Berry.

STYLE PROFILE

"JOHNNY B. GOODE" (ROCK AND ROLL)

Rhythm	*Moderately fast tempo; strong backbeat; steady eight-beat rhythm in rhythm guitar; eight-beat feel in vocals and lead guitar; rest of the band in four; lots of syncopation and rhythmic play in Berry's guitar solos.*
Melody	*Verse has long, almost speechlike phrases; chorus repeats a short riff.*
Instrumentation (timbre)	*Berry's vocals, plus electric guitar, piano, (acoustic) bass, drums (and rhythm guitar, not listed in the credits).*
Performance style	*Berry's singing neither pop-pretty nor bluesy—it is too light and friendly; his guitar playing has an edge—in its basic sound, his use of double notes in solo and rhythm lines, and the occasional* **bent notes***.*
Dynamics	*Loud, given the mostly acoustic instrumentation.*
Harmony	*Blues progression throughout.*

Texture	*Strong rhythmic layer, with rhythm guitar, bass, and drums, underpins the melody and the solos.*
Form	*Blues-based verse/chorus form.*

Key Points

Berry's guitar style	*New guitar sound between jazz/pop and electric blues; double notes a trademark.*
Rhythm and blues versus rock and roll	*Rhythmic difference: eight-beat rhythm (rock and roll) versus shuffle rhythm (R&B).*
Power of the beat	*Insistent new beat attracted teens, repelled parents.*
Chuck Berry, the "architect of rock and roll"	*Berry brought both a new beat (the most basic element) and a new guitar style (the most distinctive sound) into rock and roll.*
Rock and roll versus rock	*Berry thinks in rock rhythm; others think in R&B. Rock arrives when everyone thinks in rock rhythm.*

Terms to Know

bent note	eight-beat rhythm	obbligato
blues progression	lead guitar	overdubbing

Berry and the Definition of Rock and Roll. Chuck Berry's music had evolved considerably in the three years between "Maybellene" and "Johnny B. Goode." In the process he helped rock and roll evolve from a code word through a bleached version of rhythm and blues into a distinct new style that would ultimately lead to the rock of the 1960s. The style features that would define this new music reached critical mass in "Johnny B. Goode." The music really began to sound different, not only from pop but also from R&B. And it effectively pointed out the evolutionary path that would soon lead to rock. There are three critical style features:

o Beat
o Prominent guitar
o Thick texture

The most universal element is the **beat**, a **rock beat**—eight evenly spaced sounds per measure (or two per beat)—over a strong backbeat. In "Johnny B. Goode" we hear the eight-beat rhythm in the guitar lines and the backbeat in the drums. Listen, for example, to "Rock Around the Clock" and "Johnny B. Goode," and the difference in rhythm—shuffle rhythm versus rock rhythm—is immediately apparent. Rhythm and blues and rockabilly would continue to use the heavy shuffle rhythm, whereas Berry's rock rhythm became the norm in rock and roll.

In rock and roll, the guitar is the signature instrument; it is a key rhythm instrument and the most important solo instrument. Heard simultaneously—as they are in "Johnny B. Goode"—the dual guitar roles are the foundation of rock guitar playing. The rock-defining qualities of "Johnny B. Goode" reside largely in Berry's playing. The rest of the band, especially the bassist, has not yet caught on to his innovations. When that happened, as it did in the Beach Boys' "Surfin' U.S.A.," a blatant cover of Berry's "Sweet Little Sixteen," rock and roll became rock.

"Johnny B. Goode" is one sign that a major phase in the evolution of rock and roll had ended. Aspiring rock-and-roll musicians learned songs from recordings, not from sheet music or arrangements. When they listened to a song, they could take in all of its elements, not just the words and the melody but the interplay of instruments, rhythms, and textures as well. With the advent of Berry's recordings, a new generation of musicians began to play with the basic elements of rock-and-roll style. With the record as the primary document, the gap between musical generations decreased from years to months. We next hear a particularly creative example in Buddy Holly.

Rock and Roll's Second Generation

The artists we have encountered thus far—Bill Haley, Elvis, Little Richard, and Chuck Berry—were there from the beginning. A second wave of rock-and-roll stars followed closely in their wake: Eddie Cochran, Gene Vincent, the Everly Brothers, and many more. Standing above all of these was Buddy Holly, the most creative mind in rock and roll's second generation.

Buddy Holly. Born Charles Hardin Holly in Lubbock, Texas, Buddy Holly (1936–1959) grew up in a musical family. But to hear the rock and roll he loved, he would drive with his friends to locations where he could pick up clear-channel broadcasts of rock-and-roll radio shows at night. After graduating from high school, Holly formed the Crickets. They were a big enough hit locally that they opened a show for Elvis when he came through Lubbock in 1955, but their first records went nowhere. Holly scored his first hit late in 1957 with "That'll Be the Day." It would be his biggest hit but not his most interesting.

When Holly began to play around with the still-brand-new elements of rock and roll, he found a helpful collaborator in an unlikely place. Norman Petty ran a recording studio in Clovis, New Mexico, a small town about 100 miles from Lubbock. Petty encouraged Holly and the Crickets to go for new sounds, some of which Petty created himself (he was a master of echo and reverb). Still, it was Holly's imagination that took rock and roll to a new level. We can hear this on one of his less popular but more enduring songs from 1957, "Not Fade Away."

Like the fox trot and swing, rock and roll entered popular music as a dance music. If we keep that in mind, we realize how extraordinary the beginning of "Not Fade Away" is. Most rock-and-roll songs, including the ones that we have heard, begin by laying down a clear, steady beat. Even Bo Diddley's "Bo Diddley" (which we heard earlier) meshes the "Bo Diddley beat" with a steady rhythm in the maracas. By contrast, the beat in "Not Fade Away" is hard to find. The first sounds we hear are the off-beat rhythms of the guitar and the bass, soon reinforced by the backup vocals. Even as the song gets under way, with guitar, bass, drums, and Holly's vocals all present, there is no instrument that marks the beat—rock or otherwise. Instead, we have Holly's take on the Bo Diddley beat and the drum style associated with it. The end of the song offers an ironic touch, fading away slowly even as Holly proclaims that his love will never fade away.

As in several of Holly's songs, the lyrics are similarly innovative. The words speak to a lukewarm partner. The "I" in the song is not the big man on campus but the gawky guy who loses his girl, or who never had her in the first place. Holly writes and sings for the rest of us; in his music and his appearance, he was rock and roll's first everyman.

We can understand why "Not Fade Away" was not as popular as some of Holly's other songs; most teens still wanted to dance. But we can also understand why songs like this one so profoundly influenced the Beatles and other 1960s rock groups. "Not Fade Away" is a great

CD 2:24

"Not Fade Away," Buddy Holly and Norman Petty (1957). The Crickets.

CD 2:24	Second-generation Rock and Roll (Buddy Holly and Norman Petty; performed by the Crickets)

| 0:00 | Instrumental introduction of the signature rhythm/riff—a slightly altered version of the Afro-Cuban clave rhythm (probably via Bo Diddley). |

1st Statement of the Form

0:10	Notice the alternation between unaccompanied voice and the signature riff.
	I'm a-gonna tell you . . .
0:32	The backup riff continues. Its persistence = the persistence of Holly's not-fading-away love?

2nd Statement of the Form

| 0:42 | Jerry Allison's unusually dead-sounding drum sound continues through call-and-response. |
| | *My love a-bigger . . .* |

3rd Statement of the Form

| 1:15 | Instrumental: guitar solo replaces Holly's vocal; responses are the same. |

4th Statement of the Form

| 1:42 | *I'm a-gonna tell you . . .* |

example of how creative minds like Holly's recycled the sounds of first-generation rock and roll and sent a message that it could be more than dance music. Within rock's stylistic boundaries, one can be imaginative and create a music just for listening.

STYLE PROFILE

"NOT FADE AWAY" (SECOND-GENERATION ROCK AND ROLL)

Rhythm	*Fast tempo; the dominant rhythm—heard at first just by itself—sounds like a second-generation take on the **clave rhythm** of Afro-Cuban music, that is, a slightly altered version of the Bo Diddley beat. The rhythm section (especially the drums) conforms more to this rhythm than to a regular rock or shuffle beat; there is no steady timekeeping.*
Melody	*Two short, active phrases, with space between them for the rhythmic responses.*
Instrumentation (timbre)	*Lead and backup vocals, lead guitar, acoustic bass, and drums.*
Performance style	*Holly's hiccuppy vocal style is a rock-and-roll trademark; Jerry Allison's drums sound **muted** (Petty and Holly experimented with novel sounds, for example, using pillows to dampen the drum sound).*
Dynamics	*Moderately loud and consistent throughout.*
Harmony	*Two IV-I chord pairs: the first built on IV, the second on I.*
Texture	*Open sound throughout much of the song because of unaccompanied vocal and a lack of steady timekeeping. Call-and-response: vocal and drums, answered by backup vocals, guitar, bass, and drums.*
Form	*Strophic, with a guitar solo interpolated between stanzas.*

Key Points

Teen lyrics with feeling	*Holly writes from nerd's point of view.*
Beyond dance music	*Big leap: rock and roll that is clearly not dance music.*

Rapid evolution
of rock and roll

Learning songs from records sped up the pace of change (e.g., Holly's take on the Bo Diddley beat).

Terms to Know

clave rhythm
mute

The Fall of Rock and Roll

Rock and roll ended as suddenly as it began. Elvis was drafted into the army in 1958. When he resumed his career two years later, he had lost the cutting edge that had defined his earlier work. Little Richard gave up his career to become a preacher. Jerry Lee Lewis married his thirteen-year-old cousin without divorcing his previous wife, and the ensuing scandal seriously damaged his career. In 1959 Buddy Holly died in a plane crash. That same year Chuck Berry was arrested on a Mann Act violation and eventually sentenced to a two-year jail term. By the end of the decade, most of the major figures in rock and roll were no longer active.

The **payola** scandal of 1959 also contributed to the sudden decline of rock and roll. Because they controlled airplay of records, disc jockeys wielded enormous power. Some, like Alan Freed, used it to promote the music they liked. But many, including Freed, accepted some form of bribery in return for guaranteed airplay. The practice became so pervasive that it provoked a government investigation. Also at issue was the question of licensing rights. **ASCAP**, the stronger licensing organization, reportedly urged the investigation to undermine its major competitor, **BMI**, which was licensing the music of so many black and country performers. Establishment figures viewed the investigation results as proof of the inherent corruption of rock and roll.

By the early 1960s, it seemed as though rock and roll was just a fad that had run its course. In retrospect it was just getting its second wind. British bands would soon revitalize rock and roll and help transform it into rock. Back in the United States, Bob Dylan, Roy Orbison, the Beach Boys, and even one-hit wonders like the Kingsmen (of "Louie Louie" fame) were also laying the groundwork for the rock revolution. We return to this story in Chapter 10.

RHYTHM AND BLUES, 1955–1960

If rock and roll was the baby of the blues, then 1950s rhythm and blues was the older brother that came of age as a commercial music at about the same time rock and roll was born. During this time R&B acquired a more distinct musical identity, one that often had greater crossover appeal. Several of its stars—Fats Domino, Sam Cooke, the Coasters, the Platters—appeared consistently on the pop charts, and R&B acts in general had a stronger market presence. Although it had been around longer, it came of age as a commercial music at about the same time rock and roll caught fire—the latter part of the fifties. During this time it acquired a more distinct musical identity, one that often had greater crossover appeal.

Much commercially successful rhythm and blues moved toward the pop charts by moving away from R&B. The new directions came from two well-established sources, pop and gospel, and one innovative development: producers. **Gospel** had influenced doo-wop since the late forties; what changed was the range and the extent of its influence. Now gospel had also become a training ground for solo singing stars like Sam Cooke and Ray Charles. With the focus on individual voices, differences from artist to artist were more apparent. Vocal groups, most notably the Coasters and the Platters, also developed a recognizable sound. In general, production was more elaborate: recordings often featured richer instrumental accompaniment, more-complex arrangements, and trademark sounds. Even one- or two-hit wonders like the Marcels created recordings with a distinct personality.

Doo-wop

If we judge by the number of **crossover** hits, the most popular new sound in rhythm and blues was neither strongly rhythmic nor especially bluesy: it lacked the strong beat and the bright tempo heard in jump bands, and it lacked blues form or influence. It was a new African American pop singing style featuring male (or mostly male) groups singing in **close harmony** —closely voiced chords moving in the same rhythm. Their repertoire consisted of pop standards—songs that had been popular in the 1930s and early '40s—or new songs composed in a traditional pop style.

This new sound had roots in black gospel. The **a cappella** (singing without instrumental accompaniment) male quartet was one of the staples of black gospel in the thirties and forties. The relationship among the parts—lead vocalist singing the melody, with the other three voices supplying harmony and rhythm—was typical in both fast and slow songs and carried over into the new pop style. So did the practice of slowing down the tempo. If you listen to a gospel performance of a standard hymn like "Amazing Grace," chances are the tempo will be markedly slower than one would hear in a white church service. This tempo change would carry over into popular-song performance.

The other important model for doo-wop groups was the sound of black pop vocal groups, notably the Mills Brothers (from 1931) and the Ink Spots (whose first hit came in 1939). Both were among the most popular African American performing groups in the 1950s. These groups also sang in close harmony. Their sound displayed the subtle influence of jazz and blues. It was a real pop sound, smoother than either jazz or blues but different from white pop vocal groups.

After World War II, young males banded together on urban street corners, especially in New York City, to sing for coins, attention from girls, and the chance to make a recording. The Orioles' 1948 recording "It's Too Soon to Know" was one of the first hits in this new style. By the early 1950s, there were hundreds of these groups. Almost all took group names, frequently that of birds: Orioles, Crows, Penguins, Ravens, Flamingos. By 1954 the Penguins' classic, "Earth Angel," topped the R&B charts and climbed to number 8 on the pop charts.

The Penguins,
"Earth Angel"

This new sound lasted for about fifteen years, from the late forties to the early sixties. During its heyday it went by a variety of names, most often rhythm and blues and rock and roll. Only toward the end was it referred to as **doo-wop**, the name by which we know it now. Their material may have been familiar, but the way they sang was new. We discover why as we listen to the Flamingos' 1959 recording of "I Only Have Eyes for You," written by Al Dubin and Harry Warren, for *Dames*, a 1934 film that starred Dick Powell and Ruby Keeler. The

0:00	Verse	
	My love must be a kind...	
	"Doo-wop-sh-bop" answer.	
0:36	A	Chorus
	Are the stars...	
1:10	A	(repeated)
	The moon may be...	
1:42	B	Bridge
	I don't know if...	
2:14	A	(repeated)
	You are here?	
2:57	Fade-out. "Doo-wop-sh-bop."	

song quickly became a standard; Frank Sinatra recorded it twice, in 1945 and again in 1962 with Count Basie.

The Flamingos were a Chicago-based vocal quintet: two pairs of cousins and a lead singer. They were among the more successful doo-wop groups in the late 1950s, charting steadily on the R&B charts and occasionally crossing over to the pop charts, as they did with "I Only Have Eyes for You," their biggest hit.

As originally conceived, "I Only Have Eyes for You" is a beautiful fox-trot **ballad**, very much in the style of "Heart and Soul" (Chapter 5). If we use that song as a reference point, we can hear how thoroughly the Flamingos' version transforms pop style. Two obvious differences stand out: the singers and the tempo. The sound of the lead singer, Sollie McElroy, and the close harmony of the Flamingos as a group are different from the pop singers we have heard. The tempo of the performance is much slower, about half the speed of "Heart and Soul." Indeed, the tempo is so slow that the recording, which lasts more than three minutes, includes only one statement of the chorus rather than two or three. To energize this slow tempo, the pianist plays repeated chords in a triplet rhythm. (A **triplet** is a division of the beat into three equal parts.)

Other notable differences are the "doo-wop-sh-bop" riffs of the backup vocalists during the verse and the long stretches over a single harmony. The vocal riff is the kind that earned doo-wop its name. The riff stands out in two ways: it is the main source of rhythmic energy in the song, and it replaces even the title phrase ("I only have eyes for you") as the song's melodic signature. In this respect it anticipates an important rock-era development: the distribution of melodic interest among several parts rather than concentrating it in the lead vocal line.

The harmony in this performance is bi-polar. For long stretches, such as the opening verse and the first part of the chorus, there is no harmonic change. Upon arriving at the title phrase, the harmony suddenly becomes lush, with new chords on almost every syllable of the lyric. This kind of harmonic practice is unique to doo-wop.

All four style features—the timbre of the singers, the slow tempo, the signature vocal riffs, and the static harmony—have their roots in gospel. The result of this profound gospel influence was a thorough transformation of popular song. In this respect it is in step with the

The Flamingos,
"I Only Have Eyes
for You"

move toward the recorded performance's being the primary document of a song, even though its starting point in this case is a prerock popular song.

STYLE PROFILE

"I ONLY HAVE EYES FOR YOU" (DOO-WOP)

Rhythm	*Very slow tempo. Slow four-beat rhythm with insistent triplet rhythm in rhythm section; light but audible backbeat. Signature riff is syncopated. Lead vocalist uses free rhythm during solos; strict rhythm in harmony sections.*
Melody	*The A section is built from the opening riff; the B section has a longer phrase, which is repeated.*
Instrumentation (timbre)	*Lead and backup vocals and a full rhythm section (electric guitar, piano, bass, and drums with brushes).*
Performance style	*Use of **falsetto** (head, rather than chest, singing to extend range upward) by lead vocalist; heavy **vibrato** by guitarist.*
Dynamics	*Moderately soft.*
Harmony	*Contrasts: verse sustains one harmony; chorus features rich harmony of the original song.*
Texture	*Dense texture because of several layers of background vocals: reinforce bass, sustain harmonies. Rhythm section spans a wide range: bass, guitar in the middle range, and piano high.*
Form	*Truncated verse, then one statement of **AABA** popular song form.*

Key Points

Thorough remake of pop standard	*Thorough remake of pop **standard** links prerock pop with sixties black pop.*
Slow tempo; triplet rhythm	*Tempo is more than twice as slow as original; triplets sustain momentum.*
Harmonic variety	*Nice contrast between looped three-chord progression in verse and rich harmony used for title phrase.*
Melodic diffusion	*"Doo-wop-sh-bop" also a memorable melodic idea.*

Terms to Know

AABA form	falsetto	vibrato
brushes	standard	
doo-wop	triplet	

Songs like "I Only Have Eyes for You" were the most typical doo-wop sound: pop standards or poplike songs sung in close harmony at a slow tempo. There were hundreds of doo-wop groups singing in much the same style. There was another black singing group active in the late fifties, however, that was absolutely unique. We meet them and their producers after a brief discussion of solo singers.

Solo Singers

Solo singers also fueled the growth of rhythm and blues in the late 1950s. Many, like Clyde McPhatter and Jackie Wilson, launched solo careers after starting as lead singers in doo-wop and R&B singing groups. (Both McPhatter and Wilson sang with Billy Ward's Dominos.)

Gospel had become a training ground for solo singing stars. For singers like McPhatter and Wilson, the route from the gospel choir to the pop charts went through vocal groups. Sam Cooke bypassed doo-wop, going directly from gospel to a solo career. Ray Charles, the most important R&B singer of the late 1950s, followed the most roundabout route.

Ray Charles. Born at the beginning of the Great Depression, Ray Charles (1930–2004) faced a host of personal difficulties (he was blind since the age of six and kicked a serious drug habit) to endure as an icon of popular music—the most important and influential of the gospel-inspired solo performers of the 1950s. More than any other artist, he was responsible for the synthesis of blues and gospel. His music merged the emotional intensity of both styles. His singing came not out of the relatively smooth delivery of male quartets, as Sam Cooke's had, but from the ecstatic, uninhibited shouting of holiness churches. Several of his songs, like "I Got a Woman," were thinly disguised adaptations of gospel songs fitted with new, secular lyrics.

Charles was a musician of eclectic tastes and a strong enough musical personality to put his own stamp on everything he tried. He broke through as a rhythm-and-blues artist in 1955. During this time he also explored his interest in jazz, performing at jazz festivals as well as R&B events and recording with major jazz artists like vibraphonist Milt Jackson. In this respect he was the main rhythm-and-blues link to jazz's "return to roots" movement.

Like many R&B artists of the period, Charles included a few Latin numbers in his act and helped bring Latin music into rhythm and blues. The Latin style had an obvious effect on songs like "What'd I Say," his biggest hit of the 1950s. For rhythm-and-blues musicians like Charles, Americanized Latin rhythms represented a more complex alternative to the relatively straightforward rhythms of rock and roll.

Ray Charles,
"What'd I Say"

After establishing himself as the most important, innovative, and influential rhythm-and-blues artist of the 1950s, Charles reached out to two more styles: country and pop. While growing up he had listened to country music along with various forms of pop. After occasionally including country songs on earlier albums, he recorded two albums of country songs in 1962. Both were best-selling albums; the first topped all three charts (pop, R&B, and country) simultaneously. Charles's albums brought country songs to a wider audience, inspired other noncountry performers to record country material, and influenced a number of important country musicians, including Merle Haggard and Willie Nelson.

Charles's recordings of pop standards, like Hoagy Carmichael's "Georgia on My Mind," were similarly well received and influential. He was the first major rock-era performer to record an album of standards, a practice that a generation of singers—Linda Ronstadt, Willie Nelson, and Rod Stewart—has followed.

For most of his career, Charles was in control of his own music. He charted his own direction—through jazz, R&B, country, and pop. For other R&B groups, the end result was often a partnership between performers, songwriters, and producers. We meet two such acts, the Coasters and the Shirelles, in the next section.

The Producers

The rise of the producer paralleled the shift from sheet music to record as the primary document of a song. If a song was going to be the entire sound experience captured on vinyl, it was in everyone's best interest to have someone oversee the process. The rock era has become the era of the producer. We have already met Sam Phillips in Memphis, Bumps Blackwell in New Orleans, and Norman Petty in Clovis, New Mexico. Leiber and Stoller surpassed all of them, if only because they wrote so many of the songs their acts recorded.

1950s Rhythm and Blues (Jerry Leiber and Mike Stoller; performed by the Coasters: Carl Gardner, lead vocal; Dub Jones, bass; Leon Hughes and Billy Guy, vocals; and featuring King Curtis, saxophone)

0:00	A	1st verse
		It was fe fe fi fi ...
		I smell smoke ...
		Notice the stop time here.
0:14	A	Chorus
		Charlie Brown?
		This completes one statement of the blues progression: IV-I-V-I.
0:29	A	2nd verse
		Same music, new words.
		That's him ...
0:36	A	Chorus
		Charlie Brown ...

Leiber and Stoller. "We don't write songs, we write records," said Jerry Leiber (b. 1933) and Mike Stoller (b. 1933). Knowing that they operated within strict time constraints—by their measure, no more than 3 minutes 40 seconds (3:40) and no less than 2:20 (the upper and lower time limits of a 45 single)—Lieber and Stoller wrote a song with the recording session in mind. They crafted every aspect of the song—not only the words and melody but also the sax solos, the beat, the tempo, just about every element of the recorded performance.

They began as songwriters in love with the sound of the new black music. Among their first hits was "Hound Dog," originally written for Big Mama Thornton but covered a few years later by Elvis Presley. For Presley they wrote and produced such hits as "Jailhouse Rock." They left their imprint most strongly on the recordings of the Coasters and the second incarnation of the Drifters. We consider the Coasters' "Charlie Brown" as a fine example of the Leiber and Stoller songs that offered a completely fresh sound. Nobody had ever done anything quite like it before.

The Coasters began in 1947 as yet another of the "bird groups"—the Robins—that populated the doo-wop slice of the R&B market. In 1953 they started working with Leiber and Stoller; by 1955 hits like "Smokey Joe's Café" had attracted the interest of Atlantic Records, so they switched labels. Late in 1955 the group dissolved. The two most distinctive voices, lead singer Carl Gardner and bass Bobby Nunn, went on to form the Coasters (named for the coast along their Los Angeles home base) with Leon Hughes and Billy Guy. Bass singer Will "Dub" Jones replaced Nunn in 1958, just before the group recorded "Charlie Brown."

www
The Coasters,
"Charlie Brown"

"Charlie Brown" was one of several *playlets*, a term that Leiber and Stoller coined to describe the songs they wrote for the Robins/Coasters. **Playlets** were songs that told a funny story with serious overtones; Stoller called them "cartoons." As with print cartoons, the primary audience was young people—of all races—who identified with the main characters in the story. The stories themselves were unabashed fun. In this case, Charlie Brown is the kid who can't stay out of trouble—the kid so many boys wanted to emulate but didn't have the nerve or the imagination. The lyric is miles away from the misty-eyed romantic love of the Flamingos' "I Only Have Eyes for You."

The verse and the chorus have the harmonic form of a conventional blues but not the traditional rhymed-couplet lyric.

0:51	B	Bridge

A contrasting melody; no chorus in this section.

Who's always writing . . .

1:06	A	3rd verse and chorus

Who walks in . . .

1:28   Sax chorus; solo based on blues progression. It's easier to hear the stop-time and double-time activity in the rhythm section. Notice the strong double-time backbeat.

1:51	A	3rd verse and chorus (repeated)

Who walks in . . .

2:14   Instrumental fade-out.

The musical setting is, if anything, more distinctive than the words. Such features as the double-time drum part, which injects the performance with such energy; King Curtis's sax playing; and the solo bass line, "Why's everybody always picking on me?" give the song an individual sound. The bass vocal line, rendered in the deepest possible bass voice somewhere between spoken and sung, is in fact the hook of the song. The line became a buzz phrase among teens (and preteens) as soon as the song charted.

All four points of entry—the words, the sounds (both the Coasters' voices and Curtis's sax), the melody (especially the bass solo), and the beat—are different from just about any other music of the day. At the same time, the story and the telling of it resonate with good humor, which in turn resonated with a large, integrated audience—we have no reason to assume that Charlie Brown is black.

STYLE PROFILE

"CHARLIE BROWN" (1950s RHYTHM AND BLUES)

Rhythm	*Bright tempo. Extreme contrast between **stop-time** opening (and Dub Jones's punch line) and double-time timekeeping (the drummer plays a steady rhythm and a backbeat twice as fast as a rock beat; other rhythm instruments play bass and chord on every beat). Vocals follow rock rhythm; sax riffs and solo line up with the faster rhythm.*
Melody	*Verse: long, almost chantlike phrase. Chorus: short riffs answered by sax riffs.*
Instrumentation (timbre)	*Lead and backup vocals, saxophone, electric guitar, piano, electric bass, and drums.*
Performance style	*Rough but pleasant vocal style; Dub Jones's bass voice is a wonderful novelty. King Curtis established a new R&B sax style in his recordings with the Coasters.*
Dynamics	*Loud.*
Harmony	*Blues progression except for the bridge, which includes a new chord.*
Texture	*Busy texture most of the time: harmonized melody or call-and-response riffs. Rhythm section very active with double-time rhythms. Striking contrasts between stop time and double time.*

| Form | Another verse/chorus blues form in the A section: first four measures are the verse; last eight measures are the chorus. A new non-blues-form section appears after the second chorus: the song as a whole forms a pop song–like AABA, plus a sax solo and a repetition of the last A section. |

Key Points

Funny song	Darkly humorous song with wide appeal, clear black roots.
Fun with the form	Three popular forms—AABA, blues, and verse/chorus—merged into one song.
Leiber and Stoller: the producers	Expanded concept of song to include other distinctive features: double-time drums, Curtis's sax sound.
Different kind of doo-wop	The Coasters = upbeat, funny songs. Most doo-wop groups = pop and pop-style **ballads**.

Terms to Know

ballad	rock beat
playlet	stop time

Among the first of the great rock producers, Leiber and Stoller laid the groundwork for subsequent generations of producers. Such major figures as Phil Spector, Berry Gordy, George Martin, and Quincy Jones trace their roles back to Leiber and Stoller and the other producers of the 1950s who helped transform the making of popular music.

The Girl Groups

For rhythm-and-blues musicians and their fans, the early sixties were an exciting time. Chubby Checker (in real life a Fats Domino fan named Ernest Evans) was teaching everyone from the Kennedys on down how to do the twist. Ray Charles was bringing a new, more soulful sensibility to country and pop. Leiber and Stoller were working their magic with a second incarnation of the Drifters and creating a sound quite different from the Coasters. In New Orleans a group of musicians was finding a new rock-based groove for rhythm and blues. Berry Gordy was just beginning to build his Motown empire in Detroit. Phil Spector was constructing walls of sound. And in the Brill Building, the new address for Tin Pan Alley, a new wave of songwriters—Carole King, Burt Bacharach, and others—were writing a new kind of song and finding new kinds of singers to record them. The most popular were **girl groups** like the Shirelles. We examine one of their big hits next.

The Shirelles. The Shirelles were a female vocal quartet—Shirley Owens, Micki Harris, Beverly Lee, and Doris Coley—who formed the Poquellos in 1958 while still in high school. Their rise to the top of the charts is another of the happy accidents of the rock era. The group had won over the crowd at a high school talent show with a song they wrote themselves, "I Met Him on a Sunday." A classmate, Mary Jane Greenberg, introduced them to her mother, Florence, who, after some haggling, signed them to record the song for her fledgling label, Tiara Records. It was a local hit—big enough to be picked up by Decca. When released by Decca, the song charted nationally; it was the Shirelles' first hit.

The Shirelles: Shirley Owens, Addie "Micki" Harris, Doris Kenner, and Beverly Lee (their names at the time of this publicity photo). Owens sang lead. Note the matching gowns, the required fashion for sixties girl groups.

After a few more Decca-released recordings that went nowhere, Greenberg re-formed Tiara as Scepter Records and brought in Luther Dixon to produce the group. From 1960 to 1963, the Shirelles were almost always on the charts. Their biggest hit came in 1960 with a song written by Carole King and Gerry Goffin, her husband at the time: "Will You Love Me Tomorrow."

The song and its creation give us a wonderful preview of the tumultuous changes to come in the 1960s. It was written and performed by women, and the lyric gives us a woman's perspective on the fragility of new love.

Before rock there had been few women songwriters (Kay Swift, who wrote the 1930 hit "Fine and Dandy," stands out). Moreover, the songs that they wrote were gender-neutral; there is no obvious clue in words or music that a song is written by a woman for women. Before rock we get the woman's perspective from female blues singers (Bessie Smith's "Empty Bed Blues") and country songs like Kitty Wells's "It Wasn't God Who Made Honky-tonk Angels" (1952), her famous retort to Hank Thompson's "The Wild Side of Life."

Carole King's song gives us the other side of boastful, male R&B songs ("Good Rockin' Tonight"). The man thinks only of tonight; the woman worries about tomorrow. There is no mistaking the message of the song; the lyrics are simple and clear. This kind of frankness

 2:25

"Will You Love Me Tomorrow," Carole King and Gerry Goffin (1960). The Shirelles: Shirley Owens, lead vocal; and Micki Harris, Beverly Lee, Doris Coley, vocals.

CD 2:25	**1960s Girl Group** (Carole King and Gerry Goffin; performed by the Shirelles: Shirley Owens, lead vocal; and Micki Harris, Beverly Lee, Doris Coley, vocals)

0:00	Instrumental introduction. Notice the simple, early-sixties-style version of rock rhythm.
0:07	A
	Tonight you're mine . . .
0:35	A
	Is this a lasting treasure . . .
1:03	B
	Tonight with words unspoken . . .
1:31	A
	I'd like to know . . .
1:59	A Violins play a variation of the first part of the melody.
2:13	A (continued)
	So tell me now . . .

became possible in mainstream popular music only when society, or at least the audience for popular song, could accept this kind of straight talk. That change in attitude was under way by 1960. We hear this song as a transitional step between the Donna Reed façade of 1950s pop and the confessional songs of Carole King, Joni Mitchell, and other female singer-songwriters of the 1970s.

The music reinforces the message of the lyrics, not because it presents a coherent setting but because its main components send such different messages. There are three groups of sounds: the rhythm section, the string section, and the Shirelles. The rhythm section lays down a rather mundane rock beat, one that was fashionable during these years in rock-influenced pop. It remains constant throughout the song; there is almost no variation. But the string writing is bold and demanding—the most sophisticated part of the sound. The intricate string lines stand in stark contrast to the Shirelles' vocals, especially Shirley Owens's straightforward lead.

And therein lies the charm. The instrumental backup, and especially the skillful string parts, contrasts with the naïve schoolgirl sound of the Shirelles (none of whom was yet twenty years old when the song was released). All of this meshes perfectly with King's lyrics, the song's simple melody, and the group's look. Shirley sounds courageous enough to ask the question and vulnerable enough to be deeply hurt by the wrong answer. She, like the lyric, sounds neither worldly nor cynical.

The song and the singers were both a product and an agent of change, helping close the gap between black and white. As a product the song reflected the changes in rock and roll. As an agent of change, it was written by a white woman, produced by a black man, supported with white-sounding string writing, and sung by young black women. The message of the song is colorblind: teens of all races could relate to it. The Shirelles crossed over more consistently and successfully than any of the black acts of the 1950s in part because of the changing racial climate (the civil rights movement was gathering steam) and in part because they were teens like their audience. In songs like "Will You Love Me Tomorrow," they sing peer-to-peer about a meaningful issue.

"WILL YOU LOVE ME TOMORROW" (1960s GIRL GROUP)

Rhythm	*Moderate tempo. Straightforward rock rhythm, with* **rebound backbeat** *(two taps on the snare drum rather than just one). Other regular rhythmic patterns in piano, guitar, backup vocals, and cellos (lower strings); freer rhythms in violins, at times quite active. Melody moves at a moderate pace.*
Melody	*The A section grows out of the opening rifflike phrase, forming an arch, with the peak on "so sweetly"; strong push toward the title phrase. The bridge also grows out of the first phrase, but it is more repetitive.*
Instrumentation (timbre)	*Lead and backup vocals, full rhythm (piano, bass, electric guitar, and drums), and full strings (violins and cellos).*
Performance style	*The Shirelles' singing has a girl-next-door quality: their voices are not classically trained or modeled after mature pop, blues, or jazz singing.*
Dynamics	*Moderate throughout.*
Harmony	*Mostly I-IV-V, but with some nice surprises (such as the harmony under "tonight the light").*
Texture	*Distinct layers: lead vocal, backup vocal, violins playing an obbligato, and low strings and rhythm instruments laying down steady patterns.*
Form	*A long AABA form (it takes about two minutes to get through the form once).*

Key Points

Vulnerable lyrics, vulnerable girls?	*Innocent-sounding girls' number 1 question; the Shirelles' vocal style and look enhance the question in the lyric.*
Dressing up	*String writing adds a layer of sophistication to simple vocal sounds and rhythm-section accompaniment.*
Simple rock rhythm	*The state of rock rhythm ca. 1960: straightforward rock beat in drums, slightly liberated bass line.*
Between rock, R&B, and pop	*Teen-themed song, black pop vocal style, simple rock rhythm, poplike string writing.*

Terms to Know

girl group
rebound backbeat

Look at album covers for the girl groups of the 1960s. The acts are always nicely dressed in prom dresses or evening gowns. Their hairstyles are the current fashion for both whites and blacks (and Asians); these were the days just before Afros and other "natural" looks. The look was designed to cut across racial boundaries, to appeal to the widest possible audience. The look and the sound succeeded in this objective to an unprecedented degree. Americans were becoming more aware of equal-rights issues, and many, both black and white, were determined to do something about it. It is in this climate that girl groups like the Shirelles, the Ronettes, and many of Motown's first stars flourished. Their success underscores the fact that popular music shapes—and is shaped by—its historical context. The Shirelles' brief run on the pop charts coincided with a crucial stage in one of the most volatile periods in American history. We'll return to this issue in Chapter 10.

LOOKING BACK, LOOKING AHEAD

The fifteen years between the end of World War II and the presidency of John F. Kennedy saw the birth (and the childhood) of not just rock and roll but also a number of rhythm-and-blues styles—doo-wop, electric blues, and jump bands among them.

The big noise came in mid-decade with Elvis's explosion onto the pop charts, a seemingly endless string of hits by other rock-and-roll greats (Little Richard, Jerry Lee Lewis, and above all Chuck Berry), and the crossover success of R&B artists like Fats Domino, Sam Cooke, Ray Charles, and a host of doo-wop groups.

As the decade drew to a close, rock and roll became distinct from rhythm and blues. New stars like Buddy Holly, the Everly Brothers, and Eddie Cochran picked up the baton dropped by Elvis, who had been drafted into the army, while new acts like the Coasters joined Domino and other recently emergent R&B artists, and girl groups like the Shirelles presaged the emergence of new black pop styles.

Although in 1959 rock and roll seemed dead—a trivial fad barely more enduring than Harry Belafonte's calypso—it was in fact bubbling under, ready to erupt within a few years on both sides of the Atlantic. Rhythm and blues underwent a metamorphosis just as dramatic, with Motown, soul, and much more ruling the airwaves by the midsixties. We explore the rock revolution in the next chapter.

TERMS TO KNOW

Test your knowledge of this chapter's important terms by defining the following. If you can't recall the meaning of a certain term, refresh your memory by looking up the boldfaced term in the chapter, turning to the Glossary at the back of the book, or working with the flashcards on the *Popular Music in America* Companion Web site: *http://music.wadsworth.com/campbell_2e*

a cappella	claves	outsider music
AABA form	close harmony	overdubbing
Afro-Cuban	cover version	payola
amplification	crossover	playlet
ASCAP	doo-wop	rebound backbeat
ballad	eight-beat rhythm	rhythm and blues (R&B)
beat	eight-to-the-bar	riff
bent note	electric blues	rockabilly
Billboard	falsetto	rock and roll
blues form	girl groups	rock beat
blues progression	gospel	shuffle
BMI	indie	single
Bo Diddley beat	jump band	standard
boogie-woogie	lead guitar	stop time
brushes	maracas	tremolo
chart	mute	triplet
clave rhythm	obbligato	vibrato

The Rock Revolution:
Rock and Soul in the 1960s

In 1961 Frank Sinatra had seven albums in the Top 40, three on Capitol and four on Reprise, the record company he had just formed. The top-selling album of 1962 was the soundtrack to the film version of *West Side Story*. The top album of 1963 was Andy Williams's *Days of Wine and Roses*. The number 1 single at the beginning of 1963 was Steve Lawrence's "Go Away Little Girl." Both Williams and Lawrence were smooth-voiced pop singers; their songs looked back to pop, not ahead to rock. So, the rock revolution happened suddenly—almost overnight.

The Beatles launched the British invasion as 1964 began, and Mary Wells's "My Guy" brought Motown to the top of the charts for the first time. By 1965 the Temptations were telling us about "my girl," James Brown had gotten a brand new bag, Mick Jagger was trying —and failing—to get satisfied, and the Byrds had turned a cryptic Bob Dylan song into a huge hit.

In less than two years, rock and soul had elbowed pop and Broadway off the charts—not only the singles charts but also the album charts. They took over the music industry with mind-boggling speed. And rock stayed on top. By the end of the sixties, pop was passé and rock and roll was here to stay—in its more mature form. Fifties rock and roll had seemingly been a false alarm, easily dismissed by the pop establishment soon after Elvis got drafted, when in fact it was a prelude to the real thing—a complete changing of the guard.

THE ROCK REVOLUTION: A HISTORICAL PERSPECTIVE

To this day the rock revolution still seems like the most momentous change in the history of popular music. Nothing since has transformed popular music to such a degree, and only the modern-era revolution of the 1920s has had a comparable impact. There are several reasons for this perception:

o *It happened quickly.* The revolution was effectively over in just a few years.

o *Much of the music came from "outside."* In fact, the music that made the biggest splash came from abroad. The British invasion marked the first time that music from beyond the United States became the commercially important music of a generation. Unlike Latin music, for example, or even the calypso so popular at the end of the fifties, this was not an exotic music. This was the new mainstream.

o *The memory of the music is still vivid.* The generation that grew up with it is still around, still working (and still writing books on popular music). Oldies stations continue to feature this music, which now sounds comfortable rather than challenging. We still find these CDs in record stores (and now online!), see the performers' images on television and in magazines and books, and watch their videos and films. Commercials recycle sixties hits to sell all kinds of products. Film directors continue to draw on this music to establish time and place.

o *The music grew up very quickly, and we have it all down on record.* By 1965 a new Beatles album was an event; a year later their album releases were an even bigger deal because the group had stopped touring. Their transformation over an eight-year period from the "fab four" to the creators of some of the most inspired and intriguing music of the century encapsulated the maturing of rock from music for teenyboppers into a substantial musical language. And they were not alone: the late sixties were an extraordinarily creative period in popular music, as we'll soon discover.

o *Seemingly everyone knew this new music.* Today's pop market is fragmented into many narrow niches. But in the sixties, a sizable majority of the audience knew—and liked— the top songs, whether it was the latest Motown or Beatles hit or a song by the Rolling Stones or James Brown or the Beach Boys or the Byrds.

o *The music was the soundtrack for a decade of extraordinary social change.* Civil rights, the Vietnam War, free love, the gradual empowerment of women, the environmental movement, a huge generation gap—all of this was a brutal challenge to the established social order. And it seemed even more revolutionary when held against the fifties, when the bland façade portrayed in the media promoted the American dream even as it covered up the abuses of McCarthyism, bigotry, big business, and the like.

And there are other reasons. Finally, though, it comes down to the music itself. What was it about this music that made it so revolutionary?

The rock revolution was comprehensive, not cosmetic. It affected every aspect of the music: its influences, its creative process, its authorship, its sound, its musical message, and its end product. The music took advantage of brand-new and still-evolving technology in both performance and production. It reflected significant social shifts in both words and music. And despite the range of styles, it represented a coming together musically, the most important since the 1920s.

Rock: An Integrated Music. The Rolling Stones grew out of a chance meeting of Keith Richards and Mick Jagger at a London train station. Jagger saw Richards carrying a load of American blues albums (remember that vinyl album covers were about one foot square, so it was obvious what he was carrying) and chatted him up. The encounter led eventually to the formation of the Rolling Stones. This often-told story underscores a central feature of rock: rock is an integrated music. It is not just that the music of the sixties was more profoundly influenced by African American music than any earlier mainstream style. It is also that the influence went both ways—we hear black influences in music by white bands and white influences in music by black performers. And, most important, these various influences are assimilated into a new sensibility and a new sound. Integration is about not only being together but blending together. That's what happened.

Song Ownership and the Creative Process. From the outset rock changed the relationship between composer and performer. Most of the early rock stars, such as Chuck Berry, Buddy Holly, and Little Richard, performed original material—Elvis was an interesting exception to this trend. In their music the song existed as it was recorded and performed, not as it was written, if indeed they wrote it down at all. A song was no longer just the melody and the harmony but the total sound as presented on the record: not only the main vocal line but also guitar riffs, bass lines, drum rhythms, and backup vocals.

In the midsixties rock musicians took advantage of multitrack recording, an emerging new technology, to shape the final result even more precisely. **Multitrack recording** involves recording parts of a song onto separate tracks instead of all at once, then **mixing** them together. It had been possible to record on more than one track since the late forties. Les Paul, a technological innovator as well as an outstanding guitarist, had experimented with **overdubbing** after World War II and released several records using this procedure. Multitracking didn't really catch on until the midsixties, however, when four-track consoles became more widely available and the Beatles and George Martin demonstrated its creative possibilities.

Multitrack recording made it possible to record a project in stages instead of all at once. Strands of the musical fabric could be added one at a time and kept or discarded at the discretion of the artist or the producer. This ability to assemble a recording project in layers fostered a fundamental change in the creative process. It was possible to experiment at every stage of a project, and it was normal for one person or group to stay in creative control of the project from beginning to end. Contrast that with the diffusion of creative responsibility in prerock music: a songwriter writes a song, an arranger arranges it, then a singer gives it his own interpretation, often without consulting the songwriter. In this scenario there is usually no overriding creative control. Unlike earlier generations of songwriters, musicians in the rock era had the capability of overseeing the entire creative process.

The Sounds of Rock. The sounds of rock were startlingly new. Rock and roll and rhythm and blues had laid the groundwork for these new sounds. Still, when they arrived—with Dylan and the folk rockers, the ascent of Motown, the British invasion, the "guitar gods," soul, Latin rock, proto-funk, and pop-rock—the impact was stunning.

The new sounds began with the instruments. We think of the **electric guitar** as the signature instrument of rock, and so it is. But the instrument most responsible for the transition from rock and roll to rock was the **electric bass**. The electric bass dates back to 1950, when Leo Fender put together his first "precision" bass. It came into use gradually; bassists began using it in the late fifties. By the early sixties, it was standard equipment in a rock band. With good amplification the electric bass balanced the power of the electric guitar, giving rock bands the full bass sound they lacked in the fifties, when bassists used an acoustic instrument. James Jamerson, Motown's staff bassist, showed rock musicians what could be done with it.

In addition, a new generation of smaller, more portable electric organs appeared in the sixties, and the venerable Hammond B-3, long a fixture in black churches, resurfaced in rhythm-and-blues and rock bands. Portable **electric pianos** also came into widespread use. Some, like the Fender Rhodes, merged a piano action with electronics to produce an instrument that retained the feel of a piano but added the power and tone color of electronics.

All of these instruments benefited from a huge boost in **amplification**. Marshall stacks, the amps used by the Who, Cream, and so many other rock bands, weren't even available in 1960, but by the end of the decade their sound was filling arenas. Other companies kept pace, replacing tubes with transistors and boosting output many times over. A performance at Candlestick Park in San Francisco, at the time an outdoor baseball stadium with a capacity of almost 50,000, would have been a bad idea in 1960, the year it opened; in 1966, however, it was the venue for the Beatles' last public performance.

With increased amplification and a balance of power among the instruments, what had been the background component of a band became—in many cases—the whole band. In effect, this core nucleus—guitar(s), bass, drums, and keyboard—went from a supporting role to the center of the action. This shift flipped the balance between horns and rhythm instruments: horns, when used, were usually an extra layer; they were no longer in the limelight except for the occasional saxophone solo. And particularly in white rock, they were no longer an integral part of the band.

Rock Rhythm. This core nucleus laid down a new beat: a **rock beat.** Chuck Berry had laid the groundwork in the fifties, as we noted in Chapter 9. It wasn't until the whole band began playing with a rock conception, however, that rock and roll became rock. Again, the key player was the bass: once liberated not only from the limitations of an acoustic instrument but also from the walking pattern of swing and rhythm and blues, the bass helped establish and maintain the eight-beat-based groove that defined rock rhythm. (A **groove** is a good beat, a beat that makes you want to tap your foot and move your body, that is sustained over a long period of time.)

One result of this breakthrough was that the interplay among the instruments became both more independent and more interdependent. That is, no instrument, not even the rhythm guitar, was absolutely locked in to a specific pattern, like the bass player's walking pattern, the banjo player's "chunk" on the backbeat, or the drummer's ride pattern in prerock music. At the same time, the groove was the end product of the interaction of all the rhythm instruments. Take one away, and the groove was gone.

Sharing Melody. This sharing of responsibility also applied to melody. Up to this point, the main source of melodic interest in the songs we have heard was, appropriately enough, the **melody**—the vocal line when it was sung and the lead instrumental line when it was played. That changed with rock: melodic interest was spread out to other instruments. In many of the songs we will hear in this chapter, the song is immediately identifiable from an instrumental riff: a **hook.** The hook identifies the song well before the singer enters. Typically, other instruments also had parts with some melodic interest. One result was a greater variety of texture: from delicate tapestries with a few parts to densely packed free-for-alls.

All of these changes—in instrumentation, melodic and rhythmic approach, and texture—applied to both white rock and the black music called "soul" during the sixties. The difference from one style to the next was usually a matter of emphasis or interpretation; indeed, new ideas flowed freely in both directions.

Rock Attitudes and the Musical Message. These innovations give us a musical perspective on the wholesale shift in attitude that was at the core of the revolution. Three qualities of this new attitude stand out: sixties rock was egalitarian, it was eclectic, and it was real. Until 1960 most groups had a leader who fronted the band and/or a featured performer. In the thirties it was Benny Goodman with his orchestra. After the war it was Muddy Waters, or Louis Jordan and His Tympany Five. Even Buddy Holly fronted the Crickets. Black vocal groups, from the Mills Brothers through doo-wop and the girl groups, were the singular exception.

By contrast most sixties rock bands took group names: the Beatles, the Beach Boys, the Who, Jefferson Airplane. In so doing they projected a collective identity. There was nothing in the name that said one member was more important than the others. The interplay among voices and instruments is another key: in hooking the listener with a catchy riff or in laying down the beat, no one person was consistently in the spotlight. This was usually a group effort.

The sources of the new rock style, and the way in which they made their way into rock and soul, also evidenced this new attitude. Rock took a pragmatic approach to musical borrowing: musicians took what they needed, no matter what its source, and transformed it into something new.

Contrast that with music before 1960. Pop artists gave country songs a shower and a shave before putting them on record, as a pop cover of any Hank Williams song will attest. If the recordings are any indication, neither the singers nor the arrangers made much of an effort to understand either the sound or the sensibility of country music. Similarly, rhythm and blues usually got a bleach job: the Chords' cover of "Sh-Boom" is one example among too many. Even many of the teen idols, from Pat Boone to Fabian to Frankie Avalon, dressed the part (sort of) but neglected the sound and the style of rock and roll.

And in the sixties, sounds came from everywhere: Delta blues, Indian music, symphonic strings, jazz, music hall, folk, country—if it was out there, it was available for adoption. More important, rock musicians didn't necessarily privilege any particular style or family of styles. There is no sense of connection between the social standing of a style and its use in rock, unless it's an inverted one: the grittier the source, the more it's admired, as in the case of Delta blues. The Beatles' music epitomizes this egalitarian, eclectic approach: one track can be sublime, the next can sound like a children's song.

There was a hierarchy of importance within rock, especially in the wake of the Beach Boys' *Pet Sounds* and the Beatles' *Sgt. Pepper's Lonely Hearts Club Band*. The possibility of making an artistic statement in rock has been part of its collective understanding since the midsixties. But artistic statements were typically crafted out of seemingly ordinary materials. Even when rock emulated classical music and other established traditions, it did so on its own terms: The Who's *Tommy* was a rock opera but a far cry from conventional opera. For the best rock bands, the sound world of the sixties—and *world* is the operative word here—was like a well-stocked refrigerator and spice cabinet; bands simply took what they needed to create the feast.

Finally, rock was real in a way that earlier generations of pop had not been. Rock formed a bond with its audience that was different from the connection between Tin Pan Alley popular song and its audience. Tin Pan Alley songs offered listeners an escape from reality, whereas rock songs intensified the reality of life in the present. Moreover, the message of the song reached its audience directly because rock-era songwriters usually performed their own songs. Songs were not written *for* something—such as a musical or a film—so much as *to say* something.

Rock's concern with the present, combined with its direct and often personal communication between song, singer, and audience, elevated the role of the music for many members of that audience from simple entertainment to, in the words of noted rock critic Geoffrey Stokes, "a way of life."

The Final Result. As a result of all these innovations, rock and soul redefined popular song. In earlier generations a song existed independent of any particular version of it. A performer could put his or her personal stamp on it, as we heard with Billie Holiday's version of "All of Me," but the song was not Holiday's rendition of it; others could, and did, record it.

That changed in the sixties. Not only did the song become the sounds preserved on the recording, but the recording itself became something different from a live performance of the song. In earlier generations a record generally captured to tape (or acetate) a version of the song as it would be performed in public. The setting might be optimized for recording, but the recorded performance itself would, in most cases, not differ substantially from a live show.

With *Pet Sounds* and *Sgt. Pepper,* however, recording and live performance diverged. It became increasingly difficult to replicate a recording live. And even when it was possible, the live performance copied the recording, not the other way around. As it did in so many other areas of popular music, rock inverted the relationship between the two.

This has led in our own time to the complete divorce between recording and performance. Today one needs only a computer, the right software, a **MIDI** controller, and some imagination to make interesting music. The ability to sing or play an instrument is no longer a prerequisite for recording music. Indeed, we now can "perform" recordings—and many do. So for many readers, the split between recording and performance might seem like business as usual. The point here is that it wasn't always that way. As recently as fifty years ago, recordings simply preserved performances. The redefinition of a song, and the relationship between recording and performance, occurred only in the 1960s.

Sixties rock and soul was a revolutionary music; the rock revolution is, in fact, the only widely acknowledged revolution in the history of popular music. The discussion to this point has outlined many of rock's revolutionary changes. We hear them realized in a splendid variety of ways in the songs discussed in this chapter.

COUNTRY ROADS TO ROCK

A chance meeting in 1987 between Roy Orbison and George Harrison at a Los Angeles restaurant eventually led to the formation of one of the most esteemed and unusual supergroups, the Traveling Wilburys. The group featured five top-flight singer-songwriter-guitarists from three generations of rock: Roy Orbison, Bob Dylan, George Harrison, Jeff Lynne, and Tom Petty.

The coming together of Dylan and Orbison brought belated closure to what seemed like an antagonistic relationship throughout much of the sixties and the early seventies. Although folk and country had common roots in the music of the British Isles, folk music—or at least the music of the folk revival—and country music had followed remarkably divergent paths. Their intersection with—and through—rock began in the early sixties.

As a result of its several revivals, **folk music** had become an urban music. In the forties and early fifties, it was the Lomaxes, Woody Guthrie, and—most popular—the Weavers. The Kingston Trio sparked yet another revival in the late fifties. By 1960 this old/new folk music was flourishing in coffee houses, often located near college campuses or in the more bohemian parts of major cities—Greenwich Village in New York and North Beach in San Francisco.

This new folk revival relived the history of the music that inspired it. That is, it began by re-creating folksongs and classic "folk" performances (like those of the Carter Family). Just as Woody Guthrie gave the folk sound a contemporary focus, so did folk singers like Bob Dylan, who began to write topical songs. These were social commentaries with more sting, such as Dylan's "Talking John Birch Paranoid Blues." Indeed, Guthrie was the patron saint of the folk revival; Dylan's visit to Guthrie as he lay dying in a New York hospital was a momentous event in his life.

As in the forties and fifties, the folk music scene soon moved well to the left of the political spectrum. In the early sixties, both performers and audiences embraced the social issues of the day: the image of Pete Seeger, the strongest link between the folk revivals of the forties and the sixties, leading the masses in singing "We Shall Overcome" is still vivid. Other folk performers, like Dylan and Phil Ochs, were even more outspoken. Their songs prodded a generation of young people into thinking and then acting—with massive rallies, marches on Washington, and sit-ins.

Roy Orbison. In 1964, even as Dylan approached the height of his fame and influence as a folk artist, Roy Orbison (1936–1988) scored his only number 1 hit with "Pretty Woman." Orbison, who was born in Vernon, Texas (where Vernon Dalhart got half of his name), started his recording career as a rockabilly artist. In the midfifties he worked first with Norman Petty (Buddy Holly's producer), then with Sam Phillips. He had little success with either of them, so he moved to Monument Records, an independent label based near Nashville. Orbison was the label's first important act.

Many have called Orbison the last rockabilly. The case can also be made that he was the first country rocker. More comprehensively than Jerry Lee Lewis, he brought a country sensibility into rock, and he showed country musicians how to integrate rock and rhythm and blues into country: his "Mean Woman Blues" is a superb illustration.

An even better example of Orbison's style, if only because it showcases both his voice and his songwriting skills in a more varied setting, is "Pretty Woman." The first few seconds of the song bring us immediately into the sixties: the rhythm the drummer lays down and the guitar riff suspended over the steady beat are two keys. They illustrate two features that we associate with sixties rock: a rock beat (here an **eight-beat rhythm** over strong marking of the beat) and an instrumental hook that immediately identifies the song.

Roy Orbison, "Mean Woman Blues"

3:1

"Pretty Woman," Roy Orbison (1964). Orbison, guitar and vocal.

LISTENING GUIDE: "PRETTY WOMAN"

CD 3:1   **1960s Rock Song** (Roy Orbison; performed by Orbison, guitar and vocal)

0:00	Introduction. Familiar example of opening guitar riff, the song's melodic hook.	
0:15	A	
	Pretty woman...	
	Guitar riff returns as brief interlude.	
0:40	A	
	Pretty woman...	
	Guitar riff again.	
1:06	B	
	Pretty woman, stop a while...	
1:22	B[1]	
	Pretty woman, yeah yeah yeah...	
1:35	B (extension)	
	Cause I need you...	
1:55	A[1]	
	Pretty woman, don't walk on...	
2:07	A (extension)	
	...okay	
	If that's the way it must be...	

Orbison's voice is just as easily recognized. He has a naturally bright sound—not rough, not country twang, but not pop pretty either. The fast **vibrato** is distinctive. So is its range: Orbison can sing high effortlessly. It is expressive, almost melodramatic at times—especially when the material suits it. It remains one of the unique sounds in popular music.

He uses it to good effect in this song. The sound matches well the vulnerability of the "I" in the lyric. As the drama unfolds, we are not sure—in the words, the sound of his voice, or the musical setting—whether he'll actually connect with the pretty woman he'd "like to meet" or simply watch her from afar as she passes by. The ending is a surprise, in the story and in the music, the first time we hear it.

We don't really know whether Orbison's account is based on a real incident or whether it's a fantasy, but we have a much stronger sense of the identity of "I" than we would from a thirties or forties pop singer. It's Orbison, of course; we know this not only from the sound of his voice but because it's his song and his story. The mix of desire (the growl) and indecision comes straight out of Buddy Holly; it is a more mature expression of it. Orbison was in his late twenties when this song was popular, and he was not deliberately writing to a younger audience, as Chuck Berry did.

Orbison's sprawling song, with its many twists and turns, amplifies the shifting emotions of the lyrics. Its model is the traditional pop AABA plan, but Orbison expands it by enlarging its dimensions and interpolating extra sections. This too makes the song a more individual statement.

In its use of a guitar hook, an expanded and personalized form (in the unusual interpretation of rock rhythm), and most of all in Orbison's lyrics and singing, "Pretty Woman" exemplifies the profound changes in popular music that were taking place in the early sixties. Orbison's song certainly has antecedents, and it has strong roots in country and rock and roll, but the combination of elements signal that a new era is beginning.

STYLE PROFILE

"PRETTY WOMAN" (1960s ROCK SONG)

Rhythm	*Moderate tempo. Rock rhythm, with occasional strong marking of the beat (beginning of the song). Syncopation; irregular patterns in vocal line, piano, guitar, and bass.*
Melody	*Guitar riff is a memorable melodic hook. Vocal line in the A section spins out from a short riff and its answer. The B section uses a different riff.*
Instrumentation (timbre)	*Lead and harmony vocals and full rhythm section (twelve-string guitar, electric guitar, electric bass, drums, and piano).*
Performance style	*Orbison has a distinctive tenor voice with a fluttering vibrato—one of the most recognizable rock-era singing voices. Electric guitar sound has an edge but no distortion.*
Dynamics	*Moderately loud.*
Harmony	*Basically I-IV-V, but not in any familiar pattern. A special feature of the harmony is the way in which Orbison uses the V chord to create suspense, first at the beginning, then dramatically at the end. (The opening guitar riff **arpeggiates** the V chord.) The B section contains several harmonic surprises, even as it sticks mostly to basic chords.*
Texture	*Layered. Voice, guitar, bass, and piano are fairly independent of each other, especially in the rhythm. The guitar riff is the most memorable melodic feature.*
Form	*Expansive and original form driven by the lyric. A long song—just an introduction and once through the AABA form.*

For Orbison, however, it was the end of his brief run at the top. Soon after the success of his song, he went through really rough times. A move to MGM Records in 1965 proved disastrous, his wife died in an automobile accident in 1966, and two years later his two sons died in a fire that burned down his house. The rock world rediscovered his songs in the seventies—Linda Ronstadt recorded a beautiful cover of "Blue Bayou." It rediscovered him in the eighties; the Traveling Wilburys was a fitting if belated tribute to his importance.

Bob Dylan. Even as Orbison's song ascended the charts, Bob Dylan's music was becoming more introspective. As Dylan (born Robert Zimmerman in 1941) told an interviewer in 1964: "I don't want to write for people anymore you know, be a spokesman. From now on I want to write from inside me."

A year later he went electric. He scandalized Pete Seeger and other die-hard folkies at the 1965 Newport Folk Festival; they unplugged him. And his album *Bringing It All Back Home,* released that year, featured acoustic tracks on one side of the disc and electric tracks on the other. For Dylan the decision to merge into the new rock mainstream went back to his earliest days as a musician. Although he first made his reputation as a folk singer, he had begun making music in a rock band. So his move to rock was a return as much as a new direction.

There seems to be a connection between Dylan's shift in focus from crusader to commentator and his decision to go electric. As his songs became more personal, the lyrics became more challenging. Indeed, one of the favorite indoor sports for college students in the midsixties was deciphering Dylan's lyrics. So he needed another way to communicate the general mood of the song: that became the function of the band.

Bob Dylan ca. 1965. This photo was taken around the time Dylan recorded *Bringing It All Back Home,* which included "Subterranean Homesick Blues." Note the harmonica, which we hear on the recording.

CD 3:2

"Subterranean
Homesick Blues"
Bob Dylan (1965).
Dylan, acoustic
guitar, harmonica,
and vocal.

"Subterranean Homesick Blues," one of the popular tracks from *Bringing It All Back Home*, offers a splendid example of Dylan in a peak creative period. The lyric is a proto-rap song: a stream of obscure references, inside jokes, stinging social commentary, and cinéma vérité–type images—all delivered much too fast to understand in a single hearing.

The density of the lyric and the speed of Dylan's delivery challenged listeners to become engaged; one could not listen to him casually and expect to get much out of the experience. This explains the decision to add a band. For this song Dylan added a full rhythm section

LISTENING GUIDE: "SUBTERRANEAN HOMESICK BLUES"

CD 3:2 **Bob Dylan** (Bob Dylan; performed by Dylan, acoustic guitar, harmonica, and vocal)

0:00	Rhythm section sets up honky-tonk-style two-beat rhythm.
0:09	1st chorus

Extended blues form. The blues-derived harmonic progression is shown coordinated with the lyric.

I   *Johnny's in the basement*
    Mixing up the medicine
    I'm on the pavement
    Thinking about the government
    The man in the trench coat
    Badge out, laid off
    Says he's got a bad cough
    Wants to get it paid off

IV *Look out kid*
    It's somethin' you did

I   *God knows when*
    But you're doin' it again
    You better duck down the alley way
    Lookin' for a new friend

V   *The man in the coon-skin cap*
    In the big pen

I   *Wants eleven dollar bills*
    You only got ten

0:34	Instrumental break.
0:39	2nd chorus

    Maggie comes fleet foot
    Face full of black soot
    Talkin' that the heat put
    Plants in the bed but
    The phone's tapped anyway
    Maggie says that many say
    They must bust in early May
    Orders from the D. A.

IV *Look out kid*
    Don't matter what you did

I   *Walk on your tip toes*
    Don't try No Doz
    Better stay away from those
    That carry around a fire hose

V   *Keep a clean nose*
    Watch the plain clothes

behind his acoustic guitar and harmonica. The band sets up a honky-tonk feel with a clear two-beat rhythm. At the same time, it's a free-for-all for the guitarists; their interaction evokes electric blues. The ornery mood it sets up right at the start is an ideal backdrop for Dylan's words and voice.

What's so remarkable and significant about this song and others like it is that it simultaneously elevates popular music to a higher level of seriousness and brings it down to earth by wiping away traditional forms of pretentiousness. Dylan's lyric is far more complex than any-

	I	*You don't need a weather man*
		To know which way the wind blows
1:03		Instrumental break.
1:09		3rd chorus

Get sick, get well
Hang around a ink well
Ring bell, hard to tell
If anything is goin' to sell
Try hard, get barred
Get back, write Braille
Get jailed, jump bail
Join the army, if you fail
Look out kid
You're gonna get hit
But losers, cheaters
Six-time users
Hang around the theaters
Girl by the whirlpool
Lookin' for a new fool
Don't follow leaders
Watch the parkin' meters

1:33	Instrumental break.
1:40	4th chorus

Ah get born, keep warm
Short pants, romance, learn to dance
Get dressed, get blessed
Try to be a success
Please her, please him, buy gifts
Don't steal, don't lift
Twenty years of schoolin'
And they put you on the day shift
Look out kid
They keep it all hid
Better jump down a manhole
Light yourself a candle
Don't wear sandals
Try to avoid the scandals
Don't wanna be a bum
You better chew gum
The pump don't work
'Cause the vandals took the handles

thing that had been done before. We have admired clever pop lyrics, deep blues lyrics, and meaningful country lyrics. But we have not heard anything like this. Similarly, his singing is not pretty by any conventional standard—it was ordinary enough to convince Jimi Hendrix to start singing—but it is certainly appropriate for the song. And he embeds words and voice in a down-home setting. The combination of words and music inverts the traditional pop approach to artistry. Before, those who wanted to create artistic popular music emulated classical models: George Gershwin's *Rhapsody in Blue* or musical theater productions like *West Side Story*. Dylan's music sends a quite different message: one can be sophisticated without being "sophisticated," that is, without taking on the conventional trappings of sophistication, like symphonic strings.

STYLE PROFILE

"SUBTERRANEAN HOMESICK BLUES" (BOB DYLAN)

Rhythm	*Brisk tempo. Strong **two-beat rhythm** with emphatic backbeat. Fast delivery of the words.*
Melody	*Not a conventional melody: rather, streams of words on a single note, occasionally interrupted by a rifflike idea ("Look out, kid").*
Instrumentation (timbre)	*Voice, harmonica, acoustic and electric guitar, string bass, piano, and drums.*
Performance style	*Dylan's raspy voice was a drastic departure from almost any other kind of popular singing—pop, R&B, folk, country, or blues. Blues-tinged harmonica playing.*
Dynamics	*Loud for an acoustic band.*
Harmony	*Stretched-out **blues progression**.*
Texture	*Voice plus simple accompaniment, with **riffs** and fills layered in.*
Form	*Blues form, with first and second sections extended.*

Key Points

Confrontational tone	*Provocative lyrics, delivered very quickly.*
Raising the bar	*Street poetry with a bluesy, hard-country accompaniment = serious musical statement without classical sounds.*
Blues/rock/country fusion	*Honky-tonk beat, blues sounds and form, contemporary folk lyric, blended together.*
Blues and extended blues form	*Blues form, expanded in the first and third phrases.*
Rock: style versus attitude	*Rock in attitude but not in style features (no rock beat or rock band instrumentation).*

Terms to Know

blues progression
riff
two-beat rhythm

In essence, this kind of work formed a new definition of what artistry in rock—and by extension popular music—could be. By not only giving rock credibility but also redefining what credibility in popular music was—imagine the incongruity of Sinatra singing this song in Las Vegas—Dylan raised the bar, for rock and for popular music. Overnight the music grew up. It was no longer possible to mock rock—or at least Dylan's music—as mindless music for teens. Indeed, songs like "Subterranean Homesick Blues" would have left most adults in a state of incomprehension.

Dylan's influence was profound. His work from the sixties remains a standard by which those who followed him have been measured. He inspired others not so much by providing a model that others would copy as by showing through example what could be said in rock. Others responded by elevating their music on their own terms: when asked to explain the tremendous growth of the Beatles' music from 1965 on, Paul McCartney said that the group was only trying to please Dylan.

Dylan's influence was far greater than his popularity. People knew about him, but they did not buy his records at the rate they bought Beatles records. Perhaps he was too hip. Perhaps listeners couldn't warm up to his voice. In fact, it took the Byrds to show him how to reshape one of his songs into a pop hit: their cover of Dylan's "Mr. Tambourine Man" topped the charts in 1965.

The Byrds, "Mr. Tambourine Man"

Meanwhile, Dylan was not indifferent to the Byrds' success with his song; it would influence his next few albums, although he never truly compromised his vision in pursuit of commercial success. He wanted to be popular, but he also wanted to establish the terms of his popularity. He has remained unpredictable through every stage of his career.

Summary. Even this small sample gives us some idea of the extent to which folk and country shaped rock. In Orbison we continued to follow country's evolution; a rock/country merger was the almost inevitable next step after western swing, honky-tonk, and rockabilly.

The folk music scene in the early sixties had three distinct dimensions. One was sincere re-creations of folk music, or folklike music, such as Joan Baez's renditions of Carter Family songs. Another was pop-folk: Peter, Paul and Mary's hits exemplify this trend. A third was Guthrie-esque social commentaries; Dylan led the way here.

By using rock-derived points of entry—the distinctive sound of Roger McGuinn's twelve-string guitar, the guitar hook to start a song, and a comfortable rock beat—the Byrds' folk/rock synthesis managed to be both novel and appealing. At least in the respect that it smoothed down Dylan's rough edges and made the song more poplike, the Byrds' version of "Mr. Tambourine Man" paralleled Peter, Paul and Mary's hit version of Dylan's "Blowin' in the Wind." The Byrds' setting, however, was more imaginative and forward looking.

Dylan's continuing evolution as a songwriter and a performer left all of this behind. By 1965 he had forged a new style that borrowed heavily from folk, country, blues, and rock; he transformed this mix into music of real substance. It is not too much to say that the idea of rock as a potentially serious form of artistic expression begins with Dylan. Certainly, his peers thought so, as did his audience.

Dylan's defection signaled the end of the folk revival; his shift toward a more introspective mode inspired the singer-songwriters of the late sixties and early seventies: Paul Simon (with, then without, Art Garfunkel), Joni Mitchell, James Taylor, and many others.

Dylan himself moved in yet another direction: country music. He recorded three albums in the late sixties—*Blonde on Blonde* (1966), *John Wesley Harding* (1967), and *Nashville Skyline* (1969)—using Nashville session musicians. His country excursion strengthened the connection between rock and country, just as his earlier work helped link folk and rock. This was another of Dylan's major contributions to rock in the sixties: he played the key role in bringing both folk and country into rock.

Other rock/country syntheses emerged in the late sixties and early seventies, with initiative on both sides. Groups like the Grateful Dead, the Band, and Creedence Clearwater Revival helped create an "American" rock sound in the sixties with an infusion of country elements. Southern rock bands like the Allman Brothers and Lynyrd Skynyrd blended rock, soul, and country to create their distinctive sound. A new incarnation of the Byrds with Graham Parsons would search for a real rock/country fusion. It would fly only with the Eagles, in the early seventies. Country musicians like Glen Campbell explored a pop/rock/country mix that had broad appeal. Rock elements began to creep into even the hard country of Merle Haggard and others.

All of this happened even as the audiences grew farther apart. By the end of the decade, with Richard Nixon in the White House and Spiro Agnew still in office, the conservative backlash to the radical changes of the sixties was in full swing. Nixon and Agnew identified a "silent majority" who despised the leftist, draft-dodging, war-protesting, drug-ingesting, free-loving, irresponsible, and immature kids and the rock music that they listened to. Country music often spoke for them: as Merle Haggard pointed out, "We don't smoke marijuana in Muskogee."

MOTOWN

When Berry Gordy Jr. (b. 1929) got out of the army in 1953, he returned to his hometown of Detroit and opened a record store. He stocked it with jazz, a music he loved, but he refused to carry rhythm-and-blues records in spite of a steady stream of customers asking for them. Two years later he was out of business. He would learn from the experience.

After a couple of years working on an assembly line at the Ford plant, Gordy returned to the music business, first as a songwriter, then as the founder of yet another independent record company. This time around his goal was to create the first black pop style to cross over completely—to find a large audience among blacks, whites, and everyone else. He would succeed.

Gordy's **Motown** empire blended careful planning and tight control over every aspect of the operation with inspiration and spur-of-the-moment decisions. As it developed during the early sixties, Motown's organizational structure was a pyramid. At the top of the pyramid was Gordy. Underneath him were songwriting/producing teams like Smokey Robinson and Holland/Dozier/Holland. Underneath them were the house musicians. Berry recruited his core players from Detroit's jazz clubs. He relied on the skill and inventiveness of musicians such as bassist James Jamerson (the man who liberated the bass from its pedestrian four-to-the-bar role), keyboardist Earl Van Dyke, and guitarist Joe Messina to bring to life the songs brought by the arrangers to the garage–turned–recording studio christened Hitsville U.S.A. The fourth level were the acts themselves: Stevie Wonder, Mary Wells, the Supremes, the Temptations, the Four Tops, Martha Reeves and the Vandellas, Smokey Robinson and the Miracles, and the artist we consider here, Marvin Gaye.

The **Motown sound** grew out of this pyramid structure. At its core was Gordy's guiding principle: to create music that would appeal to everyone. To that end he focused on the most universal of all subjects—love won and lost—and told the tales in everyday language. Smokey Robinson recalls Gordy telling him early in their association that a song should tell a story; Robinson (and the other Motown songwriters) followed that advice.

Gordy's songwriters followed his plan, not only in words but also in music. Motown songs set the story to a melody with memorable hooks. The songs unfold according to a proven strategy: part of the story building to the chorus containing the hook; more of the story, followed by the repetition of the chorus, still more story—if there's time—followed again by the chorus. This template was easy for listeners to follow.

The house band—the rhythm players called themselves the Funk Brothers—was responsible for much of the Motown sound. They created the beats, the grooves, the memorable riffs—we know the song discussed below within seconds, well before Gaye starts singing—and the colors. These musicians, so essential to Motown's sound and success, were virtually anonymous. Often they would go to bars after a recording session and hear on the jukebox songs they'd helped create; few if any of the patrons would know how much they contributed.

It was the singers who moved into the spotlight. Not surprisingly, they received the lion's share of Gordy's attention. He determined what songs they recorded, what clothes they wore, their stage routines, and almost everything else related to their professional lives. Many artists came from disadvantaged circumstances, and Motown ran what amounted to a charm school to polish the public personas of its stars. Gordy did everything he could to have them project a smooth, cultivated image, both on-stage and off.

The product of this multidimensional interaction among Gordy, the songwriters and arrangers, the house musicians, and the acts was the Motown sound. It was dependable; fans knew pretty much what to expect from a Motown record. Yet the individual songs were usually different enough and imaginative enough to avoid becoming predictable in every respect. Within the general design, there was room for variation, as we hear below in a truly memorable Motown hit, Marvin Gaye's version of "I Heard It Through the Grapevine."

Of all the Motown artists, none sang with more emotional intensity than Marvin Gaye (1939–1984). His turbulent life—stormy relationships with his wife and other women, drug and alcohol abuse, and his death by his father's hand—seemed to find expression in his music. Whether singing about love, as in "Grapevine," or contemporary life, as in several songs from his groundbreaking 1971 album *What's Going On,* he communicated an extraordinary range of feeling: pain, hope, joy, and frustration.

"I Heard It Through the Grapevine" is one of the great recorded performances in the history of popular music. It is a drama in miniature. It is beautifully integrated: every element blends seamlessly to convey the sense of the text, which gradually unfolds the story of love gone wrong. The opening keyboard riff, harmonized with open intervals, immediately establishes a dark mood. Other instruments enter in stages, leading to the entrance of the voice. Each statement of the melody of the song contains four sections. The first two are blueslike in that they generally stay within a narrow range and go down more than up. The third builds to the final section for the hook of the song, "I heard it through the grapevine." It is the emotional center of each statement. A Greek chorus–like commentary by the backup singers ends each section.

Marvin Gaye singing soulfully in concert ca. 1975. We know that it's post-1970 because Gaye is not wearing a tuxedo. In 1971 Gaye broke away from Berry Gordy's control both musically and visually with his landmark album *What's Going On.*

© Neal Preston/Corbis

CD 3:3

"I Heard It Through the Grapevine," Barrett Strong and Norman Whitfield (1968). Marvin Gaye, vocal; and featuring James Jamerson on bass.

CD 3:3   **Motown Sound** (Barrett Strong and Norman Whitfield; performed by Marvin Gaye, vocal; and featuring James Jamerson on bass)

0:00   Instrumental introduction: ominous introduction—electric piano in the foreground playing famous riff; other instruments layer in, most notably the French horn swoop up, just before the verse.

1st Verse/Chorus Statement

0:21   Verse, part 1
Notice how the phrases start high and end low, or at least do not rise.
Ooh, I bet you're wondering...
Verse, part 2

0:38   Bridge to chorus
Surprising chord and sudden leap up underscores "surprise" in the lyric.
It took me by surprise...

0:45   Chorus
Backup vocals, keyboard riff, and strings help bring back the mood of the opening.
I heard it through the grapevine...

2nd Verse/Chorus Statement

1:09   2nd Verse
String response figures in a low register behind the voice + backup vocal harmony + Gaye and rhythm = rich texture.
I know that a man ain't supposed to cry...

1:35   Chorus
I heard it through the grapevine...

2:01   Instrumental interlude, borrowed from introduction.

3rd Verse/Chorus Statement

2:06   *People say believe half...*
Strings begin to soar on the bridge.
Do you plan...

2:32   Chorus
I heard it through the grapevine...

2:49   Tag. Gradual fading away. The "muttering" of backup vocals helps project the despondent mood of the song.

Key Features of Motown Sound. In "I Heard It Through the Grapevine," we can identify key features of the Motown sound. The following four aspects stand out.

o   *Melodic saturation.* The song is full of melodic fragments: the lead vocal line is the most prominent, but there are many others: guitar and keyboard riffs, horn fills, string lines—even the bass lines are melodically interesting as well as supportive (that was Jamerson's breakthrough!). The presence of so much melody, all of it easily grasped, helped ensure easy entry into the song; it also was a good reason to listen over and over.

o   *A good, but unobtrusive beat.* The song uses a rock beat, but it is very much in the background. Only the backbeat is strong. The rest is more subdued: the percussion sounds include light drums (the drummer uses mallets to get a darker sound), conga drums, and tambourine; guitars do not lay down a heavy rock rhythm; the bass is the most prominent rhythm instrument. This restrained rock rhythm has the novelty of the new beat with little of its aggressiveness. (Compare the percussion here with the drums in "Pretty Woman.") Other Motown songs used different beats. What they had in common was a strong backbeat and an understatement of everything else. In particular, timekeeping in the midrange register is subdued to give greater prominence to the voices.

○ *A broad sound spectrum.* Motown recordings gave listeners a lot to listen for. The instrumental and vocal sounds cut across all social, racial, and economic lines: we hear the relatively untutored sound of the singers—Gaye's grit, plus the backup vocalists. There are sounds as simple as a tambourine and as sophisticated as the French horn swoops and the orchestral string sounds. (Note that the interlude in "Grapevine" is a written-out solo for strings rather than a sax solo. This kind of string writing, similar to what we heard in the Shirelles' recording of "Will You Love Me Tomorrow," suggests "class"; in fact, the string players on the Motown recordings were moonlighting from the Detroit Symphony.) The rhythm section typically included more than the minimum number of players: usually there were at least two guitars, several percussionists, and keyboards. With all of this richness, there were sounds for everyone, regardless of background.

○ *A predictable form.* Using only "I Heard It Through the Grapevine," we could construct a pretty reliable template for a Motown song: layered instrumental introduction, solo two-phrase verse, bridge, title phrase, and commentary. There is enough variation in the form and in the other features of the song to keep it fresh, but we can certainly anticipate the events in the story.

These four features were designed to provide easy entry into a song—and to keep us there. All four offer basic points of entry: melodic hooks, a clear backbeat, interesting and varied instrumental sounds (the electric keyboard and horns in "Grapevine"), and an easy-to-follow form. All four also surround these entry points with interesting material, so the song rewards repeated listening. This combination of easy entry and rich texture was a key element in Motown's success.

STYLE PROFILE

"I HEARD IT THROUGH THE GRAPEVINE" (MOTOWN SOUND)

Rhythm	*Moderate tempo. Rock rhythm with strong backbeat but subdued marking of the rock rhythmic layer—mainly drums and conga on deep-sounding drums. Syncopation in vocal line in both verse and chorus, also in accompanying riffs.*
Melody	*Vocal melody consists of short phrases—longer than the opening riff. Bluesy quality because of downward direction.*
Instrumentation (timbre)	*Lead and backup vocals. Rhythm section with extra percussion (electric piano, electric guitar, electric bass, drums, tambourine, and conga), and orchestral instruments (violins and the French horn just before the voice enters).*
Performance style	*Gaye sings in a high range; the strain of singing high and the grit in his voice are ideal for communicating the pain of the rejected lover.*
Dynamics	*Moderately loud, for the most part. Sudden drop in dynamics after the chorus helps return to the ominous feeling of the beginning.*

Harmony	*Minor key version of I-IV-V with a few additional chords (minor keys have often been associated with sad moods).*
Texture	*Layered texture, with some or all of the following: lead vocal line, steady percussion parts, bass line, keyboard riffs, backup vocal responses and harmony, violin obbligato lines, and occasional other instrumental parts, like the horn swoop. These are distributed over a wide range: bass and percussion are low, voices and keyboard in the middle, strings usually in a high register. Considerable variation from the empty sound of the opening to the full ensemble in the chorus.*
Form	*Motown's take on verse/chorus form: begin with layered instrumental introduction (which typically also serves as an interlude); begin to tell the story over simple harmony (the first part of the verse); build toward the chorus (second part of the verse, often called the **bridge** [different from AABA bridge]); then arrive at the chorus, which repeats a rifflike idea several times.*

Key Points

Motown sounds	*A variety of sounds, from fingersnaps to symphonic strings.*
Melodic saturation	*Melody everywhere: lead/backup vocals and background riffs.*
Motown formula	*Subtle variation on verse/chorus template.*
Words and music	*Sad story, dark musical mood (as in the keyboard riff).*
Black crossover style	*Motown was the first black style to consistently chart.*

Terms to Know
bridge
minor key
Motown sound

Motown records mined a familiar vein in popular music: the ups and downs of love. The song focuses on love lost, but there are others that convey the exhilaration of being in love. It's worth noting how well the musical setting of "Grapevine" helps project the lyric. From the first keyboard notes, the instrumental backing matches Gaye's despair. (Another version released about the same time, by Gladys Knight and the Pips, projects a quite different mood.) Some have accused Motown of being formulaic—pop music's answer to the Detroit auto assembly lines—but emotional, as well as musical, variety was possible within a consistent overall plan.

Motown updated black pop. From Louis Armstrong and Ethel Waters, through Nat "King" Cole and the Mills Brothers, into doo-wop and the girl groups—one direction in black music had been a distinctly African American take on popular song. Motown offered not just a new take on pop but a new, black popular style—and a new kind of romantic music.

In this sense Motown was heading in the opposite direction from rock. Rock tended to look at love cynically (the Beatles' "Norwegian Wood" comes to mind), lustfully (the Rolling Stones' "Satisfaction"), or not at all. Motown songs preserve the romance in the popular songs of the thirties and forties even as they bring both lyrics and music into the present. It's evident not only in the sound—the rich string writing, the understated playing of the rhythm section—but also in the look. The groups wore tuxedos and gowns, like Las Vegas acts, not tie-dyed T-shirts and jeans, like the Woodstock crowd.

Motown was one of the remarkable success stories of the sixties. A black entrepreneur with fine musical instincts and a good business sense created an empire. For the first time in history, a black style was on equal footing with white music.

Motown lost its toehold at the top in the seventies. The Jackson 5 was Motown's last big act. Stevie Wonder gained artistic freedom as a condition of his new contract, and he used it. Marvin Gaye also sought and got independence, eventually leaving Motown altogether. The company has remained an important player in pop music; and though it is no longer the dominant and innovative force it was in the sixties, its legacy is still very much with us.

THE BRITISH INVASION

On February 9, 1964, the Beatles appeared on *The Ed Sullivan Show* for the first time. Back in the fifties and sixties, when most American television viewers had only the three network channels to choose from, *The Ed Sullivan Show* was a Sunday-night fixture. Still, the audience was enormous by any measure: an estimated 73 million viewers—almost 40 percent of the U.S. population at that time—tuned in that evening. They didn't really hear the Beatles perform, however; screams from the crowd drowned out the band.

The Beatles had scored their first U.S. number 1 hit, "I Want to Hold Your Hand," less than a month before. Their first U.S. album would reach number 1 just as they arrived in New York. In little more than a month, the band had developed a passionate following, one that would surpass Elvis's: the media dubbed it "Beatlemania." Other British bands soon followed the Beatles to the United States, and within a year the **British invasion** was under way.

The roster of British bands who made an impact in the sixties is substantial: the first wave, in 1964, included not only the Beatles but also the Rolling Stones, the Kinks, the Animals, the Dave Clark Five, and several others. By the end of the sixties, many more had joined them: the Who, Cream, and Led Zeppelin stand out.

The sudden popularity of British bands in America abruptly reversed the flow of popular music between the United States and the rest of the world. Up until the early sixties, popular music had been an American export. From the minstrel show through ragtime, syncopated dance music (recall Jim Europe's European tour at the end of World War I), and several generations of jazz, popular-song, and finally rock-and-roll music—all found an audience abroad. Musicians from other countries absorbed this American music; a few transformed what they heard into new, personal sounds. Before the sixties, however, few foreign musicians playing popular music enjoyed much of a following in the United States.

All that changed with the British invasion. Of course, the music that they played had deep American roots. Many of the bands began their careers by covering songs by Chuck Berry, Buddy Holly, and other rock-and-roll acts. The Rolling Stones' name underscores the musical impact of bluesmen like Muddy Waters and Robert Johnson. But what they brought back to the United States was an altogether new music. What's more, it was never exotic, and it soon became mainstream. Indeed, the British invasion, more than any other event, fueled the ascendancy of rock in the United States during the sixties.

What is surprising is the ease with which rock—and by extension popular music—became an international music. Up to this point, popular music *in* America and popular music *from* America were pretty much the same thing. After the Beatles that was no longer true. While Americans acknowledged, even celebrated, the Britishness of the Beatles and the other invading bands, there was no sense that their music was foreign. Perhaps it was because the sounds were at once familiar (because they were so deeply rooted in American culture)

TABLE 10.1	THE BEATLES VERSUS THE ROLLING STONES	
	Beatles	Rolling Stones
Public Image	The fab four: polished whole-some public image early on: trendy, friendly	Bad boys: projected nasty image
Longevity	Together for seven years and nine months	Still going strong: longest-lived rock band in history
Musical Development	No group has ever grown more in such a short period of time	Found their groove early on and have been mining it ever since
Key Musical Element	Melody: the Beatles redefined popular song	Rhythm: the Rolling Stones showed the world how to rock
Recording and Performance	A studio band after 1966; great-est impact on record	Huge impact in performance; still a hot ticket in early twenty-first century
Role in Defining Rock	Stretched rock's boundaries	Created rock's core musical values

yet fresh (because they represented a new way of interpreting American music). Perhaps it was the open-minded spirit that seemed to pervade the sixties. Whatever the reason, their nationality was a nonissue.

Of all the bands that came from England in the sixties, the most important—in nearly every respect—were the Beatles and the Rolling Stones. Almost from the beginning, they have been paired. The Rolling Stones followed the Beatles to the top of the American charts in 1965: their first number 1 hit was "(I Can't Get No) Satisfaction." As they grew in popularity, Andrew Loog Oldham, the manager of the Rolling Stones at the beginning of their career, carefully crafted their image in opposition to the Beatles. Yet the two bands enjoyed a good relationship, at least at the start: the Stones' second single was a Lennon-McCartney song, "I Wanna Be Your Man."

In retrospect, we might understand the relationship between the two bands as yin (the Beatles) and yang (the Stones), a complementary pairing that, when taken together, forms a whole. Table 10.1 identifies several of these complementary oppositions. We can examine the musical aspects of their complementary relationship by sampling their music. First, the Beatles.

The Beatles

In the history of popular music, the Beatles—John Lennon (1940–1980), Paul McCartney (b. 1942), George Harrison (1943–2001), and Ringo Starr (born Richard Starkey in 1940)—remain one of a kind. They were surpassingly popular throughout their time together: few acts have had their staying power. They also wowed critics; that puts them in even more elite company. What makes them unique, however, is that they have remained popular. Their music has continued to delight new generations of fans and stimulate thoughtful critical commentary. Their uninterrupted commercial and critical success, from the time their career took off in 1964 to the present, is unprecedented. No other act can match it.

The group had impeccable timing. They ushered in a new era in popular music. Their music epitomized change at a time when change was a good thing. They were the center of

The Album

Indeed, it was with the Beatles that the album replaced the single as the primary unit of record sales in rock. Certainly for Dylan, the album was the main medium. But his sales never approached those of the Beatles. Moreover, the Beatles' friendly competition with the Beach Boys' Brian Wilson resulted in the first **concept album**; that is, a long-playing record containing several tracks conceived as an integrated whole rather than simply a collection of songs. Wilson's groundbreaking contribution was *Pet Sounds*. The Beatles' entry was *Sgt. Pepper's Lonely Hearts Club Band*, which remains the most popular choice for the first concept album as well as a leading candidate for the most anticipated recording of all time. As Langdon Winner, a rock critic turned political theorist, remarked, "The closest Western civilization has come to unity since the Congress of Vienna in 1815 was the week that the *Sgt. Pepper* album was released."

Tribute Bands

The versions of the two Beatles songs used on the anthology were recorded by Rain, a fine tribute band. A **tribute band** is a special kind of cover band in that they not only perform songs recorded by other bands but also try to replicate the recording as precisely as they can. Tribute bands are a rock-era phenomenon because they use the original recording—the "official" document—as their primary source.

attention, and their music was familiar to a large audience in a way that is virtually impossible in today's fragmented marketplace.

The Beatles had a superb public persona, and its most vivid expression came in 1964's *A Hard Day's Night*, their documentary-style film about their life in the spotlight. With its mix of real and imaginary scenes and frenetic pacing, the film was as innovative as their music. The four came across splendidly; they were funny, down to earth, and lovably impudent.

Finally, though, it comes down to the music. It is their work, together and apart over an almost eight-year span, that keeps us coming back. What qualities does their music have that made it so exciting when it was released and makes it still interesting today? At the time it was, above all, a sense of discovery: fans wondered what the group would come up with next. From *Rubber Soul* on, the release of a Beatles' album was an event, in part because it would be so full of surprises.

Two enduring features of the Beatles' music fueled this sense of discovery. One was their rapid musical evolution: we can chart their progression from rock-and-roll band to sophisticated and adventurous music-makers. The other was the extraordinary range of their music: it all sounded like the Beatles, but the differences from work to work were extraordinary.

We can get some sense of the music's evolutionary path by examining a pair of basic songs, "I Saw Her Standing There" and "Get Back." "I Saw Her Standing There," which was recorded and released in the first part of 1963, was one of the group's first hits. In this song, and many of the others from the same period, the Beatles are helping define rock as a style distinct from rock and roll.

In "I Saw Here Standing There" (and several other early songs), the Beatles extended and integrated two of Chuck Berry's most important musical innovations: his rhythmic approach and the edge to his guitar sound. The groove created at the outset grows out of the energetic, obvious rock rhythm by all four Beatles: a steady, straightforward rock beat from Ringo, rhythmic and melodic riffs from John and George, and a fast-moving bass line (allegedly lifted from a Chuck Berry song) from Paul.

 3:4

"I Saw Her Standing There," John Lennon and Paul McCartney (1963). Rain.

CD 3:4   **Early 1960s Rock** (John Lennon and Paul McCartney; performed by Rain)

0:00	Introduction.

1st Chorus (AABA)

0:10   A   Bass moves at rock-beat speed here.
Well, she was just 17 . . .
Switches to four-beat speed to highlight the change in melody.
So how could I dance . . .

0:34   A   The handclaps reinforce the backbeat. This rebound backbeat was a popular early-sixties pattern (also heard in "Will You Love Me Tomorrow").
Well she looked at me . . .

0:58   B
Well, my heart . . .
Falsetto singing on "mine."
And I held her hand in mine . . .

1:13   A
Whoah, we danced . . .

2nd Chorus (partial ABA)

1:37   A   Guitar solo

2:01   B   Notice the extension of the phrase on "mine."
Well, my heart went "boom" . . .

2:15   A
Whoah, we danced . . .

2:40   Tag: repeat of title phrase.

The sound of the guitars and bass is bright and aggressive—at least by 1963 standards. It has the cutting quality heard in the playing of Berry and other rock-and-roll guitarists. As such it is an ideal instrumental complement to the group's singing: energetic, a little raw, and spilling over with good humor.

Both the sound and the rhythm of the song represent not so much a revolution as a consolidation. Along with Berry himself, the Beach Boys and other surf bands, and other British groups, the Beatles are getting everyone on the same page. As this happens rock and roll becomes **rock**. This basic sound would be the springboard for the major innovations soon to follow.

Like the music, the lyrics of the song revisit the teen-themed territory of the 1950s. They retain some of the innocence of that earlier decade ("Well, my heart went boom?") and cater to the same age group. Compared with their later songs, the lyrics seem rather simple; compared with the "moon/June" lyrics in so much British and American pop, however, they were refreshingly direct. And they contain the kind of inside references that would become a Beatles trademark. The first two lines are a good example. In Great Britain, the age of consent is sixteen. That the young lady was seventeen suggests a certain worldliness. The companion line ("And you know what I mean") was John's "wink-wink" modification of Paul's original, perhaps suggesting that the singer might be able to do more than hold her hand.

CD 3:5   Later 1960s Rock (John Lennon and Paul McCartney; performed by Rain)

0:00	Instrumental introduction

1st Statement

0:09	Verse
	Notice the drum rhythm ("dum-diddy") and the alternating guitar chords.
	Jojo was a man...
0:24	Chorus
	Call-and-response between voice and instruments throughout the chorus.
	Get back, get back...

2nd Statement

0:40	Verse
	Guitar solo. "Go home" interjected into the solo.
0:56	Chorus
	Get back, get back...
1:14	Interlude: keyboard solo on the harmony of the verse.

3rd Statement

1:29	Verse
	Sweet Loretta Martin...
1:45	Chorus
	Get back...

4th Statement

2:01	Verse
	Guitar solo.
2:16	Chorus
	Notice how the song ends on the IV chord, which leaves the music hanging in midair.
	Get back...

"I Saw Her Standing There" hints at the qualities that would help define the Beatles' legacy. It is tuneful; like most Beatles' songs, it has a catchy, memorable, and imaginative melody. It has surprises—the vocal harmonies, the extension of the bridge, and a few surprising harmonies in what is mostly a three-chord song.

Six years later their approach is quite different. Even though it is a "basic" rock-and-roll song (as opposed to elaborate productions such as "A Day in the Life"), "Get Back" is considerably more sophisticated in every respect than "I Saw Her Standing There." The content and the style of the lyric show Dylan's influence: it is at once socially aware and maddeningly difficult to decode (without a crib sheet). The chorus phrase, "Get back to where you once belonged," was originally a parody of the notorious 1968 Rivers of Blood speech by Enoch Powell, a racist British politician. In the chorus of the song, Paul assumes a Powell-like persona, telling Pakistanis trying to emigrate from Kenya to return home. Perhaps he sensed that his audience would not detect his shift from first to third person. In any event he omitted more-specific details in the verse, thereby avoiding Randy Newman's "Short People" dilemma of being seen as prejudiced. The verse seems to bear no relation to the chorus—the lyric

3:5

"Get Back," John Lennon and Paul McCartney (1969). Rain.

COMPARING STYLES

1960s ROCK (EARLY AND LATER BEATLES)

"I Saw Her Standing There"	"Get Back"
RHYTHM	
Fast tempo. Basic rock rhythm actively kept by drums, bass, and rhythm guitar. Strong backbeat. Guitar riffs and vocal line are syncopated.	Moderately fast tempo. Rock rhythm marked most strongly by alternating on- and off-beat chords from the two guitars. Drummer plays a "dum-diddy" pattern throughout, while bass plays repeated notes in time with the rock rhythm. Syncopation in verse and especially in the title phrase.
MELODY	
The A section has a question/answer–type melody: question = a riff that grows into a phrase; answer = two longer phrases. The B section grows out of a repeated riff.	Verse: a long phrase with a simple rise and fall, plus its repetition. Chorus: a short riff, which eventually grows into a longer phrase, and its repetitions.
INSTRUMENTATION (TIMBRE)	
Lead and backup vocals, plus basic rock band—two electric guitars, electric bass, and drums—and handclaps.	Lead and harmony vocal, plus two electric guitars, electric bass, drums, and electric keyboard (Billy Preston on the original recording).
PERFORMANCE STYLE	
Edge to the sound, in vocals, guitar, and bass. **Falsetto** (singing in the head, rather than from the chest, to sing higher) whoops.	Understated guitar sound during solos.
DYNAMICS	
Loud.	Moderately loud.
HARMONY	
Mostly I-IV-V, but with a surprise chord on "whooh" in the A section.	Mostly I and IV; slow chord rhythm. (Guitar response in the verse is an alternative to I-IV-V.)

makes no connection between Jojo, Loretta, and those told to "get back." There is, in effect, no narrative, or at least no coherent narrative. In this respect it is the opposite of the early song, which tells its story in a straightforward manner.

The musical differences between the two songs are a measure of how quickly rock matured. There is a sense of play in the instrumental backdrop that could come only when musicians felt secure with the rhythmic assumptions of a style. The group essentially customizes rock rhythm—Ringo's "dum-diddy" rhythm and the strong off-beat guitar chords—to fit the traveling theme of the song.

The other aspects of the song are comparably subtle. The slow crescendo at the beginning (as if the train were approaching), the understated guitar solo, Billy Preston's tasteful keyboard solos, and the simple but telling three-chord response to each line of the verse—all of this seems more in tune with the verse than the chorus. Perhaps the conflicting messages are a more subtle expression of the Beatles' sense of humor.

1960s ROCK (EARLY AND LATER BEATLES)

"I Saw Her Standing There"	"Get Back"
Active, with all instruments busy underneath the voices.	Open sound: rhythm section provides steady under-current beneath vocal; call-and-response—voice/guitar answers.

FORM

AABA, with extensions.	Verse/chorus.

KEY POINTS

Teen-themed song. Lyrics targeted at adolescents.	Insiders' song. Chorus = vague reference to racial problem in Britain. Verses = no coherent story.
The bass and rock rhythm. McCartney's bass moves at rock-beat speed.	Beyond a basic rock beat. Playing with the rock beat: two guitars alternating; "dum-diddy" drum rhythm.
Early Beatles sound. Bold sounds for early sixties: edge to vocals and guitars.	Later Beatles sound. Song uniqueness from melody plus other features: accompaniment rhythms and guitar sound.
Tunefulness. Both A and B sections built from catchy melodies.	Tunefulness. Melody in forefront: long phrases in verse; short riff in chorus.
Original features. Special features include extension of B section and falsetto whoops.	Original features. Background rhythms, tuneful melody over slow harmony, and subdued guitar style.

EVOLUTION OF THE BEATLES' SOUND

Early Beatles = fresh new sound that helps create rock.	Later Beatles = each song distinctive and imaginative.

TERMS TO KNOW

falsetto	rock	rock beat

What is clear is that the Beatles were able to imprint this song with a distinct personality. Their ability to create a sound world specific to this song is evident here, even though their resources are modest (Preston's keyboard is the only added element). It makes no difference that the song doesn't seem to convey a consistent message or that it all seems like fun. By this time, this process is second nature.

By contrast "I Saw Here Standing There" is, relatively speaking, more generic; that is, it sounds more like the other songs from the same time: "I Want to Hold Your Hand," "She Loves You," and the other early hits.

Precisely because it seems so casually tossed off, "Get Back" convincingly illustrates how the Beatles almost single-handedly redefined popular song. In the generations of popular music before rock, a song was its lyric, melody, and harmony—and sometimes not even that, in that song interpreters often reshaped the melody and arrangers or accompanists redid the harmony. With the Beatles and their peers, the song becomes the entire sound world captured on record.

We have heard songs by Roy Orbison, Bob Dylan, and Marvin Gaye. In every case, we identify the song as it's recorded: we don't expect to hear "Pretty Woman" played by 101 Strings in an elevator. The Beatles, however, went a significant step beyond this: they exploited the full potential of the song as a recorded document. For them the identity of the song was not just in the words and the melody. Every aspect of it—the choice of instruments, the way they are played, the interplay among them, and more—was purposefully shaped to evoke a mood. Often the mood enhances the meaning of the lyric. Other times, as in "Get Back," there seems to be little correlation. In either case, there is little in a later Beatles song that is gratuitous; that is, done just because it's the current fashion. This sense of musical purpose remains one of the key qualities that set the Beatles' music above so much other music of the last half century. No one before or since was better at customizing a musical setting and coordinating it with text than the Beatles.

This personalizing of a song was possible because of the extraordinary range of their music. From 1965 on, Beatles songs really begin to sound different from one another, yet they all sound like Beatles' songs. How do we account for their extraordinary musical range? Here are three important reasons.

○ *Knowledge of styles.* They had firsthand familiarity with a broad range of styles. In their dues-paying years, the band performed not only rock-and-roll covers and original songs but also pop hits of all kinds. Unlike the vast majority of contemporary groups, they had a thorough knowledge of pop before rock, and they clearly absorbed styles as well as songs.

○ *Melodic skill.* Along with the Motown songwriting teams, the Beatles were the first important rock-era musicians to write melody-oriented songs that were in step with the changes in rhythm, form, and other elements that took place during this time. No one since has written so many memorable melodies.

○ *Sound imagination.* Aided by the development of multitrack recording and the consummate craftsmanship of producer George Martin, the Beatles enriched their songs by startling, often unprecedented combinations of instruments and—occasionally—extraneous elements, such as the crowd noises and the trumpet flourishes of "Sgt. Pepper."

They brought all of these qualities into play as they created their legacy. To cite just a few examples: "Yesterday" came to McCartney so suddenly that he held off recording the song for six months because he was afraid that he'd simply remembered an old song. In fact, it is very much an old-style, fox trot song in its melodic construction (built from a three-note riff) and form (an AABA ballad, with the B and last A repeated). But McCartney modernizes the sound by using a very understated rock rhythm in his guitar accompaniment and a lean string sound (his instructions to George Martin: "not like [British conductor Annunzio] Mantovani"). These more modern touches make the prerock melody evoke "Yesterday" even more powerfully.

"Eleanor Rigby" is an even bolder statement: consider how original it was to write a song about two desperate losers. Key features of the song amplify our sense of the dead-end lives of Eleanor and Father McKenzie. The choruses are huge sighs. The melody of the verse inevitably sinks, as if a millstone were pulling it down; it is a musical expression of the depressed mood painted in the lyric. The accompaniment is comparably bold: a double string quartet replaces the standard rock band; Martin's arrangement projects a kind of undirected nervous energy that supports the image of purposeless lives in the lyric.

Despite Lennon's protestations to the contrary, "Lucy in the Sky with Diamonds" certainly seems to depict the LSD experience, and we do know that Lennon was tripping on a daily basis when he wrote the song. The evidence is in the music. In the verse of the song, the group creates a dreamy mood with the help of a synthesizer, a waltz rhythm in a languid tempo, and a transparent texture. By contrast, the chorus—simply the title of the song over and over—is basic rock and roll. Most rock-era songs have one voice through both verse and chorus. Here, however, it is as if we are experiencing an LSD trip during the verse ("tangerine trees and marmalade skies") and observing it from the outside in the chorus (rock and roll = the real world).

All three songs stretch the boundaries of rock in every direction. None of them is a conventional rock song, in subject or realization. Only the chorus of "Lucy in the Sky with Diamonds" uses conventional rock rhythm and instrumentation, and there it is not by default but to send a message of normalcy.

Implicit in this expansion is a shift in attitude. With the Beatles rock becomes whatever they say it is; it doesn't have to be any particular sound. The Beatles were rock's—and popular music's—first great eclectics. They drew on their imagination, Martin's incomparable assistance, and the sound world around them to create masterpieces, much as a master chef would select ingredients and seasonings to create a gourmet feast. The nonrock features, such as the new string sounds, older-style forms, waltz rhythms, and the like, were never exotic elements. Magically, they sounded as if they belonged—as though no other choice were possible. One reason why they were able to smoothly integrate such disparate sources was that each element served an expressive musical purpose. A new sound was seldom novelty for novelty's sake, and it usually seemed to fit into the whole; the group's success ratio was extraordinarily high.

All of this is one important dimension of their genius—and of their impact on the music of subsequent generations. Another is the tunefulness of their music. Lennon, McCartney, and Harrison wrote songs that people would want to sing, songs whose melodies were a main point of entry. The quality of their songs sets their music apart from that of many of their contemporaries.

Much sixties rock and soul was not tuneful: sample the music of the Rolling Stones or James Brown to affirm this point. This is not a criticism but simply a statement of fact. Indeed, it would be inappropriate for a song like "Cold Sweat" (heard later in this chapter) to have a tuneful melody. But it does cast into relief how the Beatles created a new kind of popular song—song not only in the generic sense of a track on a recording but also in the more specific sense of a musical work with a singable melody. That too is part of their legacy.

The Rolling Stones

While the Beatles were showing the world what rock could be, the Rolling Stones—originally Mick Jagger (b. 1943), lead vocal and percussion; Keith Richards (b. 1943) and Brian Jones (1942–1969), guitar; Bill Wyman (b. 1936), bass; Charlie Watts (b. 1941), drums; plus Ian Stewart (1938–1985), road manager and sometime keyboardist—were letting everyone know what rock should be. What they (and so many bands after them) would call "rock and roll" was not a warmed-over version of the music of the fifties but the essence of rock.

They began to craft the sound that would eventually justify their billing as "the world's greatest rock-and-roll band" in 1962, when Jagger, Richards, and Jones got together to form the first incarnation of the Stones. Wyman joined the group in late 1962; Watts followed in early 1963, the year they released their first single, a cover of Chuck Berry's "Come On." Like so many groups, they began their career playing covers—of rock-and-roll songs and blues. By 1965, however, they had started to record original material, such as "(I Can't Get No) Satisfaction." The song, and *Out of Our Heads,* the album from which it came, marked a commercial breakthrough; both topped the charts that summer. *Aftermath,* released the following year, was their first album to feature only original songs by Jagger and Richards. The group briefly fell under the spell of the Beatles: their *Their Satanic Majesties Request* was an ill-advised answer to *Sgt. Pepper.* They soon returned to rock and roll, recording such rock-defining hits as "Jumping Jack Flash" (1968) and "Honky Tonk Women" (1969). With songs like these, the group had found its groove and defined its place in the history of popular music.

The Rolling Stones' brand of rock and roll grew out of fifties rock and roll and deep blues. Richards was—and is—a big Chuck Berry fan, as his role in orchestrating the Chuck Berry tribute captured in the film *Hail, Hail, Rock 'n' Roll* testifies. Jagger and Brian Jones were serious students of the blues: the group took its name from a Muddy Waters song. When they finally hit their stride in mid-decade, however, the product was more than a blend of the two styles; they had created something new.

Their conception of rock began with an attitude: sexually charged, down and dirty, swaggering, real. All of this is an extension of the bluesman's persona, and it is embodied most powerfully in Mick Jagger. Although he came from a comfortable middle-class family and was attending the London School of Economics in the early sixties, Jagger did not simply imitate the bluesmen he admired—he forged his own identity, one that resonated with their influence but was also different and credible. The rest of the band also assumed this attitude: Keith Richards's sneer is the visual counterpart to the nasty riffs for which he is so well known. Andrew Loog Oldham, who became their manager in 1964, actively promoted this image: by his own admission, he wanted them—or at least their public image—to be the opposite of the Beatles.

Their music matched their image: they built a new sound from rock and roll, blues, and their own inspiration. From Jagger's sound to Wyman's bass lines, it was all of a piece. We can examine two core components, as heard in songs like "(I Can't Get No) Satisfaction," "Jumping Jack Flash," and "Honky Tonk Women."[*]

The Rolling Stones, "Brown Sugar"

○ *The groove.* The groove begins with a strong backbeat and an eight-beat rhythm. They are most obvious in Watts's drumming (Jones's rhythm guitar is almost inaudible), and this basic rock rhythm serves as a backdrop for everything else. Far more prominent are Richards's syncopated guitar riffs (the famous fuzztone riff in "Satisfaction," which came to him in the middle of the night, or the power chords in "Jumping Jack Flash" and "Honky Tonk Women"), Wyman's free-flowing bass lines, and Watts's drum kicks. Indeed, all three songs (and many others) start with a syncopated rhythm; Watts enters only after the songs are pretty well under way. The groove grows out of the interplay between the basic rock rhythm, the backbeat, and the layers of syncopated riffs and lines. It is the product of the style beat and the riffs, much as swing is the product of riffs over a four-beat rhythm.

○ *A dark, nasty sound.* Jagger's singing—rough, highly inflected, almost drawled, and more speechlike than sung—is the most obvious expression of the nasty Stones sound. Complementing it is the thick, dark texture produced by Richards's fondness for the lower

---

[*] Several tracks from early seventies Stones albums, like "Tumbling Dice," also illustrate the characteristic Stones groove. These are available online.

register of the guitar, Wyman's bass, and Watts's use of the bass drum. Typically, the highest sound in a Stones song is Jagger's voice, which stays in a midrange. The dark sound results from a lot of activity in the lower registers. Both Jagger's singing and the thick texture come directly from the blues; in the work of the Stones, it becomes part of the sound of rock.

The compelling rhythms and the dense, riff-laden texture set the tone for the stories told in the songs. The three discussed here are very much in keeping with the group image. In "Satisfaction" Jagger vents his sexual frustration with harangues about petty matters. "Jumping Jack Flash" is a pseudo-autobiography describing a childhood of difficult-to-imagine hard times. "Honky Tonk Women" paints a vivid picture of cruising and scoring in low-life places. To an audience raised on pop, all of this had the taste of forbidden fruit—it was a far cry from the teen-themed songs of the fifties or the early Beatles or the surf music of the Beach Boys. In effect, the Rolling Stones brought a blues sensibility into the mainstream. Both words and music thrilled a new generation and repulsed an older one.

Musical interest often extends beyond the groove and the rich texture. Typically, songs will have distinctive features, which often underscore the meaning of the text. Here are a couple of samples from the three songs: In "Satisfaction" the opening guitar riff never changes; it embodies Jagger's frustration because it tries (and tries) to go somewhere but never does. Also, the sequence of verse and chorus are switched. What is usually the verse is the part that returns again and again. It builds to a peak, at which point Jagger begins to rant. This ends futilely in a drum break. This tweaking of the form also expresses Jagger's frustration. In "Jumping Jack Flash," a high guitar halo surrounds the first phrase of the chorus—a musical signal that everything is, in fact, all right. What would be the third verse in "Honky Tonk Women" is played, not sung; several horns are added to the mix. It's an aural portrait of a crowded bar. And an especially nice touch is the delayed entrance of the bass; Wyman doesn't enter until the chorus: bass and steel guitar (used to evoke the country/honky-tonk environment) sandwich the vocals.

Summary

The Beatles and the Rolling Stones played crucial roles in defining rock as the important new music of the sixties. The roles were complementary: the Rolling Stones described rock's musical essence better than anyone else, while the Beatles opened up a world of possibilities to their contemporaries and the generations that followed.

Although they were certainly aware of each other, the two groups inhabited different worlds. Brian Jones's death "by misadventure," the Altamont riot, the occasional brushes with the law—all were real-life counterparts to the world depicted in their songs. Their lives, their group persona, and their music reeked of attitude. The Beatles conveyed a different attitude: Yoko Ono, Strawberry Fields, psychedelia, sunshiny songs, several brands of humor—from satire to buffoonery—these suggested a brighter worldview and a more high-minded attitude. With the two groups, rock gets its high and low dimensions, its core, and its boundaries.

GUITAR GODS

Perhaps the greatest creative tension in rock has been the conflict between a group conception and individual expression. Rock is, at its core, a group music, one in which independent yet interdependent elements weave together to form a sum that is greater than the parts. We heard this convincingly in the music of the Rolling Stones, who have flourished for more than four decades, and of the Beatles, who are still extraordinarily popular: neither group had a strong guitar soloist.

At the same time, there were sixties rock stars who stood out because of their brilliance as soloists. Most were guitarists: Eric Clapton, Jerry Garcia, Carlos Santana, Jimmy Page, and Jeff Beck were among the elite. The most significant and influential guitarist of the sixties, however, was Jimi Hendrix (1942–1970). More than any other guitarist, he exploited the capabilities of the solid-body guitar, improved amplification, and new electronics.

The idea of a **solid-body electric guitar** dates back to the 1930s, as guitar manufacturers worked to apply electric steel guitar technology to a standard guitar. Les Paul, a fine jazz guitarist and a technical whiz, experimented with solid-body instruments—among them the "log"—as a means of reducing **feedback** (when part of a system's output signal is returned into its own input, causing a loud howl or squeal, which was considered undesirable at the time).

Commercial solid-body guitars had been available for about two decades by the time Hendrix recorded his debut album. Leo Fender, a radio repairman turned instrument maker, began building solid-body electric guitar prototypes in 1944; he introduced his Broadcaster four years later, in 1948. Fender's Broadcaster, which became the Telecaster, and his Stratocaster, introduced in 1954, became standards by which other solid-body guitars were measured. The sudden increase in amplification in the sixties made the instrument far more powerful. An array of sound modifiers, such as the wah-wah pedal, made the instrument more versatile.

Jimi Hendrix. More than any other guitarist of the sixties, Hendrix exploited the potential of the three technologies (guitar, amplification, and sound modifiers). He had grown up listening to the blues, Robert Johnson and B. B. King in particular. He had begun his career in his teens, playing behind R&B acts: between 1963 and 1965, he played lead guitar for Little Richard, who taught him a thing or two about showmanship. In 1966 he fronted his first band, Jimmy James and the Blue Flames. Chas Chandler, a musician turned musical promoter, talked Hendrix into coming to England, where he changed his first name to Jimi and teamed up with bassist Noel Redding and drummer Mitch Mitchell to form the Jimi Hendrix Experience. They made three studio albums, beginning with *Are You Experienced* (1967), which established Hendrix's reputation as a master guitarist and helped establish the solo-oriented "power trio" as a rock medium.

In essence Hendrix transformed the solid-body guitar into a new, more powerfully expressive instrument. For him it was different in kind from acoustic and hollow-body electric guitars because it was possible to sustain notes indefinitely (a note on an acoustic guitar decays quickly) and because of the vast array of available sounds.

Like so many other rock guitarists of the sixties, Hendrix used electric blues as a point of departure, but he greatly increased the range, volume, and variety of sounds, even as he helped morph blues guitar styles into the dominant rock solo style. Hendrix was the trailblazer in both his expanded vocabulary of riffs, scales, and bent notes and his use of electronics. His was a virtuoso not only in speed—his ability to move around the instrument—but also of sound—opening up a world of new sound possibilities. As described by the *Rolling Stone Encyclopedia of Rock & Roll,* "Hendrix pioneered the use of the instrument as an electronic sound source. Rockers before him had experimented with feedback and distortion, but he turned those effects and others into a controlled, fluid vocabulary every bit as personal as the blues he began with."

Tritone: The Devil's Interval?

An **interval** is the sonic distance between two pitches. The purest interval is the **octave**: the higher note vibrates twice as fast as the lower one. A **power chord** grows out of three pitches: a low note, its octave, and a third note in between that vibrates in a ratio of 3:2 with the lower interval. The interval of the two-note chord that we hear at the opening of "Purple Haze" is a **tritone**, the interval that divides the octave in half. This equal division of the octave robs the interval of additional resonance; in this respect, it is the negation of a power chord, which reverberates above and below the main notes.

In medieval times the tritone was known as *diabolus in musica,* that is, "the devil in music." It is unlikely that Hendrix consciously connected back 800 years, but the song is about being under a spell. A more explicit, if coincidental, connection between the tritone and the devil can be found in Black Sabbath's "Black Sabbath." Tommy Iommi's riff through the heart of the song outlines the tritone.

Most of Hendrix's important recordings came in a power-trio format. A **power trio** is a three-man band (guitar, bass, and drums) with a strong solo orientation, especially in live performance. Even in the studio, the guitar orientation is evident through not only the solos but also the balance between instrumental and vocal sections. For example, "Purple Haze" (1967), Hendrix's best-known recording, begins with not one but a sequence of three guitar riffs: the oscillating tritone, a second riff made from permutations of a four-note riff, and finally an extroverted double-time riff.

Songs like "Voodoo Child" and "Red House" showcase both Hendrix's deep blues roots and the astonishing reach of his artistry. "Red House" is a straightforward blues, which Hendrix begins as if in homage to his inspiration, B. B. King. But his playing is much more extroverted than King's and that of the other electric blues guitarists of the fifties. It is clear after a few seconds that the song is about the guitar, not the story, as Jimi sings, "I've still got my guitar." "Voodoo Child," while also blues based, completes Hendrix's transformation of electric blues into rock. Hendrix is all over the instrument, shifting between high and low with ease, filling gaps between vocal phrases with flamboyant licks, and showcasing many of the devices that he pioneered.

Jimi Hendrix, "Voodoo Child," "Purple Haze," and "Red House"

Like too many of his musical contemporaries, Hendrix was a drug casualty. He died of an overdose in September 1970 in the midst of plans for new projects that reportedly would have taken his music in quite different directions. While we regret his premature death, we remain grateful for his substantial legacy, made all the more impressive because it took only three years to compile.

Hendrix, like Eric Clapton with Cream, set up a powerful dialectic within **hard rock:** how to balance individual brilliance with group impact. The tradeoff is between the groove produced by the interplay of several lines (as we heard in the music of the Rolling Stones) versus the expressive power of a soloist's inspiration and virtuosity. This tension is comparable in many respects to that heard in jazz in the 1920s: New Orleans–style collective improvisation versus the overwhelming power of a Louis Armstrong solo. It also has a nice parallel in the world of sports: a star basketball player scoring by beating his defender one on one versus an easy score resulting from several well-executed passes.

Summary. Hendrix is the fourth seminally influential rock act of the sixties discussed here, joining Bob Dylan, the Beatles, and the Rolling Stones. Collectively, the four acts raised the musical standard for rock, established its core and stretched its boundaries, and opened up new sound worlds. In addition, they were instrumental in streaming into rock its primary

TABLE 10.2	ROCK INFLUENCES	
Act	Rock Source	Contribution
Bob Dylan	Folk and country	Played the lead role in merging folk and country influences and bringing them into rock
The Beatles	Pop	Created a new kind of pop—melodically oriented but contemporary in conception
The Rolling Stones	Rock and roll	Extended the innovations of Chuck Berry to the entire band; provided the model for the groove
Jimi Hendrix	Blues	Enriched blues guitar style with technical brilliance and sound innovations; transformed blues playing into the dominant rock solo guitar style

sources and transforming them into a new musical language. We summarize this aspect of their influence in Table 10.2.

This is not to minimize the importance of other significant rock stars, nor should it detract from other contributions of these major figures. Rather, it simply brings into focus the dominant stylistic influences on rock and the key role each act played in integrating them into rock.

SOUL

In the sixties *soul* was a buzzword: for much of the decade, it identified the full range of black popular music. Indeed in 1969, almost after the fact, *Billboard* changed the name of its rhythm-and-blues chart to "Soul." And much of it was popular, by any measure. The Motown success story was the most spectacular evidence of the ascendancy of black music, but Motown artists shared the charts with other black performers as well as whites: twelve of the top twenty-five singles acts during the decade were black. It was a diverse group that included James Brown, Aretha Franklin, Ray Charles, Dionne Warwick, and the Supremes; they represented not one style but several.

Black music charted a musical path different from (mostly) white rock. Although much black music crossed over to the pop charts and influenced musicians of all races (Paul McCartney claims Motown bassist James Jamerson as a primary influence), black performers did not share much common ground musically with their white counterparts. There are three main reasons for this. The first and most significant is the strong gospel tradition. Most of the major African American performers of the sixties had grown up singing in church. There is no better example than Aretha Franklin, the "queen of soul": Aretha's father was pastor of one of the largest churches in Detroit, and she sang at his services from early childhood.

Another was the growing division between rock and roll and rhythm and blues. As we heard in Chapter 9, the differences between the two styles increased toward the end of the decade, not only because of the gospel influence in the singing but also because of differences in rhythm, instrumentation (horn sections were the rule in R&B but not in rock and roll), and texture (the bass was in the foreground, the guitar typically more in the background). Those black artists who began their careers in the sixties had also been listening to the major rhythm-and-blues artists of the fifties. Their work continued the blues/gospel/pop syntheses of these artists.

A third reason for the array of distinctly black styles in the sixties was the artistic control of a few key producers. Berry Gordy was one. Another was Jerry Wexler, who had helped build Atlantic Records into a major pop label. Memphis-based Stax Records relied more on the musical intuition of its house musicians, who included Booker T. and the MGs and the Memphis Horns, to create a "house" sound.

Soul was more than a musical term. It came into use as an expression of the positive sense of racial identity that emerged during the decade: "black is beautiful" was the slogan of many politically active members of the African American community. This shift in attitude, among both blacks and some whites, was the social dimension of the relentless pursuit of racial equality. It went hand in hand with the enfranchisement of so many African Americans through the Civil Rights Act of 1964 and the Voting Rights Act of 1965.

Black music was both an agent and a product of the enormous social changes that grew out of the civil rights movement. For whites it opened the window into the African American community a little bit wider: now it was not so much a matter of individual performers, like Louis Armstrong or Nat "King" Cole, as it was styles: the girl groups, Motown, and Stax/Volt. The cultural penetration of black music during the sixties was unprecedented.

As the drive for racial equality peaked, then deflated in the wake of the assassination of Martin Luther King Jr., black music occasionally became a vehicle for social commentary. James Brown released a series of exhortations, beginning with the 1968 song "Say It Loud— I'm Black and I'm Proud." Marvin Gaye's landmark album *What's Going On* appeared in 1971. But most of the music did not contain overt references to social conditions or racial issues. More often it dealt with the subjects that so frequently transcended race: love won and lost and the good and bad times that resulted.

Black music also benefited from white America's increased awareness of black Americans and sensitivity to racial issues. Open-mindedness toward black cultural expression paralleled open-mindedness toward political and social concerns. It didn't hurt that the music provided such accessible points of entry.

Another important factor was the deepening influence of African American music on mainstream pop. Fifties rock and roll represented a major infusion of rhythm and blues; much sixties rock went several steps further in that direction, as we have noted. Because of this, black music—even music without a strong pop orientation—sounded less different to sixties ears than Muddy Waters would have sounded to fifties ears. It is hard to imagine James Brown finding his new bag or finding a substantial white audience in the midfifties. A decade later, both happened.

With the passage of time, our view of *soul* has changed. In retrospect **soul** refers to the emotionally charged black music of the sixties, music that draws deeply on gospel and the blues. It is best exemplified by the music that came from two southern cities—Memphis, Tennessee, and Muscle Shoals, Alabama—and two performers, Aretha Franklin and James Brown. This was music of real commitment: Percy Sledge bares his soul when he sings "When a Man Loves a Woman," and James Brown was, among other things, the "hardest working man in show business." The music expressed deep feelings, with little or no pop sugarcoating: when Aretha asks for respect, she spells it out.

The soul music of the mid- and late sixties came in two speeds: fast and slow. In either case, the music was raw. There was nothing particularly pretty about the voices of Otis Redding, Sam and Dave (Sam Moore and Dave Prater), Percy Sledge, or James Brown, but there was no mistaking the energy or the emotion. The instrumental sounds were painted in primary colors: strong bass at all times, powerful horns, vibrant sax solos, drums, guitar, and keyboard. Power won out over finesse.

The soul band of the sixties was an updated version of the jump bands of the late forties and the early fifties and Ray Charles's bands of the late fifties. Fast songs, propelled by agile bass lines, had a relentless rhythmic drive. Slow songs provided a more subdued accompaniment; they surrounded the singer with a rich halo of sound.

Sam and Dave, "Soul Man"

Soul classics, like Sam and Dave's "Soul Man" and Otis Redding's "Can't Turn You Loose," typically begin with several layers of riffs: first from the rhythm section, then from the horns. At the Stax studios in Memphis, where both of these recordings were made, there were no preplanned arrangements; the musicians would find the right riffs through trial and error, which became easier through years of working together. As in the music of the Rolling Stones, there is tremendous rhythmic energy. This energy is also the product of rhythmic play: a decisive backbeat, steady timekeeping, and lots of syncopated riffs. The balance within the band is different from the Stones: most of the syncopation comes in the bass line and the horn parts; compared with rock, the guitar part(s)—usually there's only one guitarist—is typically less prominent.

Vocalists like Redding rose to the challenge of singing over this powerful and relentless backing. They sang, shouted, growled, moaned, and groaned. Their singing—laced with explosive consonants and short vowels—is almost percussive.

The songs continue to mine a familiar vein in rhythm and blues: in his sexual potency, and his willingness to brag about it, Sam and Dave's "Soul Man" is a direct descendant of Arthur Crudup's "mighty, mighty, man" and so many other rhythm-and-blues heroes.

James Brown

James Brown (b. 1933) at once epitomized the "soul man" and stood apart from the other male soul singers. Not shy about positioning himself in the popular-music pantheon, Brown billed himself as "soul brother number 1" and the "godfather of soul." As with the Rolling Stones' claim to be the world's greatest rock and roll band, Brown's claim was based on fact: he *was* the most important soul artist of the sixties.

The innovations that transformed Brown's music (and catapulted him to stardom) happened almost overnight. He had been working actively since the midfifties—his first R&B hit came in 1956—but he did little to set himself apart from other R&B artists until his breakthrough 1965 hit, "Papa's Got a Brand New Bag." (In sixties slang a *bag* is an area of expertise.) Brown's new bag was a breakthrough in rhythm. Somewhat surprisingly, fifties R&B bands had been reluctant to adopt rock rhythm; they preferred the hard shuffle popular since the late forties. Only around 1960 did a version of rock rhythm become commonplace in R&B.

We have detailed how the groove—the interplay that makes a rock beat a good beat—depends on the mix of regular timekeeping and syncopations and other patterns that create conflict with the underlying rhythms. We have heard this kind of rhythmic interplay in most of the music discussed in this chapter and most prominently in the music of the Rolling Stones, the Jimi Hendrix Experience, Motown, and soul. Brown and his band go significantly further in this regard.

Brown creates his unique kind of rhythm by addition and subtraction. He has a good-sized band—drums, bass, guitar, and keyboards (when Brown chooses to play on recordings)—plus a full horn section: trumpets, saxophones (including a baritone sax), and trombone. This is the addition: his backup band is larger than most rock bands. Except for the bass, however, all the instruments have a reduced role. Guitar and drums are in the background, and often only the drummer supplies any kind of steady rhythm. The bass line is typically the most active and varied. The horns play riffs; the baritone sax part is usually just a note or two every eight beats. Brown sings only now and then; we imagine his footwork in the silences. This is the subtraction: less vocal and less involvement from most of the instruments.

All of this—more instruments doing less—creates an irresistible rhythm and an airy, open texture. It is first realized in songs like "Papa's Got a Brand New Bag" and "I Got You (I Feel Good)," also a 1965 hit. Brown takes this basic approach a big step further two years later in "Cold Sweat," one of the most influential recordings of the decade. Here he focuses on rhythm and texture rather than harmony and melody. For the most part, there are just three chords in the song, one for the opening section and its repetitions and two alternating during the bridge. There is no melody to speak of; even more than with the soul singers, Brown's voice almost becomes a **percussion** instrument—especially in the nonverbal sounds. We hear this from the start when he counts off the song. (Try to emulate his voice and you'll find that your voice will explode and die away quickly, like many percussion sounds do.)

The interest comes in the interaction among the instruments. The beat and the rock rhythm are felt more than heard; everything else is over or against the time. It is a complex, if repetitive, rhythmic texture. And it is very close in principle to the rhythms and textures of West African music; small wonder that African musicians of the seventies preferred Brown's music over the music of all other African Americans.

CD 3:6

"Cold Sweat," James Brown and Albert Ellis (1967). James Brown and His Orchestra.

LISTENING GUIDE: "COLD SWEAT"

CD 3:6   **Soul** (James Brown and Albert Ellis; performed by James Brown and His Orchestra)

0:00		Count off—James presents the song as if in live performance.
0:05		Introduction: rhythm section groove and horn riffs.
0:13	A	
		Everything happens over one chord: call-and-response with short riffs between voice and horns.
		I don't care (ha) . . .
0:48	B	(bridge)
		Here, everything happens over two alternating chords. The second chord is sustained by the horns.
		When you kiss me . . .
		The title phrase, with stop time.
		I break out—in a cold sweat . . .
1:18	A	
		The sound is open in the center: strong bass, choked guitar, busy drums, no keyboard.
		I don't care about your wants . . .
2:01	B	
		Everything is riffs or rhythm: voice, horns (listen to the baritone sax), and rhythm section.
		When you kiss me . . .
2:22		*I break out — in a cold sweat heh!*
2:31	A	
		Sax solo, with commentary by Brown. (Maceo Parker is the saxophonist.)
		Mercy on me . . .
4:27		Drum solo: much more active against the steady rhythm. Bass line extremely syncopated.
5:39		Return to instrumental introduction.

"COLD SWEAT" (SOUL)

Rhythm	*Moderate tempo. Rock rhythm, with little marking of the beat or rock beat layer (drummer's hi-hat). Backbeat marked but not strongly. Almost everything else plays against the beat: choked guitar, horn riffs, and James Brown's vocal.*
Melody	*Isolated riffs in vocal line; not a continuous flow.*
Instrumentation (timbre)	*Voice, horn section (trumpets, saxophones, and trombone), and rhythm section (electric guitar, electric bass, and drums).*
Performance style	*About James Brown's singing: it's percussive, highly inflected, and straddling the boundary between speech and song at times. The **choked guitar** (strings partially depressed to make the strumming more percussive) sound is used extensively.*
Dynamics	*Loud.*
Harmony	*One chord in the A section; mostly two chords in B; last chord of B is complex.*
Texture	*Active, open, layered sound. Rhythm instruments play busy lines/parts; bass is prominent. Horns play riffs; baritone sax has a separate part much of the time. Open sound because chord instrument is in the background.*
Form	*Novel take on verse/chorus form. The lyrics suggest that A is the verse and B is the chorus, but there is no sense of arriving at a goal when the song reaches the title phrase. Instead, A seems like home base.*

Key Points

Soul band	*Rhythm section and mixed horn section (brass and saxes).*
James Brown's singing	*Grainy, percussive, and inflected.*
The groove	*Brown's new black groove: light rock rhythm and lots of **syncopation**.*
Static harmony	*One chord in the A section; two chords through most of the B section.*

Terms to Know

choked guitar	soul
percussion	syncopation

Brown is one of popular music's truly important innovators. His bold new approach to rhythm and texture was as far-reaching in its influence as Hendrix's guitar playing, Dylan's lyrics, the Stones' rock-defining groove, and the Beatles' soundscapes. More than any other act of the sixties, he has shown the way to the newest music of the latter part of the century; funk, rap, disco, and much of the pop and rock that has grown out of these styles (Red Hot Chili Peppers, for example) trace their roots back to him.

Aretha Franklin

For the most part, real soul music was a man's world. The most spectacular exception was Aretha Franklin (b. 1942), the "queen of soul" and one of the singular talents of popular music. Aretha grew up in a privileged yet painful environment. Her father was C. L. Franklin, pastor of one of the largest churches in Detroit and one of the most admired preachers in the African American community. Through him she came in contact with some of the great names in music: for example, gospel great Mahalia Jackson was a family friend. Aretha grew up in a hurry: singing in her father's church and then on the road as a child; a mother at sixteen; a pop/jazz singer on Columbia Records at nineteen (which turned out to be a dead end); and a series of abusive relationships.

Aretha translated all of these experiences into music of astounding range and depth. Few female singers have matched her soulfulness—her depth of feeling. Among those we have heard, only Bessie Smith and Billie Holiday are comparable. And although she was the queen of soul, she was much more than a soul singer. She was equally at home singing romantic ballads, swinging jazz standards, or returning to her gospel roots. Compared with James Brown or Otis Redding, she has a far greater emotional range. She can be tough when necessary (for example, "Think," which she sings in bedroom slippers in the 1979 film *The Blues Brothers*). But she can also show her more vulnerable side, as she did on her 1973 version of Stevie Wonder's "Until You Come Back to Me."

Jerry Wexler jumpstarted her career in 1967 when he signed her to Atlantic Records and took her to Fame Studios in Muscle Shoals, Alabama, where Rick Hall had previously recorded such soul hits as Percy Sledge's "When a Man Loves a Woman." From the first note, Wexler knew he had something special: when the recording session ended disastrously (too much liquor) and Aretha went into hiding, he tracked her down, brought her musicians to New York, and finished the album. It was a huge success; it established her reputation as one of the supreme talents in popular music, which continued with hits like "Respect," a 1967 number 1 on both the R&B and pop charts and an anthem for the women's movement.

In terms of artistic and commercial success, Aretha has had an uneven career. A series of label switches produced mixed results. Still, she remains a pop icon and one of the great talents of the twentieth century. At her best she far outshines the pretenders to her throne, as she so convincingly demonstrated in the 1999 "divas concert" taped for HBO.

Aretha Franklin, "Respect"

The Decline and the Legacy of Soul

The soul movement went into a slow decline with the assassination of Martin Luther King Jr. in 1968. King's death touched off a series of inner-city race riots, which put a damper on the drive toward integration. James Brown and Aretha Franklin continued to perform and record successfully, but racial tension seemed to affect the chemistry within the interracial house bands at Stax in Memphis and Fame in Muscle Shoals, and between the bands and the performers they backed. There were still successes: Isaac Hayes produced "hot buttered soul" in Memphis, and Al Green, another exceptional voice, enjoyed considerable success in the early seventies. But Green, who had grown up singing gospel, left the pop world behind to become a minister after an incident at one of his concerts. His defection effectively brought the era of soul music to a close.

Soul music lasted less than a decade on the charts. The first soul hits appeared in 1965; by 1975 only James Brown was still carrying the soul banner. Its influence, however, has been evident ever since. Soul brought a more contemporary version of the deep feeling of the blues into black music. In this respect it is the insider's counterpart to the British blues bands: a new view of blues sensibility by those who grew up with it, as opposed to an outsider's take. In her range, use of **melisma** (several pitches sung to a single syllable), variety of timbre, and —more important—expressive use of these tools, Aretha Franklin remains the benchmark for African American female singers. James Brown's influence is even more profound: more than any other artist of the sixties, he led the way in the continuing rhythmic evolution of popular music. And we still listen to—and enjoy—so much of this music.

THE DIVERSITY OF ROCK: SAN FRANCISCO IN THE LATE 1960s

Rock in the sixties was an international music. It was a democratic music, not privileging any particular sound or style. And it was an eclectic music, open to influences from around the world and from high and low. Precisely because of this, rock had become an incredibly diverse music by the late sixties. No earlier period of change, no previous revolution in style and sound had produced anything approaching rock's extraordinary variety.

At the end of the sixties, there was no better place to experience this diversity than San Francisco. The city had become the hippie capital of the world: Haight and Ashbury (an intersection in a heretofore ordinary neighborhood) had become the destination for thousands of young people who wanted to make love, not war, and travel the fast route to higher consciousness by tripping on psychedelic drugs.

Promoter Bill Graham turned the Fillmore Ballroom, a musty building in a rather seedy part of town, into a mecca for rock bands and their fans. Audiences flocked there for endless concerts; "live at the Fillmore" albums appeared regularly in record stores. The venue was so successful that Graham named its New York counterpart Fillmore East.

Because of Haight-Ashbury, flower power, and the other trappings of the hippie scene, it is easy enough to think of San Francisco during this period as simply the home of psychedelic rock, but a list of bands active in the San Francisco Bay Area during 1969 quickly alters that view. At the center of it was a trio of acid-rock bands: Jefferson Airplane, Quicksilver Messenger Service, and the Grateful Dead (of course, the Dead soon ranged far beyond acid rock). But there were other groups as well:

- Creedence Clearwater Revival, one of the great singles bands of the era, playing down-to-earth rock and roll
- Janis Joplin, who sang the blues with power and passion, fronting her Kosmic Blues Band
- Santana, Carlos Santana's one-band foray into Latin rock
- Sly and the Family Stone, whose music provided the crucial link between soul and funk

We consider two of these acts next: Santana and Sly and the Family Stone.

Santana and Latin Rock. The emergence of rock hybrids within and outside of rock was a natural outgrowth of the eclectic attitude of its musicians. Within rock, subgenres sprouted like mushrooms: acid rock, rock opera, hard rock, art rock, soft rock, and heavy metal, for starters. From rock outsiders came **jazz rock**, pop-rock, country rock, and the rock musical. A fascinating third option was the Latin rock of Carlos Santana, which integrated the music of two cultures.

Carlos Santana (b. 1947) was born and raised in Mexico. He moved to San Francisco in 1962. He made his first impression as a blues-inspired rock guitarist; his first commercial recording came from a live 1969 performance with blues guitarist Mike Bloomfield. That same year he acknowledged his Hispanic heritage by forming Santana. Latin music has its roots in Cuba, as noted in Chapter 8. Most Latin musicians at the time came from Spanish-speaking Caribbean countries or had roots there; New York was the American home of this music. The music of Mexico (and of Santana's father, a **mariachi** musician) is quite different. Nevertheless, Santana connected with **Afro-Cuban** music and took a lead role in integrating it into rock, in songs like Tito Puente's "Oye Como Va."

What distinguishes Latin rock from rock? More than anything else, it is the sheer quantity of percussion instruments and the persistence of Puente's clavelike rhythm that betrays Latin influence. There is no mistaking the emphasis.

Carlos Santana,
"Oye Como Va"

Sly and the Family Stone on tour in England in 1968. Note that it is a fully integrated band and that they're having a truly bad hair day.

In much sixties rock and R&B, however, the influence of Latin music is more subtle. The cowbell that opens the Rolling Stones' "Honky Tonk Women" or the conga drum heard on Marvin Gaye's "I Heard It Through the Grapevine" and so many other Motown songs are Latin instruments; they sound so natural in their contexts that we may not even connect them to their Latin roots. The open rhythmic texture of James Brown's music may not have direct Latin antecedents, but certainly the percussive emphasis and rhythmic play heard in so much Latin music was in the air; Brown could hardly have missed it.

Santana was Latin rock's lone star. New York–based Latin musicians also attempted rock/Latin fusions: bugalú was a minor sensation in the Latin community during the sixties and the early seventies. But none of this music had the crossover appeal of Santana's early music. In the midseventies, Santana gravitated toward jazz fusion, and Latin rock faded away. The influence of Latin music, however, especially via Cuba and Brazil, would be even more pronounced and more seamlessly integrated in the seventies and eighties.

Sly and the Family Stone. Fun has been a part of popular music from the beginning. We encountered it in the music for the minstrel show; and if we were to venture back a century earlier, we would encounter it in John Gay's *Beggar's Opera,* a still-popular British stage entertainment that parodied the grand opera of the time. Ragtime brought a different kind of fun; it grew out of the infectious rhythms that so many found invigorating. This in turn gave way to the frenetic excesses of the animal dances, the high spirits of the Charleston, and the bouncy fox trot songs of the late twenties. Blues opened up new possibilities: even as Bessie

Smith moaned the blues, she used metaphors for the sexual act (coffee grinder, deep sea diver) that merit at least a knowing smile. With the emergence of ragtime, jazz, and blues, popular music could be fun, in both what it said and how it felt.

In the rock era, musicians discovered many more ways to have fun. In just the music of the Beatles, we can hear the good, clean fun of "A Hard Day's Night," Lennon's self-deprecating humor in "Norwegian Wood," and outright silliness in "Yellow Submarine." Much of the black music of the sixties seemed restrained by comparison: for Motown acts every move was choreographed. James Brown worked, even when he felt good. It remained for Sly and the Family Stone to reintroduce a completely uninhibited sense of play into black music.

Musicians speak admiringly of a "tight" band: when they do, they are referring to a band that plays with great precision. James Brown's band was tight; he would fire musicians who missed cues or cracked notes. By contrast Sly and the Family Stone was a loose band. This too can be an admirable quality; it produces a quite different feel.

The band was the brainchild of Sly Stone (born Sylvester Stewart in 1944), a disc jockey turned producer and bandleader. More than any other band of the era, Sly and the Family Stone preached integration. The lineup included two of Stone's siblings—his brother Freddie and sister Rosie—Cynthia Martin on trumpet, and several others, including trend-setting bassist Larry Graham: the band members were both black and white and women as well as men.

CD 3:7

"Thank You (Falettinme Be Mice Elf Agin)," Sylvester Stewart (1970). Sly and the Family Stone.

In a series of hits spanning a five-year period (1968–1972), Sly and the Family Stone created an exuberant new sound. We hear it in "Thank You (Falettinme Be Mice Elf Agin)," one of their three number 1 hits. The music of James Brown is the direct antecedent of this song and this style: like Brown's music there is a groove built up from multiple layers of riffs played by rhythm and horns; there is no harmonic movement—instead of two chords, there is only one; and the vocal part is intermittent, with long pauses between phrases.

Sly and the Family Stone, however, create a sound that is much denser and more active than that heard in "Cold Sweat." Although the drummer marks off a rock beat along with the backbeat, the basic rhythmic feel of the song is twice as fast—what is now called a **16-beat rhythm** (by analogy with two-, four-, and eight-beat rhythms). We sense this faster-moving layer in virtually all the other parts: the opening bass riff, the guitar and horn riffs, and—most explicitly—the "chuck-a-puck-a" vocalization. The more active texture opens up many more rhythmic patterns that can conflict with the beat. Sly's band exploits several of them.

And instead of Brown's spare, open texture, there are plenty of riffs: bass, several guitars, voice, and horns. Moreover, there is a spontaneous aspect to the sound, as though it grows out of a free-for-all over the basic groove. It is this quality that gives the song (and Stone's music) its distinctive looseness—looseness that implores listeners to "dance to the music."

If we just listen to the music, it can hypnotize us with its contagious rhythm. When we consider the words, however—the opening lines are "Lookin' at the devil, grinnin' at his gun; Fingers start shakin', I begin to run"—we sense that the band may be laughing to keep from crying or from burning down the house. As with many other Sly and the Family Stone songs, there is a strong political and social message: we sense that the music is the buffer between the band and society, a restraint against violent activism. This is the first example of what would become a growing trend in black music from both the United States and abroad: powerful lyrics over a powerful beat. There is an apparent contradiction between the sharp social commentary in the lyrics and the seduction of the beat. They seem to be operating at cross-purposes: full attention and response versus surrendering to the groove. Perhaps that's so; however, it is possible to interpret this apparent conflict in other ways. One is to view the music as a tool to draw listeners in, to expose them to the message of the words. Another is to

CD 3:7   Proto-funk (Sylvester Stewart; performed by Sly and the Family Stone)

0:00	Instrumental introduction: electric bass the lead instrument at the beginning, with guitar and drums; other rhythm, horns, and voice layer in. This creates the groove that is sustained throughout the song.
0:19	1st verse
	Lookin' at the devil ...
0:55	Chorus
	(I want to) thank you ...
1:13	Instrumental interlude.
1:22	2nd verse
	Stiff all in the collar ...
1:58	Chorus
	(I want to) thank you ...
2:16	Instrumental interlude.
2:25	3rd verse
	Dance to the music ...
3:02	Chorus
	(I want to) thank you ...
3:20	4th verse
	Flamin' eyes of people fear ...
3:39	Chorus
	(I want to) thank you ...
4:30	Fade-out over the chorus.

understand the music as a means of removing the sting of the conditions described in the lyrics: lose yourself in the music, to avoid simply losing it.

In both musical substance and attitude, the music of Sly and the Family Stone was the bridge between James Brown's soul and seventies funk and especially the music of George Clinton's groups, Funkadelic and Parliament. In effect, his music is the main antecedent of funk: a **proto-funk** style.

STYLE PROFILE

"THANK YOU (FALETTINME BE MICE ELF AGIN)" (PROTO-FUNK)

Rhythm	*Moderate tempo. Rock rhythm with sharp **backbeat**. Many layers of rhythmic activity, including several double-time (based on a rhythm twice as fast as the rock beat) rhythmic figures. Almost everything is syncopated.*
Melody	*Repetitive melodies made up of short riffs in both the verse and the chorus.*
Instrumentation (timbre)	*Vocals (group singing most of the time), electric bass, electric guitar, drums, keyboards, and horns (trumpet and saxophone).*
Performance style	*Innovative electric bass techniques: slapping, thumping, and plucking the strings to make a more percussive sound (evident in the opening).*
Dynamics	*Loud.*
Harmony	*One chord throughout the entire song.*

Texture	*Dense, layered texture, made up of riffs in rhythm instruments and horns underneath the vocal. Texture remains much the same throughout the song.*
Form	*Verse/chorus.*

Key Points

Dark lyrics, upbeat music	*Words and music = conflicting messages? Party-time groove versus sobering portraits of ghetto life.*
Emphasis on the groove	*Focus is on rhythm and texture. Harmony = one chord; melody = repeated riffs.*
New bass sounds	*New, more percussive style: string is plucked, slapped, or thumped.*
Bridge from James Brown to funk	*Common threads include the great groove, static harmony, and percussive sounds.*

Terms to Know

backbeat	groove
electric bass	proto-funk

Sly and the Family Stone became popular after the assassination of Martin Luther King Jr. and after the backlash from the civil rights movement had built up steam. Civil rights legislation removed much of the government support for the racial inequities in American life, but it did not eliminate prejudice or racial hatred as many hoped it would. Nor has it disappeared in the decades that followed, here and elsewhere.

We find this same combination of strong rhythm and sharp words in Jamaican **reggae**, seventies funk, calypso from Trinidad, and, from the late seventies on, rap. Increasingly, the musical mood has become darker: much rap, for example, strips away the bright sounds from the horns, guitars, and keyboards. In these styles there is a hardness to the sound; the fun is over.

The music provided one way to escape the pain of prejudice. Drugs were another. Sly Stone used them to excess and torpedoed his career in the process. He became increasingly unreliable, often not showing up for engagements, so promoters stopped booking his band. Once again, drugs had silenced a truly innovative voice.

The Bass as Percussion Instrument

The "percussionization" of the bass was part of a general trend toward more-percussive sounds in the late sixties and early seventies. Another expression of this trend was the choked guitar sound—where a guitarist depresses the strings only part of the way—heard early on in Hendrix's "Voodoo Child" and persistently in the music for *Shaft* and other early seventies blaxploitation films and later in disco. A third came from new keyboard instruments, like the clavinet heard on so many Stevie Wonder recordings.

In turn, this trend toward more-percussive sounds is one aspect of the growing emphasis on rhythm over melody as the century progressed. It would reach its logical end in rap.

RESONANCES FROM THE REVOLUTION: POPULAR SONG IN THE ROCK ERA

In 1960 the term *pop-rock* might have been considered an oxymoron. A decade later it was reality. As the sixties began, the ascendancy of rock was not the forgone conclusion it now seems to be. It was not just that the pop establishment (Frank Sinatra, Steve Lawrence, Rodgers and Hammerstein) was doing well; there was also a new generation of songwriters and performers seemingly poised to maintain the status quo. Versatile film/TV composer Henry Mancini scored several times over with music as diverse as the title song from the 1964 film *The Pink Panther* and the romantic waltz "Moon River" from the 1961 film *Breakfast at Tiffany's.* Johnny Mathis led a new generation of pop singers into the sixties with such hits as his 1957 "Chances Are." Mathis had a new pop sound and attracted a large following, especially among those teens not fully committed to rock and roll. Ray Charles seemingly turned his back on R&B in the early sixties, venturing into country music, then revisiting pop. His version of Hoagy Carmichael's "Georgia on My Mind" remains a classic; even more far-reaching, it opened a new interpretive path for popular song.

Then the bottom fell out. As rock grew up almost overnight, pop seemed to age—it certainly went out of fashion. There was still an audience for it, but prerock music suddenly sounded dated.

Rock's increasing dominance forced artists working within established prerock styles to confront a difficult choice: to rock or not to rock. For jazz, Latin, country, and pop musicians and for musical theater composers, "rocking" meant incorporating elements of rock style into their respective genres. The rock component could be purely cosmetic, such as giving a Tin Pan Alley–type song a simple rock beat. "Winchester Cathedral," a song by the otherwise-forgotten New Vaudeville Band that topped the charts briefly in 1966, illustrates this approach. At the other extreme, it could involve redefining a genre through the thorough integration of rock attitudes as well as elements of rock style. *Hair,* the landmark rock musical, is a noteworthy example. So is Miles Davis's fusion-defining work in the late sixties.

Nowhere was this choice more difficult than in pop and musical theater, if only because of the contrast between the old guard and the new order. Latin, country, and jazz were still **outsider music**. Pop was the establishment. Its values were conservative, and so was the music much of the time. The pop establishment fought hard to preserve the status quo, as its role in the payola investigations that brought down Alan Freed demonstrates. Much of the establishment's music looked to the past (as in the Rodgers and Hammerstein musicals), looked up toward classical/art status (as in *West Side Story*), or simply dissipated into pap. With few exceptions the music had lost its cutting edge.

Pop and musical theater also had the most to lose: money (it was expensive to mount a Broadway production or film a musical), status, control—and face. Some, like Sinatra, had belittled rock and roll; they had to eat crow when the music matured commercially and musically. So for many in the industry, acknowledging and accepting rock was a sign of capitulation. It did not go down easily.

In the end, though, everything happened—there was a full spectrum of reactions to rock by pop musicians. Several forged new approaches to established styles by absorbing elements of rock into their music. Others continued to stay the course and remain completely outside of rock. Still others moved back and forth between old and new. We sample one of the most innovative of these possibilities following.

A New Kind of Pop

Before the Beatles the path of popular song from first inspiration to final product was clear: songwriters wrote songs, arrangers arranged them, and performers sang or played them. The boundaries between song and performance, and between songwriter and performer, were clearly drawn. The song was what the songwriter wrote; it existed independent of any specific arrangement or performance of it. With the help of George Martin, the Beatles consolidated this entire creative sequence into a single organic process, as we have seen. In Motown there was a division of labor—songwriters, arrangers, house band, and acts—but Berry Gordy oversaw the entire process to ensure a consistent product. By the midsixties, then, there was a continuum of possibilities for creating and performing popular song: from the complete separation of songwriting and performance inherited from the past to the complete integration of composition and performance.

We consider another quite different response here: the music of Burt Bacharach, the most innovative pop composer of the sixties.

Burt Bacharach. By 1960 Tin Pan Alley, originally a section of West 28th Street in New York, seemed to have shrunk to a single address: 1619 Broadway, otherwise known as the Brill Building. The building was home to several music publishers, most notably AlDon Music (named for partners Al Nevins and Don Kirshner), a company that set out to bridge the gap between rock and roll and traditional popular song. Staff songwriters included future star singer-songwriters Carole King, Neil Sedaka, and Neil Diamond.

The most inventive of the Brill Building–style songwriters was the team of lyricist Hal David (b. 1921) and songwriter Burt Bacharach (b. 1928). Bacharach came to popular song with a rich background in jazz, classical music (he studied composition with esteemed French composer Darius Milhaud), and traditional pop (he was serving as Marlene Dietrich's musical director even as he was turning out hits like the Shirelles' "Baby It's You"). He teamed up with lyricist Hal David in 1957; they recruited Dionne Warwick to sing their songs in 1963, and she was their voice for the rest of the sixties.

Warwick sang most of the Bacharach/David hits. Their association represented a kind of middle option between the singer-songwriters (like his Brill Building partners) and the songwriter/singer separation of traditional pop. Hal David said that he and Bacharach had the sound of her voice in their ears when they wrote. Bacharach was not nearly as capable a singer as he was a songwriter-composer and arranger. By using Warwick consistently, in songs like "Alfie" and "Do You Know the Way to San Jose," and with his arrangements, Bacharach and David were able to gain a considerable degree of control over the final result, close to what the Beatles and Motown enjoyed.

"The Look of Love," Burt Bacharach and Hal David (1967). Dusty Springfield, vocal.

Among Bacharach's most enduring hits has been "The Look of Love," a song written not for Warwick, but for *Casino Royale*, a 1967 spoof of the immensely popular James Bond films —the *Austin Powers* of the sixties. For the soundtrack Bacharach used British pop singer Dusty Springfield, whose breathy voice seems ideally suited to the song and the steamy atmosphere that words and music evoke.

David's lyric is understated; that gives it its power. What he says is mild enough, at least on the surface: "the look of love is in your eyes"; "take a lover's vow and seal it with a kiss." Because of what he doesn't say and because of Bacharach's setting, we can imagine that love goes beyond a look and a kiss—especially in the late sixties and in a James Bond film, even a spoof.

Bacharach's music reveals many of the qualities that set his music apart from everyone else writing during that time. Here are a few:

1st Chorus

0:00	A
	Spare accompaniment.
	The look of love . . .
0:20	A^1
	String obbligato added.
	The look of love . . .
0:46	B (chorus)
	I can hardly wait . . .

2nd Chorus

1:02	A
	You've got the look . . .
1:22	A^1
	Be mine tonight . . .
1:47	B
	I can hardly wait . . .
2:04	A
	Sax solo overlaps end of the second chorus.
2:24	A^1
	Sax solo continues.
2:49	B
	I can hardly wait . . .
3:05	Extended tag.

o *A carefully constructed arrangement,* with little sound hooks embedded in the texture. There are many details—the way in which the first few notes of the melody are clipped short, the scrape of the guiro (a Cuban percussion instrument), and the lush string line weaving a beautiful countermelody around Dusty Springfield's voice. These kinds of features, which go well beyond the traditional songwriter's level of control, make Bacharach's arrangements of his songs the pop counterpart to the Beatles' sound world.

o *Unusual harmonies.* A Bacharach song typically contains harmonic surprises, and this song is no exception. Even in the first phrase, the sequence of chords is unique to this song. In this respect it takes the harmonic language several steps further, and it is far removed from more-formulaic patterns, like the evergreen "Heart and Soul" progression. At the same time, it is different from the new harmonic approaches heard in the Beatles.

o *Rhythmic surprises.* Almost every pop song maintains a consistent grouping of beats from beginning to end. If there are four beats in the first measure, there will be four beats in every other measure. Not so with Bacharach. If he feels that there is a musical need to change the length or the number of beats, he does. In this song there is a relatively mild example: "how long I have waited." The compression of the line into six beats gives the melody an urgency that underscores the sense of the text.

- *Innovative forms.* Song forms, like beats and measures, tend to be predictable. A typical prerock pop song will contain four 8-measure sections in an AABA pattern; a 12-bar blues will contain three 4-measure phrases. The new songs of the sixties were less uniform, but listeners could still expect a verse and a chorus. In this song Bacharach makes a bold departure from formal stereotypes. The first phrase is conventional enough: a series of two-note riffs spanning eight measures. This leads us to expect another statement of the phrase, with a more conclusive end. But Bacharach expands the melody and extends the phrase over ten measures, then joins it at the hip to a new six-plus-measure phrase that is the climax of each section.

Bacharach obviously took a purely musical delight in investing his music with such unique touches, but it also seems clear that these features all help the music echo the crescendo of passion that inevitably follows a look of love. That they were purposeful, rather than clever for their own sake, makes them powerful.

STYLE PROFILE

"THE LOOK OF LOVE" (1960s POP-ROCK)

Rhythm	*Moderately slow tempo. Light, Latin-tinged rock beat. Backbeat present at times. Break in the rhythm at "how long I have waited" (six beats instead of four). Melody gently syncopated.*
Melody	*Melody spins out from a two-note riff. The second A section ranges more widely and becomes more active. The B section is the most active.*
Instrumentation (timbre)	*Vocal, plus rhythm section (piano, electric bass, drum, and guiro), strings, and solo saxophone.*
Performance style	*Wispy singing style; wispy sax sound.*
Dynamics	*Subdued, but building slightly to the B section.*
Harmony	*Rich harmonies with surprises (such as the second and third chords in the first A section).*
Texture	*Transparent layered texture: voice in the middle, bass on the bottom, strings usually in a high range, and piano fills behind voice; percussion constant and discreet.*
Form	*Integrated verse/chorus form: A, A¹ are the verse; they flow easily into the climactic B section, which serves as the chorus.*

Key Points

New kind of pop	*A pop song for and by adults: contemporary lyric, new pop sounds.*
Modernizing popular song: rhythm	*Understated, Latin-tinged rock beat.*
Modernizing popular song: melody and harmony	*Innovative development of melody from a short riff; surprising harmonies replace pop conventions.*
Modernizing popular song: form	*A well-connected verse/chorus form in which each section links to the next.*
Bacharach's imagination	*Stretching pop conventions: extended measure ("how long I have waited"); varied length of sections.*

Terms to Know

pop-rock

Bacharach's song, like so much other music we have heard, is a real period piece, as much a part of that slice of the sixties as Sean Connery's portrayals of James Bond. But, like Connery as Bond, the song does what it sets out to do very well indeed. That is why both have endured.

Because it is very much a product of the sixties, both the song and its performance here by Dusty Springfield may seem quite different from contemporary fare. Indeed, in a time when pop stars like Justin Timberlake, Janet Jackson, and Mary J. Blige seem to require personal trainers to prepare them for the frenetic movements that accompany their singing, it may be hard for contemporary listeners to imagine—or appreciate—a time when the performance of a pop song did not require histrionics, when singers simply stood in front of a microphone and sang. These pop stars invest their performances with extraordinary energy, but they forsake the possibility for intimacy in the process. It would be difficult to imagine them gazing at an imaginary partner with a look of love; they can't stay still long enough. It wasn't always that way.

Bacharach's Significance. Burt Bacharach and Hal David thoroughly transformed popular song into something quite different from the songs that Frank Sinatra, Johnny Mathis, and Tony Bennett were singing at the beginning of the decade. Although Bacharach's imagination and craft certainly played a big part in the transformation, there is no question that rock-era music, and especially Motown, played a crucial role in shaping Bacharach's new sound. It's particularly evident in the rhythm, the texture, the use of instrumental hooks, and the end-weighted form.

It's clear that the "The Look of Love" is miles away from Dylan or the Rolling Stones in attitude and style, and it is directed to a different, more mature audience. This fact should not obscure the larger point, however, which is that if the rock revolution had not taken place, Bacharach's song would have sounded quite different. "The Look of Love" shows the trickle-down effect of the rock revolution: the way in which rock elements blended into other styles, reshaping and revitalizing them in the process. It reminds us that the impact of the rock revolution was felt not only in depth but also in breadth—that we gauge the extent of its influence not only by how dramatically the new music differed from the music that it replaced but also by how widespread that influence was.

The Bacharach/David style would profoundly influence the next generation of pop-rock songwriters, among them Barry Manilow, Paul Williams, and Marvin Hamlisch. One product of their efforts was **soft rock**, which blended the emphasis on melody and clear forms of Tin Pan Alley song with an understated rock rhythm. This style flourished throughout much of the seventies, most notably in the recordings of the Carpenters, one of the top singles acts of the decade, and in the music of Barbra Streisand.

THE SIGNIFICANCE OF THE ROCK REVOLUTION

The sixties saw the wholesale transformation of popular music. It was not just that rock was a radically different kind of music. It was that everything about the music—how it was conceived and created, the tools with which it was made, the content of both words and music, the dynamics within musical groups and between musicians and their audience, and even what the music was—underwent significant change.

By the end of the sixties, the rock era was well under way. Rock was the dominant music in almost every domain. Virtually every other kind of music that was not rock or rock-influenced was out of fashion.

Rock era is a term that we still use freely to describe this period in popular music. Given its wide currency, it might seem that there would be a clear understanding about exactly what rock is, but that is not the case. Like so many other labels in popular music—blues, jazz, ragtime—rock has been burdened with multiple connotations. Here are some of them, and they range from restrictive to inclusive:

o *Rock and roll.* This is the core rock style, one in which the features that most consistently define the style—the beat, the instruments, the rhythmic interplay, and the assertive vocal and instrumental sounds—are consistently present. The Rolling Stones' hits discussed previously exemplify this narrow view of rock.

o *Music by rock musicians.* This encompasses not only music that is obviously rock because of its instruments, rhythms, and other style features but also music that lacks these features but is rock by either attitude or provenance. Dylan's "Subterranean Homesick Blues" does not have a rock beat or the verse/chorus form so common in rock-era songs, but it is indisputably a rock song because it is electric-era Dylan and because of the attitude it projects. In a different direction, the Beatles' "Eleanor Rigby" lacks basic rock instruments, but it is a rock song mainly because it is by the Beatles.

o *Rock as opposed to soul/rhythm and blues.* The visible evidence of this distinction is, of course, race: rock musicians are typically white; R&B musicians are usually black. The audible evidence, however, is in the music: variation in singing style, instrumentation, texture, and the like. Exceptions like Jimi Hendrix underscore the fact that the contrasts between the two style families have more to do with musical differences than racial ones.

o *Rock hybrids.* As rock took over the popular-music marketplace, some musicians in established styles—jazz, country, pop, musical theater, and the like—began incorporating elements of rock into their music. The absorption ranged from a cosmetic overlay—giving a pop song a rock-influenced beat, as Frank Sinatra did in his 1968 hit "Something Stupid"—to a seamless integration, as we noted in Santana's version of "Oye Como Va." The key point here is not that Sinatra is singing in a rock style; he isn't. It's that his hit sounds different than it would without the influence of rock. In attitude and style, this music is miles away from the music of Dylan and the Stones, but it is part of rock-era popular music because it has been touched by rock style.

o *Music of the rock era.* Any comprehensive account of rock in the sixties will include most of the music mentioned previously: rock, soul, and perhaps some of the hybrid rock styles. There are musical as well as generational links that identify these diverse styles as rock-era music, in opposition to music linked to earlier styles. Motown is not rock in the more restrictive connotations presented previously, but it is certainly rock-era music, and it is connected to rock in ways that Louis Armstrong's version of "Hello, Dolly"—a number 1 hit in 1964—is not.

We can gauge the extent to which rock took over popular music by measuring both the depth and the breadth of its impact. The music that we have discussed in this chapter defined rock as a revolutionary new music. As we listen to it in relation to music from earlier periods, we easily hear the wholesale shift in every aspect of the music. This is the depth of its impact. Just as telling, however, is the penetration of rock style into other genres. This music may lack a rock attitude, but it still evidences rock influence. This is the breadth of its impact.

By 1970 rock music had become extraordinarily diverse, as even our small sampling of musical styles suggests. Collectively, it defined a new mainstream, a new dominant style—or, in this case, a family of styles. In this respect it paralleled the coming together of popular music in the late twenties: the blend of fox trot song, jazz, and blues. But the range of styles within this new mainstream was much broader than in that earlier time. This is a reflection of the openness of rock musicians toward music of all kinds—and the openness of the rock audience toward musicians and music of many different kinds.

Rock music, in the broadest view, would become even more varied in the seventies, as we discover in the next two chapters.

LOOKING BACK, LOOKING AHEAD

The Beatles were the poster boys of the rock revolution. Their invasion of America sparked it: their commercial and musical impact was crucial to rock's ascendancy. By the time they disbanded, the revolution was complete; the new music that they had helped usher in now ruled the popular-music business. The Beatles played a key role in reshaping the music and the industry that supported it. Among the most significant developments to which they contributed: establishing rock as the new popular music, making rock an international musical language, creating a new kind of popular song, proposing rock as art, confirming the recording as the primary musical document, and expanding the range of musical influences and sounds, from sitars and calliopes to tape loops and crowd noises. These and other changes radically transformed popular music in the sixties.

The death of the Beatles as a group and the deaths of so many important rock stars—Jimi Hendrix, Janis Joplin, Brian Jones, and Jim Morrison—might superficially seemed to have echoed the troubles that plagued rock and roll at the end of the fifties. Although the losses were significant and tragic, rock didn't miss a beat. The revolution that had toppled pop was over. Rock was now big business and would grow even bigger in the coming decade.

As the seventies began, rock and rhythm and blues were comfortable. The industry had undergone a changing of the guard: record labels like Atlantic and Motown were major players, films started using rock in soundtracks, and radio was about to experience a new, more conservative, and more lucrative form of programming. The new musical language of rock and soul had quickly become common currency among musicians, which led to refinement (the superbly crafted recordings of Steely Dan), retrenchment (the rock-confirming grooves of the Rolling Stones and Lynyrd Skynyrd), expansion (the bigness and bombast of Black Sabbath, Barry White, and Bruce Springsteen), and new directions (Led Zeppelin's heavy eclecticism and David Bowie's androgynous glam). We survey these developments in the next chapter.

TERMS TO KNOW

Test your knowledge of this chapter's important terms by defining the following. If you can't recall the meaning of a certain term, refresh your memory by looking up the boldfaced term in the chapter, turning to the Glossary at the back of the book, or working with the flashcards on the *Popular Music in America* Companion Web site: *http://music.wadsworth.com/ campbell_2e*

. . . .

16-beat rhythm	groove	percussion
Afro-Cuban	hard rock	pop-rock
amplification	hook	power chord
arpeggio	interval	power trio
backbeat	jazz rock	proto-funk
blues progression	mariachi	reggae
bridge	melisma	riff
British invasion	melody	rock
choked guitar	MIDI	rock beat
concept album	minor key	soft rock
eight-beat rhythm	mixing	solid-body electric guitar
electric bass	Motown	soul
electric guitar	Motown sound	syncopation
electric piano	multitrack recording	tribute band
falsetto	octave	tritone
feedback	outsider music	two-beat rhythm
folk music	overdubbing	vibrato

. . . .

Rock and Rhythm and Blues in the 1970s

On May 13, 1971, Stevie Wonder (born Steveland Morris in 1950) turned 21. On that day his contract with Motown Records expired. The arrangement had been good for both parties: Wonder was a child star, and Motown reaped the rewards. When he came of age, however, Wonder took the $1 million in royalties that Motown had been holding in trust for him, formed his own record and publishing companies (Taurus and Black Bull, respectively), and negotiated a new record deal with Motown. For Wonder the crucial clause in the contract was complete artistic control. In effect, he made his records and Motown sold them.

Wonder assumed artistic control in an unprecedented way. He immersed himself in electronics, learning how to use synthesizers and electronic keyboards, a new and rapidly evolving technology at the time. With these newly developed skills, he played most—and sometimes all—of the parts on many of his recordings. On Wonder's recordings a single artist with a lot of equipment replaced the multilevel Motown production pyramid (discussed in Chapter 10). The string of albums that he produced in the early seventies did well enough that he was able to renegotiate his contract with Motown in 1975. The new deal gave him a $13 million advance and a 20 percent royalty rate.

Wonder's emancipation from Motown illustrates three key features of rock and rhythm and blues after 1970: First, this new music had become a big business. Second, important artists were determined to go their own ways, no matter which direction it took them. Finally, technology would play an increasingly important role in shaping the sound of popular music.

The conflict between art and commerce was just one of the oppositions and contrasts during the seventies. Musically, it was a time of consolidation and innovation. Rock and R&B musicians went to school on the great music of the sixties, and during the seventies they purified the groove. As we listen to memorable sixties music, we sense the excitement of discovery. As we listen to the music of the seventies, we admire the craftsmanship and the mastery of the best acts, from the studio perfection of Steely Dan and Stevie Wonder's studio-aided one-man band to the smoothness of the Eagles and Fleetwood Mac and the power and refinement of Led Zeppelin.

Musical innovation came from both the inside and the outside. In the early seventies, rock and R&B split off in numerous directions. The new styles are extraordinarily diverse, from singer-songwriters and country rock to funk/jazz fusion, heavy metal, art rock, and the Philadelphia sound; these and many others grew out of sixties music. Other music came from outside or began on the fringes of the industry; reggae, rap, punk, and disco stand out in this regard. Technology would drive other trends: techno and ambient music trace back to the midseventies.

Innovators came from everywhere, especially toward the end of the seventies and into the early eighties: Eddie Van Halen greatly expanded the vocabulary of the rock guitarist; Brian Eno single-handedly created a new genre based on technology that had not been readily available ten years earlier; and Grandmaster Flash turned the turntable into a musical instrument.

Yet another contrast was the one between big and small. There were big bands, big crowds, big amps (which made small bands sound big), big venues, big record sales, and big record deals. There was an enormous expansion in the variety of sounds available: the diversification of rock and R&B, already well under way at the beginning of the seventies, continued through the decade and into the eighties.

Even as Elton John was selling millions of records and selling out arenas, four-piece punk bands like the Ramones were working in crowded back rooms like the one at CBGB, the spiritual home of New York punk; and DJs were working the turntables at discos not far away. Even here the contrast between big and small was not clear-cut: a disco double-LP would become the biggest-selling record of the rock era, and punk would have an impact far greater than its market share might suggest.

In the discussion that follows, we explore the dominant themes of this period—consolidation, expansion and diversification, and innovation—first in the industry and then through a wide-ranging survey of several seventies styles. We turn our attention to the new styles of the late seventies in Chapter 12.

THE POPULAR-MUSIC INDUSTRY IN THE 1970s

In the seventies rock traded tie-dyed T-shirts for three-piece suits. In so doing it turned its core values upside down. From the beginning rock had portrayed itself as a music of rebellion: rock took over popular music with a revolution. But as the market share of rock and R&B grew, so did the financial stake. It cost more to create and promote a record, to put on a concert, and to operate a venue. There was more money to be made but also more to be lost.

The Business of Rock

Not surprisingly, a corporate mentality took over the business side of rock. It was evident to some extent in the music itself in that some artists seemed to put commercial success as the highest priority and let that shape their music (nothing new here!). Elton John, the best-selling rock star of the seventies, was the poster boy for this path. His early albums showed him to be a **singer-songwriter** of considerable gifts. Within a few years, however, he crossed over to the mainstream. He immersed himself in Top 40 while adopting a Liberace-like stage persona, donning elevator shoes, flamboyant costumes, and outlandish eyewear. His songs found the middle of the road, and he found megastardom. Somewhere along the line, he lost some of his musical individuality, trading it for familiarity and accessibility, and his visual identity at times deflected attention away from his real talent.

John was not alone in this regard; others went down his yellow brick road to superstardom. Still there were entire genres that followed paths guaranteed to keep them off the air and off the top of the charts. Heavy metal flew under the radar for the entire decade, at least so far as airplay and critical attention were concerned, and funk had only a fraction of the audience that more pop-oriented artists—black and white—enjoyed.

The impact of profit-oriented thinking was far more telling behind the scenes. It determined to a great extent which music would get promoted and how. Its impact was most evident in the media and in the use of new market strategies designed to maximize sales.

Media and Money. No medium showed the impact of the big-business mindset more than radio. In the early years of rock, radio had been an important part of the music's outsider image—witness Alan Freed and other like-minded disc jockeys in the fifties and "underground" FM stations in the sixties. In the seventies, however, the most significant new trend was **AOR (album-oriented radio)**. In this format disc jockeys could no longer choose the songs they played. Instead program directors selected a limited number of songs designed to attract a broad audience while offending as few as possible. Often stations bought syndicated packages, further homogenizing radio content. Freeform radio all but disappeared, and so did the adventurous spirit that it symbolized. As a result, distortion was out; tunefulness was in. Acts like Barry Manilow, the Carpenters, Stevie Wonder, Chicago, the Eagles, Fleetwood Mac, Paul McCartney and Wings, and of course Elton John got a lot of airplay and topped the charts.

The Emergence of Cable TV. This mentality also penetrated into new media. With the launch of cable television in the late seventies, a host of new networks emerged, looking to carve out a piece of the market. Among them was MTV, which went on the air in 1981. For the better part of three years, the network featured only white acts. In one particularly notorious incident, Herbie Hancock had to play off-camera because of network policy against presenting blacks on-camera. It took the tremendous demand for Michael Jackson to break through MTV's unwritten color barrier. Afterward, the station offered the self-serving excuse that they were only giving the audience what it wanted.

Another significant trend was the consolidation of the record industry. The scores of independent labels that recorded so many of the early R&B and rock acts were a key chapter in the story of early rock. By the end of the seventies, however, many of the independent labels had merged or had been gobbled up by a major label. As the eighties began, six companies produced half of the popular-music recordings worldwide.

Cross-marketing. A major business innovation of the seventies was **cross-marketing**. In pursuit of greater financial rewards, record companies used tours to help promote record sales. With improved amplification, the stadium or large-arena concert became commonplace. More ritual than musical event, these concerts usually confirmed what the audience already knew about the music of a particular band. As a rule there was little, if any, spontaneity in performance. Bands performed songs, usually from current or recent albums.

Often the performances were more about show than sound, although there was plenty of both. Flamboyance had been part of rock from the start—Elvis, Little Richard, Jerry Lee Lewis, Chuck Berry. Major acts like Jimi Hendrix and Pete Townshend of the Who raised the stakes: Hendrix by setting his guitar on fire; Townshend by destroying both guitars and amps at the end of a show. By the early seventies, spectacle had become part of the business and included lights, fog, costumes, makeup, pyrotechnics, and the like.

Such productions were almost a necessity because performers had to seem larger than life in such huge venues. At its most extreme, outrageous dress, makeup, and stage deportment replaced musical substance as the primary source of interest. Acts like Kiss epitomized this theatrical aspect of seventies rock.

With *Saturday Night Fever*, producer Robert Stigwood adapted cross-marketing to films. His approach to promotion was mutual reinforcement: let the film promote the songs, and let the songs promote the film. It worked: the film briefly made disco a mainstream music, and the Bee Gees briefly owned the charts. The *Saturday Night Fever* record became not only the biggest-selling soundtrack but also the best-selling album up to that time.

Rock as Big Business. The seventies proved that there was money to be made in rock and R&B on a scale that was hard to imagine even a decade before. Record sales had increased enough that the Recording Industry Association of America (RIAA) created a new category in 1976, the platinum record, which signified the sale of 1 million units. (The gold record represented sales of 500,000 units.) Moreover, the album had replaced the single as the primary unit, so revenues were even higher.

The increased sales, which occurred during a long economic recession, certainly reflect the deeper bond between music and listener, the "rock as a way of life" state of mind. But there were other causes. The ever-growing diversity of the musical landscape meant that there was music for almost everyone's taste. Technology also played a role: the development of new playback formats made the music more accessible.

Technology and Music

One of the fruits of the Allied victory in World War II was the acquisition of a magnetic tape recorder that German scientists had developed. When brought to the United States after the war, it served as the prototype for the reel-to-reel tape recorders developed by Ampex and others. These reel-to-reel tape recorders belonged to the production side of the music business. They were expensive, difficult to use, and hard to tote around—factors that outweighed their superior fidelity for all but the most dedicated and well-heeled audiophiles. In an effort to make tape playback devices more accessible to consumers, RCA developed the first tape cartridge in 1958.

Tape Players. In the sixties two important tape-based consumer formats emerged. One was the four- or eight-track tape. These tape players began to appear in cars (and Lear jets—Bill Lear had the technology developed for his line of corporate jets) in 1965 and remained popular through the seventies. The other, more enduring playback device was the audiocassette. A number of manufacturers, most notably Philips, Sony, and Grundig, worked to develop cassettes and cassette players and to come up with an industry standard. By the seventies this new technology had caught on: cassette sales grew much faster than LPs (vinyl) and by 1982 exceeded them.

This new format had many advantages. The units were smaller and so were the playback devices. Some were portable; others went into car consoles. By the midseventies boom boxes had appeared, offering a portable and low-priced alternative to the home stereo. The first Walkman came from the Sony factory in 1979; other companies quickly followed suit. All of these devices made listeners' personal recordings as accessible as the radio.

Cassette players also made it possible for consumers to assemble their own playlists, using blank tapes. With improvements in recording quality, most notably the Dolby noise-reduction technology, there was less loss in quality during duplication. People could now take their music with them wherever they went.

We reap the benefits of these innovations today. It's likely that most of you reading this book can burn your own CDs. Many of you carry around an iPod or other personal playback device, where you store hundreds if not thousands of songs. This technology is so common-place that most of us take it for granted. But it wasn't always so, nor always so easy. Personal, portable playback became a reality only in the late seventies; it has developed much further since that time.

Synthesizers. Most of the new sounds of the seventies came from synthesizers. A **synthesizer** is a device that creates sounds electronically. In early synthesizers a tone generator would gen-erate a sound wave, which other devices would modify. A pianolike keyboard was the most popular way to input the information necessary to generate a particular sound, but other devices, such as finger-activated metal bands, were also used.

Synthesizers are the ultimate musical application of electric technology. The most basic is the **microphone**, which converts any sound into an electric signal. The **pickup**, such as those used on hollow-body electric guitars, does much the same task, but it eliminates any interfer-ence between the sound and the microphone interface. Once the sound is converted into an electric signal, it can be modified: the distortion that is so crucial to rock guitar, and especially heavy metal, is produced by surrounding a note or chord with a halo of white noise. (**White noise** is a random sampling of all audible frequencies; it is also the sound one hears between radio stations.) Still, the sound begins as if on a conventional instrument: the guitarist must pluck or tap the string to generate a sound. With synthesizers every aspect of the sound, from generation to final result, can be controlled electronically. Even the use of a conventional interface, such as a piano/organ keyboard, does not impose limits on the resulting sound in the way that a guitar does.

Synthesizers opened up a new sound world to musicians. Some of the sounds replicated the timbres of existing instruments, such as the violin. (That is why early synthesizers are called **analog synthesizers**: they create an analogue, or likeness, to a conventional instru-ment.) Other sounds were simply not possible on acoustic instruments. They could be abra-sive or soothing, simple or complex. The options were—and are—limitless.

The first synthesizers were cumbersome. The Moog synthesizer, as used by Wendy Carlos in her landmark 1968 recording *Switched-On Bach,* looked like an old-fashioned telephone switchboard, with plugs connecting the various oscillators. Carlos's recording, more than any other of that time, opened up the previously arcane world of electronic synthesis to the gen-eral public.

The synthesizer became a practical instrument for studio and performance with the application of transistor technology. Early synthesizers used vacuum tubes, but by the early seventies transistors were making them faster, smaller, and more flexible. These more stream-lined synthesizers could now operate in real time, a crucial breakthrough for using them eas-ily in live performance.

The first portable synthesizers were capable of performing only a single line, like a voice or saxophone does. But as transistors became smaller and more powerful, improved models capable of playing several sounds simultaneously began to appear. Another improvement was the ability to change sounds on the fly, rather than having to stop and reset the parameters. These two changes made the instrument even more useful both in the studio and in concert.

By 1980 digital technology was on the horizon. We discuss this technological revolution in Chapter 14.

THE MUSIC OF THE 1970s: POINT AND COUNTERPOINT

One can view the years between the disbanding of the Beatles and 1980 as one long point/counterpoint. In the early and midseventies, the dominant trends built on the music of the sixties: musicians consolidated, expanded, and diversified it. Much of it became more professional in every way. By contrast, much of the vibrant and influential music of the latter part of the seventies—punk, disco, funk, electronica, and rap—came from the outside. Some of this music, like punk, emerged in opposition to the increasingly slick rock of the seventies. Other styles, such as funk, rap, and disco, emerged as alternatives for alternative audiences (black, Hispanic, and gay).

Professional Versus Amateur. We might explain the opposition of these two currents as the opposition of professional and amateur. Both *professional* and *amateur* have multiple connotations, all of which apply. A professional is a person who performs a skilled task well enough to earn a living from it. Professionals can be physicians or plumbers, athletes or attorneys; they can also be musicians or the people behind the musicians. *Professional* can also imply not only the monetary reward but also a high level of craft. When we say to someone, "that's a professional job," we are usually complimenting the person for a job well done.

Amateur and *amorous* come from the same source: the Latin word for "love." Originally, an amateur was someone who worked at a skill because he or she loved it. The term has evolved to mean a comparatively unskilled performance of a task: an "amateurish" attempt.

Craft Versus Passion. Rock and rhythm and blues began as passionate and—in comparison with the pop of the era—amateurish music. Rock lore is filled with stories that depict this: Sam Phillips, Ike Turner, a blown speaker cone, the 1951 No. 1 R&B hit "Rocket 88," and the beginning of distortion; indie label owners selling their records out of the trunks of their cars; Norman Petty recording Bobby Allison, Buddy Holly's drummer, on pillows; the endless string of one-hit wonders. It seems almost as though rock and roll came about through a series of happy accidents. The mystique of the garage band, and the enthusiastic amateurism that it implies, is still very much with us.

Professionals often work with passion, but oftentimes it is in the service of their craft. Mastery of any kind generally requires prolonged periods of intense study. Such concentrated work can produce spectacular results like the guitar wizardry of Eddie Van Halen and the "perfect" recordings of Steely Dan. Those lacking such mastery often compensate with enthusiasm and daring; the Sex Pistols epitomize this path.

Much of the music from the first part of the seventies shows great craft, often at the expense of the kind of passion and personal connection that made rock so revolutionary. It could be grandiose, theatrical, comfortable, powerful, clever, or virtuosic. The best of it is admirable.

By contrast there is a grassroots aspect to so much of the music of the late seventies: punk bands learning on the job; the DJ as the performer at a disco; rap MCs using the turntable as a performing instrument. And the undercurrent of the entire period—and beyond—is heavy metal, which often fuses craft and passion.

The point of this discussion is not to privilege craft over enthusiasm or vice versa. Rather it is to suggest that we as listeners have to be able to shift perspective, to meet each style on its own terms—to appreciate the difference in intent as well as the final result, and to connect the two.

Musical Trends in the Early and Mid-1970s. If one had to reduce the relationship between sixties and early-seventies music to a single word, that word might well be *more*. Whatever happened in the sixties happened more in the seventies. Rock became diverse in the sixties; it became more diverse in the seventies as styles and substyles proliferated. Sixties musicians found the new grooves of rock and soul. Seventies musicians found them more easily; rhythms were freer and more daring (for example, "Black Dog" and "Give Up the Funk") or more powerful ("Born to Run"). The sounds of bands got even bigger in the seventies through more-powerful amplification and additional instruments.

Contrasts between styles also became more pronounced: the seventies heard the intimate confessions of the singer-songwriters and witnessed the bombast of David Bowie's grand spectacles; sometimes these contrasts even appeared in the same song; Led Zeppelin's "Stairway to Heaven" is a memorable example. Some music was highly personal—Bruce Springsteen and Neil Young, for example. Other acts hid behind a mask: Kiss, Bowie—in his various personae, even Elton John. The attitudes that acts represented grew more diverse: consider Black Sabbath versus the Carpenters, Barry White versus David Bowie, or the Jackson 5 versus Pink Floyd.

We can get a sense of the extent of these developments with a tour through several early-seventies styles.

THE MAINSTREAM BROADENS

According to chart guru Joel Whitburn, there were five acts active at the beginning of the seventies who were among the Top 20 artists of the decade on both the singles and the album charts: Elton John, Paul McCartney and Wings, Stevie Wonder, Chicago, and Neil Diamond. It is a diverse group; at first hearing there is not a lot of overlap from one to the next or even, in some cases, from one song to the next.

Perhaps the strongest common bonds among all these artists are the accessibility and the craft of their music. Their impressive list of hits is built on the successful pop of the sixties. The songs were tuneful, not only in the sung melody but also in the use of instrumental hooks and melodic background lines. They continued to use the central harmonic language of twentieth-century pop, with a surprising twist now and again. They had good beats—clear, playful, toe-tapping. They had rich, often lush, accompaniments; there was usually a lot going on. Most of the instruments were conventional and conventionally played; Stevie Wonder's cutting-edge keyboards were the relatively rare exception. Heavy distortion and throat-ripping vocals were not part of the sound.

A mix of the accessible and the clever was one formula for pop success in the seventies, as both Chicago and Steely Dan proved. There were others: the soft rock of the Carpenters, the chameleon-like character shifts of Elton John, and McCartney's flights of melody. We consider yet another formula next.

BLACK MUSIC IN THE EARLY 1970s

With Motown and soul, African Americans gained a firm toehold in the popular-music market during the sixties. As the seventies began, they dug in more deeply even as they spread out. As with white rock, there was greater variety and a strong presence despite the inevitable backlash from the advances of the civil rights movement.

The largely integrated music scene of the sixties gave way to a more segregated and white-dominated industry. This was true at every level: the audience divided into black and white to a greater extent than before. the industry, and especially AOR radio, encouraged this. Entire genres—such as glam rock, art rock, and soft rock—lost their connection to rock's roots.

Still the place of black music within the industry was secure. Black artists continued to appear on the pop charts, with both album and singles, and black music found its way into film and television (for example, Quincy Jones's music for the popular *Sanford and Son*). We survey some of these developments next.

Black Issues, Black Voices

The sixties, which had begun with such promise for African Americans, ended dismally. The assassination of Martin Luther King Jr., the riots at the Democratic National Convention in 1968, the legal troubles of the Black Panthers, the election of Richard Nixon and the subsequent shift to more-conservative attitudes—all of this and more replaced hope with disillusionment.

One might expect that this frustration would surface in black music, and it did in various ways. Marvin Gaye's landmark 1971 album, *What's Going On,* was his most extended and successful effort in this direction. The music of Sly and the Family Stone grew darker as the seventies dawned. James Brown continued to stir black pride in songs like "Get Up, Get Into It, Get Involved." Stevie Wonder periodically put an edge on his songs; "Living for the City" talks about tough times in the ghetto. George Clinton wove his double-edged black humor (black as in dark; black as in African American) into early funk rhythms as he sought to get one nation under a groove.

Soul, the most powerful expression of a black sensibility during the sixties, continued its late-sixties decline. Al Green was the only major new voice of the seventies; as it turned out, he was the last of the great soul singers. His decision to leave the entertainment world for the ministry effectively closed the book on soul. During the seventies, however, black gospel music took on a more contemporary sound and gained a bigger audience. The Staples Singers, a family gospel group that also recorded R&B hits, was the most successful.

Film scores by Isaac Hayes (*Shaft,* 1971) and Curtis Mayfield (*Superfly,* 1972) were a different kind of musical commentary on the black experience. *Shaft* and *Superfly* were the first big-budget **blaxploitation** films, a genre that presented a black take on the action movies of the sixties. The lead roles featured a hero (Richard Roundtree as Shaft, a private eye) and an antihero (Ron O'Neal as a drug dealer). Both were set in the ghetto, a gritty backdrop that resonated well with black audiences. The music of Hayes and Mayfield contributed to this ambience. Both the scores and the theme songs were hugely successful.

Still this was not the main message of black music. Most of it talked about love, a theme universal enough to blur racial boundaries.

Black Romantic Music

Among other things, Motown made it clear that there was a big market for fresh black pop sounds. Not surprisingly, the early seventies saw the emergence of several new black pop styles. Motown presented new acts like the Jackson 5 even as sixties stars like Diana Ross, Marvin Gaye, and Stevie Wonder continued to chart and explore new directions.

Others built on the black pop style that Motown had developed. The most substantial results came from Philadelphia-based producers like Thom Bell and the team of Kenneth Gamble and Leon Huff. They expanded on the Motown formula, and Gamble and Huff were generous enough to make MSFB, their backup band, into an act that purveyed the sound of Philadelphia. (Keep in mind that the house musicians at Motown were virtually unknown outside the industry.)

Barry White went even further. Backed by his forty-piece Love Unlimited Orchestra, he undulated endlessly about love. Roberta Flack, both by herself and with Donny Hathaway, offered a mellower kind of love song. We consider one of their biggest hits, the 1972 song "Where Is the Love."

Roberta Flack (b. 1937) survived a scathing appraisal of her singing ability by her voice teacher at Howard University to become a major star. Her 1969 debut album included her first big hit, "The First Time Ever I Saw Your Face." The song reached number 1 in 1972 with help from Clint Eastwood, who used it in his 1971 film *Play Misty for Me.* Flack continued to chart into the eighties, both as a solo performer and partnered with compatible artists like Donny Hathaway, a classmate at Howard. (Hathaway fell to his death in 1979. It was officially listed as a suicide, although his friends—Flack among them—insisted that he would not kill himself despite career problems.)

The recording is an elegant, sophisticated, and expressive take on black pop. Perhaps because the title is a question that is never answered, the song flows from one section to the

Roberta Flack and Donny Hathaway, "Where Is the Love"

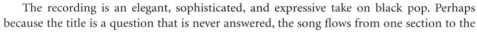

LISTENING GUIDE: "WHERE IS THE LOVE"

Sweet Soul (Ralph McDonald and William Salter; performed by Roberta Flack and Donny Hathaway)

0:00   Introduction: title riff.
Where is the love [seven times]

1st AB Statement

0:17   A   Sung as a duet here.
Where is the love . . .

0:33   B   A more intense section: longer phrases, higher range.
You told me . . .

2nd AB Statement

0:50   A   Elaborate string line behind the vocals.
Where is the love . . .

1:07   B   Wide spacing: bass low; voices, drums, and sustained chords in the middle; strings very high = open sound.
If you had had . . .

3rd AB Statement

1:26   A   Instrumental/wordless vocal. Voice and vibraphone have the melody; keyboard comps.

1:42   B   Long extension of the end of the phrase.
Oh how I wish . . .

Ending

2:04   The title riff, with fade-out.
Where is the love [many times]

next, never coming to rest. Both the chorus and the two more narrative sections are open-ended, leading to the next sections. The song ends with the chorus; it fades away even as the question remains unanswered.

The setting—light, steady drums and percussion; a sparse, syncopated bass line; lush, then active, string parts; keyboard and vibes providing subtle chording—provides a restrained accompaniment for Flack and Hathaway's expressive duet. Both have soulful, pleasant voices: they exemplify what was at the time called **sweet soul**.

STYLE PROFILE

"WHERE IS THE LOVE" (SWEET SOUL)

Rhythm	*Moderate tempo. Light rock rhythm, kept mainly by the drummer. Rhythms of the melody and the bass line are somewhat syncopated.*
Melody	*The A section melody continues from the title riff, descending slowly; the B section has four longer phrases.*
Instrumentation (timbre)	*Vocal duet. Drums, electric bass, keyboard, **vibraphone** (pitched percussion instrument), and strings (mainly violins).*
Performance style	*Gospel-influenced vocal style (especially Hathaway), with expressive inflection ("mine, oh mine").*
Dynamics	*Moderate but building toward the end of the B section.*
Harmony	*Rich harmonies that go some distance beyond I, IV, and V.*
Texture	*Layered, open sound, often with three well-defined registers: low = bass; middle = voices, keyboard, and vibraphone; high = strings much of the time.*
Form	*The main part of the song simply alternates two sections; both have new words with each statement. The title phrase riff serves as a frame when repeated and as an interlude when developed.*

Key Points

Adult orientation	*Failing relationship, older-sounding voice = more mature orientation.*
Gospel-influenced singing	*Flack's and Hathaway's vocal quality and inflection show a gospel connection.*
Lush instrumental background	*Vibraphone, strings, and light, active rhythm section provide a rich backdrop for vocals.*
Black romantic music	*Flack was one of many black pop singers singing about love in a mature way—**black romantic music** was a new sound in the early seventies.*

Terms to Know

black romantic music

sweet soul

vibraphone

Crossroads: The Harmonic Intersection of the 1970s

"Where Is the Love" helps illustrate how traditional harmony remained the language of romantic love in black music. For their harmony the romantic popular songs of the modern era (the 1920s through the 1950s), both white and black, drew on long-familiar chord progressions, such as the ever-popular "Heart and Soul" progression. This harmonic language became part of distinctively black music mainly through doo-wop and gospel. Most doo-wop recordings were either new versions of modern-era hits (like the Flamingos' "I Only Have Eyes for You") or new songs based on pop models (like "Earth Angel"). Black gospel also used traditional harmony extensively because its main artists sang white hymns or wrote gospel songs using the harmonic language of hymns.

All of this begs the question *Why is traditional harmony so appropriate for both romantic song and religious song?* Both secular love and sacred love are based on hope and the realization of that hope. We hope we find a partner with whom we can live happily ever after; we hope to find salvation in the Lord. Traditional harmony helps realize this musically because it creates a pattern of tension and release. The tension begins as we move away from the home chord; the release comes when we return to the home chord via the familiar path. If we stop the "Heart and Soul" progression in the middle or take it in another direction, we do not communicate the comfort and certainty that completing the progression gives. Eventually bringing it back home does express that certainty and comfort in both gospel and romantic pop.

Motown and other black pop in the sixties made use of traditional harmony; so did much of the black pop of the seventies and beyond. We hear a sophisticated version of it in "Where Is the Love"; we can also find it in the music of Stevie Wonder, the Philadelphia acts, Barry White, and others.

Blues Harmony and White Rock. There is another, quite different approach to harmony within African American music: it comes from the blues. Delta blues—as epitomized by Robert Johnson and Muddy Waters—uses the minimal three-chord blues progression or no harmony at all. In its purest form, blues harmony is not a progression like "Heart and Soul" because the harmony simply shifts from one chord to the next. It leaves and returns to the home chord, but the sequence of chords is not conventionally directed toward the home chord. As a result, blues harmony does not create the kind of tension and release that is inherent in the "Heart and Soul" progression and others like it. There is not the sense of moving toward a goal chord along the established path as there is in traditional harmony.

This basic blues harmony was the catalyst for the new harmonic approaches of so much sixties rock, especially that coming from Great Britain. This continued to evolve in the seventies: **power chords** replaced the standard pop harmonies, and new chord sequences carved out quite different paths.

What's significant is that the most rebellious white music of the seventies—heavy metal and punk—made the most use of this different harmonic approach. The avoidance of traditional harmony underscores the dark or depressing messages of the songs, whether it's the satanic excursions of Black Sabbath or the "no future" of the Sex Pistols. This was a radical transformation of the realness of the blues in both message and harmony.

Harmony in Black and White. Two features of these contrasting harmonic approaches are especially fascinating. The first is the seeming role reversal. At the turn of the twentieth century, harmony belonged to white music—and to black interpretations of a white style, like ragtime. The most African-like music in the United States—field hollers and work songs—had no harmony at all.

By the seventies and early eighties, however, traditional harmony played a bigger role in black music than it did in white music because black pop had a far bigger market share than funk, and rock was exploring many nonpop options. So we have the curious situation of whites abandoning their history in favor of a black-derived alternative and vice versa.

The second feature is the clear association of harmony and musical message. As used in pop—black as well as white—traditional harmony is the language of love and hope, as we have noted. Musicians who wanted to send a different, often darker message took a different harmonic path, as we discover next.

HEAVY METAL

Sound is the source of our most immediate reaction to music. Before we've heard even a few notes of a melody or heard enough rhythm to find the beat, we have already reacted to the sounds: distorted guitar, country fiddle, honking saxophone, silky vocal. Nowhere is this more evident than with heavy metal.

Distortion. The sound signature of **heavy metal** is **distortion**—a halo of white noise (a random sampling of the entire range of audible frequencies) surrounding pitched notes. Together with over- and undertones, distortion can create enormous sonic space around a simple power chord. There's an easy way to test this: sing the famous opening riff to Deep Purple's "Smoke on the Water" or play it as a single line on an acoustic instrument—guitar or piano. Then listen to the recording. The sound on the recording is much fuller and more powerful. By analogy, if we think of our version of the riff as a line drawn with a pencil, the same riff, as played by Deep Purple, is like painting over the pencil line with a 4-inch-wide brush.

For listeners, distortion has been like a powerful magnet: depending on their polarity, it has attracted or repelled them. The evolution of heavy metal suggests that musicians and fans alike find distortion as addictive as any drug: more-recent metal styles feature much more distortion than we encounter in the first metal recordings. For those not drawn to heavy metal, on the other hand, distortion repels—to the point that they often fail to go beyond this fleeting first impression to discover what else is going on in the music.

Heavy Metal: Simplicity and Skill. Heavy metal is as contradictory as the reactions it evokes. In some respects it is simple—and about as subtle as a sledgehammer. For the most part, it is unremittingly loud and tends to be rhythmically obvious. In other respects it is a music requiring great skill and sophistication: heavy metal claims the vast majority of rock's virtuoso guitarists.

By the most reliable accounts, the term *heavy metal* came into rock via Steppenwolf: the lyrics to their song "Born to Be Wild" included the phrase "heavy metal thunder," which they borrowed from William Seward Burroughs, author of *Naked Lunch*. It began to designate a new, blues-derived form of rock around 1970.

Three groups—Black Sabbath, Deep Purple, and Led Zeppelin—were responsible for giving heavy metal its identity in sound and image. Of these Black Sabbath offered the purest form of the music. The music of Led Zeppelin ranged far wider than a typical heavy metal band, whereas Deep Purple straddled the boundary between heavy metal and art rock.

Black Sabbath

Black Sabbath was a four-man group: Ozzy Osbourne, vocals; Tommy Iommi, guitar; Geezer Ward, bass; and Bill Ward, drums. The guitar-bass-drums instrumentation connects them directly to late sixties **power trios** like Cream and Jimi Hendrix Experience. (In the studio **overdubbing** turns them into a two-guitar band.) Osbourne's presence as both vocalist and frontman adds an extra dimension.

Early songs like "Black Sabbath" and "Paranoid" (the title tracks from their two 1970 albums) offer a tutorial in metal basics. Using them as examples, we expect to find the following musical features:

Black Sabbath,
"Black Sabbath"
and "Paranoid"

- *Distorted guitar sounds* and their vocal counterpart, Osbourne's sung/screamed vocals.

- *Straightforward rhythms.* "Paranoid" and the fast section of "Black Sabbath" have a quick rhythm hammered out with little or no syncopation. The slow section of "Black Sabbath" repeats one basic rhythm over and over.

- *A high ratio of instrumental sections to vocal sections,* including at least one guitar solo.

- *Power chords in new progressions.* As they are used here, the chord is in effect a static object: guitarists simply slide their hand up and down the neck of the guitar without changing its shape. Power chords shift up and down, but they do not flow smoothly, one to the next, like jazz or pop chords do.

- *A big conception.* Bands like Black Sabbath liked to tackle big, dark themes in their music (as they do here). The music supports this not only with sound but also with bold musical gestures and large-scale forms. In the original studio version, "Black Sabbath" begins with what could be the soundtrack to a Vincent Price horror movie—the sounds of a dark and stormy night. The guitar riff that is repeated over and over outlines the **tritone**, an interval that in medieval times was called "the devil in music" (*diabolus in musica*); there is no more fitting way to evoke the dark side than that. And in lieu of a conventional verse/chorus pattern, there are two distinct sections: the foreboding one with the devil's riff and what sounds like the chase. One can imagine more skillful musical settings, but that does not detract from the fact that Black Sabbath takes on, and tries to convey, heavy subjects.

Over the years heavy metal has split into seemingly dozens of substyles: thrash metal, death metal, speed metal, and so on. These diverse forms of heavy metal retain the metal-defining features heard in these two songs—and other music by Black Sabbath. One still expects these basic features in heavy metal recordings: not only the distortion but also the direct rhythms—often at breakneck tempos—loud dynamics; power chords; and big, sprawling forms.

We next discuss a more adventurous approach to this style in the music of Led Zeppelin.

Led Zeppelin

Like Black Sabbath, Led Zeppelin began as a power trio plus lead vocalist: Jimmy Page, guitar; John Paul Jones, bass; John Bonham, drums; and Robert Plant, vocals. And like Black Sabbath, they made excellent use of the overdubbing capabilities of **multitrack recording**. Page was one of the stalwarts of the British blues scene, having played with the Who, the Yardbirds, the Kinks, and several other bands.

The group came together in 1968; legend has it that Keith Moon, the drummer for the Who, suggested the name Led Zeppelin. The group's first album was released the following year. By the early seventies, they were one of the biggest attractions in rock in both the United States and the United Kingdom, their home base.

The album that secured Zeppelin's place in rock's pantheon was the untitled fourth album, known variously as Led Zeppelin IV, Zoso, or the Runes LP. The best-known song on the album, and the best known of all their songs, is "Stairway to Heaven." The song—more than eight minutes long—is one of the anthems of AOR. We can understand why: it combined accessible music, with something for everybody, with lyrics nobody could definitively decode. The melody with which the song begins sounds very much like a folksong. The recorder trio and Page's guitar reinforce that impression: it evokes the airs of Elizabethan times. It builds slowly but inexorably to the big climax, all over another hooklike riff, before receding to the original peaceful state.

Throughout we are left wondering, *What is this song about?* One can find Christian and diabolical interpretations, another take that suggests that the song is a grand metaphor for heroin addiction, and there are many others. The larger point is that the music is deliberately obscure. Page was fascinated with the occult and the misty early history of Britain; the album cover communicates that, as do the recorders. So it should not surprise us that "Stairway to Heaven," which is so accessible and appealing musically, would feature a cryptic lyric.

"Black Dog," another track from the album, tells us more about Led Zeppelin's connection with heavy metal and about rock's continuing development. The similarities between the Black Sabbath songs and "Black Dog" are immediately apparent: the instrumentation, the distortion, and the volume level. The more interesting features are the differences. Perhaps the most obvious is Robert Plant's stratospheric vocal range—substantially higher than Ozzy Osbourne's and most everyone else's. But consider how the song begins:

o   A noodle on the guitar
o   Plant singing without accompaniment
o   The band playing an extended, blues-based melodic line, without a vocal

If we compare this to so many memorable sixties **hard rock** songs, we notice a big difference. Typically, rock songs start with a guitar riff that sets the tempo. Other instruments layer in, setting up the groove. ("Jumping Jack Flash" and "Purple Haze" are two good examples of this approach.) That doesn't happen here. Early on we feel the beat strictly from Plant's vocal line. The silence that follows and the strung-out instrumental line make it difficult to group the beats into measures.

The point here is this: in the four or five years between 1967–68 and 1972, top rock musicians like Page, Jones, Bonham, and Plant became so comfortable with the rock groove that they could play with it boldly. Even the choruslike riff under Plant's "Oh, yeah" is completely syncopated. The song has a great beat throughout, but the timekeeping that does take place happens very much in the background.

Earlier we discussed how musicians settle into a style a few years after a new beat becomes common currency, to the extent that they can take its basic features for granted and begin to play with it. We heard it with both the fox trot and swing in the 1930s; we could find it also in the freer rhythms of bop and postbop jazz in the 1940s and '50s. We hear it again in the music of Led Zeppelin. One would be hard-pressed to find a sixties song that matches this one in rhythmic daring.

The extended instrumental lines in "Black Dog" also point up another feature of Led Zeppelin's approach to rock—one that would profoundly influence heavy metal bands to come. In effect they harness sololike lines within a tight group conception. Guitar solos in rock can be spectacular displays, but they can also undermine the collective conception that is at the heart of a rock groove. Page's solution was to work out sololike lines and integrate them into a group conception. For future heavy metal bands, this aspect of the recording was key. One of the marvels of a good heavy metal performance is the tight ensemble of a band as they negotiate challenging and intricate passages. We can hear its roots in this recording.

Heavy metal flourished early in the seventies, went out of favor later in the decade, then came on strong again in the eighties with a wave of new bands. We consider heavy metal's second generation in Chapter 12.

DRESSING UP: ROCK AS ART AND THEATER

The most memorable album cover of the sixties has to be the Beatles' *Sgt. Pepper's Lonely Hearts Club Band.* It was visually arresting and a great puzzle—who are all those people and why are they on the cover?—and it symbolized rock's coming of age on its own terms.

The cover featured not only the Beatles in full dress but also pop icons of the past and present. Among the many faces are those of Karl Marx and Albert Einstein, Marlon Brando and Marilyn Monroe, Stan Laurel and Oliver Hardy, H. G. Wells and Edgar Allen Poe, and, of course Bob Dylan and Dylan Thomas. This aggregation certainly seemed to suggest that past and present and "high" and "low" culture had come together. The uniforms worn by the Beatles and the absence of masks seem to symbolize the juxtaposition of reality and the escape from reality that we hear in songs like "A Day in the Life" and "Lucy in the Sky with Diamonds."

There were four messages in the cover and the album itself that resonated through British rock in the early seventies. The first was that rock could be art. The second was that an artistic statement in rock could grow out of a concept, an idea that would unify a series of musical statements into a larger entity. The third was that rock was an eclectic art, one that drew on any sources as needed. The fourth was that an artistic statement could involve assuming a persona. We sample this new direction in the music of Pink Floyd and David Bowie.

Pink Floyd

Pink Floyd's album *The Dark Side of the Moon* first appeared on the Top 200 album charts on March 31, 1973. It stayed on the chart for 740 more weeks—almost twelve and a half years. In the process it broke the record for chart longevity, previously held by Carole King's *Tapestry* album, by almost four years.

Pink Floyd, "The Dark Side of the Moon"

How do we account for its extraordinary staying power? Why were people still buying this album in the early eighties? Clearly, it offered more than novelty, though it was novel in many respects. And although it certainly seems to reflect the pervasive pessimism in Great Britain during the seventies, it transcends time and place.

The Dark Side of the Moon is a big album in every important respect. It tackles big themes, as several track titles suggest: "Breathe," "Time," "Us and Them," and "Money." And it presents a bleak vision of life. By the end the album's antihero has gone mad; he and the brain-swapping doctors seem to be a metaphor for young people and an oppressive government. The forty-three minutes of music are conceived of as a continuous, extended work. Each track flows into the next without interruption, and certain key musical gestures appear in several tracks.

Pink Floyd was formed in 1965 by guitarist Syd Barrett, bassist Roger Waters, percussionist Nick Mason, and keyboardist Richard Wright. David Gilmour replaced Barrett in 1968, and the lineup remained intact through 1982. On *The Dark Side of the Moon,* all four band members contributed to the tracks; Waters wrote all the lyrics.

The record borrows from *Sgt. Pepper* not only the idea of a **concept album** but also the collagelike techniques that are evident in both music and cover. In this work Pink Floyd goes even further.

We might group the sonic events in *The Dark Side of the Moon* into five categories:

o   Rock band sounds: vocals, guitar, bass, drums, and keyboard
o   Other conventional popular music sounds: the saxophone solos and backup vocals
o   Spoken comments—seemingly random snippets of conversations
o   Everyday noises: the ring of a cheap alarm clock, a cash register opening
o   Electronic sounds generated by the VCS3, billed at the time as the first portable synthesizer

At times they are discrete: the switch from conventional instrumentation to electronic sounds helps define the transition from "Breathe" to "On the Run." In other situations they are merged: we discover that the seemingly arbitrary money-handling sounds at the beginning of "Money" lay down an irregular rhythm when the instruments join in. (Beats are grouped by sevens: four, then three.)

Because so much of the work is instrumental—there are long electronic interludes and extended improvised sections on several tracks (as in "Any Colour You Like")—there are no standard vocal hooks serving as a chorus. Instead the character of each track comes from other features: tempo, instrumentation, timekeeping, dynamics, and harmony. The closest thing to a chorus in this extended work is not a melodic idea but a two-chord progression. We hear it first in "Breathe," then in "Time," "The Great Gig in the Sky," and "Any Colour You Like."

The use of this particular chord sequence as a recurrent theme says a lot about both the intent of the album and its enduring popularity. Melody is personal and specific: melodic ideas have distinctive rhythms and explicit patterns of rise and fall. Even the simplest ideas can have a distinct personality, as we have experienced again and again ("Heaven . . . I'm in heaven . . ."). Words make them easier to remember, but even instrumental riffs, like the ones we heard in so many sixties tunes, identify a song immediately.

By contrast the two-chord progression is at once familiar but not specific. We have encountered it many times as part of the "Heart and Soul" progression and others like it. It is, in effect, the equivalent of the faceless everyman, a sound image that seems to match the bleak mood of the album.

There's more: When we first hear the two-chord progression in "Breathe," it seems to represent the key chord and a common companion. In the course of the album, it is repeated over and over, whether underneath a vocal or as the harmonic underpinning of extended solos. The repetition of the chord pair suspends time, or at least our sense of time "goals." Moreover, it is ambiguous because the chords, their association, and their specific context here send conflicting signals. By recontextualizing this familiar sound and bringing it to the foreground, Pink Floyd manages to give listeners something familiar yet different to hook onto.

And it is all of a piece. Every aspect of the album—the heartbeats that frame it, Waters's lyrics and the spoken asides, the fascinating blend of conventional and electronic sounds, the integration of individual tracks into a larger whole, the extended instrumental sections, and more—signals that the album is making a statement, one that far transcends the scope of three-minute songs broadcast over AOR stations. One can argue whether the band succeeded in this task and to what extent, but there is no question about the seriousness of their intent.

Pink Floyd's album represents one expression of rock as art. Still another was David Bowie's first concept album, *Ziggy Stardust.*

David Bowie as Ziggy Stardust

One can use a large river as a metaphor for the continuing evolution of rock in the seventies. Certainly, there is a parallel between the tributaries that flow into a river, making it broader, and the musical influences that helped shape rock. But there was more to rock's evolution than the proliferation of styles and substyles. Even by the midsixties, rock had become a wildly diverse music rather than a single sound. As artists continued to develop rock in varied, and often conflicting, directions, the music seemed to simultaneously turn back on itself and move forward. We might describe rock in the early seventies more aptly as a bad hair day rather than as a delta fanning out as it meets the gulf, in the sense that trends, when played out over time, can reverse an evolutionary path. Exhibit A of this new metaphor might well be David Bowie as Ziggy Stardust, which undermined rock's realness and its masculinity.

By the midsixties rock was a lot of things: string ensembles as backup bands (in the Beatles' "Eleanor Rigby"), Dylan's dissing ("Like a Rolling Stone"), technology battles (Brian Wilson's "Good Vibrations" versus *Sgt. Pepper*), even Frank Zappa's satire, sophisticated and slapstick by turns, that included a sendup of *Sgt. Pepper* complete with a parody of the album cover. At its core, however, was rock and roll.

This core music was real—and male. Often it was blatantly sexual: Mick Jagger complaining that he can't be satisfied (although he apparently found some satisfaction with Bowie, whose wife caught the two of them in bed together) or the Kinks telling the world that "You Really Got Me." In this context the electric guitar, slung low and thrust out, became an obvious phallic symbol. In other settings its protagonists confronted the dangerous and nightmarish: Lou Reed "I'm Waiting for the Man," Jim Morrison describing the horror of "The End," or Ozzy Osbourne wrestling with the devil. In all these cases, the music was potent and immediate; music and message were very much in the here and now.

By the early seventies, hard rock—in all its forms—reeked of machismo, whether it involved sexuality or danger or both. It is in this context that we can understand how David Bowie's incarnation as Ziggy Stardust turned rock values on their head.

The idea of assuming a persona—in name, appearance, and action—has been part of rock since the beginning—one needs only to look at Elvis or Little Richard to verify this. In these cases and in the cases of other early rock stars, the persona was a larger-than-life version of the artist's off-stage self. It took David Bowie to go beyond that, to raise the use of a persona to art.

Bowie's persona begins with names. Bowie was born David Robert Jones in 1947. By the midsixties he was active in the London club scene. He changed his name from David Jones to David Bowie in 1966 to avoid being confused with Davy Jones of the Monkees. That was

David Bowie in concert at the Hammersmith Odeon, in the persona of his alter ego Ziggy Stardust, July 4, 1973.
As Ziggy, Bowie is in full androgynous mode. Ziggy Stardust was the first of many Bowie personas.

certainly understandable; what is provocative is that he took his new surname from the bowie knife, which is named after Jim Bowie, the American frontiersman.

Bowie's breakthrough came in 1972 with the release of the album *The Rise and Fall of Ziggy Stardust and the Spiders from Mars* and the production of the stage show based on it. He had begun to create the character the previous year. His manager convinced RCA Records (now part of BMG) to bankroll the stage show to promote the album; both were a success. (Bowie's show was an early example of the cross-marketing discussed earlier in this chapter.)

Apparently, the name and the character came from obscure sources. According to an interview, *Ziggy* came from a London tailor shop, and *Stardust* was inspired by the "Legendary Stardust Cowboy," a country singer wannabe named Norman Carl Odom whose talent was so far below his perception of it that audiences thought he was trying to be funny when he was dead serious.

A classic case of rock-and-roll crash and burn inspired the character of Ziggy Stardust: an Englishman born Brian Holden but using the name Vince Taylor had a career in France as an Elvis impersonator, beginning in the late fifties. By the midsixties he was on a drug-driven trip to megalomania—he claimed to be the son of God—and lunacy. In interviews Bowie recalled meeting him and becoming immediately aware that Taylor was "Totally flipped. The guy was not playing with a full deck at all."

Creating a character out of such obscure sources was a stroke of genius: it was extremely unlikely that anyone would see Ziggy Stardust as anything more than a product of Bowie's fertile imagination. And in fact Ziggy was far more than the sum of these disparate influences.

The Rise and Fall of Ziggy Stardust and the Spiders from Mars chronicles the brief career of an alien who arrives on Earth, becomes a rock superstar, and eventually becomes a victim of his success. Ziggy, an androgynous, cross-dressing, lavishly made-up alien, was the complete opposite of the stereotypical rock star macho man. It is hard to imagine a more radical transformation of the core attitude and image of rock. Instead of being right here, Ziggy is literally from out there; instead of being more than a man, he is so much less masculine that his sexuality is in doubt.

Bowie was courageous in being outrageous. The gay rights movement, using the examples set by civil rights and women's rights activists, was just gathering steam. Indeed the term *gay*, now the word of choice to describe the culture of homosexual men, was just entering mainstream culture, replacing more pejorative terms like *queer* and *homo*. Alternative images of gender remain difficult at the beginning of the twenty-first century; they were far more so at the beginning of the seventies.

What made Bowie's portrayal of Ziggy even more provocative was its ambiguity. Cross-dressing and other typically feminine aspects of appearance don't guarantee an alternative sexuality, although they often provide a clue (e.g., Little Richard's penchant for mascara). We do not know whether Ziggy Stardust was an extension of Bowie's personality or a complete fabrication—a put-on on a grand scale. We do know that it was a bold step.

As radical as Ziggy was, what was even more radical was Bowie's music. The songs for the album were not so much rock and roll as rock about rock and roll. There is a huge difference in perspective.

David Bowie, "The Rise and Fall of Ziggy Stardust and the Spiders from Mars"

In several discussions, we have mentioned the realness of rock and its communal aspect. Rock bands forge a group identity, as their names indicate, and a group conception. The act of performance becomes almost a ritual in which musicians and audience unite in an eternally present experience. By contrast, in the musical theater examples we have studied, the composers necessarily wrote in the third person: they composed music for others to sing. Moreover, the performers were clearly playing a role.

In *The Rise and Fall of Ziggy Stardust and the Spiders from Mars*, Bowie replaces the we/thee togetherness between musicians and audience with detachment. He does this by disguising the "I." We sense from the songs that Bowie has switched the voice from the real and present first person ("I Can't Get No Satisfaction," "You Really Got Me") to a less clearly defined voice. When he sings we don't know who he is: Is he Bowie singing about Ziggy? Is he Ziggy? Is he a third person commenting on Ziggy?

In this respect Bowie is using rock for theatrical purposes, much like musical theater composers—Sondheim, Rodgers, Webber—used popular music in service of a theatrical goal. This is in itself a jarring departure from conventional rock-era practice, although there are certainly precedents—*Tommy, Hair, Jesus Christ Superstar,* and of course *Sgt. Pepper.*

Two other aspects of *Ziggy Stardust* further complicate the picture. One is that Bowie, like any self-respecting rock musician, wrote the songs for the show. This blurs the boundary between the real first person and the fictional third person of theater. Ziggy is, of course, fictional, but Bowie is not, and the songs obscure, rather than clarify, where Bowie stops and Ziggy begins. The other is that *Ziggy Stardust* marked Bowie's entrance into the big time. He became a star in the United States only after his *Ziggy Stardust* tours. So American audiences did not have a "real" Bowie with whom to compare Ziggy.

All of this works because of the songs. On one level they're a collection of excellent songs, one quite different from the next: compare "Soul Love" with "Starman" or "Lady Stardust" with "Hang On to Yourself." Most have good hooks (Bowie commented that he "borrowed" the big leap that begins the chorus in "Starman" from "Somewhere over the Rainbow"), catchy beats, and interesting sounds, including the good guitar playing of the Spiders' lead guitarist Mick Ronson. On another level they're like theater songs, designed to help tell the story: *Ziggy Stardust* is one of the important concept albums in rock. In this regard musical gestures acquire another level of meaning: To what extent do they help portray the character and tell the story? To that end there are sharp contrasts not only from song to song but also within songs (e.g., "Starman").

It is hard to overestimate how radical a departure Bowie's theater piece was. His androgyny—the fact of it and the outrageousness of it—was the most obvious departure. It seemed to lead inevitably to the gender-blending personas of top pop stars in the eighties: most notably Michael Jackson, Prince, Madonna, and Boy George, as well as the over-the-top antics of punk bands.

Even more far-reaching was Bowie's adoption of a mask. Instead of opening himself up to his audience, he obscured his real self behind the character he had created. In so doing he reversed a trend almost a half century old. From the late 1920s through the early 1970s, popular music had become progressively more personal. It began with the intimacy of Bing Crosby's singing and the warmth of Louis Armstrong's singing and playing. Song interpreters —Billie Holiday, Frank Sinatra, Nat "King" Cole, and others—took the next step, using someone else's song as a way to express their feelings. Rock musicians made their music even more personal by expressing their emotions in both the song and its performance. The confessional songs of Joni Mitchell and other singer-songwriters represent the final step in this evolutionary process.

Bowie abruptly reversed this trend. He was not alone. The **glam rock** movement to which Bowie was linked included such acts as Alice Cooper, Mott the Hoople, Queen, and T. Rex, which featured Bowie's friend and rival Marc Bolan. At about the same time, the four members of the heavy metal band Kiss carefully hid their real selves by appearing in public only with cartoonish face paint. Elton John started wearing elaborate costumes in public performance. No one, however, approached Bowie in style, sophistication, or vision.

Ziggy Stardust was the first of several Bowie characters. Not surprisingly, Bowie has also had a significant acting career. He remains one of the most fascinating figures in rock history.

Rock as an Elite Music

Pink Floyd and David Bowie represent two quite distinct approaches to creating rock-based art music. Pink Floyd's music aspired to art; Bowie's was built on artifice; both are elite tendencies. Another important development was the music of groups like Yes, Deep Purple, King Crimson, and Emerson, Lake and Palmer, which was known variously as **art rock** or progressive rock. Their work continued the mainly British effort to raise rock to the level of art, heard in the music of the Beatles, the Who, and others.

Why this is so is a provocative question. Music critic John Rockwell speculated that the roots of this elitist tendency in U.K. rock has to do with the deep class divisions in English society and its citizens' fascination with the upper classes and the social and cultural world they inhabit. At the beginning of the twenty-first century, England remains the world's most prominent monarchy. The House of Lords, whose membership is based on heredity, remains a working part of the parliamentary government. The deeds and misdeeds of the royals remain fodder for tabloids worldwide. In this context it is not surprising that British musicians would explore so many different ways to create rock-based art music.

DRESSING DOWN: IT'S STILL ROCK AND ROLL

The end of the sixties marked the beginning of a new decade and the death of rock, or so it might have seemed. Death claimed several top stars. Jimi Hendrix, Jim Morrison of the Doors, and Janis Joplin died in 1970. Brian Jones of the Rolling Stones—the soul of the band in the opinion of some—had died the year before. They were but four of the many casualties of the drug culture.

It was another death—this time of a band—that seemed to symbolize the end of an era. The Beatles epitomized the excitement of rock. The pace of their innovations left audiences breathless with anticipation and delighted with the results. Their breakup was the downer of the decade. Each of the ex-Beatles established a solo career. As we have seen, McCartney was by far the most active and commercially successful, but both Lennon and Harrison also had notable successes. Still, none achieved singly what they had achieved collectively.

Still, rock was far from dead, as the discussion to this point has intimated. Even as most British bands explored new territory—art rock, glam rock, heavy metal—the Rolling Stones reaffirmed the core of rock with two major albums, *Sticky Fingers* (1971) and *Exile on Main Street* (1972). Many critics have regarded the latter album as their finest. The Stones took a dimmer view of their subsequent work, ironically titling a retrospective collection of their music from this period *Sucking in the Seventies*.

In North America rock and roll saw a changing of the guard. Among the casualties of the early seventies were Creedence Clearwater Revival, who broke up in 1972, and the Allman Brothers, who lost guitarist Duane Allman in a 1971 motorcycle accident. The Band continued to work, but they had peaked by the beginning of the decade. The Grateful Dead kept leading the Deadheads around the country for their endless jams. New acts, from Aerosmith to ZZ Top, reaffirmed the central place of rock and roll. We consider two of them here: Bruce Springsteen and Lynyrd Skynyrd.

Bruce Springsteen and the E Street Band in 1975, the year that he recorded "Born to Run," his breakthrough hit. Contrast Springsteen's everyman appearance (and that of his band members) with Bowie's look.

Bruce Springsteen

Asbury Park is a New Jersey beach town about an hour's drive from New York City. Bruce Springsteen (b. 1949) grew up in and around the town. Early on he forged the musical split personality that has been his trademark: he worked with bar bands close to home and also played solo gigs in Greenwich Village clubs, where he mingled with Patti Smith and other early punk rockers. This helps account for the huge swings in his music, from the all-acoustic *Nebraska* album to the hard-rocking *Born in the U.S.A.*

His enormous success comes in part from his ability to integrate seemingly contradictory aspects of his life and work. He is a superstar and a man of the people, a musician who plays to sold-out arenas and shows up unannounced to sit in with local bands. Throughout his career he has stayed close to his working-class roots and has written songs that reflect their concerns. At the same time, he is larger than life—the "Boss" to his fiercely loyal fans.

In 1974 rock critic Jon Landau went to a Springsteen concert at the Harvard Square Theatre. In a long, rambling review, he wrote, "I saw rock and roll's future and his name is Bruce Springsteen." Landau turned his words into action, becoming Springsteen's manager and disentangling him from a messy business relationship with Mike Appell, Springsteen's manager at the time.

Landau's evaluation was right on the mark in the sense that Springsteen became the biggest star of the next two decades to consciously continue the core tradition of rock. While others branched off in new directions, Springsteen stayed close to his rock-and-roll roots even as he updated and expanded the sound. For example, his first big hit, the 1975 song "Born to Run," features an oversized band (several guitars, saxophone, keyboards, bass, and drums), an extended guitar hook, a sprawling form, and a powerful, obvious beat.

Bruce Springsteen, "Born to Run"

In this song Springsteen connects directly to recent American culture. It builds on Dylan's electric phase: the same concern for the primacy of the words in the midst of a dense, loud accompaniment pervades his music. Springsteen's singing also connects his music with Dylan: his quasi-spoken, rough-edged vocal style borrows directly from Dylan's delivery.

The lyric, and the attitude it conveys, goes back another decade, to Hollywood images of rebellion: Marlon Brando astride his motorcycle in *The Wild One* (1953) and James Dean in *Rebel Without a Cause* (1955).

"Born to Run" is at once down-home and downtown. It is easy to imagine Springsteen dressed in faded jeans and a T-shirt, wearing his trademark bandanna, seated on a Harley and ready to ride off into the sunset with his girl. Certain aspects of the music—Springsteen's singing, the beat, the big guitar riff—communicate this look in sound. Such features as the bell-like effects just before the title phrase, however, and the complex harmonies and the slithering scale of the instrumental break suggest a level of sophistication far higher than one would expect from the average bar band. Springsteen brings it off: he integrates these contrasting signals into a song with real impact.

Springsteen's stature has grown since this early success. He has been one of rock's superstars since the early eighties and one of the few whose integrity and passion seem unflagging. From *Nebraska* and *Born in the U.S.A.* through the 1995 *Ghost of Tom Joad* (with its allusion to Steinbeck's *Grapes of Wrath* and connection with Dylan's idol Woody Guthrie) and his response to 9/11, *The Rising* (2002), Springsteen has continued to express his ideas honestly.

Southern Rock

As a noun *boogie* initially referred to boogie-woogie, the piano style first popularized in the late 1920s. As a verb *boogie* means to dance to rock music or to party (another noun turned verb) or—often—to do both. As an adjective *boogie* identifies the kind of rock band that plays party music.

Today, one can find boogie bands all over the world. In the early seventies, however, most of them were based in the South. The reason for this seems to be the fact that the basic sound of a boogie band is a blend of blues, rock, country, soul, and R&B—in other words, the music that an open-minded southerner would hear growing up.

The sense of regional identity of this music raises the always-provocative issue of the connection between cultural environment and musical result. In this case it generates questions like these: *Could the good-time feel of boogie rock have emerged only in the southern United States? Is this a kind of music that could be made only by musicians who had grown up hearing all this music?* Here it is a matter of race and geography.

In the sixties it was the British musicians who were serious about the blues, immersing themselves in it during their formative years as musicians. Out of that came an absolutely new kind of rock, one that was indebted to the blues yet apart from it. *Serious* is the operative word. Whether it's Mick Jagger's posturing, Eric Clapton's passion, or Jimmy Page's probing of the occult, this blues-based music is serious business. It's hard to imagine any of them—at least at the time—simply letting the good times roll. Contrast that with the music of southern bands like Lynyrd Skynyrd, who offer real blue-jeans rock. The only statement they're trying to make is *Let's have a good time.*

Whether it's due to growing up with blues, country, and the other genres or simply a fortunate coming together of these influences, this is rock at its most comfortable and down-home. This particular—and particularly American—blend is characteristic of southern rock, though the proportions may vary from band to band. Early Allman Brothers recordings are heavy on the blues because of Duane Allman's devotion to electric blues. By contrast, the music of Marshall Tucker and Charlie Daniels has a stronger country flavor. But it all seems to spring forth from the same source.

Southern rock seemed to go out of fashion, as punk, disco, and other hot new styles deflected attention away from it. But in a very real sense, this music is never out of fashion. Groups like Lynyrd Skynyrd perfected the kind of groove that will be as timeless as the music itself. This is old-time and good-time rock and roll.

British Versus American Rock

We have discussed songs by Pink Floyd, David Bowie, Bruce Springsteen, and Lynyrd Skynyrd. Pink Floyd and Bowie are of course British; Springsteen and Lynyrd Skynyrd are American. Granted, these are only four of hundreds of notable seventies acts, but they still suggest a growing division between U.K. and U.S. versions of rock.

Where the British examples suggest an elitist tendency, the American examples show a populist streak. Springsteen's song portrays himself apart from mainstream society but not above it. Lynyrd Skynyrd's "What's Your Name" is without pretense, as far from the glamour and artifice of Bowie's show as one could get in rock.

Still, there was plenty of **cross-pollination** between the United Kingdom and the United States (and Canada). Elton John remained a big star. Fleetwood Mac enjoyed tremendous success, especially with *Rumours,* which topped the charts for more than half a year in 1977. Pink Floyd hit big again in 1980 with *The Wall.* The most extensive common ground, however, came with punk and new wave music. We explore these and other late-seventies and early-eighties styles in Chapter 12.

LOOKING BACK, LOOKING AHEAD

The seventies trends discussed in this chapter—mainstream pop, black romantic music, heavy metal, rock as art and theater, and the persistence of rock and roll—represent important continuations of the rock and R&B of the sixties. Some of these trends included acts that were surpassingly popular: Elton John, Stevie Wonder, and Led Zeppelin. Some acts charted spectacular new directions (David Bowie), created more-mature versions of an existing style (Roberta Flack), or reaffirmed the past (Lynyrd Skynyrd). With all of them, there is a sense of continuity between the sixties and the seventies, a sense that the music of the seventies not only grows out of major trends in the sixties and expands their range but also combines one or more of them.

By contrast the music in the next chapter seems to come from the outside. With reggae the outsider status is geographic—Jamaica is not on the U.S./U.K. axis. Punk was at once an intensification of sixties realness and a reaction to the ascendancy of rock and the commercialization that was the inevitable consequence. Funk was a continuation of the music of James Brown and Sly and the Family Stone—more rhythmic, less melodic, and farther from the mainstream as a result. Disco cultivated an audience of minorities—at least until it caught on. We survey these next.

TERMS TO KNOW

Test your knowledge of this chapter's important terms by defining the following. If you can't recall the meaning of a certain term, refresh your memory by looking up the boldfaced term in the chapter, turning to the Glossary at the back of the book, or working with the flashcards on the *Popular Music in America* Companion Web site: *http://music.wadsworth.com/ campbell_2e*

. . . .

analog synthesizer	distortion	power trio
AOR (album-oriented radio)	glam rock	singer-songwriter
art rock	hard rock	sweet soul
black romantic music	heavy metal	synthesizer
blaxploitation	microphone	tritone
concept album	multitrack recording	vibraphone
cross-marketing	overdubbing	white noise
cross-pollination	pickup	
	power chord	

. . . .

Counterpoint:
New Trends of the Late 1970s

Much of the new and newly emergent music of the late seventies and early eighties—punk, reggae, disco, funk, techno, ambient, and, toward the end, rap—began as a reaction or an alternative to the trends of the first part of the decade rather than as a continuation of them.

Punk, for example, was an "anti" music in several respects: It was anti-commercial (although Malcolm McLaren, the man behind the Sex Pistols, certainly capitalized on the success of the band); anti-establishment (they took dead aim at authority); and anti-professional (punk rockers sought a return to garage-band simplicity). Disco, by contrast, emerged rather suddenly from the underground club scene as the hot new dance music of the late seventies. Dancing, so much a part of fifties rock and roll and early sixties rock and soul, seemed to disappear during the first part of the seventies. Disco helped bring it back.

The images we have of these various styles—the Ramones, with T-shirts and sunglasses, making a big noise in a small club; Rastafarian dreadlocks; the glitter of the disco ball and the platform shoes of disco dancers; the outrageous outfits worn by George Clinton and the members of his bands, Parliament and Funkadelic; the absence of a performance-related image for early techno—highlight the considerable differences from style to style.

Still they share some common ground. None of these styles carved out and kept a significant share of the popular-music market. Disco was the most commercially successful style, but only the Bee Gees (who were an established act before *Saturday Night Fever*) and Donna Summer sustained any kind of chart presence. For the most part, all of these styles were outside the commercial loop. Second, all were extraordinarily influential and would resonate through the music of the eighties. Several important new trends resulted from the fusion of two or more styles, such as the **punk/funk/disco fusions** heard in some eighties pop. Other new sounds came about through the guiding hand (and ear) of specific individuals, such as Brian Eno's role with U2 and George Clinton's mentoring of the Red Hot Chili Peppers.

The third common feature is strictly musical: all of these styles have more-active rhythms than rock. Reggae has a strikingly new, multilayered beat. In the case of punk, it is tempo driven; punk tempos are brisk. The others use a new, busier beat. We begin our survey with reggae.

REGGAE

For much of the twentieth century, from NBC's first network broadcast in 1925 through MTV's debut in 1981, radio has been integral to the development of popular music. It has had the ability to collapse distances, either through network hookups or clear-channel broadcasts. It created a West Coast audience for the New York–based Benny Goodman band; his Los Angeles following was large enough to kick off the swing era. The Saturday-night broadcasts of the *Grand Ole Opry*, sent out weekly from Nashville's powerful WSM, helped make country music a music for much more of the country than the South. Radio is the stuff of rock-and-roll legend: we read about Buddy Holly driving around in his car late at night, trying to find the best location to pick up his favorite R&B station.

Radio ignores borders; it is limited only by distance and wattage. Powerful transmitters just south of the Texas-Mexico border spread country music throughout the United States. Hank Snow, a top country star via Nova Scotia, Canada, first encountered country music via clear-channel broadcasts from the United States.

So it should not surprise us that Jamaicans tuned in their radios to American stations in the years after World War II. Kingston, the capital city, is just over 500 miles from Miami as the crow flies and about 1,000 miles from New Orleans. Stations from all over the southern United States were within reach, at least after dark. Like Buddy Holly, many young Jamaicans listened to rhythm and blues; for them, it replaced **mento**, the Jamaican popular music of the early fifties.

Sound Systems and Street Parties. Sound systems, the mobile discos so much a part of daily life in Jamaica, offered another way to hear new music from America. Sound systems were trucks outfitted with the musical necessities for a street party: records, turntables, speakers, and a microphone for the DJ. Operators would drive around, pick a place to set up, and begin to play the R&B hits that enterprising operators had gone to the United States to fetch. Between songs, DJs delivered a steady stream of patter. Much of it was topical, even personal: they would pick out, and sometimes pick on, people in the crowd that had gathered around.

This practice was called **toasting**. It became so popular, and so much a feature of the sound system party, that Jamaican record producers like Lee "Scratch" Perry began releasing discs in which the B side was simply the A side without the vocal track. The instrumental track would then serve as the musical backdrop for the DJ's toasting. Toasting is a direct forerunner of rap: both initially featured topical, humorous commentary over pre-existing music. Rap's first hit, the SugarHill Gang's 1979 "Rapper's Delight," followed this model, using Chic's "Good Times" as the musical background.

Ska: A New Jamaican Music. By the end of the 1950s, Jamaican music had begun to absorb, and then transform, the R&B brought to the country. The first wave of new Jamaican music was ska. **Ska** emerged around 1960 and was the dominant Jamaican sound through the first part of the decade; its most distinctive feature is a strong afterbeat: a strong, crisp *chunk* on the latter part of each beat. This was a Jamaican take on the shuffle rhythm heard in so much fifties R&B. It kept the basic rhythm but reversed the pattern of emphasis within each beat. In the shuffle rhythm, the note that falls on the beat gets the weight; the afterbeat is lighter. In ska it is just the opposite, at times to the extent that the note on the beat is absent—there is just the afterbeat. Whether this was an intentional decision by ska musicians such as Derrick Morgan and Prince Buster, a product of the relatively primitive recording studios in Jamaica during this time (recall that early electrical recording did not pick up bass sounds very well), or the lack of bass instruments and people to play them, we don't know; perhaps it was a combination of all of these factors. Whatever its sources, the strong afterbeat remains the aural trademark of ska and part of the rhythmic foundation of reggae.

Responses to Colonialism

Most Jamaicans are of African descent—about 90 percent at the turn of the twenty-first century. Most trace their roots back to slavery; like the United States, Cuba, and Brazil, Jamaica was a destination for the slave traders. More than 600,000 slaves arrived in Jamaica between 1665 and 1838, the year in which the slave trade ended. British colonial rule continued for more than a century. Great Britain gradually transferred authority to Jamaicans, with the final step—independence—taken in 1962. Redress of the economic and social inequities of colonialism, however, did not keep pace with the political changes. One result was a great deal of social unrest in the sixties.

Rastafarianism. Two midcentury movements that responded to Jamaican social inequities stand out. One—the better known and more enduring—is Rastafarianism. Rastafarianism was an important consequence of Marcus Garvey's crusade to elevate the status of people of African descent. Garvey, born in Jamaica, agitated for black power in the United States during the 1920s in response to the dire poverty and discrimination that the vast majority of blacks living in the New World faced. His efforts blended church and state: even as he pressed for an African homeland to which former slaves could return (it never materialized), he prophesied that Christ would come again as a black man. After serving half of a five-year sentence in an Atlanta prison, he was exiled from the United States and returned to Jamaica.

For centuries African slaves and their descendants had been confronting the historically inaccurate image of Jesus as a pale-skinned Caucasian. Moreover, it was inevitable that they would connect this image with the colonial empires that brought it to them. At the same time, those slaves who had become Christians saw parallels between the Jews' years in slavery to the Egyptians and the slavery of Africans in the New World. African American spirituals are rich with such connections. In this context Garvey's prophesy about Christ's second coming and his emphasis on the Jewish/African slavery connection was a logical, if controversial, extension of these circumstances. In effect they were the religious analogue to his black nationalism.

Rastafarians took Garvey's ideas several steps further. They claimed that Jesus had indeed come again, in the person of Haile Selassie (Prince Ras Tafari), the former emperor of Ethiopia. Selassie claimed lineage back to King Solomon, which Rastafarians have taken as further proof of Selassie's divine status. In line with Selassie's personal genealogy, Rastafarians also claim to be descendants of the twelve tribes of Israel.

These beliefs, which have never come together as "official" doctrine—as has happened in organized religions—are the religious dimension of Rastafarians' efforts to promote a more positive image of Africa and Africans. This has largely come from within the movement. For those on the outside, the most vivid impressions of Rastafarianism are images and sounds: dreadlocks, ganja (marijuana, which they ingest as part of their religious practice), and music. To Jamaican music they gave a sound—Rastafarian drums—and reggae's one superstar, Bob Marley.

Rude Boys. The other response to the social unrest during the transition to independence was more violent. It came in the form of "rude boys," disenfranchised young black Jamaicans who grew up in the most disadvantaged sections of Kingston. They were sharp dressers and often carried sharp knives. For many Jamaicans, including the police, they were outlaws. Others, however, saw them as heroes, much as the James Brothers and Billy the Kid were heroes to earlier generations of Americans or as today's gangsta rappers are to some young people. Ska, then **rock steady**, and finally reggae was their music. We hear echoes of the rude boys and the social conditions that created them in one of the classic reggae songs, Jimmy Cliff's "The Harder They Come."

Jimmy Cliff and the Sound of Reggae

CD 3:9

"The Harder They Come," Jimmy Cliff (1972). Cliff, vocal.

Jimmy Cliff (born James Chambers in 1948) was one of reggae's first stars. By the time he landed the lead role in the film *The Harder They Come*, he had gained an international reputation as a singer-songwriter. His appearance in the film, and the songs that he recorded for the soundtrack, cemented his place in popular-music history. In *The Harder They Come*, Cliff plays Ivan O. Martin, a musician who becomes a gangster. Although his character is loosely based on a real-life person from the 1940s, Cliff's title song brings the story into the present. The lyric resonates with overtones of social injustice and police oppression and brutality even as it outlines how the character will respond: "I'm gonna get my share now of what's mine."

The musical backdrop for Cliff's lyrics is reggae. Like many other Latin and Caribbean styles (samba, calypso, salsa), **reggae** is an Afro-centric people's popular music with a distinctive, intoxicating rhythm. Unlike the samba, which had a long history, reggae was a new sound of the late sixties and the early seventies. We have previously noted that the distinctive rhythm of ska is the result of the strong afterbeats. As ska evolved into rock steady in the latter half of the sixties, musicians added a backbeat layer over the afterbeats. This created a core rhythm of afterbeats at two speeds, slow and fast: the characteristic off-beat *ka-CHUN-ka* rhythm of reggae. (In this recording we hear this rhythm formed from the interaction of two instruments: an organ playing the off-beats and a keyboard playing the backbeats.) Because the bass had no role in establishing and maintaining this rhythm, bass players were free to create their own lines, and the best ones did. As rock steady evolved further into reggae, other rhythmic layers were added. The absence of beat marking, the midrange reggae rhythm, the free-roaming bass, and the complex interplay among the many instruments produced a buoyant rhythm, as we hear in this song.

Reggae as Topical Music

In "The Harder They Come," we are faced with the seeming contradiction between words and music. The lyrics are dark, even menacing, but the music nevertheless brings a smile to one's face and a body movement somewhere. This is happy music, in its rhythm, in the lilt in Cliff's voice, in the form (a carbon copy of Motown's verse/bridge/chorus formula), and in the gently undulating melody. We are left to ponder whether the music is the candy that entices us to listen to the message of the lyrics, or a way to forget for the moment the situation that the lyrics depict, or some other possible relationship. What we do know is that many of the songs that put reggae on the international musical map, like this one and Bob Marley's "I Shot the Sheriff" and "Get Up, Stand Up," embedded hard messages within the music's infectious rhythms and sounds.

The use of popular song as a vehicle for social commentary was a rock-era phenomenon. There were isolated examples in modern-era popular songs—Andy Razaf and Fats Waller's 1929 song "Black and Blue," a lament on the disadvantages of dark skin color, is a memorable

0:00	Introduction. Keyboards prominent.

1st Verse/Chorus Statement

0:10	1st verse
	Off-beat rhythms at two speeds define reggae sound. (One organ and bass accent the back-beat; the other organ plays mainly on the afterbeat.)
	Well they tell me . . .
0:30	Chorus
	The transition (bridge).
	So as sure as the sun . . .
	The hook.
	And then the harder . . .
	Repeated for emphasis.
	Ooh the harder . . .

2nd Verse/Chorus Statement

0:59	2nd verse
	Well the officers . . .
1:18	Chorus
	So as sure . . .
1:46	Break. Introduction, but expanded.

3rd Verse/Chorus Statement

2:04	3rd verse
	And I keep on fighting . . .
2:22	Chorus
	So as sure . . .
3:00	Tag. The interplay among the instruments is easier to hear here than in any other section.

example. But songs like these were the exceptions. What topical music there was in the thirties and forties came mostly from singer-commentators like Woody Guthrie and, to a lesser extent, the blues (for example, some maintain that Nat "King" Cole's "Straighten Up and Fly Right" is an allegory on race relations). The music of Bob Dylan and the other folk singers of the early sixties brought topical song into popular music and reshaped it in the process, as we have seen. During the sixties and early seventies, a few black performers—most notably James Brown and Sly Stone among popular musicians, as well as jazz saxophonists John Coltrane and Archie Shepp—dealt powerfully with racial issues and their emotional consequences. But the efforts of all these musicians represented only a fraction of their total output and an even smaller fraction of the musical activity in rock and soul.

Reggae was different in that it first became known outside of Jamaica as a music with a message. The music of Bob Marley, Jimmy Cliff, Peter Tosh, and other early reggae stars called attention to the social inequities in Jamaica. Moreover, it came at a time when rock had largely forsaken its role as a vehicle for social commentary. Marley would help fill that void, becoming a powerful voice on social issues.

In this respect reggae anticipated both punk and rap. And like those later styles its musical features soon found their way into songs that had no literal or emotional connection to the social issues that the first hits introduced.

STYLE PROFILE

"THE HARDER THEY COME" (REGGAE)

Rhythm	*Moderate tempo. Rock-based rhythm with distinctive reggae feel. Considerable syncopation and lots of activity, some of it double-time (moving twice as fast as the rock rhythm).*
Melody	*Long phrases, which are repeated, in the verse and the first part of the chorus (bridge); the title phrase is a short riff. All have fairly flat contours.*
Instrumentation (timbre)	*Lead vocal, two keyboards (with organ sounds), piano, electric bass, drums, and electric guitar.*
Performance style	*Cliff's vocal style, with its use of **falsetto** and **melisma**, seems inspired by sixties American music. **Choked guitar** sound.*
Dynamics	*Moderately loud.*
Harmony	*I-IV-V, but with a slow chord rhythm and in unusual sequences.*
Texture	*Densely layered, with several chord instruments, plus busy bass and drums behind the vocal.*
Form	*Verse/chorus form.*

Key Points

Reggae as protest music	*Jamaican people's music: it came from them, and it spoke to them and for them, in direct, uncompromising language.*
Reggae rhythm	*The interaction of the two organs produces the distinctive* ka-CHUN-ka *rhythm of reggae heard mainly in two organ parts.*
Words and music; words versus music	*Combines lyrics that describe the harsh conditions in which the black underclass lives with irresistible, joyous music.*

Terms to Know

choked guitar	melisma
falsetto	reggae

Reggae as an International Music

Reggae's popularity outside of Jamaica owed much to the heavy concentrations of Jamaicans in England. As part of the transition from colonialism, Great Britain opened its doors—or at least its ports—to people from its colonies. More arrived from the Caribbean than from any other former colony—around 250,000 in the late fifties and early sixties. By the end of the sixties, the British government had put into effect legislation that severely restricted immigration. By that time, however, several generations of Jamaicans were already in England, where they re-created much of their culture. All the Jamaican music of the sixties and the seventies found a supportive audience in England, among Jamaicans eager for this link to their homeland and among British whites intrigued by this quite different music.

For a new generation of British musicians in search of "real" music, reggae (and ska) provided an at-home alternative to the blues. Eric Clapton, who had immersed himself so deeply in the blues during the sixties, led the way with his cover of Marley's "I Shot the Sheriff"; the recording topped the charts in 1974. A wave of new British acts, among them the Clash, Elvis Costello, UB40, and the Police, wove the fresh sounds of reggae into their music.

Reggae's path to America seems unnecessarily roundabout. The music didn't find an audience in the United States until after it had become popular in England. Once known, however, its influence was even more diverse—and more divorced from the music's social context. For example, we hear echoes of the distinctive reggae rhythm in the Eagles' huge 1977 hit "Hotel California." It had a deeper and more lasting impact on African American music in two quite different ways. One was its influence on rap: the toasting of Jamaican DJs soon evolved into rapping. The other was on the black romantic (and anti-romantic) music of the late seventies and eighties. In Chapter 10 we noted how important bassists like James Jamerson and Larry Graham liberated bass lines from a restrictive role. Because reggae embedded the pulse of a song in its distinctive midrange rhythms, bass players were free to roam at will, largely independent of a specific rhythmic or harmonic role. Because of this, reggae offered eighties black romantic music the next step beyond the advances of Motown and the Philadelphia sound. We hear its influence in such diverse hits as "Sexual Healing," Marvin Gaye's 1982 ode to carnal love, and in Tina Turner's cynical rejection of it, her 1984 hit "What's Love Got to Do With It."

Bob Marley was reggae's greatest ambassador. With his death from cancer in 1981, reggae lost an important world presence. Reggae is still a dominant music in Jamaica, and its sounds and rhythms have shaped diverse styles in the last quarter century—and so has its look, it seems: Rastafarian dreadlocks are still fashionable. It is ska, however, its antecedent, that has enjoyed a resurgence in popularity in both Great Britain and the United States.

FUNK

Like *blues, jazz, rock, soul,* and *rap, funk* is a one-syllable word from African American culture that began as non-musical slang, then found its way into music, and eventually became a style label.

"Funk" originally targeted not the ears but the nose. As far back as the early twentieth century, *funky* meant foul or unpleasant: a person who neglected to bathe for several days usually gave off a funky odor. Over time it acquired another meaning: hip. Stylish clothes were "funky threads." When James Brown sings "Ain't It Funky Now," he is referring to the ambience, not the smell.

Funk and *funky* came into popular music through jazz. Beginning in the midfifties, *funk* referred to a simpler, more blues-oriented style—a "return to roots" and a departure from the complexities of hard bop. By the sixties it had also come to mean soulful. (It also retained the other meanings; context and delivery determined which meaning was appropriate.) By the early seventies, **funk** had come to identify a particularly rhythmic strain of black music.

James Brown was the "father of funk" as well as the "godfather of soul"—and the "grandfather of rap." Funk musicians built their music on both the basic concept of Brown's music and many of its key features. Whether he was talking about feeling good or exhorting his listeners to get up and get involved, Brown embedded his message in a powerful **groove**. Those who followed his path—first Sly and the Family Stone, then the funk bands of the seventies—expanded both the range of messages and the musical resources. Brown's music was relentlessly upbeat; Sly and the Family Stone and funk bands occasionally expressed the gloomier side of the black experience. Funk bands used the same basic lineup—vocal, horns, and rhythm instruments—but they were bigger. Not surprisingly, textures thickened and rhythms became even denser and more complex.

George Clinton and Funk

Nowhere are these developments more evident than in the music of George Clinton (b. 1940). Clinton was the mastermind behind two important funk bands, Parliament and Funkadelic. While still a teen, he formed Parliament, but as a doo-wop group. They signed with Motown in 1964 but did not break through. When Clinton left Motown, he had to relinquish the Parliament name, so he formed Funkadelic while battling Motown to regain ownership of his group's name. Funkadelic represented a major change of direction. As the group's name implies, it brought together funk and psychedelic rock: James Brown and Sly Stone meeting Jimi Hendrix. When Clinton regained control of the Parliament name in 1974, he used two names for the same band. He recorded the more outrageous material under the Funkadelic name and the tighter, more polished material as Parliament.

The formation of Funkadelic signaled Clinton's transformation into Dr. Funkenstein (he also referred to himself as Maggot Overlord); the title of his 1970 album *Free Your Ass and Your Mind Will Follow* shows another side of his funky sense of humor. Although Clinton certainly enjoyed being provocative and playing with words, there is in many of his songs a sense that he is laughing to keep from crying. He tucks his darker messages inside humorous packages set to a good-time groove. When he tells listeners to "Tear the roof off the sucker," he could be urging them to party hard—or to riot.

Without question there is an escapist aspect to his work: his many aliases, the flamboyant costumes he and his bands wore in performance, and the sci-fi world he created (the "Mothership Connection").

In a very real way, this is the opposite of punk in both attitude and music. There is no doubt about the message of a punk song like "God Save the Queen," in either words or music, which hammers the listener. By contrast, Clinton seems to invite listeners to become "one nation under a groove": surrendering to the rhythm offers momentary relief from the pain of daily life as a black person in the United States. Whatever the motivation there is no question that Clinton's groups could create a powerful groove. We experience this in his 1976 hit, "Tear the Roof off the Sucker (Give Up the Funk)," which his band recorded as Parliament.

"Tear the Roof off the Sucker." The song shows Clinton's debt to James Brown and Sly and the Family Stone as well as the ways in which his music went beyond theirs. The instrumentation is similar—vocal, horns, and rhythm—but the sound is fuller than either James Brown's or Sly Stone's because there are more instruments and all of them are busy. Clinton's debt to Brown goes beyond these general features. After 1975 his roster included two significant James Brown alumni: bassist Bootsy Collins and saxophonist Maceo Parker. They were key members of his large band, which included as many as twelve musicians.

Like Brown and Stone, Clinton creates the groove over static harmony: this is a one-chord song. The texture is dense: there are riffs and sustained chords from both horns and keyboards, high obbligato lines from a synthesizer, an active but open bass line, lots of percussion, and voices—both the choral effect of the backup singers and Clinton's proto-rap. Clinton gives Bootsy Collins a chance to stretch out. Collins's lines are active, syncopated, and melodic, calling attention to the increasingly prominent role of the bass in this branch of black music.

CD 3:10

"Tear the Roof off the Sucker (Give Up the Funk)," George Clinton, Bootsy Collins, and Jerome Brailey (1976). Parliament.

CD 3:10   **Funk** (George Clinton, Bootsy Collins, and Jerome Brailey; performed by Parliament)

0:00	Introduction.
	Tear the roof off...
	Layer in horn riffs and synthesizer chords.
	Tear the roof off...
0:19	A 1st chorus
	Lots of riffs, percussion in the background.
	You've got a real type of thing...
0:37	B 2nd chorus
	Ow, we want the funk...
0:55	C 3rd chorus
	Band keeps the "Give up the funk" riff.
	La la la la la...
1:13	A 1st chorus
	You've got a real type of thing...
1:32	B 2nd chorus
	Ow, we want the funk...
1:50	C 3rd chorus
	La la la la la...
2:08	Break. Also over the "Give up the funk" riff.
	We're gonna turn...
2:17	A 1st chorus
	Bass is even more active in this section.
	You've got a real type of thing...
2:53	B 2nd chorus
	Ow, we want the funk...
	Recording continues for another 2:36 in much the same vein.

The rhythm has a 16-beat feel over the eight-beat rhythm laid down in the drum part. Clinton's raplike introduction moves at this faster rhythm, and so do the horn riffs, the bass line, and the guitar parts. This is the same approach heard in the music of Brown and Stone, but it is a thicker sound because there is so much more going on. It is a darker sound as well, mainly because of Clinton's voice and the prominence of the bass.

Clinton's various bands—Parliament and Funkadelic were recording for two different labels, and there were other offshoots in addition to these two—ran into trouble in the late seventies, mainly because of bad money management, sloppy business practices, and drug abuse. By 1981 Clinton had consolidated the two versions of the band under one name, the P-Funk All Stars. And with the emergence of rap, his music became sampled again and again, more than any artist except James Brown.

Funk, by Clinton's band and other groups, never crossed over to the pop mainstream in its pure form. "Tear the Roof off the Sucker" was Parliament's highest-charting song, and it made it only to number 15. The music would prove to be enormously influential, however. It helped shape disco and other black styles, and, with the advent of digital technology, rappers sampled Clinton's music mercilessly.

"TEAR THE ROOF OFF THE SUCKER (GIVE UP THE FUNK)" (FUNK)

Rhythm	*Moderate tempo. The basic beat is a rock rhythm, but many parts move twice as fast as rock (the opening "rap," the bass patterns, and the conga part). Lots of syncopation in the instrumental background.*
Melody	*Melody derived from blues-inflected modal scale. First melody: long, unbroken descending line. Second melody: short riffs. Third melody: long sustained phrase. All three melodies are simply repeated several times; there is no development.*
Instrumentation (timbre)	*Voices, electric bass, drums, conga drum, electric guitars, synthesizers, and horns.*
Performance style	*Proto-rap at the beginning.*
Dynamics	*Loud.*
Harmony	*No harmonic change: decorative harmonies (in voices and synthesizer) derived from modal scale.*
Texture	*Dense texture, with voices, percussion, bass, sustained chords on horns and synthesizers, and high synthesizer lines and chords. Strong contrast from section to section: ("Give up the funk" = voices, bass doubling the melody, and percussion.)*
Form	*The song consists of three choruslike sections (both words and music are repeated) that are restated several times.*

Key Points

Rhythm over melody	*The rhythm, which features complex interactions among the various instruments, is more interesting than the melody, which doesn't develop at all.*
The bass and black music	*Completely liberated bass: little timekeeping; instead, intricate patterns and riffs, occasional doubling of melody.*
In the groove/ in the moment	*The only focus is to give up the funk. No story, no goal.*
Road to rap	*The emphasis on rhythm and the chantlike melodies are a prelude to rap and techno.*

Terms to Know

funk

Among the bands that borrowed heavily from funk was the leading black act of the late seventies, Earth, Wind & Fire.

Earth, Wind & Fire: A Black Music Synthesis

Like *rock,* the term *rhythm and blues* has been inclusive. Precisely because it has identified such a wide range of music, it has not been—indeed, cannot be—completely accurate. From the time Jerry Wexler coined the term, *rhythm and blues* has also embraced not only rhythmic and bluesy music but also black pop, which emphasizes melody and harmony over strong rhythm and a "deep blues" feeling.

Two Streams in Black Music. From doo-wop through Motown to the several streams of black romantic music in the early seventies, black pop had grown dramatically—in presence, in variety, and in market share. During the same time frame, more rhythm-and-blues-oriented black music had also grown, musically and commercially, from the big-beat music of the fifties through soul in the sixties and funk in the seventies.

These two paths were the most significant trends in black music during the third quarter of the century. And throughout their twenty-five-year history, there has been a clear distinction between the two—at least in retrospect. James Brown didn't sing black pop; Diana Ross didn't sing soul. Similarly, Roberta Flack and George Clinton inhabit different musical worlds.

Only a few artists have successfully fused these two streams; among them are two truly great performers: Ray Charles and Aretha Franklin. Both brought soul into pop and vice versa. In the early seventies, Marvin Gaye and Stevie Wonder, the two newly independent Motown artists, found a fruitful middleground between funk and romantic pop. Gaye's music in the seventies ranged from the bleakness of "Inner City Blues" and "Trouble Man" to the rapture of "Let's Get It On" and "Got to Give It Up." Wonder's music ranged from funky songs like "Superstition" to romantic ballads like "Send One Your Love." In the latter part of the decade, Earth, Wind & Fire joined them. All three acts moved easily between the two styles and at times blended them within a single **funk-pop** song.

Earth, Wind & Fire. Maurice White (b. 1941), the founder and leader of Earth, Wind & Fire, named the group after his astrological sign. He is a Sagittarian: the sign contains three of the four elements—earth, wind, and fire, but not water.

After a successful career as a session drummer at Chess Records and with jazz pianist Ramsey Lewis, White set out in 1969 to create a new kind of group. By 1971 they were Earth, Wind & Fire. The next year they moved to Columbia Records (now Sony) and continued to move up the charts. By 1975 they had become one of the elite groups of the decade, both on record and in live performance, and they remained a top act through the end of the decade.

Earth, Wind & Fire was a big group. In this respect they were in step not only with black acts like George Clinton's funk bands, Barry White's Love Unlimited Orchestra, and the various Philadelphia groups, but also the rock groups like Bruce Springsteen's E Street Band. As many as fourteen musicians could be on-stage; the nucleus of the band was White, who sang and played a **kalimba**, an African thumb piano; his brothers Verdine on bass and Freddie on drums; and singer Philip Bailey.

The band was comparable in many respects to George Clinton's groups, and they created great grooves by layering piles of riffs on top of **16-beat rhythms**. But there was a marked difference in attitude, as we hear in their first number 1 single, the 1975 hit "Shining Star."

The title and the chorus line of this song project the optimistic, hopeful mood that runs through so many of the group's songs: "Shining star for you to see, what your life can truly be." The song itself has a clear division between verse and chorus. The verse sets up a complex funk-style groove over a single chord, much like that heard in "Tear the Roof off the Sucker," but the chorus underpins a more coherent, riff-based melodic line with rapidly changing harmonies. As in gospel and love songs, rich harmony is used to send a message of hope; that also seems to be the case here.

One aspect of Earth, Wind & Fire's crossover success was their ability to meld funklike grooves with more melodious material. This versatility is evident in the range of their hit songs, from soulful ballads like "That's the Way of the World" to funkish grooves like "Serpentine

3:11

"Shining Star," Maurice White, Philip Bailey, and Larry Dunn (1975). Earth, Wind & Fire.

CD 3:11	**Funk-pop** (Maurice White, Philip Bailey, and Larry Dunn; performed by Earth, Wind & Fire)

0:00	Instrumental introduction. Guitars, then bass.
0:10	Drums and brass enter: clear 16-beat rhythm at this point.

1st Verse/Chorus Statement

0:19	1st verse
	When you wish upon . . .
0:47	Chorus
	You're a shining star . . .
0:57	Instrumental interlude. Keyboard, then electric guitar.

2nd Verse/Chorus Statement (extended)

1:13	2nd verse, part 1
	Shining star come into view . . .
1:41	2nd verse, part 2
	This is in effect another verse without a chorus in between.
	Yeah, found I had to stand . . .
2:09	Chorus
	You're a shining star . . .
2:18	Chorus, repeated, with the addition of brass.
	You're a shining star . . .
2:27	Repeated again.
	You're a shining star . . .
2:36	Notice that the instruments drop out—all but bass, then finally the bass.
	Shining star . . . [three times]

Fire." Few seventies acts were at home in both funk and black pop styles; fewer still succeeded in blending the two. Earth, Wind & Fire was one of them.

STYLE PROFILE

"SHINING STAR" (FUNK-POP)

Rhythm	*Moderate tempo; 16-beat rhythm, kept most consistently in the conga drum and the rhythm guitar, with a strong backbeat. Dense rhythmic texture, with lots of activity, much of it syncopated.*
Melody	*Both the verse and the chorus grow out of flat-contoured **riffs**; they are repeated, initially with little variation, but more freely as the song progresses.*
Instrumentation (timbre)	*Lead and backup vocals, several keyboards, electric bass, electric guitars, drums, percussion, and horns.*
Performance style	*Bailey's falsetto singing is a trademark of the group. Rhythm instruments (guitars and keyboards) favor percussive sounds.*
Dynamics	*Loud for the most part; a nice drop in dynamics at the beginning of the chorus.*
Harmony	*One chord in the introduction and the verse; a chord progression under the chorus melody.*
Texture	*Dense texture with lots of activity under the melody.*
Form	*Verse/chorus form.*

Inspirational message	*"Power of positive thinking" lyrics are rare in seventies songs. Rhythm and high vocals reinforce the lyrics.*
Funk-pop	*Verse is funklike: a lot of riffs over one chord. Chorus is more like pop: a riff repeated over constantly changing harmony.*
16-beat rhythm	*Heard in the background; background rhythms, riffs, and syncopations in the melody also move at 16-beat speed.*
Stacks of riffs	*Vocal over a deep stack of riffs—high brass figures; lower keyboard and guitar riffs.*

Terms to Know

16-beat rhythm	funk-pop
falsetto	riff

DISCO

Disco is short for *discothèque.* (It is also easier to spell.) *Discothèque* is a French word meaning "record library" (by analogy with *bibliothèque,* meaning "book library"). It came into use during World War II, first as the name of a nightclub—Le Discothèque—then as a code word for underground nightclubs where jazz records were played. Because of the German occupation, these clubs were run like American speakeasies during the Prohibition era.

The Roots of the Club Scene. Discothèques survived the war, becoming increasingly popular in France. The first of the famous discos was the Whiskey-a-Go-Go in Paris, which featured American liquors and American dance music, both live and on record. Others sprung up in the postwar years, eventually becoming a favored destination of jet setters. By 1960 the idea of a discothèque had moved to New York. The Peppermint Lounge, where Chubby Checker and the rich and famous did the twist, opened in 1961.

This rags-to-riches-and-back-to-new-rags story would become the recurrent theme of dance music in the latter part of the century. As dance fads like the twist moved out of the clubs and into mainstream society, the original audience sought out new music in different, less exclusive, and less pricey venues.

By the end of the sixties, a new club culture was thriving. It was an egalitarian, nonrestrictive environment. The new, danceable black music of the late sixties and early seventies provided the soundtrack: Sly and the Family Stone, Funkadelic, Stevie Wonder, Marvin Gaye, Curtis Mayfield, Barry White, and above all the Philadelphia acts, such as the Spinners, the Stylistics, the O'Jays, and Harold Melvin and the Blue Notes. Clubbers included not only blacks but also Latinos, working-class women, and gays, for whom clubbing had become a welcome chance to come out of the closet and express themselves. Despite the gains of the various "rights" movements in the sixties and seventies, these were still marginalized constituencies.

The Mainstreaming of Disco. By mid-decade, however, **disco** had begun to cross over—at both ends of the business. Integrated groups like KC and the Sunshine Band, which exploded onto the singles charts in 1975, began making music expressly for discos. *Saturday Night Fever* was the commercial breakthrough for the music. Almost overnight what had been a largely underground scene briefly became the thing to do.

In New York the favored venue was Studio 54, a converted theater on 54th Street in Manhattan. It became so popular that crowds clamoring to get in stretched around the corner. It was the place to see and be seen. Writing about Studio 54 at end of the seventies, Truman Capote noted, "Disco is the best floor show in town. It's very democratic, boys with boys, girls with girls, girls with boys, blacks and whites, capitalists and Marxists, Chinese and everything else, all in one big mix."

Disco and Electronics. Meanwhile, the discothèque scene continued to flourish in Europe. The new element in the music there was the innovative use of synthesizers to create dance tracks. Among the most important musicians of this trend were Kraftwerk, a two-person German group, and Giorgio Moroder, an Italian-born, Germany-based producer and electronics wizard who provided the musical setting for many of Donna Summer's disco-era hits.

Kraftwerk and Moroder exemplified the increasingly central role of the producer and of technology. Disco became a producers' music, even more than the girl groups of the sixties. Just as Phil Spector's "wall of sound" was more famous than the singers in front of it, so did the sound of disco belong more to the men creating and **mixing** the instrumental tracks than the vocalists in the studio. Here, the wall of sound was laced with electronic as well as acoustic instruments. Singers were relatively unimportant and interchangeable; there were numerous one-hit wonders.

The Village People: Disco out of the Closet

No group brought all of these elements together more completely—and more humorously—than the Village People. The group was the brainchild of Jacques Morali, a French producer living in New York. Morali's various accounts of the formation of the Village People are conflicting, but what is certain is that he recruited the men who fronted his act literally off the street and in gay clubs.

The public image of the Village People was six guys dressed up as macho stereotypes among gays: the Indian (in full costume, including headdress), the leather man (missing only the Harley), the construction worker, the policeman, the cowboy, and the soldier. These expressions of hypermaleness were, in effect, gay pinups. Their look was more important than their sound, although after a disastrous appearance on *Soul Train* Morali fired five of the six men and replaced them with new recruits.

The whole act was an inside joke. Morali and gay audiences laughed behind their hand while straight America bought their records by the millions and copied the look—mustaches, lumber jackets, and the like. Many listeners were not aware of the gay undertone to the lyrics —or if they were, they didn't care.

CD 3:12

"Y.M.C.A.," Jacques Morali, Henri Belolo, and Victor Willis (1978). The Village People.

The group's song "Y.M.C.A.," their biggest hit on the singles charts (number 2 in 1978), shows the macho men at work. In most cities and towns around the United States, a YMCA (established by the Young Men's Christian Association) is a place for families to participate in an array of activities. Some are athletic—basketball, swimming, and gymnastics; others are social and humanitarian, such as meals for senior citizens. In larger cities YMCAs can also accommodate residents. In cities like New York, these became meeting places for gays.

The lyrics of the song have fun with this situation. Seemingly innocuous lines like

They have everything for men to enjoy
You can hang out with all the boys

Village People with Jacques Morali and Henri Belolo, 1979. The photo depicts a role reversal of sorts in that Morali and his partner, Belolo, were the men behind the Village People; the public saw only the six men behind them.

take on a quite different meaning when understood in the context of the Y as a gay gathering place.

The music is quintessential disco. Here are some of its characteristic features:

- *The tempo.* Most disco songs had a tempo right around 120 beats per minute—the same speed as a Sousa march—so that the DJ could seamlessly segue one song into the next.

- *Four-on-the-floor bass drum.* Many disco songs featured a rock-solid beat marked on the bass drum (or its drum-machine counterpart). This song is no exception.

- *Active, 16-beat-based rhythms.* The conga drum most clearly marks the 16-beat rhythmic layer. Often the bass line and the drums add a *dum-diddy* rhythm. And the drummer plays on the off-beat of every beat. The rhythm in disco songs like "Y.M.C.A." derives its density and activity from both funk and dance-oriented black pop. The biggest difference is that the beat is much more obvious, not only from the beat-keeping bass drum but also from the bass line and the other rhythm instruments. Compared with funk, there is not much syncopation.

- *Rich, almost orchestral, accompaniment,* featuring an augmented rhythm section, electronic instruments, and strings. This song has all of that, with brilliant string lines, horn parts, plus "solos" for the synthesizer in the dance mix version.

- *Catchy tune*, delivered in chunks and sung without much finesse. This is a simple verse/chorus song, put together in short phrases. The vocalists are enthusiastic but not very skilled.

- *Repetitive harmony.* Disco songs often cycle familiar progressions endlessly, the better to suggest the endless disco experience—with continuous music, no clocks on the wall, or any other method of marking time. Here the harmony is a stretched-out version of that perennial favorite, the "Heart and Soul" progression, in both verse and chorus. When simply recycled, as it is here, it loses its sense of direction to a home chord; it recontextualizes the progression into something quite different in meaning: from clear boundaries to no boundaries.

LISTENING GUIDE: "Y.M.C.A."

CD 3:12 **Disco** (Jacques Morali, Henri Belolo, and Victor Willis; performed by the Village People)

0:00 Introduction. Slick disco sound: brass, high strings, strong drums marking beat. March tempo = approximately 120 beats per minute.

1st Verse/Chorus Statement

0:11 1st verse, part 1
Bass joins drums marking the beat underneath the vocal.
Young man, there's no need . . .

0:26 1st verse, part 2
"Heart and Soul" harmony underneath; each chord lasts eight beats.
Young man, there's a place . . .

0:44 Chorus, part 1
"Chorus" effect in chorus: backup singers join in on "Y-M-C-A."
It's fun to stay . . .

0:59 Chorus, part 2
Bass shifts to dum-diddy rhythm in the chorus.
It's fun to stay . . .

2nd Verse/Chorus Statement

1:15 2nd verse, part 1
Notice the sustained strings and the brass riffs behind the vocal.
Young man, are you listening . . .

1:31 2nd verse, part 2
Orchestral-like background is part of the disco message.
No man does it all by himself . . .

1:48 *It's fun to stay . . .*

2:03 *It's fun to stay . . .*

3rd Verse/Chorus Statement

2:19 *Young man, I was once . . .*

2:35 *That's when someone came up . . .*

2:52 *It's fun to stay . . .*

3:09 *Y-M-C-A . . .*

3:24 *Y-M-C-A . . .*

"Y.M.C.A." (DISCO)

Rhythm	*Disco tempo (about 120 beats per minute). Bass drum thuds out the beat; backbeat is also strong. Melody moves at a moderate pace with some syncopation. String and brass figurations often move four times as fast as the beat (16-beat speed).*
Melody	*Melodies in verse and chorus develop from riffs: verse = statement ("young man")/response; chorus reverses this ("it's fun to stay at the/Y-M-C-A).*
Instrumentation (timbre)	*Voices (a lead vocal, plus others occasionally reinforcing the lead line), drums, tambourine, handclaps, electric bass, keyboard, violins, and brass (especially trumpets).*
Performance style	*Everyday singing voice. Demanding figuration in the violin and trumpet parts.*
Dynamics	*Loud.*
Harmony	*Updated versions of the "Heart and Soul" progression (verse and chorus are slightly different). The progression cycles through the entire song; it never resolves.*
Texture	*Rich, layered texture: low = bass and bass drum; midrange = voices, sustained strings, some brass riffs, and percussion sounds; high = brass riffs and string figuration. Always a thick sound.*
Form	*Verse/chorus form with a fade-out ending.*

Key Points

Coded lyric	*NYC YMCA = gay meeting place. Lyric is full of inside jokes.*
Disco, a multiple-minority music	*Disco's original audience included gays, blacks, and Latinos; provoked homophobic and racially prejudiced reactions.*
Slick dance music	*Amateurish singing, relentless dance beat, and fancy strings.*
Funk, disco, and the beat	*Funk and disco are close musical relatives, but the more obvious beat in disco made it more popular.*
Rise of the producer	*With disco the producer assumed the main creative responsibility. Singer(s) were primarily for image.*

Terms to Know

disco

Dance Fads and the Influence of Disco

Although most disco artists came and went—Donna Summer was the biggest star, Chic the most successful band—disco was widely popular during the latter part of the seventies. During that three-year window, it spread from urban dance clubs to the suburbs, and its audience grew considerably. Disco had clear and strong gay associations, as "Y.M.C.A." makes clear, but it was more than music for gays and blacks. In this respect *Saturday Night Fever* was a slice of life: there were many working-class urban youth who used disco dancing as an outlet.

Disco was more than the music or even the culture that had produced it. For many it became a lifestyle. It was hedonistic: dancing was simply a prelude to more intimate forms of contact. It was exhibitionistic: fake Afro wigs; skin-tight, revealing clothes; flamboyant accessories; platform shoes; everything glittering. And it was drug-ridden: with disco cocaine became a mainstream drug; the logo for Studio 54 showed the man in the moon ingesting cocaine from a silver spoon.

Reactions Against Disco. All this, plus the inevitable stream of mindless disco songs (the ratio of chaff to wheat in any genre is high; disco was no exception), gave disco's detractors plenty of ammunition. They trashed the music and the culture. Ostensibly, it was simply a reaction against disco's many excesses, but there was also a strong homophonic undercurrent. Perhaps the most notorious disco-bashing incident occurred in Chicago during the summer of 1979. Steve Dahl, a disc jockey at a local rock station, organized Disco Demolition Night. Fans who brought a disco record to a Chicago White Sox doubleheader got into the park for 98¢. They spent the first game chanting "Disco sucks"; after the first game, they made a pile of records in centerfield. An attempted explosion turned into chaos.

Twentieth-Century Dance Fads. When disco disappeared from the charts and the radio, there was an "I told you so" response from those who hated it. But in retrospect it would have been surprising if it had lasted much longer. All the major dance fads in the twentieth century have had short life spans: the Charleston and the black bottom in the early 1920s, jitterbugging and Lindy hopping around 1940; the twist and other rock-and-roll dances around 1960. The Charleston and the twist were dance fads that caught on somewhat after the introduction of new rhythms: the two-beat fox trot in the teens and early twenties and the eight-beat rhythm of rock and roll in the fifties. Disco, like the jitterbug, was a dance fad that came with the division of popular music into two related rhythmic streams. In the thirties it was sweet (two-beat) and swing (four-beat). In the seventies it was rock (eight-beat) and disco (16-beat).

The swing and disco eras were brief periods when the more active rhythms of black and black-inspired music became truly popular. In both cases much of the music was rhythmically more obvious than the music that had spawned it. Many of the hits of the swing era, especially by the white bands, laid down the beat but lacked the rhythmic play of music by Count Basie, Duke Ellington, or Benny Goodman. Similarly, disco was more rhythmically straightforward than funk or black pop, as we have discussed. This made it accessible to a greater number of dancers but sacrificed musical interest in the process.

The Influence of Disco. It shouldn't be surprising that disco faded away so quickly. It was following much the same path as the other dance fads that signaled the arrival of a new beat. And it should not be surprising that a new beat took root following disco's demise. In this way disco was influential, far more so than its brief life span would suggest.

Disco has also had a more underground influence—on two levels. It was, more than any other popular style, the gateway for the wholesale infusion of **electronica**. And it created a new kind of underground dance-club culture, which would continue through the eighties and flower in the nineties. We explore both of these trends in Chapter 14. For now we turn our attention to punk.

PUNK

CBGB is a small club located in the Bowery section of New York. Originally, it was the bar in the Palace Hotel. By 1973, the year that CBGB opened, the hotel had gone from palatial to poverty-stricken: it was a cheap rooming house for the alcoholics and druggies who inhabited the neighborhood.

CBGB stands for *country, bluegrass, and blues.* Owner Hilly Kristal's original plan was to book these kinds of acts into his new club, but an encounter with Richard Hell, Richard Lloyd, and Tom Verlaine of Television—Kristal was repairing the awning over the club entrance when the three band members walked by and struck up a conversation with him—led Kristal to hire the band for a gig at his club, followed by second gig with another newly formed band, the Ramones. Neither show attracted much of a crowd.

Nevertheless, Kristal persevered and promoted. After some success with Patti Smith in early 1975, he decided to present "A Festival of the Top 40 New York Rock Bands." He scheduled it in the summer to coincide with the Newport Jazz Festival, a bigtime event. It was a gamble—he spent a lot of money on advertising—that paid off. Critics came to hear the bands, and the audience for punk exploded almost overnight.

About the same time, Malcolm McLaren came to the United States to attend a boutique fair. Three years earlier McLaren had opened a clothing boutique with Vivienne Westwood on Kings Road in London that sold clothing suitable for rebels, anarchists, and other like-minded sorts. While in New York, he met the New York Dolls, a glam rock group dying of drugs and ineptitude. He agreed to design their outfits—red leather with a hammer and sickle—and tried to convince them to come to London.

McLaren could not persuade them to come, so he put together a band from hangers-on at his boutique—guitarist Steve Jones, bassist Glen Matlock, and drummer Paul Cook, and they became the Sex Pistols. McLaren recruited Johnny Rotten (John Lydon), who sneered better than he sang, to front the band. Sid Vicious (John Ritchie) replaced Matlock in 1977. The Sex Pistols managed to stay together for a little more than three years, until Lydon and McLaren

The Sex Pistols live in Atlanta, Georgia, in January 1978. Band members (left to right) are Sid Vicious on bass, drummer Paul Cook, singer Johnny Rotten, and lead guitarist Steve Jones.

had a falling-out. (McLaren wanted to provoke the establishment and make money at the same time; as manager of the Sex Pistols, he succeeded, ripping off the group in the process.) In their brief career, however, they made a lot of noise and gave the U.K. punk movement a real shot in the arm (before a different kind of shot in the arm brought them down—Vicious died in a New York hotel room from a herion overdose).

The Message of Punk

That a boutique owner and fashion designer would form and manage Britain's seminal punk band says a lot about the movement. At least in McLaren's realization of it with the Sex Pistols, **punk** was part of a larger package. It was only one component of a presence designed to stand out, outrage, and affront those on the outside. Hand in hand with the noise of punk went the hostile attitude and—even more obvious from a distance—the look: spiked hair in a rainbow of colors, tattoos and body piercings, heavy military-style boots, and torn clothes ornamented or even held together with safety pins.

While a student at a string of art schools, McLaren had become enamored with the Situationist International movement, a small group based in France. Situationists advocated the use of provocative acts that would simultaneously serve as political statement and performance art. With the Sex Pistols, he could not have done better. Certainly, the most inflammatory statement occurred in the summer of 1977 during Queen Elizabeth's silver anniversary celebration. McLaren rented a barge, got the Sex Pistols set up to play, and sailed down the Thames during the ceremony with the band playing "God Save the Queen." The lyrics contained lines like "the Fascist regime," "She ain't no human being," and "No future," the motto of British punks.

The Aesthetics of Early Punk. The punk movement has been a unique occurrence in the history of rock, the kind of thing that could truly happen only once. This is because it was inherently contradictory. Punk was both innovative and reactionary. It sought to shock and simplify. In the minds of some of its creators, it wanted to make rock "dangerous" again. The path they chose was to take the most dangerous elements—the noise, the beat, the attitude, and the lyrics—and intensify them to the point that they generated a strong reaction, both pro and con. In this respect the music was innovative.

At the same time, they sought to return rock to the seeming simplicity of its early years—the time when anyone could learn three chords and join a rock band. This was, in essence, a populist reaction against not only the commercialization of rock but also the increasing sophistication of the music—the sophistication of musicians, producers, and engineers.

For these reasons the music went forward and backward simultaneously. Its reactionary rebellion could not happen *within* rock until rock had become the commercially dominant style and lost its confrontational edge. For mainstream seventies rock, punk was a slap in the face. At the same time, it brought to rock a concentrated intensity, a distillation of its most powerful aspects. That was a major step forward.

Punk Reverberations. This kind of reaction has, of course, been a recurrent theme in rock since the emergence of punk. The various alternative movements—grunge, neo-punk styles, and various punk fusions—have been part of the musical landscape in recent years. But these are reverberations from punk's explosion. This reactionary movement—in all senses of the term—could happen for the first time only once. It is inconceivable that any new trend would be as shocking as punk was and still be legal.

The contradictions inherent in punk reflected deeply rooted contradictions in everyday life in both the United States and Britain during the seventies. The "we" mindset of the sixties —the sense of collective energy directed toward a common goal—gave way to a "me" mindset, where everyone looked out for himself. The various rights movements and the move toward a more democratic society eroded class distinctions at a rapid rate: McLaren's stunt on the barge would have been absolutely unthinkable during Elizabeth II's coronation in 1952. Still, there was a strong conservative backlash in both countries. At the same time, a prolonged recession, fueled in part by the absence of fuel due to the Arab oil embargo, gave working- and middle-class people little opportunity to take advantage of their new social mobility; and sky-high interest rates and inflation created the fear that today's savings would be worth far less in the future. "No future," the nihilistic battle cry of the Sex Pistols, was in part a product of this bleak economic outlook.

The Power of Punk

The Sex Pistols, "Anarchy in the UK," "God Save the Queen"

One can get on a rooftop or on a sound system in an arena or auditorium and shout the lyrics to a Sex Pistols song like "Anarchy in the UK" or "God Save the Queen." No matter how strong the voice or how powerful the sound system, the words would have only a fraction of the impact that they have within the songs.

Ultimately, the power of punk resides in the music itself. People can see a punk—hair, clothes, body piercings, and tattoos—and simply look away if they don't like what they see. Sound invades one's space in a way that visual images don't. It requires more effort to reject a sound. Punk immerses listeners in sound; one cannot but react to it, pro or con.

Before we hear a word and without seeing an image, we sense the hostility seething below the surface, ready to explode. This is a product of intensifying the following "dangerous" aspects of rock:

o *The tempo.* Tempos in punk songs are typically faster than the tempos of more-conventional rock songs. They are faster than we normally move—walking, dancing, tapping our foot. The breakneck tempos of punk demand a reaction: we either get with it or reject it by not connecting.

o *The sound.* Punk is a loud music. Subtlety is not part of the equation; neither is contrast in volume. Typically, it's full-bore volume for two to three minutes.

o *The noise.* Punk guitarists use distortion. It is as much a part of punk as it is of heavy metal.

o *The singing.* Rock opened the door to rough, untrained singing styles, and punk barged through. It was a matter of chutzpah over expertise. Indeed, the lack of skill and sophistication was a virtue—and a requirement; one couldn't credibly croon a punk song. Part of the message was that anyone could sing a song if they had the nerve and the sense of outrage.

o *The beat.* The punk version of a rock beat was the most idiomatic aspect of the music and the most influential. We might describe the essential punk beat as a **saturated rock rhythm**. In a song like "Anarchy in the UK," everybody is playing in "eight": rhythm guitar, bass, and drums are all marking the eight-beat rhythmic layer as directly as possible. Moreover, rather than play a riff, guitar and bass repeat the same chord or note over and over, which makes the rhythm even more insistent.

Recall that what made rock and roll stand apart from rhythm and blues was this insistent eight-beat layer. When Chuck Berry introduced it on the guitar, he did it alone. The bass player continued to walk. In the sixties and the early seventies, rock musicians played with this eight-beat layer, as we have heard again and again. Punk bands distilled this essential rhythmic feature of rock and let it saturate the musical fabric: the entire band was dedicated to pounding it out.

Rock rhythm was confrontational in part because it raised the level of rhythmic activity. Punk's version of a rock beat was even more confrontational because this insistent rhythm was the most dominant aspect of the music.

As embodied in the music of groups like the Sex Pistols, the Ramones, Television, Iggy Pop and the Stooges, and Richard Hell and the Voidoids, punk was powerful but limited music. Punk was an ideal vehicle for expressing outrage, rebellion, and anarchic messages. Its frenetic rhythms were a perfect counterpoint to the seemingly mindless lyrics of Ramones songs like "Blitzkrieg Bop" and "I Don't Want to Go Down to the Basement." Because punk bands opted for shock value and simplicity instead of subtlety and sophistication, however, punk was not particularly useful for setting love songs, or getting down, or offering thoughtful social commentary. It was the "Wham, bam, thank you ma'am" of rock music.

New Wave

Punk was the most extreme form of a new wave of music that began to emerge around the middle of the seventies. Some of it developed concurrently with punk: Patti Smith had an ardent following and a good run at CBGB before the Ramones or Television attracted notice. The Talking Heads were regulars at the same club by the midseventies. Ohio was an unlikely locale for this new wave, but Cleveland and Akron were home to Pere Ubu and Devo, respectively. England saw the emergence of such different talents as Elvis Costello and the Clash.

The music of these **new wave** bands shared some common ground because of both what it was and what it wasn't. It was a reaction against the expansion and the commercialization of mainstream rock. The focus was on the words; lyrics were in the forefront. Words and ideas were provocative, quirky, arresting, arousing, challenging, or just plain weird (Pere Ubu's "Modern Dance" or the Talking Heads' "Psycho Killer"). They were linked by what they weren't: standard pop fare.

To support the clear delivery of the lyrics, bands favored a stripped-down, streamlined sound. Many groups were garage-band graduates. They kept their basic three- or four-piece instrumentation: guitar(s), bass, and drums, with the occasional keyboard. (Elvis Costello seemed fond of cheesy-sounding synthesizers.) The rhythmic texture was relatively clean: lots of reinforcement of the eight-beat rhythmic layer—the saturated rock rhythm was very much part of the sound—with little syncopation or rhythmic interplay. This energized the songs without overpowering or deflecting attention from the vocal. Instrumental solos were at a minimum; the primary role of the music was to enhance the words.

Within these relatively general boundaries, there was considerable variation in content and result. Elvis Costello brought the imagination and storytelling ability of a great singer-songwriter into new wave. The Clash rebelled against all establishments—political, social, and musical—with greater authority and articulateness than the Sex Pistols. Not surprisingly, they incorporated reggae, the most socially charged music in Great Britain during the seventies, and transformed it by giving it a punk edge. (Costello and the Police also absorbed elements of reggae.) Devo (the group took their name from a film entitled *The Truth about*

De-Evolution) gave this new sound a wickedly humorous twist: it is hard to imagine the Sex Pistols tongue in cheek, and it is hard to imagine Devo as anything but. The Talking Heads covered a lot of territory; David Byrne's quavery voice was ideally suited to convey a person who has drunk way too much coffee or is simply over the edge.

One of the major distinctions between the "pure" punk of the Ramones and the Sex Pistols and the new wave styles that emerged at about the same time is the aim of the music: punk aims for the gut; new wave aims for the brain—or perhaps the funny bone. The Sex Pistols' biggest songs are about rage. The lyrics of Ramones songs seem calculated to deflect attention away from the words to the high-energy sounds; we hear them, but we don't process them as a coherent statement. By contrast the music of the new wave acts demand attention to the words: Patti Smith was a published poet before she became a rock star.

From Punk to Pop. Elements of punk eventually filtered into pop. One conduit was the music of Blondie, the band fronted by peroxide-blonde leader and lead singer Deborah Harry. Although Blondie performed at CBGB with other new wave bands, the group had begun as a kind of cover band that remade hits of sixties girl groups. So it was not surprising that Blondie's music would have a pop orientation or that Harry's look would be, if anything, more important than her singing to the success of the group.

The most widespread and obvious musical feature that pop borrowed from punk and new wave was its new rhythmic conception: the clean, saturated eight-beat rhythm. This became one of the freshest sounds of the early eighties. It appears, transformed but still recognizable, in good pop hits like the Police's 1983 "Every Breath You Take" and Van Halen's "Jump," from their album *1984*.

Inevitably, pop subverted the attitude that had fueled punk. In assimilating some (but not all) of its musical features, it defanged and declawed it. There is probably no better example of this than "We Got the Beat," a 1982 hit by the all-female group the Go-Go's. It is hard to imagine a less dangerous song than this one. As has happened again and again, pop influences neutralized the threat of a dangerous music—blues, jazz, bop, rock and roll, and rock—by co-opting it.

The Go-Go's, "We Got the Beat"

Punk in the Eighties. Punk and new wave made their big splash in the late seventies. By the early eighties, punk had lost its novelty and notoriety and had become commonplace in shopping-mall suburbia. Nevertheless, both the attitudes and the musical substance continued to reverberate through rock, most obviously in a wave of alternative music, then in various neo-punk and punk-fusion styles from the early nineties to the present. It is safe to say that punk helped rock recapture the edge that had defined it in the sixties. Much of the music that captured that edge—whether pop, alternative, metal/punk fusions, grunge, or some other style—shows the influence of punk.

LOOKING BACK, LOOKING AHEAD

The music discussed in this chapter provides a cautionary tale for those who would measure the impact of a style by its chart position. None of the genres discussed here—reggae, funk, disco, or punk—had much chart success. Disco was the most successful, with about a three-year run on the charts; and Earth, Wind & Fire's funk-pop made them a top act in the latter part of the seventies. But punk's notoriety far outstripped its audience size, funk found a mostly black audience, and of the top reggae acts, only Bob Marley had a strong, sustained international presence.

All of this music, however, would prove far more influential in shaping the rock of the eighties than the chart-topping music of the seventies. The new rhythms of the eighties had their strongest links to these styles: the 16-beat rhythms heard in disco and funk, the clean eight-beat rhythm of punk, and the rhythmic play of reggae. They appeared singly, and in combination, in an extraordinary variety of music: the pop of Michael Jackson and Madonna, rap, the serious rock of U2, and the early alternative music of R.E.M.

Electronic sound generation, a big part of disco, became increasingly important in pop production. So did producers, which led not only to Quincy Jones's superbly crafted albums with Michael Jackson but also the Milli Vanilli travesty, when it was discovered that the group's lead singers had not sung on their recordings.

Time would smooth the edges off punk, at least for a while, but the anger and anti-establishment attitudes it embodied would resurface in the late eighties and continue to the present.

We survey several of these trends in Chapter 14, after a brief tour of a family of styles even farther outside the mainstream. We revisit the roots and fruits of Anglo-American folk music next.

TERMS TO KNOW

Test your knowledge of this chapter's important terms by defining the following. If you can't recall the meaning of a certain term, refresh your memory by looking up the boldfaced term in the chapter, turning to the Glossary at the back of the book, or working with the flashcards on the *Popular Music in America* Companion Web site: *http://music.wadsworth.com/campbell_2e*

16-beat rhythm	groove	punk/funk/disco fusion
choked guitar	kalimba	reggae
disco	melisma	riff
electronica	mento	rock steady
falsetto	mixing	saturated rock rhythm
funk	new wave	ska
funk-pop	punk	toasting

Country and Beyond:
The Roots and Fruits of Folk Music

Toward the end of 1991, *Billboard* magazine, the keeper of the charts, began using a new, more accurate method of calculating record sales. This new method, called SoundScan, tracked sales through the use of barcodes scanned at registers in retail centers and record stores throughout the United States. Around the same time, the music industry started using computers to track radio airplay. In combination the two information sources provided much more precise—and eventually more reliable—data about popularity.

Not coincidentally, the market share of country music just about doubled between 1990 and 1993: from 9.6 percent to 18.7 percent. This alerted industry executives on both coasts to something that country fans had known for decades: country music was much more popular than the music industry thought it was.

The dramatic jump in market share (which has since declined somewhat) was just one indication that country music had become a major player in the popular-music industry. Country music television networks, country stars in advertisements, the emergence of Nashville as an important music center, crossover chart success—these also show the growing presence of country music.

Although country was unquestionably a popular music by the latter part of the century, it hadn't lost sight of its roots: after all, the music is still called "country." Country music continues to acknowledge its musical connection to the folk music from which it came.

In earlier chapters we explored the transformation of the folk music of the Appalachians into popular music by two main routes: country and folk. In this chapter we continue to trace the development of both genres. We also explore two other folk/country connections. One is contemporary Celtic music, which connects us to Ireland and the European roots of American folk music. The other is closer to home: the Cajun music of Louisiana.

COUNTRY, FOLK, AND ROCK

For someone interested in the connection between a culture and its music, the tenures of country and folk is a fascinating study. Country has maintained its identity for the better part of a century, even though it has come a long way since Ralph Peer's excursions through the

Appalachians in search of talent. There is a connection between Jimmie Rodgers and Garth Brooks, a sense of continuity despite the enormous changes in every aspect of the music.

By contrast, the biggest of the folk revivals—the one in the late fifties and the early sixties—lasted less than a decade. The music of the folk revival was planted in alien soil and did not take root: the Carter Family couldn't grow in the sidewalks of New York. Then too it was a static entity—a "found" body of music. Moreover, there was the powerful presence of Bob Dylan, abruptly jerking the music into the present by both example and inspiration. Whatever the reasons, this preservationist movement quickly mutated into an important new direction in rock: the singer-songwriters. Shortly after, again following Dylan's lead, rock musicians began exploring rock/country mergers. We sample both below.

Singer-songwriters in the 1970s

Singer-songwriter is a generously general label. In its broadest interpretation, it could encompass at least one member of just about every rock band because most bands perform original material. It has had a more specific connotation, however: **singer-songwriter** has identified a cluster of solo performers who sang their own songs, accompanying themselves on a chord instrument. Typically, their songs tell a story or paint a picture. Often the songs are in the first person, and the stories may relate actual events in the songwriter's life. Words and melody are the primary focus; accompaniments tend to be in the background.

The first wave of singer-songwriters appeared in the late sixties in the wake of Dylan's seminal midsixties albums. Some, like Dylan, came out of the folk revival; others were songwriters who began to sing their own songs. In the latter group were musicians like Carole King, Laura Nyro, and Randy Newman. Piano was typically their instrument of choice. Among the major figures to emerge from the folk movement were Paul Simon, James Taylor, and Joni Mitchell. True to their folk background, these singer-songwriters play the guitar.

Joni Mitchell. Among the most intriguing of these singer-songwriters is Joni Mitchell (born Roberta Anderson in 1943). She was born in Alberta, Canada, and got her musical start playing in folk clubs while studying art in Calgary. She moved to Toronto and then to Detroit in 1965 after marrying Chuck Mitchell, also a folk singer; they split up a year later. Shortly after, her career as a songwriter took off, when Tom Rush and Judy Collins successfully covered her songs. Success as a performer of her own work soon followed in a series of releases that included *Blue* (1971), one of the truly enduring albums of the rock era.

Among the most persistent criticisms of rock and roll was the mindlessness of the songs: simple, even inane, lyrics set to simple three-chord accompaniments and obvious, repetitive rhythms. Old-guard critics compared such songs with the sophisticated lyrics and melodies of the great songwriters and songwriting teams—Cole Porter, Rodgers and Hart, Ira and George Gershwin—and found them sorely lacking.

The classical art song presented an even higher standard for the merger of lyric and melody. An **art song** typically begins with a poem of high quality; a composer then sets it to music of comparable quality, with piano as the accompanying instrument. The art song emerged in German-speaking Europe around the turn of the nineteenth century; it became a significant genre within a generation, in the songs of Franz Schubert and, later, Robert Schumann. It remained a viable genre throughout the nineteenth century, not only in Germany and Austria but also in France and even Russia. Rock musicians and their supporters were certainly aware of this classical tradition: concept albums like the Beatles' *Sgt. Pepper* were compared to the song cycles of Schubert and Schumann.

It is in this context that we can best appreciate the work of Joni Mitchell, especially early in her career. The lyrics of her songs are substantial enough to stand alone, apart from their musical setting: critics and academics discuss them as poetry. At the same time, the melodies are inherently interesting, enough so that musicians like pianist Keith Jarrett perform them as instrumentals. As interesting as the words and the music of her songs are in isolation, they are even more effective in combination.

The songs are written in the first person and are almost certainly rooted in her personal experience. Her marriage and divorce from Chuck Mitchell was just one in a series of tumultuous relationships. As an exceptionally intelligent and creative woman who was strong willed enough to forge a significant musical career, she clearly found it difficult to sustain a relationship and still maintain her integrity as an artist. The lyrics are more stream-of-consciousness associations than story, and the music is full of surprises. We can hear her break free from conventions to form a highly personal style.

The questing nature on display in *Blue* has resonated through her subsequent career. By the midseventies she had gone beyond the simple settings in her first albums. She began drawing on other genres: her collaboration-turned-tribute to jazz bassist Charles Mingus is a notable example. More recently, she has returned to the visual arts as well; she has exhibited widely as a photographer.

Other Singer-songwriters. Mitchell was not the only singer-songwriter to move away from the simple strum-along folk style of the early sixties. James Taylor has enjoyed considerable success not only with his own music but also with covers of songs like Marvin Gaye's "How Sweet It Is." Paul Simon began expanding his world—in sound and in place—upon becoming a solo artist. From his early-seventies albums, which make use of groups like the Dixie Hummingbirds (a fine black gospel quartet), to later albums that feature South African musicians, Simon has incorporated diverse influences into his music. Few have done it more creatively.

The singer-songwriter movement peaked in the early seventies, then went into a period of decline as other genres came to the fore. More recently, Tracy Chapman, Tori Amos, Ani DiFranco, and a few others have revived the folk-based singer-songwriter movement. Although their work has come some distance from the folk music that inspired it, what connects them is the story and a musical setting that puts words and melody at the forefront.

Country and Rock

Country and rock have been entwined from the very beginning. Bill Haley was a rockabilly; so was Elvis before he became rock and roll's first big star. As rock became a national, then an international, music, rock and country seemed to part ways. Bob Dylan played a major role in bringing them together, and he was not alone; Roy Orbison couldn't help blending the two. And Graham Parsons, first with the Byrds and then with the Flying Burrito Brothers, made the development of country rock his personal crusade. Emmylou Harris, his partner shortly before his death, continued his legacy into the seventies. Southern rockers like the Allman Brothers and Lynyrd Skynyrd grew up hearing country, rock, and rhythm and blues, and it all came out in their music; the same was true of the Band, Dylan's occasional partners. At the same time, country musicians, especially those with a pop orientation, began to assimilate elements of rock style into their music: Glen Campbell stands out in this regard.

By the early seventies, country and rock had come together in three distinct ways: rockers with country roots bringing them into their music (Roy Orbison); country musicians updating their sound; and rock groups like the Eagles adding country elements to their music.

OUTSIDE THE LAW: KEEPING COUNTRY PURE

Country music began crossing over to the pop charts more consistently in the years after World War II. Country artists like Hank Williams, Eddy Arnold, and Tennessee Ernie Ford appeared on the pop charts, and pop artists started covering country songs—Patti Page's version of Pee Wee King's "Tennessee Waltz" is an outstanding example.

The Nashville Sound. Nashville's tastemakers noted how the pop versions of country songs sold much better than the originals. Their response was to make country more like pop. The result was the **Nashville sound**, the dominant style in country music during the late fifties and the early sixties. The singing of Jim Reeves, Patsy Cline, and Eddy Arnold was closer to pop than it was to Hank Williams or Lefty Frizzell, and the background, with sumptuous strings and smooth-voiced choirs, smacked more of easy-listening music than country. A small number of musicians, including guitarist Chet Atkins, pianist Floyd Cramer, and vocalist–choral director Anita Kerr, played or sang on many of these Nashville recordings. Their continuing presence also contributed to the development of a consistent style.

Although Reeves and Arnold were among the most successful country performers of their time, there were those who felt—and rightly so—that country music was losing its identity in its quest for crossover success. The most prominent were the "outlaws," notably Merle Haggard, Johnny Cash, Willie Nelson, and Waylon Jennings. They made their case away from Nashville: Haggard in Bakersfield, California; Cash in Memphis, Tennessee; and Nelson and Jennings in Austin, Texas.

Merle Haggard in concert, 1975. This photo was taken a few years after he recorded "Okie from Muskogee," before he acquired his current look—beard, ten-gallon hat, and leather.

© Henry Diltz/Corbis

Merle Haggard. Bakersfield may seem an unlikely home for a country music rebellion, if only because it's about as far away from Nashville as one can get in the continental United States; but the story of country music in this city is another chapter in our ongoing account of the connection between music and audience. Bakersfield is in the heart of California's San Joaquin Valley, a fertile area where farmers grow much of the produce that we find in our grocery stores. In 1930 its population was just over 80,000. By 1960 it had almost quadrupled, in part because of the massive migration of Dust Bowl refugees to California. (John Steinbeck's 1939 novel *Grapes of Wrath* tells of the hardships these immigrants endured.)

Many of them came from Oklahoma, and among those was the family of Merle Haggard, who migrated west in 1934. Haggard was born three years later. After the death of his father when he was nine, Haggard ran wild and was more in trouble than out of it until he went to prison in 1958 on a burglary conviction. Inspired by a performance by Johnny Cash at San Quentin, the prison where he was incarcerated, he worked on his music.

By 1960 there were enough people from the South and the Southwest to support a thriving country music scene in Bakersfield. Its leader was Buck Owens; he and his band played a much harder country than the music coming out of Nashville. After being paroled in 1960, Haggard returned to

CD 3:13   1960s Hard Country (Merle Haggard; performed by Haggard, vocal and guitar)

0:00	Instrumental introduction.
0:08	1st verse
	We don't smoke marijuana . . .
0:35	2nd verse
	We don't make a party . . .
1:02	Chorus
	Uses the same melody as the verse, but with backup vocals adding harmony.
	And I'm proud to be an Okie . . .
1:29	3rd verse
	In a higher key, guitar responses.
	Leather boots are still in style . . .
1:56	Chorus
	And I'm proud to be an Okie . . .
2:22	Tag.
	And white lightnin's still . . .

Bakersfield and got involved with Owens's music (and with Owens's ex-wife, whom he soon married).

Haggard soon carved out his niche as the spokesman for the working class and the champion of middle-American values. The song that resonated most deeply with that audience was his huge 1969 hit "Okie from Muskogee." Haggard has claimed that he wrote the song as a joke, but he has sung it with no trace of sarcasm.

"Okie from Muskogee," Merle Haggard (1985). Haggard, vocal and guitar.

Haggard has said that his songs come out of his life; he sings them as if he's talking about it. His sound is gritty, not pretty, and with an unmistakable country edge. "Okie from Muskogee" paints a vivid, if stylized, picture of life in America's heartland, far removed from the excesses of the San Francisco hippies. Whether Haggard completely bought into his own lyric is open to debate, but there is no question that many Americans did.

The musical setting is **hard country**—a more contemporary version of the fundamental **honky-tonk** sound. In addition to Haggard's voice, it features a basic instrumentation—electric guitar, electric bass, acoustic guitar, piano, and drums played with **brushes** instead of sticks; there's no steel guitar or fiddle. An understated rock rhythm replaces the hard two-beat of honky-tonk. But the spirit is much the same: a plainspoken lyric set to a simple melody, with a no-frills, well-played backdrop.

STYLE PROFILE

"OKIE FROM MUSKOGEE" (1960s HARD COUNTRY)

Rhythm	*Moderate tempo.* **Country rock beat** = *light rock rhythm + honky-tonk two-beat; all understated here. Syncopated patterns in guitar parts.*
Melody	*Long phrases with mostly flat or gently descending contours.*
Instrumentation (timbre)	*Lead and backup vocals, electric and acoustic guitars, electric bass, piano, and drums (played with brushes instead of sticks).*

Performance style	*Haggard sings with a classic country sound: lean, without any vibrato. Electric guitarist plays bent notes in the last verse.*
Dynamics	*Moderately soft.*
Harmony	*I-IV-V, with a change of key just before the third verse.*
Texture	*Melody and accompaniment: voice is dominant, background includes simple bass and drums; nice arpeggiated patterns in acoustic guitar part; fills and riffs in electric guitar part.*
Form	*Verse/chorus.*

Key Points

Taking a joke seriously	*Haggard wrote "Okie" as a joke; the audience took it seriously.*
Hard country	*Haggard's vocal sound and delivery are pure country, with no hint of pop.*
Country rock beat	*Honky-tonk two-beat + clear, simple rock rhythm = country rock beat.*

Terms to Know

brushes
country rock beat
hard country

"Okie from Muskogee" was the first of many Haggard forays into social commentary. When released it was as current as the six-o'clock news. His most recent pronouncement, "That's the News" (2003), would probably horrify many of those who found his Vietnam War-era songs so uplifting.

The Outlaws: Willie Nelson and Waylon Jennings. Tradition-oriented country found another home in the seventies: Austin, Texas. Willie Nelson, who had tired of the Nashville treadmill, moved to Austin in 1971. He loosened up his image—wearing jeans on-stage and letting his hair grow long—and started a Fourth of July festival that brought together, according to one commentator, "the hippie and the redneck."

Nelson and Waylon Jennings started the **outlaw** movement, so called because of its defiance of Nashville's calculated commercialism and not because of any criminal wrongdoing on their part. As it turned out, Nelson and Jennings were more in tune with public taste than Nashville was. Their 1976 album, *Wanted: The Outlaws*, was the first million-selling country album. Their collaboration continued most noticeably on tour and in a series of "Waylon and Willie" albums.

Nelson has sung the music he likes. This has included not only traditional country material and his own music in a traditional style but also Tin Pan Alley standards (his 1978 *Stardust* album) and blues-flavored rock songs in collaboration with songwriter–rock star Leon Russell. This eclectic approach broadened his, and country's, audience considerably, making Nelson the most successful country crossover artist of the seventies.

The music of Cash, Nelson, and Haggard showed the viability of pure country music outside its traditional audience. Pure country also flourished within its own world. Many who had begun their careers in the fifties enjoyed considerable success in the seventies. We meet two of them following: George Jones and Tammy Wynette.

COUNTRY ROYALTY: GEORGE AND TAMMY

The success of the Outlaws was a sign of the times. For the first time in its history, country music attracted a large enough audience beyond its traditional constituency to make substantial inroads into the pop charts. Many of its stars gained national recognition: Merle Haggard, Johnny Cash, Tammy Wynette, George Jones, Loretta Lynn, and Willie Nelson all became household names. Dolly Parton went beyond that: she has become a pop icon, one of the handful of celebrities whose every move is grist for the tabloid mill.

There were many reasons for country music's increased popularity. Two involved politics: both the conservative backlash from the sixties and the election of Jimmy Carter gave country music a boost. Haggard's song was the tip of the iceberg; country music seemed to stand hand in hand with conservative points of view. Ironically, it also began to attract a young, non-southern, post-hippie audience—the very group that prompted the conservative backlash—at about the same time. Carter's election stirred southern pride; he was the first president from the Deep South elected in the twentieth century. The White House became a major venue for country performers during his presidency.

Throughout the late sixties and the seventies, country and its expanded audience met halfway. There was broad support for virtually the entire spectrum of country music, from updated versions of traditional styles (Johnny Cash, Merle Haggard, and Willie Nelson), pop-oriented country (Glen Campbell and Kenny Rogers), to rock/country fusions (Gram Parsons, Kris Kristofferson, and Linda Ronstadt). The clearest indicator of the strength of country's newly won popularity was the commercial success of hard-country acts. Haggard, Nelson, and other like-minded artists defied the conventional Nashville wisdom that commercial success requires diluting country with pop. More than any other trend, their broad appeal signaled country's entry into the musical mainstream.

George Jones and Tammy Wynette. From Jimmie Rodgers's blue yodels to the latest hits on CMT or GAC, country music has chronicled the good times and the bad times of men and women, together and apart. Songs have expressed almost every conceivable point of view: the faithful wife, the wandering wife, the faithful husband, the philandering husband. Often songs seemed as though they were airing dirty linen in public: in 1952 Kitty Wells answered Hank Thompson's "The Wild Side of Life" with "It Wasn't God Who Made Honky Tonk Angels." Still, country fans have also been partial to duets, especially between a man and a woman: they seem to put a face on the harmony heard in the music.

George Jones (b. 1931) and Tammy Wynette (1942–1998) embodied this dimension of country music so fully that it was difficult to discern where life ended and art began. Both were huge stars. Jones's career had begun in the late forties. His hits started coming in 1955; by the sixties he was charting regularly, both as a solo artist and in duets, mostly with women. Wynette grew up without a father. She married at seventeen and divorced before the birth of her third child.

George Jones performing in Boston in 1981, just after he recorded "He Stopped Loving Her Today." Jones had just begun to put his life back together after years of alcohol abuse.

While working as a beautician to pay the bills, she pursued a singing career. Within a year she was on her way, and by 1968 she had three number 1 country hits, including "Stand By Your Man" and "D-I-V-O-R-C-E."

The next year she married George Jones (they claimed to have married the year before). It didn't work, except on recordings. Jones was an alcoholic by this time, and his drinking and its effects on his personal and professional lives ruined their marriage and nearly ruined his career. Musically, however, they were a perfect match: both sang with real feeling and empathy; their duet recordings like "Take Me" and "Let's Build a World Together" document this. Their personal life, however, was a disaster, which Wynette alluded to in songs that barely disguised their real-life troubles.

Both excelled at expressing in song the pain of love gone wrong. They had experienced this pain firsthand and were able to translate it into music that touched listeners deeply. In songs like Wynette's "D-I-V-O-R-C-E" (1968) and Jones's "He Stopped Loving Her Today" (1980), an award-winning hit that marked the beginning of his comeback from alcohol abuse, we encounter the heartbreak of the end of a relationship. "D-I-V-O-R-C-E" tells the story in the present tense; we learn about the breakup of the marriage as it's happening. In "He Stopped Loving Her Today," the parting happened long ago (the love letters in the song are eighteen years old).

The emotional impact of these songs comes almost exclusively from the singing of Wynette and Jones. The songs are similar in approach: the story unfolds gradually; it describes a painful situation in plain language. Each has a gimmick: the spelling out of words in "D-I-V-O-R-C-E"; the fact that we learn toward the end that only death can end his (unrequited) love. Performed by less gifted performers, they could easily slip into soap-opera sentimentality.

The music is essentially neutral: there is nothing in the melody of the song that tells us about the pain—except when the singers reshape it. The accompaniments are tasteful and very much in the background. In both songs we hear steel guitar and a discreet rhythm section playing a discreet rock rhythm at a slow tempo. "D-I-V-O-R-C-E" also has a choir very much in the background, which surfaces only during the chorus. In Jones's song a string section creates a lush cushion of sound. This is Nashville at its most efficient: songs that are good vehicles for good singers, and professional musical settings appropriate to the mood of the song—here they are unobtrusive for the most part.

There would seem to be a purpose to the neutrality of the song and the setting. Nashville has many skilled songwriters capable of much more than three-chord songs. The producers, arrangers, and studio musicians are also highly skilled, even though they seldom flaunt it. Although the fruit of their work is far more involved and elaborate than "This Land Is Your Land," it seems to embody much the same philosophy as Woody Guthrie's: don't let the tune or the accompaniment get in the way of the words. In country music, however, it's not just what you say but how you say it.

The focus is squarely on the singers, and they deliver. Their singing exemplifies the most distinctively country sound of the last half century; they continue the legacy of Hank Williams, Lefty Frizzell, and Kitty Wells. The success that both have enjoyed, despite their personal adversity, and—more important—the respect that they earned from musicians and critics both in and outside of country music, remind us of an important lesson that every generation relearns.

Make up a short list of singers who stand out because of the emotional power and conviction of their singing, and it may very well include Billie Holiday, Bessie Smith, Frank Sinatra, Muddy Waters, Hank Williams, Ray Charles, and just a few others. There is no obvious art in their singing. None sings with the refined quality of a classically trained vocalist, nor do they display the vocal agility of a gospel or jazz singer. Unlike Connee Boswell, Sam Cooke, or Kenny Rogers, they do not have pleasant voices—voices that many will find immediately appealing.

Although they come from different genres, their singing shares certain qualities: it is personal, honest, straightforward, and intensely emotional. Because of this these singers can transmute even a mundane song into a moving experience.

We hear these same qualities in the singing of Tammy Wynette and George Jones. Wynette's is, on one level, so everyday that she sounds as though she could be singing along with the radio while doing someone's hair. But there is passion in her singing: she sounds at once strong and vulnerable. Throughout the song her voice sounds as though it's on the verge of breaking. The intensity of her singing tells us she has been through the experience she's singing about: in fact, her firstborn was only two and she was carrying her third child when she divorced. She is able to draw on that experience, then use the song to convey it to us: her performance is emotionally naked because it is at once plain and passionate. She is the neighbor next door and larger than life.

"He Stopped Loving Her Today" was the song that turned George Jones's career around and helped turn his life around, as well. Jones went through the seventies in a drunken stupor; as he said in his 1997 autobiography, if he was sober, he was asleep. By 1979 he was bankrupt and his career was in jeopardy. By his own account, it took much too long to record the narration at the end of the song because he couldn't talk without slurring his words when he was drunk, and he couldn't get to the studio sober.

CD 3:14

"He Stopped Loving Her Today," Bob Braddock and Claude Putman Jr. (1980). George Jones, vocal.

LISTENING GUIDE: "HE STOPPED LOVING HER TODAY"

CD 3:14   **Contemporary Country Ballad** (Bob Braddock and Claude Putman Jr.; performed by George Jones, vocal)

0:00	A	1st verse

Jones with a simple background: electric and acoustic guitar featured.
He said "I'll love you ..."

0:27	A	2nd verse

Add harmonica.
He kept her picture ...

0:54	A	3rd verse

The song moves up a key. Add soft (muted) strings, drums, and steel guitar.
Kept some letters ...

1:21	A	4th verse

I went to see him ...

1:48	A'	Chorus

More intense version of the verse melody; same harmony underneath; richer strings, choir added.
He stopped loving her today ...

2:15	A	5th verse

Choir outlines the melody while Jones talks the lyrics.
You know, she came ...

2:41	A'	Chorus

Slightly varied from earlier chorus.
He stopped loving her today ...

Despite these problems he delivered a performance of real conviction. The lyric strains our credulity: in this day and age, it is hard to imagine anyone carrying an unrequited love to the grave. But Jones's performance, which builds slowly to the climax, makes it credible. When he opens up on the chorus, he makes us feel how deeply the anonymous "he" felt about the woman who left him behind. There is not a trace of sentimentality in his singing. There is only the pain, plainly yet artfully expressed in subtle timing and—at the climax—deep inflection that says more than just the words could ever say.

Unlike Wynette, Jones is not singing this song from direct personal experience—indeed, he could not without the intervention of a medium. At best we sense the empathy of the friend who is unable to console the "he" in the song while he's alive. Perhaps Jones felt the parting from a different mistress: the bottle; around this time Jones began to dry out and put his life back together. In effect he died and was reborn—sober this time. His career has since prospered. He continues to perform and record and remains one of the enduring stars of country music.

Both Wynette and Jones sing simply and directly, like so many great popular singers before them. There is nothing mannered in their singing. Their art is in expressive nuance and timing, not histrionics. It is a lesson worth learning and relearning.

STYLE PROFILE

"HE STOPPED LOVING HER TODAY" (CONTEMPORARY COUNTRY BALLAD)

Rhythm	Slow tempo. Soft country rock beat; backbeat strong at high points in the song. No strong syncopation, but subtle rhythmic play in Jones's singing.
Melody	The verse features four medium-length phrases with pauses in between. The chorus has the same phrase structure and harmony, but the melody is higher.
Instrumentation (timbre)	Jones's voice; backup choir; acoustic, electric, and steel guitars; electric bass; drums; full string section (violin, not fiddle, sound); harmonica, and piano.
Performance style	Jones's singing has subtle timing and warmth within the straight (no vibrato) country sound.
Dynamics	Song builds to each chorus, growing louder in successive verses.
Harmony	I-IV-V-I (all the way through).
Texture	Melody is dominant. Rhythm section is in the background with a relatively simple accompaniment. Other instruments and sections (strings) play melodic background parts: figuration and sustained chords.
Form	Verse/chorus; verse and chorus have the same harmony and phrase structure.

Key Points

Telling a story simply	The **ballad** is about the story; everything else—Jones's emotionally credible sing, the gentle background—supports that.
Nashville production	Mix of country (harmonica and steel guitar) and commercial (choir and rich string writing) sounds.
Evolution of country music	Archetypical contemporary country song is a long way from "Old Joe Clark"; closer connection to Vernon Dalhart and Jimmie Rodgers.

Terms to Know
ballad

The best recordings of Wynette and Jones are evergreens—still as vital today as they were when they were released. Their singing remains a standard for those who have followed in their path. It is timeless, a continuing affirmation of the essence of country music.

REVISITING THE ROOTS

In 1980, the same year that George Jones scored with "He Stopped Loving Her Today," Dolly Parton made her feature film debut in *Nine to Five*. She played a country girl who comes to the big city to work. She has a job as a receptionist, and her co-workers regard her as a bimbo. Only well into the movie do they discover that she's on their side and is a lot sharper than they thought. Parton also wrote and recorded the title track to the film; the song briefly topped the pop charts that year.

Parton's success highlights the ever-present dilemma faced by country performers: how to find a balance between commercial success and country tradition. Other than the lyrics and her voice, there is nothing about Parton's song that sounds country. So though it's great to be a star, is it worth abandoning your roots to gain stardom?

Country music has wrestled with that problem throughout its history. Many of the most popular country performers have blended country and pop: the singing cowboys of the thirties and forties, the exponents of the Nashville sound in the fifties and sixties, and the **countrypolitan** singers of the seventies. Sometimes the balance shifts so much to the pop side that it's hard to find the country in a country song: almost any recent Shania Twain recording makes this clear. She sells records, but are her records really country?

While Parton, Twain, and others have courted popular success, other country musicians have chosen to remain closer to their roots. We discuss an example of this by Ricky Skaggs, plus three other roots-related examples. The first is a "newgrass" recording by an all-star progressive bluegrass group. The second is a traditional song by the Chieftains, a premier Celtic band. The third features the Cajun music of BeauSoleil and Michael Doucet. We begin with Skaggs's "Don't Get Above Your Raisin'."

Neo-traditional Country Music in the 1980s

In the early eighties, Ricky Skaggs (b. 1954) spearheaded country's **neo-traditional** movement, breathing fresh life into hard country and bluegrass. Older acts like George Jones found their careers revitalized, while younger artists like Skaggs, Dwight Yoakum, and Randy Travis found large and appreciative audiences. Many of the top acts moved easily between old and new. The strength of the neo-traditional movement highlights country's essential conservatism. For all its flirtations with other styles, country music—or at least a vocal minority within it—seems determined to preserve those qualities that define it.

Skaggs debuted on the country charts in 1981 with a cover of Lester Flatt and Earl Scruggs's "Don't Get Above Your Raisin'." Flatt and Scruggs had played guitar and banjo with Bill Monroe and the Blue Grass Boys before going out on their own in 1948. Scruggs was the first great banjo virtuoso, pioneering the "three-finger" technique that enabled him to highlight the melody in the middle of a shower of notes. The team brought bluegrass into the national spotlight in 1968 when they rerecorded an earlier hit, "Foggy Mountain Breakdown," for the film *Bonnie and Clyde*.

Flatt and Scruggs's original version of "Don't Get Above Your Raisin'" dates from 1958. Three years later Skaggs played with Flatt and Scruggs on their television show; he was one of country music's child prodigies. His choice of their song to launch his career was at once an act of homage and reminder of the timeliness of the message of the song.

Ricky Skaggs, "Don't Get Above Your Raisin'"

"Don't Get Above Your Raisin'" is ostensibly a song about the conflict between a good old boy and his social-climbing girlfriend, but many in country music took the song as an allegory for country's loss of traditional values in its romance with pop and rock and its need to rediscover its roots: the "gal" in the song is country music.

Musically, the song shows an eclectic mix of old and new. There is straight-ahead honky-tonk in the rhythm section; bluegrass mandolin and some excellent dobro playing; a little boogie-woogie/rock-and-roll piano; plus some rock guitar. Among the musicians on Skaggs's recording was Jerry Douglas, the modern master of the **dobro** (an acoustic guitar with a steel resonator in the sound hole). Douglas and four other virtuosos came together to form—at least on record—an all-star bluegrass group called Strength in Numbers. We meet them below.

Newgrass: Bluegrass Meets the World

From the start **bluegrass** was a virtuoso music. Tempos were breakneck fast, and musicians like Earl Scruggs navigated them with ease. And in its characteristic contrapuntal interplay of the different instruments, it showed its affinity with New Orleans jazz.

The first bluegrass groups, like Bill Monroe and the Blue Grass Boys, and Flatt and Scruggs, inspired generations of musicians. Among them were five undisputed masters of their instruments: mandolinist Sam Bush (b. 1952), dobro player Jerry Douglas (b. 1956), banjoist Bela Fleck (b. 1958), violinist Mark O'Connor (b. 1962), and bassist Edgar Meyer (b. 1961). Each has a strong connection to this music. Some grew up with it: O'Connor was a four-time fiddle champion. Others came from some distance away: Fleck, who grew up in New York City, was drawn to the banjo by hearing the theme music for *The Beverly Hillbillies*. And as children of the sixties and the seventies, their musical interests range far beyond bluegrass, old and new. Meyer is equally at home playing classical music, jazz, and bluegrass; he is the reigning virtuoso of the double bass. Collectively, they have helped modernize bluegrass by incorporating these diverse styles into the traditional sound world. Their music is most commonly called **newgrass**, or progressive bluegrass.

The catalyst for this more progressive approach to bluegrass was Sam Bush. In 1971 he formed New Grass Revival, the first progressive bluegrass group. In 1975 Bush's group made their first appearance at the Telluride Bluegrass Festival. During the winter Telluride is a ski resort in the Colorado Rockies. In the summer it hosts this festival.

The festival had been founded just the year before, in 1974. Bush has been a mainstay, appearing in every festival since, even as it has grown into a major event with dozens of acts from around the world. Fleck joined the third incarnation of New Grass Revival in 1981 and stayed with the group through most of the eighties. During this decade Bush and Fleck had the opportunity to perform with O'Connor, Meyer, and Douglas at Telluride. After performing live for several years, they came together in the studio in 1989 as Strength in Numbers, where they recorded their first and only album, *The Telluride Sessions*.

Newgrass begins with the core bluegrass instrumentation: five acoustic string instruments. In this respect Strength in Numbers is even more traditional than Bill Monroe or Flatt

CD 3:15 | **Newgrass** (Sam Bush and Jerry Douglas; performed by Strength in Numbers: Bush, mandolin; Douglas, dobro; Fleck, banjo; O'Connor, violin; and Meyer, bass)

0:00	Motto
	This riff-based section frames the piece; it also serves as a sectional divider.
0:04	Banjo vamp, plus syncopated mandolin/bass chords. Setting up the verselike passage.
0:11	Verse
	Dobro the melody instrument.
0:25	Chorus
	Fiddle takes over the lead role.
0:38	Motto
0:42	Verse
	Dobro solo over banjo vamp. Solos are like the new words of the verse.
0:56	Chorus
1:09	Motto
1:13	Interlude. Music floats: timekeeping is much lighter; banjo in spotlight.
1:41	Chorus
1:55	Motto expanded, which leads to bassist Meyer using pizzicato, despite playing fast-moving lines.
1:59	Bass breaks. Stop time in other instruments.
2:12	Interlude riff fragment.
2:27	Verse melody, varied and fragmented call-and-response: group answered by mandolin, dobro, fiddle, mandolin, dobro, mandolin, fiddle.
2:55	Chorus
	Biggest statement.
3:15	Motto
	Varied, to wrap up the performance.

and Scruggs in that Jerry Douglas's dobro is a more specifically country instrument than the guitar. With its brisk tempo, "Duke and Cookie" is probably closer to a conventional bluegrass song than any other track on their recording. The influence of outside styles is apparent in almost every other aspect of the song.

There is no vocal. Instead, a tuneful chorus with a couple of sharp syncopations acts as the melodic hook. The chorus alternates with solo turns by Douglas on dobro, Fleck on banjo, Meyer on bass, then rapid exchanges between Bush and O'Connor. Meyer's breaks are stunning because he moves around his instrument so nimbly and plays with such authentic inflection. The double bass is a big instrument. In a traditional bluegrass band, bass players were usually content to mark the beat. Meyer does much more throughout the song. It's as if he's driving an eighteen-wheeler on a Formula 1 track and staying up with the Ferraris.

The rhythmic undercurrent during the dobro solos shows the jazz influence. Fleck plays a rapid, raggy figuration, while Meyer and Bush play a clipped syncopated pattern instead of the more conventional *OOM-pah* dialogue. They have even more fun with the rhythm during Fleck's solo, which seems almost suspended in air.

CD 3:15

"Duke and Cookie," Sam Bush and Jerry Douglas (1989). Strength in Numbers: Bush, mandolin; Douglas, dobro; Fleck, banjo; O'Connor, violin; Meyer, bass.

STYLE PROFILE

"DUKE AND COOKIE" (NEWGRASS)

Rhythm	*Fast tempo. No underlying style beat; no consistent beat keeping. (Fleck's banjo vamp underlies verse.) Extreme variation in activity, from frenetic to free (in the interlude, at 1:13).*
Melody	*Verse and chorus are based on **modal** scale. The "motto" that frames the piece and the chorus are built from riffs. Verse and solos are instrumental-style melodies because they move quickly.*
Instrumentation (timbre)	*Mandolin, dobro, violin/fiddle, banjo, and acoustic bass.*
Performance style	*Douglas (dobro) and Meyer (bass) make use of slides into notes. Meyer uses **pizzicato** (plucking the strings), despite playing fast-moving lines.*
Dynamics	*Moderate, for an all-acoustic band.*
Harmony	*Verses are not harmonized; the motto has chords that elaborate IV, V, then I; the chorus has modally inflected harmonies based on I, IV, and V.*
Texture	*Varies from section to section: Motto = everyone together. Verses and chorus = melody/solo plus active, syncopated accompaniment. Interlude = open sound with little activity.*
Form	*Verse/chorus–based form, with framing motto.*

Key Points

Newgrass	*A contemporary take on bluegrass, with jazz-influenced soloing and rhythmic sophistication.*
Playing with time	*"Duke and Cookie" goes well beyond the kind of rhythmic play found in traditional bluegrass; it is closer to jazz in its defying of rhythmic gravity.*
Modal music	*The verse and chorus melodies are modal. The harmony is adapted to fit the modal scale in the chorus.*

Terms to Know

dobro	newgrass
modal	pizzicato

The newgrass of Strength in Numbers gives us another perspective on the tension between tradition and innovation. As we have noted, this tension has been part of the history of both country and folk music; indeed it is almost inherent in the style. Tradition has been central to bluegrass from the beginning, and its use of traditional instruments set it apart from other postwar trends in country music. It was, as we have noted, the first neo-traditional country style, so it should not surprise us that Sam Bush's New Grass Revival ruffled some feathers.

The Place of Bluegrass and Newgrass. Country and folk music have gone beyond their roots for a variety of reasons. Jimmie Rodgers sang the blues because that was the music he grew up hearing; it gave him a vehicle for saying what he wanted to say. Then and now the powers-that-be in Nashville have pushed country toward pop to make money: the Nashville sound, countrypolitan, and today's crossover stars. Folk singers in the early sixties quickly went from the past to the present so that they could comment on the problems in contemporary society, then they moved away from folk style in part to make money—Dylan was keenly aware of the Byrds' success with his songs. Strength in Numbers seems to have yet another motivation: they are almost like chemists in a laboratory, mixing different compounds to discover which ones combine well. There is a sense of experimentation in their efforts and an exhilaration as things come together. It is a strictly musical journey.

In these more modern forms, bluegrass has not only survived but thrived. Granted, it is a niche music—no bluegrass group is likely to crack the Top 40 or go platinum—but there is a good audience for the music, as the growth of festivals like the one at Telluride evidence.

Next, we encounter another vibrant marriage of old and new in the music of the Chieftains.

Celtic Music

Even as the folk revival was getting under way in the United States, another folk revival was taking place in Ireland. This one was not just about music but about the reclamation of a culture. Centuries ago the Celts (pronounced "kelts") had been prominent throughout northwestern Europe, but over time England asserted its authority over other regions in the British Isles, as France did in Brittany and Spain did in Galicia. After World War II, these minority cultures sought to reclaim their heritage. Celtic languages that had almost disappeared, such as Gaelic (in Ireland and Scotland), Manx (on the Isle of Man), Welsh, Cornish (in Cornwall, a region in Southwest England), Breton, and Galician, were revived and taught to younger generations. Scholars took a fresh look at the history of their cultures. People preserved or revived other aspects of their culture, as well: food, dress, dance, and of course music.

In Ireland a man born in 1931 as John Reidy played a key role in bringing back, and bringing to light, Irish traditional music. While in his twenties, he began using the Gaelic form of his name: Seán Ó Ríada. During this time he sought out Irish traditional musicians. In 1959 he went a step further and formed a traditional Irish band. Among the members was Paddy Moloney, a master of several traditional Irish wind instruments, among them Uilleann pipes (an Irish bagpipe) and the tin whistle. In 1962 Moloney formed the Chieftains, using several other members of Ó Ríada's folk group, Ceoltóirí Cualann. The Chieftains worked semi-professionally for more than ten years; by 1975 they were well enough established to become full-time professional musicians.

The Chieftains first came to the United States in 1972 as part of an Irish festival. In 1979 they appeared as the musical guests on *Saturday Night Live*. In that year they added flutist Matt Molloy, which stabilized the group's membership, and released their ninth recording, *The Chieftains 9: Boil the Breakfast Early*. For this recording the group included not only Moloney and Molloy but also Martin Fay, fiddle and bones; Seán Keane, fiddle; Derek Bell, harps; and Kevin Coneff, bodhrán and vocal. (The **bodhrán** [pronounced "*bow* (rhymes with *cow*) -rawn"] is an ancient Irish framedrum, traditionally made with a wooden body and a goat-skin head; it is played with a double-headed stick called a cipín, or beater.)

The most distinctive element of **Celtic music**, or at least Celtic dance music, is the instrumentation, which includes not only fiddle and flute but also instruments particular to Irish music: tin whistle, Uilleann pipes, harp, and bodhrán. The texture created by bands like the Chieftains—the melody played in a high range by the fiddle and a very high range by the tin whistle, the deep drumming sounds of the bodhrán, sustained sonorities on the Uilleann pipes, and other melodic lines weaving in and out—gives Celtic music its distinctive sound identity. It is in effect an orchestral version of a set of dance tunes played on a fiddle; the different combinations of instruments add variety and interest while maintaining the high energy from beginning to end.

Dance music is an important part of the repertoire of Celtic bands like the Chieftains. Dances like jigs and reels—traditional folk dances in Ireland as well as Appalachia—are typi-

CD 3:16   **Celtic Music** (Paddy Moloney; performed by the Chieftains)

0:00		Introduction, part 1
		Bodhrán (drum), then tiompaán (dulcimer-like instrument) and handclaps.
0:10		Introduction, part 2
		Melodic fragments doubled in flute/tin whistle; rhythmic response in bones; then call-and-response between flutes and fiddle.

First string of dance tunes: ABC

0:30	A	Fiddles and harp chords.
0:38	B	Flute joins the fiddles.
0:46	C	Fiddles, flute (and bodhrán).
		Dance tunes (repeated)
0:56	A	Pipes joins in on melody, harp more prominent.
1:04	B	Full band.
1:12	C	

New pair of tunes

1:20	D	Pipes solo.
1:30	E	Pipes and flute.
1:38	D	Full band.
1:46	E	Full band (continued).
1:54	D	Fiddle and flute.
2:02	E	Flute alone on melody, with pipes drone (sustained tones).

Third set of tunes

2:12	F/F	Vocal, then vocal and flute.
2:29	G/G	Vocal, then vocal and flute.
2:46	F/F	Instrumental and in a higher key.
3:03	G/G	Instrumental and staying in the higher key.
3:19	F/F	Instrumental and in a higher key.
3:36	G/G	Instrumental and staying in the higher key.

CD 3:16

"Boil the Break-fast Early," Paddy Moloney (1979). The Chieftains.

cally short, two-section pieces played at a brisk tempo. To create a longer number, musicians would string several jigs together, bringing one or more back in the course of the number. In "Boil the Breakfast Early," the title track from *Chieftains 9*, we hear three sets of tunes: one group of three and two groups of two.

STYLE PROFILE

"BOIL THE BREAKFAST EARLY" (CELTIC MUSIC)

Rhythm	*Fast tempo. Dancelike rhythms—fast-moving melodic lines recall the reel, a folk dance from the British Isles that was also popular in the United States. A strong dance beat, but little syncopation.*
Melody	*There are seven melodies, all in an instrumental style. Their fast rhythm, rapid rise and fall, and infrequent pauses would make them challenging to sing, although the boys make a good effort.*
Instrumentation (timbre)	*Voices, fiddles, drums, guitar, bass, bodhrán, flute, tin whistle, and harp.*

Performance style	*Celtic* **scat singing**: *several musicians singing two of the tunes.*
Dynamics	*Moderately loud for acoustic instruments.*
Harmony	*No harmony, except for a very occasional harp strum.*
Texture	*Ranges from a single voice or instrument to a rich texture, with multiple versions of the melody, countermelodies (usually in the harp), sustained sounds, and percussion.*
Form	*A series of short sections strung together that form a large-scale three-part form.*

Key Points

A series of dances and instrumental melodies	*"Boil the Breakfast Early" contains three sets of dance tunes; this is a typical feature of Celtic dance music.*
Celtic instruments	*Traditional Irish instruments—harp, Uilleann pipes, bodhrán, and tin whistle—are prominent throughout the song. They join fiddles and flute, played in the traditional folk manner.*
Celtic-style jamming	*Doubling of the melody in the fiddle, flute, and/or tin whistle; intricate accompaniments in the other instruments, especially the harp.*

Terms to Know
bodhrán
Celtic music
scat singing

Since the seventies the Chieftains have broadened the range of their music through numerous collaborative projects, joining forces with musicians as diverse as the Rolling Stones and classical flutist James Galway. Their sessions with American country musicians, including *Another Country* (1992) and *Down the Plank Road: The Nashville Sessions* (2002) reaffirmed the common heritage of Irish traditional music and country music.

Cajun Music

When the French settled in 1605 in what is now Nova Scotia, they called their new home Acadia. After a century and a half, they had grown into a thriving community of about 10,000; 150 years later they were driven out by the English during the war between the French and the English. Some made their way to Louisiana, another French-speaking region in North America. Over time *Acadian* became *Cajun,* and their language evolved into a distinct dialect of French.

Cajuns make up part of the Creole culture of Louisiana. *Creole* is a transformation of the Portuguese word *crioulo,* which Portuguese colonists used to distinguish slaves who had been born in the New World, as opposed to slaves who had arrived from Africa. Eventually, it came into use throughout the Caribbean and the Gulf region, including Louisiana. As discussed in Chapter 3, during slavery free persons of mixed parentage (usually black and white) were known as *Creoles of color.* After the Civil War, the term acquired a broader meaning, embracing whites, blacks, and those of mixed parentage. Still, it refers primarily to those who have Africans somewhere in their family tree. (Keep in mind that in Louisiana a person was legally black if he or she was one-sixty-fourth African—that is, if one great-great-great-great-grandparent was African.) Because of substantial intermingling of the races, through intermarriage and extramarital activity, a clear distinction arose between those who were clearly of mixed

CD 3:17	Cajun Music (Michael Doucet; performed by Doucet and BeauSoleil)

| 0:00 | Introduction. Eerie beginning with violin, other instruments layering in, wild yell. |

First Statement

0:15	A	Instrumental version of the first melody.
0:25	B	Instrumental version of the contrasting section; country beat begins here.
0:34	A	Violin and accordion.
0:43	A	Notice multiple versions of the melody here and above.

Second Statement

0:53	A	
		All along the bayou . . .
1:03	A	
		Bayou's hot . . .
1:12	B	
		Bayou's hot . . .
1:21	B	
		Oh we all do drink it all up . . .

race and those who were more African in appearance. From the early nineteenth century through emancipation, *Creoles of color* and *free persons of color* were more or less interchangeable terms because most free persons of color were of mixed race. With the end of slavery, all blacks were hypothetically free. But with the rollback of civil rights, all persons of color suffered under the oppressive restrictions of segregation. Since that time *Creoles of color* has referred to those of mixed race, whereas *black Creoles* refers to those with little or no white blood.

"Zydeco Gris-gris," Michael Doucet (1985). Doucet and BeauSoleil.

Two related but independent musical traditions emerged in rural Louisiana: one was white, the other was black. Both made use of the **accordion**, brought to Louisiana by nineteenth-century German immigrants (not all German immigrants ended up in Texas). The fiddle was a key instrument in the music of whites, as it has been in other styles that evolved from European folk music. It has been less widely used in the music of blacks. Instead, they have made use of a rubboard, a percussion instrument made out of tin roofing material.

The music of white French-speaking Louisianans is known as **Cajun music**. Its black counterpart has been known since the late fifties as **zydeco**. The term *zydeco* allegedly comes from the French word for "the beans": just as *Acadian* became *Cajun, les haricots* ("lay-zah-ree-co") became *le zydeco. The beans* are the first words in the title of a song popularized by accordionist Clifton Chenier, "Les Haricots Sont Pas Salés." The lyrics tell about times so hard that there was no salted meat to spice up the beans.

Cajun music was the first of these rural Louisiana styles to gain recognition, both regionally and nationally. An appearance by a Cajun band at the Newport Folk Festival in 1964 was a springboard for national recognition of this regional music. It was also a reflection of a growing interest among French-speaking Louisianans to preserve their culture. That movement has led to such developments as CODOFIL, the Council for the Development of French in Louisiana. Interest in zydeco came later, principally through the work of Chenier, the "king of zydeco" until his death in 1987.

Third Statement: Expanded because of guitar and organ solos

1:32	A	Instrumental, pretty much identical to the earlier A.
1:41	A	Continuing.
1:51	B	Electric guitar solo.
2:10	C	Organ solo over new harmonies.
2:29	A	Back to the beginning.
2:38	A	Continuing.

Fourth Statement

2:47	A	[Vocal in Cajun.]
2:57	A	
3:07	B	
3:16	B	

Ending

| 3:25 | A | Opening again, with a crisp, decisive ending. |

Like the people themselves, Cajun and zydeco have blended and borrowed from each other. We hear a nice example of this in "Zydeco Gris-gris," a song by Michael Doucet and BeauSoleil, the most popular Cajun band of our time.

Gris-gris is a local term for a voodoo spell or its opposite—a talisman, or lucky charm, that can ward off evil. One can buy gris-gris bags in New Orleans shops that stock voodoo paraphernalia. In this song it is probably the latter: the fiddle and the accordion seem to chase away the evil spirits heard at the beginning of the song, which lets the good times roll.

As befits its home base, "Zydeco Gris-gris" is a musical gumbo. Its roux—the thickening that gives the gumbo its distinctive flavor—is the sound of the fiddle and the accordion playing the melody of the dance tune. In this respect the song is certainly a cousin of "Old Joe Clark" or "Boil the Breakfast Early": a bright, active dance tune played on a fiddle. The other sounds come from everywhere: the conga drum used to evoke the evil spirits is Cuban, the rhythm section and the beat they play—a kind of two-step rock beat—would be at home behind a country singer or fiddler. The guitar solo comes right out of rock; the organ solo out of R&B. Stylistically, it is a real mix.

STYLE PROFILE

"ZYDECO GRIS-GRIS" (CAJUN MUSIC)

Rhythm	*Brisk dance tempo. Clean country-style rock beat with obvious timekeeping and a strong backbeat; melodic rhythms move briskly and typically line up with the beat.*
Melody	*Instrumental-style melody: fast-moving values, fairly long phrases, active contour (repeated notes followed by skips).*
Instrumentation (timbre)	*Vocals, fiddle, conga drums, drum set, electric bass, **button accordion** (featuring buttons on both sides, rather than buttons and a keyboard), and electric guitar.*

Performance style	*Doucet's vocal is enthusiastic but raw, much like his fiddle playing. The organ and electric guitar solos connect to late-sixties rock.*
Dynamics	*Loud throughout.*
Harmony	*The A section uses just two chords. The B section shifts down to a new key; it too relies on just two chords. Both change harmonies in a slow rhythm.*
Texture	*A thick, layered texture, with multiple versions of the melody (voice/fiddle and accordion), extra percussion, plus other rhythm instruments laying down an obvious country rock beat.*
Form	*Dance-inspired form: the alternation of two sections (neither acts as a chorus), except for the organ solo.*

Key Points

Button accordion	*This Cajun instrument is used as a lead and obbligato instrument.*
Good-time beat	*Strong country rock–style beat is one link to contemporary country music.*
Pentatonic scale	*The A and B sections use different forms of the same **pentatonic scale**.*
Regional country sound	*Language and use of button accordion are distinctly Cajun. Pentatonic, dancelike melody and country rock beat connect to traditional and contemporary country.*

Terms to Know

button accordion	pentatonic scale
Cajun music	zydeco

Cajun music is a country music. Its roots are in the rural South but in the bayous of Louisiana rather than the hills of West Virginia and the rest of the southern Appalachians. Like country music, it has made a nearby city its home base: New Orleans, the home of jazz and so much good rhythm and blues, now embraces Cajun and zydeco as well. And like country music, it has easily integrated other influences into the base style: zydeco is to Cajun music as blues has been to country.

Old Wine, New Bottles: New Sounds in Traditional Styles

In newgrass, Celtic music, and Cajun music, old and new merge in vibrant, novel ways. Their traditional orientation is evident, yet each projects a contemporary sound. We don't have the sense that we are listening to a museum piece—an attempt to replicate an earlier style. Rather, it is as though each group of musicians is breathing new life into a traditional style.

The same can be said, however, for just about all of the music in this chapter. What makes the musical examples for newgrass, Celtic, and Cajun music more traditional-sounding than the other examples? We can point to at least three reasons why:

- First, each song is clearly dance music or dance-inspired music ("Duke and Cookie" has much the same relationship to bluegrass as fifties jazz does to swing).
- Second is the showcasing of the instruments. Two of the selections have vocals, but they are not personal stories or commentaries.
- Third is the instruments themselves and how they're played. Whether it's bluegrass instruments, the Irish instruments in the Chieftains selection, or the fiddle and accordion in BeauSoleil's song, there is an immediate connection between the traditional acoustic

instruments and tradition. More-contemporary instruments, such as drums and electric bass, and even the electric guitar and organ heard in "Zydeco Gris-gris," don't sound intrusive because they are not the focus except during solos. As a result, the songs seem to resonate with the same spirit that we heard much earlier in "Old Joe Clark."

LOOKING AHEAD: COUNTRY MUSIC IN THE 1990s

Country music arrived in the nineties. It was not just the news that SoundScan tabulations provided. The music had a much stronger presence—in films, on television, in commercials, over the radio, even in the checkout lanes at the supermarket. The attitude of both musicians and audiences seemed to change. Both seem to project a newfound assurance, a sense that they don't need to apologize for liking country music: the hillbillies of the twenties had become the hunkabillies of the nineties.

The nineties saw a new generation of country stars. The biggest, like Shania Twain, Faith Hill, the Dixie Chicks, and especially Garth Brooks, have attracted huge crossover audiences. Others, like Randy Travis, Alan Jackson, Vince Gill, John Michael Montgomery, and Travis Tritt, kept country focused on its core values even as the music continued to evolve. The mentor of this latter group has been George Strait.

There was also a musical reason for country's ascendancy. As more music in other genres emphasized rhythm and sound over words and melody, many of those who wanted music with understandable words delivered in an easily understood way, with a melody one could hum, turned to country.

This chapter has surveyed not only contemporary country music but also other music that connects back to the folk music of the British Isles, either directly (the Chieftains) or after transplantation to the United States. The cross-pollination among styles has continued and has become even more diverse—consider folk/classical fusions with classical cellist Yo-Yo Ma and Mark O'Connor (*Appalachia Waltz*; *Appalachian Journey*) and the blending of African music, Celtic music, and electronica. All of this is very much part of the future as well as the past as we enter the twenty-first century.

TERMS TO KNOW

Test your knowledge of this chapter's important terms by defining the following. If you can't recall the meaning of a certain term, refresh your memory by looking up the boldfaced term in the chapter, turning to the Glossary at the back of the book, or working with the flashcards on the *Popular Music in America* Companion Web site: *http://music.wadsworth.com/campbell_2e*

accordion	Celtic music	neo-traditional
art song	countrypolitan	newgrass
ballad	country rock beat	outlaw
bluegrass	dobro	pentatonic scale
bodhrán	hard country	pizzicato
brushes	honky-tonk	scat singing
button accordion	modal	singer-songwriter
Cajun music	Nashville sound	zydeco

Rock and Black Music Since 1980

In the 2003 film *School of Rock*, Dewey Finn (actor/guitarist Jack Black) explains to a class of private-school fourth graders how to put together a rock band. The first step, he tells them, is for the prospective band members to name their influences—the groups that they listen to. His recommendation is common practice. Check bulletin boards in music stores, record shops, or university coffee houses. Often bands looking for another member or two define their sound by the bands that have influenced them. In some cases these bands may be working within a particular style—thrash metal, or a punk/ska fusion; in others there may be diverse influences.

Implicit in this short scene are two key features of musical life at the turn of the twenty-first century. One is the extraordinary variety of music to which musicians and listeners have access and the ease with which they can access it. When rock arrived in the sixties, it was an eclectic music and an international music. In the intervening forty years, it has become even more eclectic—virtually micro-eclectic—and global in its reach.

The other is that we are now in a postliterate musical world. For centuries the most reliable way to transmit musical information across time and space had been through musical notation. Mozart and Beethoven wrote down their symphonies and sonatas. Joplin wrote down his rags, which gave many Americans their first contact with an authentic African American music.

But musical notation is an imperfect tool. It can convey certain aspects of music with some precision, but others are beyond its reach. For instance, in any of the examples discussed in Chapter 12, it would be possible to notate the pitches of the vocal and instrumental parts, but there is no way to write down the vocal quality of Robert Plant or Roberta Flack. These must be heard to be understood and emulated.

Partly because of this, apprenticeship in popular music has been largely ear-based, increasingly so in recent years. Musicians learn songs and styles by listening and copying—both in person and on record. Until the rock era, however, musicians who could not read music found it difficult to structure musical time.

Notation can regulate time. Composers or songwriters can slow down, speed up, or even stop time as they create a musical work. Performers have the same luxury as they skim through or work out a piece of music.

In the early days of recorded sound—before tape recording became widely available to musicians and consumers—this kind of time control was not available. But with the advent of multitrack recording and consumer playback devices that are portable and easy to use, both musicians and listeners began to gain control of time. Creative people could assemble their music in stages, rather than record it in a single take. Listeners could easily review parts of a recording, for study or pleasure, and even slow it down to better hear details.

All of this became exponentially easier, and less expensive, with the emergence of digital technology. It gave creators and consumers the kind of control over time that only notation had previously provided but without many of its drawbacks. In addition, it has added an ever-growing array of resources that render notation unnecessary in the creation of even complex projects.

Without question, notation remains a valuable tool, but it is no longer essential to the creation of sophisticated music. For many contemporary musicians, waveforms and MIDI bars have replaced notes and rests as the primary visual image. We now explore how this happened.

THE DIGITAL REVOLUTION

What made electronic technology—the microphone, the radio, and improved recording quality—possible was the ability to convert sound waves into electrical signals, and electrical signals back into sound. What made digital audio possible was the ability to encode the waveform generated by the electrical signal into a binary format. This was accomplished by **sampling** the wave at regular intervals, with several possible gradations. On a standard CD, the wave is sampled 44,100 times per second; there are 65,536 ($16 \times 16 \times 16 \times 16$) possible gradations of the wave. This high sampling rate, coupled with the thousands of gradations, makes it possible to simulate the shape of the wave so closely that the original waveform and the digital sample of it are virtually identical.

Digital audio fools our ears in much the same way that digital images fool our eyes. Open an image on your computer and magnify it. You'll notice that it is a grid of squares, each a single color or shade of gray. Each square is so small, however, that our eyes are fooled into seeing color blends, curves, and other continuous images.

This ability to encode waveform data digitally has had several benefits. First, it eliminated signal degradation. In analog tape recording, there were inevitably some unwelcome sounds: one can hear tape hiss on predigital recordings that have not been remastered and on cassette copies of recordings. The more a tape is copied, the more pronounced the extraneous sounds become. By contrast, digital information can be copied an infinite number of times with no loss of quality, as anyone who's burned a CD or used a file-sharing service knows.

Second, it became possible to maintain quality despite unlimited use. Because of the physical contact of a stylus with a record groove, or tape with a tape head, the quality of sound recorded on these media degraded over time. A recording played for the hundredth time on a turntable or a cassette player will sound worse than the first time, no matter how much care is taken. Digital audio eliminated this problem.

Third, the high sampling rate has enabled those working with computer audio to isolate musical events with a precision that earlier generations could only dream about. Instead of shuttling a tape head back and forth to find the right starting point, those working in the digital domain can quickly identify and mark the beginning and the end of a musical event. Once isolated, they can manipulate it at will—compressing or expanding it, changing its pitch higher or lower, changing its timbre, or enhancing it with special effects.

The New Digital Technologies

It was one thing to have the capability of using digital technology; it was quite another to actually have the hardware that made it possible. After years of research and development, several crucial technologies emerged by the early eighties: the audio CD, MIDI, sampling, computer audio, and the Internet.

Audio CD. The audio CD required more than the ability to convert sound into digital data; it was also necessary to apply laser technology to encode and decode the data from the storage medium (hence the term *burn* a CD). Research on the laser dates back to a 1958 paper by a physicist at Bell Labs. By the early seventies, lasers were being used to read digital data stored on discs. By 1980 Philips and Sony, two of the leaders in audio research, had agreed on a standard for CD audio: 16-bit sampling and a 44.1 K sampling rate. (Other sampling precisions and sampling rates have since come into use: streaming audio generally uses less precise sampling [8-bit sampling produces one-sixteenth of the data of 16-bit sampling] and slower sampling rates.)

In 1984 the first CD pressing plant in the United States—in Terre Haute, Indiana—started producing CDs. The first CDs were expensive because the production process was seriously flawed; only a relatively small percentage of the CDs produced were good enough for release, so the cost of early CDs was high—higher than for cassettes or vinyl. (Not surprisingly, given the nature of the music business, the cost of a CD has remained higher than that of a cassette, even though production costs are now much less. It was too much to expect that record companies would pass their savings on to consumers.)

This initial audio CD format remains the most common method for delivering sound digitally, although, with the emergence of portable MP3 players, DVD audio, online music services, and other formats, that may soon change.

MIDI. *MIDI* stands for *Musical Instrument Digital Interface.* It is an industry standard that allows electronic instruments to communicate with one another and with a computer. In theory this seems like a natural and modest step. In practice it was a tremendous breakthrough for two main reasons. First, it enabled a single person to simulate an orchestra, a rock band, or a swing band with just one instrument. Using an instrument such as a MIDI-enabled electronic keyboard, musicians could choose from an array of MIDI-out sounds—usually no less than 128. They could play the passage as though playing a piano or an organ, but the sound coming out would be like a trumpet, or bells, or violins, or a host of others.

Second, MIDI devices could interact with sequencers. A **sequencer** is a device that enables a person to assemble a sound file track by track. Using a sequencer that can store eight tracks, a person can re-create the sound of a band: one track for the bass, another for the rhythm guitar, and so on.

Sequencers can also be used to create loops. A **loop** is a short sound file—say, a drum pattern or a bass line—that can be repeated and combined with other loops or freely created material to create a background for a song, whether it's rap, pop, techno or house, or something else. To make this process easier, loops are usually a standard length: eight beats (two measures), sixteen beats (four measures), and so on. With these kinds of resources, assembling the rhythm track to a song can be like building with LEGOs: users simply snap them into a track in their digital audio software.

Sampling. A **sample** is a small sound file. There are two basic kinds of samples in common use. One is the recorded sound of a voice or group of voices, an instrument (such as a grand piano) or group of instruments (a violin section), or some other sound. This sound can then be activated through another device. For instance, one can buy a disc with the sampled sound of several cellos playing every note on the usable range of the instrument, recorded in many different ways. Then the buyer can install it on a computer, activate it with the appropriate software, and produce a passage that sounds like a recording of the cello section of a first-rate symphony orchestra.

This kind of sampling has been available since the sixties. The first commercial "sampler" to achieve any kind of currency was the Mellotron, a keyboard instrument on which pressing a key would activate a looped tape of a string sound. It was not very flexible, but it was a cost-efficient alternative to hiring violinists. Sampling didn't really become practical, however, until digital technology.

Sampling has now reached such a level of sophistication that it is often impossible to determine whether a passage was recorded live or created using samples. In effect, this kind of sampling is a higher-tech version of MIDI playback because the sounds are more accurately rendered.

The other basic type of sampling involves lifting short excerpts from existing recordings to use in a new recording, much like a visual artist will use found objects to create a collage. This has been a staple of rap background tracks since the technology became available in the mideighties.

Computer Audio. In 1965 Gordon Moore, one of the founders of Intel, predicted that the number of transistors on a computer chip would double every couple of years. Moore's Law, as it has been called, has largely held true: the amount of computing power one can buy for $1,000 has doubled every eighteen months or so.

Because CD-quality digital audio requires more than a million samples per second, the first personal computers could not handle audio processing in real time. Fast-forward to the turn of the century, though, and it's a different story. One can burn CDs at—(I hesitate to put a number here because by the time this book gets into print it will be out of date). Digital audio workstations, sequencers, special-effects plug-ins, notation software—there is nothing in the process of creating and producing a recording that cannot be done by a computer, supported with the right software and peripherals, except the invention of original material.

Those who have come of age with this technology in place may find it to be business as usual, but for those of us who have seen it emerge it is truly awe-inspiring. For just a few thousand dollars, anyone can do in a home studio just about anything that would have required a million-dollar studio setup less than a generation ago—and a lot more!—and not have to pay for studio time.

One of the images of this era that is sure to endure is the creative person sitting not at an instrument but at a workstation, surrounded by displays, keyboards, CPUs, and other computer audio equipment. A recent example: Moby, featured on the covers of *Spin, Wired,* and *New York Times Magazine* in 2002.

The advances in computer-based digital audio have put high-end music production within almost anyone's budget. For the aspiring creative artist, the financial investment is a fraction of what it once was. The larger investment is time: not only to develop the necessary musical skills but also to master the applications necessary to create the desired result. And there are plenty of role models, from Stevie Wonder, Brian Eno, and Grandmaster Flash to Moby, Trent Reznor, Juan Atkins, Richard James, and hundreds more. And it will only get better.

The Internet. If Keith Richards and Mick Jagger had been born forty years later, chances are the Rolling Stones would never have come together. It's not just the musical changes but the circumstances of their chance encounter. Most likely, Jagger would be wearing earphones, and he would not have been clutching his treasured, hard-to-find blues LPs. He might still have treasured them, but they wouldn't be hard to find; he could go online and find Robert Johnson, Muddy Waters, Elmore James, and most of the other great bluesmen. He could hear excerpts from their recordings, buy their albums online, or access them through file sharing, both legal and illegal. And they would be stored on his iPod; there would be no album covers in sight.

For listeners the Internet has collapsed time and space. Users can listen to music from around the world and from most of the century. By way of example: Before writing this paragraph, I listened to two complete songs online. The first was "Vahsi" (pronounced "wah-shee"), a song recorded by Kesmeseker, a Turkish alternative band. It's very much in the international rock style; only the language of the vocals gives away its country of origin. The second was Cole Porter's 1928 hit, "Let's Misbehave," recorded by Irving Aaronson and his Commanders. Aaronson led one of the top dance orchestras of the late twenties and early thirties. This breadth and ease of access were unheard of in the eighties and only imagined in the early nineties.

At the risk of repeating myself, those who have grown up with this ease of access to music may not appreciate how much it changes the musical landscape. To have such extensive resources so readily available is momentous and unprecedented.

The Implications of Digital Technology

Digital technology, in all its dimensions, has made every aspect of popular music more accessible: its creation, production, distribution, promotion, and consumption. It has helped make popular music a global music that can bond people and make them more appreciative of cultural differences. The access is there; it is simply a matter of taking advantage of it.

Technology is neutral, but its use is inevitably a two-edged sword. For those who create music, the availability of so much material and the ease with which it can be used can be seductive. Why use a drummer when you can program a drum machine to play faster, more steadily, and more reliably? Why think up your own bass line or drum pattern when you can choose from hundreds or thousands of loops performed or created by skilled musicians? Why leave the flaws in the lead vocal part when you can extract clips from alternate takes and patch them in seamlessly? Why settle for anything less than a "perfect" recording when a perfect recording is possible?

The danger is that the loss of spontaneity, collective inspiration, and imagination will more than offset the gains in efficiency and production—that the perfection of the machines will make the music less human. It need not happen, but it *can* happen if these potentially wonderful resources are used indiscriminately.

Most of the popular music of the past forty or so years, from rock to rap to raprock, has prided itself on being "real." And when compared with the music of earlier generations, it has been. By contrast music making as preserved on record has moved away from being "real" since the Beatles retired from live performance. It began when recordings diverged from live performance rather than captured it. It continued when producers used machines to simulate or replace live musicians: drum machines instead of drummers, and synthesizers programmed for musical gestures and effects that are difficult if not impossible to achieve with conventional instruments (such as sections of *The Dark Side of the Moon*).

Sequencing and sampling deepened the separation between recording and performance: recordings could be constructed entirely from someone else's work. We are now in a time when a DJ can "perform" recordings live—when he can play or mix intricate rhythms and riffs, all prerecorded and stored on a hard drive, with a single touch of his finger. It is now possible for someone with no expertise as a vocal or instrumental performer to create a well-crafted, interesting performance without performers of any kind as intermediaries.

In the rock era, "real" and "personal" have usually been closely linked. A musical statement that is real has grown out of an incident in the life of the person who created it, or it expresses a personal opinion. Rock was a more real and more personal music that prerock pop because acts performed their own music and because so many acts emulated the realness of the blues and of the contemporary folk music of Woody Guthrie.

It is not just the words but also the music that is both real and personal. This is apparent in such things as the cultivation of a distinctive sound and style and the use of inflection, timing, note bending, and other expressive tools to communicate directly and personally.

Any instrument other than our voice or our body is a machine. Some are simple: a pennywhistle or a cowbell. Others are complex, beautifully crafted pieces of engineering, such as a saxophone or a grand piano. But most pitched instruments, especially those in common use, have been capable of emulating the sound of the human voice, and drums have been known to talk. As we heard, a bluesman can do many things with his guitar: strum, play riffs, or add another part. One of them has been to make his guitar sing—to emulate his voice.

Most musicians who learn to play expressively spend a good deal of time mastering their instruments. As they develop the skill, there is continuous feedback between musical ideas and their execution, until the experience becomes organic; what they do leads them to discover what more they can do. When they achieve mastery, the instrument becomes an extension of themselves; they can be as real and as personal as if they were singing. In performance they can react in real time, according to their mood and their interaction with other musicians and the audience.

The key point is this: digital technology has made it easier to make well-crafted music, for those with well-developed musical skills and those with little or no skill. But it has also made possible a less immediate kind of music making. In performance or recording, there can be a world of difference between having a drummer playing and having a drum loop playing, simply because the drummer can respond in the moment. For those who want to keep their music real, the challenge is to use the technology in ways that enhance the personal dimension of their music rather than undermine it.

Another option is to create a completely new aesthetic, one that builds naturally on the radical innovations of digital technology. We explore one such aesthetic in a discussion of electronica.

ELECTRONICA

Among the most enduring images in twentieth-century music is the singer with the guitar. The image transcends style, race, gender, locale, and theme: Blind Lemon Jefferson, Jimmie Rodgers, Gene Autry, Maybelle Carter, Robert Johnson, Woody Guthrie, Bob Dylan, Joan Baez, Joni Mitchell, and countless others; country and city, traditional and topical.

Now imagine a sound that is its complete opposite. Instead of mostly singing, there is little or no singing—and what vocals there are have been filtered through an electronic device. There is no melody with accompanying chords; instead there might be wisps of riffs or some sustained notes. Instead of the simple rhythm of the accompaniment, there is the thump of a low percussion sound marking the beat, several fast-moving patterns, plus other electronically generated loops. Instead of the strumming of an acoustic guitar, there is an array of electronic sounds, complete with special effects. Instead of a story with a beginning and an end, there is total immersion in a sound world with no apparent time boundaries. Instead of a single performer singing and playing while a few others listen, there is a DJ in his booth, surveying a dance floor filled with bobbing and weaving bodies as he mixes his music.

You will find examples of this totally opposite sound in the dance/electronica section of your favorite record store—on the street, in the mall, or online. **Electronica** has become the umbrella term for a large and varied family of styles: house, techno, trance, ambient, jungle, drum 'n' bass, industrial dance, and many more.

The almost total contrast between electronica and the folk/blues/country singer underscores how radically different the electronic-based music of the eighties, the nineties, and the twenty-first century is from so much earlier music, including much of the music of the early rock era. The differences begin with its origins and continue with its venues, its performance, and ultimately its intent.

The Antecedents of Electronica

Most popular-music genres have evolved through the influence of music from "below"; that is, music from "plain folk" who live outside and "beneath" the realm of high culture. We use the word *roots* to convey this. Electronica is different. Its origins are in the most cerebral and esoteric music of the midtwentieth century: the classical music avant-garde.

During the middle of the twentieth century, composers in Europe and the United States, using equipment as sophisticated as the first tape recorders and synthesizers and as everyday as nuts and bolts, explored virgin musical territory. Shortly after World War II, French composer Pierre Schaeffer began creating music using recorded sounds, rather than musical ideas inside his head, as raw material. The recordings could be of any sounds at all, and they could be modified or transformed in any way possible before being assembled into a music event. Schaeffer called this process *musique concrète* (concrete music).

Others, among them German composer Karlheinz Stockhausen, French American composer Edgard Varèse, and American John Cage, assembled compositions completely from synthesized sounds; they recorded and then spliced them together to form a complete composition. In 1958 Lejaren Hiller set up the first computer-music studio, at the University of Illinois. Among these new electronic works were the first examples of the recording as the creative document—with no performer involved in the creative process.

Much of this music was conceptual: it grew out of a particular idea or concept that the composer wanted to explore. The results pushed every possible extreme. American composer Milton Babbitt created works in which every musical parameter was regulated by a predetermined series: total serialism. In effect his compositions using this procedure were precomposed. At the other end of the spectrum were works by John Cage. One famous piece required the performer to sit perfectly still for 4 minutes 33 seconds; the composition was the ambient sounds in the performing space. Stockhausen composed a work for piano in which fragments of music were printed on an oversized score; the performer determined the sequence of the fragments during the performance. Cage created works in which events were determined by chance. Varèse created *Poème électronique*, an electronic piece that mixes synthesized and *concrète* sounds, for the 1958 World's Fair in Brussels. It was played over 425 loudspeakers.

All of these concepts have found their way into the various electronica styles. To cite just a few connections: The loudspeaker setup for *Poème électronique* anticipates the "total immersion" sound systems of dance clubs. Stockhausen's piano piece, where the performer switches arbitrarily from fragment to fragment, anticipates the DJ mixing on the fly. *Musique concrète* anticipates the "found" sounds that appear in so much electronica and related styles, like rap. And totally electronic pieces anticipate the countless synthesizer-generated dance tracks.

All this is not to argue for a causal connection between midcentury avant-garde music and the electronica of the past twenty-five years. Rather, it is to suggest three things: First, that even the most esoteric ideas and concepts have a way of filtering down; in this case, they made it all the way to the underground—the club scene that has nurtured this music. Second, electronica could blossom only when the necessary equipment became accessible and affordable. Third, electronica involves more than simply making dance music on computers. Its most imaginative creators have radically altered or overturned conventional assumptions about music making.

Music for Dancing, Places to Dance

The dance club is the home of electronica. The dance scene that has nurtured the music since the early eighties has been an underground continuation of disco: the music of Donna Summer and Giorgio Morodor were among the best and most successful examples of early electronica. In essence, after disco declined in popularity there were still people who wanted to dance; the club scene, and the music created for it, gave them that outlet.

Two major club scenes emerged in the Midwest: house music in Chicago and techno in Detroit. Both would have a profound influence on dance music throughout the world. **House music** was a low-budget continuation of disco: DJs like Frankie Knuckles would use bare-bones rhythm tracks as part of mixes that included disco hits and current disco-inspired songs. The Detroit **techno** scene was almost exclusively the work of three friends and colleagues, Juan Atkins, Derrick May, and Kevin Saunderson, who had known each other since junior high. Despite their Detroit base, they were more interested in techno pioneers like Kraftwerk than in Motown. Atkins said in an interview that "I'm probably more interested in Ford's robots than in Berry Gordy's music." As DJs and producers, they delivered a stark, dark kind of dance music under numerous guises, including Atkins's Model 500 and May's Rhythim Is Rhythim.

By the mideighties the music had migrated to Great Britain. The event that brought the music, the culture, and the drugs up from the underground and into the public eye was the 1988 "Summer of Love," a rave that went on for weeks. A rave is a huge dance party conducted in a large space: outdoors, an abandoned warehouse, or even a large club. Ecstasy and other "designer" drugs were very much a part of the scene; they suppressed the need to eat or sleep. (Never mind that the drugs are dangerous—even deadly—especially when consumed with alcohol.)

Ambient music, a quite different branch of electronica, dates back to the seventies. Its early history includes not only Pink Floyd, Kraftwerk, and Tangerine Dream but also Brian Eno, an electronica pioneer since the midseventies, and, among other things, the "father of ambient music." His recording *Ambient I: Music for Airports* (1979) is seminal.

As its name suggests, ambient music is more atmospheric and less dance driven, with more attention to texture and less emphasis on rhythm. As a genre within electronica, it hasn't had a home, but it has merged with both house and techno, introducing a more varied sound world into both. In these hybrid genres, it began to catch on in the late eighties and early nineties.

Fueled in part by the growth of the club scene, a host of other styles have emerged in the 1990s and the 2000s. The proliferation of styles came about not only through the combination and the recombination of existing styles (such as ambient house) but also through the absorption of outside influences, which led to an array of hardcore techno substyles. Electronica has begun appearing on the pop charts, in the music of such acts as Bjork, the Chemical Brothers, and Moby.

Hearing Electronica

Dance music has defined a new performance paradigm for popular music. The nature of the venue—the dance club rather than the arena, auditorium, night club, or coffee house—has fundamentally altered what is performed, how it's performed, how it's created, and how it's experienced.

The obvious difference, of course, is the use of recordings, rather than live musicians, to create the music being heard. That doesn't mean that there isn't the spontaneity and performer/crowd interaction that can be part of a live performance; it's just that it comes from a different source: the DJ.

The idea of stringing together a series of songs has a long history in popular music. From the thirties on, dance orchestras and small dance combos would occasionally play a **medley**, a group of songs connected by musical interludes. Often medleys were slow dance numbers; bands would play one chorus of each song, rather than several choruses of one song. But they could be any tempo.

During the early years of the rock era, medleys were harder to create in the moment because the identity of a song was more comprehensive. It was more than just the melody and the harmony; it included every aspect of the song as preserved on the recording, making it more difficult to alter songs so that one would flow easily into the next. Still, the idea of connecting songs did not disappear, as landmark albums such as *Sgt. Pepper* and *The Dark Side of the Moon* evidence.

Still it wasn't until disco that the idea of creating medleys resurfaced, in a much updated form. It was the DJ who transformed the practice of connecting songs into an art. A DJ with a two-turntable setup was able to **mix** a series of songs into a **set**, an unbroken string of songs that could last longer than even the most extended Grateful Dead jam.

The art of the DJ begins with music that he or she selects. For this reason many DJs create their own music: it helps them develop a signature style. In performance—in the dance club —the skilled DJ strings together a series of dance tracks with seamless transitions. It is not just that he blends one record into the next without dropping a beat (unless he means to). He orchestrates the sequence of songs, how much of each he'll use, and the kind of transitions he'll make to give a sense of architecture to his set. It is in this context that he can respond to the dancers' energy, building to a climactic moment as the set unfolds.

In the discussion of rock and rhythm and blues in the sixties, we noted that the record had become the document—the fullest and most direct expression of the musicians' creative intent. This changes in dance music. The musical unit is no longer the recording—which is seldom if ever played in its entirety—but the set. The recording is the raw material for the set; recordings are the building blocks—much as riffs are the building blocks of so many songs.

This in turn changes the nature of a dance track. It is not just that it is music for dancing. It is that the dance track is often created with the idea that it is a component of a larger structure—the set—rather than an entity complete unto itself—the song. This is a radical departure from mainstream rock; rock gave the song an integrity that it could not have had in earlier generations.

Moreover, music for dance clubs uses a different sonic spectrum. Since the early sixties, popular music designed for airplay concentrates on midrange frequencies because they come across better on radio than high or low frequencies do. By contrast dance clubs typically have good sound systems, so producers can take advantage of the full range of audible frequencies. Electronica styles typically make full use of this, especially low-end frequencies.

This combination of a relentless dance beat and a full sonic spectrum, all in an enclosed space, produces a kind of sensory inundation. It is virtually the opposite extreme of sensory deprivation, and it seems to have many of the same mind-altering consequences.

CD 3:18

"Nude Photo," Derrick May (1987). Rhythim Is Rhythim.

We hear an influential example of electronica: "Nude Photo" by Rhythim Is Rhythim, a good early sample of Detroit techno. "Nude Photo" establishes a characteristic techno groove almost immediately. The heart of it is the beat: a bass drum–like sound on every beat, a strong backbeat, and a fast-moving percussion part. Layered over that is some more-melodic material: complicated, syncopated synthesizer figures, one in midrange and two in a lower register. After the track gets under way, a slow-moving melodic fragment comes in and out. There is some variety: a short raplike vocal, some other vocal sounds, addition and subtraction of the various layers, and some new versions of the melodic figures toward the end. These are the musical counterparts to the disco ball: rotating, and slightly different because of that, but essentially the same throughout. The track begins and ends abruptly; one can imagine it as part of a mix where we would never hear a beginning or an end.

This example can only hint at the range of sounds, rhythms, and textures possible within the world of electronica. Still, it highlights key features of the genre: a steadily marked rhythm at about 120 beats per minute; rich, complex textures featuring electronically generated percussive and pitched sounds; very little singing; subtle changes within a generally repetitive, **modular form**; and little sense of beginning or end. These tracks are not telling a story; they're sustaining a mood.

LISTENING GUIDE: "NUDE PHOTO"

CD 3:18   **Electronica** (Derrick May; performed by Rhythim Is Rhythim)

0:00	First sound block: bass drum on every beat, backbeat, low syncopated line, midrange syncopated pattern, other percussion sounds.
0:15	Voice enters.
0:22	High slow-moving synthesizer riff added.
0:37	High riff out, then in, while midrange pattern drops out.
0:59	Midrange, high synth riff returns.
1:14	High riff out.
1:29	Strong break: active percussion at 16-beat speed, no other riffs.
1:37	Midrange riff returns.
1:44	Bass drum on the beat out.
1:51	Bass drum back while midrange riff suggests a new chord.
1:58	Like the beginning, except for the suggestion of a new chord at the end of the module.
2:16	Extra percussion, swoosh.
2:28	More sounds; low middle; high synth riff returns.

"NUDE PHOTO" (ELECTRONICA)

Rhythm	*Moderately fast beat (about 120 beats per minute); 16-beat rhythm with a strong beat (bass drum–like sound) and a stronger backbeat. Most other rhythms (pitched and percussive synthesized sounds) move at 16-beat speed; riffs and patterns map onto a rhythm moving four times the beat speed. Lots of syncopation; variation in beat keeping.*
Melody	*Pitched lines are melodic in the sense that they have a contour and do not outline chords. They are not tuneful: low and midrange patterns are too jagged and syncopated to sing; the high synthesizer line is singable but repetitive.*
Instrumentation (timbre)	*All sounds except for vocal fragments are generated electronically: drum machines and synthesizers use a variety of timbres.*
Performance style	*The music is not "performed" at any stage of the production process, so there are no performer-related style features.*
Dynamics	*Depends on the sound system—consistent throughout.*
Harmony	*No real chords: a single chord is implied throughout most of the song; a second is introduced toward the end (at about 1:52).*
Texture	*Dense, layered texture is made up of percussive and pitched patterns. The variation in texture as parts leave and return are a main source of interest.*
Form	*Modular. The track is built from four-measure sound blocks defined mainly by the low-pitched synth pattern. Other parts come and go, usually at four-measure intervals.*

Key Points

Electronic sound generation	*Where's the band? Except for voice clips, all sounds are electronically generated; no one "plays" an instrument.*
Mixing	*In a dance club "Nude Photo" would be part of a seamless mix; neither beginning nor end would be heard.*
A new way of making music	*No one has to perform in real time at any stage in the creation of the music.*
Rhythim's Rhythm	*"Nude Photo" mixes obvious beat- and backbeat-keeping with several layers of active, often complex rhythms.*
Manic minimalism	*"Nude Photo" is a high-energy music with little variation or change.*

Terms to Know

electronica

mix

modular form

Electronica has been the most faceless music of the past twenty-five years. Its creators work anonymously in studios—often alone. They assume aliases: Aphex Twin is Richard James; Rhythim Is Rhythim is Derrick May. The music they produce—largely instrumental and without the melodic points of entry common to other kinds of popular music—does little to encourage the listener to identify with them in the same way that they would identify with the lead singer or lead guitarist of a rock band. In many ways this recalls the structure of the music business at the turn of the previous century, when largely anonymous songwriters turned out reams of songs for Tin Pan Alley publishers. For the most part, DJs are the stars of electronica, but it is a very localized form of celebrity.

There are signs, however, that the music as a genre is developing a larger audience and a more mainstream presence. In the United States, Moby has put a face on electronica, in part by bringing his music closer to a mainstream pop style. This of course has provoked cries of outrage from hardcore clubbers who feel that he's selling out. Nevertheless, the genre has significantly broadened its base, and it is often a component of world beat and rap.

Although its market share remains small by pop standards, electronica has had a profound influence on popular music. Rap, pop, rock, world beat—there is hardly a contemporary sound that does not show at least some influence of the technology and the tools of dance music. It is inevitable that the radical changes to the popular-music landscape that it has brought about will filter into pop music in the twenty-first century. For now we consider its impact on rap.

RAP

Several years ago I was asked by a group of students to participate in a discussion: "Is rap music?" To get the discussion started, one of the students read a definition of music. As it turned out, rap would not have been music according to the dictionary definition, but at no time in the discussion did anyone challenge the question itself. For me the correct answer to the question is neither yes nor no. The correct answer is simply, "It doesn't matter." **Rap** is rap: a creative form of expression that uses musical sounds to help get its message across. (Indeed, one could argue convincingly that the rap video is the first total-arts genre in that it combines poetry, drama, visual arts, dancing, and music!) Whether rap is "music" should be a nonissue—and it *is* a nonissue to the millions who enjoy it.

Forerunners of Rap

The practice of talking over a musical accompaniment has a long history in popular music. Al Jolson used to talk over instrumental statements of the melody in the twenties; bluesmen and contemporary folk artists like Woody Guthrie would routinely strum and talk.

Within the popular tradition, the practice of reciting poetry over a musical accompaniment goes back to the fifties, when Beat poets such as Kenneth Rexroth presented their work backed by a jazz combo. Somewhat later, African American poets such as Amiri Bakara (LeRoi Jones) often delivered their work with jazz in the background. In the sixties, acts as different as Bob Dylan and James Brown delivered words that were both rhymed and rhythmic, using a vocal style that fell somewhere between everyday speech and singing.

The most direct antecedent of rap, however, was the **toasting** of the Jamaican DJs who ran the mobile sound systems and kept up a steady stream of patter as they changed discs. As mentioned in Chapter 12, they became so adept, and so popular, that Jamaican record companies began issuing the instrumental background of a recording as the B side of a song so that DJs could prolong their toasts. The SugarHill Gang's "Rapper's Delight," the single widely acknowledged as the first commercial rap, uses a similar approach: much of the rap takes place over a sample of Chic's "Good Times." Another source of rap, this one closer to home, was George Clinton's funk; we heard a proto-rap at the beginning of "Tear the Roof off the Sucker (Give Up the Funk)."

Rap and African American Culture

There are numerous parallels between the Mississippi Delta in the first half of the twentieth century and the South Bronx in the latter half. Both regions are heavily black. Both are heartbreakingly poor: there is either no work, or work at such low pay that one cannot make ends meet. They are violent, even lawless places. Health and living conditions are closer to life in a third-world country than the suburbs of New York or Memphis: out-of-wedlock children born to young teens; rats and roaches everywhere; and segregated, underfunded schools, where the playgrounds may become battlegrounds.

There are differences, of course. The Delta was—and is—rural. Geography, prejudice, and poverty kept the people who lived there thoroughly isolated from mainstream culture. The South Bronx is urban. Fifth Avenue in Manhattan is a short subway ride away. But it might as well have been another world for those who lived in the ghetto. In effect there has been in both cases an invisible barrier that has prohibited meaningful contact between blacks and whites. Television, however, brought the rich and famous into the living rooms of South Bronx residents, so they had a much sharper sense than their Delta counterparts of what they didn't have.

Both are depressing, demoralizing environments that can suck the hope out of one's mind, body, and spirit. So it is a testament to the resiliency of African Americans and the vitality of their culture that the Delta and the South Bronx have been home to two of the most vital, important, and influential forms of artistic expression to emerge in the twentieth century. Just as the Delta is the spiritual home of the blues, so is the South Bronx the home of rap.

Ask those who listen to rap what draws them to it. Chances are they'll say, "It's real." Like the blues, the realness of rap is not just in what it says but in how it says it. Rap gives us a window into life in the ghetto: the good, the bad, the ugly . . . and the beautiful. There is humor; bleak visions of the past, present, and future; posturing; misogyny and responses to it; slices of gang life and pleas to bring an end to it; brutal depictions of current conditions and forceful demands for action. Like other roots music—blues, folk, and country—this is music by and for its constituency. That rap has found a much wider audience is great but incidental to its original mission. The power comes from its emotional urgency. As with the blues, we can feel it's real. It has much more of an edge, in words and sound. It's as if African Americans are saying, "We're tired of this ——."

Rap is a contemporary instance of a popular style speaking to and for its audience. In a 1992 *Newsweek* article, Public Enemy's Chuck D called rap "Black America's CNN." In his view it serves as the news service of the inner city, providing information and viewpoints not available through conventional media. Chuck D feels that rap and rap videos give whites exposure to a side of African American life that they could not get short of living in a ghetto.

Rap and Hip-hop. Rap emerged as one artistic dimension of **hip-hop** culture, along with break dancing and graffiti. All three were unconventional forms of expression that required considerable skill and preparation. Break dancing is extremely athletic; its vigorous moves parallel the energy of the music to which it's performed. Graffiti artists prepared their work much like a military campaign. They would plan the graffito through a series of sketches, scout out the train yards, sneak in and paint the cars, then sneak out. Their use of trains and buses as canvases suggests that graffiti was another way to get their message out of the ghetto.

There is a kind of defiance built into all three: rap, graffiti art, and break dancing. The implicit message is: "You can put us down, but you can't keep us down. You—the Man, the

Establishment—can subject us to subhuman living conditions. You can ignore us. But you can't break our spirit. We can create something that comes from us, not you, and you can't do what we do, even though you want to." (Keep in mind that before Eminem there was Vanilla Ice.)

Rap and Technology. Rap is a fascinating blend of low- and high-tech and of the creative use and reuse of whatever is at hand. One can rap without any accompaniment at all. In this sense it is about as low-tech as one can get. The first raps happened over existing music, but it wasn't long before DJs such as Grandmaster Flash found ways to put a new (back)spin on playing discs. With Grandmaster Flash the turntable went from simple playback device to musical instrument. Equipped with two turntables, each with a copy of the record being played, DJs would **scratch** (move the turntable in a steady rhythm while the needle was still in the record groove to produce a percussive sound) and create breaks by repeating a segment of a song over and over on alternate turntables. To do this DJs had to know exactly how far back to spin the turntable. Affordable samplers have rendered this pioneering technique obsolete.

These techniques were two more in a long string of found sounds within African American music: the **bottleneck** for the guitar, the toilet **plunger** for the trumpet and trombone, the diddley bow, and the washtub bass. The resources may have been more sophisticated, but the principle remains the same: an imaginative search for new sound resources.

Rap was the freshest new direction in popular music since rock. It began on the street corners of black sections of New York City. The first hit, the SugarHill Gang's 1979 release "Rapper's Delight," came in both long and short versions: the latter was for radio airplay. Young people around the country spent hours memorizing the rap before inventing their own.

Rap evolved quickly from this point in content, style, and appeal. Among the pioneers was Grandmaster Flash. "Adventures of Grandmaster Flash and the Wheels of Steel" became a textbook for the creative possibilities of sampling. It was not just that Grandmaster Flash pasted in excerpts from Chic's "Good Times" and Queen's "Another One Bites the Dust," as well as sound fragments from other songs and sources, but that he manipulated the sounds that he brought in. In the process he completely recontextualized them. As with electronica styles, the excerpt was no longer the song but part of a larger unit. "The Message," the other groundbreaking song by Grandmaster Flash, was a brutal picture of ghetto life. Its impact came not only from the words but the bleak, empty musical setting and the "slice of life" interpolations, such as the arrest at the end of the track. Both tracks were especially influential on the next generation of rappers, but neither charted.

Rap crossed over to the mainstream with Run-DMC's version of "Walk This Way," which featured Aerosmith members Steven Tyler and Joe Perry. The new version made the charts in 1986—exactly a decade after the original. A year later, LL Cool J and the Beastie Boys (who were signed to Def Jam Records, the most prominent rap label at the time) found the charts; with their emergence rap burst out of the ghetto and into the 'burbs.

With the surge in popularity came a shift in tone. Many early raps had been "good time" music; Grandfather Flash's bleak portraits of ghetto life were the exception. Now groups like Public Enemy gave their raps a confrontational edge and supported them with dense, aggressive, sample-rich backgrounds. For example, "1 Million Bottlebags," a track from their 1991 album *Apocalypse 91 . . . The Enemy Strikes Black,* indicts both those who produce and promote alcohol consumption and those who consume it. Their anger is palpable.

At the same time, rap spread rapidly from its New York home base. Among the most prominent new centers of activity was southern California. It was the home of gangsta rap,

Public Enemy,
"1 Million
Bottlebags"

the most commercially significant new trend of the late eighties and nineties. Acts like Dr. Dre, NWA, and Ice Cube became household names. Gangsta rap became the most confrontational and controversial rap genre because of the messages of the raps and the language used to convey it. Some heard it as a no-holds-barred portrait of life in the 'hood; others denounced it as a cartoonish parody. There was ample evidence for both points of view.

As rap entered the mainstream, it began to filter into other styles. Both the sound and attitude of rap appeared regularly in both R&B and rock. At the same time, rap producers sampled widely, drawing on such diverse sources as Latin music, funk, and fifties jazz.

Nas Among the new rap stars of the mid-nineties was Nas (Nasir Jones, b. 1973). The son of jazz trumpeter Olu Dara, Nas grew up in Queensbridge, a massive, dangerous, and desolate housing project in New York. Despite dropping out of school in the eighth grade, he developed into one of the more thoughtful and literate rappers of the nineties. *Illmatic,* his 1994 debut album recorded when he was only 20, drew widespread praise as a quintessential example of "street flow," a seemingly endless stream of inventive and provocative observations about life in the projects.

"Life's a B****," one of the most admired tracks on the CD, contains two raps, one by AZ (Anthony Cruz) and the other by Nas, with a refrain by AZ tying them together. The raps express powerfully a fundamental contradiction in rap. Both title and content portray the

despair of life in the projects, and the rappers' complex response to it. They stress that life is short and get what you can while you can; as one reviewer noted, the message is not "life's a b**** and then you die" but "life's a b**** because you die." The raps are full of conflicting messages: Nas celebrating the first quarter of his life even as both acknowledge that living the rest of it is unlikely; AZ proclaiming an amoral value system while acknowledging sinners; Nas matter-of-factly describing his early encounters with sex and drugs yet seeming to put it behind him.

However, the biggest conflict is between the content of the raps and the fact of them. That AZ and Nas would devote the time, energy, and passion to create meaningful statements about their lives is an affirmation of their lives and their culture. It is, in the most fundamental way, vital. It says that they have chosen to spend at least part of their lives creatively rather than giving in completely to the "sin" ("cause all of us turned to sinners") that has brought so many of their peers down. It suggests the

Nas (Nasir Jones) in a 1996 photograph, staring thoughtfully into the camera. This serious expression and simple attire suggest a maturity well beyond his years—he was 22 at the time of this photo.

CD 3:19

"Life's a B****,"
Anthony Cruz,
Nasir Jones, Oliver
Scott, Ronnie
Wilson (1994). AZ
(Anthony Cruz)
and Nas, Olu Dara
(trumpet).

0:00	"Conversation" between AZ and Nas, over an unvarying instrumental background
0:21	1st verse
	Visualizin' the realism of life and actuality
1:04	Chorus
	*Life's a b**** and then you die . . .*
1:24	2nd verse
	I woke up early on my born day, I'm twenty years of blessing.
2:18	Chorus
	*Life's a b**** and then you die . . .*
2:43	Trumpet solo
	The muted trumpet recalls Miles Davis's sound.

same spirit as those community gardens one occasionally finds growing in an empty lot in a rundown neighborhood. In this respect, rap is the post-modern urban counterpart to the blues: just as a bluesman sings the blues to chase away the blues, so does a creative rapper rap to convey hope in an environment of despair.

Is rap music?   Rap is more than the poetry; the musical setting is integral to its presentation and impact. Here, the understated, unchanging backdrop—dark bass and percussion, a pair of chords that never resolves, and a high string synthesizer sound, all at a slow tempo—immediately sets a gray mood. Moreover, it does not change, as if to suggest that the environment is permanent. The accompaniment sets up a powerful contrast between the brevity of life and the endlessly hopeless environment that makes lives short. The mournful muted trumpet at the end, by Nas's father Olu Dara, sustains the bleak mood through the end of the track.

STYLE PROFILE

"LIFE'S A B****" (RAP)

Rhythm	*Slow tempo. Subdued eight-beat rhythm with a strong backbeat; rap moves at 16-beat speed. Syncopated bass line, keyboard chords.*
Melody	*Because it's a rap, there is no melody in the vocal parts. The trumpet*
Instrumentation (timbre)	*raps by AZ and Nas, bass, sampled keyboard chords, sustained high synthesizer sound, percussion sounds; muted trumpet solo at the end.*
Performance style	*Rap is more than speech and less than singing.*
Dynamics	*Moderately soft.*
Harmony	*Two-chord progression that is repeated; it never resolves.*
Texture	*Spare, widely spaced instrumental backdrop provides sound cushion for the raps and trumpet solo.*
Form	*Verse/chorus, introduction and tag.*

Key Points

Drum and bass: distilling a dark sound	*Rap showcases two of the most enduring instrumental trends in black music: increased emphasis on percussion and increased prominence of the bass.*
Voice as a percussion instrument	*In rap the voice has become a percussion instrument: definite rhythm but indefinite pitch.*
Sampling	*The songwriting credits identify two members of the Gap Band, a ca. 1980 funk band, suggesting that parts of the song were sampled from one of their recordings.*
Soul, funk, and rap	*Rap is the ultimate consequence of James Brown's new rhythmic bag.*
Is rap music?	*It doesn't matter. Rap need only be judged on its own terms: whether it communicates its message effectively.*

Terms to Know

rap

sampling

Still, the fact that the rap is the most prominent part of the texture has prompted rap's detractors to dismiss rap as "not music"—and by implication an inferior form of expression—simply because it does not have a melody. The hotly-debated question "Is rap music?" should be a non-issue. Instead, we should aim to understand rap for what it is—poetry integrated into a rich, rhythmic musical setting—rather than what it isn't—a conventional popular song. The most valid answer to the question "Is rap music? is not "yes" or "no," but "It doesn't matter." Rap is what it is, an innovative mix of poetry and music.

Rap and the "Percussionization" of Popular Music. In the larger view of things, we can understand rap as the logical end result of a process that had been going on for most of the twentieth century: the "percussionization" of popular music. It began shortly after the turn of the century, with the formation of the syncopated dance orchestra, which included a drummer. It continued with the development of the drum set and the more percussive approach to banjo playing—the crisp backbeat of the fox trot. Next was the plucking of the string bass, instead of bowing it, as was customary in orchestral playing. (Plucking—**pizzicato**—is exceptional.) Rhythm-and-blues and rock musicians soon found ways to extract percussive sounds from new instruments of the rock era: the choked guitar and the slapping techniques on the electric bass. Rhythm-and-blues recordings often featured extra percussion instruments, especially conga drums. New keyboard instruments, such as the clavinet (heard on Stevie Wonder's "Superstition") produced percussive sounds. Synthesizers and drum machines expanded the range of percussive sonorities.

With rap the voice becomes a **percussion** instrument. Like many other percussion instruments, a rapper's voice has resonance (more so than normal speech) and a general sense of high and low. But the rapper does not sing definite pitches as a singer does. James Brown was a primary source for this because even his singing is percussive—listen to how syllables explode and then die away quickly when he sings a phrase like "I Feel Good." As an all-percussive genre, rap has taken this trend about as far as it can go. In this respect it is the sound parallel to the increased activity in the style beats of popular music.

Rap remains a vital segment of the popular-music world, as a trip to any record store makes clear. Moreover, one hears rap, or raplike passages, in R&B, electronica, pop, and other contemporary styles. In addition, numerous rap fusions have surfaced in the past two decades: rap-metal, rap-rock, and rap-punk.

Like so many other genres with aggressive postures and outsider status (heavy metal, punk, techno), rap has gotten its share of bad press. Its critics focus on the language, the lifestyle, the lyrics, and the emergence of substyles like gangsta rap to condemn the entire genre. There is no denying rap's edge—the speed and the tone of the rap and the busy rhythms underneath virtually guarantee it. Nevertheless, rap is inherently content-neutral. It can be, and has been, used to deliver a variety of messages—not only dark gray portraits of life in the 'hood and expletive-filled rants but also humor and hope.

The impact of rap goes beyond the genre itself. Its influence on other genres is apparent not only in the mix of singing and rapping within a song but also in the more prominent role of rhythm in so much music of the eighties and beyond.

POP IN THE 1980s

Perhaps it's a karmic balancing act. Coincidence or not, it is certainly intriguing that the three biggest pop acts of Ronald Reagan's presidency were Michael Jackson, Prince, and Madonna. In an era of political and social conservatism, all three presented complex, provocative, and at times confusing images of race and gender. Michael Jackson's gradual metamorphosis to paleness, questions about his sexual preferences, and his erratic behavior have been tabloid fodder for more than two decades. Prince, the child of an interracial couple, alternated between blatant eroticism in performance and total withdrawal from the public eye—to the extent that he even retracted his name. Madonna broke down barriers on-stage, in the media, and behind the scenes. People noticed what she did and what she thought; both were often controversial. More telling, she was the first female pop star to chart her own career path.

Two of them have ascended to one-name celebrity status. Michael Jackson might well have if it weren't for an even more prominent Michael J.

All three have been extraordinarily visible; what people can see has been very much a part of their success. Michael Jackson broke through first. He appeared as the scarecrow in the 1978 film *The Wiz*, a black take on *The Wizard of Oz*. There he met producer/composer Quincy Jones, who was instrumental in shaping his career. He made his mark in a series of landmark music videos that displayed the full range of his talents.

In 1984 Prince had a surprise hit with the semi-autobiographical film *Purple Rain*. By that time Madonna's career was well under way; she would star in music videos, stage musicals, and films, such as *Desperately Seeking Susan* (1985).

Madonna (Madonna Louise Ciccone) on tour in 1985 to promote her second album, *Like a Virgin*. This was a good year for her: both album and singles charted very well in the United States and Britain, and her acting role in *Desperately Seeking Susan* received critical acclaim.

All three capitalized on a newly emergent genre—the music video—that became a staple on a new network—MTV—in a new medium, cable television.

MTV and Music Videos

Those who have grown up with hundreds of networks may find it difficult to imagine a time when television viewing options consisted almost exclusively of three networks: NBC, CBS, and ABC. Larger metropolitan areas had public television and a few independent stations, but until the early seventies most viewers had only the three major networks from which to choose.

Cable TV is almost as old as commercial broadcasting. The first cable TV services were launched in 1948; a well-situated antenna brought television signals to homes in remote rural regions. There was some growth during the fifties and sixties, but cable TV as we currently know it didn't get off the ground until the seventies. Two key developments—the launching of communications satellites and significant deregulation of the broadcast industry—made cable television economically viable.

Cable changed the economics of the television industry and transformed it in the process. Networks relied exclusively on advertising for their revenue; the signal was free. Cable TV services charged subscribers a fee and passed on a percentage of that fee to the channels that they offered their subscribers. This new source of revenue made possible the fragmentation of the television market. A network that could command only 1 or 2 percent of the market would have no chance for success against the major networks; but that same 1 or 2 percent of the cable market could provide enough income to make the network viable.

MTV. Among the first of these new cable networks was MTV. The network began broadcasting in 1981. Symbolically, the first music video that MTV broadcast was "Video Killed the Radio Star." The original format of the network was analogous to Top 40–style radio stations: videos replaced songs, and VJs (video jockeys) assumed a role similar to radio disc jockeys.

Perhaps because cable originally serviced mainly rural parts of the country, MTV took an AOR-type approach to programming. For the first couple of years, programming targeted a young, white audience: bands were almost exclusively white—Duran Duran, a British pop group with a keen visual sense, was one of the early MTV bands. Black acts cried "racism" with some justification.

It was Michael Jackson who broke MTV's color barrier. The demand for his spectacular music videos—made in conjunction with his 1982 album *Thriller*—was so overwhelming that the network changed its policy.

The Cable Act of 1984 effectively deregulated the television industry. In its wake the cable industry wired the nation. With new revenues came new and improved programming. MTV started VH1 in 1985 and diversified its programming in several ways, adding documentaries, cartoons, and talk shows and continuing to broaden its programming. In particular, its segments on rap helped bring it out of the inner city.

MTV has affected both consumers and creators. The network has become a key tastemaker for young people around the world. It has influenced not only what they listen to but also many other aspects of youth culture: dress, looks, body language, vocabulary, and attitudes. The fact of MTV has also reshaped the sound of pop, as we consider shortly.

Music Videos. Rock had been a look as well as a sound from the start. Elvis was a sensation on television, then in films. Other rock-and-roll stars made their way into films as well, although not as stars: the 1956 film *The Girl Can't Help It*, which starred Jayne Mansfield, featured Little Richard, Gene Vincent, and Fats Domino. The Beatles' breakthrough film feature, *A Hard Day's Night* (1964), showed the power of film to enhance music, especially when the visual element was so well in tune with the music and the spirit of the band.

It wasn't until the late sixties, however—the twilight years of the Beatles' career—that the idea of using videos to replace live performance began to emerge. At the same time, live performances were captured on video or film: documentaries of the 1967 Monterey Pop Festival and Woodstock in 1969 remain treasures. Further experiments, especially by new wave acts like Devo, moved closer to the integration of sound and image that characterizes contemporary music video. With the arrival of MTV, the music video became such a key component of the music industry that it redefined the relationship among story, image, and sound.

The Impact of Music Videos. The music video inverted the conventional relationship among story, image, and sound. In musical theater and film musicals, songs were written for the story, ideally enhancing those moments when what the character felt was too much for mere words. In earlier music videos, the relationship was the opposite: the visual element was designed to enhance the song. Now the music video is such an essential component of pop success that acts create song and video as an integrated whole. In either form it is a relatively new expressive medium.

The most obvious, and most widely discussed, consequence of music videos was the suddenly increased emphasis on the look of a band, and the look of the video, as a determinant of success. Certainly, looks and clever video production could compensate for inferior music and dramatically enhance a good song.

The Transformation of Pop. The impact of music videos went beyond packaging a song, at least in the work of Michael Jackson and Madonna, the two stars who defined music video in the eighties. Both are sensational, innovative dancers, and both were in touch with the new dance music. Madonna started her career in the New York club scene. *Off the Wall* (1979), Michael Jackson's first big post-*Wiz* success, drew on disco, and much of his eighties music had a punk/funk/disco–derived edge. Neither has the voice of a great pop or R&B singer.

The new sound of pop that emerged in the eighties was, more than anything else, the confluence of three developments: the emergence of MTV and music videos, the more active rhythms and richer textures of dance music, and the return of the all-around performer. (Michael Jackson's most direct predecessor would be Fred Astaire.) The result was a new kind of pop in which much of the momentum in the song shifted from the melody to the dance track–like rhythms. At the same time, dancer-singers like Michael Jackson and Madonna put on exhilarating displays. The songs were still tuneful, but they left room for plenty of movement. Even when everyone knows that the vocal is overdubbed, it still strains our credibility to imagine Michael or Madonna singing soulfully through their vigorous dancing.

Michael Jackson, "Thriller"

The title track to *Thriller* shows the musical side of these changes. It is a long song by pop standards, in part because of the buildup at the beginning and the voiceover at the end by Vincent Price, one of Hollywood's masters of the macabre. But the heart of the song is a Disneyesque version of scary: Michael's voice, the skillful orchestration, the security of the four-on-the-floor bass drum and the heavy backbeat, and the busy rhythms—all ensure a cartoonish kind of pop more reminiscent of Scooby Doo than *Friday the 13th*. This is not to say that it wasn't well done or was undeserving of its enormous popularity. But compared with the Black Sabbath version of a scary night, this one is safe—at least until the music drops out and Price has his last laugh.

Today the pop singer who simply stands in front of a microphone and sings a tuneful melody is the exception, not the rule, especially at the top of the charts. Vigorous movement is in, whether it's groups like the Backstreet Boys and 'N Sync or solo acts like Mary J. Blige, Janet Jackson, Britney Spears, and Ricky Martin. The music matches the movement. Much of it draws on the 16-beat rhythms of dance music and rap. An overlay of tuneful melody and pleasant voices cannot obscure the fact that the new acts of the eighties took pop in a new and visually exciting direction.

The Persistence of Love

The more traditional black pop, the one that charted the ups and downs of romantic love, got a makeover in the eighties. A new generation of singers—among them Lionel Richie, Whitney Houston, and Luther Vandross—were among the brightest stars of the eighties and nineties. Top acts from the past continued to make great music: Tina Turner, Marvin Gaye (until his untimely death in 1984), Aretha Franklin, Stevie Wonder, and Diana Ross stand out.

The new sound of the eighties resulted mainly from two significant changes: the use of synthesized sounds to replace most, if not all, of the traditional instruments, and more-adventurous rhythms. The sumptuous backgrounds that were so much a part of the sound of later doo-wop, Motown, Philadelphia, and Barry White are part of this updated black pop sound. The difference is that producers use electronic analogues to the strings, horns, and even rhythm instruments. Their function is much the same, but the sounds are new. This fresh new sound palette gives the music a more contemporary flavor.

LISTENING GUIDE: "DON'T WANT TO BE A FOOL"

CD 3:20   **1990s Black Pop** (Luther Vandross and Marcus Miller; performed by Vandross, vocal)

0:00	Instrumental introduction. Notice two layers of melodic riffs.
0:10	1st verse, part 1
	No steady timekeeping under Vandross; mostly sustained chords.
	Love, what have you done . . .
0:30	1st verse, part 2
	Bass and more percussion sounds added.
	I once believed . . .
0:50	Chorus, part 1
	Buildup to title phrase.
	Each time around . . .
	Chorus, part 2
	Title phrase riff.
	I just don't want . . .
1:30	Instrumental interlude.
1:41	2nd verse, part 1
	Backup vocals preview the hook ("he doesn't feel the shame").
	Whenever a fool's in love . . .
2:01	2nd verse, part 2
	Richer texture than the 1st verse.
	He looks at love . . .

The other major change had to do with rhythm. By the beginning of the eighties, 16-beat rhythms were the norm throughout popular music, and especially black music, as we heard in both dance music and rap. The most obvious difference between 16-beat and rock rhythms has been the greater activity: 16-beat rhythms are busier. At comparable tempos, however, they also offer many more opportunities for rhythmic play simply because there are so many more combinations of sound and silence.

We hear all of this in Luther Vandross's "Don't Want to Be a Fool," a track from his successful 1991 album, *Power of Love*. Like so many black pop singers, Vandross (b. 1951) grew up singing gospel. He began his career largely out of the limelight, composing jingles and doing session work as a backup singer for numerous top acts. A guest appearance on an album by Change, *The Glow of Love* (1980) led to a recording contract and jumpstarted his solo career. By the middle of the decade, he had become one of the most prominent of the new generation of black pop singers.

"Don't Want to Be a Fool" shows the innovations in rhythm and instrumentation right from the start. The introduction and the first phrase of the verse have almost no timekeeping from percussion instruments; we hear mainly electronic keyboards and Luther's voice. Things get busier as the song builds to the refrain. By the refrain the fast rhythm is present but spread out among several different percussion sounds. The bass line moves occasionally in these quicker rhythms, but there is never a time when the 16-beat rhythm is hammered out, as it so often is in rap and dance music. Indeed, the heart of the song—Luther's vocal, the background vocals, and the background instrumental harmony and melodic riffs—is in the eight-beat rhythm of a rock song for the most part.

CD 3:20

"Don't Want to Be a Fool," Luther Vandross and Marcus Miller (1991). Vandross, vocal.

2:24	Chorus, part 1
	Buildup to title phrase
	Next time around . . .
	Chorus, part 2
	Title phrase riff.
	I just don't want . . .
3:04	Bridge
	Intense moment: high register, rapid exchanges between lead and backup vocals.
	(No way . . .)
3:24	Chorus, part 1
	New, more active version of the transition to the hook.
	(I can't love anybody . . .)
	Chorus, part 2
	Title phrase riff.
	I just don't want . . .
4:05	Tag. Gentle fade-out.
	Never, never again . . .

This combination of the two rhythmic levels—eight- and 16-beat rhythms—plus the more implicit approach to timekeeping seems to match the mood of the song better than the more explicit, active rhythms of dance music. It would be harder to focus on the words and the story they're telling if they had to compete with insistent dance rhythms.

STYLE PROFILE

"DON'T WANT TO BE A FOOL" (1990s BLACK POP)

Rhythm	*Moderately slow tempo. Strong backbeat (once the song is well under way). Free 16-beat rhythms layered over a steady rock beat; most are syncopated.*
Melody	*The title phrase hook is a simple, catchy riff. Phrases in the verse are moderate in length with pauses in between. The verse develops nicely from the opening phrase. Fast dialogue in the bridge.*
Instrumentation (timbre)	*Lead and backup singers, electric bass, guitar, electronic keyboard, string, and percussion sounds.*
Performance style	*Vandross has a rich, expressive, wide-ranging voice with strong gospel overtones. Lead and backup vocals also gospel inspired.*
Dynamics	*Moderate, building to the title phrase each time through the form.*
Harmony	*I-IV-V enriched by harmonic excursions to other keys.*
Texture	*Active, open texture with multiple layers: several percussion parts, bass, sustained stringlike sounds, mid- and mid-upper-range riffs and melodic fragments in keyboards and guitar. Considerable variation from section to section. Gradual increase in layers to title phrase hook.*
Form	*Classic Motown form: two-part verse, chorus composed of buildup (transition) to hook, plus a "bridge" (identified this way on liner notes), which is the most intense section of the song.*

Key Points

The music of romance	*Song continues and updates the black romantic song tradition of doo-wop and Motown.*
Updating Motown: the formula for love music	*A more expansive version of a classic Motown **verse/chorus form**.*
Updating Motown: an electronic sound world	*Electronic counterparts to most conventional instrumental sounds, plus new timbres (such as bell-like sounds) update Motown/seventies black pop accompaniment.*
Updating Motown: rhythms	*Strong backbeat and discreet rock beat most of the time underpin other freer, more active and syncopated rhythms.*

Terms to Know

verse/chorus form

We can hear this rhythm as a more sophisticated continuation of the rhythms in the black pop of the sixties and the seventies. Recall that one of Motown's innovations was a more implicit approach to rock and shuffle rhythms: the bass was strong but free, while the mid-range timekeeping was very much in the background: the song still had a great beat, but rhythm did not overpower the melody and the rich accompaniment. The rhythms heard in "I Don't Want to Be a Fool" take this innovation several steps further.

Like the black romantic music of the seventies, the romantic music of the eighties and nineties was a mature music, for a generally older audience. It held on to love, that most persistent of themes, and the musical values that had expressed it for generations—tuneful melodies, rich harmony and backgrounds, foot-tapping but noninvasive rhythms—while updating its sounds and rhythmic strategies. In this way it—along with smooth jazz, its instrumental counterpart—retained its niche in the marketplace.

RESTORING ROCK'S CONSCIENCE

Rock and soul provided the soundtrack for the social protest of the sixties. These strong musical voices were an integral part of the movement that transformed society. In the seventies it seemed that "we" disappeared and "me" took over: the collective identity and energy of the sixties mutated into a more self-oriented set of attitudes.

In the eighties rock and rhythm and blues rediscovered its conscience and its sense of social significance. This happened on several levels. One was a series of benefit concerts and recording sessions. Among them were the all-star USA for Africa, which produced the 1985 single and video "We Are the World"; Band Aid and Live Aid, the U.K. counterpart to USA for Africa, which produced its own hit single, "Do They Know It's Christmas?/Feed the World"; and John Mellencamp's Farm Aid.

A second was the evocation of the glory days of the sixties in the work of a new generation of singer-songwriters like Tracy Chapman, Suzanne Vega, Tori Amos, and Ani DiFranco. A third was a punk-inspired return to the relative simplicity and meaningfulness of sixties rock, as heard in the music of early alternative bands like R.E.M. Other acts continued to produce music that made a statement: Bruce Springsteen's music stands out in this regard.

U2. If any band epitomized the return to social awareness, it would be the Irish group U2. Formed in 1977 U2 comprises vocalist Bono (born Paul Hewson in 1960), guitarist The Edge (born David Evans in 1961), bassist Adam Clayton (b. 1960), and drummer Larry Mullen (b. 1961). By the early eighties, they had become a significant act in Europe; success in the States soon followed. Early hits like "Gloria" (1982) made their position clear; appearances by band members at Band Aid and Live Aid concerts further strengthened their association with significant causes.

Brian Eno began producing their albums in 1984, and that collaboration would extend into the nineties. He was able to enhance their sound, giving it a polish and a distinctiveness that would set it apart from every other eighties band and make U2 one of the truly significant bands of the decade.

Their best work from the eighties amply demonstrates how powerful rock can be when message and music are on the same page. It is one thing to embed a powerful message in the lyric of a song; it is a much bigger step to have the message resonate in every aspect of the music.

With their 1983 album *War,* U2 had developed a new, serious rock sound for the eighties. Sometimes the musical message is overt: gunshots from drummer Larry Mullen resound through "Sunday Bloody Sunday," a lament for the victims of the never-ending civil war in Ireland. But it was more than that. The group, especially after their association with Brian Eno, developed a big, rich sound that sounded important. It worked well behind both the songs with socially aware lyrics, such as "Pride (In the Name of Love)," a 1984 tribute to Martin

U2, "Where the Streets Have No Name"

Luther King Jr., and those with more-personal statements, such as "Where the Streets Have No Name," a track from the 1987 Grammy-winning album *The Joshua Tree*.

The key components of this sound are striking contrasts in range and speed as well as insistent, subtly varied rhythms. The contrast in range comes both from The Edge and Eno. The Edge plays rhythm guitar–like patterns—fast, repeated chords—in a range that is well above the standard range. Most rhythm guitar parts are below the vocal line; The Edge's patterns are typically at or above Bono's quite high vocal range. As a result, there is a lot of distance between bass and guitar—or guitars; overdubbing is the norm. This gives the sound a spaciousness that typical rock songs don't have.

A second contrast is between fast and slow. Typically, both the drums and the guitar insistently mark 16-beat rhythms, especially in climactic passages; but the rhythm of the melody is slow as are the chord rhythms and the occasional sustained sounds. Again, this strong contrast imparts a bigness to the sound.

U2's approach to rhythmic play is subtle. We are most aware of the insistent rhythms from all three instruments: guitar, bass, and drums. The guitar part is almost always fast. The bass moves more slowly, and the drumming is often both fast and slow simultaneously. The Edge embeds asymmetrical patterns, which are usually built from slightly varied chords, into his fast-moving part. This resembles in principle minimalist-style paintings, which at first glance seem to be simply a solid color but which on closer inspection reveal subtle variations in hue and texture that make the surface more vibrant and distinctive.

Bono has a marvelous sense of pacing. The basic melody seems straightforward rhythmically, and it usually moves at a speed between the two extremes. But Bono anticipates a little here or holds back a little there, so that the flow is not mindlessly metrical.

This is not funky music; there isn't the kind of obvious rhythmic play that one hears in southern rock, for example. And for good reason: the good-time feel of a great rock groove would undermine the seriousness of intent; it would be in conflict with the intense sound of Bono's singing. Instead, words and music work together: Bono's singing, the bigness of the sound, the subtle timing and pattern variation, and the deep contrasts—all amplify the sense of the lyric. No one else sounded quite like this, and only Springsteen stirred the same kind of admiration.

This happy marriage of message and music gave U2 a status that few rock-era acts have achieved. Their success comes in part from transcending rock's most basic attraction: the beat. Instead, they fused the edge and blatant rhythms of punk with the high activity of disco and postdisco dance music. By integrating this rhythmic approach into a spacious sound environment, they were able to communicate serious messages in both words and music. It was a significant new direction for rock.

ALTERNATIVES

The outside/inside story of popular music is a cross between David and Goliath and Jonah and the whale. Whether it's four fellows sitting around a hotel room deciding to become a minstrel troupe (the Virginia Minstrels), ragtime pianists playing in bars and bordellos, jazz bands playing speakeasies, fiddlers straight out of the hills selling magic elixirs between songs, Woody Guthrie on the road, bop musicians playing their music in dingy clubs, blues musicians plying their trade in juke joints, R&B bands packing in a car to drive from gig to gig and independent record companies recording them and selling singles from the trunks of cars, folkies singing protest songs in Greenwich Village cafés, or punk bands sweating through a set at CBGB—new movements start out small and on the fringes. They're the Davids.

The Goliath is, of course, the established structure: not only the music business but also societal attitudes. They battle, and at first it seems like no contest: it's all Goliath. But as the marginal style gains a following, Goliath morphs into the whale and swallows David, who has become Jonah.

The tension between inside and outside has played out on several levels. There is the matter of social acceptance. Outsider styles have invariably gotten a chilly reception from the musical establishment: typically the powers-that-be denigrate or ignore these styles, those who create them, and those who support them. Money is on the side of the establishment; musicians and the people behind them usually scuffle.

When the second half of the story begins—that is, when the establishment starts co-opting the outsider style—two other tensions emerge. The first is musical: whether to remain true to one's roots or artistic vision or adapt it by blending it with more-familiar material. One finds this issue in eighties heavy metal: bands had to decide whether to become more mainstream to attain popular success (Van Halen, Def Leppard, Guns N' Roses) or try to preserve the purity of the genre (Metallica, Motörhead, Pantera). The second is its corollary: whether to remain true to the core audience that has supported the music or abandon them in search of fame and fortune—effectively, to sell out.

There were three major "outsider" movements in the eighties. Each grew out of an outsider style of the late seventies. Techno was the underground reverberation of disco. Rap came out of funk and reggae. The third, alternative, was a continuation and expansion of punk.

Alternative Rock

The elevator-trip version of alternative rock: In the sixties rock mattered; in the seventies it sold out—except for punk; in the eighties alternative bands mattered; in the nineties they sold out.

Such a simple paradigm cannot but distort the reality of the situation. Integrity is not incompatible with popular success, as the Beatles and many other acts have demonstrated. Nor is all pop necessarily bad. But there was no question that the bottom-line mentality of the major players in the music business has made mainstream pop more calculating and less daring. In this respect the paradigm rings true.

What the paradigm does describe with greater accuracy is the "us versus them" attitude of those who inhabited the world of alternative rock. Those who created alternative rock and those who supported it believed passionately that their music mattered. For them rock was a way of life, as it had been in the sixties.

Control was the key. Bands sought the artistic freedom to make the music they wanted to make, uncorrupted by a corporate mindset. In support of this goal, a self-contained world developed: small, independent record companies; venues that held hundreds instead of thousands; a support system of critics, fanzines, college radio stations, and small-time promoters; and—above all—the fans. It was a grassroots movement to restore integrity and importance to rock.

Because it started out on such a small scale, the world was far more personal. Fans, writers, and others who supported the music felt a sense of ownership. Usually, they had gone the extra mile or two to seek out bands to follow. They bought their recordings. Perhaps they had gotten to know members of the band, done some of the grunt work, or written for a fanzine.

The sense of connection went beyond the music: as the Minutemen, one of the pioneer alternative bands, sang, "Our band could be your life."

So when a band caught on—signed with a major label; played on big, well-organized tours; made videos; appeared on MTV—they felt betrayed. Success was also a concern for the musicians: Kurt Cobain was troubled by the new fan base Nirvana acquired with *Nevermind*. He didn't feel the same connection with them as he did with those who supported Nirvana before their breakthrough.

Ultimately, however, the only meaningful question should have been whether the band's music changed as a result of their success.

There is some irony in the fact that "rock that mattered" became an alternative to mainstream music, rather than the heart of it, in less than two decades. Even though many of the sixties artists whose music mattered the most—from Dylan and the Who through Lou Reed, Janis Joplin, and Jim Morrison—were never mainstays on the charts, there was a sense of common purpose between them and acts, such as the Beatles and the Rolling Stones, who did have a real pop presence. Moreover, they had the support of those behind the scenes, from major label contracts to free-form radio and festivals like Woodstock.

That was not the case in the eighties. For the most part, the mainstream had evolved away from this change-the-world attitude. Acts like Springsteen and U2—acts that said something important to a lot of people—were the exception, not the rule. Most of the other integrity-first bands were simply an alternative to the mainstream.

Musically, alternative rock has been defined as much by what it isn't as by what it is. It isn't mainstream pop—or at least it wasn't until 1991. The earliest alternative bands—the Replacements, Sonic Youth, Hüsker Dü—built their attitude and their sound on punk. Most projected a sense of alienation. Tempos were fast, rhythms were busy, and volume was generally loud—and sounded louder because of the small spaces in which they played. The instrumentation was that of a typical nuclear rock band: a guitar or two, bass, and drums. Beyond that, and the fact that bands flew under the radar of big music, there was little common ground. *Alternative* was an umbrella term for the music and the culture that continued to reverberate from punk.

Nirvana: Alternative Breaks Through

The pivotal song in the history of alternative rock was Nirvana's "Smells Like Teen Spirit" from their 1991 album, *Nevermind*. For this recording Nirvana consisted of singer-guitarist Kurt Cobain (1967–1994), bassist Chris Novoselic (b. 1965), and drummer Dave Grohl (b. 1969). Grohl replaced the drummers on their first album *Bleach* (1989), which the group made for $600. In the wake of its surprising success, Nirvana signed with Geffen Records. As a result, *Nevermind* was a far more elaborately produced album.

The album soared to number 1, dethroning Michael Jackson, whose *Dangerous* album had been on top of the charts. "Smells Like Teen Spirit" got incessant airplay from MTV. All of a sudden the nineties had an anthem: it is still among the best-known songs of the decade. Alternative had crossed over.

Nirvana's particular brand of alternative was called grunge. **Grunge** fused punk disaffection with the power and distortion of heavy metal. Like so many other alternative styles, it started on the fringes—literally: Cobain and Novoselic formed Nirvana in Aberdeen, Washington. Aberdeen is a coastal city—the fringe of North America. It is a gray place; there is nothing to stop the fog that rolls in much of the time. The group's first single appeared on one of the many **indie** labels: the appropriately named Sub-Pop, which was based in Seattle. Nirvana's sudden success made Seattle the mecca for grunge, but the sound had already surfaced in several locations around the United States.

Nirvana, "Smells Like Teen Spirit"

In retrospect it is easy to understand the enormous appeal of "Smells Like Teen Spirit," especially to its target audience: angry young people who were not ready to buy into the system. The lyrics jerk from image to idea like a trigger-happy video editor. Their power comes not from their coherence but from the jarring juxtapositions—*mulatto, albino, mosquito, libido; hello, how low.*

The music amplifies this sense of dislocation. The song begins with a distinctive four-chord pattern. It is barely amplified; it sounds almost as if Cobain is trying it out for a song he's writing. Suddenly, we hear the same riff, this time with the whole band in heavy metal mode. Just as suddenly, the middle falls out—we are left with just bass, simple drum timekeeping, and a haunting two-note riff, which serves as an introduction to the verse; it continues underneath Cobain's singing. The two-note riff speeds up under "hello/how low." The two-note vocal riff that sets "hello" then becomes the raw melodic material for the climactic section of the refrain. Here Cobain sings as if his throat is being ripped out. A short instrumental interlude, which interrupts the four-chord progression, bridges the refrain and the verse that follows.

We hear this same sequence of events, then a loud instrumental version of the verse and the "hello" section. Instead of the refrain, however, the song shifts to a third verse; we hear the entire verse/bridge/refrain sequence again, followed by primal screams on the word "denial."

"Smells Like Teen Spirit" is a dark song. Everything about it conveys that message; its enormous impact comes in part from the reinforcement of this mood on so many levels. The chord progression does not follow a well-established path; because of this we respond more to its rise and fall. It is like a hole that one cannot climb out of: every time the band arrives at the fourth and highest chord, they drop back down. Because the bass line/outline runs through almost all of the song, despite all of the contrasts it seems to suggest a depressed state of mind that's impossible to shake. In this context the instrumental break following the refrain sounds absolutely demonic; it is really, purposefully ugly, even mocking.

The big innovation—and perhaps the biggest stroke of genius—is the almost schizophrenic shift from section to section. Nirvana creates sharply defined sound worlds within each section of the song. They are haunting, mocking, and angry in turn. They create sharp contrasts from section to section: the kind one would more likely encounter between one song and the next, rather than within a song. When combined with the relentless chord progression and the repetition of the two two-note melodic fragments, they project a mood of utter despair: one can rage against the wind—or the machine—or fall into an almost apathetic state, but it is impossible to shake off the dark mood.

"Smells Like Teen Spirit" is a remarkable synthesis of several different, almost contradictory elements. The melodic material, especially the instrumental hooks, the "hello" section, and the vocal refrain, embed themselves in the listener's ear; they offer immediate points of entry. At the same time, they don't sound like music calculated to be appealing—they seem to be a direct expression of the mood of the song; that they are catchy at the same time is a bonus.

The heavy metal power chords and distortion pack a terrific punch, even more than usual because they contrast with the more austere sections. With this, the uncompromising tunefulness, the austerely beautiful sound worlds—all sharply contrasting yet ultimately integrated into a bleak portrayal of the darkest depression—it is easy to understand why "Smells Like Teen Spirit" was the song of the nineties. And it makes Cobain's subsequent suicide even harder to take; it is as if he let us into his mind so that we can feel his despair.

Especially since Nirvana's emergence, alternative rock has been a much more economically viable alternative. The interest of major labels, the stronger market position of indie labels (shades of the late forties and fifties!), the Internet, and the enterprising spirit of so many acts—Ani DiFranco has been a role model here—have seen alternative and other outsider styles become very much a part of the contemporary music scene.

Not surprisingly, "Smells Like Teen Spirit," and Nirvana's music in general, had a major influence on other alternative bands. One aspect of Nirvana's style that caught on quickly was the abrupt contrast within sections. Many alternative bands became adept at re-creating a wide range of styles; they displayed this mastery within songs as well as across them. We explore a fine example of this in the next section.

HIGH BROW/LOW BROW: TWO PERSPECTIVES ON 1990s ROCK

In the spring of 1993, the British band Radiohead released their first album, *Pablo Honey*. At first the album did better in the United States than in the United Kingdom, mainly because the single "Creep" received a lot of airplay on alternative radio stations. The band's next album, *The Bends* (1995), earned them elite status: critics mentioned Radiohead in the same breath as the Beatles and U2. Fans looked forward to their subsequent albums with the kind of anticipation that the Beatles had enjoyed. Each release promised something really new—something to stretch the ear and the mind.

The Dave Matthews Band (DMB) also recorded their first album in 1993. It was drawn from a live performance and issued on the group's own label, Bama Rags. From start to finish, it showed the kind of energy and enterprise for which the band is famous. It sold well enough that the band could choose with which of the majors they would sign: they opted for RCA (now BMG, and there are rumors of yet another big merger). By the end of the decade, their albums started at the top of the charts. In the fall of 2003, they played to a crowd of 85,000 in New York's Central Park to raise money for the New York City school system.

The two bands have some common ground. Both have enjoyed sustained success at the highest level. Both make their home base in a university town: Oxford, England, for Radiohead and Charlottesville, Virginia, for the Dave Matthews Band. Both have kept the same personnel through their long run. Both brought fresh sounds into nineties music: Radiohead mainly through imagination, and Dave Matthews mainly through instrumentation and improvisation.

The differences between them are more striking. Radiohead took their name from "Radio Head," a song from the Talking Heads' 1986 album *True Stories*. The song blends disparate influences (reggae rhythms, accordion) into a "brave new (musical) world." This seems to presage the path that Radiohead has chosen. By contrast the Dave Matthews Band is a WYSIWYG-type name: Dave Matthews and four others. Its simplicity harks back to the fifties, when acts were identified by their names: Elvis, Jerry Lee Lewis, Buddy Holly, Chuck Berry. Together they epitomize the yin and yang of rock in the nineties. We explore this next.

Radiohead

The five members of Radiohead—bassist Colin Greenwood (b. 1969); his brother Jon (b. 1971), who plays guitar and keyboards; drummer Phil Selway (b. 1967); singer-guitarist Ed O'Brien (b. 1968); and lead vocalist and guitarist Thom Yorke (b. 1968)—formed the group while attending Abingdon School in Oxford, a private school that dates back to the twelfth century. They dissolved for several years while band members attended different universities, then came together again; they signed their first record deal in 1991.

Their first album made it quite clear that the group would find their own direction. The album name, *Pablo Honey,* came from a bit by the Jerky Boys, a comedy group whose CDs consist of irritatingly funny phone calls. "Creep," the single that got them noticed, is very much in the spirit of the times: it is Buddy Holly, deeply depressed. Musically, however, it does little to predict the group's future.

The alienation that marked Radiohead's early work becomes even more pronounced in subsequent albums. This is apparent before the first sound: the liner notes for *OK Computer* (1997) contain the lyrics displayed almost randomly amid collagelike images. Both words and images are hard to decode. *Kid A* (2000) is even more frugal with content: there are simply fragments of images and no lyrics. It is as if the group is challenging its audience: we have something of value to say to you, but you have to work hard to discover what it is. This attitude extends to their music, which is among the most distinctive new sounds of the nineties.

Their work contains conflicts and discontinuities within the words, within the music, and between the words and the music; these demand that listeners engage with the song in more than a casual way. In particular, the music is complex and rich enough—even though it is also quite accessible—to admit multiple levels of meaning. Not since the Beatles' demise has a group blended accessibility, challenge, sound imagination, and sound variety so artfully. This is rock aspiring to significance.

The Dave Matthews Band

In 1986 Dave Matthews (b. 1967) moved to Charlottesville, Virginia. He is from South Africa, but his parents moved to New York in 1969. By the end of the eighties, he was tending bar in a jazz club, admiring musicians like saxophonist LeRoi Moore and keeping his music to himself. After a trip home to South Africa, he returned to Charlottesville and decided to record some songs that he'd written. To help make a demo, he recruited several jazz musicians, several of whom he'd heard in the club where he'd worked. Four of the musicians on his demo— violinist Boyd Tinsley, saxophonist LeRoi Moore, drummer Carter Beauford, and bassist Stefan Lessard—remain the nucleus of his band. Guitarist Tim Reynolds, although not an official band member, has remained a longtime collaborator.

The Dave Matthews Band played their first gig in 1991 and quickly built a large and enthusiastic fan base. This led to more touring and the release of their first record, which went gold without a major label contract. Still more touring led to a deal with RCA; as the new millennium began, DMB was one of the hottest bands in the United States. Each new album has topped the charts. The appearance in Central Park simply confirmed their status as one of the most popular bands of recent years.

The musicians that Matthews chose for his band set it apart from so many other bands on the outside looking in. It has the guitar/bass/drums nucleus, but both Beauford and Lessard are skilled jazz musicians who brought a jazzlike freedom to their playing. The two lead instruments, saxophone and violin, are the trademark solo instruments of rhythm and blues and country music, respectively. Both get plenty of space to solo. The influence of jazz, not only in the instrumental interludes but also in the interplay of the rhythm section, plus the R&B and country connections, give the Dave Matthews Band an all-American sound.

Summary

If the music of Radiohead evoked the experimentation and boldness of the sixties, the music of the Dave Matthews Band reminds us of rock and roll—the time when the music was fresh and fun and had a great new beat. Both reverberate with the energy of the sixties, when rock simultaneously solidified its core and stretched its boundaries.

Their complementary relationship updates several of the themes in previous chapters. There is the elitist/populist polarity, which seems to emerge from the difference in cultural heritage. The United Kingdom has been home to the Beatles, the Who, David Bowie, Led Zeppelin, art rock, and U2. The United States has produced Bob Dylan, Creedence Clearwater Revival, the Grateful Dead, Bruce Springsteen, and Southern rock. Although Dave Matthews is South African by birth, he grew up in the States. For the better part of two decades, his home base has been in the South. His music seems to build on that special blend of R&B, country, and rock that we noted as present in the music of Lynyrd Skynyrd and other southern rock bands, infusing it with the spontaneity and inventiveness of jazz.

Radiohead epitomizes craft and imagination. In their complexity and sonic imagination, they are closer to classical compositions than pop songs. By contrast the Dave Matthews Band lives as a live act. They tour relentlessly, and they thrive on it; even the studio recordings seem to ring with crowd noise.

We are at the end of a long evolutionary cycle. Recall that the modern era lasted about fifty years, from the 1910s through the early '60s. From an evolutionary point of view, the rock era may well be coming to a close. Certainly, it is harder now to develop a genuinely new voice than it was forty years ago, when the Beatles and Brian Wilson were slugging it out in the studio. Nevertheless, both Radiohead and Dave Matthews have found new ways of synthesizing existing ideas and materials; it helps explain why they continue to prosper as they enter their second decade in the public eye.

WORLD MUSIC

We live in a musically extraordinary time. For the first time in the history of civilization, there is a universal expressive language. It has long been said that music is the universal language. There is some truth to that: the fact that audiences in Beijing can appreciate the music of Beethoven and audiences in London can enjoy the music of Ravi Shankar suggests that music has the power to transcend geographical and cultural boundaries.

This kind of universality, however, is akin to the study of Latin or classical Greek. Both classical music and classical Indian music are long-established traditions. In western culture, "classical" music is largely a fixed or, at best, a slowly evolving repertoire. Beethoven has been dead for almost 200 years. While performances bring his music to life, they do not change what he wrote (travesties like Walter Murphy's "A Fifth of Beethoven" notwithstanding) or add to his output. Beethoven's music may speak to nonwestern listeners, but it is not changed in the process.

By contrast, contemporary popular music is a living musical language. It is not just that Malaysians enjoy Michael Jackson or that Russians respond to Radiohead. It is that regional dialects of contemporary music are emerging around the world—by combining electronic resources and the international (U.S./U.K.) rock/R&B tradition with local music—and that artists from around the world are coming together to make new kinds of music by combining musical elements from different regions.

The Roots of the World Music Movement

The global music of the past twenty years has grown out of a movement that, in the United States, dates back to the early fifties in the music of the Weavers. Among their biggest hits were songs from Israel ("Tzena, Tzena, Tzena") and South Africa ("Wimoweh"). Later in the decade, Harry Belafonte would enjoy comparable success with his versions of calypso songs like "Banana Boat (Day-O)." Although their music doesn't sound much like authentic versions of the songs, their advocacy of folk music from then-exotic locales and their effort to capture something of its spirit played a large part in creating the open-minded attitude that has characterized rock-era music. Belafonte also played a key role in introducing South African singer Miriam Makeba to U.S. audiences. She would enjoy a long run in the sixties, but her success did not lead to widespread interest in South African music.

Brazilian music and the Beatles played a big part in expanding the popular-music world view. Brazilian music was an early example of an international/regional fusion: jazz met samba and returned as bossa nova. The Beatles spearheaded a more inclusive musical attitude on several levels. One was the simple fact of their success. The British invasion of the midsixties made rock—and by extension popular music—an international music. It didn't matter that the Beatles were from Liverpool instead of Los Angeles; audiences went wild over them. Bands in Britain and the States listened to and learned from each other: Paul McCartney acknowledged the influence of Motown bassist James Jamerson on his playing and of Bob Dylan on the group's songwriting.

The second level of influence was their musical daring: they were not afraid to try anything or to use music from any source. By their example they nurtured the open-mindedness of rock and folk artists; specifically, they helped bring Indian music to a much wider western audience. George Harrison's flirtation with the sitar and his use of it in songs like "Norwegian Wood" helped open the door for Indian musicians like Ravi Shankar.

Reggae was the most prominent **outsider music** to emerge in the seventies. Like Brazilian music it involved a regional transformation of popular music from the United States. But because of the emigration of Jamaicans to Great Britain and its close association with political and social causes, reggae has had a more powerful impact there than in the States. During the same decade, musicians such as guitarist Ry Cooder branched out from rock and blues into roots music, first within the United States, then throughout the world. And recall from Chapter 13 that the Chieftains began to attract interest outside of Ireland toward the end of the seventies.

The Emergence of World Music

All of this laid the groundwork for the world music movement that flowered during the eighties. Four key ingredients were in place: the development of regional popular styles, deep interest from a few mainstream popular musicians, the drive to reclaim folk heritages around the world, and audience interest.

Reggae was the first of the Afro-centric popular styles to gain notice. It had several advantages: strong musical connections to R&B yet its own distinctive sound; an audience base in England because of the Jamaicans who had moved there; a powerful message; and—perhaps most important—lyrics in English.

Other Afro-centric music followed reggae's path to international recognition. The eighties saw a renewed interest in calypso and soca (soul calypso, a regional/international hybrid that had emerged during the seventies) from Trinidad, zouk and cadence from the French

Caribbean, samba from Brazil, Afro-pop styles like juju from Nigeria and highlife from Ghana (King Sunny Ade was the best-known Nigerian musician), mbadax from Senegal (Youssou N'Dour was the first to achieve international recognition), plus a variety of music from South Africa.

None of these styles has succeeded on the same scale as reggae—many, especially the West African styles, must overcome the language barrier—but all have an international presence. Most were already in existence well before the eighties (calypso, for example, dates back to the teens, highlife to the twenties). Their emergence in the eighties reflects both the changes in the music—a more updated sound through the addition of electronic instruments and the incorporation of elements from the international style—and the interest of musicians and audiences in new sounds.

The complement to regional musicians' blending elements of the international style with their local music was mainstream musicians' bringing these regional styles into their music. Three musicians stand out: Paul Simon, David Byrne, and Peter Gabriel. All played an active role in promoting world music by using regional musicians on their recordings (Ladysmith Black Mambazo with Paul Simon; Youssou N'Dour with Peter Gabriel) and by seeking out and promoting regional music (David Byrne assembled several anthologies of Brazilian music; Gabriel co-founded WOMAD, the world festival of music, art, and dance).

The eighties also saw a revival of folk traditions around the world. Chief among them was Celtic music, but other regional folk and folk/international styles found enthusiastic international audiences: music from Bulgaria (Le Mystère des Voix Bulgares, clarinetist Ivo Papasov), flamenco (the Gipsy Kings), contemporary Native American music, and indigenous Australian music.

Technology and the media played a crucial role in building audiences for this music. Affordable and portable recording equipment made it possible to record music almost anywhere in the world: folk musicians benefited from this, just as rap and techno artists did. Cable television, and especially networks with a global reach (most notably CNN), raised awareness of other cultures. It is the Internet, however, that provided the real breakthrough. Today those with a computer and a decent broadband connection can seek out, read about, and hear music from anywhere in the world without leaving their chair.

World Beat

Today's world music scene is a dizzying array of musical styles. It ranges from traditional music captured on record (Tibetan monks, Bulgarian women's choir) through regional popular musics (soca, juju) to many different kinds of **fusions** (jazzlike blendings of different musics).

Among the most exciting developments is **world beat**, which is not so much a particular style as an attitude: to blend regional and international, old and new, popular and folk into new kinds of music. We sample one, a song by Angélique Kidjo.

In much of the music by African artists who have enjoyed international success, there is something of the atmosphere of a family reunion. It is not so much a coming together of people as of styles and cultures—music from the mother continent meeting up with its American offspring. We hear a fine example of this in the music of Angélique Kidjo. Kidjo (b. 1960) is a native of Benin, a small West African country on the gulf of Guinea. Benin was formerly a French colony, and French is still the official language. Kidjo moved to Paris in 1983 to further her training; at a jazz school there, after giving up on classical vocal training, she discovered singers like Billie Holiday. By 1989 she had a recording contract and a career in Europe. Within a few years, she had become the best-known African female vocalist since Miriam Makeba.

In 1998 Kidjo recorded *Oremi* with several top jazz and R&B musicians—among them saxophonist Branford Marsalis, keyboardist Kenny Kirkland, and guitarist Wah Wah Watson —as well as South African singers and African percussionists. Among the tracks is "Itche Koutche."

The title of the song, which is also the refrain, means "bad behavior" in Yoruba, one of the main languages of Nigeria (the eastern neighbor of Benin). The lyric, written by Kidjo, explains that a woman who is about to introduce her boyfriend to her mom is more interested in finding out how much he makes than whether he loves her. She wrote it to call attention to the differences in attitudes toward relationships between the African and American cultures.

Chances are we won't understand the lyric, but we will understand that a riff is a riff and a groove is a groove on both sides of the ocean. The jazz flavor comes from Marsalis, who cowrote the song. Everyone sounds at home together; only the language, the South African background vocals, and Kidjo's strong voice betray the African element.

It is remarkable how easily Kidjo and her musical associates work together. Although there is certainly an underlying affinity between West African and African American music, there are still pronounced differences between the two style families. One reason for this ease is that Africans sought out the internationally popular music: Kidjo recalls listening to the Beatles and James Brown—indeed Brown's music was better known and better received throughout West Africa than that of any other African American artist.

CD 3:21

"Itche Koutche," Jean Louis Hebrail, Angélique Kidjo, and Branford Marsalis (1998). Kidjo, vocal; and Marsalis, saxophone.

STYLE PROFILE

"ITCHE KOUTCHE" (WORLD MUSIC)

Rhythm	Moderate tempo; 16-beat rhythm with a crisp backbeat; many layers of activity, most of it playing against the time.
Melody	Verselike section and transition: moderate-length phrases with much repetition. Chorus: a repeated riff within a narrow range. Most melodic material is based on the **pentatonic scale**. Saxophone "chorus" is a jazzlike instrumental line: too angular and fast to sing easily.
Instrumentation (timbre)	Three vocal sounds: Kidjo, female backup singers, and male backup singers; soprano saxophone (soprano sax operates in a high register), overdubbed at times; large rhythm section: bass, drums, percussion, guitars, and keyboards, including organ.
Performance style	Kidjo's singing is powerful and hard (no vibrato or soft edges). The male vocal sound is heard throughout sub-Saharan Africa. Percussive sounds from chord instruments, especially **choked guitar** keeping the 16-beat rhythm. Opening "percussion" vocal is a fresh sound.
Dynamics	Moderately loud.
Harmony	Basically one chord throughout the instrumental sections. Alternation of I and IV in the vocal sections.
Texture	Many layers, most in low to mid-upper range (saxophone and organ parts are generally the highest-pitched instruments). Despite many layers, the sound is relatively open because most of the parts are simple riffs or percussion patterns. Melody dominates in vocal and saxophone line sections.

STYLE PROFILE *(cont'd)*

Form *Verse/chorus form with extended instrumental interludes (which also have a verse/chorus–like pattern); however, there is no new text for the verselike section.*

Key Points

"Itche Koutche" *According to Kidjo, the song title means "bad behavior"; she's talking about men's bad behavior.*

World beat music *Here, contemporary world music blends regional elements (language and vocal sounds) with important international styles (R&B and jazz).*

Jazz influence *Marsalis's choruslike line, improvised episodes (especially bass and saxophone), and organ fills show jazz influence.*

Modal melody *Vocal melody and saxophone line are modal, with strong pentatonic orientation.*

Terms to Know

choked guitar	pentatonic scale
fusion	world beat

LISTENING GUIDE: "ITCHE KOUTCHE"

CD 3:21 **World Music** (Jean Louis Hebrail, Angélique Kidjo, and Branford Marsalis; performed by Kidjo, vocal; and Marsalis, saxophone)

0:00 Introduction. Vocal percussive sounds, then vocal "response" figure.
Ou yéyé, o yéyé...

1st Statement of the Form: Two-part instrumental introduction, then verse/transition/chorus

0:12 Instrumental groove: guitars, bass, drums, percussion, and keyboard.
0:23 Jazzlike saxophone line that returns regularly; organ, voices in the background.
0:42 "Verse"
Like the verse in a Motown song, but the text doesn't change.
Oko to fé n'ko...
1:01 Transition
Building to the hook.
Ofé gba owo étan...
1:10 Chorus
Title phrase means "bad behavior."
Itche koutche...

2nd Statement of the Form

1:30 Instrumental: the opening groove returns to the spotlight.
1:39 Jazzlike saxophone line that returns regularly; organ, voices in the background.
1:59 Verse
Same lyric as before.
Oko to fé n'ko...

Summary

Kidjo's song is just the tip of the iceberg. Go almost anywhere in the world and you can hear local/international fusions: J-pop in Japan, trance music from Pakistan, Turkish rock —the possibilities are limitless. In some cases only the language gives away the regional identity; in others—including the example just discussed—regional influences are very much in the forefront.

For many this new musical world has been an exciting development, but not everyone has received these musical fusions warmly. Among them are the purists who consider any type of intermingling of styles a degradation of the native style. One can understand and sympathize with that point of view. A traditional music is a living document of a culture. It helps the people preserve their heritage, and it gives those outside the culture some sense of what it is like. At the same time, most musical traditions are not static; they evolve. Recall that the Carter Family's "Wildwood Flower" started out as a parlor song that found its way into the hills and then back to the city in a cover by Joan Baez. What is different about our time is the rate of change, which is much faster.

It is likely that both directions will flourish: some will work to preserve earlier traditions and succeed; others will make new sounds out of old. There is new enthusiasm for old cultures and their artifacts, largely since the sixties, and it is expressed in numerous ways. In classical music one of the hottest trends has been the re-creation of historically accurate

2:18	Transition
	Ofé gba owo étan...
2:28	Chorus
	Itche koutche...

3rd Statement of the Form: More expansive because of extended instrumental groove

2:48	Extended jam over instrumental groove (bass out at the beginning, then solos).
3:07	Saxophone line returns.
3:26	Verse
	Oko to fé n'ko...
3:46	Transition
	Ofé gba owo étan...
3:55	Chorus
	Itche koutche...

Extended Instrumental Ending

4:15	Instrumental groove: bass solo, then bass/saxophone duet, then saxophone duet and voice-over.
4:53	Saxophone line; Marsalis overdubs a solo on top of the riff; Kidjo joins in on the riff; other voices layer in.
5:32	Groove returns, gradual fade-out, wry ending.

Angélique Kidjo performing with Latin rock guitarist Carlos Santana during the "We Are the Future" charity concert in Rome's ancient Circus Maximus, May 16, 2004. The concert, organized by Quincy Jones (who had overseen "We Are the World" almost twenty years prior) raised money for children's centers in six war-scarred cities.

performances of older music, complete with instruments of the times—"period instruments." In western Europe languages that were almost lost have been resurrected and are now being taught again. Gaelic, Welsh, Cornish, and Manx have made a comeback. So have Breton and Provençal in France, and Catalan and Galacian in Spain. In the United States and Canada, Native Americans have worked to reclaim their heritage and revive their traditions. The western world is, on balance, more sympathetic to cultural diversity than it was fifty years ago, when the phrase *cultural diversity* would probably have received a quizzical look instead of a knowing nod.

At the same time, the impulse to rub out boundaries has never been stronger. Musicians like Wynton and Branford Marsalis, Edgar Meyer, and Keith Jarrett are equally expert in classical and popular styles. The Kronos String Quartet covers Jimi Hendrix, and classical pianist Christopher O'Riley is touring with his versions of Radiohead tracks as I write. Yo-Yo Ma, the leading classical cellist of our time, recorded *Appalachian Waltz* and *Appalachia Journey* with bassist Edgar Meyer and violinist Mark O'Connor (whom we heard in Strength in Numbers in Chapter 13), as well as a song by Antonio Carlos Jobim with top Brazilian musicians.

Couple this with folk/electronic fusions, with Rod Stewart and Queen Latifah becoming the latest rock stars to record pop standards, with Branford Marsalis guesting on Angélique Kidjo's album, and with countless other **cross-pollinations**: the boundaries between genres that seemed so clearly drawn at the beginning of the rock era—classical, pop, Broadway, jazz, folk, and rock and roll—are blurring to the point where it is difficult to locate them.

Both directions are healthy; indeed they complement each other. Together they open up new sound worlds to discover—discoveries that were difficult, if not impossible, a generation ago. The opportunity to do so is truly a blessing.

SOME FINAL THOUGHTS

CD 3:22

"Yarum Praise Song"/"Niles," Fra Fra Tribesmen/ Cornelius Claudio Kreusch (1998). BlackMudSound.

In the first edition of this book, I presented a series of musical examples featuring West African musicians. Among them was "Yarum Praise Song," a field recording of musicians from Ghana. The recording was made before 1970, probably well before; it captures the sound of the traditional music of the Fra Fra tribe, untouched in any obvious way by contemporary music. The point of the excerpt was to show how key features of West African music had found their way into popular music.

I include it here in two versions to make much the same point from a different perspective. The first part of the track is the original field recording. The second part is "Niles," the first track from *Scoop* (1998), a recording by the German jazz pianist Cornelius Claudio Kreusch. Kreusch describes his music, which he calls BlackMudSound, as a blend of world-Afro-jazz-funk and pop. To strengthen the ethnic dimension, he engaged musicians from West Africa, the Caribbean, South America, and the Middle East as well as North American–based jazz players.

"Niles" begins with a sequenced excerpt from "Yarum Praise Song." As the song unfolds, Kreusch layers in other instruments: piano, bass, percussion, whistle, and saxophone. Meanwhile the excerpt runs through the entire song. The key point is this: there is no musical discontinuity. It is as though these obscure men from Ghana are jamming with Kreusch and his group. The inferior quality of the field recording is the only obvious clue that the tribesmen aren't at the recording session.

Kreusch's mix of his fusion music with a Ghanaian field recording is a powerful statement, not because it is an isolated example—which it may be—but because it needn't be. One could sample numerous field recordings like the "Yarum Praise Song" and mix them into much of the music we have heard in this chapter, and they would sound very much at home.

LISTENING GUIDE: "YARUM PRAISE SONG"/"NILES"	
CD 3:22	**World Music Fusion** (Fra Fra Tribesmen/Cornelius Claudio Kreusch; performed by BlackMudSound)
0:00	Fra Fra Tribesmen: shaker, pitched instrument playing a riff, vocal "commentary."
0:07	Pitched instrument settles into a riff, which is repeated with slight variation.
0:37	Original "Yarum Praise Song" fades out; "Niles" begins with the same music.
0:41	Drums enter.
0:45	Bass, then piano overlay a simple three-note riff.
0:55	Whistle, piano improvisation over three-note riff (with sax added) and "Yarum Praise Song" loop.
	The track continues in much the same vein: "Yarum Praise Song" loop, three-note riff repeated regularly, whistle, and piano improvisations followed by brief pause.

Imagine how incongruous the same recording would be with songs from the first part of the century, like "Take Me Out to the Ball Game," or from the previous century, like "Old Folks at Home."

STYLE PROFILE

"YARUM PRAISE SONG"/"NILES" (WORLD MUSIC FUSION)

Rhythm	*Slow tempo; 16-beat rhythm in African excerpt; drummer lays rock beat over it; other rhythms are syncopated or fast-moving lines.*
Melody	*African example has only a simple riff repeated with some variation. "Niles" adds a three-note slow-moving riff, plus a fast, wider-ranging figuration in piano and whistle.*
Instrumentation (timbre)	*"Yarum Praise Song": Unknown pitched instrument, shaker, voice. "Niles": "Yarum" plus drums, bass, saxophone, piano, and high whistle.*
Performance style	*Jazzlike inflection in the piano solo; voice (in background of "Yarum Praise Song") is everyday singing.*
Dynamics	*Moderately soft.*
Harmony	*No chord; grounded over same note throughout.*
Texture	*Distinct layers, first in "Yarum Praise Song," then additionally with bass, piano, and other instruments. Open sound because of sparse activity in most parts.*
Form	*One stream: no internal checkpoints.*

Key Points

Old and new African values	*The shaker rhythm and rifflike figures heard in "Yarum Praise Song" are staples of contemporary popular music.*
World fusion	*Here it comes completely from Kreusch—a true integration of folk and nonfolk music.*
Modal and pentatonic	*Kreusch's piano musings fill in the pentatonic scale used for the African and contemporary riffs to create a **modal** scale.*
Meditating on African music	*"Niles" does not use a standard form (such as verse/chorus form); it simply starts and stops (Kreusch meditating on African music?).*

Terms to Know

cross-pollination

modal

pentatonic scale

What this tells us is the extent to which popular music has evolved from musical styles that were completely European in inspiration (such as Henry Russell's "Woodman, Spare That Tree") to music that is very much in tune and in time with African music.

One of the most remarkable aspects of this evolutionary journey is that no individual or group of individuals seems to have consciously guided the music in this direction. It is as if black Americans have drawn on their collective cell memory throughout the twentieth century to reclaim their African heritage. As society accepts the new music of a generation, African American trailblazers push the music toward a more African sensibility. In this century we have gone from ragtime, syncopated dance music, and swing to rap, techno, and world beat. As we listen to "Niles" and the interplay between the Ghanaian musicians recorded a half century ago and Kreusch and his contemporary musicians, there is a sense that the music not only has moved forward but has come home.

To put all of this in perspective: there was little change in the sound of mainstream popular music between 1800 and 1900. The music of the minstrel show had given popular song a dance beat and a more accessible form. Still, songs from the 1800s and 1900s spoke much the same musical language. By contrast the differences between the waltz songs of the early twentieth century and the music we have just listened to are so profound and so far-reaching that they might as well come from two completely different cultures.

As we have documented throughout this book, the transformation of popular music through the course of the twentieth century has been a gradual yet relentless and surprisingly regular process. There have been periods of significant change: from the midteens to the early thirties, and from the midfifties to the early seventies. And there have been numerous tangents—bop and the jazz that followed from it; heavy metal from the early seventies to the present; the musicals of Stephen Sondheim; newgrass. But there is no denying the end result: a hundred years ago, popular music was mostly about melody. Today it is mostly about rhythm and sound.

This profound change is mainly the product of two century-long developments: the infusion of African elements into the prevailing popular styles and the advances in technology that have revolutionized every aspect of the music business.

It has been a remarkable story.

TERMS TO KNOW

Test your knowledge of this chapter's important terms by defining the following. If you can't recall the meaning of a certain term, refresh your memory by looking up the boldfaced term in the chapter, turning to the Glossary at the back of the book, or working with the flashcards on the *Popular Music in America* Companion Web site: *http://music.wadsworth.com/ campbell_2e*

. . . .

alternative	medley	sample
bottleneck	MIDI	sampling
choked guitar	mix	scratch
cross-pollination	modal	sequencer
electronica	modular form	sequencing
fusion	outsider music	set
grunge	pentatonic scale	techno
hip-hop	percussion	toasting
house music	pizzicato	verse/chorus form
indie	plunger	world beat
loop	rap	

. . . .

I, IV, and V The chords of the blues progression (and many other songs); Roman numerals for 1, 4, and 5. *See* **blues progression**.

12-bar blues form The most widely used form for one chorus of a blues song. It is defined principally by its chord progression, which features I, IV, and V in a consistent pattern over twelve bars: I(1), I(3) / IV(5), I (7) / V(9), I(11). The 12-bar blues form is used in both vocal and instrumental songs. In sung 12-bar blues songs, the typical lyric is a rhymed couplet, with the first line repeated:

I write these words to try to explain the blues	*1st line of couplet*
Yeah, I write these words to try to explain the blues	*1st line of couplet repeated*
Hope these words are something you can use.	*2nd line of couplet, the rhyme*

16-beat rhythm A style beat in which the fastest rhythmic layer moves four times the speed of the beat: 4 times per beat × 4 beats = 16-beat rhythm. First popularized in disco and funk, it has been the most widely used style beat since the early 1980s.

A&R (artists and repertoire) The person in charge of a recording session, who advises the performer(s) on choice of repertoire.

a cappella Singing, usually by a group, without instrumental accompaniment.

AABA form A four-part form in which the first, second, and fourth sections (A) are identical, and the third (B) is different. AABA was the most widely used song form between 1920 and 1955.

ABAC form A four-part form in which the first and third sections (A) are identical, and the second (B) and fourth (C) sections are different from A and from each other. It was the most widely used song form between 1910 and 1925 and was the most common alternative to AABA form after 1925.

accent A musical event that stands out from its neighbors because of a change in one or more musical elements. The most common sources of accent are intensity (the event is louder), duration (longer), density (the event contains more parts), or pitch (higher or lower).

accordion An instrument in which sound is produced by forcing air past reeds through hand-operated bellows. The accordionist changes pitch through either a keyboard or buttons, located at either end of the bellows mechanism.

acoustic instrumentation Instrumentation featuring only acoustic instruments (no amplifiers or electronically generated sounds).

acoustic recording An early recording process in which sound vibrations were transferred directly to the recording medium (cylinder or disc) by means of a large horn or cone. In 1925 it was replaced by electric recording.

Afro-Cuban Cubans of African descent.

alternative An umbrella term for the music and the culture that continued to reverberate from punk. Stylistically, alternative is defined by what it *isn't*—mainstream pop—more than by what it is.

amplification The process of increasing the intensity of a performer's sound by external means.

amplifier A piece of equipment that can increase the strength of an electric signal.

analog synthesizer A synthesizer in which musical variables are controlled by adjusting voltages. In many cases the waveforms generated in this manner were similar (i.e., analogous) to the waveforms of acoustic instruments; hence the designation *analog* synthesizer. Analog synthesizers were used until the early 1980s, when they were gradually replaced.

Anglo-American An American of English, Scottish, Welsh, or Irish ancestry.

AOR (album-oriented radio) A type of FM radio format that emphasized a restricted playlist.

aria An independent vocal solo that is part of a larger work, such as an opera or oratorio.

arpeggio A chord whose pitches are performed one after the other instead of simultaneously. Also called *broken chord.*

art music Music created strictly for concert listening. It serves no functional purpose; its value lies solely in its inherent musical worth. Classical music is, by and large, art music; so is much jazz and some musical theater and rock.

art rock A rock substyle that sought to elevate rock from teen entertainment to artistic statement, often by drawing on or reworking classical compositions (e.g., Emerson, Lake, and Palmer's version of Mussorgsky's *Pictures at an Exhibition*). Art rock was often distinguished by the use of electronic effects and mood music–like textures far removed from the propulsive rhythms of early rock.

art song A setting of a poem of high quality for voice and piano. It has been an established genre in classical music since the early nineteenth century. Rock musicians and their supporters were certainly aware of this classical tradition: concept albums like the Beatles' *Sgt. Pepper* were compared to the song cycles of the classical composers Schubert and Schumann.

ASCAP Stands for *American Society of Composers, Authors, and Publishers;* a membership organization that protects the rights of its members by licensing and distributing royalties for the public performances of their copyrighted works.

backbeat A percussive accent occurring regularly on the second beat of beat pairs: 1 *2* 1 *2* or 1 *2* 3 *4.*

bajo sexto an oversized Mexican twelve-string guitar that typically served as a bass instrument in small groups, or *conjuntos.*

ballad In twentieth-century popular music, a popular song performed at a slow tempo.

bandoneón A button accordion (i.e., buttons used to change pitch in both hands) popular in Argentina.

banjo A four- or five-stringed instrument, with a skin head stretched over a wooden or metal hoop, that is strummed or plucked. It was used principally in minstrel show music, early jazz and syncopated dance music, and old-time music and bluegrass.

bar See *measure.*

bass The generic term for the lowest-pitched instrument in a popular-music ensemble.

bass drum pedal A foot-operated device used to beat a bass drum.

beat (1) The rhythmic quality of a piece of music that invites a physical response ("that song has a good beat"). (2) The (usually) regular marking of time at walking/dancing/moving speed (usually between 72 and 144 beats per second). (3) The rhythmic foundation of a style or substyle, distinguished by the consistent use of regular rhythms and rhythmic patterns: a two-beat, a rock beat, a shuffle beat.

bebop *See* bop.

beguine In American popular music, an Americanized form of the Cuban rumba. It has a similar rhythmic feel but lacks the clave rhythm heard in authentic Afro-Cuban music.

belt A loud, vigorous singing style widely used by singers in musical theater.

bent note A slight alteration of the pitch of a note for expressive purposes. It is used by both singers and instrumentalists, especially in blues and blues-influenced styles.

big band The large jazz ensemble of the swing era that typically contains a complete rhythm section and three horn sections: three to five trumpets, three to five trombones, and four to five saxophones.

big-band swing Swing-era or swing-style music performed by a big band.

Billboard A prominent music business magazine. *Billboard* is the primary source for chart information for a variety of musical styles.

black romantic music A term used here to describe post-1970 love ballads sung by black artists.

blackface Entertainment using white performers who smeared burnt cork on their faces to portray themselves as blacks.

blaxploitation A term used to describe early-seventies films set in the ghetto and featuring black stars, like *Shaft* with Richard Roundtree and *Superfly* with Ron O'Neal.

bluegrass An updated version of country's old-time string band music. Bluegrass developed in the late 1940s under the guidance of mandolinist Bill Monroe.

blue note An African-inspired alteration of certain conventional scale tones.

blues (1) A melancholy mood or feeling ("I've got the blues"). (2) A style characterized principally by highly inflected, often speechlike melodic lines. (3) A song in blues form. *See also* **country blues; electric blues.**

blues form A standard blues form consists of a rhymed couplet, with the first line repeated. Each line lasts four measures, so each couplet is matched to twelve measures of music. Each twelve-measure unit forms one chorus; a typical blues song contains several choruses.

blues progression The defining chord progression of a 12-bar blues. Here is a typical version of the progression, measure by measure:

1	2	3	4	5	6	7	8	9	10	11	12
I	I	I	I	IV	IV	I	I	V	IV	I	I

BMI Stands for *Broadcast Music Incorporated*. BMI was founded in 1939 to license the performing rights of popular musicians excluded by ASCAP, especially jazz, country, and blues musicians.

Bo Diddley beat A distinctive rhythm that is virtually identical to the clave rhythm. *See* clave rhythm.

bodhrán An ancient Irish framedrum, traditionally made with a wooden body and a goat-skin head; it is played with a double-headed stick called a cipín, tipper, or beater. The modern Irish word is pronounced "*bow* [rhymes with *cow*] -rawn."

bones Literally bones, or bonelike sticks, used as a percussion instrument in the minstrel show.

bongos A pair of small single-headed drums played with the hands. They are an integral part of an Afro-Cuban percussion battery.

boogie-woogie A blues piano style characterized by repetitive bass figures, usually in a shuffle rhythm.

book The script for nonmusical sections in a musical theater production.

bop A jazz style that developed in the 1940s, characterized by fast tempos, irregular streams of notes, and considerable rhythmic conflict.

bossa nova A samba-based, jazz-influenced Brazilian popular-song style that became popular in the United States in the early 1960s.

bottleneck Originally the neck of a beer bottle worn over a finger of a guitarist's left hand; when placed in contact with the strings, it produced a sliding or whining sound, ideally suited to accompanying the blues. Later, narrow metal cylinders replaced bottlenecks. Also, used generally to describe a guitar played using a bottleneck or bottleneck-like device. Also called *slide*.

brass bass *See* tuba.

brass section The section including all brass instruments, usually trumpets and trombones.

breakdown An up-tempo fiddle tune for dancing.

bridge (1) A wooden arch that conducts the vibrations of a string instrument to the resonating cavity. (2) The B, or contrasting, section of a song in AABA form.

British invasion A term used to describe the influx of British rock bands in the midsixties, including the Beatles, the Rolling Stones, and the Animals.

broadside A topical text sung to a well-known tune. Broadsides were, in effect, an urban folk music with printed words.

broken chord See *arpeggio*.

brushes Two groups of thin wires bound together to make narrow fans. Brushes are used by percussionists in lieu of sticks when a more delicate sound is desired.

B-side The side of a 78 or 45 rpm record expected to be the less popular side. Also called *flip side*.

burlesques In a minstrel show, humorous parodies of cultivated material.

button accordion An accordion in which both hands change pitch by pressing buttons, rather than keys.

cadenza A place in a musical work where accompaniment stops so that a soloist may improvise (or play in an improvisatory manner), usually in a virtuoso style.

Cajun music The characteristic music of white French-speaking residents of Louisiana.

cakewalk A dance fad of the 1890s; also the music to accompany the dance.

call-and-response A rapid exchange, usually of rifts, between two different timbres: solo voice and guitar; solo voice and choir; or saxophones and trumpets.

calypso The most widely known traditional music of Trinidad.

Celtic music The traditional folk music of Ireland. Celtic bands often feature traditional Irish instruments such as the harp, Uilleann pipes, the bodhrán, and the tin whistle.

cha-cha-cha A Latin dance that became popular in the 1950s. Its name comes from the signature rhythm that ends each phrase.

Charleston The most popular of the vigorous new dances of the early 1920s.

chart A list of the most popular songs during a given time period. Charts have been compiled from sheet music and record sales as well as radio airplay. There are separate charts for different types of music.

choked guitar A playing technique in which the strings are partially depressed to make the strumming more percussive.

chop-chord style In bluegrass, a mandolin accompaniment characterized by a heavy backbeat.

chord A group of pitches considered as a single unit. The notes of a chord may be played simultaneously, or they may be played in a series as an arpeggio.

chord progression A sequence of chords. Many of the chord progressions in popular music follow well-used patterns, such as the chord progressions for "Heart and Soul" and "La Bamba."

choreographer A person who designs dances and dance routines.

chorus (1) A large singing group. (2) In verse/chorus and rock songs, that part of a song in which both melody and lyrics are repeated. (3) In blues and Tin Pan Alley songs, one statement of the melody.

citybilly Someone who performs country music in a more urban (i.e., more mainstream) style.

clarinet A mid- to high-range woodwind instrument. It was the high front-line instrument in New Orleans jazz and a solo instrument in thirties jazz.

classical music Art music by such European composers as Bach, Mozart, Beethoven, and Stravinsky; or music by any composer in the European tradition of music for concert performance.

classic blues The popular blues style of the 1920s, which typically featured a woman singing the blues (e.g., Bessie Smith) accompanied by one or more jazz musicians.

clave rhythm The characteristic rhythm of Afro-Cuban music. It can be represented as:

//X x x X x x X x // x x X x X x x x //

The x's indicate an eight-beat rhythm; X's are accented notes. To create a *reverse* clave rhythm, switch the two measures.

claves Two cylindrical sticks about 1 inch in diameter used to tap out the clave rhythm.

close harmony A singing style in which the other notes of the chords are near in pitch to the melody note, with all parts typically moving in the same rhythm.

collective improvisation An improvisational context in which more than one performer is improvising a melody-like line. Collective improvisation is standard practice in New Orleans jazz, free jazz, and much rock-era jazz fusion.

comping In bop jazz style, chordal accompaniment played in rhythmically irregular or unpredictable patterns.

composition Creating music, especially music of some complexity, to be performed at a later date—as opposed to improvisation, where the music is created at the time of performance. The music is usually notated.

concept album A recording comprising several songs that explore a single theme. The term came into use in the 1960s to describe albums like the Beatles' *Sgt. Pepper.*

concert band A band (woodwinds, brass, and percussion instruments) that performs in a concertlike setting (seated on-stage, in front of an audience) rather than while marching.

conga drum A large (2 feet 6 inches high), cigar-shaped drum, which is open at the bottom and covered by a drum head at the top. It is one of the essential instruments of Afro-Cuban music and has been used in addition to or in place of drum sets during the rock era.

conjunto The Spanish word for a small ensemble.

coon song A turn-of-the-twentieth-century popular-song genre, usually with racially stereotyped lyrics (*coon* is derogatory slang for an African American) and some syncopation.

cornet A trumpetlike instrument that was widely used in military bands and early jazz. It is stockier than the trumpet, and the sound is not as brilliant.

country A commercial form of the music of white southerners, which began with the advent of commercial radio in the early 1920s. The different styles of country music mix elements of the traditional folk music of the South with other popular styles, such as jazz, pop, and rock.

country blues A family of African American folk blues styles that flourished in the rural South. Country blues differs from commercial blues mainly in its accompanying instrument—usually acoustic guitar—and its tendency toward less regular forms.

country rock A hybrid style that merged country music and rock. Country rock developed in the late 1960s, chiefly through the efforts of Gram Parsons.

country rock beat Most characteristically, a strong honky-tonk two-beat combined with a clear, simple rock rhythm.

countrypolitan The country/pop/soft rock combination popularized by Kenny Rogers and others in the 1970s.

cover version A version of a song by someone other than the original artist.

cowbell A cowbell (a bell worn by cows) from which the clapper has been removed. It is widely used in Afro-Cuban music; two cowbells are part of the typical setup for *timbales.*

crooner A male singer who sings with a sweet sound in a conversational, low-key manner. Amplification made crooning possible. Bing Crosby was the most successful of the early crooners.

cross-marketing The practice of using media in tandem so that each helps promote the other. The practice began in the early 1970s, when rock bands toured to promote a newly released recording. Robert Stigwood, producer of *Saturday Night Fever,* was the first to adapt this promotional strategy to film in a big way by using songs from the soundtrack to spark interest in the film.

cross-pollination The stylistic interchange between different musical styles, such as European-derived and African-inspired music.

crossover A term used to identify a song or artist associated with one popularity chart (e.g., rhythm and blues) who attains popularity on another chart. Early in his career, Elvis was the ultimate crossover artist, placing songs on the pop, rhythm-and-blues, and country charts.

cubop A fusion of bop and Latin rhythms. It developed in the late 1940s, primarily under the guidance of trumpeter Dizzy Gillespie.

cymbal A metal, circular plate, with a slightly raised indentation, often mounted on a pole, that, when struck, makes a ringing or bell-like sound.

delineator A black minstrel performer who purported to portray African Americans in an authentic manner. Delineators were popular members of minstrel troupes after the Civil War.

density The measure of the amount of musical activity occurring simultaneously in a composition.

disco A dance music that rose to popularity in the midseventies. Disco songs typically had a relentless beat; a complex rhythmic texture, usually with a 16-beat rhythm; and rich orchestration, typically an augmented rhythm section with horns and strings.

distortion Electronic timbral alteration. In some rock styles, distortion is intentional; intense distortion is the most immediately identifiable feature of heavy metal.

Dixieland jazz *See* New Orleans jazz.

dobro An instrument associated with country music, with the body of an acoustic guitar and a resonating device placed in the sound hole. Like the steel guitar, the dobro is typically played horizontally, and the strings are stopped with a metal bar.

doo-wop A pop-oriented R&B genre that typically featured remakes of popular standards or pop-style originals sung by black vocal groups. Doo-wop died out in the early 1960s with the rise of the girl groups and Motown.

doubling (1) The practice of switching from one instrument to another, e. g., from saxophone to clarinet. (2) Two or more instruments on the same part.

downtown Latin style A watered-down version of Afro-Cuban music intended for the white American market.

drone notes A single note sustained for an extended period of time.

drum kit *See* drum set.

drum set A group of percussion instruments set up so that they can be played by a single performer. The standard drum set includes a bass drum, struck by a pedal operated by the drummer's right foot; a snare drum; two or more tom toms; a hi-hat operated by the drummer's left foot; and two or more suspended cymbals. Also called *drum kit* and *trap set*.

duration The length in time of a musical event.

dynamics Levels or changes in intensity. The dynamic level of a Ramones song is very loud.

eight-beat rhythm A rhythm that divides each beat of a four-beat measure into two equal parts. It is the characteristic rhythmic foundation of rock. Also called *eight-to-the-bar*.

eight-to-the-bar See *eight-beat rhythm.*

electric bass A solid body, guitar-shaped bass instrument. It is tuned like a string bass. The electric bass came into widespread use in popular music around 1960.

electric blues A post–World War II blues style characterized by the use of a full rhythm section, including electric guitar. It is the most popular form of contemporary blues.

electric guitar An electrically amplified guitar. The first electric guitars retained the hollow body of an acoustic guitar and added a pickup to convert the string vibration into an electric signal. By 1960 the solid-body guitar, with no resonating cavity, had emerged as the primary design for electric instruments.

electric piano A keyboard instrument popular in the 1960s and '70s that combines electronic sound generation with a piano-like action. The most popular model was the Fender Rhodes. With the application of microchip technology, digital keyboards have largely replaced electric pianos.

electric recording A recording procedure developed in the 1920s that converts sound into an electric signal before recording and then converts the electric signal back into sound for playback. With its far superior sound quality, it immediately made acoustic recording obsolete.

electric steel guitar Invented in the early 1930s, it soon replaced the dobro as the instrument of choice for lap guitarists.

electronica The umbrella term for a large and varied family of musical styles: house, techno, trance, ambient, jungle, drum and bass, industrial dance, and many more.

endman A comic in a minstrel troupe. Minstrel performers sat in a semicircle on-stage; an endman sat at one end or the other.

event song A song that tells the story of a noteworthy event, often a catastrophic one (e.g., "The Wreck of the Old 97"). Event songs have a long history in folk and country music.

"exchange" rhythm The rhythm created by the call-and-response between sections.

falsetto Head, rather than chest, singing, used by a male singer to extend his range upward.

feedback A partial return of the electric signal from guitar to amplifier, which can cause distortion.

fiddle The informal name given to the violin by folk musicians. Fiddle tunes are the traditional dance tunes played primarily in the southern Appalachians.

flute A metal wind instrument in the shape of a tube. It is open at one end and has a hole at the other that the performer blows across.

folk music Music made by a group of people (e.g., Cajuns, Navahos, or whites from rural Appalachia), mostly without formal musical training, primarily for their own amusement or for the amusement of others in the group. Within the group, folk music is transmitted orally. Within the popular tradition, folk music has also referred to folksongs sung by commercial musicians (e.g., the Kingston Trio) or music with elements of folk style (e.g., the folk rock of the late 1960s).

form The organization of a musical work in time.

four-beat rhythm A rhythmic foundation in which each beat receives equal emphasis; the common rhythmic basis for jazz.

fox trot A popular dance created in the teens by Irene and Vernon Castle. Also, a song with a two-beat rhythmic foundation suitable for dancing the fox trot.

free form Not using a conventional song form.

front line The horns (or other melody-line instruments, such as the vibraphone) in a jazz combo. The term comes from the position of the horn players on the bandstand: they stand in a line in front of the rhythm instruments.

functional music Music created to support some other activity. Dance music, marching music, and exercise music are all functional.

funk An R&B-derived style that developed in the 1970s, primarily under the guidance of George Clinton. It is characterized mainly by dense textures (bands may include eight or more musicians) and complex, often 16-beat rhythms.

funk-pop The style of a few seventies acts that were at home in both funk and black pop styles; fewer still succeeded in blending the two. Earth, Wind & Fire was one of those that did.

fusion A term applied to much of the jazz rock interactions since the 1970s. Fusion often combined the improvisational fluency and harmonic interest of jazz with an eight- or 16-beat rhythmic foundation and a group-oriented, rather than solo, approach.

genre A body of music linked by such features as instrumentation and form. A genre, such as blues, can appear in several different styles.

girl groups A term used to identify the all-female singing groups popular in the early 1960s.

glam rock A rock style of the early 1970s in which theatrical elements—makeup, outlandish dress—were prominent. David Bowie, in his various incarnations, is considered by many to be the major figure in glam rock.

gospel A family of religious music styles: there is white and black gospel music. Black gospel music has had the more profound influence on popular music by far. Created around 1930 by Thomas Dorsey and others, gospel has influenced popular singing, especially rhythm and blues, since the early 1950s.

griot In West African culture, the tribe's healer (witch doctor), historian (preserver of its history in his songs), and, along with the master drummer, most important musician.

groove A good beat, which makes you want to tap your foot and move your body, that is sustained over a long period of time.

grunge A rock substyle that emerged around 1990 that fused punk disaffection with the power and distortion of heavy metal.

guitar A six-stringed instrument that is either strummed or plucked. In popular music guitars come in many forms, both acoustic and electric.

habanera A dance created in Cuba during the early nineteenth century that became popular in both Europe and South America. Its characteristic rhythm resurfaced in the Argentine tango and the cakewalk.

hambone rhythm An African American version of the Afro-Cuban clave rhythm: "shave and a haircut, two bits." Bo Diddley popularized this rhythm in his hit "Bo Diddley." *See also* **clave; patting juba.**

hard country An updated version of honky-tonk style, popular since the late 1960s.

hard rock A family of rock styles characterized by loud dynamic levels; a strong beat; aggressive, blues-influenced vocal styles; and prominent guitar lines, often with distortion and other modifications of the basic sound.

harmony Chords and the study of chord progressions.

heavy metal A hard rock style that developed in the early 1970s. Its most distinctive feature is heavy distortion.

hi-hat A pair of cymbals attached to a vertical stand. A pedal operated by the drummer's left foot brings the cymbals together, then apart. Also called *sock cymbal.*

hillbilly A derogatory term for white rural southerners. *Hillbilly* also identified early country music.

hip-hop A term used to describe the African American culture from which rap emerged. Its artistic expressions include not only rap but also break dancing and graffiti.

honky-tonk (1) A working-class bar. (2) Country music associated with honky-tonks. It developed around 1940 and was distinguished from other country music of the period in its use of drums, a heavy backbeat, and electric guitar.

honky-tonk beat A countrified two-beat: clear *OOM-pah* rhythm with a crisp backbeat.

hook A catchy melodic idea in a rock-era song. It usually comes in the chorus, where it can be repeated frequently.

horn A generic term for wind instruments. The horn section of a funk band, for example, may contain saxophones, trumpets, and trombones.

horse opera A slang expression for a film that featured singing cowboys like Gene Autry and Roy Rogers. The first horse operas appeared on-screen in the 1930s.

house music An early techno style based originally in Chicago; it was a low-budget continuation of disco.

improvisation The act of creating music spontaneously rather than performing a previously learned song the same way every time. Improvisation is one of the key elements in jazz.

indie Slang for *independent;* it refers to small record labels not affiliated with one of the major record companies.

inflection Moment-to-moment changes in dynamic level. Aretha Franklin sings in a highly inflected style.

inspiracion In Afro-Cuban music, the section of the song where percussionists improvise.

instrumentation Literally, the instruments chosen to perform a particular score; broadly, the instrumental and vocal accompaniment for a recording.

intensity The degree of loudness of a musical sound.

interlocutor The straight man in a minstrel show. The interlocutor would sit in the middle of the semicircle and ask questions of the endmen, who would give comic replies.

interpolation The insertion of a song into a musical comedy for which it was not written. Interpolation was common in the early years of musical comedy, when producers would insert a song into a show simply because it was a hit.

interval The sonic distance between two pitches.

jazz A group of popular related styles primarily for listening. Jazz is usually distinguished from the other popular music of an era by greater rhythmic freedom (more syncopation and/or less-insistent beat keeping), extensive improvisation, and more-adventurous harmony. There are two families of jazz styles: those based on a four-beat rhythm and those based on a rock or 16-beat rhythm.

Jazz Age A term reportedly coined by the writer F. Scott Fitzgerald to identify the new spirit of the 1920s.

jazz rock A sixties style that mixed jazz and rock in varying proportions. By the early 1970s, jazz rock was more commonly known as *fusion.*

jubilee choir African American choirs, originally formed from students of newly founded black colleges, who performed spirituals and other sacred music. They were popular in the years following the Civil War.

jump band In the late 1940s, a small band—rhythm section plus a few horns that played a rhythm-and-blues style influenced by big-band swing and electric blues. Saxophonist/vocalist Louis Jordan was a key performer in this style.

kalmiba An African thumb piano.

keyboard A generic term for an instrument—piano, organ, synthesizer—played by depressing keys. It also refers specifically to electronic keyboard instruments, especially synthesizers.

lead guitar The guitarist in a rock band who is playing the melody, the most prominent riff, or a solo.

librettist One who writes text for a sung stage production.

libretto The text for a sung stage production, from opera to musical comedy.

licks Slang term for musical ideas.

loop A short sound file—say, a drum pattern or a bass line—that can be added to a track in a song to supply a rhythm, harmony, riff, or other similar element.

lyricist The person who writes the words for a song.

mainstream A term commonly used to identify the most popular style(s) during a given time period.

mambo A Latin dance fad of the late 1940s and '50s that combined the rhythms of the Afro-Cuban *son* with the horn sounds of big-band jazz.

mandolin A small plucked string instrument of European origin. It is used chiefly in bluegrass.

maracas A percussion instrument made by putting handles on dried, seed-filled gourds; the shaking of seeds against the interior walls makes the distinctive sound.

march Music composed in regularly accented, usually duple meter that is appropriate to accompany marching; a composition in the style of march music.

march form A multisectional form commonly used in marches and march-influenced music, such as rags and early jazz compositions. A standard march typically contains four distinct sections, each of which is repeated. A typical march form: AA/BB// (trio) CC/DD.

march rhythm A steady, obvious *OOM-pah* pattern with beats grouped by two.

mariachi A Mexican ensemble usually containing trumpets, guitars, and violin.

marimba A pitched percussion instrument. It has wooden bars laid out like a piano keyboard, with resonators under each bar. The bars are struck with mallets.

measure A consistent grouping of beats. A waltz has measures containing three beats; a march has measures with two beats. Also called *bar*.

medley A group of songs connected by musical interludes.

melisma Several pitches sung to a single syllable. In popular music melisma has been most widely used by African American musicians, especially blues and gospel-influenced artists.

melodic idea A fragment of melody, often used as a point of departure for longer melodic units.

melodic phrase A standalone unit of melody, longer than a riff, but less than a section.

melody The most musically interesting part of a musical texture. The melody is typically distinguished from other parts by the interest and individuality of its contour and rhythm.

mento The Jamaican popular music of the early 1950s.

microphone A device that converts sound waves into an electric signal. The microphone has been in use in popular music since the 1920s.

MIDI Stands for *Musical Instrument Digital Interface;* a protocol that enables digital devices such as instruments and computers to communicate.

minor blues A blues in a minor key.

minor key A key that uses a minor scale (a different, darker-sounding scale).

minstrel-spiritual A post–Civil War popular-song genre that merged the typical minstrel show song with the African American spiritual.

minstrelsy A form of stage entertainment distinguished by cruel parodies of African Americans. Minstrelsy was popular from the early 1840s to the end of the nineteenth century.

mix A series of songs or dance tracks seamlessly connected by a disc jockey.

mixing The process of integrating the many tracks from a multitrack recording into a finished recording.

modal A term that identifies scales and harmonies different from the conventional scales heard in nineteenth- and early-twentieth-century popular music.

modular form One section in a musical piece that does not necessarily imply what follows.

montuno In Afro-Cuban music, a syncopated accompanying figure, usually played on the piano, that is repeated indefinitely.

Motown Slang for *Detroit.* Also the music produced there in the 1960s and early 1970s, chiefly by Berry Gordy Jr. for his record label of the same name.

Motown sound A consistent set of characteristic style features heard in sixties Motown recordings.

mountain vocal style A term used to describe the vocal style of singers like bluegrass legend Bill Monroe; the "high lonesome sound."

multisectional form Compositions (usually instrumental) with three or more sections. Marches and rags typically use multisectional form.

multitrack recording The process of recording each part of a performance separately, then mixing them into a complete performance. The Beatles, along with their producer George Martin, were among the first to take full advantage of multitrack recording techniques.

musical comedy A form of sung dramatic stage entertainment originally characterized by a lighthearted, loosely organized plot, generally about a contemporary situation familiar to its audience. Since *Show Boat* it has become more substantial musically and dramatically.

musical theater Drama enriched by popular song. Generally refers to musicals that make a serious effort to integrate drama and music, such as *Show Boat* and *Oklahoma!*.

mute (1) A device to dampen or reduce the sound of an instrument, altering it in the process. Brass instrumentalists use a variety of mutes, including such "found" devices as toilet plungers and hats.

Nashville sound A pop-oriented country style that enjoyed a vogue in the late 1950s and early 1960s, featuring sumptuous orchestrations and sweet-voiced singers in place of fiddles and other identifiably country sounds.

neo-traditional A style that offers a new take on an established, or traditional, style.

New Orleans jazz Style of jazz performance based on the early bands that performed in and around New Orleans; revived in the late 1940s, it is based on collective improvisation and quick tempos. The front-line instruments usually include cornet or trumpet, clarinet, and trombone, with a rhythm section partial or complete. Also called *Dixieland jazz*.

new wave The "back to basics" movement within rock beginning in the late 1970s, featuring simplified instrumentation and basic chords and melodies. An early new wave band was the Talking Heads.

newgrass A term used to identify the progressive bluegrass music of the 1970s and beyond.

obbligato A second melody playing under the main melody

octave The interval between two pitches that vibrate in a 2:1 ratio. Pitches that vibrate in such a simple ratio to each other share the same letter name.

old-time music The earliest recorded country music of the 1920s and '30s; refers in general to the style and repertory of older country musicians.

olio The second section of a minstrel show—the variety portion that featured a wide range of unrelated acts, much like the later vaudeville shows.

opera A musical drama in which the entire libretto (text) is sung.

operetta Originally a kind of European musical drama that was less serious than opera, with speech instead of singing between songs, but with more dramatic integrity than musical comedy. Generally, plots told a fairy tale–like story. European operettas were popular in the United States through World War II. *Show Boat* began an American operetta tradition.

oral tradition Elements of a group's culture—songs, stories, and the like—that are passed from generation to generation by singing, talking, or playing, rather than in written form.

outlaw A term that came into use in the 1970s to describe the music of Willie Nelson, Waylon Jennings, and other like-minded country artists who rejected Nashville and its slick production style.

outsider music Music outside the mainstream, i.e., the most popular music of a particular period.

overdubbing The process of recording an additional part onto an existing recording.

parlor song A song to be sung at home in the parlor, like Stephen Foster's "Beautiful Dreamer," popular through most of the nineteenth century. Also called *home songs* and *piano bench music.*

patriotic song A song with a patriotic theme.

patter song A song in which the lyrics proceed at a rapid pace. The operettas of Gilbert and Sullivan include numerous humorous patter songs.

patting juba A practice among slaves in which they tapped out tricky rhythms on their thighs, chests, and other body parts.

payola The practice of record companies' bribing disc jockeys to secure airplay for their records.

pentatonic scale A scale with five notes per octave. Two pentatonic scales are used widely in popular music: the Anglo-American pentatonic scale, heard in minstrel songs (Foster's "Oh, Susanna" begins with such a scale) and some country music; and the African American pentatonic scale, heard in blues and blues-influenced styles.

percussion A family of instruments whose sounds are produced primarily by striking some kind of vibrating medium. There are two branches of the percussion instrument family: instruments with indefinite pitch, like drums and cymbals; and instruments with definite pitch, like marimbas and vibraphones.

performance style The way the musicians sing and play.

piano bench music *See* parlor song.

piano rag A marchlike, syncopated composition for the piano.

pickup A device that connects an acoustic string instrument to an amplifier, allowing the instrument to be amplified directly instead of through a microphone.

pitch The relative highness or lowness of a musical sound, determined by the frequency with which it vibrates.

pizzicato A style of playing a stringed instrument in which the strings are plucked rather than bowed or strummed.

plantation song A minstrel show song that mixed the subject of a minstrel song with the slower, more melodious, and more sentimental parlor song.

playlet A term coined by producers Jerry Leiber and Mike Stoller to refer to a song that told a funny story with serious overtones; Stoller called them "cartoons."

plunger The business end of a toilet plunger, used as a horn mute.

pop-rock A rock-era substyle that grafted elements of rock style onto prerock popular song.

popular-music industry The business establishment surrounding popular music, comprising not only musicians but also managers, record companies, radio stations, music journalists, and music distributors and retail stores.

power chord A chord containing three pitches: a low note, its octave, and a third note in between that vibrates in a ratio of 3:2 with the lower interval. *See also* **tritone**.

power trio A three-man band (guitar, bass, and drums) with a strong solo orientation, especially in live performance.

proto-funk A style that anticipates rhythms and textures of funk.

punk A rock style that emerged in the late 1970s characterized musically by relatively simple instrumentation, rhythms, and production. The Ramones and the Sex Pistols were among the best-known punk bands.

punk/funk/disco fusion Music from the 1980s (e.g., much of Prince's music) that combines the hard edge and drive of punk with the greater rhythmic and textural complexity of funk and the strong beat of disco. Several important new trends resulted from the fusion of two or more styles, such as the punk/funk/disco fusions heard in some eighties pop.

race record A term that came into use in the early 1920s to describe recordings by African American artists intended for sale primarily in the African American community.

ragtime A popular style at the turn of the twentieth century that mixed European forms, harmony, and textures with African-inspired syncopation. Ragtime began as a piano music, but soon the term was applied to any music—song and dance as well as piano music—that had some syncopation.

rap A musical style of the 1980s and '90s characterized by a rhymed text spoken in a heightened voice over a repetitive, mostly rhythmic accompaniment.

rave A huge dance party conducted in a large space: outdoors, an abandoned warehouse, or even a large club. Ecstasy and other "designer" drugs were very much part of the scene.

refrain *See* chorus.

reggae The most widely known Jamaican popular music, it has a distinctive, intoxicating rhythm. It emerged around 1970 in the music of Jimmy Cliff, Bob Marley, and others.

response Typically a riff that "answers" another riff or melodic idea.

reverse clave rhythm A version of the clave rhythm, in which the second half of the pattern comes first.

revue A type of stage entertainment popular in the first third of the century. Revues were topical; they often lampooned prominent public figures. They had a flimsy plot, designed to link—however loosely—a series of songs, dance numbers, and comedy routines.

rhapsody An extended musical composition that does not use a conventional form.

rhymed couplet Two lines of poetry that rhyme.

rhythm The time dimension of music. The cumulative result of musical events as they happen over time.

rhythm and blues (R&B) A term used since the midforties to describe African American popular styles, especially those influenced by blues and/or dance music.

rhythm section The part of a musical group that supplies the rhythmic and harmonic foundation of a performance. Usually includes at least one chord instrument (guitar, piano, or keyboard), a bass instrument, and a percussion instrument (typically the drum set).

rhythmic play Rhythmic events—syncopations, irregular patterns, and the like—that do not line up with the beat.

ride cymbal The cymbal on which a bop or post-bop jazz drummer plays a ride pattern, most commonly *dummmmm, dump a dummmmm. . . .*

riff A short (two to seven pitches), rhythmically interesting melodic idea.

rip In trumpet or trombone playing, a slide up to a high note.

rock (1) An umbrella term to describe the family of styles that share an eight-beat rhythmic foundation. (2) Music made by musicians associated with rock. (Many of the Beatles' songs, for example, do not use a rock beat, but they are classified as rock because they are by the Beatles.)

rock and roll A transitional style that emerged in the midfifties as the precursor of rock.

rock beat Eight evenly spaced sounds per measure (or two per beat)—over a strong backbeat.

rock musical A musical that uses rock rhythms and generally incorporates some of its ideas and attitudes. *Hair* was a prototypical rock musical.

rock steady A Jamaican music popular in the latter part of the 1960s. It effected the transition from ska to reggae.

rockabilly According to Carl Perkins, a country take on rhythm and blues, performed mainly by white Southerners, that combined elements of country music with rock and roll. Rockabilly was most popular in the midfifties.

romantic ballad A popular song with a romantic theme, performed at a slow tempo.

rumba An Afro-Cuban-inspired dance popularized in the United States during the early 1930s.

salsa A term that came into use in the 1960s and '70s to describe an updated form of the mambo. It is now the most popular traditional form of Afro-Cuban music in both the United States and Cuba.

samba The most popular Afro-Brazilian dance music of the twentieth century in Brazil and elsewhere. The samba has been popular in the United States since the early 1930s. The 16-beat rhythms of samba influenced the new jazz and African American popular styles of the 1970s and '80s.

sample A small sound file. There are two basic kinds of samples in common use. One is the recorded sound of a voice or group of voices, an instrument (such as a grand piano) or group of instruments (a violin section), or some other sound. This sound can then be activated through another device. The other main kind of sampling involves lifting short excerpts from existing recordings to use in a new recording, much like a visual artist will use found objects to create a collage or assemblage.

sampling A recording technique used since the early 1980s, in which a short excerpt from an earlier recorded performance is recorded ("sampled") and interpolated into a new recording.

saturated rock rhythm A version of rock rhythm in which all of the main instruments (guitars, bass, and drums) reinforce the eight-beat rhythmic layer. It is prominent in much punk and punk-influenced rock styles.

saxophone A family of keyed brass instruments with clarinet-like mouthpieces. The saxophone came into the United States during the 1920s and has been used extensively in popular music since that time.

scale A conventional arrangement of pitches in a series separated by small intervals. The two most widely used families of scales in popular music are *diatonic scales,* with seven pitches per octave, and *pentatonic scales,* with five pitches per octave.

scat singing A type of wordless singing, usually at a fast tempo, in which the singer uses nonsense syllables in place of lyrics. Typically scat singers imitate instrumentalists.

scratching A sound produced by rotating an LP record back and forth on a turntable while the needle is in a groove. The tone arm picks up the vibration as if the record were spinning. The performer can control both the pitch and the rhythm of the sound produced in this way by the speed and duration of the movement. Scratching is part of the sound world of rap and other African American popular styles of the 1980s and '90s.

sequence Repeating a melodic idea at a higher or lower pitch.

sequencer A device that enables a person to assemble a sound file track by track. Using a sequencer that can store eight tracks, a person can re-create the sound of a band: one track for the bass, another for the rhythm guitar, and so on.

sequencing A recording technique in which an excerpt of music (such as a rhythm track) is recorded several times in succession. When it is played back, it gives an unvarying texture to the accompaniment.

set A group of songs performed by a band or presented by a disc jockey. Popular and jazz musicians play a set of songs, then take an extended break. A DJ may mix songs into a set that provides continuous music for a half hour or more.

sheet music Music in notated form. Popular songs were sold exclusively in sheet music until the advent of recording in the 1890s.

shuffle A four-beat rhythm in which each beat is reinforced with a long/short pattern. Shuffle rhythms were most common in post–World War II jump styles and rhythm and blues.

singer-songwriter A term that came into use around 1970 to describe songwriters who performed their own music. The music of singer-songwriters was generally characterized by an emphasis on melody, a folklike accompaniment, and a relatively low dynamic level.

single A recording containing one song per side (before digital recording) or a single song on a CD.

ska The dominant Jamaican popular music through the first part of the 1960s. The most distinctive feature of ska is a strong afterbeat: a strong, crisp *chunk* on the latter part of each beat.

slide *See* bottleneck.

sock cymbal See *hi-hat.*

soft rock A family of rock styles characterized mainly by sweeter singing styles; more melodious, even Tin Pan Alley–esque vocal lines; richer instrumentation; and a gentle dynamic level. Soft rock blended the emphasis on melody and clear forms of Tin Pan Alley song with an understated rock rhythm.

solid-body electric guitar An electric guitar that does not have a hollow resonating cavity. Without amplification, a solid-body electric guitar makes almost no sound.

son The most characteristic style of Afro-Cuban music, popular in Cuba during the early part of the twentieth century. Some of the Cuban musicians who migrated to New York in the 1930s and '40s blended *son* with big-band swing to produce the mambo.

sonero The lead singer in a *son* band.

song interpreter Singers, like Billie Holiday, Hank Williams, and Frank Sinatra, who transform popular song into personal statements, often thoroughly altering the contour and the rhythm of the melody.

song plugger A publishing-house pianist who could play a new song for a professional singer or a prospective customer.

soul A term used widely in the 1960s by both white and black Americans to describe popular music by African Americans, particularly music, like that of James Brown, marginally influenced by pop or white rock styles.

speakeasy A nightclub in which alcoholic beverages were illegally sold; despite their illegal status, they flourished during Prohibition.

spiritual A kind of religious African American folksong that flourished in the nineteenth century. Spirituals were introduced to white audiences after the Civil War by groups like the Fisk Jubilee Singers.

standard A song that remains popular well after its initial appearance; songs that live on in recordings, films, and live performances.

steel guitar An electric version of the Hawaiian guitar that has been a popular instrument in country music since the mid-1930s. It rests on the performer's knees or on a stand just above the knees. The strings are stopped with a metal bar held in one hand and plucked with the other. A more modern and complex version is the pedal steel guitar, which may have several necks as well as foot-activated pedals and knee-operated levers that allow for changing the pitch or volume.

stop time The periodic interruption of steady timekeeping by the rhythm section.

strain A section of a march or marchlike composition.

stride piano An offshoot of ragtime that typically featured a more complex bass/chord accompaniment and elaborate figuration in the melody.

string band A small group in early country music, consisting mainly of string instruments of various types; fiddle, banjo, and guitar were the most widely used.

string section That part of an orchestra or ensemble containing violins and other string instruments.

strophic A song form in which two or more verses of text are sung to the same melody. A hymn is strophic.

style The set of those common features found in the music of a time, place, culture, or individual.

sweet As opposed to swing, so-called sweet bands played songs in a two-beat rhythm, with little syncopation, slow tempos, and flowing melodies.

sweet soul A term originally used in the seventies to refer to pop-oriented black music.

swing (1) The sense of rhythmic play—the result of various kinds of rhythmic conflict—that characterizes good jazz performance. (2) Music, often jazz or jazz-influenced, based on a clearly marked four-beat rhythm.

swing era The era in popular music extending from about 1935 to 1945 that featured big bands playing swing-based songs.

syncopated dance music A post-ragtime orchestral dance music popular in the 1910s and early '20s, characterized by the use of syncopated rhythms over a two-beat rhythm.

syncopation Accents that come *between* the beats of a regular rhythm, rather than *with* them.

synthesizer A family of electronic instruments in which sounds are produced electronically, either by generating a waveform within the machine or by digitally recording acoustic sounds (e.g., the tones of a piano). Most, but not all, synthesizers are operated by a keyboard.

tag A short section added to the end of the song.

Tambo and Bones Nicknames for the endmen in a minstrel show, so called because one usually played a tambourine and the other a pair of bones.

tambourine A shallow one-headed drum with loose metallic discs at the sides.

tango An Argentine dance seemingly based on the habanera that has been popular in Europe and the United States since the 1910s. In the United States, it was the first of the Latin dance fads.

tango nuevo Literally, *new tango.* A term associated with the music of Astor Piazzolla, who radically transformed the traditional tango.

techno Post-disco dance music in which most or all of the sounds are electronically generated.

Tejano A Texan of Mexican ancestry; something, especially music, connected with Tejano culture.

tempo The speed of the beat.

texture The relationship of the parts in a musical performance.

thumb-brush style An early country guitar style in which the performer plays the melody on the lower strings and, between melody notes, brushes the chords on the upper strings. It was first popularized by Maybelle Carter.

timbales A pair of shallow, single-headed drums tuned to different pitches. Timbales are a customary component of the percussion section of an Afro-Cuban band.

timbre The distinctive tone quality of a voice or an instrument.

Tin Pan Alley A nickname for a section of East 28th Street in New York City, where many music publishers had their offices. Also, the styles of the songs created in the first half of the century for these publishers: a *Tin Pan Alley song* refers to songs by Irving Berlin, George Gershwin, and their contemporaries.

toasting The practice developed by Jamaican disc jockeys of delivering a steady stream of patter. Much of it was topical, even personal: they would pick out, and sometimes pick on, people in the crowd that had gathered around. Toasting is a direct forerunner of rap: both initially featured topical, humorous commentary over pre-existing music.

traditional country vocal sound The flat, nasal, relatively uninflected vocal sound associated with country music.

trap set *See* drum set.

tremolo Time kept in the melody only.

tribute band A cover band that not only performs songs recorded by another band but that also tries to replicate the recording as precisely as possible.

trio (1) A group of three musicians. (2) The second half of a march, rag, and other composition in multisectional form. In a march the melody of the trio is often lyrical.

triplet A division of the beat into three equal parts.

tritone The interval that divides the octave in half. It is the negation of a power chord, which reverberates above and below the main notes. In medieval times the tritone was known as *diabolus in musica,* that is, "the devil in music." *See also* **power chord.**

trombone The tenor and baritone voices in the brass section. Trombones use slides (instead of valves) for changes in pitch. The trombone was a staple of the marching band, early jazz bands, and prerock dance orchestras. It appears occasionally in contemporary horn sections.

trumpet The high voice in the brass section. The trumpet consists of a mouthpiece and a long, slightly conical tube that bends back on itself and then out in the original direction, where it ends in a flared bell. Valves permit a trumpeter to make adjustments in pitch.

tuba The bass voice of the brass section. The tuba contains a long, wide bored tube, which gives it a mellow sound. It has been used infrequently in popular music, most significantly as the bass instrument of the rhythm section during the 1920s. By 1930 it had been replaced by the string bass. Also called *brass bass.*

tumbao A syncopated bass pattern characteristic of Afro-Cuban music.

turkey trot A popular animal dance of the early twentieth century. Like many of the other "animal dances" of the period, the turkey trot was considered scandalous because it encouraged "lingering close contact" between the dancers.

twelve-bar blues See *blues form.*

two-beat rhythm The division of the measure into two primary beats or accents; the rhythmic basis of the fox trot and other early syncopated instrumental styles.

two-step A social dance popular around the turn of the twentieth century.

unison Two performers playing the same pitch.

uptown Latin style The sound of authentic Afro-Cuban music in the 1940s and '50s.

vaudeville A form of stage entertainment popular from the 1880s to about 1930. It consisted of a series of acts: singers, dancers, novelty performers, and comics. It differed from the revue and musical comedy in that there was no attempt to link vaudeville acts into a dramatically coherent whole.

vernacular Common everyday speech, usually rich in slang.

verse That part of a song in which the same melody is sung two or more times with different words. In the chorus, by contrast, words and melody are the same in every repetition.

verse/chorus form The most popular song form of the late nineteenth century. The verse tells a story in several stages (this section is strophic, i.e., different words are set to the same melody), whereas the chorus, which comes at the end of each verse, repeats both words and melody to reinforce the main message of the song. In early verse/chorus songs, the chorus was often sung by a small group, usually a quartet.

vibraphone A pitched percussion instrument. The vibraphone consists of a group of metal bars arranged like a piano keyboard, with tubular resonators underneath. Dampers, activated by a foot pedal, allow the player to control how long each note sounds. The vibraphone has been used mainly in jazz as an alternative to horns in the front line.

vibrato A slight oscillation in the basic pitch of a musical sound. Vibrato is used by most popular singers and instrumentalists (except for pianists and percussionists).

violin A high-pitched stringed instrument that is usually played with a bow. In popular music the violin has been used in several quite different ways. It has been played fiddle-style by early minstrels and country performers. It is played in the classical manner in sweet dance orchestras, film soundtracks, richly orchestrated pop-vocal arrangements, and other situations in which a lush, warm sound is desirable. It has also been used as a solo jazz instrument.

walkaround The conclusion of a minstrel show, featuring the entire troupe in a grand finale of song and dance.

walking bass A bass line in which the performer plays one note every beat.

waltz rhythm A dance rhythm with three beats per measure and a strong accent on the first beat. Typically, a waltz moves at a fairly rapid tempo.

waltz song A type of song popular around 1900 in which a flowing melody is supported by a simple, waltz-time accompaniment.

western song A song associated with the singing cowboy of the 1930s and '40s.

western swing A Texas country style popular in the 1930s and early 1940s. Western swing added drums, horns, piano, and steel guitar to the instrumentation of the standard country band. This horrified traditionalists but delighted others.

white noise A random sampling of all audible frequencies; it is the sound one also hears between radio stations.

wind section That part of a musical ensemble that includes wind instruments: trumpets, clarinets, and the like.

world beat A general term to describe the rhythms in music that fuse a prevailing international style with a regional music, such as rhythm and blues plus a regional African style.

Your Hit Parade A popular radio show from 1935 to 1955.

zydeco The music of black French-speaking Louisianans.